1997

The Oryx Guide to Distance Learning

A Comprehensive Listing of Electronic and Other Media-Assisted Courses

William E. Burgess

With a foreword by Eric H. Boehm

ORYX PRESS
1994

*The rare Arabian Oryx is believed to have inspired the myth of the unicorn. This desert
antelope became virtually extinct in the early 1960s. At that time several groups of
international conservationists arranged to have 9 animals sent to the Phoenix Zoo
to be the nucleus of a captive breeding herd. Today the Oryx population
is nearly 800, and over 400 have been returned to reserves
in the Middle East.*

Library of Congress Cataloging-in-Publication Data

Burgess, William E., 1939–
    The Oryx Guide to distance learning: a comprehensive listing of electronic and other
media-assisted courses / William E. Burgess.
        p. cm.
    Includes indexes.
    ISBN 0-89774-823-9 (alk. paper)
    1. Distance education—United States—Directories.   2. University extension—United
States—directories.   3. Distance education—United States—Curricula.   4. University
extension—United States—Curricula.
I. Title.
LC5805.B87 1994   94-10004
378'.03'02573—dc20   CIP

Contents

Foreword
Whither Distance Learning

The last decade and the first years of the 1990s were just a sampler of the bewildering pace of change and the concomitant turbulence we will continue to experience in the remainder of this decade and in the millennium to come. Not surprisingly, many of the changes are reflected in "distance learning"—be it in the education or the training modes.

The predominant mode of delivery to students is by broadcast television, either on standard channel broadcast or by cable telecast. The second major delivery system supplies course materials accompanied by videocassette. The third delivers course materials through audiocassette supplements, popular for language and music appreciation courses. Not surprisingly, interactive/video, computer conferencing, computer tutorials, and satellite networks represent the low volume in delivery.

It is likely that newly developed high technology will play an ever more significant role. Peter G.W. Keen, a distinguished authority in information technology, makes the case for use of electronic technology in education when he says:

> Education is expensive, and first-rate teachers are scarce, especially in the information technology field. Releasing people to attend a three-day course can sometimes be justified but is disruptive and inefficient on a regular basis, and bringing the best, and busiest teachers to a firm or to a nearby conference center is often not practical. It is much more efficient and eminently practical to bring the students and educators together electronically. (*Shaping the Future: Business Design Through Information Technology*, Harvard Business School Press, 1991, p. 104)

An example of the widespread use of computer communication is computer conferencing, also known as computer-mediated instruction. This frequently used method of delivery was selected by The International School of Information Management (ISIM), the educational institution for which this writer serves as Chairman of the Board. Among the many new technologies available to distance education, this delivery mode has three critical characteristics: (1) it encourages extensive communication among all participants, (2) it is effective in enhancing the learning outcome, and (3) it costs relatively little.

The computer—linked through modems and communcation software to a telephone network—is ubiquitous and inexpensive. It can be used by participants in a course either at their own choice of time, like electronic mail (e-mail), "asynchronously," or simultaneously, "chat mode."

Providers of distance education through electronic means may also be at the threshold of committing to multimodal delivery modes, rather than the current prevailing preference for one electronic delivery mode, often at the exclusion of others. This new trend would not preclude the use of traditional modes of delivery where applicable. But traditional educational institutions need to recognize that technological changes occurring today are altering the realities with which they have been dealing. Widespread availability of powerful electronic learning tools will probably raise the level of expectation in education, as indeed they are now doing extensively in the field of training for workforce preparedness.

Computer communication such as e-mail, having become a growth industry, is now used by millions. According to an article in *Forbes* April 13, 1992, p. 84, computer networks are now the fastest growing part of the computer industry. The National Information Infrastructure (NII), conveyed to the public as the "Information Superhighway," stimulates the visioning communication throughout the United States. This technological advancement is expressed in the market realities, in the form of rapid growth in private computer usage and in the spectacular growth in the use of Internet and e-mail or bulletin board services (BBSs). Similarly, the explosive growth of "edutainment" methods and electronic publishing, principally the growth in use of CD-ROM in education and entertainment, will transform the separation of current delivery methods into a seamless whole where the distinction between distance education and resident education may steadily become less significant.

Thus, in the future, as we continue to see rapid changes in technology, we can anticipate new applications in education. For instance, the aforementioned *Forbes* article suggests that the telephone, television, and computer are going to merge into a "telecomputer." This "intelligent box" will be linked to the rest of the world by high-capacity smart wires.

In conclusion, the distribution of modes of delivery in a future *Guide* will probably reflect the electronic age even more extensively and also will reflect a move toward more sophisticated use of tools, both in the amalgam of delivery modes and their more effective or better applications.

Eric H. Boehm, Chairman
The International School of Information Management

Introduction

Distance learning is not a new phenomenon. Correspondence courses have been offered by various postsecondary institutions for over a hundred years. Pennsylvania State University, for example, offered its first agricultural courses in the 1890s and added credit correspondence courses for professional engineers in 1918. Today, the availability of academic, professional, and continuing education opportunities from colleges and universities is boundless.

Traditional *correspondence study*, also known as *home study* or *independent study*, is offered by an educational institution that provides lesson materials by mail, prepared in a logical and sequential order. Upon completion of a lesson, the student sends the assigned work to the school for correction, grading, comments, and subject guidance by qualified instructors. Upon successful completion of the course, the student is granted college credit that may be applied to a degree program. Noncredit participation is also possible, whereby the student receives a certificate or diploma for successful completion of a course or series of courses. As a logical progression of this mode of study, a variety of modern media methods are used to deliver courses to students. The media include audiocassettes, audio conferencing, broadcast television, computer conferencing, teleconferencing, videocassettes, and other forms to enhance the learning possibilities in a multitude of disciplines.

SCOPE

The Oryx Guide to Distance Learning provides information on 298 institutions offering over 1,500 media-assisted courses for which academic credit can be earned. These include 116 main entries for universities or colleges, consortiums, public broadcasting stations, and statewide telecommunications services. Additionally, there are 182 entries for institutions that participate in consortiums, public broadcasting services, and telecommunication services. These participating organizations are identified by name and location and include a cross-reference to their parent or related organization. Participating organizations are also cited in the Institution Index.

Methodology

All of the institutions listed in this directory were queried by mail or telephone with a request for detailed information regarding their mode of operation and the distance learning media-assisted courses available. Subsequent editions of this directory will inevitably increase in size as the number of institutions offering media-enhanced instructional courses grows. Many states are currently developing statewide educational telecommunications systems, a complex task requiring the resolution of many issues, one of which is the economic barrier. Some groups of states have begun to share resources, thus preventing duplication of programs and reducing operational costs.

Accreditation

This *Guide* includes only those media-assisted courses for which academic credit is awarded by fully accredited postsecondary institutions. Accreditation has been granted by one of the following agencies:

- American Association of Bible Colleges (AABC)
- Distance Education and Training Council [formerly National Home Study Council] (DETC)
- Middle States Association (MSA)
- North Central Association of Colleges and Schools (NCA)
- New England Association of Schools and Colleges (NEASC)

- Northwest Association of Schools and Colleges (NASC)
- Southern Association of Colleges and Schools (SACS)
- Western Association of Schools and Colleges (WASC)

Degree Programs

Academic credit earned through media-assisted distance learning can be applied toward a degree program and can also, in many cases, be transferred to another institution depending upon the applicability of the course to the student's academic program. Generally, only a certain number of credits earned through distance learning courses can be applied toward an associate or baccalaureate degree.

However, in institutions whose focus is on distance or alternative education programs, a full degree program can be pursued solely through distance learning, and detailed descriptions of the available programs are included in this *Guide*. In particular, Colorado SURGE, Mind Extension University, National Technological University, International School for Information Management (ISIM), and Nova University offer graduate and/or undergraduate degree programs that can be completed via interactive audio/video, computer conferencing, satellite network, and videocassette media. Formal admission procedures and academic credentials are required and are so noted in the entries.

Alternative and *external degree* programs are offered by various postsecondary institutions throughout the nation. An *alternative degree* program offers the student a variety of choices in pursuing a degree. These can include a combination of short residence sessions (usually during summer) or night classes, plus the successful completion of distance learning courses and recognition for other academic achievements as evidenced through credit-by-examination. An *external degree* program is one in which almost all requirements may be completed without formal classroom attendance. Credits, earned either by previous formal classroom attendance or distance learning, may be accepted in transfer from other institutions. Other requirements can be met through credit-by-examination and the successful completion of distance learning courses.

Courses listed in this directory have applicability for students working in both alternative and external degree environments. For a complete listing of institutions offering degree programs to which distance learning courses may be applied, see *The Adult Learner's Guide to Alternative and External Degree Programs* by Eugene Sullivan, The Oryx Press, 1993.

Although tuition fees are provided in this *Guide*, prospective students should always contact the institution of choice to determine current tuition fees and other costs. Because of escalating economic conditions, these fees are often subject to increase on a semester basis. Also, the availability of courses is subject to change. Many courses may be offered in rotation depending on demand.

Users of this *Guide* should bear in mind that all information has been supplied either by the institutions or through public sources. The editors have assumed all information supplied by the institutions to be factual and accurate. Listings are not meant to be comparative in nature nor is a listing in this directory meant to be an endorsement of any institution by The Oryx Press.

Glossary of Delivery Systems Used in Distance Learning

The information age has introduced new methods of delivering study materials to the student and classroom. Modern equipment such as the VCR and the portable audiocassette player, satellite communications and interactive video, plus the professionally produced educational television series have enhanced the capabilities for the distance learner. Although distance learning courses still require a textbook and study guide and completion of assigned lessons, midterm exams, and a final examination, the potential for learning has increased dramatically. Following is a glossary of delivery systems, all of which are included in this *Guide*.

Audiocassette

Audiocassettes are used extensively in foreign language courses but also enhance courses in English literature where the likes of Julie Harris or John Gielgud can be heard in readings and dramatizations of great works in poetry and literature. English-as-a-Second-Language programs, high school completion courses in both English and Spanish, music appreciation courses, and other subject areas utilize the audiocassette as supplementary and, in many cases, required material.

Audio Conferencing

Similar to the conference call used by companies in the business world, an audio conference can involve a group of distance learning students and an instructor, all interacting with one another by means of the telephone. Although not a formal class setup, the audio conference gives students, each with a common goal in a specific course, the opportunity to ask questions of their instructor and to explore ideas with other course members.

Audiographic Conferencing

An audiographic conference is one in which participants at various locations have a means of graphic support so that they can talk, look at visual images, and draw visual images.

Broadcast Television

No longer aired on just the "sunrise semester," academic courses are now presented over the multitude of Public Broadcasting System (PBS) television stations throughout the nation—and at almost any hour of the day. These courses, commonly called telecourses, are sponsored by various local universities and community colleges. The participating student is enrolled by an institution, often by telephone registration, and upon the successful completion of the telecourse (usually 26 half-hour programs), fulfillment of lesson assignments, and a final examination, is granted academic credit. This delivery system is the most prevalent at the present time. Telecourse participation does require a personal discipline necessary for independent study but also gives those students unable to meet the restrictions of a structured college-attendance requirement the freedom to study at their own pace. Students have a significant array of subject area courses available on broadcast television, all of which have been produced by professional educators and organizations.

The producers of telecourses are many and varied, ranging from the British Broadcasting Corporation (BBC) to the Southern California Consortium for

Community College Television (INTELECOM), from WGBH/Boston to the Wisconsin Foundation for Vocational, Technical, and Adult Education, Inc. These and many other organizations are responsible for the development of the telecourse and many are joint efforts. Some have been funded by the Annenberg/CPB Project. The telecourses, as prepared by the various producers, may be used in total as the offering of the college or university, or only a part of the series may be included in the course. Under most circumstances the college or university will offer the telecourse with modification by a faculty member. The amount of credit awarded is determined by the institution granting that credit. The required textbook(s) and study guide, always purchased by the student, may have been written expressly to accompany the telecourse series sequence.

Telecourses are available throughout the United States via public broadcasting stations. The courses offered are generally those developed by various producers and require the use of textbooks and study guides. To avoid superfluous repetition of similar telecourse offerings, only representations of regional institutions may be listed in this *Guide*. It is recommended that the student note the title and description of a telecourse of interest and then contact the local television station, community college, or university to determine its availability. Telecourse scheduling is usually on a semester basis, and the number of courses available for broadcast varies from semester to semester.

Computer Conferencing

The advent of the personal computer and modem has made it possible for students to interact with other students and the instructor. Students in nationwide, even worldwide locations can be networked to a central computer and participate in "seminars" and other group activities. Computer conferencing is similar to electronic mail, but all messages can be read by the students in the order they were received.

Electronic Mail

A computer and modem are necessary to transmit mail through telephone lines. Commonly called e-mail, this delivery system permits students to submit lesson assignments to the electronic mailbox of the instructor. Feedback to the student is also possible,

provided he or she has been assigned an electronic mailbox and code.

Interactive Audio/Video

A form of closed circuit television that transmits video and audio, it is usually limited to a single building on a campus or to specific off-campus sites. Students at all sites are able to see and talk to the instructor or talk to students at other sites viewing the same presentation.

Online Services

The past 20 years have seen the emergence of online services that by means of data storage of massive quantities of information (bibliographic and full-text), make it possible for the student to go "online" with a personal computer. This connection requires a telecommunications modem and log-in protocol to gain access via telephone lines to the database of choice. Using a search strategy, the user then has the results displayed. In the context of course participation, online services are usually the entrance key to the resources of the academic library.

Radio Broadcast

A radio presentation of a distance learning course is broadcast over a local radio station and is usually a replay of an instructor's lectures that were prerecorded on the campus. It may also be the audio portion of a videotaped telecourse.

Satellite Network

Communications satellites orbiting the earth receive electronic signals that are beamed back to earth at various locations. The communication method is used extensively by, among others, the Adult Learning Service of PBS, Mind Extension University, and the National Technological University.

Teleclasses

This type of distance learning involves the presentation of a course in a specially designed classroom where students view a lecture given by the instructor. No interaction between students and the instructor takes place. The presentation can be either a broadcast over the college or university cable system or a replay of a video series.

Telephone Contact

Students participating in a distance learning course almost always have the telephone number of the instructor and may make direct contact on a regularly scheduled basis.

Videocassette

Many of the courses televised by PBS stations are also available on videocassette. Licensing fees and lease arrangements are made by the institution offering the course with the producer or distributor of the video series. Further, many institutions videotape an instructor's formal class lectures, and the videocassette may become a required supplement to the lesson assignments. A videocassette course requires that the student rent or purchase the videotapes and view them at his or her convenience. A time limit for the completion of a course may be based on the semester or quarter system or the student may be given 12 months to complete the course requirements. Textbooks and study guides are used to assist the student throughout the sequence. Another option is for the student to view the videotapes in the audiovisual department on the campus. This department is most often found in the Library Resources Center or campus library.

How to Use This *Guide*

ARRANGEMENT

Institutions in this *Guide* are arranged geographically by state and, within state, alphabetically by name of institution. Entries are indexed by course subject areas, methods of delivery, and institution name. An appendix of institutions that provide nationwide or worldwide access is included. Generally, institutions are colleges or universities. In other cases, the institution may be an umbrella organization that airs television courses for a number of local area colleges and universities (e.g.,WGBH/Boston), or an official state organization that oversees the educational telecommunications activities for the statewide area (e.g., North Dakota Interactive Video Network).

INDEXES

It is recommended that the Subject Index be used as the entry point to this *Guide*. This index lists the subject areas (Accounting, Adult Education, Advanced Technology, Management, etc.) for which there are courses. Entries in the subject index are arranged by subject, by state, and then by institution name. Citations under subject refer the user to the institution, its city, and its state. The state identification appears in boldface for easy reference to the alphabetical arrangement by state in the Main Entry section.

The Delivery System Index refers the user to institutions that use the delivery systems cited (Audio Conferencing, Audiocassette, Audiographic Conferencing, Broadcast Television, etc.). This index is valuable to the user who is seeking a course of study in a particular delivery mode. The name of the appropriate institution and its city and state are listed under each delivery system. Entries are in order alphabetically by delivery system, by state, and then by institution name.

The Institution Name Index is useful for those prospective students who have identified the institution in which they wish to enroll for a course. The names of the institutions appear in alphabetical order and give the city and state.

All three of the above indexes indicate with an asterisk those institutions that provide nationwide or worldwide access. Because some institutions offer course participation only to regional areas, this feature eliminates the need for a perusal of the main entries to find those institutions geared to a nationwide or worldwide audience. An Appendix of Institutions Providing Nationwide or Worldwide Course Access lists only those institutions asterisked in the three indexes.

The sample entry on the following page identifies the various components of a main entry.

Sample Entry

Name of institution or organization offering distance learning courses

University of Iowa
Division of Continuing Education
Center for Credit Programs
116 International Center
Iowa City, IA 52242-1802
(800) 272-6430

Address, phone number, and fax number

Region in which courses are available

Geographic Access: Iowa for Broadcast Television, nation-wide for audio- and video-enhanced courses.

DELIVERY SYSTEMS

Audiocassette
Audio-enhanced courses require access to an audiocassette player/recorder.

Videocassette
Video-enhanced courses require the use of a VCR.

Broadcast Television
Telecourses are broadcast over Iowa Public Television throughout the state of Iowa.

Modes of media-assisted course delivery used

INSTITUTION DESCRIPTION

General description of institution or organization

The University of Iowa is located in the southeastern section of the state. The university was established in 1847, very soon after the Iowa Territory became a state. Instruction began in 1855 and nontraditional educational opportu-

Accreditation: NCA

Accrediting organization. *See* Introduction for list of abbreviations

Contact person for distance learning information

Official/Contact: Leonard Kallio, Assistant Director

Admission Requirements: Open enrollment. Students must be at least high school juniors.

Requirements for admission to distance learning courses

Tuition: $64 per semester hour plus a $15 nonrefundable enrollment fee per course. Additional fees required for audio- and video-enhanced courses. Royalty fees may apply for public

Tuition and fees

Applicability of distance learning credits toward a degree

Degree Credit: Credit for successful completion of courses may be applied toward a degree.

Grading: Letter grades (A-F) are assigned. D- is the minimum passing grade. Exams must be proctored. Credit is awarded in semester hour units.

Grading and exam policy

Library services/resources available to distance learning students

Library: All courses are designed to be self-contained. University of Iowa facilities are not available for nonresident students.

COURSES OFFERED

Subject of course

Anthropology

Faces of Culture

Name of course

This telecourse embraces cultures from all continents, high-lights major human subsistence patterns, and illustrates hu-

Description of course

Main Entry Section

Alabama

Southeastern Bible College
External Studies
3001 Highway 280 East
Birmingham, AL   35205

(205) 969-0880

Geographic Access: Nationwide

DELIVERY SYSTEMS

Audiocassette
Audiocassettes are utilized in most of the courses listed below. Student must have access to an audiocassette player.

Videocassette
An optional videocassette tape is available for the course Greek I, described below.

INSTITUTION DESCRIPTION

Southeastern Bible College was founded in 1935 and offers Christian higher education in a Biblical framework. The college takes its place with similar institutions throughout the country in offering training with a high academic standard coupled with a balanced spiritual emphasis. The college is nondenominational.

The External Studies Department began at Dallas Bible College in Texas in 1959. The department was transferred to Southeastern Bible College in January 1986.

The courses listed and described below are college-level courses enhanced with videocassette presentations.

Accreditation: AABC

Official/Contact: Ray E. Baughman, Dean of External Studies

Admission Requirements: High school graduation or GED. Enrollment is restricted to students in the United States, the Armed Forces, and U.S. missionaries.

Tuition: $60 per semester hour. Textbooks, study materials, and videocassettes must be purchased by the student.

Degree Credit: All credits awarded for successful completion of a video-enhanced course may be applied toward an external degree program at Southeastern Bible College and may be accepted in transfer to another institution. Students should check with their home institution to determine the applicability of the course for transfer of credit.

Grading: Students are requested to have a responsible nonrelated adult supervise examinations. This could be a pastor, Sunday school teacher, or friend and must be approved by Southeastern Bible College. Letter grades (A, B, C, D, F) are assigned. Credit is awarded in semester hour units.

Library: Students are encouraged to utilize the library facilities of their local communities.

COURSES OFFERED

Counseling

Counseling
This course surveys counseling theories, examines the role of the Christian counselor, and introduces the student to the basic techniques and methods of personal counseling. Problem areas that will be studied include anxiety, depression, suffering, guilt, loneliness, rejection, self-discipline, and personal relationships. Audiocassette tapes: $10. (2 credits)

English

English Grammar and Composition

This is a course in grammar, correct usage, and punctuation. Three types of writing assignments are covered during the course. Audiocassette tapes: $2.50. (3 credits)

English Composition

A continuation of the above course with emphasis on composition. The analysis of compositions and writing of short compositions are preparation for the writing of a research paper. Lessons emphasize style, organization of materials, research techniques, documentation of sources, and bibliographical preparations. Audiocassette tapes: $2.50. (3 credits)

Family Relations

Marriage and Family Counseling

Principles and techniques available to the counselor are explored and evaluated. A part of this course is made up of selected tape lectures from counseling seminars. Audiocassette tapes: $10. (2 credits)

Marriage and Family

In an age of changing values, this course introduces the student to what the Bible says about marriage and the family. The student will study the role of the husband and wife, communication in the home, parent-child relationships, dating and courtship, and perils to marriage and the family. Eight key lectures by Mervin Longenecker, selected reading assignments, and several short research projects are required. Audiocassette tapes: $7.50. (2 credits)

Greek

Greek I

This course gives an introduction to New Testament Greek and Greek language tools. It is a practical course designed to enrich a teaching and preaching ministry. Many memory helps are supplied. The course studies the alphabet, parts of speech, sentence structures, verb tenses, and substantive cases. Optional videocassette tape rental: $50. Audiocassette tapes: $7.50. (3 credits)

Greek II

A continuation of Greek I. Each lesson will include four areas of study: a review of grammar, analysis of selected Greek verses, translation exercises, and vocabulary study. Audiocassette tapes: $7.50. (3 credits)

Hebrew

Introduction to Biblical Hebrew

This is a practical course designed to enrich a teaching and preaching ministry. Studied are the alphabet, parts of speech, word formation, sentence structures, and synonyms. A unique method of verb identification is presented. Audiocassette tapes: $5. (3 credits)

History

History of Christianity

This course briefly traces Christianity's history from Pentecost to the Reformation. It then emphasizes the period from Reformation to the present. Major divisions center around the Reformation, nineteenth-century religious liberalism, and the development of Christianity in America. The student will learn of the theological antecedents that affect the church scene today. Audiocassette tapes: $5. (3 credits)

Human Development

Introduction to Human Development

This course is an introduction to the self-actualization of a person so that he/she is doing what he/she is best fitted to do. Spiritual, psychological, and social aspects of human development are studied. The student will take the Daisy Temperament Analysis and Ministry Quotient Analysis to help understand him/herself. The student will learn how to develop personal relationships and reach out to others. Audiocassette tapes: $10. (3 credits)

Mathematics

College Math

This course is designed for those working toward teacher certification in elementary education, for those who need a math course in elementary education, or for those who need a math course in their program. It presumes little prior knowledge of mathematics and is presented in a semiprogrammed work-text format that allows students to progress at their own pace. Audiocassette tapes: $2.50. (3 credits)

Psychology

Introduction to Psychology

This course is a study of human behavior and mental activity. Major theories of behavior are explored and evaluated. Assignments include personal applications and experiments. Modern methods of educational theory are used in this course. Audiocassette tapes: $7.50. (3 credits)

Educational Psychology

The scientific study of learning and other human behavior that is relevant to education. Educational objectives, learner characteristics, learning theories, learning principles, creativity, motivation, discipline, memory, measurement and evaluation, and educational innovations are studied. Audiocassette tapes: $10. (3 credits)

Religious Studies

Bible Study Methods

In this course the student will study eight different methods of Bible study and then learn to correlate them into the mastery of a Bible book. Audiocassette tapes: $5. (3 credits)

Bible Survey I

The student will study Bible history and prophecy in order to have a framework in which to study each book of the Bible, understand its relationship to other books of the Bible, and to see the Bible as a whole. There is also an emphasis upon Bible geography. Audiocassette tapes: $5. (3 credits)

Bible Survey II: Old Testament

Attention is given to the theme, principal teachings, background, author, recipients, date, and geography of each book. Audiocassette tapes: $5. (3 credits)

Bible Survey III: New Testament

Attention is given to the theme, principal teachings, background, author, recipients, date, geography, and how the New Testament relates to the Old Testament. Audiocassette tapes: $5. (3 credits)

Bible Exposition: Acts

From the ascension of Christ and the birth of the church to the end of the first church generation in A.D. 63, the unfolding revelation of God is studied in its chronological order and in its geographical and historical setting. The emphasis is put upon studying the Scripture itself. This is accomplished by the use of certain Bible study methods and the interaction of the student with resource materials. Audiocassette tapes: $10. (3 credits)

Bible Exposition: Daniel

This course is a detailed, analytical study of the Book of Daniel. This book gives a basic framework for the study of prophecy. Audiocassette tapes: $2.50. (2 credits)

Bible Exposition: Exodus

This course leads the student into a detailed study of the "Book of Redemption." It shows how God redeemed His people from Egypt by blood and by power. It also illustrates many of the conflicts, trials, and testings that a believer experiences. Audiocassette tapes: $2.50. (2 credits)

Bible Exposition: Genesis

The Book of Genesis is of primary importance because it is the "seed plot" of the Bible. The student will study the historical, geographical, and chronological settings, the covenants, key people, and key events: creation, temptation, fall, flood, and entrance into Egypt. Key chapters are studied in detail. Audiocassette tapes: $2.50. (3 credits)

Bible Exposition: Hebrews

The Book of Hebrews is the great transitional book for the Jewish Christian. This course is designed to explore many of the Old Testament theological concepts and relate them to the New Testament. Audiocassette tapes: $7.50. (2 credits)

James and Galatians

This course is an expositional study of these Bible books. Audiocassette tapes: $2.50. (4 credits)

Bible Exposition: Gospel of John

This book of the Bible will be studied verse by verse. Audiocassette tapes: $7.50. (2 credits)

Bible Exposition: Joshua

A detailed analytical study that examines the development of Israel as a theocratic nation as it enters and possesses the promised land. This will include the historical background, the military campaigns, the tribal allotments, and the character qualities of Joshua and other persons in this period. Audiocassette tapes: $5. (2 credits)

Luke and John

In this course, instruction is given in Bible practicum series. The practicums unite analytical Bible study and Christian ministry. Audiocassette tapes: $2.50. (4 credits)

Bible Exposition: Revelation

A detailed analytic study of Revelation with special emphasis on the historical and eschatological significance of the book as it relates to the premillennial, pretribulational, dispensational system of interpretation. Audiocassette tapes: $5. (3 credits)

Bible Exposition: Romans

The Book of Romans is a doctrinal treatise of supreme importance. It is really a condensed doctrinal course in the subjects of grace, propitiation, righteousness of God, justification, reconciliation, identification, adoption, sanctification, spiritual gifts, and glorification. Audiocassette tapes: $5. (3 credits)

I & II Thessalonians, Philippians

Emphasis is given to the principles of evangelism, care of new believers, spiritual life, the Lord's return for His church, the Day of the Lord, and the doctrine of Christology. Audiocassette tapes: $2.50. (2 credits)

I & II Timothy Practicum

This course is an analytical study of the two pastoral epistles that Paul sent to Timothy. Audiocassette tapes: $2.50. (4 credits)

Life of Christ

A presentation of the Lord's earthly life in both a chronological and geographical order. Audiocassette tapes: $10. (2 credits)

Missionary Methods in Acts

This course is an inductive study of the Book of Acts. There is a special emphasis upon the philosophy and methods of the church as it begins to fulfill the great commission. Audiocassette tapes: $2.50. (3 credits)

Personal Evangelism

This course is a study of the theology, principles, and methods designed to equip students to share with others a saving knowledge of Jesus Christ. A part of the course is related to the follow-up of a new Christian. The student will listen to eight lectures by Evangelist James Dixon and will submit a tape of a presentation of the gospel. Audiocassette tapes: $7.50. (2 credits)

Pastoral Practicum

This practicum is designed to give the student guided experiences on the qualifications of a pastor, the call, licensing/ordination, pitfalls, and visitation of church members, prospects, shut-ins, bereaved, and nursing home and hospital patients. A plan for pre-marital counseling will also be prepared. Audiocassette tapes: $2.50. (2 credits)

Introduction to Missions

This course is a study of the biblical and theological basis for missions as given in the Bible. Consideration is given to the missionary call and stress is placed upon the biblical response to universalism and syncretism. The history of missions is surveyed through missionary biographies. The course examines the basic means and opportunities of missions, selected ministries through church and parachurch entities, and trends in missions today. Audiocassette tapes: $5. (2 credits)

Doctrine: Bible Introduction Practicum

This course is divided into three basic parts: the various doctrines of inspiration, canonicity or determining what books should be in the Bible, and how the message of the original autographs has been transmitted to us today. Audiocassette tapes: $2.50. (4 credits)

Doctrine: Eschatology

This is a study of biblical prophecy, the basis of interpretation, God's plan of the ages, biblical covenants, dispensations, prophecies of this age and its end, the tribulation, the second advent, the kingdom, and the eternal state. A study of the relationship of this life to positions and activities of eternity. Audiocassette tapes: $5. (2 credits)

Doctrine: Spiritual Life

This course introduces the student to the promise of the Spirit-filled life and the ministry of the Holy Spirit to the believer. There are practical helps given to help pray more effectively, to enjoy Bible study, to meet temptation victoriously, to witness, and to find God's will for one's life. Audiocassette tapes: $7.50. (2 credits)

Doctrinal Summary

This course is a systematic study of the whole field of Christian doctrine: Bibliology, Theology, Christology, Soteriology, Anthropology, Pneumatology, Ecclesiology, Angelology, and Eschatology. Audiocassette tapes: $7.50. (3 credits)

Speech

Speech

Basic principles of effective speech are studied with emphasis on voice, general appearance, method of delivery, and preparation of various types of speeches. The assigned speeches will vary from 3 to 10 minutes and are to be given in connection with a church ministry or civic club. Cassette tapes are used for instruction in voice development, to give examples of the different kinds of speeches, to record the student's speeches, and to record the instructor's evaluation of the student's speeches. Students may submit speeches on audio or VHS videocassettes. Audiocassette tapes: $10. (3 credits)

Theology

Theology I

This course is a systematic survey of Bible doctrines: Bibliology, Theology Proper, Christology, and Pneumatology. It is designed to carefully orient the student in the field of Systematic Theology and to help relate the studies to one's personal life. Audiocassette tapes: $5. (3 credits)

Theology II

A continuation of Theology I. A systematic survey of Bible doctrines: Angelology, Satanology, Anthropology, Harmatiology, Soteriology, Ecclesiology, and Eschatology. Audiocassette tapes: $5. (3 credits)

University of Alabama
College of Continuing Studies
Office of Educational
Telecommunications
128 Martha Parham West
Box 870388
Tuscaloosa, AL   35487-0388

(205) 348-9278 *Fax:* (205) 348-9246

Geographic Access: Alabama, Arkansas, Louisiana, Mississippi, Texas

DELIVERY SYSTEMS

Videocassette
QUEST's delivery mode enables working professionals to continue their education without leaving their jobs or disrupting their lives. This program delivers classes via videotape to a student's place of employment or a conveniently located QUEST open site.

INSTITUTION DESCRIPTION

The University of Alabama covers 850 acres in the heart of Tuscaloosa, a city of 75,000 residents in west central Alabama. As a comprehensive university, the University of Alabama offers many programs and activities with its 16 major components. Quality University Extended Site Telecourses (QUEST) is one of the newest avenues of delivery of courses for the university.

QUEST was initiated in fall 1991 as the University's first totally video-based graduate/undergraduate program and now includes six studio classrooms in various academic departments. The videotapes provide working professionals with the means to continue their education without giving up their jobs. The purpose of QUEST is to make quality, up-to-date education available in a flexible, convenient manner. Students choosing this program may enroll in a variety of courses in engineering, computer science, commerce and business administration, and nursing. Other disciplines are added as studios are opened.

Accreditation: SACS

Official/Contact: Carroll Tingle, Director, QUEST

Admission Requirements: All students enrolling in the QUEST program must be admitted to the University of Alabama. An individual who is interested in earning graduate credit, but who is not an applicant for a graduate degree, may be admitted for nondegree studies with the approval of the department or program in which the course is offered.

Tuition: Tuition for QUEST courses is determined by the governing board of the University of Alabama. Tuition changes, if any, become effective with the fall semester each year. Tuition $125 per semester hour. An admission fee of $20 for undergraduate and $25 for graduate students is paid by all new students. There is no nonresidency charge to off-campus students. Students may audit a QUEST course at a cost equivalent to one semester hour. Textbooks can be ordered from the QUEST office or may be purchased at the University Supply Store or a local bookstore. MasterCard, VISA, and Discover Card accepted.

Degree Credit: Degree programs through QUEST courses are offered through the College of Engineering, College of Commerce and Business Administration, and the Capstone College of Nursing. The Department of Aerospace Engineering offers an opportunity to pursue a master's degree without on-campus residence.

Registered nurses who wish to earn a bachelor of science in nursing will find that QUEST regularly offers courses applicable toward the B.S.N.

Grading: Examinations must be proctored. Letter grades are assigned. Credit is awarded in semester hour units.

Library: Students have access to all library facilities of the University of Alabama.

COURSES OFFERED

Business

Labor Law
A study of contemporary statutory and case law affecting employees, employers, and labor organizations. Includes intensive analysis of recent issues that are of interest because of their impact on public opinion and on management-employee relations. Topics for discussion include the legal aspects of union activity among public employees and questions arising under recent equal employment opportunity laws. (3 credits)

Engineering

FORTRAN Programming
Basic concepts of FORTRAN programming. Student must have the availability of a computer with the ANSI 90 FORTRAN compiler or any other FORTRAN 77 compiler which handles character data. The course will be taught using a microcomputer under the DOS operating system. (3 credits)

Computer Management Information Systems
The nature of computerized information systems, problems created by the computer relative to personnel, components of computer systems, programming and application of computers to business problems. (3 credits)

Microcomputer Applications
Familiarization with DOS, fundamental and intermediate word processing commands, spreadsheet applications, and database management. (3 credits)

Engineering Statistics
Probability and basic statistical concepts, discrete and continuous distributions, the central limit theorem, sampling distributions, point and interval esti-

mation, hypothesis testing, regression and correlation analysis, analysis of variance. (3 credits)

Engineering Materials I - Structure and Properties
Basic structure of ceramics, alloys, composites, metals, and polymers. Relationships between the structure of materials and mechanical, electrical, magnetic, thermal, and chemical properties. (3 credits)

Finite Element Analysis
Finite element method applied to truss, frame, and continuum structures. (3 credits)

Optimal Control
Optimal control of dynamic processes, calculus of variations, Hamilton-Jacobi theory, Pontryagin's maximum principle, dynamic programming. (3 hours)

Statistical Applications in Civil Engineering
Frequency analysis of physical and experimental data, extreme value theory, point and interval estimation, concepts of statistical inference, correlation and regression, simulation and data synthesis. (3 credits)

Structural Analysis
Theory and principles of structural analysis of determinate and indeterminate structures. (3 credits)

Process Calculations
Quantitative study of physical and chemical processes and chemical reactions, calculations for gases/vapors/humidity and process material balances. (3 credits)

Analysis of Operating Systems
Implementation of operating systems. (3 credits)

Control Systems Analysis
Classical and modern feedback control system methods, stability, Bode/root locus/state variables, and computer analysis. (3 credits)

Engineering Economics
Annual cost, present worth, rate of return, and benefit-cost methods of determining prospective differences between or among design alternatives. Includes fixed and variable costs, and retirement and replacement problems. (3 credits)

Integer Programming
Optimization in integer variables by cutting planes, branch-and-bound, group theoretic, and implicit enumeration. (3 credits)

Manufacturing Systems Design Computer-Aided Manufacturing

Introduction to computer technology and applications in manufacturing, including CAD, group technology and computer-aided process planning, artificial intelligence, numerical control and robot technology, computer-integrated production management systems, and computer interfaces and networks. (3 credits)

Introduction to Computing

Introduction to computer science for graduate students with limited computer science backgrounds who wish to major or minor in computer science. Includes high-level languages, programming techniques, machine organization, assembly language, and data structures. (6 credits)

Production Planning and Control

Forecasting and estimation, aggregate planning, charts and network models, resource allocation, inventory control, sequencing and scheduling, dispatching, flow control, bills of materials, and requirements planning. (3 credits)

Statistical Quality Control

Use of statistical tools and techniques in the control of quality of manufactured products. Shewhart control charts, single/double/multiple sampling inspection plans. (3 credits)

Work Design and Human Performance

Design and evaluation of human-machine systems and working environments to optimize human productivity and performance, with emphasis on the industrial environment. (3 credits)

Operations Research

Model construction, linear programming, network models, dynamic models, stochastic models, queueing theory, and decision theory. (3 credits)

Human Information Processing

Human mental capabilities and limitations, human-machine interfaces, mental workload, human-computer interfaces, human error, and system design. (3 credits)

Network Optimization

Theories, algorithms, and applications for networks and graphs, shortest path, K-shortest, traveling salesman, multiterminal flow, minimum cost flow, and multicommodity problems. (3 credits)

Advanced Dynamics of Machinery

Modeling and analysis of dynamic systems, with emphasis on Newtonian and Lagrangian techniques applied to the three-dimensional motion of rigid bodies. (3 credits)

Advanced Analytical Methods in Heat Transfer

Advanced treatment of conduction heat transfer, using classical mathematical techniques and numerical methods. (3 credits)

Statics

Forces and couples and resultants of force systems, free-body diagrams, equilibrium, problems involving friction, centroids, center of gravity, distributed forces. (3 credits)

Mechanics of Materials I

Concepts of stress and strain, analysis of stresses and deformation in bodies loaded by axial, torsional, and bending loads, combined loads analysis, statically indeterminate members, thermal stresses, columns, and thin-walled pressure vessels. (3 credits)

Dynamics

Kinematics of particles and rigid bodies, Newton's laws of motion, and principles of work-energy and impulse-momentum for particles and rigid bodies. (3 credits)

Fluid Mechanics

Fluid statics, application of conservation laws to simple systems, dimensional analysis and similitude, and flow in open and closed conduits. (3 credits)

Genetic Algorithms in Optimization and Machine Learning

Theory and application of genetic algorithms, schema processing, and implicit parallelism. Computer implementation and current applications in parameter and combinatorial optimization and optimal control genetics-based machine learning systems. (3 credits)

Neural Networks

Theory, implementation, and applications of learning automata and neural networks. Early applications from psychology and biology. Current applications in engineering and machine learning. (3 credits)

Metallurgical Process Calculations

Mathematical quantitative relations of chemical reactions and physico-chemical processes, principles of overall mass and energy balances and the application of these principles to metallurgical systems. (3 credits)

Management

Organizational Theory and Behavior
A course designed to help students understand organizational theory, interpersonal communication, and other behavioral science concepts and then integrate them into managerial tools for effective use in business, industry, and public-sector organizations. (3 credits)

Introduction to Human Resources Management
Introductory course surveying problems and issues in labor economics, personnel management, and labor relations. Emphasis is placed on public policies affecting management and union representatives and on the role of the human resources manager in the organization. (3 credits)

Nursing

Cardiac Electrophysiology
Opportunity to expand knowledge of cardiac arrhythmias and dysrhythmias and to identify basic deviations from the normal 12-lead EKG. Discussions directed toward application of knowledge gained from hypothetical case situations. (3 credits)

Introduction to Nursing Research
Utilization of theory and scientific methodology in the review of research. Provides an opportunity to critique current nursing research and requires the student to use critical inquiry methodology and to become a discriminating consumer of research. Writing proficiency is required for a passing grade in this course. (3 credits)

Human Pathology, 1st and 2nd Terms
Examination of disruptions in adaptive mechanisms of human beings throughout the life span. (4 credits)

AIDS: A Caring Response
Opportunity to increase knowledge of all aspects of AIDS as a catastrophic illness affecting individuals, families, and society. Emphasis on prevention and detection of AIDS and associated multidimensional well-being requirements. (3 credits)

Pharmacology
Investigation of the role of pharmaceutical agents in assisting the individual's physiologic and psychologic adaptation to stressors. Classifications of pharmaceutical agents are discussed in regard to mechanism of action, adverse side effects, and nursing implications. (3 credits)

Alaska

University of Alaska
Center for Distance Education
College of Rural Alaska

130 Red Building
Fairbanks, AK   99701

(907) 474-5353 *Fax:* (907) 474-5402

Geographic Access: Worldwide

DELIVERY SYSTEMS

Electronic Mail
Students may submit lessons by Fax (907) 474-5402 for an additional $25 fee per course. Assignments may also be submitted by BITNET. The Center's user id is SYCDE@ALASKA. Instructors may or may not return comments via BITNET depending on their particular situation.

Videocassette
Some courses utilize videotapes as supplementary material. *See* Courses Offered.

INSTITUTION DESCRIPTION

The Center for Distance Education and Independent Learning offers its academic resources to people who seek a college education but cannot for a variety of reasons attend on-campus classes. The maximum time for completion of a course is 12 months from the date of enrollment, including the final examination. Students may submit lessons by mail, fax, or BITNET.

Accreditation: NASC

Official/Contact: Jim Stricks, Director

Admission Requirements: Enrollment in the program does not require, nor does it constitute, formal admission to the University of Alaska, Fairbanks. Any person who has the proper prerequisites for a specific course may be enrolled. Students have the responsibility for selecting courses that will satisfy their degree requirements.

Tuition: $58 per credit hour plus a $20 service fee per course. Textbooks and learning materials must be purchased by the student. Students located outside the United States must submit payment in U.S. dollars and will be charged an extra $20 materials handling fee per course to cover additional postage charges.

Degree Credit: Full-time students at the University of Alaska, Fairbanks may enroll in one independent learning course per semester and the course must be completed by the end of the semester. Credit may be applied to the degree program being pursued.

Grading: Most courses require that the student complete proctored examinations, one of which is the final exam. The letter grading system (A, B, C, D, F) is used. Credit is awarded in semester hour units.

Library: For students in Alaska but outside the Fairbanks area, a toll-free number (800) 478-5348 to the UA Fairbanks Rasmuson Library is available for interlibrary loan of materials.

COURSES OFFERED

Accounting

Elementary Accounting I
An introductory course in accounting concepts and procedures for service businesses and for merchandising businesses owned by a single proprietor. 13 lessons, 3 exams. (3 credits)

Elementary Accounting II
A continuation of introductory accounting concepts and procedures emphasizing the problems of busi-

nesses organized as partnerships or corporations and performing manufacturing operations. 16 lessons, 4 exams. (3 credits)

Alaska Native Studies

Alaska Native Claims Settlement Act

A general survey of the Alaska Native Claims Settlement Act (ANCSA). It will include a brief historical overview of land claims of various tribes in the Lower 48 and in Alaska leading to the Settlement Act of 1971. Examines the current status of the various Native corporations, including regional, village, and nonprofit corporations. Special attention is given to the discussion of future issues related to implementation of ANCSA. 14 lessons, 2 exams. (3 credits)

Anthropology

Introduction to Anthropology

An introduction to the study of human societies and cultures based on the findings of the four subfields of the discipline: archaeological, biological, cultural, and linguistic. 19 lessons, 4 exams. (3 credits)

Native Cultures of Alaska

An introduction to the traditional Aleut, Eskimo, and Indian (Athabaskan and Tlingit) cultures of Alaska. Comparative information on Eskimo and Indian cultures in Canada is also presented. Includes a discussion of linguistic groupings as well as the cultural groups. Presents population changes through time, subsistence patterns, social organization, and religion in terms of local ecology. Precontact interaction between native groups of Alaska is also explored. A general introductory course presenting an overall view of the cultures of Native Alaskans. 17 lessons, 4 exams. (3 credits)

World Ethnography: Indian Sikhs

Cultural heritage, social systems, modes of economic adaptation and cultural change for human populations in major geographic regions of the world. Focus on the Sikhs of India. 10 lessons, 2 exams. (3 credits)

Art

Two-Dimensional Design

Fundamentals of pictorial form, principles of composition, organization, and structure. This course utilizes videocassettes and thus requires access to a videocassette recorder. 14 lessons, no exams. (3 credits)

Aviation Technology

Private Pilot Ground School

Study of aircraft and engine operation and limitations, aircraft flight instruments, navigation computers, national weather information and dissemination service. Federal Aviation Regulations, flight information publications, radio communications, and radio navigation in preparation for FAA Private Pilot written exam. 14 lessons, 2 exams. (4 credits)

Biology

Natural History of Alaska

Aspects of the physical environment peculiar to the north and important in determining the biological setting. Major ecosystem concepts to develop an appreciation for land use and wildlife management problems in both terrestrial and aquatic situations. 15 lessons, 1 project, 2 exams. (3 credits)

Introduction to Marine Biology

A general survey of marine organisms, evolution of marine life, habitats and communities of ocean zones, productivity, and marine resources. 9 lessons, 1 exam. (3 credits)

Business

Basics of Investing

This course covers personal financial planning, goal setting, and investing. Also, a study will be made of stocks, bonds, trusts, securities, options, real estate, and other investment vehicles. The topics of inflation, taxes, interest rates, retirement, and selecting financial planners are covered. 16 lessons, 1 project, 2 exams. (3 credits)

Real Estate Law

A practical course surveying the various kinds of deeds and conveyances, mortgages, liens, rentals, appraisals, and other transactions in the field of real estate and the law. 15 lessons, 2 exams. (3 credits)

Applied Business Law I

A survey of the legal aspects of business problems including basic principles, institutions, and administration of law in contracts, agency, employment and personal sales and property ownership. 14 lessons, 3 exams. (3 credits)

Applied Business Law II

A survey of legal aspects of business problems including basic principles, institutions, and administration of law in insurance, suretyship (negotiable instruments), partnerships, corporations, trusts, wills, bankruptcy, torts, and business crimes. 15 lessons, 2 exams. (3 credits)

Child Development

Child Development

Study of development from prenatal through middle childhood including the cognitive, emotional, social, and physical aspects of the young child. Course includes child observations. Emphasis is on the roles of heredity and environment in the growth process. 14 lessons, 2 exams. (3 credits)

Computer Science

Introduction to Computer Programming

Concepts of structured programming and algorithm design within the syntax of the PASCAL programming language. Requires access to an MS-DOS computer. 9 lessons, 2 exams. (3 credits)

Economics

The Alaskan Economy

A broad introductory examination of economic problems in Alaska. Analysis of historical trends and current patterns of economic growth. Particular emphasis on present and future alternative economic policies. 14 lessons, 2 exams. (3 credits)

Principles of Economics I: Microeconomics

Theory of prices and markets, income distribution, contemporary problems of labor, agriculture, market structure, pollution, etc. 22 lessons, 1 exam. (3 credits)

Principles of Economics II: Macroeconomics

Analysis and theory of national income, money and banking, and stabilization policy. 22 lessons, 1 exam. (3 credits)

Education

Literature for Children

Criteria for evaluating children's books and applications of criteria to books selected by student. Study of outstanding authors, illustrators and content of specific categories of literature, book selection aids,

and effective use of literature to promote learning. 10 lessons, 3 projects, 1 exam. (3 credits)

Diagnosis and Evaluation of Learning

Detailed information about the teaching/learning process in the classroom emphasizing making teaching decisions. The student will learn the strengths and weaknesses of various forms of diagnosis and evaluation of learning, with particular emphasis on problems encountered in cross-cultural settings. Attention will be given to informal, formal, process, and product assessment. 12 lessons, 1 exam. (3 credits)

The Exceptional Learner

An overview course which develops the foundation for understanding, identifying and serving the exceptional learner in rural and urban settings. A special emphasis is placed on working with exceptional learners in the regular classroom. The unique needs of exceptional students in rural settings from bilingual/multicultural backgrounds are covered. 8 lessons, 1 exam. (3 credits)

Building a Practical Philosophy of Education

A study of philosophy as a distinct discipline with its own terminology, concepts, and processes and how it functions in the field of education. Special emphasis is given to an application of philosophy of education to cross-cultural situations in Alaskan classrooms. 10 lessons, 2 exams. (3 credits)

English

Methods of Written Communication

Instruction in writing expository prose, including generating topics as part of the writing process. Practice in developing, organizing, revising, and editing essays. 10 lessons, 2 exams. (3 credits)

Intermediate Exposition with Modes of Literature

Instruction in writing through close analysis of literature. Research paper required. 14 lessons, 2 exams. (3 credits)

Introduction to Creative Writing: Poetry

A study of the forms and techniques of poetry for beginning students. Discussion of students' work. 10 lessons, no exams. (3 credits)

Frontier Literature of Alaska

Study of representative works of fiction, verse, and nonfiction which deal with Alaska and the Yukon Territory. 11 lessons, 2 exams. (3 credits)

Geography

Introductory Geography

World regions, an analysis of environment with emphasis on major culture realms. 12 lessons, 4 exams. (3 credits)

Elements of Physical Geography

Analysis of the processes that form the physical environment and the resulting physical patterns. Study of landforms, climate, soils, water resources, vegetation, and their world regional patterns. 13 lessons, 2 exams. (3 credits)

Geography of Alaska

Regional, physical, and economic geography of Alaska. Special consideration of the state's renewable and nonrenewable resources, and of plans for their wise use. Frequent study of representative maps and visual materials. 16 lessons, 3 exams. (3 credits)

Geology

Principles of Geology

Provides an understanding of earth processes (both on the earth's surface and at depth) and origin and classification of major rock types. Other topics include factors that have shaped the Earth, geologic events and processes occurring today, and ideas of future occurrences. 14 lessons, 2 exams. (3 credits)

Health

Science of Nutrition

This is an introductory course in which the principles of nutrition and how they relate to the life cycle are studied. The effect this course has upon the student's thinking relative to nutrition and upon the student's dietary habits is an important outcome. An objective is improvement, if needed, in the student's nutritional status. 18 lessons, 2 exams. (3 credits)

History

Western Civilization I

The origins and major political, economic, social, and intellectual developments of western civilization to 1500. 16 lessons, 2 exams. (3 credits)

Western Civilization II

Major political, economic, social, and intellectual developments of western civilization since 1500. 16 lessons, 2 exams. (3 credits)

Alaska, Land and Its People

A survey of Alaska from earliest days to present, its peoples, problems, and prospects. 11 lessons, 2 exams. (3 credits)

History of the U.S. I

The discovery of America to 1865: colonial period, revolution, formation of the constitution, western expansion, Civil War. 20 lessons, 2 exams. (3 credits)

History of the U.S. II

History of the U.S. from Reconstruction to the present. 15 lessons, 2 exams. (3 credits)

History of Alaska

Alaska from prehistoric times to the present. Research methodology and use of archival resources relating to Alaska's past. 14 lessons, 2 exams. (3 credits)

Maritime History of Alaska

A survey of Alaska's maritime history with emphasis on exploration and resource utilization by Natives, Russians, and Americans. 13 lessons, 2 exams. (3 credits)

Polar Exploration and Its Literature

A survey of polar exploration efforts of all Western nations from 870 A.D. to the present and a consideration of the historical sources of this effort. 16 lessons, 2 exams. (3 credits)

History of the American Military

This course is a history of the military's place in American life and society from the Colonial era to the early 1980s. 19 lessons, 2 exams. (3 credits)

History of U.S. Foreign Policy

Analysis of the evolution of U.S. foreign policy with emphasis on the post-World War II period and the emergence of a bipolar distribution of power. Includes major discussion of the Vietnam War, American policy in the Middle East, and the foreign policy views of the Kennedy, Nixon, Carter, and Reagan administrations. 19 lessons, 2 exams. (3 credits)

Journalism

Introduction to Mass Communications

History and principles of mass communications and the role of information media in American society. Introduction to professional aspects of mass communications, including print and broadcast. 18 lessons, 1 project, 2 exams. (3 credits)

Introduction to Broadcasting

Principles of broadcasting as they relate to the people of the United States, including history, government involvement, and social effects. 19 lessons, 4 projects, 3 exams. (3 credits)

Journalism and Yearbook Production and Theory

Writing, editing, and production techniques for high school publications including short courses on desktop publishing, basic and electronic photography, advertising, management, and legal liabilities. The value of First Amendment rights to our form of government. Access to a University of Alaska network provides communication with other teachers. 12 lessons, 1 project, no exams. (3 credits)

Linguistics

Nature of Language

The study of language: systematic analysis of human language and description of its grammatical structure, distribution, and diversity. 14 lessons, 2 exams. (3 credits)

Marketing

Principles of Advertising

Advertising including strategy, media use, creation and production of advertisements, and measurement of advertising effectiveness. 22 lessons, 2 exams. (3 credits)

Principles of Marketing

Role of marketing in society and economy. The business firm as a marketing system and management of the firm's marketing effort. 22 lessons, 3 exams. (3 credits)

Mathematics

Basic College Mathematics

Operations with whole numbers, fractions, decimals, and signed numbers. Percents and ratios. Evaluating algebraic expressions. Introduction to geometric figures. 16 lessons, 3 exams. (3 credits)

Elementary Algebra

First year high school algebra. Evaluating and simplifying algebraic expressions, solving first degree equations and inequalities, integral exponents, polynomials, factoring, rational expressions. 16 lessons, 3 exams. (3 credits)

Review of Elementary Algebra

This course is designed to assist students in reviewing material covered in the course described above. 6 lessons, 1 exam. (1 credit)

Intermediate Algebra

Second year high school algebra. Operations with rational functions, radicals, rational exponents, complex numbers, quadratic equations, and inequalities. Cartesian coordinate system and graphing, systems of equations, determinants and logarithms. 15 lessons, 3 exams. (3 credits)

Review of Intermediate Algebra

Reviews materials covered by the course described above. 6 lessons, 1 exam. (1 credit)

Review of Basic Geometry

High school geometry without formal proofs. Topics covered: basic definitions, measurements, parallel lines, triangles, polygons, circles, area, solid figures, and volume. 6 lessons, 1 exam. (1 credit)

Elementary Functions

A study of algebraic, logarithmic, and exponential functions, together with selected topics from algebra. 16 lessons, 2 exams. (3 credits)

Trigonometry

A study of the trigonometric functions. 16 lessons, 2 exams. (3 credits)

Concepts and Contemporary Applications of Mathematics

Applications of math in modern life, including uses of graph theory in management science. Probability and statistics in industry, government, and science. Geometry in engineering and astronomy. Problem solving emphasized. Requires access to a videocassette recorder. 15 lessons, 3 exams. (3 credits)

Concepts of Math

Mathematical thought and history for students with a limited math background. Mathematical reasoning rather than formal manipulation. May include number theory, topology, set theory, geometry, algebra, and analysis. 20 lessons, 3 exams. (3 credits)

Calculus I

Techniques and application of differential and integral calculus, vector analysis, partial derivatives, multiple integrals, and infinite series. 20 lessons, 3 exams. (4 credits)

Calculus II
Techniques and application of differential and integral calculus, vector analysis, partial derivatives, multiple integrals, and infinite series. 24 lessons, 3 exams. (4 credits)

Calculus III
Techniques and application of differential and integral calculus, vector analysis, partial derivatives, multiple integrals, and infinite series. 20 lessons, 3 exams. (4 credits)

Mathematics for Elementary School Teachers I
Elementary set theory, numeration systems, and algorithms of arithmetic, divisors, multiples, integers, introduction to rational numbers. Utilizes videocassettes. 15 lessons, 3 exams. (3 credits)

Mathematics for Elementary School Teachers II
A continuation of the course described above. Real number systems and subsystems, logic, informal geometry, metric system, probability, and statistics. 15 lessons, 3 exams. (3 credits)

Mineral Exploration

Mineral Exploration Techniques
This course covers the modern, scientific exploration and prospecting techniques utilized in Alaska since the 1970s. Exploration design, ore deposit models, exploration geochemistry, geophysics, drilling sampling, and geostatistics will be studied. 13 lessons, 2 exams. (3 credits)

Mineralogy

Minerals, Man, and the Environment
A general survey of the impact of the mineral industries on man's economic, political, and environmental systems. 13 lessons, 3 exams. (3 credits)

Music

Music Fundamentals
An introductory study of the language of music. Includes basic notation, melodic and rhythmic writing, scales, bass and treble clefs, and basic harmony. 15 lessons, 3 exams. (3 credits)

Appreciation of Music
A guide to the richer enjoyment of classical music through a study of the main periods, styles, and composers from the time of Gregorian chant to the present. Utilizes videocassettes and self-correcting audio listening exercises. 8 lessons, 2 projects, 2 exams. (3 credits)

Petroleum Technology

Fundamentals of Petroleum
This course is designed to give an overall view of the petroleum industry in terms that are understandable by the layperson as well as the professional. Included are lessons on petroleum geology, prospecting, leasing, drilling, production, pipelines, refining, processing, and marketing. 10 lessons, 2 exams. (3 credits)

Political Science

Introduction to American Government and Politics
Principles, institutions, and practices of American national government. The Constitution, federalism, interest groups, parties, public opinion, and elections. 15 lessons, 2 exams. (3 credits)

Psychology

Introduction to Psychology
Fundamentals and basic principles of general psychology, emphasizing both the natural science orientation and the social science orientation and including the cultural, environmental, heredity, and psychological basis for integrated behavior. Visual perception and its sensory basis. Audition and the other senses. Motivation and emotion. Basic processes in learning, problem solving, and thinking. Personality and psychological disorders and their prevention, treatment, and therapeutic strategies. 19 lessons, 2 projects, 5 exams. (3 credits)

Developmental Psychology in Cross-Cultural Perspective
The development of persons is examined from both a psychological and cross-cultural perspective. Key topics will be the development of cognition, personality, and social behavior with attention to relevant research on those cultures found in Alaska. 18 lessons, 8 exams. (3 credits)

Drugs and Drug Dependence
A multidisciplinary approach to the study of drugs and drug abuse emphasizing acute and chronic alcoholism, commonly abused drugs, law enforcement and legal aspects of drug abuse, medical use of drugs, physiological aspects of drug abuse, psychological and sociological causes and manifestations

of drug abuse, recommended drug education alternatives and plans, and the treatment and rehabilitation of acute and chronic drug users. 21 lessons, 6 exams. (3 credits)

Sociology

Introduction to Sociology

An introduction to the science of the individual as a social being, emphasizing the interactional, structural, and normative aspects of social behavior. An attempt is made to construct a cross-cultural framework in understanding and predicting human behavior. 18 lessons, 2 exams. (3 credits)

Social Institutions

Application of the concepts learned by developing and carrying out short surveys of sociological phenomena. Institutions of society, such as family, political and economic order, are examined, including their operation in the Alaska rural and cross-cultural milieu. 15 lessons, 2 exams. (3 credits)

The Family: A Cross-Cultural Perspective

The study of comparative patterns of marriage and family relationships. Various approaches such as the developmental, systems, and social psychological

are used to analyze these relationships. The family is followed through the stages of the family life cycle, such as mate selection, marriage, early marital interaction, parenthood, the middle and later years, and possible dissolution. Attention is given to cross-cultural differences in Alaska as well as in other parts of the world. 17 lessons, 2 exams. (3 credits)

Statistics

Elementary Probability and Statistics

Descriptive statistics, frequency distributions, sampling distributions, elementary probability, estimation of population parameters, hypothesis testing (one and two sample problems), correlation, simple linear regression, and one-way analysis of variance. Parametric and nonparametric methods. 14 lessons, 2 exams. (3 credits)

Travel Industry

Tourism Principles and Practices

Forces which influence the international and domestic hospitality, leisure, travel, and recreation industries. Socioeconomic models and measure of regional impact, demand, and supply. 16 lessons, 2 exams. (3 credits)

Arizona

Rio Salado Community College
Distance Learning Office
Department of Instructional Technology

640 North 1st Avenue
Phoenix, AZ   85003

(602) 223-4206

Geographic Access: Worldwide

DELIVERY SYSTEMS

Audio Conferencing
These classes are "live" interactive sessions connecting students from many locations by telephone. The instructor and students become a "universal" class brought together by telephone lines. The class may be taken from the student's own phone or from a conference site nearby. Conference-call classes link Rio students with other students all over the world.

Audiocassette
These courses are similar to print-based classes, but include supplementary information on audiocassette tapes to help with studies. Students can read lessons, then listen to additional information provided by the instructor or subject experts. The tapes are mailed to the student at no additional cost (there is a charge for failure to return tapes).

Broadcast Television
A wide variety of courses are broadcast every semester on local television channels 3, 8, and some educational cable channels. If a lesson is missed, the student may reserve that lesson on tape through Rio's Library/Media Department.

Computer Conferencing
The student may use a modem to connect a personal computer to the college's mainframe computer to gain access to assignments, fellow students, and instructor. Students without their own computers may take these classes from any of Rio's computer lab sites.

Interactive Audio/Video
Students, separated by location, can join together with each other and their instructor, using video technology with cameras and monitors. A special "pad camera" allows visual images to be viewed in a full-screen format.

Videocassette
In addition to printed materials, a "lecture" portion of these classes is provided on videotapes. The videotapes will be mailed at no cost with other course materials (there is a charge for failure to return tapes).

INSTITUTION DESCRIPTION

Rio Salado Community College was founded in 1978 and is a noncampus college of the Maricopa County Community College District. Courses and programs, both credit and noncredit, are provided at community facilities, in the plants of business and industry, and through television, cable, radio, video conferencing, and audio- and videocassettes.

Rio Salado offers courses in several alternative delivery formats for students who, because of time, distance, or limited mobility, do not have easy access to traditional classes. Each course offered in these formats is equivalent to the same course offered in a classroom setting and is transferable as such. In every class, students have an opportunity for telephone or in-person contact with the instructor.

Accreditation: NCA

Official/Contact: Betsy Frank, Coordinator

Admission Requirements: Open enrollment.

Tuition: $29 per semester hour credit plus a $5 nonrefundable registration fee. Textbooks must be purchased by the student and can be obtained only from the Rio Salado bookstore located on the South Mountain Community College campus. Books may be ordered by phone. MasterCard and VISA accepted.

Degree Credit: It is possible to earn a two-year degree by taking the courses offered through the various delivery systems of Rio Salado Community College.

Grading: Most courses have midterm and final examinations that must be taken at a designated site. Students who are unable to attend regularly scheduled exams may schedule other proctored arrangements upon the approval of the college. Letter grades are assigned. Credit is awarded in semester hour units.

Library: The Library/Media Department supports all officially registered students.

COURSES OFFERED

Art

Art History: Prehistory to Gothic
An audiographic-conference class. (3 credits)

Business

Import/Export Business
An interactive audio/video class. (1 credit)

Communications

Introduction to Human Communication
An audio-conference class. (3 credits)

Economics

Macroeconomic Principles
An audiographic-conference class. (3 credits)

Education

MCCCD Certification Course
An audiocassette course. (3 credits)

English

Fundamentals of Writing
An audiocassette course. (3 credits)

19th Century American Fiction
An audiocassette course. (3 credits)

Creative Writing
A computer-conference class. (3 credits)

Family Life

The Modern Family
A broadcast television course over KAET-TV Channel 8. (3 credits)

Geology

Introduction to Physical Geology I: Physical Lecture
A broadcast television course over KAET-TV Channel 8. (3 credits)

Health

Healthful Living
A broadcast television course over KAET-TV Channel 8. (3 credits)

Humanities

Human Origins and the Development of Culture
A computer-conferencing class. (3 credits)

Information Systems

Business Systems Analysis and Design
A computer-conferencing class. (3 credits)

Management

Owning and Operating a Small Business
A broadcast television course over KAET-TV Channel 8. (3 credits)

Human Relations in Business
An audio-conference class. (3 credits)

Marketing

Principles of Marketing
A broadcast television course over KAET-TV Channel 8. (3 credits)

Mathematics

Intermediate Algebra
A videocassette course. (3 credits)

College Algebra
A videocassette course. (3 credits)

Philosophy

Business Ethics
An audio-conference class. (3 credits)

Psychology

Introduction to Psychology
A broadcast television course over KAET-TV Channel 8. (3 credits)

Reading

Critical and Evaluative Reading
An audiocassette course. (3 credits)

Sociology

Introduction to Sociology
An audiocassette course. (3 credits)

Statistics

Business Statistics
An interactive audio/video class. (3 credits)

Wastewater Management

Water/Wastewater Operational Concepts
An interactive audio/video class. (3 credits)

University of Arizona
VideoCampus
Extended University

1955 East Sixth Street
Tucson, AZ   85719

(800) 955-8632 *Fax:* (602) 621-3269

Geographic Access: Nationwide

DELIVERY SYSTEMS

Broadcast Television
Courses are broadcast on People's Choice TV and may be recorded on student's VCR.

Satellite Network
Some courses are offered on the satellite network of the National Technological University.

Videocassette
Videotapes supplement study guides and textbooks.

INSTITUTION DESCRIPTION

The University of Arizona is a state institution and land-grant college. It was established in 1885. The VideoCampus is part of the opportunities offered by the University of Arizona Extended University.

Through the VideoCampus, students can take University of Arizona courses for credit or enrichment in the comfort and convenience of home or workplace. VideoCampus courses are taught by University of Arizona faculty and carry all the academic credibility of the University of Arizona. Using video technology—videotape, live interactive microwave, cable, and satellite—VideoCampus delivers courses to Tucson, Sierra Vista, and locations around the world. The majority of course offerings are technically oriented to appeal to engineering students. Students can work on degrees in optical sciences, electrical engineering, and reliability and quality engineering by taking a few courses each semester on VideoCampus.

Businesses and organizations throughout the world use the University of Arizona VideoCampus for training and education. Employees receive university credit toward their degrees, earn professional certificates, and use special video courses customized for their needs. Site coordinators are assigned to work with the students.

Accreditation: NCA

Official/Contact: June Dempsey, Director, Extended University

Admission Requirements: If studying for credit, formal admission to the University of Arizona is necessary.

Tuition: Fees for VideoCampus credit and noncredit courses vary. $140 per unit of credit for in-state employee-students under a corporate plan, $420 per unit of credit for out-of-state employee-students. Tuition for in-state University of Arizona students $93 per unit, out-of-state students $420 per unit. Other fees may apply. Tape delivery charges may also be added. Textbooks must be purchased by the student.

Degree Credit: VideoCampus courses can apply to academic programs, including Bachelor of Arts degree (interdisciplinary studies major), Professional Certificate Award or Master of Science degree in reliability and quality engineering, Master of Science degree in optical sciences, Master of Library Science degree, Graduate Certificate in School Librarianship.

Grading: If the student is taking a VideoCampus course in the Tucson area, examinations may be taken at the University of Arizona Extended University office. Students taking courses at company sites have examinations proctored by their site coordinator. Credit is awarded in semester hour units.

Library: Students residing in the Tucson area have access to all library services of the University of Arizona.

COURSES OFFERED

Aerospace and Mechanical Engineering

Reliability Engineering
Time-to-failure, failure-rate, and reliability determination for early, useful and wear-out lives. Equipment reliability reduction, spare parts provisioning, reliability growth, reliability allocation. (3 units)

Probabilistic Mechanical Design
Application of probability theory and statistics to mechanical and structural design, modern mechanical reliability methods, design philosophy. (3 units)

Anthropology

Culture and the Individual
Cultural and psychosociological dimensions of human development and human behavior. (3 units)

Bilingual Reading and Writing

Bilingual Reading and Writing
Analysis of reading and writing situations encountered by bilingual students. Phonological, semantic, and syntactic aspects of instruction. Methods and materials. (3 units)

Electrical Engineering

Active and Passive Filter Design
Approximation methods for realizing Butterworth, Chebychev, Thomson, and Elliptic filters. Verification and testing of realizations. (3 units)

Digital Signal Processing
Discrete-time signals and systems, z-transforms, discrete Fourier transform, fast Fourier transform, digital filter design. (3 units)

Fundamentals of Device Electronics
Introductory device aspects of semiconductors. Crystal structures, one-dimensional quantum theory, parabolic bands, carrier statistics, SRH centers, drift and diffusion. (3 units)

Solid State Circuits
Introduction to unit step processes in semiconductor manufacturing. Introduction to various semiconductor processes, with emphasis on process and device integration issues for major integrated circuit processes. Basic circuit and design techniques including subsystem design and device scaling. Fundamentals of chip layout and integrated circuit design methodology for solid state circuits. (3 units)

Energy Conversion
Principles and operating characteristics of rotating machinery and electromagnetic transducers, single-phase and polyphase transformer operation, laboratory demonstrations and tests of transformers and rotating machinery. (3 units)

Random Processes for Engineering Applications
Probability, random variables, processes, correlation functions and spectra with applications to communications, control, and computers. (3 units)

Digital Image Processing
Image statistics, models, transforms. Enhancement and restoration, coding, tomography. (3 units)

Synthesis of Control Systems
State feedback control, stabilization and pole placement, observers, optimal control by calculus of variations and Pontryagin's minimum principle, dynamic programming. (3 units)

Analog Integrated Circuits
Non-switching aspects of analog integrated circuits using bipolar or CMOS technologies. Biasing, DC behavior, small signal behavior. Emphasis on use of physical reasoning, identification of circuit func-

tions, and use of suitable approximations to facilitate understanding and analysis. (3 units)

Electronic Packaging Principles

Introduction to problems encountered at all levels of packaging. Thermal, mechanical, electrical reliability, materials and systems integration. Future trends in packaging. (3 units)

Power Electronics

Design and analysis of switching converters: topologies, state-space averaging, feedback, power bipolar transistor and MOSFET characteristics, magnetic modeling and design. (3 units)

Engineering Applications of Graph Theory

Terminology, algorithms, and complexity analysis will be included. Application areas will include but are not limited to communication networks, VLSI routing and layout, analog circuits, and mapping of sequential and parallel algorithms onto computer architectures. (3 units)

Modern Computer Architecture

Overview of uniprocessor architectures, introduction to parallel processing, pipelining, vector processing, multiprocessing, multicomputing, memory design for parallel computers, cache design, communication networks for parallel processing, algorithms for parallel processing. (3 units)

Fundamentals of Computer Networks

Introduction to computer networks and protocols. Study of the ISO open systems interconnection model, with emphasis on the physical, data link, network, and transport layers. Discussion of IEEE 802, OSI, and Internet protocols. (3 units)

Judaic Studies

Women in Judaism

Images of Jewish women in Jewish and other texts. Texts include religious, historical, and literary genres from biblical, medieval, and modern sources. The course will deal with Jewish women as mothers, leaders, stereotypes, and current feminist viewpoints. (3 units)

Library Science

Literature for Children's Librarians

Literature for younger children, including picture books. Traditional literature for use with children. Reference materials. Fantasy, humor, realistic fic-

tion, poetry, classics, informational books. Criticism and reviewing of children's literature. (3 units)

Literature for Adolescents

Literature to meet recreational and developmental needs of the junior and senior high school age, including some books for adults. Reviewing and book talks. (3 units)

School Library Administration and Organization

Services, finances, personnel, evaluation, facilities, organization and technical services in the school library. (3 units)

Library Collection Development

Principles of collection development, evaluation and review of materials, selection tools, acquisition of materials, problems in selection, including censorship. (3 units)

Organization, Cataloging, and Classification of Materials

Cataloging library materials, filing, and searching automated bibliographic databases. (3 units)

Basic Reference

Survey of general reference sources, discussion of reference technique. (3 units)

Optical Sciences

Electromagnetic Waves

Maxwell's equations, Vector and scalar wave equations. Vector and scalar potentials and gauges. Green's functions and boundary value problems. Reflection and refraction. Optics of isotropic materials. Optics of crystals. (3 units)

Fourier and Statistical Optics

Mathematical background, convolution, the Fourier transform, linear filtering, two-dimensional operations, diffraction, image formation, probability and random variables, stochastic processes, random data. (4 units)

Digital Image Processing

Image statistics, models, transforms, enhancement and restoration, coding, tomography. (3 units)

Russian

Russian Civilization and Culture: Pre-Christian Era to the Present

Selected topics in Russian culture and civilization: architecture, film, fine art, literature, music and theater within their artistic, historical, ideological, and sociological contexts. Taught in English. (3 units)

Spanish

Second-Semester Spanish
Uses the oral approach. Assumes the student has had some contact with the language. (4 units)

Second Year Spanish
Uses a thematic approach to studying the language with emphasis on expanding communication skills. (4 units)

Special Education

Behavior Principles for the Handicapped
Use of behavior principles to modify the behavior of handicapped persons, especially moderately and severely handicapped. (3 units)

Language Development for the Exceptional Child
Pragmatic, semantic, and syntactic aspects of prelinguistic and linguistic development in exceptional children and youth. Cognitive and social bases of language development. (3 units)

Statistics

Statistics for Engineering and the Physical Sciences
Probability theory, point and interval estimation, hypothesis testing and regression analysis, applications to quality control and reliability theory. (3 units)

Systems and Industrial Engineering

Engineering Statistics
Statistical methodology of estimation, testing hypotheses, goodness-of-fit, nonparametric methods and decision theory as it relates to engineering practice. Significant emphasis on the underlying statistical modeling and assumptions. (3 units)

Expert Systems
Building, testing, and evaluating expert systems. Computer systems that emulate the human and draw conclusions based on incomplete or inaccurate data. Each student will build an expert system using commercially available expert system shells. (3 units)

Women's Studies

Women in Western Culture
Examines the various ways in which women have been depicted in western philosophy, literature, and the arts from the classical Greek period to the present. Explores women's cultural expressions and representations of themselves. (3 units)

Women in Judaism
Images of Jewish women in Jewish and other texts. Texts include religious, historical, and literary genres from biblical, medieval, and modern sources. The course will deal with Jewish women as mothers, leaders, stereotypes, and current feminist viewpoints. (3 units)

Arkansas

Arkansas Telecommunications Consortium
Arkansas Technical University

Tucker Hall, Suite 21
Russellville, AR   72801

(501) 968-0278

Geographic Access: Arkansas

DELIVERY SYSTEMS

Broadcast Television
Telecourses are broadcast over the Arkansas Education Television Network which airs throughout the state.

INSTITUTION DESCRIPTION

The Arkansas Telecommunications Consortium (ATC), in a joint effort with the Arkansas Education Television Network (AETN), selected a core group of telecourses to offer at regular intervals. These classes were selected to meet the basic/general education requirements at the universities and colleges across Arkansas. ATC and AETN offer five courses per semester and three during the summer term. Although the courses are aired at off times (e.g., 5:30 AM, etc.), students record the episodes for later viewing and study.

The participating institutions and personal contacts are:

- Garland County Community College (Hot Springs National Park AR), Dr. Alan Hoffman, (501) 767-9371
- Henderson State University (Arkadelphia AR), La-Juana Mooney, (501) 246-5511
- Mississippi County Community College (Blytheville AR), (501) 762-1020
- North Arkansas Community College (Harrison AR), Dr. Gordon Watts, (501) 743-3000
- Phillips County Community College (Helena AR), Dr. Gene Weber, (501) 338-6474
- Southern Arkansas University - Main Campus (Magnolia AR), James Genandt, (501) 235-4000
- Southern Arkansas University Tech (Camden AR), Judy Harrison, (501) 574-4500
- University of Arkansas at Little Rock, Lifelong Education (Little Rock AR), (501) 569-3000
- Westark Community College, Off-Campus Credit/Continuing Education (Fort Smith AR), (501) 785-7004

Accreditation: All participating institutions are accredited by NCA.

Official/Contact: Barbara A. Berry, President, ATC

Admission Requirements: Open enrollment. Requirements may vary among the member institutions. Contact the college of choice for proper procedure.

Tuition: Contact the college of choice for current information regarding tuition, fees, and other materials costs. Textbooks may be purchased at any of the college bookstores.

Degree Credit: Credit earned by successful completion of a telecourse may be applied to a degree program. Students anticipating transfer to a four-year institution should determine beforehand if the credits earned will transfer.

Grading: Letter grades are assigned. Examinations must be taken on campus or under the supervision of an approved proctor. Credit is awarded in semester hour units. The courses described below generally carry three semester credits.

Library: Students have access to the library resources of the institutions in which they are officially enrolled.

COURSES OFFERED

Gerontology

Growing Old in a New Age
This gerontology and health sciences series helps students understand the process of aging and its impact on the lives of individuals and society. The programs draw upon the expertise of social and biological scientists, medical professionals, and the personal experiences of retired individuals to compel students to re-examine their attitudes toward aging. The series is hosted by broadcast journalist Susan Stamberg and features conversations with more than 75 older adults. Available through the University of Arkansas at Little Rock. 13 one-hour video programs. (3 credits)

History

Americas
The programs in this telecourse examine the contemporary history, politics, and social structures of the countries of Latin America and the Caribbean. They feature the dilemmas of national development, authoritarianism and democratization, urbanization, race, religion, and revolutions as well as the Latin American presence in the United States. Available through the University of Arkansas at Little Rock. 10 one-hour video programs. (3 credits)

Humanities

Humanities Through the Arts
Maya Angelou, noted poet-author, is host of this diverse examination of seven major art forms: film, drama, music, literature, painting, sculpture, and architecture. This multimedia humanities survey is an exciting blend of sights, sounds, impressions, and ideas that teach students both the history and elements of each art form. 30 half-hour video programs. (3 credits)

Political Science

Government By Consent
This American government survey provides students with an understanding of democracy, the U.S. Constitution, political parties, the three branches of government, due process, and more. The series marries political science instruction with examples of how students can involve themselves in government. Program topics include federalism, PACs, congress, the legislative process, domestic policy, foreign policy, the judiciary, first amendment freedoms, and rights of the accused. 26 half-hour video programs. (3 credits)

Psychology

The World of Abnormal Psychology
This abnormal psychology series helps students distinguish the typical from the abnormal and the functional from the dysfunctional. It examines the complex factors that cause behavioral disorders and demonstrates the psychological, biological, and social approaches to treatment and discusses current research. The programs feature actual patient case studies, and the interviews with these patients provide an invaluable perspective on the emotional toll paid by those who suffer from behavioral disorders. Commentary by therapists and other mental health professionals presents the multiple approaches to treatment. 13 one-hour video programs. (3 credits)

Psychology: The Study of Human Behavior
An introductory psychology telecourse designed for adult students seeking general education psychology instruction from colleges and universities. The course introduces students to the basic content of psychology: the facts, theories, perspectives, and terminology. It encourages critical thinking about issues in psychology and promotes an appreciation of the diversity of human beings and human behavior. The programs put student viewers in contact with individuals who are deeply involved in the lesson's subject. The distant learner is exposed to authorities whose research has helped shape modern psychology. 26 half-hour video programs. (3 credits)

Spanish

Destinos: An Introduction to Spanish, Part 1
This introductory Spanish language series teaches students how to listen, speak, read, and write in Spanish. The programs use the powerful appeal of the "telenovela" to make the language come alive. A mystery story encourages basic language skills as well as understanding of gestures and cultural clues that enrich communication. The series also exposes

students to the diverse cultural contexts in which Spanish is spoken as the story unfolds in Spain, Argentina, Mexico, Puerto Rico, and other countries. 26 half-hour video programs. (3 credits)

Garland County Community College
See **Arkansas Telecommunications Consortium**

Henderson State University
See **Arkansas Telecommunications Consortium**

Mississippi County Community College
See **Arkansas Telecommunications Consortium**

North Arkansas Community College
See **Arkansas Telecommunications Consortium**

Phillips County Community College
See **Arkansas Telecommunications Consortium**

Southern Arkansas University - Main Campus
See **Arkansas Telecommunications Consortium**

Southern Arkansas University Tech
See **Arkansas Telecommunications Consortium**

University of Arkansas at Little Rock
See **Arkansas Telecommunications Consortium**

Westark Community College
See **Arkansas Telecommunications Consortium**

California

Allen Hancock College
See **INTELECOM**

American River College
See **Northern California Telecommunications Consortium**

Antelope Valley College
See **INTELECOM**

Bakersfield College
See **INTELECOM**

Barstow College
See **INTELECOM**

California Institute of Integral Studies
Transformative Learning Online Integral Studies Doctoral Program
765 Ashbury Street
San Francisco, CA   94117

(415) 753-6100; *Fax:* (415) 753-1169

Geographic Access: Worldwide

DELIVERY SYSTEMS

Online Services
Transformative Learning Online (TLO) is supported by the Electronic University Network, a rich learning environment for collaborative learning. Computer-mediated activities link students and faculty and provide a central focus for the development of learning communities. These activities include academic courses, private cohort group conferences, exchange of papers and projects, ongoing feedback through online dialogue, student advising and technical support, library services, student lounge, issues forums, learning center, and guest faculty presentations and discussions.

INSTITUTION DESCRIPTION

The California Institute of Integral Studies is a nonprofit, nonsectarian graduate school. It was founded in 1968 by Haridas Chaudhuri and was originally known as the California Institute of Asian Studies. In 1980 the present name was adopted to indicate the Institute's commitment to a unifying vision of humanity, nature, world, and spirit. The use of the term "integral" stems form the integral yoga of Sri Aurobindo (1872-1950), poet, philosopher, political activist, and sage of India, and from the integral philosophy, psychology, and yoga of Dr. Chaudhuri, who extended Aurobindo's work.

In fall 1992 the School for Transformative Learning was established within the California Institute of Integral Studies. The school is devoted to defining, researching, and promoting integral approaches to learning and creative social change. Its primary mission is to form a community of thought and practice that can support integral learning within both the institute and the community at large. The school applies Haridas Chaudhuri's principles of integralism to education, focusing on learning which permits people to develop simultaneously the intellect, the spirit, and the imagination, and to incorporate affective and experiential as well as conceptual learning. It will cultivate educational approaches that encourage: (1) a variety of learning modalities, (2) interdisciplinary work in fields such as science, literature, social science, and the arts, and (3) a valuing of both cultural diversity and cultural coherence.

The TLO doctoral program offers an innovative approach to studying and researching transformative change in individuals, groups, communities, and cultures. Using collaborative approaches in study and research, students and faculty participate together in developing theoretical models and research methods that support the study and practice of transformative change. TLO is supported by the Electronic University Network, a learning environment for collaborative learning. Upon enrollment in TLO, each student is grouped in a learning community: a cohort of students and others who work and learn together. This cohort engages their courses at a distance via electronic communication, supplemented by written, audio, and visual materials. Each cohort has a primary faculty person who works with the group throughout the two-year duration of the cohort.

Accreditation: WASC

Official/Contact: Dr. Steve Eskow, TLO Faculty Leader

Admission Requirements: Candidates for admission must possess: extensive experience creating contexts to evoke transformative learning and change; demonstrated capacity to learn and work both independently and collaboratively; interest in participating in an ongoing experimental venture in learning that will require abilities to tolerate ambiguity and search for new directions as new paths are opened and uncertainties in the intellectual journey encountered; interest in research that uses the student him/herself and the members of the learning team as subjects of inquiry; a completed Master's degree (exception made only for candidates of high promise who agree to take additional coursework in order to complete this requirement).

Tuition: 1994 tuition $265 per quarter unit. Students "meet" with their cohort group in the online community for a period of two years. During this period students enroll for a minimum of six quarter units per quarter. Students will then continue to enroll for additional courses and independent study, including a dissertation project, at their individual pace until they complete the required 90 quarter units for graduation. An application fee of $60 due with application; enrollment deposit of $200 due upon acceptance of application into the program (credited to tuition); registration fee of $60 due per quarter.

Degree Credit: In the online Ph.D. program, each learning community develops specific curricula and modes of learning appropriate to individual and group goals. Students complete a total of 54 units over a two-year period as participants in a learning community. Upon completion of the 54 units, a qualifying assessment of the student's progress is required. The remaining units for the dissertation, language requirements, and electives, are completed independently. The 90 credits required for the degree are distributed among areas of learning as follows: core studies, 36 units; milieu studies (individual and group learning contracts, 18 units; language, 6 units, electives 15 units, dissertation colloquium, 3 units; dissertation, 12 units.

Grading: Qualifying assessment of a student's progress is accomplished upon the completion of the various unit requirements.

Library: Students may gain access to the various bibliographic and full-text searching services.

COURSES OFFERED

Transformative Learning

Foundations of the Integral Worldview
The courses in this component explore the philosophical perspectives that give rise to an integral vision of learning and change, analyze the influence of culture and community on the processes of creating meaning, and examine theories of human development within individuals, groups, institutions, and communities. Courses I, II, III, IV, V, and VI are two-unit courses pursued over a two-year period, one course per quarter.

Design and Conduct of Inquiry
These courses investigate conflicting paradigms in social science research and pursue mastery of qualitative research methods relevant to issues surrounding transformative learning and change. Courses I, II, III, IV, V, and VI are two-unit courses pursued over a period of two years, one course per quarter.

Learning and Change in Human Systems
Courses in this component explore transformative learning and change as both content and process within individuals, small groups, and larger systems. Attention is given to critical and creative thinking, the development of self, the development of collaborative processes within the learning group, and the ongoing process of the learning community in reaching its goals. Emphasis is placed on cognitive, affective, intuitive, physiological and spiritual dimen-

sions of individual experience, and on parallel dimensions within groups, institutions, communities, and cultures. Courses I, II, III, IV, V, and VI are two-unit courses pursued over a two-year period, one course per quarter.

Cerritos College
See **INTELECOM**

Citrus College
See **INTELECOM**

Coast Community College District
See **INTELECOM**

College of Alameda
See **Northern California Telecommunications Consortium**

College of Marin
See **Northern California Telecommunications Consortium**

College of San Mateo
See **Northern California Telecommunications Consortium**

College of the Canyons
See **INTELECOM**

Columbia College
See **Northern California Telecommunications Consortium**

Compton Community College
See **INTELECOM**

Consumnes River College
See **Northern California Telecommunications Consortium**

Contra Costa College
See **Northern California Telecommunications Consortium**

Crafton Hills College
See **INTELECOM**

Cuyamaca College
See **INTELECOM**

DeAnza College
See **Northern California Telecommunications Consortium**

El Camino College
See **INTELECOM**

Evergreen Valley College
See **Northern California Telecommunications Consortium**

Foothill College
See **Northern California Telecommunications Consortium**

Fullerton College
See **INTELECOM**

Glendale Community College
See **INTELECOM**

INTELECOM
Intelligent Telecommunications
College Credit Telecourses
Plaza Centre
150 East Colorado Blvd., Suite 300
Pasadena, CA   91105-1937

(818) 796-7300

Geographic Access: Southern California

DELIVERY SYSTEMS

Broadcast Television
INTELECOM uses a variety of broadcast and cable channels to reach the large viewing served. The Community College Instructional Network (CCIN) is an instructional delivery system owned and operated by INTELECOM. It is designed primarily to allow the feeding of college-level instructional television programming to all cable companies in the Southern California area. PBS stations that broadcast telecourses are KCET Channel 28 in Los Angeles, KOCE Channel 50

in Orange County, KVCR Channel 24 in San Bernardino, and KPBS Channel 15 in San Diego. SDITV is The Learning Channel in San Diego.

INSTITUTION DESCRIPTION

Since the fall of 1970, over 605,000 Southern California residents have enrolled in college credit telecourses offered by INTELECOM, a nonprofit corporation. Telecourses are offered through the cooperative efforts of 42 community colleges. When a student enrolls in a course, he/she becomes a student at one of these colleges. An on-campus instructor serves as a contact for the course, answers questions, provides review opportunities, and evaluates examinations or study projects. Telecourses offered via INTELECOM are described in the Courses Offered section. Prospective students should contact the community college nearest them for enrollment procedures. The INTELECOM member colleges with telephone number contacts are:

- Allen Hancock College (Santa Maria CA) (905) 922-6966, Ext. 475
- Antelope Valley College (Lancaster CA), (805) 943-3241, Ext. 222
- Bakersfield College (Bakersfield CA), (805) 395-4535
- Barstow College (Barstow CA), (619) 252-2411, Ext. 220
- Cerritos College (Norwalk CA), (310) 860-2451, Ext. 455
- Citrus College (Glendora CA), (818) 914-8881
- Coast Community College District (Costa Mesa CA, (714) 241-6142
- College of the Canyons (Santa Clarita CA), (805) 259-7800, Ext. 330
- Compton Community College (Compton CA), (310) 637-2660, Ext. 2535
- Crafton Hills College (Yucaipa CA), (909) 888-6511, Ext. 1131
- Cuyamaca College (El Cajon CA), (619) 670-1980, Ext. 444
- El Camino College (Torrance CA), (310) 715-3313
- Fullerton College (Fullerton CA), (714) 992-7023
- Glendale Community College (Glendale CA), (818) 240-1000, Ext. 5149

- Irvine Valley College (Irvine CA), (714) 559-3262
- Long Beach City College (Long Beach CA), (310) 420-4133
- Los Angeles Community College District (Los Angeles CA), (213) 666-4488
- Mira Costa College (Oceanside CA), (619) 727-2121, Ext. 262
- Moorpark College (Moorpark CA), (805) 378-1404
- Mt. San Antonio College (Walnut CA), (714) 594-5611, Ext. 5410
- Oxnard College (Oxnard CA), (805) 986-5814
- Palomar College (San Marcos CA), (619) 744-1150, Ext. 2430
- Pasadena City College (Pasadena CA), (818) 585-7108
- Rancho Santiago Community College (Santa Ana CA), (714) 564-6725
- Riverside Community College (Riverside CA), (909) 684-3240, Ext. 328
- Saddleback College (Mission Viejo CA), (714) 582-4518
- San Bernardino Valley College (San Bernardino CA), (909) 888-6511, Ext. 1131
- Southwestern College (Chula Vista CA), (619) 421-6700, Ext. 302
- Ventura College (Ventura CA), (805) 654-6465
- Victor Valley College (Victorville CA), (619) 245-4271, Ext. 263

Accreditation: All member colleges are accredited by WASC.

Official/Contact: Gretchen Plano, Member Services Coordinator

Admission Requirements: Open enrollment. Registration for a course can be accomplished by telephone.

Tuition: Generally, $13 per unit of credit. Contact the college of choice for current information regarding tuition and other fees. Textbooks and study materials must be purchased by the student.

Degree Credit: INTELECOM is not a degree-granting institution. Credit earned is awarded by the institution in which the student enrolls and may be applied toward a degree and/or used in transfer to a four-year institution.

Grading: Examinations must be proctored. The grading system of the member colleges may vary, but standard letter grades are the norm. Credit is awarded by the college of choice, usually in semester hour units.

Library: Officially registered students have access to the learning resources facility of their college. Students are also encouraged to use their local community libraries.

COURSES OFFERED

Anthropology

Faces of Culture
Discover the customs, cultures, and societies the world over and how our own culture integrates into this broad range of human possibilities. 26 programs. Broadcast over KCET, KOCE, KVCR, SDITV, and CCIN.

Astronomy

Project Universe
Easy-to-understand, yet comprehensive exploration of the solar system, stars, galaxies, and the universe. 30 programs. Broadcast over KOCE, KVCR, and CCIN.

Business

Business and the Law
Explores and illustrates how the law and the legal system interface with the many facets of business, including sales, contracts, employment practices, and government regulations. 30 programs. Broadcast over KOCE and CCIN.

The Business File
Introduces how business operates and functions within our economic system. Organization, management, interaction, productivity, and technology are discussed by industry and business leaders nationwide. 28 programs. Broadcast over KOCE, KVCR, and CCIN.

Child Development

Time to Grow
A comprehensive look at child development, embracing issues of biology, experience, development stages, and guidance. 26 programs. Broadcast over KCET, KOCE, KVCR, SDITV, and CCIN.

Computer Literacy

The New Literacy
Practical approach to computers including terminology and methods of data processing, as well as computer applications in a broad range of settings and applications. 30 programs. Broadcast over KOCE and CCIN.

Economics

Economics U$A
Introduces the tools and concepts of economic analysis including income, inflation, unemployment, banking, competition, wages, and tariffs. 28 programs. Broadcast over KCET, SDITV, and CCIN.

English

Literary Visions
Dramatizations and conversations with contemporary writers explore fiction, poetry, and drama with emphasis on plot, characters, style, symbolism, and more. 26 programs. Broadcast over KCET, SDITV, and CCIN.

Geology

Earth Revealed
Examines how the Earth's dynamic and interacting geologic systems relate to the development of life and the delicate secrets of our environment. 26 programs. Broadcast over KCET, KOCE, KPBS, and CCIN.

Government

Government By Consent
Seeks to encourage participation and involvement in government by dissolving the perception that government is a remote and larger-than-life process. 26 programs. Broadcast over KOCE, KVCR, and CCIN.

Family Life

Portrait of a Family
Examines the forms and changing definitions of the family in the closing decade of the 20th Century. 26 programs. Broadcast over KOCE, KVCR, and CCIN.

Finance

Personal Finance and Money Management
The basics of personal budgets, buying, home ownership, investing, insurance, wills, and more. 26 programs. Broadcast over KOCE and CCIN.

History

America in Perspective
Great location, photographs, and personal interviews with historians and eye-witnesses to historical events combined to reveal the history of the United States. 26 programs. Broadcast over KOCE and CCIN.

American Adventure
Illustrates how wars, treaties, elections, and legislation have shaped the government and the people of the United States from its beginning through 1877. 26 programs. Broadcast over KCET, KOCE, KVCR, SDITV, and CCIN.

Humanities

Humanities Through the Arts
The humanities as expressed through film, theatre, music, literature, art, and architecture, highlighting the meaning and evaluation of individual artists and their works. 30 programs. Broadcast over KOCE, SDITV, and CCIN.

Management

Taking the Lead: The Management Revolution
Emphasizing the major functions of management such as planning, organizing, staffing, directing and controlling, this series presents topics of current importance and proves that the strategies of the 80s are no longer relevant in the challenging environment of the 90s. 26 programs. Broadcast by KCET, KOCE, KPBS, and CCIN.

Marketing

Marketing
Provides the student with insight into the complex interrelationships behind the marketing process, by showing how real-life marketing managers handle the full range of real world marketing problems. 26 programs. Broadcast over KOCE and CCIN.

The Sales Connection
From identifying prospects to closing the deal, provides novice or seasoned salespeople with tools and insight into today's markets. 26 programs. Broadcast over KCET, KVCR, and CCIN.

Oceanography

Oceanus: The Marine Environment
An Emmy Award-winning series focuses on the marine environment as a truly unique feature of planet earth. 30 programs. Broadcast over KOCE, KVCR, and CCIN.

Psychology

Psychology: The Study of Human Behavior
Designed to provide a diversity of viewpoints, this series emphasizes critical thinking while presenting everyday applications of psychology. 26 programs. Broadcast over KOCE, KVCR, SDITV, and CCIN.

Small Business Management

Something Ventured
Provides present and future entrepreneurs with the tools they need to compete effectively in the world of commerce. 26 programs. Broadcast over KOCE and CCIN.

Sociology

Sociological Imagination
Illustrates major sociological concepts through an in-depth look at groups, communities, institutions, and social situations. 26 programs. Broadcast over KCET, KOCE, KVCR, SDITV, and CCIN.

Irvine Valley College
See **INTELECOM**

Laney College
See **Northern California Telecommunications Consortium**

Long Beach City College
See **INTELECOM**

Los Angeles Community College District
See **INTELECOM**

Mendocino College

See **Northern California Telecommunications Consortium**

Merritt College

See **Northern California Telecommunications Consortium**

Mira Costa College

See **INTELECOM**

Modesto Junior College

See **Northern California Telecommunications Consortium**

Monterey Peninsula College

See **Northern California Telecommunications Consortium**

Moorpark College

See **INTELECOM**

Mt. San Antonio College

See **INTELECOM**

Northern California Telecommunications Consortium

2595 Capitol Oaks Drive
Sacramento, CA   95833-2926

(916) 565-0188

Geographic Access: Northern California

DELIVERY SYSTEMS

Broadcast Television
Telecourses are aired over stations KRCB/Channel 22, KQED/Channel 9, and KVIE/Channel 6.

INSTITUTION DESCRIPTION

Since 1972, Northern California residents have enrolled in college credit telecourses offered by the Northern California Telecommunications Consortium (NCTC) through the cooperative efforts of many Northern California community colleges. Over fifty courses have been offered at community colleges from Weed to Coalinga, Susanville to Fresno, and the San Francisco Bay area. When students enroll in a course, they officially become a student at one of these cooperating colleges. An instructor on campus will serve as the personal contact for each course, answering questions, providing review opportunities, and evaluating midterm and final examinations or study projects.

Availability of courses varies from semester to semester and campus to campus. Students should determine the course(s) desired and contact the nearest college for information on availability for enrollment.

The following colleges are participants in the consortium. If the prospective student is unsure which community college is the closest to home, contact the NCTC office at (916) 565-0188 for assistance.

- American River College (Sacramento CA), (916) 484-8011
- College of Alameda (Alameda CA), (415) 522-7221
- College of Marin (Kentfield CA), (415) 883-2211
- College of San Mateo (San Mateo CA), (415) 574-6161
- Columbia College (Columbia CA), (209) 533-5100
- Contra Costa College (San Pablo CA), (415) 235-7800
- Consumnes River College (Sacramento CA), (916) 688-7300
- DeAnza College (Cupertino CA), (408) 864-5678
- Evergreen Valley College (San Jose CA), (408) 274-7900
- Foothill College (Los Altos Hills CA), (415) 960-4600
- Laney College (Oakland CA), (415) 834-5740
- Mendocino College (Ukiah CA), (707) 468-3100
- Merritt College (Oakland CA), (415) 531-4911
- Modesto Junior College (Modesto CA), (209) 575-6067
- Monterey Peninsula College (Monterey CA), (408) 646-4010
- Sacramento City College (Sacramento CA), (916) 449-7111
- San Joaquin Delta College (Stockton CA), (209) 474-5051

- Santa Rosa Junior College (Santa Rosa CA), (707) 795-8038
- Solano Community College (Rohnert Park CA), (707) 864-7000
- Vista College (Berkeley CA), (415) 841-8431
- West Valley College (Saratoga CA), (408) 867-2200
- Yuba College (Marysville CA), (916) 741-6700

Accreditation: All member institutions are accredited by WASC.

Official/Contact: Sandra Scott-Smith, Operations Manager

Admission Requirements: Deadlines for registering in a telecourse vary. When the prospective student has determined the course(s) desired and where they are being offered, refer to the telephone number listed above and contact the institution.

Tuition: Contact the college of choice for up-to-date information regarding tuition, fees, and charges for other materials. Textbooks may be purchased from any of the college bookstores.

Degree Credit: Credit earned for successfully completing a telecourse may be applied toward a degree program. Questions about transferability will be answered by the college in which the student is enrolled.

Grading: The grading system is the option of the college. Normally, letter grades are assigned. Examinations must be taken at testing sites on the college campuses or under the supervision of an approved proctor. Credit may be awarded in semester or quarter hour units depending on the policy of the institution.

Library: The library facilities of the college in which the student is enrolled are available. Local community libraries are also a resource for student research.

COURSES OFFERED

Anthropology

Faces of Culture
This introductory cultural anthropology series features dramatic film footage from around the world. The programs embrace cultures from all continents, highlighting major lifestyles and illustrating human adaptation to environment from the beginnings of the human species to the present. Topics include language and communication, marriage and the family, kinship and descent, economics, religion and magic, the arts, and cultural change. 26 half-hour programs.

Art History

Art of the Western World
This survey of Western art provides unusual perspectives on seminal paintings, sculptures, and architectural structures. Beginning with ancient Greece, the series presents major works within the religious, intellectual, and social contexts of their day. 9 one-hour programs.

Astronomy

Project Universe
This presentation of introductory astronomy includes awe-inspiring footage from NASA and JPL. The telecourse includes authoritative coverage of significant discoveries and developments in the discipline. Among topics treated are the search for satellites of the planets Uranus and Neptune, high-energy phenomena, IRAS, SETI, expanded treatment of Kepler's and Newton's laws, and universal gravitation, as well as significant theories and cosmological models. 30 half-hour programs.

Biology

Introduction to Biology
Designed as an introductory, non-laboratory general biology course. The living world of animals and plants around the viewer is related to human existence to help the student realize the unity of all life forms. The vital role of man in the total ecology of this planet is presented. 36 half-hour programs.

Business

Business and the Law
This series emphasizes contracts and the legal system. Students will learn from modules on the law of sales, commercial paper, agency, and property as well as from discussions of such critical legal topics as government regulation, employment, and consumer and environmental protection. 30 half-hour programs.

The Business File
This series provides a comprehensive overview of the contemporary business environment. Using a

news interview format, the programs present leading scholars and corporate executives discussing business theory and its practical application. The series encompasses five general areas: (1) American business, foundation, and forms. (2) Organizing and managing a business. (3) The internal workings of a business. (4) The environment of a business. (5) The challenge of business. Topics include marketing, finance, accounting, and management. 28 half-hour programs.

Career Guidance

Voyage: Challenge and Change in Career/Life Planning

A basic course in career/life planning that focuses on the process by which students may plan effective and satisfying relationships between work and life. Among vital topics addressed in the course are: self-assessment, dealing with change, decision making, people environments, lifestyle balance, values and career decisions, finding jobs, and setting goals. 30 half-hour programs.

Chemistry

The World of Chemistry

This series takes the student into industrial and research laboratories nationwide to observe chemistry's applications to everything from cosmetics to genetics. Highly reactive experiments and effective computer simulations demonstrate chemical principles clearly and safely through video. 26 half-hour programs.

Computer Literacy

The New Literacy

This introductory survey of data processing prepares students to use computers in their personal and professional lives. The series introduces students to terminology and examines how the computer can be applied to a range of organizational settings. Topics include data representation, storing data, personal computing, system analysis and design, programming languages, and more. 26 half-hour programs.

Computer Science

ComputerWorks

This telecourse gives students the chance to gain familiarity with different types of software programs and computers. Students can use and evaluate word processing, spreadsheet, graphics, database, accounting, communications, and publishing programs. 16 half-hour programs.

Earth Science

The Earth Revealed: Introductory Geology

In this telecourse, students will examine how interacting geological systems impact the earth and the environment. Dramatic footage shows geological features and phenomena driven by plate tectonics, earthquakes, mass wasting, and more. 26 half-hour programs.

Planet Earth

This telecourse takes the student on travels with noted scientists as they seek out clues by peering into outer space and beneath the polar ice caps. This course will help viewers grasp the complexity of the many systems operating within our planet. 7 one-hour programs.

Economics

Economics U$A

This foundation course covers basic macro and micro principles: supply and demand, competition, efficiency, the business cycle, fiscal policy, inflation, deficits, and more. Interviews with leading economists and business leaders as well as case studies of major business events illustrate economic principles. 28 half-hour programs.

English

Literary Visions

This English series brings literature to life with dramatizations, readings, and commentary from scholars and writers. By placing a strong emphasis on writing about literature, the series also teaches advanced compositional skills. Contemporary authors James Dickey, August Wilson, Maxine Hong Kingston, and Tillie Olson among others discuss their inspiration and the craft of creative writing. 26 half-hour programs.

Voices and Visions

The passion and spirit of 13 American poets are skillfully realized in this course. The programs bring out the visual nature of the poems by Eliot, Pound, Dickinson, and others and capture the environments in which they were created. 13 one-hour programs.

Environmental Science

Race to Save the Planet

This telecourse explores the relationships between human society and the earth's natural resources. From fossil fuels to rain forests, from intensive agriculture to industrial pollutants, the course demonstrates how dramatically human activities are influencing the global web of ecosystems. The course examines the major environmental questions facing the world today, among them deforestation, the loss of species' diversity, soil erosion, and climate change. 26 half-hour programs.

Finance

Personal Finance and Money Management

Designed for the nonbusiness major, this course studies the basics of budget and buying, the intricacies of home ownership, income tax, and investment, and the wise use of insurance, wills, and trusts. 26 half-hour programs.

French

French in Action

This French language series is an innovative, effective, and entertaining way to learn a foreign language. The programs combine video, audio, and print to teach French using the innovative, "immersion method" developed by Professor Pierre Capretz of Yale University. Each program is entirely in French and features stories and vignettes that explain new lexical and grammatical topics. The programs also contain clips from French television and cinema and everyday situations from contemporary French culture. Parts 1 and 2, each part 26 half-hour programs.

History

American Adventure

This American history series starts with Columbus' discovery and the early colonial settlements and ends with the Civil War and Reconstruction. Filmed at historic sites in 23 states plus Mexico, the series weaves together historic facts with the people, places and events of the American past. 26 half-hour programs.

America in Perspective: U.S. History Since 1877

This telecourse provides an analytical frame of reference for U.S. events after the Civil War. Historical analysis is provided by over 40 renowned scholars. Topics include Native Americans, immigrants, minorities, Spanish-American War, World Wars I and II, the Great Depression, the Cold War, the civil rights movement, the Vietnam War, the conservative resurgence, the 1980s, and the end of the Cold War. 26 half-hour programs.

The Western Tradition

These programs examine the cultural and philosophical movements that have shaped the Western world from ancient times to the present. Parts 1 and 2, each part 26 half-hour programs.

The Africans

Examines the history and contemporary life of Africa through its triple heritage: what is indigenous, what was contributed by Islam, and what was acquired from the West. 26 half-hour programs.

The Chinese: Adapting the Past, Building the Future

This telecourse combines the talents of internationally known television producers and directors, senior China scholars, and media education experts to provide an engaging, in-depth examination of China as it seeks modernization after a century of cataclysmic change. 26 half-hour programs.

Horticulture

The Home Gardener

This telecourse provides students with fundamental skills necessary for planting and maintaining gardens and lawns either as a hobby, a necessity, or a means of saving money. It will stimulate interest in particular kinds of gardening or in the cultivation of certain plant varieties, demonstrate ways in which established gardens can be improved, and demonstrate techniques for reducing expenses of landscaping and maintaining the home garden. 30 half-hour programs.

Humanities

Humanities through the Arts

Maya Angelou, noted poet-author, is host of this examination of seven major art forms: film, drama, music, literature, painting, sculpture, and architecture. This multimedia humanities survey is an exciting blend of sights, sounds, impressions, and ideas that teach students both the history and elements of each art form. 30 half-hour programs.

Interior Design

Designing Home Interiors

This telecourse emphasizes the planning of residential interiors that will satisfy individual and family needs, values, and lifestyles. The course also focuses on responsibilities of and career opportunities for interior design professionals. Consumer education regarding selection of home furnishings is stressed as well. 26 half-hour programs.

Management

The Business of Management

This telecourse provides a valuable introduction to the theories of management and business. Especially designed for managers without formal business training and undergraduates interested in a business career, the course provides essential information on planning, staffing, directing, decision making, motivating, and communicating. 26 half-hour programs.

Marketing

Marketing

This course involves the basic principles of marketing as they apply to small business and large corporations. It focuses on the application of successful marketing strategies. The course visualizes marketing at work—planning, research, consumer behavior, physical distribution, promotion, and pricing strategy. 26 half-hour programs.

Oceanography

Oceanus: The Marine Environment

This telecourse focuses on the marine environment as a unique feature of the planet Earth and investigates areas of intense scientific and public concern: the pervasiveness of the ocean and its effect on the Earth's weather, its stunning physical size and diversity of contained life forms, its contributions to the physical and historical development of man, its impact on geopolitical and economic matters, the impact of oceanic pollutants, and the potential of exploitation of marine resources. 26 half-hour programs.

Philosophy

Ethics in America

The programs in this telecourse deal with business, government, the military, law, journalism, and medicine. Prominent judges, journalists, politicians, and others debate provocative ethical questions. 10 one-hour programs.

Joseph Campbell: Transformations of Myth Through Time

The programs from this course were selected from over 50 hours of lectures by Joseph Campbell. Topics include origins of man and myth, gods and goddesses, philosophy of the east, the Tibetan *Book of the Dead*, Arthurian legends, Tristan and Isolde, the Parsifal legend, and more. 14 one-hour programs.

Photography

The Photographic Vision

This telecourse takes students beyond basic photographic principles to possibilities for self-discovery and expression through photography. It explores the historical tradition of photography and emphasizes the impact this medium has had on our way of understanding and experiencing the world. The course teaches techniques for responding to photographic images, analyzing aesthetics and structure, and understanding the historical context of hundreds of images. 20 half-hour programs.

Political Science

Government By Consent

This American government survey provides students with an understanding of democracy, the U.S. Constitution, political parties, the three branches of government, due process, and more. Program topics include federalism, PACs, congress, the legislative process, domestic policy, foreign policy, the judiciary, first amendment freedoms, and rights of the accused. 26 half-hour programs.

Psychology

Discovering Psychology

This introductory psychology series covers the fundamental principles of psychology including: brain and behavior, sensation and perception, conditioning and learning, cognitive processes, psychopathology, social influences, therapy, and more. 26 half-hour programs.

Psychology: Study of Human Behavior

An introductory psychology telecourse designed for adult students seeking general education psychology instruction from colleges and universities. The course introduces students to the basic content of psychology: the facts, theories, perspectives, and terminology. It encourages critical thinking about issues in psychology and promotes an appreciation of the diversity of human beings and human behavior. 26 half-hour programs.

The World of Abnormal Psychology

This series helps students distinguish the typical from the abnormal and the functional from the dysfunctional. It examines the complex factors that cause behavioral disorders and demonstrates the psychological, biological, and social approaches to treatment, and discusses current research. The programs feature actual patient case studies, and the interviews with these patients provide an invaluable perspective on the emotional toll paid by those who suffer from behavioral disorders. Commentary by therapists and other mental health professionals presents the multiple approaches to treatment. 13 one-hour programs.

Small Business Management

Something Ventured

This small business management series provides entrepreneurs with the tools they need to compete effectively in the world of business. Students observe a variety of small businesses in action and gain a first-hand look at how to start a small business, evaluate business opportunities, market products or services, manage personal and fiscal demands, and more. 26 half-hour programs.

Sociology

The Sociological Imagination: Introduction to Sociology

This introductory sociology series features mini-documentaries that are emotionally strong illustrations of issues such as socialization, social control, sex and gender, aging, collective behavior, and social change. Expert commentary from noted sociologists provides an academic framework for sociological issues such as group dynamics, deviance, social class, religion, and family. 26 half-hour programs.

Portrait of a Family

This interdisciplinary series takes a look at marriage and the family. Several themes are developed: tension between the individual and the societal environment, contradictory cultural values, and the diversity of patterns of living and decision making people face. Documentary footage and commentary show the fascinating mosaic of family forms that exist today. Programs cover relationships, marriage, and the family in transition. 26 half-hour programs.

Spanish

Destinos: An Introduction to Spanish

This Spanish language series teaches students how to listen, speak, read, and write in Spanish. The programs use the appeal of the "telenovela" to make the language come alive. The series also exposes students to the diverse cultural contexts in which Spanish is spoken as the story unfolds in Spain, Argentina, Mexico, Puerto Rico, and other countries. Parts 1 and 2, each part 26 half-hour programs.

Statistics

Against All Odds: Inside Statistics

With this innovative, introductory statistics course, students learn key statistical processes from the perspective of real people doing real statistical work. The programs focus on practical applications, and teach statistics through location footage and state-of-the-art computer graphics. 26 half-hour programs.

Writing

The Write Course

This English composition and rhetoric series teaches writing from a "process" point of view. The programs are ideal for freshman English students as they present deliberate pre-writing and revision strategies. Most of the nation's leading authorities on the teaching of composition are interviewed along with well-known writers. Students are encouraged to develop individual writing processes with particular emphasis on skills needed for academic and business writing. 30 half-hour programs.

Oxnard College
See **INTELECOM**

Palomar College
See **INTELECOM**

Pasadena City College
See **INTELECOM**

Rancho Santiago Community College
See **INTELECOM**

Riverside Community College
See **INTELECOM**

Sacramento City College
See **Northern California Telecommunications Consortium**

Saddleback College
See **INTELECOM**

San Bernardino Valley College
See **INTELECOM**

San Joaquin Delta College
See **Northern California Telecommunications Consortium**

Santa Rosa Junior College
See **Northern California Telecommunications Consortium**

Solano Community College
See **Northern California Telecommunications Consortium**

Southwestern College
See **INTELECOM**

University of California
Center for Media and Independent Learning
University Extension
2223 Fulton Street
Berkeley, CA   94720

(510) 642-3245 *Fax:* (510) 643-8683

Geographic Access: Worldwide

DELIVERY SYSTEMS

Electronic Mail
Students enrolling in the electronic mail option can submit assignments by modem. To do so, the student must have an electronic mail address on the Internet, Bitnet, or UUCP networks, or they can purchase one on the UC system running UNIX. To use the UC system, the student must have access to a terminal or a personal computer (IBM or compatible PC) with a serial card, modem, and communications software plus a telephone line to dial-up and log-in to an individual account.

Videocassette
Available as supplementary material to a printed text and other materials. These can be rented or purchased (see below with course description).

Audiocassette
Used in language courses. These can be rented or purchased (see below with course description).

Broadcast Television
Courses available are offered through the Mind Extension University via local television channels.

INSTITUTION DESCRIPTION

The Center for Media and Independent Learning is the distance learning division of UC Extension, the continuing education arm of the University of California. It was established more than 75 years ago to extend the resources of the university throughout the community. The independent learning courses listed below utilize audio- or videocassettes to supplement and enhance study.

The center has joined with Jones Intercable, through its Mind Extension University (ME/U), to make courses available nationally via cable television. Students who live in an area where their cable system subscribes to ME/U can access the video portions of the courses directly. Students who live outside cable service areas with ME/U can arrange to obtain the video segments on videocassette directly from ME/U. For more information on the courses available, contact ME/U at 1-800-777-MIND or *see* Mind Extension University in this directory.

Accreditation: WASC

Official/Contact: Mary Beth Almeda, Director

Admission Requirements: Courses are open to all interested adults; California residence is not required. Courses may be taken for credit or noncredit. Credit earned is accepted at the University of California and at other accredited institutions. Acceptance of credit earned toward degree requirements is under the jurisdiction of the college or university that is to grant the degree. Students may enroll at any time and have one year from the date of enrollment to complete a course.

Tuition: The cost per course is listed below with the course description. VISA or MasterCard accepted. The cost of textbooks is not included in the tuition and may be purchased locally or ordered through the Center for Media and Independent Learning. Audiocassettes supplied with course materials are not returnable. Videocassettes may be purchased or rented. See course descriptions below.

Degree Credit: Credit for courses may be applied to a degree program.

Grading: Students enrolled for credit take final examinations under the supervision of a proctor. Students in California select proctors from a list of authorized examination centers throughout the state. Students outside California have examinations proctored by any one of the following in their area: a high school principal or administrator, a college or university faculty member or administrator, or U.S. embassy or consular officers. Students in the Armed Forces may have examinations proctored by a chaplain, an Information and Education Officer, or any of the options mentioned above. The grading system is A-F; the minimum passing grade is D. There is no academic penalty for failure to complete a course. Credit is awarded in semester hour units. Some courses have credit awarded in quarter hour units and are so identified at the end of the course description. *See* Courses Offered.

Library: Students have access to any University of California Library. Use of local libraries is encouraged.

COURSES OFFERED

Astronomy

Introduction to General Astronomy

An essentially nonmathematical description of modern astronomy with emphasis on the structure and evolution of stars, galaxies, and the universe. The course includes discussion of studies of pulsars, quasars, and black holes. The solar system and space exploration of the planets. *Fee:* $330. *Understanding Space and Time Series* has four 28-minute parts. Purchase optional, $125. Single tape, $39. (3 semester credits)

Biology

Modern Biology

The course covers structures and activities fundamental to all forms of life. The student examines the organization and function in the human as a representative vertebrate, reproduction and development, principles of heredity, evolutionary processes, kinds of living things, adaptations of organisms, and relationships of plants and animals, including humans, to each other and to their physical environment. *Fee:* $310. *How Scientists Know About Punctuated Equilibria* is a video of 20 minutes duration that explores the development of a new theory that explains how evolution takes place. The video features paleontologists Niles Eldredge and Stephen Jay Gould. Purchase optional, $39. (3 semester credits)

Plants and Civilization

In this course the student explores the biology, selection, use of plants for human purposes, and the interrelation between the evolution of domesticated plants and human cultural evolution. *Fee:* $310. *How Scientists Know About Human Evolution*, a video of 18 minutes duration explains evolutionary theory by showing how scientists study human fossils and use them to draw conclusions about human biological and cultural evolution. Purchase optional, $39. (3 semester credits)

Plant Life in California

This course focuses on the vegetation, plant communities, and life zones of California. It examines influences on patterns of vegetation, origin of California flora, plant distribution throughout the state, and basic ecological concepts. *Fee:* $310. *Wild California: The Land*, a video of 19 minutes duration explores the wildlife and ecology of six terrestrial habitats of California and the West through four seasons. Purchase optional, $39. (3 semester credits)

Chinese

Elementary Chinese: Course I

This course provides the student with the foundations of vocabulary and grammar for Modern Standard Chinese (Mandarin), emphasizing reading and writing. Speech practice can be gained through listening and responding to tapes. Five audiocassette tapes are provided with the course materials. *Fee: $370. A Taste of China* is a series of four videos that introduces traditional Chinese culture by using Chinese cuisine as a "window" for Western audiences. The series includes *Masters of the Wok, Food for Body and Spirit, The Family Table, Water Farmers.* Each video is of 29 minutes duration. Purchase optional. Series price, $125. Single tape, $39. (5 semester credits)

Computer Science

Concepts of Data Processing

This introduction to data processing and computer science includes computer history, computer applications and their impact on society, and career opportunities in this rapidly expanding field. The course also covers other topics such as hardware, input/output, problem definition, and computer languages. Access to a computer is not necessary. *Fee: $320. Computers at Work* is a ten-part video series that employs numerous case studies to show what computers are, how they work, and how they are used to solve problems in a diverse group of work settings. Each video is 30 minutes in length: *The Information Age, The Computer System, Computer Hardware, Computer Software, Business Systems Development, Computer Communications, Database Systems, Microcomputers, Computers and Society, Artificial Intelligence and the Future.* Purchase optional. Ten-video series, $250. Single tape, $39. (3 semester credits)

Introduction to Progamming with BASIC

This course introduces BASIC system commands and program statements and explains how they are used to carry out data processing operations. Course topics include how to design a program, how to operate a computer, system descriptions, entry of BASIC instructions, input and output, branching, looping, mathematical functions, subroutines and strings, arrays, file processing, and matrix commands. Access to a computer is necessary. While the text specifically addresses VAX systems, the Apple IIe and the Macintosh, the IBM PC and the Radio Shack TRS-80 Model 4 computer systems may be used. *Fee: $320. Basic Power* is an eight-part video series that demonstrates the essentials of BASIC, approximately 20 minutes duration each. The series includes *The Basics of BASIC, Arithmetic Operation, Defining Variables, Program Structures, Subscripted Variables and Arrays, Subroutines and Functions, Input and Output, File Structures.* Purchase optional. Eight-part video series, $195. Single tapes, $39. (3 semester credits)

French

French: Elementary Course I

This beginner's course concentrates on grammar, reading, and writing. Speech practice is provided through listening and responding to tapes. Ten audiocassette tapes are provided with the course materials. *Fee: $350. French Language Videotapes* is a nine-video supplement and may be used with any text. Each video is produced entirely in French with native speakers only. The series concludes with a thorough review. Purchase optional. Nine-video series, $250. Single tape, $39. (3 semester credits)

French: Elementary Course II

The emphasis in this continuation of the above course is on sentence structure and composition with extensive speech practice provided by the tapes. Fourteen cassette tapes are provided with the course materials. *Fee: $365.* (3 semester credits)

Geology

Introduction to Physical Geology

This course acquaints the student with the principles and concepts of physical geology. It covers the origins of crustal materials, especially rocks, volcanoes, earthquakes, plate tectonics, and the erosional processes and their role in landscape development. Important areas of geological interest, especially those in the western United States, are emphasized in examples. *Fee: $310. When the Bay Area Quakes* is a video of 20 minutes duration. Computer graphics and television news footage of the 1989 Loma Prieta earthquake are used to illustrate the four main geologic effects of California earthquakes: ground shaking, liquefaction, landslides, and ground ruptures. Purchase optional, $39. (3 semester credits)

Geology of California

The geological framework of California and the history and origin of rocks and landscapes are examined. Each geological province is studied: The Sierra Nevada, the Basin-Ranges, the Mojave and Colorado deserts, the Transverse and Peninsular ranges of southern California (including the Los Angeles and Ventura Basins), the Coast Ranges, the Great Valley, the Klamath Mountains, the Cascade range, and the Modoc Lava Plateau. The course covers the rocks and structure of each province, the fault patterns and their structural and earthquake history, and natural areas of great human interest. *Fee:* $305. *When the Bay Area Quakes* is a video of 20 minutes duration. Computer graphics and television news footage of the 1989 Loma Prieta earthquake are used to illustrate the four main geologic effects of California earthquakes: ground shaking, liquefaction, landslides, and ground ruptures. Purchase optional, $39. (4 quarter credits)

German

German: Elementary Course I

Development of the four basic language skills: reading, writing, understanding, and speaking. The informative textbook compares German and American geography and cultural institutions. Six audiocassette tapes are provided with the course materials. *Fee:* $365. (3 semester credits)

German: Elementary Course II

A continuation of developing the four basic skills: reading, writing, understanding, and speaking. The textbook contrasts north, middle, and south Germany and its former East and West political divisions. It also describes the lives of Germany's greatest writers, Goethe and Schiller. Four cassette tapes are provided with the course materials. *Fee:* $325. (3 semester credits)

German: Elementary Course III

The focus in this course is on refining the four basic language skills. The textbook surveys the history of Germany and its social structure, characterizes two major German writers (Heine and Thomas Mann), and briefly describes the other German-speaking countries (Austria and Switzerland). Three audiocassette tapes are provided with the course materials. *Fee:* $320. (3 semester credits)

History

While Soldiers Fought: War and American Society I

This course explores the social, political, economic, and cultural impact of war on American society. The course covers the American Revolution, the Civil War, the Spanish American War, and World War I. The course is offered via the Mind Extension University on three videotapes. *Fee:* $345. (3 semester credits)

While Soldiers Fought: War and American Society II

A continuation of the above course covering World War II, the Korean Conflict, and Vietnam and its legacy. The course includes four videotapes. *Fee:* $342. (3 semester credits)

Italian

Elementary Italian I

This course teaches the fundamentals of Italian grammar, reading, and writing and introduces the elements of Italian culture. Speaking practice is gained through listening and responding to the nine audiocassette tapes provided with the course material. *Fee:* $335. (3 semester credits)

Elementary Italian II

In this course, the student continues building Italian language skills. Speaking is practiced and Italian culture is learned with the aid of eight audiocassette tapes provided with the course materials. *Fee:* $330. (3 semester credits)

Marketing

Principles of Marketing

The role of marketing concepts in business decisions, marketing methods, and the effect of marketing on company profitability and image are covered in this course. The course explores the complex interrelationships between product, price, promotion, distribution, customer service, packaging, and market research. Additional topics include market segmentation, consumer buying behavior, and international marketing. *Fee:* $320. *The Ad and the Id: Sex, Death, and Subliminal Advertising* is a videocassette of 28 minutes duration showing how advertisers use powerful subliminal images to influence and motivate consumers to buy. Purchase optional, $39. (3 semester credits)

Physics

General Physics

This elementary course in physics covers mechanics, wave motion and sound, heat, and thermodynamics. *Fee:* $290. *Understanding Space and Time Series* is a video series produced by the BBC. It includes topics in physics for the general audience in the first nine parts of 28 minutes each: *Ground Control to Mr. Galileo, As Surely as Columbus Saw America, Pushed to the Limit, Conflict Brought to Light, Marking Time, E=MC Squared, An Isolated Fact, Royal Road, At the Frontier.* Purchase optional. Nine-part series, $225. Single tape, $39. (2 semester credits)

Political Science

American Institutions

This course examines the basic workings of the Constitution and the institutions of the federal government (Congress, the presidency, the bureaucracy, and the judiciary), the American system of electoral politics (including parties, interest groups, social movements, public opinion, and participation), and several areas of public policy (defense, foreign policy, civil liberties, civil rights, the rights of minorities, social spending, welfare reform, and the political aspects of the economic system). Discussion of these aspects of American politics is organized around the theoretical questions of democracy and justice. *Fee:* $330. A 38-minute video, *From the Floor of the Convention*, presents a grassroot view of a presidential nominating convention and follows three first-time delegates (including Apple Computer founder Steve Wozniak) to the 1984 Democratic National Convention. The video provides a unique behind-the-scenes look at the American political process in action. Purchase optional, $39. (3 semester credits)

Psychology

Psychology of Communication

This course focuses on why people communicate the way they do and how they can communicate better. It considers the practical applications of theory and research to personal and professional communication. Topics include the role of information in modern life, the importance of communication in building and maintaining relationships, special problems of communicating within groups and organizations, the uses and effects of television and mass media, and communication and the future of society. *Fee:* $310. *The Interpersonal Perception Task*, a 40-minute video, is an acclaimed study of nonverbal communication showing common social interactions, each followed by a multiple-choice question about the interaction. Purchase optional, $39. (3 semester credits)

Developmental Psychology

An overview of child development, including prenatal development, birth and the newborn, physical, cognitive, language, emotional, and social development during infancy, preschool years, and middle childhood. *Fee:* $305. Two videos are available to supplement the course materials. *Brandon and Rachel: Patterns of Infant Development* is of 34 minutes duration. The principles of motor, language, and personality development are demonstrated through the behavior of two seven-month-old infants. Purchase optional, $39. *Mother-Infant Interaction Series* is a six-part series filmed at the City University of New York Child Development Research Project. The series illustrates the maternal influence on the emotional and cognitive development of infants: *Forms of Feeding at Six Weeks, Feeding and Frustration Tolerance at Six Months, Feeding and Object Relations at One Year, Feeding and Function Pleasure in the First Year of Life, Feeding and Object Cathexis in the First Year of Life, Resemblances in Expressive Behavior.* Tapes (black and white) are of 40 to 49 minutes each. Purchase optional. Six-part series, $150. Single tape, $39. (4 quarter hours)

Social Psychology

This course explores how an individual's behavior, feelings, and thoughts may be influenced by others. Topics include interpersonal attraction, prosocial and antisocial behavior, nonverbal communication, social influence, attitude change, environment and behavior, and research methods. *Fee:* $310. *A World of Gestures* is an informative video exploring gestures from cultures worldwide. The 28-minute video examines the meaning and function of gestures as a form of nonverbal communication and studies their origins and emotional significance. Purchase optional, $39. (3 semester credits)

Reading

Literature for Children

This course considers strategies for evaluating and selecting literature for children from preschool through adolescence and presents approaches to improving children's response to literature. Ways are explored to use literature in school reading programs and in specific subject areas. Also explored are ways to discover what children want to read and how to become familiar with the works of authors, illustrators, and current publications. *Poetry is Words that Sing!* is a 28-minute video. The Pacific Poetry Ensemble teaches poetry to children by demonstrating its most basic power: the power to enchant. The video shows how the Ensemble develops and presents a spellbinding classroom presentation. Purchase optional, $39. (3 semester credits)

Spanish

Spanish: Elementary Course I

This beginner's course provides a foundation of vocabulary and grammar. Through written and aural/oral exercises, the student builds a knowledge of the language. Eight audiocassette tapes are provided with the course materials. *Fee:* $340. (3 semester credits)

Spanish: Elementary Course II

A continuation of the above course providing a study of Spanish vocabulary and grammar, in combination with writing and listening/speaking exercises. Eight audiocassette tapes are provided with the course materials. *Fee:* $335. (3 semester credits)

Spanish: Elementary Course III

A continuation of the above course that further develops knowledge of vocabulary and grammar and includes a thorough review of Spanish by written and aural/oral means. Five audiocassette tapes are provided with the course materials. (3 semester credits)

Spanish: Intermediate Course I

This continuation of the above course reviews vocabulary, grammar, and sentence structure. It provides further study in pronunciation and composition. Five audiocassette tapes are provided with the course materials. *Fee:* $330. (3 semester credits)

Spanish for the Professions: Course I

This course enables the student to quickly attain a working knowledge of the Spanish language. A vocabulary is built that is most suited to the student's needs. The study options are Spanish for Teachers (three audiocassette tapes) and Spanish for Medical Personnel (four audiocassette tapes). *Fee:* $310. (2 semester credits)

Spanish for the Professions: Course II

This course is a continuation of building Spanish language skills and applying them to one's professional needs. Communication skills for the workplace are improved and review and practice for language proficiency examinations are accomplished. The study options are Spanish for Teachers (four audiocassette tapes) and Spanish for Medical Personnel (four audiocassette tapes). *Fee:* $330. (2 semester credits)

University of Phoenix - San Francisco
Online Programs

100 Spear Street
Suite 200
San Francisco, CA   94105

(415) 541-0141; (800) 388-5463 *Fax:* (415) 541-0761

Geographic Access: Worldwide

DELIVERY SYSTEMS

Online Services

Prior to the student's first class, he/she will be guided through an online orientation to become familiar with Alex, the online program's computer conferencing system. The online campus is open 24 hours a day, seven days a week.

INSTITUTION DESCRIPTION

The University of Phoenix was founded in Phoenix, Arizona, in 1976. The University offers professional level undergraduate business, management, and nursing degrees, and graduate degrees in business, management, nursing, and education. The Online Programs are offered from the San Francisco branch of the University.

Unlike traditional semester- or quarter-based schools, the University of Phoenix Online program is structured linearly so that a student can begin a course of study any month of the year. Online's sequential format accommodates program interruptions and occasional breaks that are sometimes necessary to handle personal or professional responsibilities. Online students have access to a full range of student services including transcript evaluations, technical assistance, an electronic library, and financial aid. A private electronic mailbox is also issued to each student which makes it possible to send confidential messages to any faculty member, student, or University official.

Online degree programs available include the Bachelor of Science in Business Administration, the Bachelor of Arts in Management, the Master of Business Administration, and the Master's in Management.

Accreditation: NCA

Official/Contact: Annette Fajardo, Enrollment Counselor

Admission Requirements: High school diploma or equivalent; minimum of 50 semester credits from a regionally accredited college or university; cumulative GPA of 2.0 or better; minimum of 2 years of full-time, post-high school work experience providing exposure to organizational systems and management processes; acceptable score on the TOEFL for non-native speakers of English; completion of the University of Phoenix proctored Comprehensive Cognitive Assessment; current employment or access to an organizational environment appropriate for the application of theoretical concepts to relevant workplace issues.

Tuition: Application fee $58. Tuition $325 per credit. Books must be purchased by the student and the costs vary per course. Materials shipping fee $10 per course.

Degree Credit: The *Bachelor of Science in Business Administration* is a two-year, 47-credit degree completion program designed for the working professional who has already earned a minimum of 50 college credits. The program coursework in marketing, finance, computer information processing, economics, accounting, business law, and communications satisfies the major course of study requirement and is comparable to the traditional junior and senior years of study. The *Bachelor of Arts in Management Program* is a two-year, 41-credit degree completion program designed for the working professional who has already earned a minimum of 50 college credits. The program coursework in personnel management, finance, information processing, organizational behavior, accounting, business law, and communications satisfies the

major course of study requirement and is comparable to the traditional junior and senior years of study. This program focuses more on the specific abilities it takes to run a successful department. The *MBA Program* is a 40-credit broad-based curriculum composed of a sequentially structured set of courses designed to equip the student with the practical analytical and decision-making tools necessary to successfully compete in the complex business world. From legal considerations to marketing principles, the student is exposed to all the disciplines which influence the decision-making process. The *Master's in Management* program is a 40-credit graduate program designed to fill the educational needs of the majority of mid-career professionals seeking to further develop and refine their management skills. In contrast to the MBA with its heavy emphasis on quantitative analysis, this program focuses more on the human aspects of management science. From understanding the structure and behavior of organizations to forming a departmental budget and strategic plan, the student will be equipped with the knowledge and skills required to be an effective manager of both people and projects.

Grading: Letter grades are assigned upon completion of a course. Credit is awarded in semester hour units.

Library: Students have access, via the Alex system, to the resource materials available in the electronic library of the university.

COURSES OFFERED

Business Administration

Management and Leadership
This course focuses on the planning, organizing, staffing, leading, and controlling functions of the manager. Students are exposed to effective employee motivation techniques and acquire tools useful in the solving of frequently encountered management problems. 5 weeks. (3 credits)

Business Communications
This course covers models of communication process, routine business correspondence, international business communication, editorial process, presentation techniques, and interviewing strategies. 5 weeks. (3 credits)

Business Law
In this course, students examine the role of manager in dealing with issues related to the law. Federal and

state court systems, civil litigation, and consumer and antitrust law as they relate to the conduct of business are covered. 5 weeks. (3 credits)

Computers and Information Processing

This course focuses on the effective use of information systems in the management process. Students examine ways in which computers can improve the productivity and efficiency of an organization. 5 weeks. (3 credits)

Business Research Project

This course is divided into three parts. Together, they cover the uses of business research, research methods, report writing, instrument design, measurement criteria, interviewing techniques, and empirical analysis. 12 weeks (8 credits)

Statistics in Business

Students learn how to apply the concepts of probability, sampling, and hypothesis testing to the solution of business problems. Various forms of statistical analysis, including correlation and regression, are covered. 10 weeks. (6 credits)

Economics for Business

Structured to equip students with the ability to analyze a wide array of economic indicators and to evaluate the implications of those indicators on their own business or discipline. Business cycles, money supply, taxation, productivity, supply and demand, governmental policies and controls, and international trade are covered. 10 weeks. (6 credits)

Financial Accounting

Covers accrual accounting concepts, analysis of financial statements, annual report analysis, inventory valuation analysis, financial controls, depreciation of operational assets, and accounting theory. Students learn how to integrate and make use of accounting information in their planning and control responsibilities. 10 weeks (6 credits)

Managerial Finance

Covers working capital management, leveraging, long-term financing, and financial forecasting. Students are provided an overview of the fundamentals of financial administration which make it possible to understand the financial consequences management decisions have on an organization. 10 weeks. (6 credits)

Marketing

This course covers marketing strategies, opportunity analysis, new product development, pricing, and the product life cycle. An emphasis is placed on the relationship of the marketing function to other managerial and organizational functions. 5 weeks. (3 credits)

Quantitative Analysis in Business

In this course, students learn how to apply the concept of probability, sampling, and rational decision analysis to the solution of various business problems. Descriptive statistics, forecasting, correlation, and regression analysis are also covered. 6 weeks. (3 credits)

Management

Personnel Management

In this course, students examine some of the critical issues and responsibilities involved with managing people. Performance appraisal methods and strategies, staff training and development, wage and salary structures, and legal responsibilities are among the topics addressed. 5 weeks. (3 credits)

Finance and Accounting for Managers

These courses specifically address the needs of managers who are not directly involved in the financial or accounting area but must integrate and make use of accounting and financial information in their planning and control responsibilities. Students are provided an in-depth overview of financial and accounting principles which affect common managerial and organizational decision-making processes. 10 weeks. (6 credits)

Contemporary Issues in Management

This course examines a broad array of contemporary issues facing today's managers. Topics include ethics, prejudice, manager/employee communications, harassment, conflict of interests, and values. Students have the opportunity to analyze the relationship of these and other issues to the management function within their own organizations. 5 weeks. (3 credits)

Strategic Planning

This course covers strategic planning and implementation, strategy analysis models, and contingency planning. Students study the internal forces which shape strategy, develop long-term goals, and draw up corresponding operational plans. 6 weeks. (3 credits)

Human Resource Management

In this course students examine employee recruitment strategies, staff training and development issues, benefits and compensation packages, and other responsibilities of the human resource department. 6 weeks. (3 credits)

Managing Information

Students explore different ways in which information is managed and how information needs and flow are evaluated. The course focuses on the manager as an end user and the role a manager plays in evaluating the components and effectiveness of an information system. 6 weeks. (3 credits)

Budgeting

In this course, students study the relationship of the budgeting process to the organization's strategic plan and objectives. Forecasting, evaluation and control, and cost/expense allocation are covered. 6 weeks. (3 credits)

Advanced Budgeting

A continuation of the above course. Addresses such issues as financial controls, data analysis, spreadsheet application, and the application of key financial ratios. 6 weeks. (3 credits)

Decision Making

This course covers individual and group decision-making processes, goal setting, and the relationship of decision making to personal and organizational values. Students examine how to apply different decision-making models to job situations. 6 weeks. (3 credits)

Project Management

This course examines the key components necessary to effectively manage projects. Students study production and performance evaluation, quality control, and work flow analysis. 6 weeks. (3 credits)

Applied Management Science Project

This course is in two parts. Together they cover the uses of business research, research methods, report writing, instrument design, measurement criteria, interviewing techniques, and empirical analysis. 9 weeks. (4 credits)

Applied Managerial Statistics

In this course, students learn how to apply the concepts of probability, sampling, and hypothesis testing to the solution of business problems. 6 weeks. (3 credits)

Marketing for Customer Satisfaction

Students examine the context in which the manager assumes a marketing role within the organization. Pricing policy, product life cycle, marketing research, and ethics are covered. 6 weeks. (3 credits)

External Environment of Business

Through case study analysis, students examine the ways in which the external environments of government regulation, economy, technology, and competition affect the conduct of business. 6 weeks. (3 credits)

Fundamentals of Executive Management

This course focuses on the role of executive management in directing an organization and improving organizational performance. Students analyze the basic functions of management and their interrelationships. 6 weeks. (3 credits)

Human Relations and Organizational Behavior

In this course, students analyze how individuals and groups function within the context of the organization with an emphasis on motivation and productivity, decision making and problem solving, and interpersonal relations. 6 weeks. (3 credits)

Legal Environment of Business

This course covers the American legal system as it relates to the regulation of business, organizational structure, commercial property, and consumer law. Through case study analysis, students examine the role of the manager in dealing with issues related to the law. 6 weeks. (3 credits)

Information Management in Business

This course covers centralized and decentralized data processing and system development and implementation. Students examine the strategic and operational uses of management information systems and learn how to evaluate cost effectiveness of systems and development. 6 weeks. (3 credits)

Advanced Managerial Economics

This course covers macro- and microeconomic principles and concepts as applied to the management of a business enterprise and the evaluation of business problems. Students learn how to analyze a wide array of economic indicators and to evaluate the implications of those indicators on their own organization. 6 weeks. (3 credits)

Advanced Managerial Accounting

Covers the knowledge and skills necessary for managers to integrate and employ accounting information in their planning and control responsibilities. Annual report analysis, costing methods, internal control systems, and ratio analysis are examined in relationship to their role in effective decision making. 6 weeks. (3 credits)

Advanced Managerial Finance

This course examines stocks and annuities, cash management, leverage, and debt financing. An emphasis is placed on the knowledge necessary to fund growth, manage liquidity, and formulate investment strategies. 6 weeks. (3 credits)

Advanced Marketing Management

In this course, students learn the skills necessary to prepare a comprehensive marketing plan. The relationship of the marketing function to other managerial and organizational functions is presented. Students examine the basic principles and objectives of market research, including the application of social and behavioral science to the solution of marketing problems. 6 weeks. (3 credits)

Strategy Formulation and Implementation

This course examines how the formulation of strategic objectives and operational goals impacts organizational structure, corporate culture, reward systems, and linked control systems. Students analyze the forces internal to an organization which contribute to the shaping of strategy and the development of long-term goals. 6 weeks. (3 credits)

International Business Management

This course covers sociocultural analysis techniques, risk analysis and evaluation, international legal and financial systems, and government-to-business relations which affect international trade. 6 weeks. (3 credits)

Management of the Total Enterprise

This capstone course is designed to integrate and focus all of the subject matter covered in the MBA program coursework. Through case study analysis, students are able to examine how the microcosm of a particular business relates to and is affected by the macrocosm of the external environment. 6 weeks. (3 credits)

Ventura College
See **INTELECOM**

Victor Valley College
See **INTELECOM**

Vista College
See **Northern California Telecommunications Consortium**

West Valley College
See **Northern California Telecommunications Consortium**

Yuba College
See **Northern California Telecommunications Consortium**

Colorado

Adams State College
See **KRMA/Denver**

Arapahoe Community College
See **KRMA/Denver**

Colorado Mountain College
See **KRMA/Denver**

Colorado Northwestern Community College
See **KRMA/Denver**

Colorado State University
Telecourses
Division of Continuing Education
Spruce Hall
Fort Collins, CO   80523

(800) 525-4950 *Fax:* (303) 491-5288

Geographic Access: Worldwide

DELIVERY SYSTEMS

Broadcast Television
Telecourses are broadcast over the following channels: Channel 6 (KRMA-TV Denver), Channel 25 (Fort Collins (repeat schedule on Columbine Cable), Channel 8 (KTSC-TV Denver), Channel 12 (KBDI-TV Denver).

INSTITUTION DESCRIPTION

Continuing Education began at Colorado State University in 1972 by providing adults of all ages the opportunity to continue learning. Whether adults are entering the workforce, training for new careers, seeking career advancement, striving to keep up with current professional information, or interested in learning for personal enjoyment and satisfaction, the Division makes every effort to provide high quality instruction for each individual student.

Telecourses are approved Colorado State academic courses. Enrollment and the grade earned will be recorded on an official Colorado State transcript upon course completion. Telecourses are credit courses. Each telecourse is a full-fledged college course that integrates video and print components. This delivery technique represents a flexible, responsive, and convenient method of bringing knowledge to students. Telecourses are designed for busy people who find the broadcast delivery of instructional materials more convenient to their needs.

There are four elements in a telecourse: a series of television programs (usually two half-hour programs per week), a study guide, a textbook, and an on-campus faculty member. The telecourses listed below are representative of those available. Other courses are offered during the various semester and summer sessions. Contact the Telecourse office for up-to-date offerings and schedules.

Accreditation: NCA

Official/Contact: Richard Thomas, Distance Learning Coordinator

Admission Requirements: Open enrollment. Some courses may require prerequisites. Courses are approved for the DANTES program. Eligible military personnel should process DANTES applications through their Education Officer.

Tuition: Varies by course. Tuition and fees are listed below with the course descriptions. Students must purchase textbooks either locally or through the Colorado State University Bookstore. MasterCard and VISA accepted for both tuition/fees and the purchase of textbooks.

Degree Credit: Credits earned may be applied toward a degree at Colorado State University.

Grading: The grading system is A, B, C, D, F with pluses and minuses recorded and averaged. The minimum passing grade is D. Examinations must be proctored. Credit is awarded in semester hour units.

Library: Students officially enrolled in a telecourse may use the CSU Library.

COURSES OFFERED

Geology

Introduction to Geology: The Earth Explored
  This course is part of the Annenberg/CPB Collection entitled *Earth Revealed: Introductory Geology.* It is a comprehensive study of the Earth's physical processes and properties with emphasis on understanding the scientific theories behind the geological principles. These principles are vividly documented with the assistance of on-location footage at major geological sites around the world. Presented are both the dramatic forces—volcanic activity and earthquakes—as well as the more subtle and ever present elements of the geological process. The video also illuminates the often unrealized link between human activity and geological change. Tuition $195 plus a $25 fee. (3 credits)

Human Development and Family Studies

Marriage and Family Relationships
  Prerequisite: General Psychology or General Sociology. This course is produced by the California Consortium and is designed to acquaint the student with the major themes of marriage and family: cultural influences on the individual in relationships, mate selection, marriage and family types, parenting, and family change and crisis resolution. A cross-cultural approach to marriage and family will be utilized to familiarize the student with the variety of forms and functions in human relationships including single life, heterosexuality, homosexuality, racial and ethnic variations, and individual family form(s). Tuition $195 plus a $25 fee. (3 credits)

Philosophy

Ethics in America
  This introductory-level philosophy course examines contemporary ethical conflict and provides students with the intellectual tools to analyze moral dilemmas in the fields they choose to pursue—and in the society in which all of us must live. At the core of the course is a prime-time television series that places experts from government, the press, medicine, law, business, and the military directly in the line of fire. Guided by the probing questions of skilled lawyers, luminaries from C. Everett Koop and T. Boone Pickens to Antonin Scalia, Peter Jennings and Jeane Kirkpatrick grapple with moral concerns that arise in both personal and professional life. Tuition $195 plus a $30 fee. (3 credits)

Psychology

General Psychology
  This course is an introduction to the diverse field of psychology, exposing the student to leading researchers and the latest developments in the field. It will help the student develop an understanding of the variety of approaches to the study of human nature while encouraging curiosity and critical thinking. Beginning with the foundations and progressing to more complex extensions and applications, the course integrates historical and current perspectives with emerging theories, paradigms, and significant new fascinating studies of the mind and behavior. Tuition $195 plus a $25 fee. (3 credits)

Computer-Mediated Instruction for General Psychology
  If the student has access to a personal computer and telephone modem, Section 861 of General Psychology may be chosen. This section is available to students who are interested in taking advantage of Bulletin Board electronic two-way communication with the course instructor. Tuition $195 plus a fee of $25. (3 credits)

Developmental Psychology Across the Life Span
  Another of the Annenberg/CPB Collection entitled *Seasons of Life,* this course examines the drama of human development that unfolds under the influence of three "clocks": a physical clock, social clock, and a psychological clock. Following real people

through pivotal events in their lives, such as the birth of a child and the death of a spouse, the television and audio programs present provocative insights emerging from recent research in psychology, biology, anthropology, and sociology. The television programs provide a chronological overview of stages of the life span, while the audio programs concentrate on specific topics. Tuition $195 plus a fee of $40. (3 credits)

Abnormal Psychology

Prerequisite: General Psychology. This course is part of the Annenberg/CPB Collection entitled *The World of Abnormal Psychology.* This is a new telecourse that explores the complex causes, manifestations, and treatment of common behavior disorders. Interviews with patients give students an invaluable perspective on the emotional toll paid by those who suffer from behavior disorders. In addition, analysis by therapists and other mental health professionals presents the multiple approaches to treatment. The course introduces abnormal behavior in the context of psychological well-being to show these behaviors along a continuum from functional to dysfunctional. Tuition $195 plus a fee of $25. (3 credits)

Sociology

Sociology of Rural Life

Prerequisite: General Sociology. This course is part of the Annenberg/CPB Collection entitled *Rural Communities: Legacy and Change.* This course addresses the challenges facing rural America by traveling to 15 rural regions and examining various facets of community life: rural life in the U.S. and third world societies, analysis of sociocultural systems, social differentiation, social institutions, and problems of social change. Tuition $195 plus a $25 fee. (3 credits)

Social Work

Introduction to Social Work

This course is an introduction to the profession of social work, the historical events that led to the creation of a social welfare institution in the United States, and an overview of the knowledge, values, intervention skills, practice settings, and population groups served by social workers. Tuition $260 plus a $50 fee. (4 credits)

Colorado SURGE
Division of Continuing Education
Colorado State University

Spruce Hall
Fort Collins, CO 80523

(800) 525-4950 *Fax:* (303) 491-7886

Geographic Access: Worldwide

DELIVERY SYSTEMS

Teleclasses
Students may view videotapes alone, or preferably in a small group, at their convenience. Potential course offerings are listed below but actual course availability will depend upon the number of off-campus students registering and the availability of classrooms and/or recording capability.

INSTITUTION DESCRIPTION

Colorado SURGE (State University Resources in Graduate Education), headquartered at Colorado State University, is an innovative method of delivering graduate education to working professionals who cannot attend regular on-campus classes. It was established in 1967 as the first video-based graduate education program of its kind in the United States.

An average of 80 courses are taught each semester via SURGE, representing 17 departments in the Colleges of Agricultural Sciences, Applied Human Sciences, Business, Engineering, Natural Sciences, and Veterinary Medicine and Biomedical Sciences. Currently, over 600 students are enrolled at over 90 open and corporate sites throughout Colorado and the nation. During its successful 25-year history, over 350 students have completed graduate degrees.

Regular on-campus courses, taught by Colorado State graduate faculty, are videotaped in specially equipped classrooms. This "teleclass" format ensures that the information being presented is timely and up-to-date. The tapes, along with handouts, are sent via UPS to participating site coordinators. Site coordinators make these tapes and materials available to students, provide information about the program, supply registration forms, proctor exams, and return the tapes. Tapes are *not* sent to individual students.

Accreditation: NCA

Official/Contact: Debbie Sheaman, SURGE Registrar

Admission Requirements: Baccalaureate degree from an accredited college or university. Submit application form; have two official transcripts sent to the department in which study is planned; three references; Graduate Record Examination data (test scores must have been earned within five years of application).

Tuition: In-state $250 per credit; out-of-state student $350 per credit. Textbooks may be ordered through the Colorado State University Bookstore. MasterCard, VISA, American Express, and Discover Card accepted.

Degree Credit: The SURGE program offers required courses for master's degrees in: Agricultural Engineering, Business Administration, Chemical Engineering, Computer Science, Electrical Engineering, Engineering Management, Environmental Engineering, Industrial Engineering, Systems Engineering and Optimization; M.S. with specialization in Management, Mechanical Engineering, Statistics. In general, a minimum of 32 credits must be earned at Colorado State University, 21 of which must be earned after formal admission to the Graduate School. However, it is not necessary for students to be enrolled in a degree program or contemplating a graduate degree to register for SURGE courses.

Grading: Exams are sent directly to the site coordinator by the instructor. A cover sheet will be attached with the appropriate information regarding time limits, use of calculators, etc., for each exam. SURGE students have only two grading options, traditional (A, B, C, D, F) or audit. Thesis credits are graded as satisfactory or unsatisfactory. Credit is awarded in semester hour units.

Library: SURGE students have the privilege of using the Colorado State Morgan Library on campus. A registration status letter will be sent each term to all students. Computer dial-up access to library holdings is also available to SURGE students with a personal computer and modem via CARL (Colorado Association of Research Libraries).

COURSES OFFERED

Accounting

Managerial Accounting
The course objective is to provide the student with an awareness and understanding of the accounting procedures, techniques, concepts, and reports available for use by management in setting, implementing, and evaluating long- and short-term goals. Course content: short-run and long-range planning, control, and reporting. (3 credits)

Adult Education

Processes and Methods
Processes and methods including helping theories used by adult learning facilitators. (3 credits)

Adult Teaching and Learning I
Theory, research, and practice of adult teaching and learning. Concepts of behavior related to adults as learners in contrast to the young. (3 credits)

Agricultural Engineering

Soil-Water Engineering
Control of the plant-soil-water environment, irrigation and drainage, soil and water conservation. (4 credits)

Environmental Law
The environmental laws and regulations which affect the practicing engineers and environmental consultants, including the following: (1) environmental protection of water resources, including the Clean Water Act, wetlands protection and groundwater pollution, conflicts between water quality regulation and Western water rights and the Safe Drinking Water Act, (2) solid toxic and hazardous waste regulations, (3) air quality control, (4) wildlife protection, (5) toxic and environmental tort litigation, (6) environmental audits. (3 credits)

Drainage Engineering
Course deals with the flow of water in soils, drainage problems and investigations, drainage theory, design of drainage systems, installation and maintenance procedures, interaction of subsurface drainage systems. Coursework will include reading assignments, homework problems, and exams. (3 credits)

Hydraulic Design of Farm Irrigation

Hydraulic design of small irrigation structures used at the farm level to obtain water control. (3 credits)

Groundwater Quality and Contaminant Transport

Analysis of hydrochemical data. Advection with and without mixing. Retardation of reactive solutes. Design of groundwater quality investigations. (3 credits)

Flow in Porous Media

Advanced course in the mechanics of multiphase flow in porous media. Analyses of steady and unsteady flow of two fluids in horizontal and vertical flow systems. Applications to seepage through layered systems and classical imbibition and infiltration problems. (3 credits)

Agriculture

Agricultural and Resource Economics

Law as it governs acquisition of water rights under riparian and appropriations systems, interstate waters, and agencies of distribution. (3 credits)

Agronomy

Agricultural Experimental Design

Design of agricultural experiments and statistical analysis of resulting data. (3 credits)

Business

Managerial Economics

The course objective is to provide the student with an awareness and understanding of the accounting procedures, techniques, concepts, and reports available for use by management in setting, implementing, and evaluating long- and short-run goals. Course content includes short-run planning, control, reporting, and long-range planning, control, and reporting. (3 credits)

Business Policy

Formulating and executing top-level business policies. (3 credits)

Production Administration

The course includes a critical study of specific industries and representative firms therein. The focus is on methods and methodology pertaining to the effective planning/scheduling and control of operating systems in the acquisition and movement of materials and the utilization of resources in a manu-

facturing organization. Topics will cover operating strategies of selected manufacturing organizations with an emphasis on micro applications and their potential strategic impact. Students should have a prior knowledge of MRP and JIT before taking this class. (3 credits)

Business Information Systems

Computer Applications in Decision Making

Quantitative techniques analysis for business problems solved by computer utilization. Application of traditional management science techniques and decision support software. Study of information systems technology for strategic purposes. Access to a personal computer required. Class format includes PC assignments, case discussion, and application project. (3 credits)

Advanced Systems Design

Procedures used in successful design and implementation of an information system. (3 credits)

Chemical Engineering

Unit Operations and Transport Phenomena II

Mass transfer operations, simultaneous heat and mass transfer, equilibrium stage operations. (3 credits)

Chemical Engineering Thermodynamic Fundamentals

Topics to be covered include: (1) thermodynamic properties of pure fluids: the equations relating the thermodynamic properties (P, V, T, U, H, S, G, A) of a homogeneous single-phase system are reviewed, (2) thermodynamic properties of homogeneous mixtures: the concept of partial molar properties is introduced and the distinction between ideal and nonideal solutions is illustrated through consideration of volume changes and heat effects due to mixing, (3) phase equilibria: basic concepts such as the criteria for equilibrium, the phase rule, and Duhem's theorem are developed, (4) chemical reaction equilibria: basic concepts such as the criteria for equilibrium and the relationship between equilibrium coefficient and the standard free energy change of reaction are presented. (3 credits)

Process Control and Instrumentation

This course is aimed at providing fundamental knowledge on how to control a chemical process. Laplace transform principles are reviewed. Mathematical models of simple systems are derived. Open loop and closed loop systems are analyzed. Frequency response methods are used to design controllers. Some practical applications of feedback control are discussed. Other control techniques such as feedforward, ratio, cascade decoupling, and model-based control are introduced. The course includes two lab experiments to demonstrate control principles. (3 credits)

Advanced Reactor Design

A brief review of fundamentals in chemical reaction engineering is followed by a deeper exploration of more advanced areas such as heterogeneous catalysis and multiphase reaction. Emphasis is placed upon gas-solid reactions and kinetic mechanism with examples from the microelectronics industry. (3 credits)

Civil Engineering

Basic Hydrology

Study of hydrologic cycle, precipitation processes, soil moisture, infiltration, groundwater, rainfall-runoff processes, utilization of water resources. (3 credits)

Engineering Hydrology

Hydrologic design under uncertainty, conventional and remote sensing, design flows and storms, river routing, reservoir design, watershed models. (3 credits)

Modeling Watershed Hydrology

Development and application of watershed models, structure, calibration, evaluation, sensitivity analysis, simulation. (4 credits)

Residuals Management

Planning and design for processing and disposal of residuals including solid wastes, sludges, hazardous wastes. (3 credits)

Aqueous Chemistry

Principles of solution chemistry applied to aquatic systems. (3 credits)

Unit Processes of Environmental Engineering

Water and wastewater treatment processes, disinfection, aeration, activated sludge, trickling filters, anaerobic digestion, ponds. (4 credits)

Water Resource Systems Analysis

Applications of systems analysis and optimization techniques in water resources planning and manage-

ment. Weekly homework assignments, including instruction on and use of available computer software for IBM PC and compatible microcomputers on simulation and optimization of water resource systems. Available software includes linear programming, dynamic programming, and network flow algorithms for complex problems in water resources planning and management (provided free with course registration). (3 credits)

Earth and Earth-Retaining Structures

Load on conduits, retaining walls, braced cuts, sheet pilewalls, slope stability, embankments. (3 credits)

Fundamentals of Vibrations

Free and forced vibrations of single, two, and multiple degree of freedom systems. Closed-form and numerical solutions. (3 credits)

Advanced Design of Wood Structures

Characteristics of structural products and their consideration in design, behavior of glulam members, wood trusses, and other wood structural systems. (3 credits)

Urban Water Management

Modern techniques for analysis, management, and control of water supply, wastewater and urban drainage, and flood control systems. (3 credits)

Infrastructure Engineering and Management

Infrastructure program planning, management, and engineering. Problems, tools of analysis, solution strategies. Use of decision support systems. (3 credits)

Wind Effects on Structures

Analysis of wind effects on buildings and structures, deterministic and probabilistic methods, aerodynamic loading and response, codes and standards. (3 credits)

Computational Fluid Dynamics

Unique fluid mechanics aspects of advection, boundary conditions, and turbulence models. Solution of elliptic, parabolic, and hyperbolic problems. (3 credits)

Open Channel Flow

Steady/uniform/non-uniform flow, backwater curves, flow through bridge piers/transitions/culverts, spatially varied and unsteady flow. (4 credits)

Hydraulics of Closed Conduits

Pipe transmission and distribution systems design including flow control, flow measurement, energy dissipation, pump selection, transients, cavitation. (3 credits)

Water Quality Hydrology

Effects and dispersion of natural, municipal, industrial, toxic, and other water pollutants on natural and impounded waters. (3 credits)

Solutions to Groundwater Problems

Numerical flow models, finite difference and finite element methods, parameter identification, stochastic modeling, advanced analytical solutions. (3 credits)

Design of Dams

Design of earth and concrete gravity dams, structural, soil mechanics, seepage, earthquake, wind waves, and site selection considerations. (3 credits)

Foundations of Solid Mechanics

Analysis of stress and strain in solids emphasizing linear elasticity and plasticity, introductions to creep, viscoelasticity, and finite deformations. (3 credits)

Finite Element Method

Theory and application in elasticity, porous flow, heat conduction, and other engineering problems. (3 credits)

Advanced Structural Analysis

Development of the finite element method for nonlinear structural analysis, stability of structures. (3 credits)

Advanced Design of Metal Structures

Behavior of steel, aluminum, and cold formed members. Development of elastic and inelastic code provisions, LRFD design methods, building systems. (3 credits)

River Mechanics

Characteristics of rivers, mechanics of sediment and water discharge emphasizing alluvial systems, channel stabilization, control, response. Problems related to river mechanics and river engineering. Major research-oriented project meeting the following objectives: literature review on a selected topic, analysis of field or laboratory data leading to the comparison of new technology with existing methods. (3 credits)

Stochastic Analysis in Water Resources

Stochastic processes applied to various water resources problems. Synthetic data generation, forecasting, Kalman filtering, kriging. Topics will include time series analysis of hydrologic processes, physically based stochastic hydrology, stochastic modeling of hydrologic time series (univariate and multivariate), disaggregation and aggregation of hydrologic processes, modeling of short-term rainfall data generation, and forecasting of hydrologic processes. (3 credits)

Computer Science

Computer Organization

Digital logic, digital systems, representation of data, assembly level organization, memory system organization and architecture. (4 credits)

Algorithms and Data Structures

Data structures, complexity analysis, sorting, searching, numerical computing, file systems, databases, graphics. (4 credits)

Discrete Structures

Machine logic, data structures, spanning trees, machines and languages, Boolean algebra, algebraic structures, recursive algorithms. (4 credits)

C Programming Module

Data types, expressions, program structures and idioms, I/O, libraries. (2 credits)

Comparative Programming Languages

Virtual machines, data types, sequence control, programming paradigms, storage management, grammars and translation, semantics. (4 credits)

Foundations of Computer Science

Formal languages, automata, algorithms, complexity classes, computability and decidability, process coordination, algorithms for artificial intelligence. (4 credits)

Software Development Methods

Methods used to develop large-scale software projects in industry emphasizing design, implementation, and testing. (4 credits)

System Architecture and Software

Memory organization, I/O control, alternative architectures, multitasking, process control, security, networking, distributed computing. (4 credits)

Introduction to Computer Graphics

This course will give the student an understanding of the fundamentals of computer graphics necessary to create images of two- and three-dimensional objects. Outline: graphics output devices, clippin algorithms, 2D and 3D coordinate transformations, hierarchical object definitions, 3D viewing projections, hidden line and surface removal, curve and surface representations. This course requires that the student have access to a computer system with a graphics CRT display capable of printing a copy of the graphics screen. (4 credits)

Introduction to Artificial Intelligence

Class discussions range from Lisp and Prolog fundamentals to philosophical issues in artificial intelligence. The bulk of the course is between these two extremes. The languages Lisp and Prolog are used to illustrate basic data structures and programming techniques used in the field of artificial intelligence. Problem-solving search methods, logical reasoning techniques, production-rule systems, semantic nets, and frames will be implemented as programming assignments. An overview of other topics, such as neural networks and genetic algorithms, is included. (4 credits)

Data Communications

This course examines the principles of data communication. Local area networks are discussed including the components used to construct them. Most of the course material will be presented within the framework of the OSI Reference Model, including a variety of communication protocols. Internet and ISDN will also be discussed. The student should have access to a C compiler on a PC or workstation in order to complete lab assignments. (4 credits)

Computer Graphics

The objective of this course is to learn the fundamentals of producing realistic views of three-dimensional objects. Algorithms for performing perspective transformations, generating surfaces, and shading surfaces are introduced. Access to a workstation running X Windows will be useful. (4 credits)

Artificial Intelligence

The course is structured around a comparison between traditional methods in artificial intelligence and neural network connectionist models. Specific topics include natural language understanding, memory organization, planning, and machine learning. Knowledge of C required. (4 credits)

Algorithmic Language Compilers

Compiler instruction, lexical analysis, parsing, semantics, code generation, and error detection. Students will write a C compiler in the class. Must have access to Yacc and Lex software or their equivalents,

as well as a C compiler. This course will require 15 to 20 hours per week of student programming effort. (4 credits)

Advanced Computer Architecture

Models of computation, cache memories, pipelined execution, vector execution, VLIW and superscalar architectures. (4 credits)

Parallel Processing

The main course topics include parallel processing paradigms (SIMD, distributed or shared memory and dataflow), example architectures, interconnection networks, performance analysis and evaluation of parallel and distributed systems, and the hardware/software interaction in parallel computing. (4 credits)

Performance Evaluation and Modeling

This course will present the major techniques in evaluating the performance of computer systems, concentrating on analytic methods. Real applications, especially those drawn from multiprocessor systems, will drive the presentation. Review of required probability and other subjects will be included. (4 credits)

Architecture of Advanced Systems (Optical Communication Networks)

The course will take a critical look at the recent developments in technology, network architectures, protocols, and applications for optical communication networks operating at gigabit rates. The course is designed for engineers and computer scientists who are interested in finding out about the state-of-the-art as well as technical challenges in this area. Topics cover introduction to communication networks, gigabit network applications, modulation, multiplexing and switching techniques, optical communication networks—topologies and MAC protocols, future of networking. (3 credits)

Earth Resources

Modeling Watershed Hydrology

Development and application of watershed models, structure, calibration, evaluation, sensitivity analysis, simulation. (4 credits)

Electrical Engineering

Introduction to Microprocessors

Microprocessor organization, assembly language, I/O techniques, real-time interfaces, applications, hardware/software. Student must be able to attend a lab section either on campus or arrange to complete at work site. (4 credits)

Digital Control and Digital Filters

FIR and IIR digital filter design, analog and digital invariance and direct digital control algorithms, hybrid systems analysis. (3 credits)

Communications Systems

This is a course in basic modulation techniques, such as AM, FM, and digital modulation. The course will pay special attention to the performance of these systems in the presence of noise. In addition, some discussion of information theory, error correcting codes, and channel capacity will be included. The student should have access to a computer with graphics and a high-level language such as Pascal, C, or FORTRAN. (3 credits)

MOS Integrated Circuits

MOSFET device physics, inverters, logic/shift register/memory circuits. Integrated circuit design rules and layout. NMOS and CMOS. Student must have access to integrated circuit CAD system for NMOS and CMOS. (3 credits)

Operational Amplifier Circuits

Active filter implementations with operational amplifiers, nonideal amplifier, cascade/multiple feedback, leapfrog implementations, switched capacitor filters. (3 credits)

Microwave Theory and Component Design

Fundamentals of microwave engineering, components, devices, and measurements. (3 credits)

Digital Optical Computing

Optical devices, optical disks, holographic memories, interconnection networks. Optical systems for numerical and nonnumerical data processing. (3 credits)

Optical Materials and Devices

Semiconductor light emitters and detectors, dielectrics, and light reflection from, and progration through, anisotropic dielectrics. (3 credits)

Testing of Digital Systems

The objective of this course is to provide students with the background of the techniques of testing digital systems, with the emphasis on CMOS logic circuits. Fault modeling will be introduced. Various test generation algorithms for static and dynamic CMOS circuits will then be presented. Also covered will be important topics in CMOS testing, such as test invalidation, design for robust testability, and self-checking circuits. Each student is required to do a project on the subject chosen by the student, in consultation with the instructor. (3 credits)

Estimation and Filtering Theory

Optimal Kalman filter estimators, smoothing and prediction, applications to communications and controls. (3 credits)

Design Automation

Advanced logic design methods, digital system modeling/simulation/testing, design for testability, CAD systems. (3 credits)

Multidimensional Digital Signal Processing

Multidimensional signals and systems, 2-D transforms, stability methods, design and implementations, spectral factorization, and image modeling. (3 credits)

Performance Evaluation and Modeling

This course will present the major techniques in evaluating the performance of computer systems, concentrating on analytic methods. Real applications, especially those drawn from multiprocessor systems, will drive the presentation. Reviews of required probability and other subjects will be included. (4 credits)

Architecture of AVLSI System Design II

This course is designed for students who are interested in high-level VLSI design techniques. Many important issues in VLSI design methodology will be covered to enhance students' understanding of VLSI design. Course topics include VLSI design trajectory, behavioral and functional design, logic and circuit design, chip design, interconnection and packaging, and VLSI testing and yield estimation. (3 credits)

Topics in Electromagnetics

Applications of wave propagation and scattering to microwave radar, Doppler radar, meteorological radar applications. (3 credits)

Topics in Solid State Electronics

Advanced principles of microwave devices, solar cells, theory of solids, or transport in materials. (3 credits)

Engineering

Linear Programming and Network Flows

Optimization methods, linear programming, simplex algorithm, duality, sensitivity analysis, minimal cost network flows, transportation problem. (3 credits)

Nonlinear Programming

Theoretical, computational, practical aspects of nonlinear programming (NLP), unconstrained/constrained NLP, quadratic programming, large-scale NLP. (3 credits)

Engineering Decision Support and Expert Systems

The student is introduced to modern tools for analyzing complex engineering decision problems under conflicting objectives and uncertainty. A number of techniques are presented for aiding in the analysis of a wide range of complex engineering problems. Basic concepts of expert systems are presented to show an essential synergy between decision support systems and expert systems for development of decision support structures that allow inclusion of heuristics and symbolic information. (3 credits)

Finance

Financial Environment and Operations

The objective of this financial management course is to provide the student with an introduction to the problems faced by corporate financial managers and to suggest methods for resolving the problems. The course will emphasize financial planning. That is, what are the problems faced by financial managers in a dynamic economic environment and what steps can the manager take to resolve the problems. The course draws heavily on economic theory. In addition, the disciplines of accounting and statistics are heavily used to formulate and solve the problems faced by financial managers. (3 credits)

Financial Markets

Analysis of money and capital markets and their relevance for the business decision-making process. Topics include term structure of interest rates, import of Federal Reserve policy, hedging techniques (futures, options, and swaps), international capital flows, and the continuing evolution of the structure of financial institutions. (3 credits)

Forest Sciences

Advanced Design of Wood Structures

Characteristics of structural products and their consideration in design, behavior of glulam members, wood trusses, and other wood structural systems. (3 credits)

Industrial Science

Cost, Productivity, and Financial Control

Optimizing time-cost restraints, controlling expenditures, account code designations, reporting systems. (3 credits)

Research Methods

Identification, analysis of research problems in applications of technology. (3 credits)

Management

Management of Organization Development

Methods for managing organizational change. (3 credits)

Management

Moves beyond basic management concepts to probe management values, philosophies, practices, and concepts from both traditional and modern viewpoints. (3 credits)

Managerial Planning and Control

The purpose of this course is to develop student understanding of the process of globalization taking place in the world economy and to develop a conceptual knowledge base about international business. (3 credits)

Basic Business Statistics

The intent of the course is to provide training and understanding in the techniques and methods of statistical analysis of data as used in the business environment. Course content includes review of statistical measures, discrete probability distributions, continuous probability distributions, sampling distribution theory and applications, estimation of parameters, sampling procedures and applications, statistical decision making I (classical hypothesis testing), statistical decision making II (chi-square-goodness of fit, contingency tables—one way), regression and correlation—simple linear, index numbers, time series analysis. (3 credits)

Marketing

Marketing Systems

The course objective is to provide an introduction to and a comprehensive analysis of macro- and micro-marketing for graduate students with nonbusiness undergraduate degrees. Students should develop an understanding of the structural characteristics of marketing organizations, the role of marketing in society, the managerial elements, and the problems inherent in the marketing organization. Course content includes the marketing system, market demand, product decisions, place decision, promotion decisions, price decisions, planning/implementing/controlling marketing activities, international marketing, marketing's social responsibility. (3 credits)

Mathematics

Discrete Structures

Machine logic, data structures, spanning trees, machines and languages, Boolean algebra, algebraic structures, recursive algorithms. (4 credits)

Linear Programming and Network Flows

Optimization methods, linear programming, simplex algorithm, duality, sensitivity analysis, minimal cost network flows, transportation problems. (3 credits)

Nonlinear Programming

Theoretical, computational, practical aspects of nonlinear programming (NLP), unconstrained/constrained NLP, quadratic programming, large-scale NLP. (3 credits)

Applied Mathematics II

Fourier series, Fourier integrals, partial differential equations, Bessel and Legendre functions, Laplace transforms, and finite differences. (3 credits)

Mechanical Engineering

Design of Models for Decision Making

Design of decision-making models for industrial engineering. (3 credits)

Manufacturing Engineering

Casting, forming, machining, and welding processes used in manufacturing operations. (3 credits)

Materials Engineering

Structural engineering materials and their selection on basis of property, processing, and economic considerations. (3 credits)

Statistics

Engineering Statistics

Probability and distribution theory, estimation and testing, correlation and regression, applications to engineering and manufacturing. (3 credits)

Design and Data Analysis for Researchers II

This course is intended for graduate students who need to have knowledge of how statistical approaches and methods can help solve problems and answer questions. Second of the two-semester sequence covers (1) the interrelationship between science and statistics with an introduction to problem-solving techniques, (2) exploratory data analysis with emphasis on graphical methods, (3) basis inferential procedures, and (4) design and analysis of experiments. Several mainframe and micro-based computer packages will be used. (3 credits)

Mathematical Statistics

Sampling distributions, estimation, testing, confidence intervals, exact and asymptotic theories of maximum likelihood and distribution-free methods. (3 credits)

Linear Statistical Models I

Multivariate normal, properties of quadratic forms, noncentral F, t, X (squared), Gauss-Markov theory, full rank/multiple/polynomial regression models. (3 credits)

Vocational Education

Human Resource Development

Human resource development foundations and techniques related to vocational training and development for industry, business, education, and government. (3 credits)

HRD and Training Needs Assessment and Analysis

Identify and evaluate human resource development training and education activities and strategies in response to organization performance issues. (3 credits)

Community College of Aurora
See **KRMA/Denver**

Community College of Denver
See **KRMA/Denver**

Front Range Community College

See **KRMA/Denver**

International School of Information Management, Inc.

50 South Steele Street
Denver, CO   80209

(800) 441-4746 *Fax:* (303) 752-4044

Geographic Access: Worldwide

DELIVERY SYSTEMS

Online Services
Instruction is delivered through ISIMnet, an educational computer conferencing environment. Students use a personal computer to connect to ISIMnet three or four times a week, at their own convenience. Students interact with one another and with their instructors online by posting and receiving messages on ISIMnet, their "virtual classroom." Use of a common integrated software package makes it possible for students and instructors to exchange ideas and information in graphic, word processor, database, and spreadsheet form. ISIMnet also provides electronic mail for private messages.

INSTITUTION DESCRIPTION

The International School of Information Management, Inc. (ISIM) and two related corporate entities, ABC-CLIO and INTELLIMATION, form an educational alliance dating back to 1953, with offices in Santa Barbara, Denver, and Oxford, England. ABC-CLIO and INTELLIMATION provide award-winning multimedia services and products to libraries and schools worldwide.

ISIM was founded in 1987. Its mission is to provide working adults with flexible opportunities to study business and information management, and to acquire the skills and knowledge they need to succeed in a rapidly changing and fiercely competitive world. With a focus on information management, current offerings include accredited Master of Business Administration (MBA) and Master of Science (MS) degrees and a variety of corporate training courses.

ISIM courses are application-oriented to better pre-

pare students for the demands of today's workplace. Special emphasis is placed on the leadership functions of decision making, team building, and communication in dealing with the people, environment, process, and project aspects of an enterprise. Students work individually and in teams to complete assignments and master course content. Through discussion, students and instructor share experiences, insights, and questions related to course content; everyone learns from everyone else. To participate in ISIMnet's learning community, students must have access to a computer with a communications capability.

Accreditation: DETC

Official/Contact: Mary Adams, Vice President

Admission Requirements: Applicants must submit the following documents: application for admission; evidence of bachelor's degree from an accredited or state-approved college or university, or an equivalent certified degree from a recognized foreign college or university (ISIM may conditionally accept applicants in their final year of bachelor's degree studies); official transcripts of all previous college study; resume of employment and professional accomplishments; three letters of recommendation (one preferably from current employer); a goals statement reflecting academic, professional, and personal goals that the applicant hopes to achieve through ISIM's MBA or MS program. In addition, successful applicants should have the following: an awareness of new skills needed for further career growth; a basic understanding of the principles and practices of management; an ability to write clearly and conduct research; functional familiarity with word processing or text editing and online communications technology. Admission is based on an assessment of each applicant's potential for successfully completing the program of his/her choice.

Tuition: Tuition is $250 per unit (subject to change). Total tuition costs for the 50-unit MBA or MS program are $12,500. A study guide for each course is included in the tuition fee. Books, software, materials, and online charges are not included. The following items should be budgeted into the total degree cost: books ($500-$1000); graduation fee ($100); communications software ($150); integrated software package ($100); online tutorial ($150); online charges ($500-$1000); materials shipping and handling ($150 @ $15 per course). Payment plans are available.

Degree Credit: The Master of Science in Information Management and the Master of Business Administration with emphasis on Information Systems and Technology programs each require the completion of 50 units of credit.

Grading: A letter grade of A, B, or U (unsatisfactory) is assigned for student performance in each course. Academic credit is granted on the basis of courses passed. Courses not passed (graded U) may be repeated.

Library: The Internet provides access to databases and academic library collections around the world. ISIM provides information about accessing the Internet.

COURSES OFFERED

Business Administration

Management

This course focuses on the foundations of sound management theory, and on the processes and techniques of decision making. Subjects discussed include the process of management, communication, motivation, leadership, behavior, control, and application. Not included in this course are topics of specific ISIM courses focusing on strategic planning, management information systems, and international competition.

Accounting

A course that focuses on accounting concepts and builds to a level in which the student can perform accounting-related functions in a corporate environment. Topics include principles and practices for recording business transaction data. Construction and interpretation of financial statements: balance sheet, income statement, and cash flow. Accounting and legal requirements in preparing financial statements. The use of accounting data for strategic and management purposes, emphasis on profitability: cost prevention and reduction, and revenue.

Quantitative Analysis

The understanding and ability to utilize quantitative analyses is a most valuable process for decision makers and professionals responsible for guiding their organizations into a dynamic environment where change and the internationalization of businesses are constant. The field of quantitative analysis is undergoing constant change in response to shifts in needs of the end user of the information.

This course focuses upon the foundations of calculus, statistics, and econometric forecasting. Subjects discussed include limits, continuity, differentiation, integration, statistics, probability, law of large numbers, central tendency, theorem, regression, correlation, and forecasting.

Finance

This course focuses on the foundations of financial theory and techniques of financial decision making. Subjects discussed include financial analyses of liquidity, debt, and profitability. Short-term, intermediate-term, and long-term financing. Working capital and cash management. Credit management and capital budgeting, costs of raising various forms of capital, operational and financial leverage, dividend theories and policies, optimal capital structure, profit planning, and reorganization of the firm.

Marketing Management

This course focuses on marketing and marketing management concepts and builds to a level in which the student can manage marketing and related functions in a corporate environment, thereby enabling the student to become a more productive member of the management team. Subjects include market research and analysis, developing an effective marketing strategy including segmentation, targeting, and positioning. Implementing marketing strategy with the marketing mix: product, pricing, distribution, and promotion.

Managerial Economics

A course that focuses on the application of economic analysis to the managerial decision-making process. Topics include demand functions, marginal revenue functions, elasticities of demand, consumer behavior, costs of production, and international dimensions of demand production and cost, linear programming, monopolistic competition, oligopoly and rivalrous market structure, economic forecasting, and pricing and profit strategy.

Strategic Planning

Strategic planning is a systematic, generally formal effort of an organization to define its purpose and align itself with its current and future environment. This course is designed to provide students with the tools for developing strategic plans. Each student will be required to prepare a strategic plan based on his/her organization.

Strategies for Change

This course focuses on the identification of and adaptation to ongoing changes brought on by information technology. Special consideration is given to developing strategies for managing the change.

Emerging Technologies

State-of-the-art and emerging technologies in information processing are examined in this course which includes a survey of recent advances in software development (such as OOP and CASE), hardware (ranging from PCs and workstations to a survey of the latest supercomputing technology), and computer networking strategies.

Capstone Project

The Capstone Project allows students to apply the knowledge and skills acquired in their courses to the work environment. This project is completely individualized. Students are encouraged to select work-related projects that are of particular interest to them and that will result in professional growth. Work on the project should begin upon completion of the core courses.

Specialization

Specialization (two 5-unit courses) beyond the MBA is available in health care, entrepreneurship (with focus on intellectual property, information management, and telecommunications.

Information Management

Managing in a Rapidly Changing Environment

This course sets the stage for ISIM's MS degree program consisting of 50-units of six 5-unit core courses, three 5-unit electives, and a 5-unit project. The course focuses on the need for organizations to respond efficiently and effectively to the rapid, worldwide changes that are occurring now and will continue into the 21st century. Management techniques for promoting a culture that facilitates change are presented, and discussion includes the dynamics of growth and change and their impact on the success of technology-intensive organizations.

Management of Information Systems

The focus of this course is on planning, organizing, and controlling user services, and on managing the information systems development process. Additional topics covered include the organizational learning curve, dealing with vendors, budgeting, accounting, management reporting, and legal considerations.

Information Systems Strategic Planning

The relationship of information systems planning to overall organization goals, policies, plans, and management style are explored. Guidelines for selecting systems projects, assessing the installation's current state, and determining processing and financial needs are also discussed.

Technology Ethics and Social Responsibility

This course challenges students' awareness of the ethical issues inherent in business and professional decisions and examines the relationship between the individual, the firm, and society, especially with respect to the development and implementation of new technology.

Telecommunications

This comprehensive overview of the telecommunications industry includes a brief history, a look at the field's structure and regulation, information on networks and telecommunications services, the basics of traffic engineering, and an introduction to the primary concepts of data communications systems and the underlying functions and principles of telecommunications management.

Emerging Technologies

State-of-the-art and emerging technologies in information processing are examined in this course which includes a survey of recent advances in software development (such as OOP and CASE), hardware (ranging from PCs and workstations to a survey of the latest supercomputing technology), and computer networking strategies.

Capstone Project

The Capstone Project allows students to apply the knowledge and skills acquired in their courses to the work environment. This project is completely individualized. Students are encouraged to select work-related projects that are of particular interest to them and that will result in professional growth. Work on the project should begin upon completion of the core courses.

Information Technology

Data Communications

This course provides essential skills and knowledge for designing communication systems. Network protocols and wide- and local-area networks are covered in detail. Topics include the seven-layers of the OSI model, client-server technology, and comparison of different network architectures.

Systems Design

Formalization of information systems analysis and design processes allow exploration of state-of-the-art techniques for systems specification and design. Topics include real-time structured analysis and design, and object-oriented analysis and design.

Telecommunications Policy

This course explores alternative forms of regulation of AT&T and the RBOCs, rate structure and tariffs, computer inquiries and open network architecture, wireless technologies and related policy issues, and current issues in telecommunications policy.

Telephony

This course provides a detailed look at voice telephone systems. Topics include characteristics of speech, network hierarchy, customer premises equipment, transmission systems and impairments, multiplexing, signaling, altering and supervision, traffic engineering, network optimization, and switching fundamentals.

Management

Customers, Markets, and Technology in Technology-Intensive Organizations

This course focuses on the relationship between technology-based products and the consumers of these products. Students investigate methodologies for designing, developing, and delivering technology-based products that solve real-world problems.

Information Systems Policy

Designed to provide an understanding of the overall information needs of an organization and the role of computer-based information systems, this course covers management of computer-center and technical personnel, systems development management, and enterprise analysis.

Planning for Information Networks

This course presents a methodology for planning telecommunications networks from the perspective of a technical manager. General planning principles are covered, and during the course students develop a general model based on structured analysis techniques. Related topics of network architectures, risk analysis, and disaster recovery are discussed.

Technology and the Global Environment

The focus of this course is on the impact of globalization on technological innovation and infusion. Students interpret the technological activities of organizations in their global context and analyze the likely impact of these activities on technological choices and opportunities.

KRMA/Denver
Council for Public Television
1089 Bannock Street
Denver, CO   80204

(303) 892-6666

Geographic Access: Colorado, Wyoming

DELIVERY SYSTEMS

Broadcast Television
Telecourses are aired over KRMA/TV, Channel 6.

INSTITUTION DESCRIPTION

The telecourses aired by KRMA/TV are academically proven, well-produced television series developed by college faculty, scholars, practitioners, and instructional design specialists. Because taking a telecourse requires only a minimum (if any) of on-campus attendance, it has become one of the most popular alternatives to traditionally taught courses.

A telecourse is a coordinated learning system based on a series of television programs supplemented by print materials (text, study guide, readings) and local faculty involvement in the form of lectures and/or consultation. The choice of discipline, amount of credit, course level/requirements and tuition cost for each telecourse may vary from one institution to another. Prospective students should contact the institution of their choice to determine the availability of the courses listed below. Participating institutions and telephone contacts are:

- Adams State College (Alamosa CO), (800) 548-6679
- Arapahoe Community College (Littleton CO), (303) 797-5604
- Colorado Mountain College (Glenwood Springs CO), (800) 621-9602

- Colorado Northwestern Community College (Rangely CO), (303) 675-3273
- Colorado State University (Ft. Collins CO), (800) 525-4950
- Community College of Aurora (Aurora CO), (303) 360-4743
- Community College of Denver (Denver CO), (303) 556-3386
- Eastern Wyoming College (Torrington WY), (800) 658-3195
- Front Range Community College (Westminster CO), (303) 466-8811
- Laramie County Community College (Cheyenne WY), (307) 634-5853
- Metropolitan State College of Denver (Englewood CO), (303) 721-1313
- Morgan Community College (Fort Morgan CO), (800) 622-0216
- Northeastern Junior College (Sterling CO), (303) 522-6600
- Pikes Peak Community College (Colorado Springs CO), (800) 825-0401
- Red Rocks Community College (Lakewood CO), (303) 988-6160
- Trinidad State Junior College (Trinidad CO), (800) 621-8752
- University of Northern Colorado (Greeley CO), (800) 776-2434
- Western State College (Gunnison CO), (303) 943-2885

Accreditation: All participating institutions are accredited by NCA.

Official/Contact: Josefina Tuason, Coordinator

Admission Requirements: Prospective students should contact the college of their choice to determine admission requirements. Generally, open enrollment for all courses.

Tuition: Tuition varies among institutions. Contact the college of choice for current tuition and fees. Textbooks must be purchased by the student and can be obtained at the college bookstores.

Degree Credit: Credits earned by successful completion of a telecourse may be applied to a degree program. Limitations as to total amount of credit may apply. Educators should be aware of school district policy, their endorsement areas and/or degree program requirements before registering. Colorado educators wishing to use community college courses may do so if the coursework applies to a new endorsement, is in the area of the teacher's assignment, extends the computer skills of the teacher, or deals with child abuse. Specific questions dealing with certification can be directed to the Colorado Department of Education at (303) 866-6628.

Grading: Examinations must be proctored. Generally, letter grades are assigned. Credit is awarded in semester hour units for most courses (normally each course is for 3 credits).

Library: Students officially enrolled for a telecourse have access to the library resources at the institution where registered.

COURSES OFFERED

Anthropology

Faces of Culture
Examines the adaptive survival mechanism within societies and the relationship between individuals and their culture. Studies marriage and family, social stratification, kinship, and descent. (3 credits)

Business

The Business File
Takes a comprehensive view of the contemporary business world from internal functions to international operations. Explores the complexities of both large and small businesses in various areas of operation. (3 credits)

Business and the Law
Provides a comprehensive overview of law and the world of business. Includes law of sales, commercial paper, agency and property. (3 credits)

Economics

Economics U$A
Examines major historic and contemporary events that have shaped 20th-century American economics. Establishes a clear relationship between abstract economic principles and concrete human experience through interviews, commentary, and analysis. (3 credits)

Education

Education of the Gifted and Talented
Surveys the history, philosophy, and potential research directions of gifted education. Helps identify the characteristics of gifted learners, state their general educational needs, evaluate various program models and apply techniques learned. (3 credits)

Teaching Problem Solving in Mathematics
Illustrates how diverse instructional strategies, materials, and resources can be used in the classroom to develop student problem solving. (3 credits)

English

Literary Visions
Brings literature to life with dramatizations of individual works and readings of literary passages. Organized around three major genres of literature—short fiction, poetry, and drama. (3 credits)

Environmental Science

Race to Save the Planet
Provides a dynamic report of the current outlook for the global environment, describing the threats that different natural systems face and dissecting the complex web of interconnections that bind human society to the environment. (3 credits)

Geology

Earth Revealed
A comprehensive study of the earth's physical processes and properties with emphasis on understanding the scientific theories behind the geological principles. (3 credits)

Planet Earth
Unlocks the secrets of the earth and solar system, visualizing dynamic, cyclical processes. Provides close-hand looks at some of the great forces which continue to sculpt our planet and cause changes in the universe. (3 credits)

History

The American Adventure
Focuses on the human story, as well as the political and economic stories of America, from Columbian contact to the Civil War and Reconstruction. (3 credits)

The Western Tradition
Weaves together history, art, literature, religion, geography, government, and economics to provide an understanding of the pendulum swings of history and the evolution of human institutions. (3 credits)

Management

Taking the Lead
Provides an overview of management in the nineties, with an emphasis on the competencies that are essential for success. Based on the major functions of management—planning, organizing, staffing, directing, and controlling. (3 credits)

Marketing

Marketing
Offers a thorough introduction to marketing as it relates to contemporary living and society's changing needs. Includes such topics as consumer markets, planning, and forecasting, product adoption, wholesaling, retailing, advertising and publicity, pricing strategy, selling, and international marketing. (3 credits)

The Sales Connection
Designed to provide aspiring salespeople, and those already involved in sales, with the tools and insight they need to compete in the age of long-term, consultative-style selling. (3 credits)

Mathematics

College Algebra: In Simplest Terms
An introductory course that takes the student step-by-step to a thorough understanding and working knowledge of the concepts and practical, real-life applications of algebra. (3 credits)

Philosophy

Ethics in America
Examines contemporary ethical conflicts and provides a grounding in the language concepts and traditions of ethics. (3 credits)

Political Science

Government by Consent
Integrates political science instruction with examples of how students involve themselves in government. Attempts to change common perception of

government as a removed, larger-than-life process which seems inaccessible to citizens. (3 credits)

The Pacific Century

A survey of the modern history, economics, politics, and cultures of the Pacific Basin region. Explores how the region has evolved to emerge as a principal political and economic center of the upcoming century. (3 credits)

Psychology

Discovering Psychology

A study of the fundamental principles and major concepts of psychology, using original footage of classic experiments, interviews with renowned psychologists, and documentaries of emerging research. (3 credits)

Seasons of Life

Chronicles major changes in human development through voices of people in all the seasons of life and through the commentary of researchers who study the life span. (3 credits)

The World of Abnormal Psychology

Explores the complex causes, manifestations, and treatment of common behavior disorders through interviews with patients and commentary by therapists and other mental health professionals. (3 credits)

Religious Studies

Beliefs and Believers

A comprehensive look at the nature and function of the religions and secular beliefs that comprise the major "worldviews" in place today. (3 credits)

Rural Sociology

Rural Communities

Addresses the challenges facing rural America by traveling to 15 rural regions and examining various facets of community life. Includes profiles of communities confronting decisions about how much change is acceptable and necessary. (3 credits)

Sociology

The Sociological Imagination

An in-depth look at groups, communities, institutions, and social situations that illustrate major sociological concepts. Covers such issues as socializa-

tion, social control, sex and gender, aging, education, collective behavior, and social change. (3 credits)

Spanish

Destinos

Uses the powerful appeal of a uniquely Hispanic genre—the "telenovela"— to make language and culture come alive. Designed to help students develop basic language skills as well as understand the gestures and cultural clues that enrich communication. (3 credits)

Statistics

Against All Odds

An exploration of statistical processes, stressing data-centered topics rather than the more traditional path from probability to formal inference. (3 credits)

Metropolitan State College of Denver
Extended Campus Programs

Suite 116
5660 Greenwood Plaza Boulevard
Englewood, CO   80111

(303) 721-1313

Geographic Access: Colorado

DELIVERY SYSTEMS

Broadcast Television
KRMA-TV, Channel 6, airs telecourses each semester. Many of these telecourses may also be seen on KBDI-TV, Channel 12, as well as on cable.

INSTITUTION DESCRIPTION

Metropolitan State College of Denver is a state institution that shares a campus and facilities with the Community College of Denver—Auraria as well as maintaining four other centers in the metropolitan Denver area. The college was established in 1963.

Telecourses are fully accredited college classes that combine television viewing, a textbook, study guide, and class meetings or discussion groups with a qualified instructor. Classes are offered on a semester basis.

Accreditation: NCA

Official/Contact: Gwen Thornton, Director, Telecourse Program

Admission Requirements: Graduation from high school or GED.

Tuition: See course descriptions below. VISA and MasterCard are accepted. Textbooks may be purchased at the Auraria Book Center in the Auraria Student Union.

Degree Credit: Formally admitted students may apply credit toward a degree program.

Grading: Letter grades are assigned. Examinations must be proctored. Credit is awarded in semester hour units.

Library: Students have access to catalogs of all Colorado Alliance of Research Libraries (CARL) members.

COURSES OFFERED

Archaeology

Archaeology
Out of the Past is a new telecourse that uses visually dramatic on-site filming to enable students to explore how archaeologists reconstruct ancient societies and explain how and why they evolved. Research at the spectacular Classic Maya Center of Copan, Honduras, forms the core of the series, but a broadly comparative perspective includes many other civilizations and cultures, past and present, from North America, Africa, Europe, and the Middle East. Students will understand how archaeology and anthropology interact. Includes the video component as well as class meetings or discussion groups. In-state cost $263. (3 semester credits)

Chemistry

Chemistry and Society
The World of Chemistry provides a broad view of chemistry extending beyond the conventional classroom environment. On-site footage of industrial processes illustrates chemical reactions, while computer animation reveals the changes that take place at the molecular level. Interviews with distinguished scientists shed light on chemistry's historical foundations, recent developments, and future directions. The course uses computer testing and grading for independent learning. Required orientation session. Optional meetings. In-state cost $263. (3 semester credits)

Geology

General Geology
Earth Revealed: Introductory Geology vividly documents a comprehensive study of the earth's physical processes and properties, including the scientific theories behind the geological principles. The telecourse shows on-location footage at major geological sites around the world. In-state cost $346. (4 semester credits)

History

Western Civilization Since 1715
This is the second semester of a year-long telecourse, *The Western Tradition*, that begins with the end of the Middle Ages and the onset of the Renaissance, continuing through industrial modernization to the present. By weaving together history, art, literature, religion, geography, government, and economics, the course helps students recognize the pendulum swings of history and identify parallels in the modern world. In-state cost $263. (3 semester credits)

Mathematics

College Algebra
College Algebra: In Simplest Terms takes the viewer step-by-step to an understanding of algebra. Real-life applications of algebra will be covered through on-location documentary segments. In-state cost $346. (4 semester credits)

Introduction to Statistics
Against All Odds: Inside Statistics is an introductory exploration of statistical processes stressing data-centered topics rather than the more traditional path from probability to formal inference. This telecourse combines state-of-the-art sequentially animated graphics, on-location footage, and face-to-face interviews in a masterful blend of exposition and entertainment. In-state cost $346. (4 semester credits)

Philosophy

Ethics in America

Through a series of ten case studies, this telecourse examines contemporary ethical conflicts and the process involved in ethical decision making. In each program a moderator leads a panel of distinguished Americans through a hypothetical, ethical dilemma involving business, government, law, journalism, the military, medicine, or scientific research. On the panels are such well-known individuals as Geraldine Ferraro, Peter Jennings, Jeane Kirkpatrick, Antonin Scalia, and C. Everett Koop. In-state cost $263. (3 semester credits)

Political Science

American National Government

Government by Consent is a government survey telecourse that focuses on teaching students how to access their government. The course combines political science instruction with examples of how students involve themselves in government, in the interest of changing students' perceptions of government as a removed, larger-than-life process that seems inaccessible to most citizens. In-state cost $263. (3 semester credits)

Contemporary Latin America

Americas is an examination of the contemporary history, politics, culture, economics, religion, and social structure of Latin America and the Caribbean. From Mexico to the Malvinas, the series and course explore the stories behind the limited images and incomplete information that catch our attention in newspapers and popular magazines. *Americas* delves into the forces that have molded the region's past and the processes that are shaping its future. Occasional meetings. In-state cost $263. (3 semester credits)

Psychology

Introductory Psychology

Discovering Psychology is a telecourse that takes viewers into the working laboratories of leading scholars and researchers to learn about the fundamental principles and concepts of psychology. Topics include brain and behavior, sensation and perception, conditioning and learning, motivation and emotion, life-span development, the self and identity, sex and gender, testing and intelligence, psychopathology and therapy, stress and health issues,

and new directions. Class meetings. In-state cost $263. (3 semester credits)

Abnormal Psychology

This telecourse examines the complex factors that cause behavioral disorders, looking at biological, psychological, and environmental influences. Students will learn the professional vocabulary for describing psychological disorders, approaches to their treatment, and current research. Class meetings. In-state cost $263. (3 semester credits)

Sociology

Introduction to Sociology

Sociological Imagination is an innovative telecourse structured as a documentary, featuring interviews with people in their family settings, at work, school, worship, and play. It deals with issues such as socialization, social control, sex, gender, and aging and includes expert commentary from leading sociologists. Class meetings. In-state cost $263. (3 semester credits)

Portrait of a Family

This telecourse examines contemporary marriage and the family, including traditional and single-parent families, step-families, the dynamics of adult development, and the personal decisions required to create and maintain a marriage. Orientation meeting. In-state cost $263. (3 semester credits)

Mind Extension University
The Education Network

9697 East Mineral Avenue
P.O. Box 3309
Englewood, CO   80155-3309

(800) 777-6463

Geographic Access: Nationwide

DELIVERY SYSTEMS

Broadcast Television

Students will receive Mind Extension University (ME/U) courses on their cable systems as part of their basic service. If ME/U is unavailable by cable, other alternatives are satellite dish on Galaxy V, Transponder 21, or a tape rental service available to students enrolled for credit. Students taking courses through ME/U should have a television monitor, playback unit (VCR), and an ample supply of 1/2" VHS videotapes. Students tape the classes and review them at a more convenient time.

INSTITUTION DESCRIPTION

The ME/U Education Network is devoted solely to education via distance learning. Established in 1987 by Glenn R. Jones, ME/U is a basic cable network offering 24-hour daily delivery of educational programming, including classes for personal and professional development, K-12, certificate programs, and bachelor's and master's degrees. ME/U is available to satellite dish owners and affiliated cable companies nationwide by satellite transmission from Englewood, Colorado on Galaxy V, Transponder 21.

The network launched its programming in November of 1987 with the cooperation of its flagship school, Colorado State University, and approximately 50 Jones Intercable systems across the country. Programming was available only four hours per day in the middle of the night. Shortly thereafter, the network expanded to 12, then 24 hours of educational programming per day. By its fourth year it had become the fastest growing cable network in the country. Today the network is affiliated with more than 800 cable systems nationwide and more than 24 nationally known universities and colleges as well as students and viewers representing all 50 states.

All degrees, programs, and courses offered on the network are supported by universities and colleges holding regional and program-specific accreditation. The partnerships between ME/U and its affiliate schools include the careful coordination of their separate and distinct roles. The role of the affiliate schools is to develop and evaluate programming and to provide academic functions. ME/U delivers programming, provides administrative support, and offers necessary student services via the ME/U Education Center.

Programming delivered by ME/U is produced by major universities and some of the world's best known educational production authorities.

The ME/U academic year consists of three semesters: Fall, Spring, and Summer. Registration begins four to six weeks before each semester.

Accreditation: Regional and program-specific

Official/Contact: Glenn R. Jones, Chairman and Chief Executive Officer

Admission Requirements: The ME/U Education Center in Englewood, Colorado is the central administrative unit linking students, universities, and the network. Registration advisors at the Center can be reached through the toll-free number (800) 777-MIND from 9:00 AM through 11:00 PM Eastern Time, Monday through Friday, and 9:00 AM through 7:00 PM Eastern Time, Saturday and Sunday. The Center's registration advisors are available to answer registration, admissions, advising, financial aid, and scheduling questions. They accept college course registrations and fulfill textbook orders. Upon enrollment, students will receive course packets that include cablecast schedules and other important information relating to the course.

Tuition: Varies depending on the course (see course descriptions below). Payment for tuition, fees, and books are accepted by credit card (MasterCard, VISA, Discover, American Express), money order, personal check, or purchase order number.

Degree Credit: Programs leading to the completion of a bachelor's degree, bachelor's management degree, bachelor's social science degree, and a bachelor's degree in animal science are available through ME/U. At the master's degree level, students may pursue degrees in business administration, education and human development administration, and library science.

Grading: Students must choose a proctor to administer examinations. This proctor must be carefully selected and approved by the appropriate school. The grading system is selected by the various colleges and universities. Credit is generally awarded in semester hour units.

Library: A "missed tape service" is available for a fee to registered students who miss taping a lesson. Orders should be placed within 24 hours of the missed taping to ensure minimum delay in coursework.

COURSES OFFERED

Accounting

Introductory Financial Accounting
Fundamentals of the collection, recording, summarization, and interpretation of accounting data. Tuition and fees: $375. (3 credits)

Animal Science

Animal Products Option Completion Program

This degree program of Kansas State University is designed primarily for students who have completed the equivalent of the first two years of college. The degree offers courses to prepare for production, management, marketing, distribution, and sales applications in the food industry at all levels. It will build on a liberal arts foundation with a concentration in animal science, but also substantial coursework in agriculture, biological and physical sciences, mathematics, statistics and computer science, business, and economics. A total of 127 credits is required for the degree. Students participating in this degree completion program must complete standard KSU admission procedures through ME/U. Individuals not enrolled in the degree program may wish to take selected courses for personal or professional growth.

Baccalaureate Degree Completion

Bachelor's Completion Degrees from NUDC

The National Universities Degree Consortium (NUDC) consists of nine major land-grant and state universities from across the nation that have joined together to offer Bachelor's Completion Degrees through the ME/U distribution network. These universities include Colorado State University, Kansas State University, University of Maryland University College, University of New Orleans, University of Oklahoma, Oklahoma State University, University of South Carolina, Utah State University, and Washington State University. Undergraduate course offerings of ME/U are listed under the appropriate subject heading.

Biology

Introduction to Biology

This course is a general study of the basic concepts of biology including the human body and the environment. Emphasis is on the characteristics of plant and animal life, human body systems, health, genetics, and the interaction of organisms in their environment. Tuition and fees: $300. (3 credits)

Business Administration

MBA Program

The Master of Business Administration (MBA) program provides a broad business education which develops fundamental skills in finance, marketing, organizational structure and change, human resource management, accounting and management systems. The College of Business at Colorado State University requires 33 credit-hours minimum to fulfill the requirements of the MBA degree in addition to any common-body-of-knowledge requirements. This requirement is applicable to all MBA candidates of Colorado State, including those pursuing the degree through ME/U. The student has the option of pursuing a general MBA program or an MBA with a concentration program (Computer Information Systems, Management, Finance, Quality Improvement). The general MBA program requires the completion of tool courses and general courses. The tool courses, each earning 3 credits, include Computer Applications in Decision Making, Managerial Economics, Business Research, and Statistical Decision Making. The general courses, also earning 3 credits each, include Managerial Accounting, Financial Management: Theory and Case Studies, Marketing Strategy, Management, and Production Administration. Tuition and fees: $300 per credit or $900 per course. A one-time registration fee of $25 is collected with the first enrollment. For students who do not have satellite or cable reception available in their area, courses may be delivered by videotape at an additional fee of $175 per course.

Business Management

Legal and Regulatory Environment of Business

General concepts regarding the nature of the legal system, ethical issues in business decision making, dispute resolution processes, basic constitutional limitations on the power of government to regulate business activity, the nature of government regulation and fundamental principles of tort and contract law. From the telecourse *Business and the Law*. Tuition and fees: $465. (3 credits)

World Economic Development

The economics of the developing nations: a review and analysis of common problems and issues. Tuition and fees: $465. (3 credits)

International Business

This course was developed to provide students in business and related fields an introduction to the international environment and its impact on business activity. The course will touch on a variety of topics in the areas of political, economic, and cultural analysis and will examine the managerial responses appropriate in international business. Tuition and fees: $440. (3 credits)

Industrial and Labor Relations

Basic course in industrial and labor relations. Broad coverage of the institution of collective bargaining and its environment, the goals and operation of labor unions, the impact of unions on management, and labor relations law. Tuition and fees: $400. (3 credits)

Leadership and Management in an Age of Diversity

This course examines the challenges to effective leadership and management encountered by the contemporary manager in a rapidly changing environment. Focus is on leadership styles and motivational techniques conducive to high performance in various organizational settings with a very diverse work force. Includes organizational design issues, the corporate/organizational culture, job design and enrichment, and organizational communication. Tuition and fees: $573 ($618 outside Maryland). (3 credits)

Accounting for Managers

A survey course in accounting principles for non-accounting majors who will need to make managerial decisions using accounting information. Includes financial planning and reporting, internal controls, financial statement analysis, elements of managerial cost accounting and budgets. Tuition and fees: $573 ($618 outside Maryland). (3 credits)

The Global Business Environment

This course examines current economic issues that have international consequences. Focuses on how the global economic and political environment affects domestic business and public policy decisions. Includes managing the multinational corporation and the growth of international marketing and competition. Tuition and fees: $573. (3 credits)

Organizational Communication

A framework for understanding the structure of organizational communication. Analyzes problems, issues, and techniques in communication through cases, exercises, and projects. The goal is for students to become more effective communicators and organizational negotiators. Tuition and fees: $573 ($618 outside Maryland). (3 credits)

Principles of Marketing

An overview of the field of marketing. Topics include marketing strategies, marketing research, consumer behavior, selecting target markets, developing/pricing/distributing/promoting products, services and nonprofit marketing, international marketing, and social and ethical issues related to marketing today. Tuition and fees: $573 ($618 outside Maryland). (3 credits)

Marketing for Managers

This course presents creative managerial approaches to marketing, sales, and business development. Compares and contrasts examples of marketing successes and marketing failures. Includes marketing research, competitor analysis, market segmentation, marketing planning, product/service development, distribution, pricing, advertising and sales promotion, and sales and program implementation. Tuition and fees: $573 ($618 outside Maryland). (3 credits)

Total Quality Management

This course surveys the methods of applying total quality management in a variety of organizational settings to improve quality and productivity. Includes development and description of total quality standards and specifications, numerical control methods, work measurement, work-distribution analysis, time study, process flow and operations auditing, and other techniques. Tuition and fees: $573 ($618 outside Maryland). (3 credits)

Managerial Planning and Competitive Strategies

This capstone course provides an overview of the continuous, systematic process of managerial planning, environmental scanning, and developing plans and strategies to gain competitive advantage. Tactical and strategic management issues will be highlighted through use of case studies, class projects, and discussion. Tuition and fees: $573 ($618 out of state). (3 credits)

Child Development

Psychological Foundations of Childhood

The interplay of biological factors, individual personality, social structure, and other environmental forces in shaping the growing child. Tuition and fees: $360. (3 credits)

Criminal Justice

Strategies of Crime Control

Analysis of social and organizational contexts, ideologies, and standards which influence the making, implementation, and impact of crime control policies. Focus on advocated reforms of specific current crime control practices and policies, e.g., community policing, selective incapacitation, gun control, exclusionary rule or victims' rights. Tuition and fees $440. (3 credits)

Criminal Law

Criminal Law

An examination of the principles, functions, and limits of substantive criminal law. Also includes a study of basic crime categories, and state and national legal research materials. Tuition and fees: $440. (3 credits)

Economics

Survey of Economic Issues

This course is designed to give an understanding of the workings of the economy as a whole (macroeconomics) as well as of the individual markets of which it is composed (microeconomics). From the telecourse *Economics U$A*. Tuition and fees: $300. (3 credits)

Introduction to Microeconomics

Goals, incentives, and outcomes of economic behavior with applications and illustrations from current social issues. Operation of markets for goods, services, and factors of production. The behavior of firms and industries in different types of competition, income distribution and international exchange. From the telecourse *Economics U$A*. Tuition and fees: $360. (3 credits)

Education

Educational Technology Leadership

The objective of this Master of Arts in Education and Human Development program is to provide students with the knowledge and skills necessary to become leaders in the dynamic field of educational technology. The program curriculum includes 36 hours of coursework. Required courses, each earning 3 credits, include Computers in Education and Human Development, Educational Hardware Systems, Managing Computer Applications, Power/Leadership and Education, Policy-Making for Public Education, Quantitative Methods II: Research Procedures, Applying Educational Media and Technology, and Design and Implementation of Educational Software. The remaining 12 hours of required electives may be selected from the following: Media Services Management, Introduction to Interactive Multimedia, Telecommunications in Education, Developing Interactive Media. Students applying for degree candidacy in this program must meet the admission requirements of the School of Education and Human Development of The George Washington University. Tuition and fees: $594 per course, plus an interactive computer bulletin board fee. A one-time $25 fee will be payable at the first registration.

Family Life

Marriage

Consideration of courtship and marriage with special emphasis on building a healthy paired relationship. Communication and decision making. Coping with such problems as money, sex, role taking, in-laws, and children. From the telecourse *Portrait of a Family*. Tuition and fees: $465. (3 credits)

Geography

Environment and Culture

This course is designed for postsecondary study. The series begins with an overview of geography's central issues: the interaction between people and the environment and the extent to which geography may be said to influence human behavior and vice-versa. From the telecourse *Introduction to Geography*. Tuition and fees: $300. (3 credits)

History

American South Comes of Age

A study of the changes in the American South's economy, politics, and race relations in the three decades that followed the beginning of World War II. The purpose of this course is to develop an understanding of this transformation and to place it in historical perspective. Tuition and fees: $489. (3 credits)

History of Islam

Survey of the history of Islamic civilization in the Near East, North Africa, India, and Malaysia from the advent of the prophet to the modern period. Tuition and fees: $465. (3 credits)

History of Modern Japan Since 1800

Japan's response to the West, with emphasis on the opening of Japan, the Meiji Restoration, modernization, imperialism, intellectual currents and recent economic growth. Tuition and fees: $465. (3 credits)

Twentieth-Century Russia

Analysis of Russia's development of political, social, economic, and cultural characteristics and experiences during the period of its modern transformation—roughly 1900 to the present. Though these subjects are interesting in themselves, the larger objective is to gain an appreciation and better understanding of Russia's present position and role in the world community. Tuition and fees: $375. (3 credits)

The Presidents and the Cold War

A special view of American history, seen from the perspective of the national leaders who fought the Cold War. The course will deal with the presidents from Franklin D. Roosevelt to George Bush, and focus on the emergence, the evolution, and the end of the Cold War. Tuition and fees: $375. (3 credits)

Western Civilization to 1500

History of western civilization from the ancient world to the Reformation. From the telecourse *Western Traditions*. Tuition and fees: $360. (3 credits)

Western Civilization After 1500

History of western civilization from the Reformation to the present. Tuition and fees: $360. (3 credits)

Human Resources Management

Management of Human Resources

This course provides a review of the human resource management system. Topics include the nature and challenge of personnel management, from mechanics to social responsibility, the organization of a culturally diverse workforce, current issues such as the Americans with Disabilities Act and total quality management. Tuition and fees: $495. (3 credits)

Humanities

Introduction to Art

An introduction to the analysis and interpretation of visual arts. Visual, emotional, and intellectual aspects of art in painting, sculpture, printmaking, and architecture. Tuition and fees: $360. (3 credits)

The Humanities Through the Arts

Provides an introduction to film, drama, music, literature, painting, sculpture, and architecture. The course stresses an awareness of self and society as it can be encouraged through a study of western art. Tuition and fees: $548. (4 credits)

Interdisciplinary Social Science Degree Completion

Interdisciplinary Social Science Degree Completion Program

Kansas State University offers a degree completion program designed primarily for students who have completed the equivalent of the first two years of college. The social science disciplines include anthropology, economics, geography, history, political science, psychology, and sociology. Students participating in this degree completion program must complete standard KSU admissions procedures through ME/U. Individuals not enrolled in the degree program may take selected courses for personal or professional growth.

Library Science

Master of Arts in Library Science

The Master of Arts in Library Science degree requires 38 units of graduate credit: 26 on video and 12 on the University of Arizona campus at Tucson. Only students who take courses at designated sites in participating states can enroll in the program. Students interested in earning the Master of Arts should request a graduate admission packet by calling 1-800-955-UofA. Tuition and fees: $13 ME/U registration fee plus $120 per credit in WICHE states and $155 per credit outside the WICHE region. Tuition of $80 per credit plus $20 per credit remote fee for Arizona graduate students. Courses available and applicable to the program are listed below.

Introduction to the Organization of Information

An introduction to the theories and practices used in the organization of information and cataloging of materials. Overview of standards.

Library Collection Development

Principles of collection development, evaluation and review of materials, selection tools, acquisition of materials, problems in selection including censorship.

Foundations of Library and Information Services

Elements of librarianship, historical backgrounds, types of libraries, the role of the library in American life, current issues.

Basic Reference

Survey of general reference sources, discussion of reference technique.

Research Methods

Need and opportunities for research in librarianship, types of research, research methodology, study of research design, elementary statistics.

Library Management

Introduction to management concepts, the organizational structure of libraries, systems analysis, financial administration, and the utilization of library personnel.

Trends in Library Management

Fundamentals of management issues in the public sector affecting all types of libraries and information centers including management principles, theories, philosophies, practices, and research finding.

Introduction to Information Science

Methods, theories, and technology of information science. Elements of computer programming and systems design. Implementation and management of computer systems in libraries and information centers.

Information Storage and Retrieval

Student involvement in online, interactive systems.

Library Systems Analysis

Introduction to quantitative methods for the design, analysis, and control of library systems.

Public Librarianship

Administration of tax-supported libraries serving the general public, including problems of governmental relationships, community responsibilities, financial support, buildings, personnel, and collections.

Academic Librarianship

Present trends in academic libraries, including financial administration, collection evaluation, personnel requirements, and building needs.

Special Librarianship

Mission, organization, and administration of the special library.

Human Factors in Information Systems

Study of the human-information system interface: libraries, computers, human-information processing, physical-psychological factors in design and operation of information systems.

Literature for Children's Librarians

Literature for younger children, including picture books. Traditional literature for use with children. Reference materials. Fantasy, humor, realistic fiction, poetry, classics, informational books. Criticism and reviewing of children's literature.

Management

Management

The course explores management principles and decision making as applied to management systems, organizations, interpersonal relationships, and production. From the telecourse *Business of Management*. Tuition and fees: $360. (3 credits)

Management Degree Completion

Management Degree Completion Program

The University of Maryland University College offers the opportunity to obtain a bachelor's degree in management. This degree completion program is designed primarily for students who have completed the equivalent of the first two years of college. The management concentration stresses the integration of contemporary management theory and practice. The concentration is particularly appropriate for adult students who want management courses that emphasize the manager's perspective. Themes common to the required core management courses are the global nature of business, managing diversity, leadership, problem solving and critical thinking, communication skills, ethics in business, planning and competitive strategies, and the application of the material to current issues. A minimum of 120 semester hours of credit is required for graduation.

Marketing

Advertising and Promotion

This course presents an overview of the role of advertising and sales promotion in today's business climate. Particular emphasis is put on determining where these elements fit in the overall marketing mix. Students will learn to evaluate advertising and develop creative strategies for a product. The world of media will be explored with emphasis on the strengths and weaknesses of each advertising medium. Tuition and fees: $495. (3 credits)

Mathematics

Statistical Methods for the Natural Scientist

Statistical concepts and methods basic to experimental research in the natural sciences: hypothetical populations, estimation of parameter confidence intervals, parametric and nonparametric test of hypotheses, linear regression. Correlation, one-way analysis of variance, T-test, chi-square test. Tuition and fees: $400. (3 credits)

Mathematics in the Social Sciences

Basic entry-level mathematics course for the liberal arts curriculum. Topics include management science, statistics, social choice, size and shape, and computer science. By exploring mathematics application in different fields, this course shows mathematics as the language of modern problem-solving. In addition, computer graphics, animation sequences, and location shooting enliven the presentation of mathematics concepts and methods in a real-world contest. Tuition and fees: $300. (3 credits)

Philosophy

Ethics in America

This introductory-level philosophy course examines contemporary ethical conflicts and provides the intellectual tools to analyze moral dilemmas in the fields we choose to pursue—and in the society in which all of us must live. At the core of the course is a prime time television series that places experts from government, the press, medicine, law, business, and the military directly in the line of fire. Guided by the probing questions of skilled lawyers, luminaries from C. Everett Koop and T. Boone Pickens to Antonin Scalia, Peter Jennings, and Jeane Kirkpatrick grapple with moral concerns that arise in both personal and professional life. Tuition and fees: $300. (3 credits)

Physics

Basic Physics and Physical World View

This course is intended to cover what is traditionally a college course in general physics. The development of the physical principles of how the universe operates is treated from a historical and cultural perspective that illuminates the essential humanity of the subjects. The course treats the development of mathematical tools necessary for the search for understanding and insight into processes. From the telecourse *The Mechanical Universe*. Tuition and fees: $300. (3 credits)

Political Science

Gender and Politics

This course will focus on the participation of women in American politics—both historically and in the contemporary period. It will include an emphasis on women's recent successes as candidates at both the state and national levels. In addition, the course will include a careful analysis of many public policies which particularly impact women within American society, such as reproductive choice, women in the workplace, and family law. Tuition and fees: $440. (3 credits)

Problems of Government

This course documents key chapters in the story of the nuclear age, exploring not only events of the period, but also the underlying issues of nuclear policy, strategy, and technology. It will provide students with a foundation for understanding issues of the past, debates of the present, and implications for the future. From the telecourse *War and Peace in the Nuclear Age*. Tuition and fees: $465. (3 credits)

Psychology

Industrial Psychology

A study of the application of psychological principles, methods, and techniques in business and industry. Tuition and fees: $465. (3 credits)

General Psychology

Principles of psychology, emphasizing empirical approaches, theories and research on learning, individual differences, perception, and social behavior. From the telecourse *Discovering Psychology*. Tuition and fees: $300. (3 credits)

Psychology Across the Life Span

This course examines the drama of human development which unfolds under the influence of three "clocks": a physical clock, a social clock, and a psychological clock. The television and audio programs present provocative insights emerging from recent research in psychology, biology, anthropology, and sociology. The programs provide a chronological overview of stages of the lifespan, while the audio programs concentrate on specific topics. From the telecourse *Seasons of Life*. Tuition and fees: $300. (3 credits)

Social Sciences Degree Completion

Social Sciences Degree Completion Program

Washington State University (WSU) offers a degree completion program designed primarily for students who have completed the equivalent of the first two years of college. The Bachelor of Arts in Social Sciences is a liberal arts degree and provides students with multiple options and emphases in the social sciences. Students participating in this degree completion program must complete standard WSU admissions procedures including providing transcripts of all previous college work. Individuals not enrolled in the degree program may wish to take selected courses for personal or professional growth. WSU requires the completion of at least 120 credits for the BA degree, 40 of which must be at the upper-division level.

Sociology

Law and Society

This course deals with social factors in the emergence and operation of law: impact of law on society. It has been said that for those who live in modern society, every possible human act can be related to law—a particular act may be required, merely permitted, or prohibited. This course uses a metaphor of law as civil contract as a guide to understanding the relationship between law and society. Tuition and fees: $440. (3 credits)

Legal Ethics

A thorough consideration of the American Bar Association's "Code of Professional Responsibility" and "Code of Judicial Conduct." A paralegal's conduct and responsibilities in different legal settings in relation to the above listed codes. A paralegal's conduct and relationships with attorneys' clients, and other persons, emphasizing the paralegal's limitations in addition to overall legal ethical considerations. Tuition and fees: $375. (3 credits)

Dealing with Diversity

Prepares students to function more effectively in a multicultural society. Helps students explore the identities, values, and interaction of diverse groups in our culture, such as those distinguished by race, ethnicity, gender, class, sexual orientation, and age. Tuition and fees: $336 (undergraduate), $348 (graduate). (3 credits)

Statistics

Elementary Statistics

An introductory course in the theory and methods of statistics. Descriptive measures, elementary probability, samplings, estimation, hypothesis in testing, correlation and regression. From the telecourse *Against All Odds*. Tuition and fees: $360. (3 credits)

Morgan Community College
See **KRMA/Denver**

National Technological University

700 Centre Avenue
Fort Collins, CO   80526-9903

(303) 495-6421 *Fax:* (303) 484-0668

Geographic Access: North America

DELIVERY SYSTEMS

Satellite Network

The network operates on G-STAR 1 with one modern Ku-band transponder to provide up to 12 compressed digital video channels 24 hours a day. The signal is received by subscribers through medium-size (usually 3.6 meters or larger) downlinks located near the professionals and managers viewing the broadcasts. Telephone lines from the receiving sites to the campus classroom provide for faculty-student interaction. This interaction is supplemented by electronic and regular mail, computer teleconferencing, and telephone office hours.

INSTITUTION DESCRIPTION

National Technological University (NTU) is a private, nonprofit institution founded in 1984 to serve the advanced educational needs of today's busy, highly mobile engineers, scientists, and technical managers. NTU is a consortium of 45 leading engineering schools. It offers programs of study leading to M.S. degrees in computer engineering, computer science, electrical engineering, hazardous waste management, health physics, manufacturing systems engineering, engineering management, materials science and engineering, management of technology, software engineering, and special majors. The courses comprising these curricula are selected from among the best courses offered by the member schools. The classes originate on the campuses of the participating universities and are delivered via satellite directly to technical professionals and managers at their work sites.

Today there are over 440 receive sites in more than 130 sponsoring organizations. In 1992 there were over 4,500 course enrollments at the graduate level. Major users include AT&T, Digital Equipment, Eastman Kodak, Hewlett-Packard, IBM, Martin Marietta, Motorola, NCR, and the U.S. Navy.

In addition, NTU produces and distributes a broad array of noncredit short courses and seminars on topics of special interest and value to the technical community. From July 1, 1991 through June 30, 1992, the number of enrollments in these noncredit programs exceeded 105,000.

The frequency of course offerings depends upon the programmatic priorities of the institution where the course is taught, student demand, and program needs. Students should consult the official applicable class schedule published for each term of instruction for a listing of the courses offered during any given term.

NTU also offers a Certificate of Completion Program that is designed to recognize the achievements of students who design their own courses of study to meet the specific needs of their individual careers.

Accreditation: NCA

Official/Contact: Donald M. Yeager, Vice President

Admission Requirements: Students are admitted to the program by application to a coordinator at the member institution/company sponsoring the courses. Interested persons my contact NTU at the above address for more information regarding site availability and other admission procedures.

Tuition: There is a one-time fee for access to the NTU network that does not include the tuition and registration fees for courses taken at the sites. There are four different types of one-time access fees, payable over the initial two years: (1) Corporate/Agency. Fees range from $65,000 for less than 20,000 domestic employees to $260,000 for greater than 100,000 domestic employees. (2) Site: Credit and Noncredit. A one-time fee, payable over the initial two years of $4,000 for 250 or less employees on site to $24,000 for greater than 2,000 employees. (3) Site: Noncredit Only. A one-time fee, payable over the initial two years of $2,400 for less than 250 employees on site to $14,400 for greater than 2,000 employees. (4) Consortiums. The subscription for a single site consortium formed to access both the credit and Advanced Technology and Management programming would be $24,000; a noncredit only, single-site consortium would pay $14,400. Academic courses for credit for both matriculated or nonmatriculated students is $489 per semester credit hour. Prospective candidates are advised to contact NTU for other pertinent information regarding all fees and tuition charges.

Degree Credit: Master of Science degree programs are available in the United States, Canada, and Mexico. An annual *NTU Bulletin* lists approximately 900 courses from the participating universities in the various master's curricula. Undergraduate bridging courses for nonmajors wishing to enter the M.S. programs in computer engineering, computer science, and electrical engineering are also available.

Grading: Examinations are proctored at the delivery site. Grades are entered on the students NTU transcript.

Library: The latest information on each course is available on the NTU Electronic Information System. The NTU system is connected to Internet; the name of the system is NTUPUB.NYU.EDU. To connect to the system, use either telnet (telnet ntupub.ntu.edu) or rlogin (rlogin ntupub.ntu.edu-l ntur). Enter NTU at the Login and Password prompts. The system will prompt for all additional necessary information. If inquirer has no Internet access, dial-in using (800) 634-4329. Communication parameters are 8 data bits, 1 stop bit, no parity, 1200 bps.

COURSES OFFERED

Advanced Technology and Management

Advanced Technology and Management
Master of Science programs are offered in the following concentrations: computer engineering, computer science, electrical engineering, engineering management, hazardous waste management, health physics, management of technology, manufacturing systems engineering, materials science and engineering, software engineering, and special majors. Undergraduate bridging courses for nonmajors wishing to enter the M.S. programs in computer engineering, computer science, and electrical engineering are also available. Credits are awarded in semester hour units. CEUs are now offered for a variety of Advanced Technology and Management Programs. Contact site coordinator or NTU for details.

Northeastern Junior College
See **KRMA/Denver**

Pikes Peak Community College
Telelearning
Division of Extended Studies
5675 South Academy Boulevard
Colorado Springs, CO   80906-5498

(719) 540-7112

Geographic Access: Colorado

DELIVERY SYSTEMS

Broadcast Television
Telecourse programs are broadcast on KTSC-TV Channels 8 and 15 in Pueblo and Colorado Springs or KRMA-TV Channels 6 and 63 in Denver. The video programs are incorporated with a text, study guide, assignments, and examinations. Students interact with their instructors via mail, telephone, and/or periodic meetings.

Interactive Audio/Video
These classes are narrowcast over the Instructional Television Fixed Service (ITFS) at the same time that they are being taught on campus. ITV students watch the lectures on television and interact with their instructor via telephone. Students can call in with questions or comments and receive immediate feedback from the instructor. ITV courses are aired on American Telecasting of Colorado Springs Channel 103. PPCC also has regular access to Tri-Lakes Cable Channel 6 and Channel 23 on Big Sandy Telecommunications.

INSTITUTION DESCRIPTION

In 1967 the Colorado General Assembly established El Paso Community College in the west area of Colorado Springs as a state educational institution. Classes began in 1969. The name of the college was changed in 1977 to Pikes Peak Community College in recognition of the college's role in providing educational services beyond El Paso County.

Telelearning courses are the same as on-campus, regular semester courses. They begin and end within published dates and the courses offered vary each semester. Those courses described below are indicative of the subjects offered. Orientation sessions are required for every student enrolled in a telelearning course.

Accreditation: NCA

Official/Contact: Paul Romero, Telelearning Coordinator

Admission Requirements: If the applicant for admission to a telelearning course is not a continuing student at PPCC, an Application for Admission must be filed.

Tuition: $50 per credit hour. There is also a $25 producer's fee for each course. Textbooks must be purchased by the student.

Degree Credit: Credit earned may be applied to an associate degree program at PPCC.

Grading: Examinations must be proctored and taken on-campus. Letter grades are assigned. Credit is awarded in semester hour units.

Library: Officially registered students have access to all of the facilities and materials of the Learning Resources Center. Also, PPCC has developed a microcomputer-based network to enhance instruction. Students use the Local Area Networks (LAN). This network is coupled with telecommunications which provide instruction from across the state.

COURSES OFFERED

Biology

Environmental Biology
A Telelearning Course. (3 credits)

English

College Spelling Skills
Designed for students who have difficulty in spelling and in avoiding common pitfalls in word use. Syllabication, dictionary use, spelling rules, and vocabulary in context. Supplemental computer-assisted instruction available. An ITV course. (3 credits)

Review of Writing
Produce logical, well-developed compositions with no mechanical errors. Practice development, revision, and completion of single paragraphs, summaries, critiques, and compositions. Computer used for word processing. An ITV course. (4 credits)

Geology

Earth Science
A Telelearning Course. (3 credits)

History

The Civil War
This telecourse encompasses Civil War social history in all of its aspects: dramatic battles, experiences of common soldiers, sectional politics, military strategy, blacks and women in the war, and the war's effects on America. Students will take exams on the award-winning films and text and will write a paper on a Civil War topic of interest to them. A Telelearning Course. (3 credits)

Mathematics

Developmental Mathematics
Addition, subtraction, multiplication, and division of whole numbers, decimals, and fractions. Ratios, proportions, and percent. Placement is determined by diagnostic testing. Supplemental computer-assisted instruction is available. An ITV course. (4 credits)

College Algebra
Includes a brief review of intermediate algebra, equations and inequalities, functions and their graphs, exponential and logarithmic functions, linear and nonlinear systems, graphing of the conic sections, introduction to sequences and series, permuations and combinations, the binomial theorem, and theory of equations. An ITV course. (4 credits)

Philosophy

Transformations of Myth
A Telelearning Course. (3 credits)

Statistics

Introduction to Statistics
Data presentation and summarization, introduction to probability concepts and distributions, statistical inference-estimation, hypothesis testing, comparison of populations, correlation, and regression. A Telecourse. (3 credits)

Red Rocks Community College
See **KRMA/Denver**

Trinidad State Junior College
See **KRMA/Denver**

University of Northern Colorado
See **KRMA/Denver**

Western State College
See **KRMA/Denver**

Connecticut

Capital Community-Technical College

See **Connecticut Community-Technical College System**

Connecticut Community-Technical College System
Televised Instruction
CCIT Cable Network

61 Woodland Street
Hartford, CT   06105-2392

(203) 566-8760

Geographic Access: Connecticut

DELIVERY SYSTEMS

Broadcast Television
Various cable systems throughout Connecticut are affiliated with the CCIT network. CCIT broadcasts fifteen hours a day, seven days a week, 8AM to 11PM. The daily schedule begins on Monday and ends on Sunday.

INSTITUTION DESCRIPTION

Since the fall of 1973, the Connecticut Community-Technical Colleges have been offering college credit courses on public television and, as of 1983, on their own CCIT Instructional Cable Network. Over the past two decades, thousands of adults have availed themselves of the opportunity to enroll in almost 100 courses.

As a service to hearing-impaired students, the telecourses are closed captioned. For those taking advantage of this means of receiving the courses, a decoder connected to the television set will print the spoken word on the lower third of the TV screen. For those without a decoder, a special broadcast with open captioning is often scheduled.

Students desiring to enroll for a course should contact the college of choice. The colleges associated with the televised instruction program are:

- Capital Community-Technical College (Hartford CT), 203/520-7846
- Gateway Community-Technical College (New Haven CT), 203/789-7043
- Manchester Community-Technical College (Manchester CT), 203/647-6242
- Northwestern Connecticut Community-Technical College (Winsted CT), 203/738-6309
- Norwalk Community-Technical College (Norwalk CT), 203/857-7070
- Tunxis Community College (Farmington CT), 203/679-9590

Accreditation: All participating colleges are accredited by NEASC.

Official/Contact: Daniel G. McAuliffe, Director of Televised Instruction

Admission Requirements: Telecourse enrollment is open to any Connecticut citizen, including high school students who may bank credits.

Tuition: $163.25 per 3-credit course.

Degree Credit: Credit earned by successful completion of a course may be applied toward an associate degree and may be accepted in transfer to a four-year college.

Grading: Examinations must be proctored. Letter grades are assigned. Credit is awarded in semester hour units.

Library: Students are encouraged to use the resources of the Learning Resource Centers on the campuses of the community colleges.

COURSES OFFERED

Business

Something Ventured

This course presents an entrepreneurial approach to small business management. It provides a unique opportunity to observe a variety of small businesses in operation—in both rural and suburban communities, as well as large metropolitan areas—to get an "over-the-shoulder," first-hand look at what it is like to start and operate a small business. (3 credits)

Geology

Introductory Geology

The *Earth Revealed* telecourse offers a comprehensive study of the Earth's physical processes and properties, with emphasis on understanding the scientific theories behind the geological principles. Presented are both the frantic forces—volcanic activity and earthquakes—as well as the more subtle and ever-present elements of the geological process. The telecourse also illuminates the often unrealized link between human activity and geological change. (3 credits)

Gerontology

Social Gerontology

Growing Old in a New Age is an introductory-level gerontology telecourse that provides an understanding of the process of aging, old age as a stage of life, and the impact of aging on society. Students are given a unique opportunity to witness firsthand a developmental picture of the elderly as they discuss their triumphs, relationships, losses, health, and personal views on aging. Experts' commentary complements the elders' interviews, with in-depth examination and analysis of the physiological, psychological, and social aspects of aging. (3 credits)

History

Americas: Modern Latin American History

Americas is a revealing examination of the contemporary history, politics, economics, religion, culture, and social structures of the countries of Latin America and the Caribbean. From Mexico to the Malvinas, the series and course explore the stories behind the limited images and incomplete information that capture public attention in newspapers and popular magazines. (3 credits)

Pacific Century

This telecourse in modern Asian history provides students with a better understanding of how the rich and varied cultures of Northeast Asia (China, Japan, Korea, and the Soviet Far East) and Southeast Asia (Indonesia, Malaysia, the Philippines, Singapore, Thailand, and Vietnam) have merged to form modern nations. Throughout the series, four major themes emerge: modernity versus tradition, the conflict between East and West, the United States in the Pacific, and democracy, political authority, and economic growth. (3 credits)

Humanities

Eyes on the Prize

This telecourse presents a comprehensive history of the people, the stories, the events, and the issues of the civil rights struggle in America, focusing on the period of American history from World War II to the present. The period of the contemporary civil rights movement is one of the most significant in our history. It made America a more democratic society which transformed the face of American culture and changed those who participated in it. (3 credits)

Marketing

The Sales Connection: Principles of Selling

This business telecourse has been designed to provide aspiring salespeople, and those already involved in sales, with the tools and insight they need to compete in the age of long-term, consultative-style selling. In each program, several of our nation's top sales experts will offer valuable information and advice about identifying sales prospects, as well as developing and maintaining good sales relationships. Students will be able to see those theories and processes put to practical use through the first-hand stories of professional salespeople, from retail, wholesale, manufacturing, and service industries. (3 credits)

Philosophy

Ethics in America

This telecourse teaches students the skill of moral reasoning, enabling them to identify, analyze, deliberate, and ultimately solve moral dilemmas for themselves. By exposing students to a wide range of ethical positions and examining the rationales on which they are founded, the course encourages students to question their own ethical positions. Students learn the vocabulary, paradigms, and metaphors through which the conversation in Western ethics has proceeded for the past 2500 years and also how to apply that discussion to the resolution of today's moral conflicts. (3 credits)

Psychology

Time to Grow

This telecourse covers all aspects of children's physical, cognitive, and psychosocial growth and development from birth through adolescence, including the most recent theoretical and applied perspectives about effective ways of caring for and working with children. (3 credits)

Gateway Community-Technical College

See **Connecticut Community-Technical College System**

Manchester Community-Technical College

See **Connecticut Community-Technical College System**

Northwestern Connecticut Community-Technical College

See **Connecticut Community-Technical College System**

Norwalk Community-Technical College

See **Connecticut Community-Technical College System**

Tunxis Community-Technical College

See **Connecticut Community-Technical College System**

Florida

Florida West Coast Public Broadcasting, Inc.
Instructional TV

1300 North Boulevard
P.O. Box 4033
Tampa, FL   33677-4033

(813) 254-9338 *Fax:* (813) 253-0826

Geographic Access: Florida

DELIVERY SYSTEMS

Broadcast Television
Telecourses are broadcast on a regular basis by WEDU Channel 3. A broadcast schedule can be obtained from WEDU or the college of choice.

INSTITUTION DESCRIPTION

Florida West Coast Public Broadcasting owns and operates WEDU Channel 3 and airs telecourses to the Tampa Bay viewing area. The Community/Junior College Consortium is a group of six colleges that award credit for successful completion of a telecourse broadcast by WEDU. The member institutions are:

- St. Petersburg Junior College (St. Petersburg FL), (813) 341-3600
- Hillsborough Community College (Tampa FL), (813) 253-7000
- Polk Community College (Winter Haven FL), (813) 297-1000
- South Florida Community College (Avon Park FL), (813) 453-6661
- Pasco Hernando Community College (Dade City FL), (904) 567-6701
- Manatee Community College (Bradenton FL), (813) 755-1511

Accreditation: SACS

Official/Contact: Annette DeLisle, Educational Projects Manager

Admission Requirements: Open enrollment. For credit to be applied toward a degree, formal admission to the college of choice is required.

Tuition: Tuition and other fees vary among the member institutions. Prospective students should contact the college of choice for up-to-date information.

Degree Credit: Credit earned for successful completion of a course may be applied to a degree program.

Grading: Examinations must be proctored and normally are taken on the campus. Letter grades are assigned. Credit is generally awarded in semester hour units.

Library: Access to the Library Resource Center of the college in which the student is officially enrolled is available.

COURSES OFFERED

Business

The Business File
From the basic principles of organizational structure and management to the challenges of business on an international scale, this series provides a comprehensive overview of the contemporary business environment. Using a news interview format, the programs present leading scholars and corporate executives discussing business theory and its practical application. The series encompasses five general areas: American business, foundation, and forms.

Organizing and managing a business. The internal workings of a business. The environment of business. The challenge of business. Topics include marketing, finance, accounting, and management. Produced by Dallas Telecourses. 28 half-hour programs.

Health

Living with Health

This introductory health series focuses on the lifestyle components that encourage wellness. The programs encompass all areas of health: the physical, emotional, social, intellectual, and spiritual. One-fourth of the programs focus on individual health including emotional and intellectual well-being, fitness, exercise, and diet. The other episodes explore the impact of relationships on health, illness, injuries, substance abuse, current health issues, public health, healthcare providers, and aging. Produced by Dallas Telecourses. 26 half-hour programs.

History

American Adventure

This American history series starts with Columbus' discovery and the early colonial settlements and ends with the Civil War and Reconstruction. Filmed at historic sites in 23 states plus Mexico, the series weaves together historic facts with the people, places, and events of the American past. The programs feature interviews with renowned historians who provide academic analysis as well as narratives drawn from diaries, letters, and music of the period. Produced by Dallas Telecourses. 26 half-hour programs.

Oceanography

Oceanus: The Marine Environment

Focuses on the marine environment as a unique feature of the planet Earth and investigates the areas of intense scientific and public concern: the pervasiveness of the ocean and its effect on the Earth's weather, its stunning physical size and diversity of contained life forms, its contributions to the physical and historical development of man, its impact on geopolitical and economic matters, the impact of oceanic pollutants, and the potential of exploitation of marine resources. 26 half-hour programs.

Political Science

Government by Consent

This American government survey provides students with an understanding of democracy, the U.S. Constitution, political parties, the three branches of government, due process, and more. The series marries political science instruction with examples of how students can involve themselves in government. Program topics include federalism, PACs, congress, the legislative process, domestic policy, foreign policy, the judiciary, first amendment freedoms, and rights of the accused. Produced by Dallas Telecourses. 26 half-hour programs.

Psychology

Discovering Psychology

This introductory psychology series covers the fundamental principles of psychology including brain and behavior, sensation and perception, conditioning and learning, cognitive processes, psychopathology, social influences, therapy, and more. The host for the series, Philip Zimbardo of Stanford University, weaves the thread of each topic through original footage of classic experiments, interviews with renowned psychologists, and segments on emerging research. He takes students into working laboratories and introduces leading scholars and researchers who seek to improve the quality of human life and our understanding of the mind. Produced by WGBH/Boston. 26 half-hour programs.

Sociology

Sociological Imagination

This introductory sociology series features mini-documentaries that are emotionally strong illustrations of issues such as socialization, social control, sex and gender, aging, collective behavior, and social change. Expert commentary from noted sociologists provides an academic framework for sociological issues such as group dynamics, deviance, social class, religion, and family. Produced by Dallas Telecourses. 26 half-hour lessons.

Hillsborough Community College
See **Florida West Coast Public Broadcasting**

Manatee Community College
See **Florida West Coast Public Broadcasting**

Miami-Dade Community College
Open College

300 Northeast Second Avenue
Miami, FL   33132-2297

(305) 237-3123

Geographic Access: Florida

DELIVERY SYSTEMS

Audiocassette
Students must have access to an audiocassette player.

Videocassette
Access to a VHS video player/recorder is required. Students may also view the videocassettes in the audiovisual center of any Miami-Dade Community College campus.

INSTITUTION DESCRIPTION

Miami-Dade Community College was founded in 1960 and was recognized in 1985 as the number one community college in America. Various campuses include the North Campus, Kendall Campus, Mitchell Wolfson New World Center Campus, Medical Center Campus, and Homestead Campus.

The Open College offers college credit courses that utilize videocassettes, audiocassettes, and independent studies. Students are required to visit the campus two times per semester. The courses are academically equivalent to those offered on campus.

Accreditation: SACS

Official/Contact: Castell V. Bryant, Dean, Student Services

Admission Requirements: Open door admissions policy. Degree-seeking students must have high school graduation or equivalent and be formally admitted to the college.

Tuition: Florida residents $33.20 per credit; nonresidents $115.50 per credit. Additional fees apply for supplementary materials. Textbooks must be purchased by the student.

Degree Credit: Credits earned by the successful completion of an Open College course may be applied toward the associate degree.

Grading: Letter grades A - F are assigned. Examinations must be taken on campus or under the supervision of an approved proctor. Credit is awarded in semester hour units.

Library: Open College students are entitled to the same privileges as on-campus students, including the use of audiovisual services and libraries.

COURSES OFFERED

Earth Science

Introduction to Earth Science
Selected concepts and principles of earth science taken from the areas of astronomy, geology, meteorology, and oceanography. (3 credits)

English

English Composition 1
A required general education core course in college-level writing. Students will write unified, coherent essays using various methods of development and review sentence and paragraph structures and writing fundamentals. (3 credits)

English Composition 2
A continuation of the above course. Students will compose informative and persuasive essays, write responses to a variety of readings, and produce a documented paper based on research. (3 credits)

Advanced English Composition 1
A general education distribution course in college-level writing. Students will compose essays in response to a variety of readings and demonstrate critical thinking. (3 credits)

Humanities

Humanities
An integrated approach to the humanities: creative ideas, works, and accomplishments of various cultures from the areas of art, architecture, drama, music, literature, and philosophy are presented. (3 credits)

Mathematics

General College Mathematics
Addresses essential mathematical competencies at the levels of algorithms and problem solving within

such areas as geometry, probability and statistics, algebra, computer literacy, and sets and logic. (3 credits)

Intermediate Algebra

Topics include operations with algebraic expressions, linear equalities and inequalities, quadratic equations, exponents and exponential equations, radicals and radical equations, algebraic fractions, applications, graphing, and introduction to functions. (3 credits)

Environmental Science

Energy in the Natural Environment

Investigation of the physical environment using energy as a theme to demonstrate the impact of science and technology on the environment and on the lives of people. (3 credits)

Psychology

Introduction to Psychology

Blends classic material with the most recent developments in psychological theory. Provides an understanding of human behavior as a natural phenomenon subject to scientific study. (3 credits)

Individual in Transition

Main themes include person and self, society and culture, development and the life cycle, and the maintenance of physical and psychological health. (3 credits)

Social Science

The Social Environment

An interdisciplinary course that emphasizes the cultural, political, and global dimensions of societies. Its main objective is to promote knowledge of contemporary and historical forces that shape our social environment and engage students on a life-long process of inquiry and decision making. (3 credits)

Spanish

Elementary Spanish 1

A multimedia approach to acquire proficiency in the basic skills—listening/understanding, reading, speaking, and cross-cultural awareness. Emphasis on practical vocabulary and accurate pronunciation. (4 credits)

Spanish for Native Speakers 1

Writing, spelling, punctuation, sentence structure, and reading selections for vocabulary expansion as they are relevant to the training of individual students. (3 credits)

Nova University
Center for Computer and Information Sciences

3301 College Avenue
Fort Lauderdale, FL   33314-9987

(305) 475-7352

Geographic Access: Worldwide

DELIVERY SYSTEMS

Online Services
Students use an IBM-compatible personal computer system. It is the student's responsibility to determine that the clone is fully compatible. Courseware development is based on MS DOS 4.0 or higher. DOS 2.0 and higher may be used for online work, but local work using Nova-generated diskettes may not always run on earlier versions of MS DOS. Support for Apple II e/c/GS series computer system is very limited. Students are advised to contact the Central CCIS office if they anticipate purchasing a new system prior to joining the program.

INSTITUTION DESCRIPTION

Nova University is an independent, nonsectarian university chartered by the State of Florida in 1964. It is located on a 200-acre main campus west of Fort Lauderdale with additional locations in downtown Fort Lauderdale, Coral Springs, and Port Everglades. Nova University has become a major force in educational innovation. It is distinguished by its commitment to provide breadth and depth of knowledge as the basis for quality education that keeps pace with rapidly changing professional and academic needs.

The Master of Science in Computer-Based Learning program offers a curriculum of core courses completed through a computer-based learning delivery system available to students in their locale. Online interactive learning methods and teleconferencing are used throughout the instructional sequence. In addition, each student will complete two specialty courses and a practicum. The practicum enables students to investigate a situation directly related to activities within their own institutions or organizations and translate course theory into practice. Master's students are also required to attend two institutes in Florida, prior to graduation. The summer institute is held in July or August and the winter institute in January. Both comprise sessions that are usually scheduled from Monday through Sunday. Institutes feature scheduled courses taught by distinguished full-time faculty and by experts in the field who generally hold the doctoral degree.

The Master of Science in Computer Information Systems is also offered in an institute, computer-based format.

Accreditation: SACS

Official/Contact: Edward R. Simco, Dean

Admission Requirements: Formal application with transcripts of all college and university work completed. Baccalaureate degree required for the Master of Science degree program. Students are required to demonstrate UNIX competency prior to registration.

Tuition: $260 per credit. $60 yearly registration fee. Included in the tuition are study guides and instructional materials. Students must purchase their own textbooks. Students receive 10 hours of online time per course included in the tuition. Additional time can be purchased at the rate of $15 per hour. This cost includes both the time on the Nova host computer and the cost of Tymnet. Students must purchase their own computer equipment and modem.

Degree Credit: Master of Science in Computer-Based Learning, Master of Science in Computer Information Systems. Each program requires the completion of 36 credit hours. The MS in Computer-Based Learning requires the completion of a common core of eight courses. In addition, each student will complete two specialty courses and the practicum. Up to six graduate credits may be transferred from a regionally accredited institution.

Grading: Examinations are scheduled online and during institutes. The grading system includes: A, Excellent; B, Satisfactory; C, Marginal Pass; F, Failure; P, Pass (used for practicums); I, Incomplete. Credit is awarded in semester hour units.

Library: The Information Retrieval Service of Nova University does computer searches and is available to all students. The service has access to ERIC and more than 350 other databases, including many social and behavioral science databases. Students may contact the service to request a literature search.

COURSES OFFERED

Computer-based Learning

Online Information Systems

This course examines different information handling and retrieval systems and technologies. Special emphasis is placed on investigating the dimensions of CD-ROM and related optical disc technology for delivery of large textual databases and facilitating imaginative manipulations of electronically-stored words and pictures. Strategies and approaches for online information retrieval to access source databases and for assessing the role of database vendors and producers are also explored in depth. (3 credits)

Statistics, Measurement, and Quality Control

Total Quality Management (TQM) has become persuasive to the decision-making process in industry and education. This course is organized to serve as an introduction to the world of statistical analysis. Attention will be given to how descriptive and inferential statistical analysis serves as an important tool in the overall decision-making matrix of a TQM environment. Analyses are facilitated through the use of software available to the Novavax community. The issues of data integrity, reliability, and validity are emphasized. There is also a major emphasis on research design. (3 credits)

Database Management Systems

The Ingres relational DBMS is used to assist students in the development of databases for use in professional settings. Topics include database concepts, data dictionaries, data directories, query languages, database administration, management of data, menu design, and database planning. (3 credits)

The Theory of Human Factors

This course focuses on the dynamics of human-computer interaction. The student is given a broad overview of the human factors field and specific background relating to the role of human factors information systems, education, and training applications. Areas to be tied to the course include, but are not limited to human factors design goals, the merging of computer and communication technologies, anticipated developments in human factors products, the study of personal computer software tools, the office of the future, and trends in human factors and ergonomics research. (3 credits)

Systems Analysis and Design

An introduction to basic system analysis and design concepts, techniques and types of information modeling, data modeling, fourth-generation languages, and integrated computer-aided software emerging (I-CASE) techniques. The course involves a comprehensive study of the information systems—strategic planning (Enterprise Model), analysis, systems design, and implementation. It also covers the details of process modeling and data modeling techniques to integrate the new techniques in the system development environments with emphasis on information, architectural design, and implementations. (3 credits)

Strategic Management, Leadership, and Finance

The methods of strategic management are used in this course to provide opportunities for students to demonstrate skills in the management of work organizations: strategic planning, portfolio analysis, strategy formulation, leadership, and strategies for changing structures are presented. (3 credits)

Case Analysis

Cases from the Harvard Business School Case Service are used by students to develop creative approaches to training program design. Emphasis is placed on designing alternative systems through use of the following methodologies: brainwriting, cross-impact analysis, critiques of science fiction stories, and scenario writing. Computer conferences are used to promote discussion. An online (searchable) database of a case prepared by students serves as a learning resource in this course. (3 credits)

Special Topics in Computer-Based Learning

This seminar will focus on the professor's current research interests. (3 credits)

Computer Education

Practicum Proposal in Computer Education (Part I)

Students are required to produce a proposal of publishable quality for a project in computer education. Upon approval of their proposal, students will be able to produce the final practicum report. (3 credits)

Practicum Report in Computer Education (Part II)

Students are required to produce a final report of publishable quality for a project in computer education. This report will become part of the online student practicum database. (3 credits)

Introduction to Structured Programming in Pascal

Students will develop a systematic approach to problem solving that will result in a plan that can be coded in the Pascal programming language. (3 credits)

Advanced Computer Programming in Pascal

Building on a foundation in structured programming, students will select an appropriate area for the educational application of computers. They will then create a usable Pascal problem that incorporates advanced techniques to meet an identifiable need. (3 credits)

Information Management

Practicum Proposal in Information Technology and Resource Management (Part I)

Students are required to produce a proposal of publishable quality for a project. Upon approval of their proposal, students will be able to produce the final practicum report. (3 credits)

Practicum Report in Information Technology and Resource Management

Students are required to produce a final report of publishable quality for a project on a CBL design. This report will become part of the online student practicum database. (3 credits)

Telecommunications in Information Technology and Resource Management

Topics include computer-based information telecommunications networks, electronic mail, packet switching, GTE Telenet and Tymnet, multiplexing modems, handshaking, satellite communications, file protection, and data encryption (security). (3 credits)

Emerging Technology in Information Technology and Resource Management

The implications of emerging computer architectures and work stations for information technology and resource management is the subject of this course. Topics include computer-based information, telecommunications networks (OCLC, BRS, Dialog), CD-ROM and optical disk technologies, and satellite communications, teleconferencing, data security, and encryption schemes. (3 credits)

Information Systems

Practicum Proposal in Information Systems (Part I)

Students are required to produce a proposal of publishable quality on a project in information systems. Upon approval of their proposal, students will be able to produce the final practicum report. (3 credits)

Practicum Report in Information Systems (Part II)

Students are required to produce a final report of publishable quality on a project in information systems. This report will become part of the online student practicum database. (3 credits)

Planning and Policy Formulation in Management Information Systems

This course is specifically designed to provide a thorough background on information systems planning. Topics include the overall information needs of organizations and the role of information systems in providing them, the relationship between administrative and management issues and the administration of the information systems functions, and the relationship between the information systems project and the external environment. (3 credits)

Emerging Technologies in Information Systems

An introduction to computer architecture, computer operating systems, and their interrelations are presented in this course. Topics include structured programming concepts, data organization, and file processing, hardware and software requirements in relation to information systems, and fourth-generation languages and their applications to information systems. (3 credits)

Operations Research

An introduction to the theory and methodology of mathematical programming (linear and nonlinear), optimization theory, deterministic and probabilistic models, scheduling models (simulation), and queuing methods. The student will learn to apply mathematical models and their implications for the control of complex systems and processes. (3 credits)

Information Systems in Organizations

This course provides a framework for understanding and analyzing information in organizations. Topics covered include the role of information systems in organizations, systems theory, systems concepts, information concepts, information system applica-

tions, system evaluation and selection, and management considerations in constructing, installing, monitoring, and maintaining information systems. (3 credits)

Database Management Systems

The methodologies and principles of database analysis and design are presented. Topics include conceptual modeling and specifications of databases, database design process and tools, functional analysis and methodologies for database design, entity-relationship model and advanced semantic modeling methods. The auxiliary concepts and theories of database systems will also be discussed in this course. (3 credits)

Information and Systems Analysis

Topics include application development strategies, problem identification, feasibility assessment, requirements analysis, logical specification of the planned system, project management, documentation and standards, and the new object-oriented methods of systems analysis. (3 credits)

Data Communication Systems and Networks

This course focuses on the principles and applications of data communications. Topics covered include an examination of basic concepts and major components in a data communications system, hardware requirements and equipment, systems design considerations, network architecture, LANs, common carrier services, network management, standards, and the regulatory environment. (3 credits)

Modeling and Decision Systems

This course introduces students to the principles and techniques needed for using an information system in decision making. Topics include problem representation, structured and unstructured decision making, model formulation, decision theory, linear programming, queuing, simulation, risk analysis, cost-benefit analysis, idea generation, delphi techniques. (3 credits)

Expert Systems

Topics include program identification and feasibility, choice of platform (program "shell" and hardware), techniques of knowledge acquisition, verification, and some theoretical subjects such as methods of reasoning, knowledge representation, inference engines, and backward and forward chaining. Students will use a commercial shell to build a working expert system. (3 credits)

Information Systems Management

The course focuses on strategies for translating information requirements into an installed system that satisfies organizational goals and objectives and is accepted by its users. Tasks that are required to convert the information design into a working system are examined. (3 credits)

Survey of Fourth-Generation Languages

This course surveys several of the commercially available platforms (hardware/software) for fourth-generation languages. Mainframe and PC-based fourth-generation languages are included. (3 credits)

Office Automation Systems

This course focuses on strategies for utilizing technology to handle the information used in the office to improve the quantity, content, and format of work performed. (3 credits)

Legal and Ethical Aspects of Computing

This course focuses on issues that involve computer impact and related societal concerns. (3 credits)

Computer Integrated Manufacturing

This course provides a framework for understanding how functional organization structure impacts the design of a management information system in a manufacturing setting. Special emphasis will be on marketing, manufacturing, and financial information systems. (3 credits)

Computer Graphics for Information Managers

This course presents computer graphics as an aid to information managers who need a clear means of presenting the analysis of information. Topics include basic graphic techniques (e.g. histograms, bar charts, pie charts), the theory of graphic presentation of information, desktop publishing software, presentation software, graphics monitors (EGA, CGA, VGA, RGB, composite), laser printers, computer screen projection systems, and standards. (3 credits)

Distributed Database Management

Students will study information storage and retrieval in a distributed environment. (3 credits)

Computer Security

This courses provides a foundation for understanding computer and communications security issues and a framework for creating and implementing a viable security program. Topics covered include hardware, software, and network security. The regulatory environment, personnel considerations, protective measures against a variety of potential threats including hackers, disgruntled insiders, and software viruses. Techniques for responding to incidents not prevented. (3 credits)

Decision Support Systems

Examines concepts of decision support in both a non-automated and automated environment. Emphasis will be placed on structures, modeling, and the application of various decision support systems in today's corporate environment. Additional emphasis will be placed on the use of executive information and expert system applications. Case studies will be used to look at existent applications of each of these types of technology. (3 credits)

System Design Process

Focuses on the information system design process and methodology. Among the issues addressed are the user-oriented application description, functions to be performed by the application system, logical and physical design, outputs, hardware and software selection, planning to accommodate change, and audit and control processes such as quality assurance, program development testing, and maintenance. (3 credits)

Computer-Aided Software Engineering

Topics include a critical comparison between computer-aided software engineering (CASE) and fourth-generation languages (4GLs), upper CASE (analysis/design), lower CASE (code generation and testing), toolkits, workbenches, methodology companions, platforms, completeness and consistency checking. (3 credits)

Human Factors in Computing Systems

This course focuses on the dynamics of human-computer interaction. The course provides a broad overview of the human factors field and offers specific background relating to the role of human factors in information systems applications. (3 credits)

Data Center Management

This course stresses information center methods for building systems between users and analysts. The traditional life-cycle development will be reviewed. The role and services of the information center will be discussed within the context of these issues: user support, goals in terms of user education and training, promoting systems support and development services, and promulgating and monitoring use of standards for software and for protection of data resources. Other topics include principles of application generators, prototyping, and user and provider roles in an information center. (3 credits)

Pasco Hernando Community College
See **Florida West Coast Public Broadcasting**

Polk Community College
See **Florida West Coast Public Broadcasting**

St. Petersburg Junior College
See **Florida West Coast Public Broadcasting**

South Florida Community College
See **Florida West Coast Public Broadcasting**

Southeastern College
Continuing Education Department

1000 Longfellow Boulevard
Lakeland, FL 33801

(813) 665-4404

Geographic Access: Worldwide

DELIVERY SYSTEMS

Telephone Contact
The Guided Instruction via Telephone and Mail format is utilized in all of the courses listed and described below. In this format, the student interfaces with the instructor by telephone as frequently as desired.

Videocassette
The use of videocassettes as supplementary course material is indicated where appropriate with the course description below.

INSTITUTION DESCRIPTION

The mission of the Continuing Education Department of Southeastern College is to provide to the adult learner the opportunity for personal or professional development as related to biblical, ministerial, and theological studies utilizing independent study delivery systems. The college is affiliated with the Assemblies of God.

Courses are offered in the Guided Instruction Via Telephone and Mail format. The student is provided with a course syllabus that includes course requirements, texts, outline, test procedures, grading structure, and an annotated bibliography.

Accreditation: SACS, AABC

Official/Contact: Thomas G. Wilson, Director, Continuing Education

Admission Requirements: For credit courses, graduation from an approved high school or equivalent. Anyone may register for courses on a noncredit basis but may not be changed at a later date to credit status.

Tuition: $60 per credit hour. Textbooks must be purchased by the student.

Degree Credit: Credit earned may be applied to an external degree program and may be accepted in transfer by other institutions. Students should check with their institutions if planning to transfer credit for a course.

Grading: All courses include final examinations that are supervised by a proctor (pastor, public school principal or teacher, college instructor, commissioned officer). The Independent Studies Program reserves the right to reject any proctor. Letter grades (A, B, C, D, F) are assigned. Credit is awarded in semester hour units.

Library: Students have access to the Southeastern College library by either on-campus visits or by mail. Up to five books may be withdrawn by mail for a period of four weeks. Students are encouraged to identify and use local library resources.

COURSES OFFERED

Astronomy

Astronomy
Introduction to the astronomy of the solar system, astrophysics, and constellations. Small telescopes utilized for celestial observation. The course assumes no physics or mathematics background. (2 credits)

Christian Education

Children's Ministries
A specialized study of children's ministry as it pertains to specific programs such as Children's Church, Kids' Crusades, Story Hour, Vacation Bible

School, camps, retreats, etc. Involves special emphasis on the principles of Christian Education as applied to these areas. (2 credits)

Family Ministries

A course designed to equip a leader with the knowledge and skills of how to minister to families in the church. It includes an analysis of trends and issues of the contemporary family, formulation of strategies, and administration of family ministries. (2 credits)

Christian Leadership Development

Leadership Development

A theological rationale based upon the doctrine of the priesthood of the believer and the gifts of the Holy spirit is developed with practical application for the recruitment and development of lay persons for ministry within the congregation and the community. The course focuses on the identification of individual gifts and talents that persons may possess and the training of those individuals for various ministries. Styles of leadership, administrative functions, and multistaff relationships are considered. (2 credits)

Organizational Behavior and Leadership Styles

A theology of leadership is developed upon which current trends in church organization and leadership are assessed. The history of organizational and management theory is developed, as well as organization, leadership, and group process theories. (3 credits)

Conflict Management

Based upon biblical and behavioral concepts, this course is designed to equip religious leaders with an understanding of conflicts, and the skills to deal with them. It is based upon the premise that conflicts are inherent in being human and that salvation does not involve the absence of conflicts, but the realization of redemptive outcomes in conflicts. The goals to be achieved are interpersonal acceptance and group effectiveness. (2 credits)

Counseling and Contemporary Issues

Course content deals with controversial issues of the so-called "alternative lifestyles." These include homosexuality, occultism, drug and alcohol addiction, divorce, and remarriage. (3 credits)

Christian Missions

Missionary Field Work

A short-term missionary field project supervised by the college. The project involves literature distribution and evangelism of the community, children and youth programs, and ministry in the churches. (3 credits)

Theology of Missions

An introduction to the theology of the Christian Mission in the Old Testament and New Testament, and a study of the responsibility of the individual, the pastor, and the church in its implementation. (3 credits)

Area Study: Latin America

A general introduction to the area in matters of geography, historical development, religious and cultural development, and the spread of the gospel and development of the church. (3 credits)

History of Missions

A survey of the expansion of the church from apostolic times to the period of Carey (19th century). Study is made of the historical background, and contributions and methods of the principal missionaries of this period. (3 credits)

Modern Missions Survey

A historical survey of missions during the 19th and 20th centuries noting the problems and challenges of today's church. Attention will be given to the development and spread of Assemblies of God missions. (3 credits)

Anthropology

A survey of man and his culture. Special study is made of primitive groups in the world today. (3 credits)

Missionary Methods

This course deals with the administration of the missionary enterprise of the Assemblies of God under both the Foreign and Home Missions Departments and the missionary's relationship to these, as well as the modern missionary methods, problems and trends, and the indigenous church. (2 credits)

Area Study: Europe

A general introduction to the area in matters of geography, historical development, religious and cultural development and the spread of the gospel and development of the church. (3 credits)

The Urban Context for Ministry

An analysis of the city from a standpoint of demographics, lines of communications, slow and rapid change, which provides the backdrop for the church planting and church revitalization. Examples of various cities in foreign countries will be used also to enhance an awareness of the necessity for flexible strategies. (2 credits)

Area Study: Middle East

A general introduction to the area in matters of geography, historical development, religious and cultural development, and the spread of the gospel and development of the church. (3 credits)

Area Study: Far East

A general introduction to the area in matters of geography, historical development, religious and cultural development, and the spread of the gospel and development of the church. (3 credits)

Area Study: Africa

A general introduction to the area in matters of geography, historical development, religious and cultural development, and the spread of the gospel and development of the church. (3 credits)

Contemporary Issues in Missions

This course allows specialized studies of issues related to the field and to Church Missions interaction. A formal research paper is required. (3 credits)

Cross-Cultural Communications

A study of problems encountered by a Westerner in communicating with people in a foreign setting. (3 credits)

Education

Exceptional Student Education

A course designed to equip the regular classroom teacher with the knowledge and skills needed in working with exceptional students. Emphasis on causes, terminology, diagnosis, characteristics, problems, and educational implications. (2 credits)

Teaching Language Art Skills

Approaches in building a language arts program. Focus on skills in teaching handwriting, spelling, oral and written communications. (2 credits)

Teaching Health and Physical Education

A consideration of healthful school services, health instruction, and their relationships to the growth and development of the child and the learning process. (2 credits)

Instructional Media for Education

A course designed to develop skills and techniques needed for the utilization and production of classroom instructional materials and equipment. (1 credit)

Media Practicum

Laboratory work on the college newspaper and yearbook, media projects and/or programs for churches, schools, and other ministries. (1 credit)

Teaching Reading in the Content Areas

The study of methods, materials, and techniques of teaching reading in the content areas, focusing on the incorporation of vocabulary, comprehension, and study skills into the content curriculum. (2 credits)

Teaching English in the Secondary School

A study of instructional methods, content, objectives, and materials for teaching secondary level English. Field-based pre-student-teaching experiences required. (2 credits)

Early Childhood Education I

Consideration of basic concepts, goals, and principles underlying program planning. Focus upon role of teacher, records, reporting to parents, planning for individual and group activities. Observation and participation in early childhood settings required. (3 credits)

Early Childhood Education II

Exploration of early childhood curriculum, emphasizing effective learning environments, curriculum content, methods, materials, and appropriate activities for the age level. (3 credits)

Special Methods of Teaching Secondary Subjects

Planning for teaching in the secondary subject areas of English, social studies, science. Study of methods, materials, and processes specific to the student's teaching area. Focus on teacher behaviors and teaching strategies. Field-based pre-student-teaching experiences required. (2 credits)

Teaching Social Studies in the Elementary School

Curriculum instructional approaches and materials for teaching social studies in grades K-6. Emphasis placed on helping prospective teachers acquire background and skills in developing and teaching units of work. (2 credits)

Teaching Social Studies in the Secondary School

A study of the objectives, organization of materials, and methods of teaching social studies in the secondary school. Emphasis is given in the program to development of content materials, and current issues and trends. Field-based pre-student-teaching experience required. (2 credits)

Introduction to Reading

An approach to teaching reading utilizing diagnosis, prescription, assessments, and a management system. Phonics terminology and procedures for teaching skills in the following areas are presented: auditory discrimination, visual discrimination, word recognition, comprehension, and reference and study skills. Opportunities for demonstration of eight teacher competencies are provided. (3 credits)

Diagnosis and Remediation of Reading

This course explores evaluation of student strengths and weaknesses in the elementary classroom through the use of criteria-referenced assessments and norm-referenced tests. Teacher-made activities to be used for remediation are developed and commercial materials are selected for use in the instructional process. Field-based pre-student-teaching experiences required. (3 credits)

Teaching Art for the Elementary Teacher

Art through laboratory practice in painting, drawing, design, graphics and various crafts with particular reference to their appropriateness for teaching in the elementary school. (2 credits)

Teaching Science in the Elementary School

Emphasis is placed on service content, methods, and materials as related to teaching science in elementary schools. (2 credits)

Music for the Elementary Teacher

A course designed for elementary education majors to give the teacher a knowledge of music teaching methods and materials for use in the classroom. (2 credits)

Curriculum Design K-12

An overview and evaluation of school programs and the underlying philosophy of curriculum K-12, with emphasis on the teacher's role in the organizational structure, techniques, and problems of curriculum development at the primary (K-3), elementary (1-6), middle grades (5-9), and secondary (6-12) levels. (2 to 3 credits)

Organization and Administration of Christian Schools

A study of the basic organization and administration of Christian schools. Emphasis placed on the areas of organizing, staffing, and financing, as well as on the functions of various departments. (3 credits)

English

Major British Authors

An analytical introduction to the major writers of British literature that focuses on the lives and times of the authors as well as on their writings. (3 credits)

Advanced Grammar

This course is designed to enable students to develop proficiency in analyzing almost all types of sentences and grammatical structures. The traditional method of diagramming sentences is used extensively. (3 credits)

Contemporary Literature

A study of selected American, English, and world literature of the twentieth century with emphasis given to literature of the last three decades. (3 credits)

Contemporary Christian Writers

A critical study of fictional works by selected authors: C.S. Lewis, Graham Greene, Alexsandr Solzhenitzyn, Walker Percy, Flannery O'Connor, Frederick Buechner, and Harold Fickett. (3 credits)

Introduction to Shakespeare

A course designed to introduce students to Shakespeare's comedies, histories, tragedies, and romances by the studying of selected plays. (3 credits)

The American Novel

A course designed to familiarize the students with the growth and development of the American novel beginning with early American novels and concluding with the great novelists of the 1920s (Hemingway, Fitzgerald, and Faulkner). (3 credits)

Evangelism

Healing: A Ministry of the Holy Spirit

The biblical basis for a doctrine of divine healing will be investigated. A historical survey will demonstrate the continuation of divine healing throughout the history of the church. Recent and contemporary practices related to divine healing will be addressed. (3 credits)

Evangelism and the Gifts of the Holy Spirit

A study of the use and importance of the gifts of the Holy Spirit in the evangelism of the New Testament church, especially in the Acts of the Apostles. After establishing the connection between the manifestation of the supernatural gifts and the spread and acceptance of the Gospel message in the New Testament, students will explore the impact these gifts could have on modern-day evangelism. (3 credits)

Modern Cults

A study of modern cults, their doctrinal positions, and defections from historical Christianity. (3 credits)

Royal Ranger Leadership Training

A course designed to train potential Royal Ranger leaders in the local church. Emphasis is placed on organizing an outpost, counseling boys, coordinating the outpost meetings, and the camping programs. (2 credits)

Worship and the Gifts of the Holy Spirit

A theology of worship will be developed based on both the Old and New Testament models. (3 credits)

Geology

Geology

Introduction to the origin and classification of earth materials and landforms with a study of minerals, rocks, and processes of the earth's crust. (3 credits)

Geophysics

Planet Earth

Seven videocassette programs reveal insights and discoveries of the past two decades as internationally known scientists share their theories about the formation of the earth and the universe beyond. Computer graphics and special effects accompany footage shot especially for the series on all seven continents, in the oceans, and in outer space. (3 credits)

History

Western Civilization I

A survey of the great epochs of civilization from early Mesopotamian and Egyptian beginnings to the beginning of the Renaissance, including the development of social, economic, religious, and political institutions. (3 credits)

Western Civilization II

A survey from the beginning of the Renaissance to the present with an emphasis on the factors which have resulted in the problems of our current world society. (3 credits)

Modern European History to 1870

A history of Europe from 1600 to 1870 with an emphasis on the factors leading to and resulting in new national monarchies and the development of world wide (European) colonialism. (3 credits)

Modern European History Since 1870

A history of Europe from 1870 to the present with an emphasis on the factors leading to the World Wars and the tension between East and West. (3 credits)

The Ancient World

A study of the Greek and Roman civilizations, considering the body of classical knowledge developed by such Greek writers as Erastosthenes, Archimedes, Protagoras, Socrates, Aristotle, Plato, Hippocrates, Thucydides, and Herodotus. A study of such Roman writers as Vergil, Tacitus, and Cicero. (3 credits)

American Church History

An examination of the development and significance of religion in the United States. Emphasis will be given to the influence of the church and society upon each other. Emphasis will also be given to American revivalism and its contribution to the Pentecostal movements of the twentieth century. (3 credits)

History of Religious Renewal Movements

A survey and analysis of revival/renewal movements and spiritual awakenings throughout the history of the Christian church. Emphasis will be given to the reasons for their development, their significance, their impact upon society, and the reasons for their continuation or decline. (3 credits)

Music

Church Music Organization and Administration

A study of the administrative role of the minister of music in a fully developed music program at the local level. (3 credits)

Pastoral Ministries

Church Jurisprudence

A study of the laws in various administrative areas affecting clergymen and churches. The study includes pastoral contracts, rights, liabilities, restrictions, negligence, taxation, administration of private schools, church and state, and laws of the church. (2 credits)

Youth Ministries

This course deals with methods of building an effective youth program, including the strategy, management, and funding of a youth ministry. Emphasis is placed on the educational and worship ministry to youth, pastoral ministry to youth, and building Christian character in youth. (3 credits)

Philosophy

Principles of Ethics

A survey of the theory of value as applied to human goals and behavior, with Christian ethics compared to other systems. (3 credits)

History of Philosophy

A survey of the ideas underlying western civilization from Thales to the present. Special emphasis is given to Descartes, Leibniz, and Kant. (3 credits)

Psychology

Applied and Community Psychology

A survey of the specialized fields of psychological practice including personnel, engineering, law, counseling, and consumer psychology. The application of psychology to rehabilitation, interpersonal skills, and related areas plus concepts of community psychology as they have developed. (3 credits)

Theories of Personality

A study of the nature, development, and adjustment of personality. Points of view representing the various systems of psychology are represented. The work of the major theorists are reviewed, evaluated, and systematized. (3 credits)

Psychological Foundations of Education

A study of psychological principles of human growth, development, and learning theory applied in teaching. A study of the exceptional child's physical, emotional, and psychological needs with implications for instructional programs. Construction, evaluation, and interpretation of formal and informal educational tests and measurements. A review of various models and methods of classroom management. (3 credits)

Developmental Psychology

A study of the human growth and development from conception to death. The course emphasizes physical, mental, emotional, social, and personality growth with special attention given to guidance toward acceptable behavior, responsible adult control of relevant phases of nurture, modes of interpersonal interaction, and the aging process. (3 credits)

Psychology of Religion

A study of historical development, the current trends, and the major contributions of the psychological studies of religious experience and development. A study of how the church has contributed to the psychological welfare of man through religious experience and how the church can function to facilitate mental health. (3 credits)

Integration of Psychology and Theology

A study of the contemporary evangelical efforts to integrate psychology and theology, focusing on the value of an integrative effort to both the theory and practice of psychology and theology. Discussion includes matters of behavior, cognition, emotion, and motivation. (3 credits)

Psychotherapy: Theory and Practice

A discussion of various theoretical approaches to the practice of counseling and psychotherapy with normal and disturbed clients. Focus will be on the psychoanalytic, cognitve, behavioral, and phenomenological approaches. (3 credits)

Social Psychology

A review of the theories of interpersonal behavior and group dynamics emphasizing the influence of groups and group membership upon individual behavior including aggressions, attitudes, attribution, conformity, altruism, communication, propaganda, morale, and other aspects of interpersonal relationships. (3 credits)

Physiological Psychology

A study of the biological basis of human behavior, including in-depth treatment of relationships between the activity of the nervous and endocrine systems and behavior. (3 credits)

Experimental Psychology

A study of methods and problems in psychological experimentation. Emphasis is on the study of techniques used with specific reference to defining variables, stating hypotheses, designing experiments with adequate controls, and reporting findings. The student is expected to carry out several experiments during the semester. (3 credits)

Marital and Family Therapy

A study of typical marriage and family problems including communications, roles, and sexual dysfunction. Various counseling techniques related to marital maladjustment and principal approaches to conjoint marital therapy and family therapy will be emphasized. An overview of family systems approach will be given. (3 credits)

Directed Readings and Research in Psychology

Provides the student with the opportunity for extensive study through in-depth reading in a specific topic of his/her choosing under the guidance of the Psychology Department. An intensive synopsis of readings or a formal research paper is required. (1 to 3 credits)

Religious Studies

Isaiah

A careful study of the life of Isaiah with emphasis given to his times, his message to Israel, and his Messianic prophecies. Attention is given to the problem of authorship. (2 credits)

Old Testament History II

An analysis of the history of Israel from the Babylonian captivity through the Maccabean period. Special attention will be given to Daniel's experiences in the exile, the reconstruction of the temple, the rebuilding of Jerusalem, the contributions of some of the minor prophets, and the impact of the foreign cultures and powers on Israel. (3 credits)

Genesis

An exegetical treatment of the first book of the Bible. (2 credits)

Jeremiah

A study of the life and ministry of the prophet Jeremiah who lived during the last days of the Jewish kingdom. (2 credits)

Hebrew Wisdom Literature

An examination of the wisdom literature of the Old Testament with special emphasis given to Proverbs and Ecclesiastes. (2 credits)

Exodus

An exegetical course in Exodus that gives consideration to the deliverance of Israel, the law, the tabernacle, and the priesthood. Israel's history and culture are discussed in the light of the theology of Ancient Israel. (2 credits)

Leviticus

An exegetical course that deals with the Old Testament covenant and the Levitical laws relating to the various offerings, the operations of the tabernacle, and the cleanliness and purity of the people of God. (2 credits)

Ezekiel

An analysis of the ministry of the man who preached to Israel during the period of exile in Babylon. (2 credits)

The Book of Job

An analysis of the problem of evil and suffering in relation to a sovereign God as presented in the book of Job. (2 credits)

Apocalyptic Literature of the Old Testament

An exegetical and historical analysis of the apocalyptic literature of the Old Testament and the nature of apocalyptic literature. (2 credits)

Matthew

A study of Matthew's gospel emphasizing the Sermon on the Mount and other discourses such as the parables of the kingdom, the church, and eschatological passages. (2 credits)

Luke

A study of Luke's gospel showing the portrayal of Jesus as the universal Savior. Topics of study include Luke's literary style, his social interest, prayer, and the Holy Spirit. (2 credits)

Earlier Epistles of Paul

An analytical study of Galatians and I and II Thessalonians, with emphasis on the relationship of faith and works, the transmission of authoritative teaching, and the teaching on the *parousia*. (2 credits)

Mark

A study of Mark's distinctive portrayal of Jesus' ministry as the servant of Yahweh and his Gentile emphasis. (2 credits)

Prison Epistles

An analytical and expository treatment of Ephesians, Philippians, Colossians, and Philemon. (2 credits)

Pastoral Epistles

An expository study of I and II Timothy and Titus. Consideration is given to the authorship, date, the threat of gnosticism, and the significance that these epistles have for church organization and for the function of the pastor in the local church. (2 credits)

Biblical Introduction

A study of the inspiration, canonization, and transmission of the Biblical text. The course includes a review of the history of the English Bible. Trustworthiness of the text is supported by a consideration of archaeological discovery and correlation with secular historical data. (2 credits)

General Epistles

An outlined study of the letters of James, Peter, John, and Jude, with special attention given to historical background, structure, and distinctive teachings of each book. (2 credits)

Revelation

An analysis of the historical setting, language, and special symbolism in Revelation. Special attention will be given to the apocalyptic language and the end-time images described in the book. (2 credits)

Epistle to the Hebrews

An expository study with a discussion of the authorship, date, and destination of this epistle. Emphasis is placed on the priestly work of Christ. (2 credits)

Social Science

World Geography

A study of the geographic regions, inhabitants, resources, physical characteristics, and economy of the world. (3 credits)

Economics

This course is designed to provide the student with an understanding of economic problems and institutions. Economic behavior of individuals, business firms, public agencies, and interest groups will be considered. (3 credits)

United States Government

A study of American politics: the constitutional basis, organization, and function of our government. (3 credits)

Theology

The Doctrine of God

An in-depth study of the doctrine of god, considering His existence, names, nature, attributes, works, and the Trinity. (2 credits)

The Doctrine of Christ

A study of the person and work of Jesus Christ, including consideration of His names, natures, humiliation, exaltation, offices, and atoning death. (2 credits)

The Doctrine of Last Things

A study of the doctrine of last things. Consideration will be given to physical death, immortality of the soul, the rapture, the second coming of Christ, the resurrection of the dead, and the final judgment. (2 credits)

University of Florida
Department of Independent Study and Distance Education

1223 NW 22nd Avenue
Gainesville, FL   32609

(904) 392-1711

Geographic Access: Nationwide

DELIVERY SYSTEMS

Audiocassette
Used primarily in language courses but also accompany other courses as supplementary materials.

Videocassette
Requires the use of a VHS videocassette player.

INSTITUTION DESCRIPTION

The University of Florida offers media-assisted correspondence courses in conjunction with the resident programs of all nine universities in Florida's State University System. These courses are part of the overall correspondence program that began in 1919.

The courses described below require the use of a VHS videocassette player or an audiocassette player.

Accreditation: SACS

Official/Contact: Sandra Scaggs, Director

Admission Requirements: Open enrollment for those not officially enrolled in a college or university. Otherwise, approval of the student's dean, counselor, or high school principal is required.

Tuition: $54.97 per semester hour for Florida residents. $213.62 per semester hour for non-Florida residents. Full tuition must accompany application at time of enrollment. VISA and MasterCard accepted. Textbooks, study guides, and other materials must be purchased by the student.

Degree Credit: Credit will be accepted by the University of Florida toward a degree.

Grading: Examinations must be proctored. They may be taken at Gainesville, Florida, or will be sent to any educational institution. Letter grades of A, B, C, D, and E (failure) are assigned. Credit is awarded in semester hour units.

Library: Students have access to the libraries of the University of Florida System. Students not in Florida should use their local community library resources.

COURSES OFFERED

Economics

Principles of Macroeconomics
The nature of economics, economic concepts, and institutions. Emphasis on the accounting, analytical, and policy aspects of national income and product, as well as public finance, money and banking, and international trade. Videotape: $6 ($6.36 for Florida residents), study guide: $19 ($20.14 for Florida residents). 22 assignments, 1 exam. (3 credits)

German

Beginning German 1
This first-semester course aims to develop the student's skills in reading, writing, understanding, and speaking German. Audiotapes: $18.15 ($19.24 for Florida residents). 21 assignments, 2 exams. (4 credits)

Beginning German 2
A continuation of Beginning German 1. Audiotapes: $14.95 ($15.85 for Florida residents). 18 assignments, 2 exams. (3 credits)

Beginning German 3
A continuation of Beginning German 2. Audiotapes: $14.00 ($14.84 for Florida residents). (3 credits)

Mathematics

Basic College Algebra
Covers techniques of algebra. Linear, polynomial, exponential, and logarithmic functions, equations, and graphs. Systems of equation and inequalities, counting, and applications. Audiotapes: $22 ($23.32 for Florida residents). 15 assignments, 3 exams. (3 credits)

Medical Terminology

Medical Terminology for the Health-Related Professions
A study of the prefixes, suffixes, and word roots which are combined to constitute the language used in medicine and the health-related professions. Terms related to disease states, diagnostic procedures, and equipment are emphasized. This course is accompanied by eight audiocassette tapes to aid the student in building listening and speaking skills. Audiotapes: $22 ($23.32 for Florida residents). 12 assignments, 2 exams. (3 credits)

Psychology

General Psychology
Introductory survey of the basic principles, theories, and methods of contemporary psychology. Audiotapes: $52.80 ($55.97 for Florida residents). 18 assignments, 1 exam. (3 credits)

Georgia

University of Georgia
Independent Study
Georgia Center for Continuing Education

1180 East Broad
Athens, GA 30602-3603

(706) 542-3243 *Fax:* (706) 542-5990

Geographic Access: Nationwide

DELIVERY SYSTEMS

Audiocassette
Used extensively in foreign language courses.

Videocassette
Students must have access to a VHS player.

INSTITUTION DESCRIPTION

The University of Georgia, a land-grant and sea-grant university, is Georgia's oldest, most comprehensive, most diversified institution of higher education. Its constituencies are numerous, and the scope of its programs in graduate, professional, and undergraduate education is the most extensive in Georgia.

Independent Study offers an extensive variety of traditional correspondence courses. Some of these courses require the use of video or audio lecture tapes or language audiotapes. The cost of each tape is given in the course description below. Tapes are not returnable.

Accreditation: SACS

Official/Contact: Edward S. Weeks, Jr., Department Head

Admission Requirements: There are no admission requirements for enrolling in Independent Study other than that the student must have completed high school or its equivalent.

Tuition: $50 per quarter hour credit. Textbooks, study materials, and audio- and videotapes must be purchased by the student.

Degree Credit: Independent Study is not a degree-granting unit of the University System of Georgia. Credits earned may be applied to a degree program and may be accepted in transfer by other institutions.

Grading: Examinations must be proctored. Letter grades (A, B, C, D, F) are assigned. Credit is awarded in quarter hour units.

Library: Students enrolled in Independent Study courses may obtain access to the University of Georgia libraries.

COURSES OFFERED

Family Relations

Development within the Family
Individual and family development during the life cycle is considered with special emphasis upon interpersonal relationships among family members. 13 lessons, 2 exams. Videotape: $20. (5 credits)

French

Elementary French (FR 101)
Conversation, grammar, fundamentals of pronunciation and reading are taught. 19 lessons, 1 exam. 3 audiocassettes: $43.75. (5 credits)

Elementary French (FR 102)
A continuation of FR 101. 18 lessons, 1 exam. 3 audiocassettes: $43.75. (5 credits)

Elementary French (FR 103)

A continuation of FR 102. 15 lessons, 1 exam. 3 audiocassettes: $43.75. (5 credits)

Intermediate French

Extensive reading of texts of literary merit. Grammar review, conversation, and pronunciation. Also prepares students to enter courses in French literature and French composition and conversation. 15 lessons, 1 exam. Audiocassette tapes: $30. (5 credits)

German

Elementary German I

Introduction to essentials of grammar, acquisition of basic vocabulary. Practice in reading, speaking, and writing. 11 lessons, 1 exam. Audiocassettes: $22.10. (5 credits)

Elementary German II

A continuation of Elementary German I with an increased emphasis on the active use of the language. 10 lessons, 1 exam. Audiocassette tapes: $22.10. (5 credits)

Elementary German III

A continuation of Elementary German II. 11 lessons, 1 exam. Audiocassettes: $23.20. (5 credits)

Latin

Elementary Latin

An introduction to the Latin language: pronunciation, fundamentals of grammar, reading, and translation. 14 lessons, 2 exams. Audiocassette tapes: $34.15. (5 credits)

Elementary Latin II

An introduction to the Latin language, continued from Elementary Latin I. 14 lessons, 2 exams. Audiocassettes: $34.15. (5 credits)

Elementary Latin III

Completion of study of Latin grammar and syntax begun in elementary Latin I and II. Introduction to reading continuous Latin passages. 14 lessons, 2 exams. Audiocassette tapes: $34.15. (5 credits)

Mathematics

Finite Mathematics I

Finite mathematics with applications. Topics include fundamental algebra, polynomial and rational models, linear systems, matrices, sets, counting, probability, and mathematics of finance. 16 lessons, 1 exam. Videotape: $20. (5 credits)

Spanish

Elementary Spanish I

Introduction to essentials of grammar, acquisition of basic vocabulary. Practice in reading, speaking, and writing. 9 lessons, 1 exam. 7 audiocassettes: $25. (5 credits)

Elementary Spanish II

A continuation of Elementary Spanish I with an emphasis on the active use of the language. 9 lessons, 1 exam. 6 audiocassettes: $25. (5 credits)

Elementary Spanish III

A continuation of Elementary Spanish II. 9 lessons, 1 exam. 3 audiocassettes: $42. (5 credits)

Intermediate Spanish

A review of Spanish grammar, reading of selected texts and particular emphasis on conversation and expansion of vocabulary. 9 lessons, 1 exam. Audiocassette tapes: $11.88. (5 credits)

Idaho

Boise State University
Continuing Education

1910 University Drive

Boise, ID   83725

(208) 385-3486

Geographic Access: Idaho

DELIVERY SYSTEMS

Broadcast Television

Telecourses are broadcast by KAID-TV, Channel 4.

INSTITUTION DESCRIPTION

Established in 1932 as a community college, Boise State University progressed to a four-year university with the first graduation in 1967. The University became part of the state system in 1969.

BSU Continuing Education, in cooperation with KAID-TV, Channel 4, offers a variety of college credit classes for viewing at home. These telecourses feature a combination of televised lectures, textbook readings, and written assignments. A BSU instructor acts as a facilitator and as an additional resource for students.

Accreditation: NASC

Official/Contact: Nancy Ness, Coordinator

Admission Requirements: Open enrollment. Participants may register in person at the BSU Library or call (800) 632-6586, ext. 1702 for a register-by-mail packet.

Tuition: $75 per undergraduate credit plus $5 per credit broadcast fee. Fees are subject to change.

Degree Credit: No more than 12 pass/fail telecourse credits may be applied toward university graduation requirements.

Grading: Examinations must be proctored. All telecourses are pass/fail. Credit is awarded in semester hour units.

Library: Officially enrolled students are permitted access to the library resources of Boise State University.

COURSES OFFERED

Environmental Science

Race to Save the Planet

This telecourse entitled *Race to Save the Planet* provides a dynamic report of the current outlook for the global environment, describing the threats that different natural systems face and dissecting the complex web of interconnections that bind human society to the environment. The course will help develop a set of intellectual tools, an understanding of the sciences involved and, ways of thinking about people and the environment that will enable students to evaluate for themselves how serious a given environmental problem might be. Three "no-video" units are required. (2 credits)

Rural Sociology

Rural Sociology: Legacy and Change

This social science telecourse visits fifteen diverse rural regions across the country, exploring the problems faced by individuals, families, and communities. Their economies are in transition, their peoples diverse, and their futures uncertain. Among the group profiles are Laotian immigrants in rural Kansas and entrepreneurs planning a world-class ski resort in California's Sierra Nevada Mountains.

These rural communities and many others inevitably confront decisions about how much change is acceptable and necessary, and what tools and techniques are most effective in assuring the vitality and maintaining the character of their community. (2 credits)

University of Idaho
Continuing Education
Extended Learning

CEB-214

Moscow, ID   83843-4171

(208) 885-6641 *Fax:* (208) 885-5738

Geographic Access: Worldwide

DELIVERY SYSTEMS

Audiocassette
Audio-enhanced courses are mainly those in the field of foreign language.

Computer Tutorials
Used primarily in microcomputer applications courses.

Videocassette
Video-enhanced courses encompass a variety of subjects, particularly the field of economics.

INSTITUTION DESCRIPTION

The University of Idaho is a state institution and land-grant college. It was chartered in 1890 and has been offering distance learning courses for the past 20 years.

In addition to the audio- and video-enhanced courses listed below, traditional correspondence courses are offered. The program is administered by University of Idaho and courses are written and graded by approved faculties at the University of Idaho, Boise State University, Lewis Clark State College, and Idaho State University. Each media-assisted course consists of the media component, a course study guide, and text(s). The study guide integrates all of the course components, details the reading assignments from the required text(s), gives the viewing or listening assignments, and contains study notes, written assignments, and/or examination information. The media compo-

nent highlights the major themes of the course and helps pace student work.

Accreditation: NASC

Official/Contact: Julie Rinard, State Coordinator

Admission Requirements: Students who do not wish to apply credit toward a college degree may register for any course in which they have an interest. Formal admission is not required and enrollment does not constitute admission to the University of Idaho.

Tuition: $53.75 per undergraduate credit hour, $75.75 per graduate credit hour. Textbooks and supplies must be purchased by the student. Partially refunded deposits are necessary for most media-assisted courses (see below with the course description). MasterCard and VISA accepted.

Degree Credit: A student desiring to apply college credit toward a degree must satisfy the requirements of the respective college.

Grading: The grading system for each course is established by the instructor. Examinations must be proctored by an approved supervisor. Credit is awarded in semester hour units.

Library: Students are encouraged to utilize their local community library. Officially registered students may use the university/college libraries when in the vicinity.

COURSES OFFERED

Economics

Principles of Economics (Macro)
Organization and operation of American economy, supply and demand, money and banking, employment and aggregate output, public finance and economic growth. This course requires a partially refundable deposit of $50 for 3 VHS tapes. 20 lessons, 4 exams. (3 credits)

Principles of Economics (Micro)
Principles of governing production, price relationships, and income distribution. This course requires a partially refundable deposit of $50 for 3 VHS tapes. 20 lessons, 4 exams. (3 credits)

Money and Banking
Analysis of the role of money, credit, and the financial system in the U.S. economy through the economics of commercial and central banking. Study of

monetary theory and monetary policy as they affect both domestic and international economic policy goals. This course requires a partially refundable deposit of $50 for 3 VHS tapes. 20 lessons, 3 exams. (3 credits)

Education

Microcomputer Applications

Computer applications course designed primarily for office administration and business teacher education students. Includes hands-on experience using word processing, spreadsheet, and database management software packages. Also some methodology, curriculum development, and classroom management techniques. 5 lessons, 4 exams. Computer tutorial component. (3 credits)

Engineering

Statics

Addition and resolution of forces, vector algebra, graphical methods, equilibrium, free body diagrams, trusses, frames, friction, centroids and moments of inertia, fluid statics, and virtual work. This course requires a partially refundable deposit of $50 for 4 VHS tapes. 25 lessons, 2 exams. (3 credits)

English

World Literature

Examination of major works and authors in historical perspective, with emphasis upon literary and cultural backgrounds. The set of audiotapes and slides requires a partially refundable deposit of $75. 16 lessons, 4 exams. (3 credits)

Library Science

Computer Applications in Libraries

Developments and trends in library automation, especially computer applications to library work and administration. A computer tutorial course. 16 lessons, 2 exams. (3 credits)

Music

Survey of Music

History and appreciation of western music from the Middle Ages until the contemporary period, with a brief introduction to jazz and folk styles. The course stresses the relationship of music to western history and culture. 8 audiocassette tapes accompany the text *Listen, Brief Edition*. 22 lessons, 2 exams. (3 credits)

Spanish

Elementary Spanish C101

Develops ability in understanding, speaking, reading, and writing. Basic grammatical structures and vocabulary. Introduces the student to Spanish culture. Audiotape purchase: $25. 10 lessons, 11 exams. (4 credits)

Elementary Spanish C102

A continuation of the above course. Audiotape purchase: $25. 9 lessons, 10 exams. (4 credits)

Special Education

Augmentative and Alternative Communication Strategies for Persons with Moderate and Severe Disabilities

Develops a process for decision making, models for assessment, strategies and implementation steps for designing communications systems. A partially refundable $100 deposit is required for 14 modules of VHS tapes. 13 lessons, 3 exams. (3 credits)

Vocational Education

Classroom Management and Student Motivation

Techniques and strategies to motivate student interest and encourage learning. A video-enhanced course. 17 lessons, 2 exams. (2 credits)

Illinois

Belleville Area College
Telecourse Office
2500 Carlyle Road
Belleville, IL   62221-5899

(618) 235-2700

Geographic Access: Illinois, Missouri

DELIVERY SYSTEMS

Broadcast Television
Some telecourses are broadcast over television Channel 9 (KETC-TV, St. Louis, Missouri) or Channel 8 (WSIU, Carbondale, IL). A detailed broadcast schedule is included in the student handbook packet.

Videocassette
All telecourse programs are available on videotape for home viewing. If a student wishes to check-out tapes to view at home, a visit to the BAC Telecourse Office is necessary. An entire set of tapes will be provided for the student. A "set" includes two to five videotapes, depending on the course. All videotapes issued must be returned undamaged at the end of the semester.

INSTITUTION DESCRIPTION

Belleville Area College (BAC) is a comprehensive public community college located 30 miles southeast of St. Louis and serves an area of 2100 square miles. The college was established as a junior college in 1946 and became a Class I junior college in 1967 under the name Belleville Junior College. In 1969 the present name was adopted.

The BAC telecourses combine televised or videotaped lessons with related textbook readings and assignments. Telecourses allow busy students to earn college credit at home, a convenient way to get a college education. Students have access to the same support services and campus privileges as on-campus students.

A mentor (BAC instructor) is assigned to each telecourse. The mentor will contact the student in the beginning of the semester to notify the student of his/her office hours. Courses listed below are representative of those offered during the year on a semester basis. Even though these courses are convenient, they do require a significant amount of self-discipline and independent study.

Accreditation: NCA

Official/Contact: Laurie Bingel, Telecourse Specialist

Admission Requirements: Proof of residency must be provided for students in the community district. Students not providing proof of residency will be billed at the out-of-district rate.

Tuition: $32 per credit hour for in-district students. Textbooks must be purchased by the student. A $25 production fee is also required which is assessed to pay for the royalties of the professionally produced programs, videotapes, and the production of the student handbooks and pertaining correspondence.

Degree Credit: Each telecourse is considered equivalent to its traditional campus counterpart. Students are advised to contact the counseling office or the college they plan to transfer to for credit transferability.

Grading: All telecourse students are required to attend the midterm and final examinations and other on-campus sessions as required. The exams are administered by the course mentor and are held at the Belleville Campus. Exam details are listed in the telecourse schedule which is included in the student handbook packet.

Library: Videotaped copies of the telecourse programs are available for students to view at the various campus and public libraries in the community college district.

COURSES OFFERED

Anthropology

Cultural Anthropology

TV title: *Faces of Culture*. A one-semester college-level television course in introductory anthropology. The telecourse, which features dramatic and unique film footage from around the world, embraces cultures from all continents, highlights major human subsistence patterns, and illustrates human adaptation to environment from the beginning of human history to the present. The course focuses on the thesis that every society is based on an integrated culture which satisfies human needs and facilitates survival. In addition to the study of many foreign cultures, this course also explores the ways in which our own culture fits into the broad range of human possibilities. 26 half-hour segments. (3 credits)

Aviation Technology

Private Pilot Ground School

TV title: *An Invitation to Fly: Basics for the Private Pilot*. Designed to help the potential private pilot to become a safe and competent pilot. Upon successful completion, the student should be able to pass the Federal Aviation Administration (FAA) written examination for the private pilot. Students will view programs which were produced by the College of San Mateo, California. 30 half-hour segments. (3 credits)

Biology

Introduction to Marine Biology

TV title: *Oceanus*. An orientation to the marine sciences including physical and chemical properties of the sea, the sea air interface, the biology of the sea and the geology of the ocean basins. Students will view programs entitled *Oceanus* that are produced by the Southern California Consortium for Community College Television. The programs feature Dr. Bernard W. Pipkin of the University of Southern California as the on-air host. 30 half-hour segments. (3 credits)

Business

Introduction to Business

TV title: *The Business File*. An introductory college-level telecourse in the fundamentals of business that provides an in-depth examination of all elements of business today. From the internal functions of a business to the challenges of business on an international scale, the course provides a comprehensive view of the contemporary environment of business. The series encompasses five general areas: American business, foundation and forms, organizing and managing a business, the internal workings of a business, the environment of business, and the challenges of business. 28 half-hour segments. (3 credits)

Computer Science

Introduction to Data Processing

TV title: *The New Literacy*. This telecourse reflects the trend toward a more practical approach in introductory computer courses. It is an up-to-date survey of electronic data processing, computer hardware and software systems, and developments that will provide the basis for further advancements in information processing. The course is designed to provide a comprehensive overview of the computer: what it is, what it can do and cannot do, how it operates, and how it may be instructed to solve problems. The course familiarizes learners with the terminology of data processing and examines the application of the computer to a broad range of settings and social environments. It also prepares learners to understand and utilize computers in both their personal and professional lives. 26 half-hour segments. (3 credits)

Economics

Introduction to Economics

TV title: *Economics U$A*. The video segments approach the subject in a journalistic style. Former CBS/ABC correspondent David Schoumacher is the investigative reporter exploring the causes and effects of major economic events of the twentieth century. He interviews participants who "were there" and enlivens each program with archival and contemporary footage, newspaper photographs and headlines, graphics, animation, and radio recordings. In each program, noted economist Richard Gill, former professor of economics at Harvard University, analyzes the principles that underlie the economic events. 28 half-hour segments. (3 credits)

Health

Health

TV title: *Here's to Your Health*. This telecourse covers a broad range of topics from puberty to menopause. It offers how-to tips for avoiding and overcoming depression and hypertension, kicking the smoking habit, coping with the effects of alcoholism, and beating drug addiction. It explores the concepts of shaping up, cancer detection and treatment, and sexual health. 26 half-hour segments. (2 credits)

History

U.S. History to 1877

TV title: *The American Adventure*. This telecourse is concerned with the development of the American civilization starting with the European background and ending with the Reconstruction Period. Includes the Age of Discovery, the period of colonization of the French, Spanish, and English. Also covers the early years of the Republic, the development of the Constitution, the War of 1812, the growth of nationalism and manifest destiny, and the Civil War and Reconstruction. 26 half-hour segments. (3 credits)

Gardening

Home Gardening

TV title: *The Home Gardener*. This course will teach basic gardening skills from soil preparation to landscape design, from vegetable cropping to hanging baskets. Students will be introduced to expert horticulturists and entomologists and will have an opportunity to see interesting and unusual botanical gardens and nurseries. Coast Community College of California produced the programs which were written and presented by John Lenanton of Orange Coast College, Costa Mesa, California. 30 half-hour segments. (3 credits)

Philosophy

Ethics

TV title: *Ethics in America*. This telecourse examines real contemporary ethical conflicts in American life and provides a grounding in the language, concepts, and traditions of ethics. The discussions in this course range from the beginnings of the ancient Greeks wondering about the source of moral obligations and the nature of the good person, through such other modern personal dilemmas as loyalty, accountability, privacy, and truthfulness. The course is designed for the beginning student in ethics and those persons who are interested in having a better understanding about how we know what is right and wrong. 10 one-hour segments. (3 credits)

Psychology

General Psychology

TV title: *The Study of Human Behavior*. Introduces facts and scientific principles of the psycho-physical activity in human behavior. Subjects include the role of heredity, maturation, environment, behavioral development, sensory processes, perception, motivation, learning and remembering, emotions, and adjustments and maladjustments. Students will view programs which are produced by Coast Community College of California. 26 half-hour segments. (3 credits)

Child Development

TV title: *A Time to Grow*. This course is a study of the interplay of biological factors, human interaction, social structure, and other cultural forces in shaping the growing child. It covers prenatal through adolescent periods. Students will view programs entitled *A Time to Grow* which are produced by Coast Community College of California and was co-produced in association with the Extension Division of the University of California at San Diego and McGraw-Hill Book Company. 26 half-hour segments. (3 credits)

Sociology

Introductory Sociology

TV title: *The Sociological Imagination*. This telecourse has been designed to give the student a transformation of consciousness—the ability to confront the ordinary with extraordinary vision. The primary goal is to develop the sociological imagination of students. The programs show people in their family settings, at work, school, church, and play. The documentaries are thought provoking illustrations of sociological issues and ideas. 26 half-hour segments. (3 credits)

The Family

TV title: *Portrait of a Family.* A close look at marriage, family, and alternative lifestyles in the closing decade of the twentieth century. This course provides a balance between the solid research and theoretical base students need and the practical examination of personal choice and decision making students want. It is a course people not only take, but an experience they share and value. 26 half-hour segments. (3 credits)

Speech

American Playhouse

TV title: *American Playhouse.* This telecourse presents a series of stage plays, musicals, book adaptations, and docudramas by American writers. The course will investigate the characters, plots, and themes in the plays viewed. 8 segments. (3 credits)

Governors State University
Center for Extended Learning
Television Courses

University Park, IL   60466-3187

(708) 534-7890

Geographic Access: Illinois

DELIVERY SYSTEMS

Broadcast Television
Many courses can be viewed on cable. Cable broadcasts are announced prior to each trimester.

Videocassette
Courses may be viewed in the University Library or checked out for home viewing.

INSTITUTION DESCRIPTION

Governors State University is specially designed to serve undergraduate transfer students and those seeking master's degrees. By offering only classes traditionally reserved for college students at the third year or higher, GSU emphasizes the development of professional expertise within the context of liberal studies. To meet this goal, Governors State gives students the opportunity to study with a faculty that has the highest proportion of doctorates to be found at any public university in Illinois.

Established in 1969, Governors State is the youngest member of the Board of Governors Universities system, but it already has distinguished itself by achieving a national reputation for the use of communications technology for instruction.

The Office of Media-Based Instruction offers television courses that present the course content on a series of videotapes with a coordinating faculty member. A study guide and one or more textbooks are required for each course. Some courses have discussion sessions scheduled through the trimester. Television courses can be viewed in the University Library or checked out for home viewing. Many courses can be viewed on cable and some are available in area libraries. All media-based courses have an orientation session to provide an opportunity for students to meet their instructor and to discuss course requirements. Orientations are held during the first two weeks of each trimester. Students can usually choose either a weekday evening or a Saturday morning session. Television course orientations are mandatory.

Accreditation: NCA

Official/Contact: Leo Goodman-Malamuth, II, President

Admission Requirements: Students not currently enrolled at Governors State University may enroll as nondegree-seeking or undeclared students. Undergraduate students must have an AA/AS degree or 60 semester hours with a C average from a regionally accredited institution. Graduate students must have a bachelor's degree from an accredited institution. Students must be in good academic standing at the last institution attended.

Tuition: Undergraduate $246 per 3-credit course, graduate $258 per 3-credit course. All study guides and textbooks, as well as the videotapes for a selected number of television courses, can be purchased or ordered by phone from Follett's GSU Bookstore.

Degree Credit: Students interested in pursuing a degree should contact the Office of Admissions and Student Recruitment at (708) 534-4490 for information.

Grading: Television course students will receive examination information at the orientation session. Generally, students must take exams on the campus under the supervision of a proctor. Letter grades (A, B, C, D,

F) are assigned. Credit is awarded in semester hour units.

Library: The University Library offers its services to students enrolled in a media-based course.

COURSES OFFERED

Accounting

Financial Accounting
Requires one orientation session and two class meetings. (3 credits)

Managerial Accounting for Health Care Organizations
One orientation session and two review sessions. (3 credits)

African Studies

African Civilizations
A study of the African people and their various cultural differences. Focuses on correcting misconceptions of Africa and Africans through readings from a wide selection of publications. One orientation session required. 2 class meetings. Book critique and final paper. (3 credits)

Child Development

Child Development
One orientation session required. 3 exams. (3 credits)

Economics

Principles of Macroeconomics
One orientation required. 3 exams. (3 credits)

Education

Foundations of Education
One orientation session. 2 exams. 3 class meetings. (3 credits)

English

Literature for Children and Adolescents
One orientation session required. 2 exams. 3 class meetings. (3 credits)

Shakespeare's Plays
One orientation session required. 1 exam. (3 credits)

Health

Contemporary Health Issues
One orientation session required. 2 exams. (3 credits)

Nutrition
One orientation session required. 2 exams. (3 credits)

History

History of Civil Rights
One orientation session required. 2 exams. 5 class meetings. (3 credits)

Management

Principles of Management
One orientation session required. 2 class meetings. 2 exams. (3 credits)

Psychology

Principles of Psychology
One orientation session required. 3 exams. (3 credits)

Personality Theories
One orientation session required. 3 exams. (3 credits)

Social Psychology
One orientation session required. 2 exams. (3 credits)

Adulthood
One orientation session required. 3 exams. (3 credits)

Religious Studies

Studies in Religion
One orientation session required. 3 class meetings. (3 credits)

Sociology

Urban Dynamics
Identifies and analyzes the social, political, economic, psychological, and physical forces in an urban community and how these affect the lives of people who live there. One orientation session required. 2 exams and a paper. (3 credits)

Dealing with Diversity
A teleclass that explores the identities, values, and interaction of diverse groups in our culture. One orientation session required. (3 credits)

Vietnam, A Television History
One orientation session required. Paper must be submitted. (3 credits)

Special Education

Survey of Exceptional Students
One orientation session required. 4 class meetings. 2 exams. (3 credits)

Statistics

Statistics
One orientation session required. Optional lab meetings. 2 exams. (3 credits)

Substance Abuse

Substance Abuse: Current Concepts
One orientation session required. 3 exams. (3 credits)

The Adolescent Substance Abuser
One orientation session required. Take-home final exam. (3 credits)

Theatre

Creative Dramatics Workshop
One orientation session required. 1 exam and final project. (3 credits)

Harold Washington College
Center for Open Learning

30 East Lake Street
Chicago, IL 60601

(312) 984-2874

Geographic Access: Illinois

DELIVERY SYSTEMS

Broadcast Television
Telecourses may be viewed on WYCC/TV, Channel 20 in the Chicago area.

Videocassette
The "Study Unlimited" cassettes are available at branches of the Chicago Public Library and certain City Colleges of Chicago campuses. Some courses are available for home rental. This option is provided by an independent service called College Video Corporation, 550 Montgomery Avenue, #1133N, Bethesda MD 20814, (800) 852-5277.

INSTITUTION DESCRIPTION

The Center for Open Learning, long part of Chicago City-Wide College, has recently become a unit of Harold Washington College. Channel 20, the City Colleges of Chicago's own television station, broadcasts a wide variety of day, evening, and weekend college credit courses.

For those whose schedules are irregular or who prefer self-paced study, many of the regular college credit courses have been recorded on videocassettes. Some courses are available for home rental to registered students for an additional fee, but they can also be viewed over NovaNET, available at City Colleges of Chicago campus locations only.

Accreditation: NCA

Official/Contact: Barbara Willis, Director

Admission Requirements: Students must register at the Chicago City-Wide College of choice. When registering for a course, the student will be mailed a course syllabus and instructions. Each course has a faculty coordinator who is available to answer questions and who conducts optional classroom review sessions before each exam.

Tuition: Chicago residents $31.50 per credit hour, Illinois residents $94.22 per credit hour, out-of-state students $128.94 per credit hour. WYCC-TV Channel 20/Study Unlimited courses have a $3 per course additional charge. Textbooks must be purchased by the student. MasterCard, VISA, and Discover Card accepted.

Degree Credit: Credit earned for successful completion of a course may be applied to a degree program.

Grading: Examinations must be proctored. Students can take exams at any of thirteen convenient locations in Chicago. For videocassette courses, exams are usually taken at the location where students study and review tapes. Exams are taken by appointment on days, evenings, or weekends. Procedures for testing are explained in detail in the course packet mailed to registered students.

Library: Registered students have access to any library in the City Colleges of Chicago.

COURSES OFFERED

Art

The Photographic Vision: All About Photography

This series presents an overview of photography both as an art and as a skill. The programs cover the technical principles, historical tradition, impact on the way we understand the world, and the aesthetics of photographs. The programs also feature interviews with renowned photographers, museum curators, historians, and critics. Each lesson includes related photographic assignments. Broadcast on WYCC/Channel 20. (2 credits)

Astronomy

Descriptive Astronomy

A videocassette course. The presentation of introductory astronomy (*Project Universe: Astronomy*) includes awe-inspiring footage from NASA and JPL. The telecourse includes authoritative coverage of significant discoveries and developments in the discipline. Among topics treated are the search for satellites of the planets Uranus and Neptune, high-energy phenomena, IRAS, SETI, expanded treatment of Kepler's and Newton's laws, and universal gravitation, as well as significant theories and cosmological models. 30 half-hour programs. (3 credits)

Biology

General Biology I and II

Introducing Biology is a an enlightening combination of rare informative film and clear comprehensible print materials prepared especially for this course. Students readily develop an understanding of the basic concepts of biology, the characteristic elements, processes, and features common to all life forms, the nature and workings of the human body, and the vital role humans play in the total ecology of the earth. Designed for the nonmajor. 36 half-hour programs. (6 credits)

Business

Fundamentals of Accounting

Utilizes the telecourse *Principles of Accounting*. Broadcast on WYCC/Channel 20. (3 credits)

Introduction to Business

This series, *The Business File*, provides a comprehensive overview of the contemporary business environment. Topics include marketing, finance, accounting, and management. Broadcast on WYCC/Channel 20. 28 half-hour programs. (3 credits)

Business Mathematics

By the Numbers is a series that explores the role business math plays in our professional and personal lives. The content evolves from mathematical foundations to basic business concepts. Students learn about the business applications of math concepts such as fractions and percents and learn how to figure interest, cash flow, cost allocations, and financial statements. Broadcast on WYCC/Channel 20. 26 half-hour programs. (3 credits)

Business Law I and II

This series entitled *Business and the Law* emphasizes contracts and the legal system. Students will learn form modules on the law of sales, commercial paper, agency, and property as well as from discussions of such critical legal topics as government regulation, employment, and consumer and environmental protection. Part I broadcast on WYCC/Channel 20, Part II on videocassette. 30 half-hour programs. (6 credits)

Child Development

Human Growth and Development

Based on the telecourse *Time to Grow*. Covers all aspects of children's physical, cognitive, and psychosocial growth and development from birth through adolescence, including the most recent theoretical and applied perspectives about effective ways of caring for and working with children. Broadcast on WYCC/Channel 20. (4 credits)

Computer Science

Introduction to Data Processing

Based on the telecourse *The New Literacy*. A videocassette course. This introductory survey of data processing prepares students to use computers in their personal and professional lives. The series introduces students to terminology and examines how the computer can be applied to a range of organizational settings. Topics include data representation, storing data, personal computing, system analysis and design, programming languages, and more. 26 half-hour programs. (3 credits)

Introduction to Microcomputers

This telecourse, entitled *ComputerWorks*, gives students the chance to gain familiarity with different types of software programs and computers. Students can use and evaluate word processing, spreadsheet, graphics, database, accounting, communications, and publishing programs. Broadcast on WYCC/Channel 20. 16 half-hour programs. (3 credits)

Economics

Principles of Economics I and II

Based on the telecourse *Economics U$A*. A comprehensive television course in macro- and microeconomics. Through the use of interviews, commentary, and analysis, the course establishes a clear relationship between abstract economic principles and concrete human relationships. Part I broadcast on WYCC/Channel 20. Part II is a videocassette course. (6 credits)

English

Composition I and II

Based on the telecourse *The Write Course*. This English composition and rhetoric series teaches writing from a "process" point of view. The programs are ideal for freshman English students as they present deliberate strategies for pre-writing and revision. Most of the nation's leading authorities on the teaching of composition are interviewed along with well-known writers. Students are encouraged to develop individual writing processes with particular emphasis on skills needed for academic and business writing. 30 half-hour programs. Part I broadcast on WYCC/Channel 20. Part II is a videocassette course. (6 credits)

Literature and Film

Based on the telecourse *Novels on Film*. Broadcast on WYCC/Channel 20. (3 credits)

Environmental Studies

Man and Environment

Based on the telecourse *Race to Save the Planet*. The programs in this course provide scientific background for workable solutions to the greenhouse effect and ozone depletion and other major environmental problems. Discusses alternative fuels and waste reduction and cleanup strategies. Broadcast on WYCC/Channel 20. Ten 1-hour programs. (3 credits)

Fine Arts

History of Painting, Sculpture, and Architecture

Based on the telecourse *Art of the Western World*. This survey of Western art provides many unusual perspectives on seminal paintings, sculptures, and architectural structures. Beginning with ancient Greece, the series presents major works within the religious, intellectual, and social contexts of their day. Broadcast on WYCC/Channel 20. Nine 1-hour programs. (3 credits)

Health

Health Education

Based on the telcourse *Here's to Your Health*. Examines today's issues and presents contemporary approaches to maintaining a well-balanced life. Personal and community health practices from birth through old age are looked at from a self-care viewpoint. Covers a broad range of topics from puberty, menopause, AIDS, and sex to the digestive system, back problems, and prescription medicines. Stresses autonomy in health maintenance—achieving and maintaining a healthy body/mind through education. Broadcast on WYCC/Channel 20. (3 credits)

History

History of the American People to 1865

Based on the telecourse *The American Adventure*. This American history series starts with Columbus' discovery and the early colonial settlements and ends with the Civil War and Reconstruction. The programs feature interviews with renowned historians who provide academic analysis as well as narratives drawn from diaries, letters, and music of the period. Broadcast on WYCC/Channel 20. 26 half-hour programs. (3 credits)

History of the American People from 1865

Based on the telecourse *America in Perspective*. This telecourse provides an analytical frame of reference for U.S. events after the Civil War. Historical analysis is provided by over 40 renowned scholars. Topics include Native Americans, immigrants, minorities, Spanish-American War, World Wars I and II, the Great Depression, the Cold War, the civil rights movement, the Vietnam War, the conservative resurgence, the 1980s, and the end of the Cold War. A videocassette course. 26 half-hour programs. (3 credits)

Humanities

General Course I

Based on the telecourse *In Our Own Image*. A videocassette course. (3 credits)

General Course II

Based on the telecourse *Humanities Through the Arts*. This course surveys seven art forms: film, drama, music, literature, painting, sculpture, and architecture. Each art form is examined from four perspectives: historical, elements of art, form/meaning, and criticism/evaluation. Broadcast on WYCC/Channel 20. (3 credits)

Management

Principles of Management

Based on the telecourse *The Business of Management*. Especially designed for managers without formal business training and undergraduates interested in a business career. The course provides essential information on planning, staffing, directing, decision making, motivating, and communicating. Broadcast on WYCC/Channel 20. 26 half-hour programs. (3 credits)

Mathematics

College Algebra

Based on the telecourse *College Algebra in Simplest Terms*. This course provides students with knowledge of algebra, helping them master problem-solving skills they need for higher mathematics as well as daily life. The programs use computer graphics and pictures to illustrate concepts such as factoring, linear and quadratic equations, circles and parabolas, functions, logarithmic equations, permutations, probability, and more. Closed captioned for the hearing impaired. Broadcast on WYCC/Channel 20. 26 half-hour programs. (4 credits)

Oceanography

Introduction to Oceanography

Based on the telecourse *Oceanus: The Marine Environment*. Focuses on the marine environment as a unique feature of the planet Earth and investigates areas of intense scientific and public concern: the pervasiveness of the ocean and its effect on the Earth's weather, its stunning physical size and diversity of contained life forms, its contributions to the physical and historical development of man, its impact on geopolitical and economic matters, the impact of oceanic pollutants, and the potential of exploitation of marine resources. A videocassette course. (3 credits)

Philosophy

General Course

Based on the telecourse *Ethics in America*. Broadcast on WYCC/Channel 20. (3 credits)

Political Science

The National Government

Based on the telecourse *Government by Consent*. A survey course that provides students with an understanding of democracy, the Constitution, political parties, the branches of government, due process, and more. Program topics include the living Constitution, federalism, local government, the power of PACs, the Presidency, the Congress, the legislation process, and first amendment freedoms. Broadcast on WYCC/Channel 20. 26 half-hour programs. (3 credits)

Psychology

General Psychology

Based on the telecourse *Psychology: The Study of Human Behavior*. An introductory psychology telecourse designed for adult students seeking general education psychology instruction. The course introduces students to the basic content of psychology: the facts, theories, perspectives, and terminology. Broadcast on WYCC/Channel 20. (3 credits)

Child Psychology

Based on the telecourse *Time to Grow*. Offers an engaging look into the world of the growing, developing child. The programs cover all aspects of children's physical, cognitive, and psychosocial growth and development from birth through adolescence.

The course looks at children from a developmental perspective. It includes the most recent theoretical and applied perspectives about effective ways to care for and work with children. Broadcast on WYCC/Channel 20. (3 credits)

Science

General Course

Based on the telecourse *Planet Earth*. This telecourse will help viewers grasp the complexity of the many systems operating within our planet. Broadcast on WYCC/Channel 20. (3 credits)

Sociology

Introduction to the Study of Society

Based on the telecourse *The Sociological Imagination*. This introductory series features minidocumentaries that are emotionally strong illustrations of issues such as socialization, social control, sex and gender, aging, collective behavior, and social change. Expert commentary from noted sociologists provide an academic framework for sociological issues such as group dynamics, deviance, social class, religion, and family. Broadcast on WYCC/Channel 20. 26 half-hour programs. (3 credits)

Marriage and the Family

Based on the telecourse *Portrait of a Family*. This interdisciplinary series takes a look at marriage and the family. Several themes are developed: tension between the individual and the societal environment, contradictory cultural values, and the diversity of patterns of living and decision making that people face. Documentary footage and commentary show the fascinating mosaic of family forms that exist today. Programs cover relationships, marriage, and the family in transition. A videocassette course. (3 credits)

Statistics

Introductory Statistics

Based on the telecourse *Against All Odds: Inside Statistics*. Current applications of data analysis show the why and how of statistics, vividly demonstrated by host presentations and computer graphic illustrations. Emphasizes the power gained by learning these methods to better understand our quantitative world. Broadcast on WYCC/Channel 20. (3 credits)

Sangamon State University
Telecourse Office

Shepherd Road
Springfield, IL   62794

(217) 786-6615

Geographic Access: Illinois

DELIVERY SYSTEMS

Broadcast Television

Most telecourses are broadcast over the CONVOCOM public television network. The broadcast channels (non-cable) are: (1) WSEC, Channel 65, Springfield, (2) WMEC, Channel 22, Macomb, (3) WQEC, Channel 27, Quincy, (4) WSEC, Channel 14, Jacksonville. When a telecourse is offered in Peoria, WTVP provides area students with access on Channel 47. Video courses are mainly those prepared and distributed by PBS.

INSTITUTION DESCRIPTION

Sangamon State University is a state institution providing upper division and graduate study only. It was established in 1969.

The telecourse operation at Sangamon is currently going through a transitionary period. It is in the beginning stages of compiling a list of eight core telecourses that will be offered at alternating times over the next year. Enrollments have ranged from 30 to 60 students per telecourse. Five or six class meetings are scheduled to provide time for discussion, taking exams, or submitting assignments.

Accreditation: NCA

Official/Contact: Heidi Waltner, Director

Admission Requirements: Open enrollment. Students in degree programs at Sangamon or other institutions are given flexibility in arranging study schedules by enrollment in a telecourse.

Tuition: Contact the Telecourse Office for current tuition and fees. Textbooks and study guides may be purchased at the SSU Bookstore.

Degree Credit: Credit earned may be applied to a degree program at Sangamon State University. Students from other institutions should contact their Registrar to determine if credits will transfer.

Grading: Letter grades (A, B, C, D, U) are assigned. Credit is awarded in semester hour units.

Library: Videocassettes are on reserve in the Sangamon State University Library or Richland Community College Library.

COURSES OFFERED

History

Eyes on the Prize

This telecourse is a comprehensive history of the people, the stories, the events and issues of the civil rights struggle in America. The course focuses on the period of American history from World War II to the present and takes the point of view that the period of the civil rights movement is one of the most significant in our history. It made America a more democratic society, gave rise to other movements which transformed the face of the American culture, changed those who participated in it, and influenced and created a new generation of American leadership. (4 credits)

Vietnam

This course documents a full record of conflict from the background of Vietnam and its people through the French presence, to a chronology of the period from 1945 to 1975, with an examination of the impact of the war on American society in the years which followed. The series places Vietnam in a historical perspective and permits viewers to form their own conclusions about the basis of conflict, what was won and lost, and by whom. (4 credits)

The Middle East

This telecourse is an interdisciplinary introduction to one of the more complex and important regions in the world. Students will gain a historical overview paying particular attention to culture and religion. The course will also examine the contemporary Middle East: Lebanon, OPEC and the oil bonanza, and the Arab-Israeli dispute. Finally, students will consider how the superpowers have influenced the affairs of this region. (4 credits)

The Pacific Century

A series of 10 hour-long television programs which highlight the impact of Western exploration and examines the larger scope of mutual transformation between East and West. Contrasts the themes of modernization and tradition. (4 credits)

Sociology

Portrait of a Family

A close look at marriage, family, and alternative lifestyles in the closing decade of the twentieth century. Balances solid research and theory with a practical examination of personal choice and decision making. (4 hours)

Western Illinois University
School of Extended and Continuing Education
Educational Broadcasting and Independent Study

305 Memorial Hall
Macomb, IL   61455

(309) 298-2182 *Fax:* (309) 298-2133

Geographic Access: Worldwide; Illinois for Public Broadcasting Service (PBS) broadcasts.

DELIVERY SYSTEMS

Broadcast Television

PBS telecourses may be broadcast on educational television channels. International University Consortium (IUC) telecourses as well as PBS telecourses require an enrollment fee (given below with course description).

Videocassette

Includes programs viewed at home or viewing sites. Available on 1/2" VHS videotapes that may be leased.

Teleclasses

Includes previously taped classroom lectures as well as readings, assignments, and examinations. Tapes may be rented for a partially refundable deposit of $70.

INSTITUTION DESCRIPTION

Western Illinois University was established as Western Illinois State Normal School in 1899 and offered first instruction at the postsecondary level in 1902. After several name changes, the current name was adopted in 1957. The main campus in Macomb supports satellite centers at 12 locations. The School of Extended and Continuing Education is responsible for the various distance learning programs.

Telecourses combine televised programs, reading assignments, and examinations. The telecourses are licensed from Public Broadcasting Service, including some produced by the Annenberg/CPB Project and the International University Consortium. In addition, WIU produces telecourses on the campus. PBS courses may be broadcast by the student's local public broadcasting station. The student is responsible for contacting them to ensure that the telecourse of choice is broadcast in the student's locale. The video programs for telecourses are also available on VHS tapes that may be leased from the Independent Study Program.

Accreditation: NCA

Official/Contact: Joyce E. Neilsen, Director

Admission Requirements: Adults who have earned a high school diploma or a GED may enroll. Courses are offered on a semester basis with registration preceding the fall, spring, and summer sessions.

Tuition: $81 per credit. Additional tape rental fees are included with the course descriptions below. Textbooks and study guides must be purchased by the student and must be ordered from the WIU University Union Bookstore.

Degree Credit: Credit earned through successful completion of a telecourse/teleclass may be applied toward a degree program at WIU. Students from other institutions should ascertain that credit earned will transfer.

Grading: If enrolled on a credit basis, letter grades (A-F) are awarded. Examinations must be proctored. Acceptable proctors include testing center personnel of community colleges and universities, school superintendents, high school principals and counselors, and education officers at correctional institutions. Credit is awarded in semester hour units. Courses may be taken for noncredit (same tuition rates apply).

Library: All registered students have access to the Western Illinois University Library.

COURSES OFFERED

Agricultural Economics

Marketing Grain and Livestock Products
   The trading of futures contracts as a basis hedge. Introductory material includes basic jargon, the use of hedging by agribusiness, and a pricing-strategy decision framework. A comparison of basis hedging and multiple hedging is considered in the context of business objectives, evaluation criteria, market risk, and profit potential. A Teleclass. 18 two-hour classes on tape. A deposit of $70 is required ($40 refunded when tapes are returned in good condition). (3 semester hours)

Commodity Markets and Futures Trading
   Multiple hedging and speculation. An introduction to the institutions and jargon of the futures market is followed by the study of technical analysis to identify trading signals: bar chart, point-and-figure, moving averages, volume and open interest, momentum, HI/LO, %R, RSI, stochastics, and DMI. A Teleclass. 17 two-hour classes on tape. A deposit of $70 is required ($40 refunded when tapes are returned in good condition). (3 semester hours)

Options on Futures
   The trading of options on futures contracts for hedging or speculative purposes. Familiarization with the jargon is followed by consideration of risk/return and effective-price profiles of option positions, hedging strategies for long and short cash positions, trading strategies, and an introduction to the Black pricing model. A Teleclass. 5 two-hour classes on tape. A deposit of $70 is required ($40 refunded when tapes are returned in good condition). (1 semester hour)

Market Logic
   The CBOT Market Profile (R). This approach to market analysis was formulated by J. Peter Steidlmayer, developed by the Chicago Board of Trade, and can be used for day-trading and overnight positions. A Teleclass. 11 two-hour classes on tape. A deposit of $70 is required ($40 refunded when tapes are returned in good condition). (2 semester hours)

English

Literature of the Americas
   An exploration of Spanish-American, African-American, and French- and English-Canadian fiction. The novels and short stories illuminate the themes common to all four cultures—the nature of myth and history, the dilemma of the intellectual, the clash of cultures, the war of the sexes—all dramatized in very different ways. A two-semester course. There is an additional $25 fee assessed by the International University Consortium for this telecourse. (6 semester hours)

Geology

Planet Earth

Explores our planet—its interior, oceans, continents, mountains and volcanoes, energy and mineral resources, climate, sun and atmosphere. As you move through the telecourse sequence, you climb from the depths of the oceans to the heights of our solar system in all its magnificence. Internationally recognized experts share their theories, models, and opinions. On-location film footage takes you to places and events you might not otherwise experience. Animation and graphic displays let you "see" more difficult concepts. A PBS Telecourse. There is an additional $15 charge. VHS tapes are available for leasing. (3 semester hours)

Psychology

Seasons of Life

This course examines the drama of human development which unfolds under the influence of three "clocks": a physical clock (the timeline our bodies follow), a social clock (the age norms dictated by family and society), and a psychological clock (each individual's unique sense of timing). A PBS Telecourse. There is an additional $15 charge. VHS tapes are available for leasing. (3 semester hours)

Indiana

Indiana State University
Independent Study
Continuing Education and
Instructional Services

Alumni Hall, Room 124
Terre Haute, IN 47809

(812) 237-2555 *Fax:* (812) 237-3495

Geographic Access: Nationwide

DELIVERY SYSTEMS

Videocassette
The video component supplements the text and study guide.

INSTITUTION DESCRIPTION

Indiana State University is a comprehensive, state-assisted institution of higher education. It was established in 1865.

Traditional correspondence courses have been offered at ISU for over 70 years. The courses listed below have a video component used as part of the course.

Accreditation: NCA

Official/Contact: Clair D. Woodward, Director

Admission Requirements: Admission to ISU is not required for enrollment in a course and registration may take place at any time during the year. Any high school graduate or equivalent is eligible to enroll in a course.

Tuition: $88 per semester hour. This fee includes all course materials with the exception of the textbook which must be purchased by the student. Videotapes may be rented at $5 per videocassette ($10 refundable deposit and a $2.50 mailing fee).

Degree Credit: Credit earned upon successful completion of course may be applied to a degree program at ISU. Students of other colleges or universities who enroll should consult the school or agency where the credit is to be used to assure that the credit will apply as intended.

Grading: Examinations must represent the student's own work and must be completed in the presence of an approved supervisor without the aid of texts, notes, devices, or outside help, unless specified otherwise in the examination directions. Letter grades are assigned. Credit is awarded in semester hour units.

Library: The video components of the courses listed below are available for viewing at the ISU Cunningham Memorial Library during regular library hours.

COURSES OFFERED

Biology

Conversational Biology: Reproduction, Growth, and Development
Emphasis is placed on the biological aspects of human reproduction, growth, and development. A video-enhanced course. No lessons, 1 exam. (1 credit)

Conversational Biology: Human Genetics
A study of basic genetic principles with emphasis on various human genetic defects. Consideration of genetic disease and counseling included. A video-enhanced course. No lessons, 1 exam. (1 credit)

Fine Arts

Visual Arts in Civilization
A topical survey of major concepts in the visual arts and their relation to the societies that produce them.

A video-enhanced course. 15 lessons, 1 exam. (3 credits)

Psychology

General Psychology

An introduction to psychology as a science, surveying learning, motivation, perception, psychobiology, cognition, intelligence, personality, etc. A video-enhanced course. 15 lessons, 2 exams. (3 credits)

Sociology

Social Conflict

An analysis of conflict and conflict resolution on interpersonal, intergroup, interorganizational, and international levels. General theories of conflict are examined in the light of selected empirical studies. A video-enhanced course. 14 lessons, 2 exams. (3 credits)

Indiana University
Division of Extended Studies
School of Continuing Studies

Owen Hall Room 001
Bloomington, IN 47405

(800) 457-4434 *Fax:* (812) 855-8680

Geographic Access: Nationwide

DELIVERY SYSTEMS

Audiocassette
Used primarily in foreign language courses.

Computer Tutorials
Computer disks accompany course materials for courses in computer science.

Videocassette
Video-enhanced courses in biology and political science are offered.

INSTITUTION DESCRIPTION

Indiana University is one of the oldest state universities in the midwestern United States. It was founded in 1820 and has grown to eight campuses.

Independent study courses have been offered by IU since 1912. In addition to traditional correspondence courses, audio- and video-enhanced courses are offered. Some courses require access to an IBM-compatible computer.

Accreditation: NCA

Official/Contact: Lawrence Keller, Director

Admission Requirements: Admission to Indiana University is not required for independent study students. Enrollment does not constitute admission to IU.

Tuition: Undergraduate $71 per credit hour, graduate $107.85 per credit hour. Textbooks must be purchased by the student. Audiocassettes and videotapes may be borrowed from the Division of Extended Studies upon payment of a deposit, refundable upon the return of the materials in good condition. Due to software copyright protection laws, software and accompanying texts may not be returned.

Degree Credit: Credit earned by successful completion of a course may be applied to a degree at Indiana University. Students seeking transfer of credit should check with their institution to validate acceptability of transfer credit.

Grading: A letter or number grade is assigned, depending upon the option of the instructor. Examinations must be proctored and may be taken at the IU examination center or at any accredited university, college, or high school under the supervision of an administrative official. Credit is awarded in semester hour units.

Library: Students are encouraged to utilize their local community libraries.

COURSES OFFERED

American Studies

Representative Americans—Special Topic: People with Disabilities

An audio-enhanced course. Americans with disabilities both from a historical and a contemporary perspective. An examination of the architectural, institutional, and attitudinal environment encountered by disabled persons. 9 submissions, 2 exams. (3 credits)

Biology

Biology of Women

A video-enhanced course. This course examines the biological basis for bodily functions and changes that take place throughout the life of females. 9 submisisons, 3 exams. (3 credits)

Classical Studies

Medical Terms from Greek and Latin

An audio-enhanced course. Basic vocabulary of some 1,000 words, together with materials for formation of compounds, enables the student to build a working vocabulary of several thousand words. Designed for those intending to specialize in medicine, nursing, dentistry, or microbiology. 6 submissions, 2 exams. (2 credits)

Computer Science

Introduction to Microcomputers and Computing

A computer-assisted course. The use of computers in everyday activities. How computers work, use of packaged programs for word processing, spreadsheets, file management, communications, graphics, etc. Students must have access to an IBM-compatible 8086/8088, 80286, or 80386 computer with 640K of memory, and two floppy drives or one floppy drive and one hard (fixed) drive. Available using 3.5 inch or 5.25 inch disks. 3 submissions, 3 exams. (3 credits)

Advanced Microcomputing: Programming with Applications

A computer-assisted course. Introduction to computer programming, utilizing languages within standard application tools. Emphasizes problem solving, interface design principles, and documentation writing. Students must have access to an IBM-compatible 8086/8088, 80286, or 80386 computer with 640K of memory and two floppy drives or one floppy drive and one hard (fixed) drive. Available using 3.5 inch or 5.25 inch disks. (3 credits)

Introduction to Programming

A computer-assisted course. Fundamental programming constructs, including pointers, structures, and files. Emphasis on modular programming, user-interface design, and documentation principles. Compares and contrasts the relative merits of two distinct languages. Applications software may be used to illustrate some concepts. Not intended for computer science majors or minors. Students must have access to an IBM-compatible 8086/8088, 80286, or 80386 computer with 640K of memory and two floppy drives or one floppy drive and one hard (fixed) drive. Available for use with 3.5 inch or 5.25 inch disks.

COBOL and File Processing

A computer-assisted course. Computer programming and algorithms. Applications to large file processing functions of an organization. Students must have access to an IBM-compatible 8086/8088, 80286, or 80386 computer with 640K of memory and two floppy drives or one floppy drive and one hard (fixed) drive. Available for 3.5 inch or 5.25 inch disks. 9 submissions, 3 exams. (3 credits)

Introduction to Computer Science

A computer-assisted course. A first course in computer science for those intending to take advanced computer science courses. Introduction to algorithm design, programming, and analysis. Using SCHEME programming language, the course covers procedural, data, and syntactic abstractions and use of several programming paradigms, including functional, imperative, logical, and object-oriented. Students must have access to an IBM-compatible 8086/8088, 80286, or 80386 computer with 640K of memory and two floppy drives or one floppy drive and one hard (fixed) drive. Available for 3.5 inch or 5.25 inch disks. (4 credits)

COBOL Programming

A computer-assisted course. Basic notions of computer programming. Problems for programming and execution on computer. Students must have access to an IBM-compatible 8086/8088, 80286, or 80386 computer with 640K of memory and two floppy drives or one floppy drive and one hard (fixed) drive. Available for 3.5 inch or 5.25 inch disks. (1 credit)

Folklore

Introduction to Folklore

A video-enhanced course. A view of the main forms and varieties of folklore and folk expression in tales, ballads, gestures, beliefs, games, proverbs, riddles, and traditional arts and crafts. The role of folklore in the life of human beings. 10 submissions, 2 exams. (3 credits)

Introduction to American Folklore

An audio-enhanced course. Folklore and traditional expressive behavior within the context of American culture. Art and traditional philosophies of folk groups found in America, including ethnic groups, occupational groups, regional groups, religious groups, etc. The function of folklore within the lives of American people. 11 submissions, 1 exam. (3 credits)

French

Elementary French I

An audio-enhanced course. Introduction to French language and selected aspects of French civilization and culture. 12 submissions, 4 exams. (4 credits)

Elementary French II: Language and Culture

An audio-enhanced course. Basic structures of the French language and selected topics of French civilization and culture. 12 submissions, 4 exams. (4 credits)

German

Beginning German I

An audio-enhanced course. Intensive introduction to present-day German and selected aspects of German life. Intensive drills for mastery of phonology, basic structural patterns, and functional vocabulary. 18 submissions, 2 exams. (5 credits)

Beginning German II

An audio-enhanced course. A continuation of Beginning German I. 18 submissions, 2 exams. (5 credits)

Humanities

Modern Literature and Other Arts: An Introduction

Analyzes the materials of literature, painting, and music, and the ways in which meaning is expressed through the organization of the materials. Investigates differences among the arts. Examples selected from the past 200 years. 7 submissions, 1 exam. (3 credits)

Italian

Elementary Italian I

An audio-enhanced course. Introduction to contemporary Italian conversation, grammar, reading, and elementary writing. 11 submissions, 5 exams. (4 credits)

Elementary Italian II

An audio-enhanced course. A continuation of Elementary Italian I. 11 submissions, 5 exams. (4 credits)

Music

Music for the Listener

An audio-enhanced course. How to listen to music. Art of music and its materials. Instruments and musical forms. 9 submissions, 3 exams. (3 credits)

Political Science

American Politics through Film and Fiction

An audio- and video-enhanced course. The recurrent theme of power in politics is explored in depth—by means of five novels and five films. From a list of selected works, students must choose and locate the novels and videos, many of which may be borrowed form libraries. Film choices include *El Norte, Reds, Citizen Kane, The Candidate, Mr. Smith Goes to Washington, All the King's Men, Executive Action, Absence of Malice, And Justice for All, Roger and Me, Do the Right Thing, Norma Rae, Network, Fahrenheit 451,* and *China Syndrome.* Selected novels include *Breakfast of Champions, White Noise, 1876, All the King's Men, The Last Hurrah, All the President's Men, The Hunt for Red October, Advise and Consent, Invisible Man, Fail Safe, The Handmaid's Tale,* and *1984.* 5 submissions, 2 exams. (3 credits)

Spanish

Elementary Spanish I

An audio-enhanced course. Introduction to present-day Spanish language and culture. Intended for those with little or no previous instruction in Spanish. 13 submissions, 2 exams. (4 credits)

Elementary Spanish II

An audio-enhanced course. A continuation of Elementary Spanish I. 13 submissions, 2 exams. (4 credits)

Speech Communication

Public Speaking

An audio-enhanced course. Theory and practice of public speaking, training in thought processes necessary to organize speech content, analysis of components of effective delivery and language. 7 submissions, 1 exam. (2 credits)

Interpersonal Communication

An audio-enhanced course. Practical consideration of spontaneous human interaction in face-to-face situations. Special attention to perception, language, and attitudes in dyads and small groups. 7 submissions, 1 exam. (2 credits)

Business and Professional Communication

An audio-enhanced course. Examines organizational communication with emphasis on skills acquisition. Developed skills include interviewing, group discussion, parliamentary procedure, and public speaking. 10 submissions, 2 exams. (3 credits)

Indiana Vocational Technical College
Distance Learning

1534 West Sample Street
South Bend, IN   46619

(219) 289-7001

Geographic Access: Indiana

DELIVERY SYSTEMS

Broadcast Television

Pre-produced videos are broadcast over Heritage Cable Channel 31 or WNIT-TV Channel 34.

Computer Tutorials

An IBM or compatible computer is required for self-directed tutorials.

Interactive Audio/Video

Classes are held at Ivy Tech campuses in South Bend, Elkhart, and Warsaw and selected area businesses or health care facilities. Instructor delivers lessons produced live in South Bend Ivy Tech's teleclassroom and delivered to the sites by closed circuit television. Students may ask instructors questions during class via an audio hookup.

INSTITUTION DESCRIPTION

Indiana Vocational Technical College, commonly referred to as Ivy Tech, was created by an Act of the Indiana General Assembly in 1963 to provide non-baccalaureate, postsecondary vocational-technical educa-

tion. There are 13 campuses located throughout Indiana: Columbus, Muncie, Kokomo, Lafayette, South Bend, Fort Wayne, Gary, Sellersburg, Madison, Evansville, Terre Haute, and Richmond.

There are three types of distance learning opportunities available from Ivy Tech: telecourses, live distance education, and computer modem courses. Telecourses involve viewing professional pre-produced video lessons at home at various times, reading textbook lessons and doing assignments at the student's convenience, and turning in assignments by mail. Questions may be asked of the instructor at specific times by phone. Students must also attend three sessions on campus (Southbend, Elkart, or Warsaw) for the first class meeting and the midterm and final exam.

Live distance education courses have classes at Ivy Tech campuses in South Bend, Elkhart, or Warsaw, or at selected area businesses or health care facilities. The student sees and hears the instructor deliver lessons produced live in South Bend Ivy Tech's teleclassroom and delivered to the student's site via closed circuit television. Students may ask the instructor questions and hear the answers during class by audio hookup.

Computer Modem Courses require the use of an IBM or compatible computer, self-directed tutorials, and a student edition of software provided with the text. Assignments are turned in and the instructor's comments are submitted by electronic bulletin board using a computer modem provided at a nominal fee. The student must attend three to four sessions on campus in South Bend.

Accreditation: NCA

Official/Contact: Carl F. Lutz, Chancellor

Admission Requirements: Open enrollment. Apply by mail or phone for telecourses to Ivy Tech Business and Industry Training, 1534 West Sample Street, South Bend, IN 46619, (219) 289-7001; 2521 Industrial Parkway, Elkhart, IN 46516, (219) 293-4657; 850 East Smith Street, Warsaw, IN 46850, (219) 267-5428. For Live Distance Education courses, apply by mail or phone to Office of Student Services at the above addresses. For computer modem courses, apply to Office of Student Services, 1534 West Sample Street, South Bend, IN 46619, (219) 289-7001.

Tuition: $50.30 per credit hour. Textbooks and lab kits must be purchased by the student.

Degree Credit: Credit awarded may be applied toward an associate degree.

Grading: Examinations are taken on campus and are proctored. Letter grades A, B, C, D, F are assigned. Credit is awarded in semester hour units.

Library: Officially registered students have access to the Learning Materials Center on any Ivy Tech campus throughout Indiana.

COURSES OFFERED

Biology

Biology

A telecourse offering an introduction to the nature and functions of the human body and the characteristic elements, process, and features common to all life forms. (3 credits)

Biology Lab

This telecourse covers experimentation and analysis of biological concepts to be carried out with laboratory materials at home. To be taken with the above course. (3 credits)

Business

Introduction to Business: The Business File

A telecourse that studies ownership, organization principles and problems, management, control facilities, administration and development practices of American business. (3 credits)

Computer Science

Electronic Spreadsheets: Lotus 1-2-3, V. 2.3

A Computer Modem course. Covers menu commands, formulas, macro commands, graphs, database, and file operations. (3 credits)

Microcomputer Database Management: dBASE IV, V. 1.1

A Computer Modem course. Teaches how to create, modify, retrieve, and report using database management system. (3 credits)

Word Processing: WordPerfect, V. 5.1

A Computer Modem course. Introduction to the word processing package. How to create and edit documents. (3 credits)

Advanced Word Processing: Advanced WordPerfect 5.1

A Computer Modem course. Covers advanced applications: footnotes, macros, merging, graphics, tables, path and line drawing. (3 credits)

English

English Composition I: The Write Course

A telecourse offering an innovative approach to learning and improving skills by presenting real-life dramatizations of the writing process at work. (3 credits)

Management

Techniques of Supervision

Basics for increasing group job performance through motivational, team-building, and problem-solving skills. A live distance education course. (3 credits)

Medical Terminology

Medical Terminology

A live distance education course that covers the basic terminology required of the allied health professional: meaning, spelling, and pronunciation. Abbreviations, signs, and symbols are included. (3 credits)

Practical Nursing

Nutrition for PNs

This live distance education course covers the basic principles of nutrition and diet therapy in wellness and illness, the role of the practical nurse in assisting patients in meeting nutrition needs. Nursing program acceptance not required. (2 credits)

Anatomy and Physiology for PNs

Structure and function of the human body, physical and chemical factors enabling human beings to maintain homeostasis. Nursing program acceptance not required. A live distance education course. (5 credits)

Psychology

Psychology

A live distance education course covering the fundamentals of the biological basis of behavior, sensation and perception, learning and memory, personality and psychological disorders. (3 credits)

Taylor University
Independent Study
Adult and Continuing Education

1025 West Rudisill Boulevard
Fort Wayne, IN   46807

(219) 456-2111

Geographic Access: Worldwide

DELIVERY SYSTEMS

Audiocassette
Audio-enhanced courses in Bible, education, preaching, and music appreciation are offered.

Videocassette
An introduction to art courses is video-enhanced.

INSTITUTION DESCRIPTION

Taylor University is an interdenominational, evangelical, Christian, undergraduate institution educating men and women for life-long learning. In 1992, Summit Christian College merged with Taylor University.

Audio- and video-enhanced courses are available. In quality and in content, all credit courses are designed to be equivalent to residence work as much as possible. Most courses have twelve to thirteen lessons. Almost all lessons involve the reading and studying of the textbooks with the student giving essay responses to thought-provoking questions related to the material covered.

Accreditation: NCA

Official/Contact: Richard Dugan, Vice President

Admission Requirements: Open enrollment.

Tuition: $50 per credit hour. Nonrefundable enrollment fee $10. Canadian students add $10 postage deposit. International students add $20 postage deposit. Textbooks must be purchased by the student.

Degree Credit: A limited number of credit hours may be applied toward a baccalaureate degree at Taylor University.

Grading: A final examination over the subject matter covered is required in most courses. All exams must be completed and graded before any transcript will be released. Credit is awarded in semester hour units.

Library: Students are encouraged to use their local community library.

COURSES OFFERED

Bible

Romans
A detailed analysis and exegesis of the teaching of Romans, with special emphasis on the development of thought throughout the entire book. An audio-enhanced course. (3 credits)

Biblical Languages

Introduction to Biblical Hebrew
A study of the fundamentals of accidence and basic syntax of Biblical Hebrew. An emphasis on translation from English to Hebrew. A translation of selected portions of the Hebrew Old Testament. An audio-enhanced course. (2 credits)

Christian Education

Christian Education of Children
A study of the ways of ministering effectively to all age groups of children within the church and of evaluating and structuring church programs so as to strengthen both the home and the church. The student will learn principles of effective, creative programming geared to helping children with their needs. An audio-enhanced course. (3 credits)

Perspectives on the World Christian Movement
An introduction to the theology, history, strategy, and priorities of contemporary evangelical mission work. (Prepared by the Institute of International Studies, Pasadena, CA). An audio-enhanced course. (3 credits)

Fine Arts

Introduction to Art

A study of art through a historical survey. This course is designed to give the student an introduction to the great masters of the past, the art periods, as well as broaden the student's appreciation for and understanding of art. This course utilizes a 9-part video series. A rental fee of $20 plus a $30 security deposit (refunded when the tapes are returned). (2 semester hours)

Music

Music Appreciation

A course designed to develop greater understanding and appreciation of music of the various historical periods. An introduction to the art of music and its materials. Considerable attention is given to listening to recordings and studying the lives of leading composers. An audio-enhanced course. (2 credits)

Preaching

Introduction to Preaching

Principles of the preparation and delivery of sermons with experience in both writing and delivery. Emphasis on expository preaching and the development of a basic sermonic process. A detailed introduction to this course is given on the first of four cassette tapes included with the course. An audio-enhanced course. (3 credits)

Iowa

Emmaus Bible School
Correspondence Study

2570 Asbury Road
Dubuque, IA 52001

(319) 588-8000

Geographic Access: Worldwide

DELIVERY SYSTEMS

Audiocassette
The courses listed and described below utilize audiocassettes as supplementary material to the study guides and textbooks. Students must have access to an audiocassette player.

INSTITUTION DESCRIPTION

Emmaus Bible College was founded in 1941 in Toronto, Ontario, Canada. For more than 50 years Emmaus has distributed self-study Bible courses throughout the world. Courses are available in over 100 languages and are presently being distributed in over 100 countries, allowing Emmaus to speak the language of 80 percent of the world's population. Presently, there is a growing penal ministry in institutions of North America and there is also a domestic ministry. An average of more than 1,400 courses distributed to students every day, or one course per minute, makes Emmaus one of the largest correspondence schools in the world.

The courses described below are audio-enhanced and require the use of an audiocassette player.

Accreditation: AABC

Official/Contact: Charles Fizer, Director

Admission Requirements: A prospective student must show proven ability to do college-level work. Anyone interested may order courses directly from Emmaus. Students outside the United States should contact a Regional Director of Emmaus Bible College in their respective countries.

Tuition: Varies, depending on the course. Contact the school for current tuition/fees. Students must purchase course materials. Audiocassette cost per course: $7.75.

Degree Credit: Credits indicate the relative difficulty of each course in the Emmaus curriculum and are not intended to indicate equivalency of college-level instruction or transferability of credit to the resident programs of Emmaus Bible School or any other school. Students desiring to transfer Emmaus credits should contact the school to which they seek transfer and determine the eligibility/acceptance of Emmaus credits. Emmaus does not award degrees by correspondence study.

Grading: All grades are in percentages. 70 percent and above is passing. Examinations are open book.

Library: Various booklets and tracts plus other informational pieces are sent to the student.

COURSES OFFERED

Religious Studies

Bible Prophecy
This introductory study helps in understanding the order of future events. By showing the distinctive positions of Israel, the church, and the nations, God's prophetic plan is made clear. (1 credit)

What the Bible Teaches
While the primary purpose of this course is the simple presentation of the gospel, it also presents a valuable systematic outline on such subjects as the

Bible, God, man, sin, Christ, salvation, heaven, and hell. (1 credit)

Guide to Christian Growth

The course offers sound, practical advice to the young believer. This simple course covers such topics as worship, scripture memorization, good works, the quiet time, and the fruit of the Spirit. (1 credit)

Personal Evangelism

In this course young believers are taught basic principles in the important matter of winning others for the Lord Jesus Christ. (1 credit)

The Gospel of Mark

Mark emphasizes "Christ came not to be served, but to serve and to give His life as ransom for many." (1 credit)

The Gospel of Luke

Luke portrays the humanity of Christ. Content rather than chronology seems to be important to him. (1 credit)

The Book of Acts

This course shows the amazing spread of the gospel and the dynamic witness of first century Christians. (1 credit)

The Epistle to the Romans

Romans deals with issues of sin and personal growth. The issues dealt with in this book are vital to young believers. (1 credit)

First Corinthians

A verse-by-verse exposition, subtitled *The Church and Its Charter*, dealing with instruction for the local church and individual believers. (2 credits)

Philippians, Colossians, and Philemon

A meaningful exposition of three of Paul's epistles from prison—Philippians, his letter of warmth, Colossians, his letter of glory, and Philemon, his letter of forgiveness. (1 credit)

The Thessalonian Epistles

A timely course for a day when the truth of Christ's return is openly denied. (2 credits)

Timothy and Titus

Paul is writing in these letters to Timothy and Titus on the subject of the shepherd care of individuals and local churches. (1 credit)

Revelation

Subtitled "Visions of Judgment and Glory," this is an introductory study of "the things which are and the things which shall be." (1 credit)

The Holy Spirit at Work

This study expounds the person and work of the Holy Spirit of God in the world, the church, and the individual believer. (1 credit)

The Lord's Supper

This course teaches the student how to follow the Lord's command, "This do in remembrance of Me." (1/2 credit)

How to Teach

This course is for anyone involved in teaching Sunday school or Bible class. (3 credits)

North Iowa Area Community College
Telecourse Department

500 College Drive
Mason City, IA   50401

(800) 392-5685

Geographic Access: Iowa

DELIVERY SYSTEMS

Broadcast Television
All courses are broadcast by Iowa Public television and can be seen on Channel 24 or cable Channel 11 in the Mason City area.

INSTITUTION DESCRIPTION

In addition to academic subjects, North Iowa Area Community College (NIACC) offers vocal and instrumental music programs, a cooperative education program in business subjects, alternating work and class periods, and a freshman program for the educationally disadvantaged. The college grants certificates, diplomas, and associate degrees.

Telecourses are broadcast by Iowa Public Television. All assignments are developed through the NIACC course instructor. Telecourses bear official

NIACC credit with some courses meeting the core requirements for a degree; others are for elective credit.

Accreditation: NCA

Official/Contact: Don Kamps, Coordinator

Admission Requirements: Open enrollment.

Tuition: $48.50 per credit hour with added fees, for a total course cost of $166.80. Texts and study materials must be purchased by the student.

Degree Credit: No degree program via telecourses, although credit earned is applicable toward a degree.

Grading: Letter grades are awarded. Examinations must be proctored. Credit is awarded in semester hour units.

Library: All telecourses are on tape with copies available at the NIACC Library on a limited basis. Students should attempt to view programs at the originally scheduled times or make arrangements for taping at home.

COURSES OFFERED

Anthropology

Faces of Culture

This course embraces cultures from all continents, highlights major human subsistence patterns, and illustrates human adaptation to the environment from the beginning of human history to the present. Individual studies enable viewers to experience cultures in depth, while more general multicultural programs promote cross-culture comparisons and analysis of general themes. 26 half-hour programs. (3 credits)

Business

The Business File

An introduction to the fundamentals of business. Provides a comprehensive view of the contemporary business environment from the internal functions of a business to challenges of business on an international scale. 28 half-hour programs. (3 credits)

Government

Government by Consent

An American government course that focuses on teaching students how to access the government. Explains ways people can become involved in the political process to find solutions to political, social, and economic problems. 26 half-hour programs. (3 credits)

Humanities

Ethics in America

An introductory-level course that examines contemporary ethical conflicts and provides an understanding of the language, concepts, and traditions of ethics. The case study approach draws examples from business, government, civil and criminal law, journalism, the military, medicine, and scientific research. 10 one-hour programs. (3 credits)

Psychology

Discovering Psychology

Covers the fundamental principles and major concepts of psychology. Concepts are illustrated through the use of original footage of classic experiments, interviews with renowned psychologists, and documentaries on emerging research. 26 half-hour programs. (3 credits)

Time to Grow

An introductory course in child development that covers all aspects of children's physical, cognitive, and psychological growth. Includes the most recent theoretical and applied perspectives on ways of caring for and working with children. 26 half-hour programs. (3 credits)

Teikyo Marycrest University
Adult Programs
1607 West 12th Street
Davenport, IA   52804-4096

(319) 326-9581

Geographic Access: Iowa

DELIVERY SYSTEMS

Broadcast Television
Telecourses are broadcast over Iowa Public Television stations. KTIN-TV, Channel 12 in Iowa City is the local access channel.

INSTITUTION DESCRIPTION

Teikyo Marycrest University is an independent coeducational university in the Catholic tradition. It was originally chartered as the women's division of St. Ambrose College in 1939 and became a separate institution in 1954. Affiliation with the Teikyo University group was accomplished in 1991.

The Adult Programs division of the university is responsible for the registration of students for telecourses. These are broadcast over the local PBS television station.

Accreditation: NCA

Official/Contact: Neala McCarthy, Coordinator

Admission Requirements: Open enrollment.

Tuition: Contact the Adult Programs Office for current tuition and fees. Students must purchase textbooks and other materials. Additional royalty fee may apply.

Degree Credit: Credit earned may be applicable to a degree program at Teikyo Marycrest University.

Grading: Letter grades are assigned. Credit is awarded in semester hour units.

Library: The Learning Resource Center is available to officially registered telecourse students.

COURSES OFFERED

Art

Art of the Western World
From ancient Greece to the present, this broadcast telecourse discusses the social values and ideals that gave birth to Western art. Explores the connection between great works and the environments that stimulated their creation. Each program covers the art of two related eras, such as Greece and Rome, or Romanesque and Gothic. 9 one-hour programs. (3 credits)

History

The American Adventure
This broadcast telecourse focuses on the human story as well as the political and economic stories of America. From Columbian contact to the Civil War and Reconstruction, this course illustrates how wars and treaties, elections and legislation affected the people of the United States and helped develop America's democratic spirit. 26 half-hour programs. (3 credits)

Americas
A multidisciplinary study of the contemporary political, economic, social, and cultural history of the countries of Latin America and the Caribbean. This series also looks at the forces of the past that have made this region of the world what it is today and how those influences will inevitably shape the future of the area. 10 one-hour programs. (3 credits)

Sociology

The Sociological Imagination
This telecourse is designed to give students an in-depth look at groups, communities, institutions, and social situations that illustrate major sociological concepts. The documentary-style programs address issues such as socialization, social control, aging, education, collective behavior, and social change. 26 half-hour programs. (3 credits)

Faces of Culture
Embraces cultures from all continents, highlights major human subsistence patterns, and illustrates human adaptation to the environment from the beginning of human history to the present. Individual studies enable viewers to experience cultures in depth, while more general multicultural programs promote cross-culture comparisons and analysis of general themes. 26 half-hour programs. (3 credits)

University of Iowa
Division of Continuing Education
Center for Credit Programs

116 International Center
Iowa City, IA   52242-1802

(800) 272-6430

Geographic Access: Iowa for Broadcast Television, nationwide for audio- and video-enhanced courses.

DELIVERY SYSTEMS

Audiocassette
Audio-enhanced courses require access to an audiocassette player/recorder.

Videocassette
Video-enhanced courses require the use of a VCR.

Broadcast Television
Telecourses are broadcast over Iowa Public Television throughout the state of Iowa.

INSTITUTION DESCRIPTION

The University of Iowa is located in the southeastern section of the state. The university was established in 1847, very soon after the Iowa Territory became a state. Instruction began in 1855 and nontraditional educational opportunities began in 1916.

The Center for Credit Programs offers audio- and video-enhanced courses, particularly in the field of foreign language. Also telecourses offered via Iowa Public Television are offered during the fall, spring, and summer sessions.

Accreditation: NCA

Official/Contact: Leonard Kallio, Assistant Director

Admission Requirements: Open enrollment. Students must be at least a high school junior.

Tuition: $64 per semester hour plus a $15 nonrefundable enrollment fee per course. Additional fees required for audio- and video-enhanced courses. Royalty fees may apply for public television broadcast courses. Textbooks must be purchased by the student. MasterCard and VISA accepted.

Degree Credit: Credit for successful completion of courses may be applied toward a degree.

Grading: Letter grades (A-F) are assigned. D- is the minimum passing grade. Exams must be proctored. Credit is awarded in semester hour units.

Library: All courses are designed to be self-contained. University of Iowa facilities are not available for nonresident students.

COURSES OFFERED

Anthropology

Faces of Culture
This telecourse embraces cultures from all continents, highlights major human subsistence patterns, and illustrates human adaptation to the environment from the beginning of human history to the present. Individual studies enable viewers to experience cultures in depth, while more general multicultural programs promote cross-culture comparisons and analysis of general themes. 26 half-hour programs. (3 credits)

Out of the Past: An Introduction to Archaeology
This broadcast telecourse provides insight into the field of archaeology and examines the tools that scientists use to study past civilizations. The spectacular classic Maya center of Copan, Honduras, provides the focus for the series, but a broadly comparative perspective includes many other civilizations and cultures. 8 programs of 60 minutes each. (3 credits)

Art

Calligraphy I
Fundamentals and exercises in the use of the broad-edged pen in the making of the Fraktur letterform. Emphasis on making letters and arranging them well, plus some practice in calligraphy as applied letterform design. A one-hour videotape is required (purchase only: $20). 6 assignments, no exams. (3 credits)

Calligraphy II
Building upon foundations of the above course, this course examines a variety of tools and letterforms, emphasizing that the look of the letter is determined by the tool that produces it. The broad-edged nib, the dip pen, the brush, and others, as appropriate, are used in the creation of the following letterforms: Merovingian, Uncial, Legend, Versals, Brushscript, Copperplate, and Dutch Caps. Use of watercolor and

techniques with calligraphic applications are explored. A four-hour videotape demonstrating techniques and letterforms is required (purchase only: $40). 8 assignments, no exams. (3 credits)

Chinese

Chinese I

An introduction to spoken Mandarin Chinese, with some instruction in writing Chinese characters. Assigned work consists of memorizing vocabulary and dialogues, reading and writing exercises, as well as oral exercises on tapes. Required set of audiocassette tapes (purchase only: $20). 7 assignments, 4 exams. (4 credits)

Chinese II

A continuation of the above course. Some instruction in writing Chinese characters. Assigned work consists of memorizing vocabulary and dialogues, reading and writing exercises, as well as oral exercises on tapes. Students will mail tapes to the instructor so their speaking ability and pronunciation can be perfected. Required audiocassette tapes (purchase only: $20). 8 assignments, 4 exams. (4 credits)

Computer Science

The New Literacy

A broadcast telecourse that is an up-to-date survey of electronic data processing, computer hardware and software systems, and developments that will provide the basis for further advancements in information processing. 26 programs of 30 minutes length each. (3 credits)

Education

Time to Grow

This broadcast telecourse is a new introductory course in child development that covers all aspects of children's physical, cognitive, and psychological growth. Includes the most recent theoretical and applied perspectives on ways of caring for and working with children. 26 one-half hour programs. (3 credits)

French

Elementary French (9:1)

This is a beginning course in the French language, intended for those who have never studied French before or who seek a thorough review. It is an introduction to French grammar, sounds, and culture through the development of communication skills in speaking, listening, writing, and reading. A set of audiocassette tapes is required (purchase price: $20). 7 assignments, 2 exams. (4 credits)

Elementary French (9:2)

A continuation of the above course. A set of audiocassette tapes is required (purchase price: $20). 7 assignments, 2 exams. (4 credits)

Geology

The Earth Revealed

A broadcast telecourse that presents an overview of the earth's physical processes and properties with emphasis on understanding the scientific theories behind the geological principles. These principles are vividly documented with the assistance of on-location footage at major geologic sites around the world. 26 half-hour programs. (3 credits)

German

Elementary German

For those who have never studied German or who seek a thorough review. Designed to develop skills in reading, writing, hearing, and speaking German, while providing an introduction to the cultures of the German-speaking peoples. Required materials include textbook, workbook, and audiocassette tapes. Computer-assisted drills are optional. 7 assignments, 2 exams. (3 credits)

Latin American Studies

Americas

This broadcast telecourse is a multidisciplinary study of the contemporary political, economic, social, and cultural history of the countries of Latin America and the Caribbean. This series also looks at the forces of the past that have made this region of the world what it is today and how those influences will inevitably shape the future of the area. 10 one-hour programs. (3 credits)

Philosophy

Ethics in America

This introductory level telecourse examines contemporary ethical conflicts and provides an understanding of the language, concepts, and traditions of ethics. The case study approach draws examples from business, government, civil and criminal law, journalism, the military, medicine, and scientific research. 10 one-hour programs. (3 credits)

Political Science

Pacific Century

This broadcast telecourse is a new interdisciplinary course that provides students with an understanding of the historical and geographic context of the development of Northeast Asia (China, Japan, Korea, and the Soviet Far East) and Southeast Asia (emphasizing Indonesia, Malaysia, the Philippines, Singapore, Thailand, and Vietnam). 10 programs of 60 minutes each. (3 credits)

Government by Consent

An American government telecourse that focuses on teaching students how to access the government. Explains ways people can become involved in the political process to find solutions to political, social, and economic problems. 26 half-hour programs. (3 credits)

Psychology

The World of Abnormal Psychology

This broadcast telecourse explores the complex causes, manifestations, and treatments of common behavior disorders. Looks at mental health issues from the patient's perspective as well as analysis from the therapist or other health care professional. 13 one-hour programs. (3 credits)

Russian

First-Year Russian

Equivalent to one semester of introductory Russian language. The course covers exactly half of the cooperative Soviet-American textbook *Russian:*

Stage I, which contains considerable cultural as well as grammatical material. A set of nine audiocassette tapes is required (purchase price: $20) in order to develop listening and speaking skills. 8 assignments, 3 exams. (4 credits)

Sociology

Introduction to Sociology: Principles

Examination of how individuals are organized into social groups, ranging from intimate groups to bureaucracies, and how these influence individual behavior. Nature and interrelationships of basic social institutions such as family, education, religion, economy. Course includes materials developed, in part, under a grant from the Annenberg/CPB Project. Required audiocassettes: $10. 9 assignments, 2 exams. (3 credits)

Special Education

Introduction to Continuing Education

This course explores the historical and conceptual foundations of the theory and practice of continuing education. This exploration will include the consideration of adult learning theory, basic terminology, the nature of adult students, and the major institutions offering educational experiences and credentials to adult learners. Adult and continuing education, in its many forms, is one of the most vibrant and fastest growing areas in all of education. Because it is a field in great flux, any serious inquiry must include the consideration of a number of controversial questions. The course will examine several of these controversies. Three types of material are required: a course anthology (purchase fee: $25), a set of audiocassettes (purchase fee: $5), and two videotapes available on a loan basis ($5 each). 14 assignments, 1 exam. (3 credits)

Kansas

University of Kansas
Division of Continuing Education

Continuing Education Building
Lawrence, KS   66045

(913) 864-4792 *Fax:* (913) 864-3952

Geographic Access: Worldwide

DELIVERY SYSTEMS

Computer Tutorials
The student must have an IBM or compatible computer to handle the computer diskettes supplied as part of the course material package.

Videocassette
Students view videos supplied with the course materials.

Audiocassette
Courses, particularly in foreign languages, require listening to audiocassette as well as recording assignments.

INSTITUTION DESCRIPTION

The University of Kansas is a major educational and research institution with over 28,000 students and 1,900 faculty members. The university includes the main campus in Lawrence, the Medical Center in Kansas City, the Regents Center in Overland Park, a clinical campus of the School of Medicine in Wichita, and educational and research facilities throughout the state. There are fourteen major academic divisions within the university.

Descriptions of media-assisted courses are given in the course listings below. Computer diskettes and video- and audiotapes are included in course fees and are part of the materials package for courses that re-

quire them. Students must furnish the audiocassette player or VCR for courses that require their use.

Accreditation: NCA

Official/Contact: Nancy R. Collyer, Director

Admission Requirements: Enrollment in a media-assisted course does not constitute official admission to the resident program of any of the seven Regents institutions. Courses may be taken by both graduate and undergraduate students, but students from institutions other than the University of Kansas are responsible for obtaining approval from their schools and advisors if credit is to be applicable to their programs. Any course may be taken on a noncredit basis without special permission. Enrollment can be accomplished at any time during the year. Students have nine months to complete a course.

Tuition: The tuition fee as determined by the Kansas Board of Regents is $67 per credit hour. This fee may be adjusted during the academic year. The postage and handling fee is $20.50 for each course. An additional charge of $17.50 per course is assessed for instructional materials and student services. This fee includes the cost of the student study guide, computer diskettes, and video- or audiotapes. Textbooks are purchased by the student and can be obtained from the Kansas Union Bookstore (800) 458-1111. MasterCard and VISA accepted for both tuition and book purchases. Total course fees are given below with each course description.

Degree Credit: Credits may be accepted and applied toward degree requirements at the University of Kansas. Students from other institutions should check with their advisors for approval and to ensure acceptance of credit toward a degree.

Grading: The grading system is determined by the course author. Final examinations must be proctored at an approved educational institution or taken at an examination site on the campuses of the university system.

Library: Students can access KU's online catalog of library holdings from computer terminals in the libraries or by remote microcomputer to the campus computer network. For the latter, the student must have an IBM or compatible computer, modem, and communications software.

COURSES OFFERED

Anthropology

Introduction to Cultural Anthropology

An introduction to the nature of culture, language, society, and personality. Included in this survey are some of the major principles, concepts, and themes of cultural anthropology. Videotape: *Anthropological Fieldwork in Polynesia*. Fee of $321 includes tuition, materials, videotape, postage and handling. (4 credits)

Myth, Legend, and Folk Belief in East Asia

A survey of the commonly held ideas about the beginning of the world, the role of the gods and spirits in daily life, and the celebrations and rituals proper to each season. This course presents the world view of the ordinary peoples of East Asia in contrast to their more sophisticated systems of philosophy, which are better known to the Western world. Eight lectures on audiotapes. Fee of $299 includes tuition, materials, audiotapes, postage and handling. (3 credits)

Art

Introduction to Art History

An introduction to art and architecture in Western culture. Basic principles and problems of the visual arts are analyzed, as are the major historical trends and periods. Style, content, and cultural background are discussed and illustrated. Videotape: *Art of the Eastern World*, a nine-part television series. Students may take either a lower or upper division version of this course. Fee of $269 includes tuition, materials, loan of videotapes, postage and handling. Students who return the videotapes in good condition will receive a $15 refund. (3 credits)

Biology

Principles of Biology

Introduces basic concepts of biology at the cellular, organismal, and population levels of organization and their applications to humans and modern society. Unifying themes include evolution, the relationship of structure to function, and laws of biological systems. Videotape: *Vole-population Dispersal*. Fee of $254 includes tuition, materials, videotape, postage and handling. (3 credits)

Communication Disorders

Survey of Communication Disorders

Provides a general understanding of normal and deviant speech, language, and hearing in adults and children. This course considers the normal development of communication behavior, the nature of communication disorders, and the interaction of speech pathology and audiology with allied fields (education, medicine, psychology, special education). Videotape on communication problems, diagnostic and remediation techniques, speech disorders, and hearing loss. Fee of $254 includes tuition, materials, videotape, postage and handling. (3 credits)

Communication Disorders

Development of oral language and processes of communicative behavior with emphasis on disorders. Consideration of problems in habilitation. Videotape on communication problems, diagnostic and remediation techniques, speech disorders, and hearing loss. Fee of $254 includes tuition, materials, videotape, postage and handling. (3 credits)

East Asian Languages and Cultures

Myth, Legend, and Folk Belief in East Asia

A survey of the commonly held beliefs about the beginning of the world, the role of the gods and spirits in daily life, and the celebrations and rituals proper to each season. The course presents the world view of the ordinary peoples of East Asia in contrast to their more sophisticated systems of philosophy. Eight lectures on audiotapes. Fee of $299 includes tuition, materials, audiotapes, postage and handling. (3 credits)

English

Introduction to Poetry

The appreciation and understanding of selected masterpieces of American Poetry. Attention is given to various poetic forms and techniques and the relationship between the poet's life and his/her works. Videotape: *Voices and Visions* in eight parts. Fee of $269 includes tuition, materials, loan of videotape, postage and handling. Students who return the videotapes in good condition will receive a $15 refund. (3 credits)

French

Elementary French I

Introduction to the French language with an emphasis on understanding and speaking in realistic, everyday circumstances. Fee of $438 includes tuition, materials, loan of audio- and videotapes, postage and handling. Students who return the tapes in good condition will receive a $45 refund for these materials. (5 credits)

Elementary French II

Promotes a proficiency in spoken French, while developing skills in listening comprehension, reading, and writing. Fee of $438 includes tuition, materials, loan of audio- and videotapes, postage and handling. Students who return the tapes in good condition will receive a $45 refund for these materials. (5 credits)

German

Elementary German I

Designed to train the student to comprehend modern German. Includes essentials of grammar, practice in speaking, reading, and writing German. The audiolingual method and training in written German are both used. Fee of $438 includes tuition, materials, loan of audiotapes, postage and handling. Students who return the audiotapes in good condition will receive a $40 refund for these materials. (5 credits)

Elementary German II

A continuation of grammar, practice in conversation, composition, and reading. Fee of $413 includes tuition, materials, loan of audiotapes, postage and handling. Students who return the audiotapes in good condition will receive a $30 refund. (5 credits)

Health

AIDS and STDs: Facts of Life

An overview of the epidemiology of AIDS and other sexually transmitted diseases. Presents the history of these diseases, factors contributing to their spread, at-risk populations, and prevention techniques. Videotape: *AIDS: A Practical Approach to Prevention.* Fee of $254 includes tuition, materials, videotape, postage and handling. (3 credits)

Music

Introduction to Jazz

A study of jazz in its historical contexts. Introduces examples of various kinds of jazz and jazz improvisations. Fee of $254 includes tuition, materials, loan of audiotapes, postage and handling. Students who return the tapes in good condition will receive a $7 refund for these materials. (3 credits)

Philosophy

Introduction to Logic

An introduction to the theory and practice of modern logical analysis. Special emphasis is placed on the logical appraisal of everyday arguments. Recommended but not required software: Computer tutorials for *Introduction to Logic*, 5 diskettes. Fee of $259 includes tuition, materials, loan of software, postage and handling. (3 credits)

Psychology

Brain and Behavior

Introduces the basics of brain organization and describes the brain's microcomponents in terms of the structure and function of individual cells and their chemical environments. Develops a conceptual framework for discussion of sensation, movement, homeostasis, biorhythms, emotion, learning, memory, thinking, consciousness, and abnormal behavior. Videotape: *The Brain*, an eight-part television series. Fee of $269 includes tuition, materials, loan of videotapes, postage and handling. Students who return the videotapes in good condition will receive a $15 refund. (3 credits)

The Mind

Introduces many of the recent discoveries about the mind and the brain. The course focuses on the mental activities that distinguish humans from other living creatures and that may be based on the unique capacities of the human mind. Videotape: *The Mind*, a nine-part television series. Fee of $269 includes tuition, materials, loan of videotapes, postage and handling. Students who return videotapes in good condition will receive a $15 refund. (3 credits)

Religious Studies

History of Judaism

An investigation of the individuals and events that shaped Judaism in the context of shifting social, economic, political, and cultural realities from the first century to the present. Videotape: *Heritage: Civilization and the Jews*, a nine-part television series. Fee of $279 includes tuition, materials, loan of videotapes, postage and handling. Students who return the tapes in good condition will receive a $15 refund. (3 credits)

Spanish

Elementary Spanish I

Introduction to the Spanish language, providing explanations of and practice in listening, speaking, reading, and writing skills. Audiotape: *Communicating in Spanish*. Fee of $423 includes tuition, materials, audiotapes, postage and handling. (5 credits)

Elementary Spanish II

A continuation of Elementary Spanish I. Audiotape: *Communicating in Spanish*. Fee of $423 includes tuition, materials, audiotapes, postage and handling. (5 credits)

Special Education

Introduction to the Psychology and Education of Exceptional Children and Youth

Current practices in the identification, placement, and education of exceptional children and youth. Emphasis on patterns of social, cognitive, language, and physical development of exceptional children. Social, political, and economic advocacy issues. Videotape: *A New Way of Thinking*. Fee of $239 includes tuition, materials, loan of videotapes, postage and handling. (3 credits)

Stress Management

Managing Stress: Principles and Techniques for Coping, Prevention, and Wellness

Covers major stress management techniques, helping others cope with stress, and promoting wellness. Theories and models of stress, psychological basis for stress, relationship between personality and stress, family and social stress, job stress, dissatisfaction, and burnout are discussed. Audiotape: *Finding Your Balance: Deep-muscle Relaxation Exercise and Meditation Exercise*. Fee of $239 includes tuition, materials, postage and handling. (3 credits)

Kentucky

Ashland Community College
See **Kentucky Telecommunications Consortium**

Cumberland College
See **Kentucky Telecommunications Consortium**

Eastern Kentucky University
See **Kentucky Telecommunications Consortium**

Elizabethtown Community College

Telecourse Administration
600 College Street Road
Elizabethtown, KY 42701

(502) 769-2371

Geographic Access: Kentucky

DELIVERY SYSTEMS

Broadcast Television
Telecourses are broadcast over WKZT-TV Channel 23 in Elizabethtown.

INSTITUTION DESCRIPTION

Elizabethtown Community College serves the citizens of Hardin County and the seven surrounding counties of Bullitt, Breckinridge, Grayson, Hart, LaRue, Meade, and Nelson. The college opened its doors in 1964.

Telecourses offered by the college are broadcast over KET, The Kentucky Network.

Accreditation: SACS

Official/Contact: Ronald Thomas, Administrator

Admission Requirements: Open enrollment.

Tuition: Undergraduate Kentucky resident $105 per 3-credit course, nonresident $315. Textbooks, study guides, and other study components must be purchased by the student.

Degree Credit: Credit earned by successful completion of a telecourse may be applied toward an associate degree.

Grading: Examinations must be proctored by an officially approved supervisor. Letter grades (A-F) are assigned. Credit is awarded in semester hour units.

Library: Officially registered students have access to the Learning Resources Center on the Elizabethtown campus.

COURSES OFFERED

Business

The Business File
An introduction to business for everyone who wants to expand their understanding of the contemporary business environment. This telecourse exposes students to the internal and external functions of businesses and to the challenges of business on an international scale. Produced by Dallas Telecourses and Dallas County Community College District. 28 half-hour telecasts (2 per week). (3 credits)

English

Literary Visions

Brings literature to life with dramatizations of individual works and readings of literary passages. Selections from contemporary and traditional works are presented with a strong emphasis on writing about literature so students can learn and use advanced compositional techniques. Organized around three major genres of literature—short fiction, poetry, and drama—the television programs examine literary elements such as character, plot, and symbolism. Developed by the Southern California Consortium in association with the Instructional Television Consortium and produced by Maryland Public television. 26 half-hour telecasts (2 per week). Closed-captioned for the hearing-impaired. (3 credits)

History

The American Adventure

This telecourse covers the first semester of American history. The series focuses on the human story as well as the political and economic stories of early American history to 1877. Taped on location in 23 states and Mexico, *The American Adventure* brings to life the conflicts and consequences of our nation's early history and illustrates how wars and treaties, elections, and legislation affected the people of the United States and helped develop America's democratic spirit. Produced by Dallas Telecourses and Dallas County Community College. 26 half-hour telecasts (2 per week). (3 credits)

Psychology

Discovering Psychology

Covers the fundamental principles and major concepts of psychology, including brain and behavior, sensation and perception, conditioning and learning, cognitive processes, motivation and emotion, life-span development, the self and identity, sex and gender, testing and intelligence, social influences, psychopathology and therapy, stress and health issues, methodology, and new directions in the field. Produced by WGBH/Boston in association with the American Psychological Association. The series is part of the Annenberg/CPB Collection. 26 half-hour telecasts (2 per week). Closed-captioned for the hearing-impaired. (3 credits)

Sociology

The Sociological Imagination

The goal of this course is to give students the perspective and intellectual tools needed to think critically about social change and the social structures in which it takes place. Produced by Dallas Telecourses and the Dallas Community College District. 26 half-hour telecasts (2 per week). (3 credits)

Hazard Community College
See **Kentucky Telecommunications Consortium**

Henderson Community College
See **Kentucky Telecommunications Consortium**

Kentucky State University
See **Kentucky Telecommunications Consortium**

Kentucky Telecommunications Consortium
KETV/Kentucky ETV

600 Cooper Drive
Lexington, KY   40502-2248

(606) 233-3000

Geographic Access: Kentucky

DELIVERY SYSTEMS

Broadcast Television

Telecourses are broadcast over KET, the Kentucky Network and transmitted to various television stations throughout the state. The courses listed below represent the entire program of courses offered over KET. Member institutions may or may not carry all courses during a semester and may vary the frequency of availability for enrollment. Contact the campus representative listed above for the current availability of telecourses for credit on their campus.

INSTITUTION DESCRIPTION

The Kentucky Telecommunications Consortium was created by the state legislature in 1978 for the purpose of providing college credit television courses to distance learners throughout the Commonwealth.

The Consortium is comprised of representatives from KET (the Kentucky Network), Kentucky colleges and universities, and the Council on Higher Education.

The Council on Higher Education serves as the administrative head and fiscal agent of the Consortium. KET provides major support by managing, promoting, and broadcasting the telecourses. Participating colleges and universities provide instructional management for telecourses on their campuses.

The Kentucky Telecommunications Consortium selects the college credit telecourses for KET broadcast. All telecourses considered by the Consortium were previewed by Kentucky colleges and universities who offer KET telecourses for credit on a regular basis. Member institutions and contact persons are listed below.

State Universities:
- Eastern Kentucky University (Richmond KY), Connie Vencill, (606) 622-2001
- Kentucky State University (Frankfort KY), Debbie C. Tillett, (502) 227-6634
- Morehead State University (Morehead KY), Wanda Littleton, (606) 783-2004
- Murray State University (Murray KY), Gerald M. Dinh, (800) 669-7654
- Northern Kentucky University (Highland Heights KY), Susan Kemper, (606) 572-5601
- University of Kentucky (Lexington KY), Nofflet D. Williams, (800) 432-0963
- University of Louisville (Louisville KY), Lowell R. Embry, (502) 588-6061
- Western Kentucky University (Bowling Green KY), (502) 745-5305

University of Kentucky Community Colleges:
- Ashland Community College (Ashland KY), Office of Admissions, (606) 329-2999
- Elizabethtown Community College (Elizabethtown KY), Ronald Thomas, (502) 769-2371
- Hazard Community College (Hazard KY), Mike Dixon, (606) 436-5721
- Henderson Community College (Henderson KY), Bob Park, (502) 827-1867
- Lexington Community College (Lexington KY), Robert E. Carter, (606) 257-3415
- Madisonville Community College (Madisonville KY), John Peters, (502) 821-2250

- Owensboro Community College (Owensboro KY), Greta McDonough, (502) 686-4400
- Paducah Community College (Paducah KY), Sherry Cope, (502) 554-9200
- Somerset Community College (Somerset KY), Tracy Casada, (606) 679-8501
- Southeast Community College (Cumberland KY), Roger C. Noe, (606) 589-2145

Independent Colleges:
- Cumberland College (Williamsburg KY), Robert Schoonover, (606) 549-2200
- Lees College (Jackson KY), Mary Sue Johnson, (606) 666-7521
- Midway College (Midway KY), George Huxel, (606) 846-5358
- Saint Catherine College (Saint Catharine KY), Stanley Katz, (606) 336-5082
- Thomas More College (Crestview Hills KY), Office of the Registrar, (606) 344-3380
- Union College (Barbourville KY), Kay Dawn McFarland, (606) 546-4151

Accreditation: All member institutions are accredited by SACS.

Official/Contact: Mary L. Olson, Higher Education Manager

Admission Requirements: Prospective students should register for a course at the institution in their area by contacting the individual listed above for member institutions. Registration can be by mail or in person on campus.

Tuition: Tuition varies by institution. Contact the campus coordinator listed above for current rates and fees. Textbooks, study guides, and other materials costs are borne by the student.

Degree Credit: Credit for courses successfully completed may be applied toward a degree program.

Grading: Examinations must be proctored according to the policy of member institutions. Grading system is the option of the institution providing the course. Credit is generally in semester hour units and the amount of credit for each course listed below is determined by the institution offering the course.

Library: Students have access to the library resources of the institutions in which they have enrolled.

COURSES OFFERED

Business

The Business File
This telecourse is an introduction to business for everyone who wants to expand their understanding of the contemporary business environment. The course exposes students to the internal and external functions of businesses and to the challenges of business on an international scale. 26 classes. Two half-hour television classes per week.

Something Ventured: Small Business Management
A business telecourse designed to provide aspiring entrepreneurs, and those already involved in a small business venture, with the tools needed to enhance their potential for success. Students are given a unique opportunity to observe a variety of small businesses in operation in both rural and suburban communities, as well as large metropolitan areas, for an over-the-shoulder look at what it is like to start and operate a small business. The documentary footage is then analyzed by a council of leading experts in the small business arena. Produced as part of the *Business Connection* by INTELECOM (Southern California Consortium). 26 classes. Two half-hour television classes per week.

Economics

Economics U$A
A comprehensive television course in macro- and microeconomics designed to address the sharply increasing demand for quality college courses in this critical field of study. The series is being offered by most participating Kentucky institutions at the graduate level for teacher educators. The television series is an absorbing documentary examination of major historic and contemporary events that have shaped 20th-century American economics. Through interviews, commentary, and analysis, the series establishes clear relationships between abstract economic principles and concrete human experiences. Produced by the Educational Film Center in cooperation with Wharton Econometric Forecasting Associates and the Southern California Consortium. The series is part of the Annenberg/CPB Collection.

28 classes. Two half-hour television classes per week.

English

Literature
Literary Visions brings literature to life with dramatizations of individual works and readings of literary passages. Selections from contemporary and traditional works are presented with a strong emphasis on writing about literature so students can learn and use advanced compositional techniques. Organized around three major genres of literature—short fiction, poetry, and drama—the television programs examine literary elements such as character, plot, and symbolism. The series host, Shakespearean actress Fran Dorn, identifies these elements within dramatizations of the representative literary works. Commentary from noted critics contributes the multiple perspectives that would be found in class discussion. Developed by the Southern California Consortium in association with the Instructional Television Consortium and produced by Maryland Public Television. 26 classes. Two half-hour television classes per week.

Geology

Physical Geology
The Earth Explored provides students with an international field trip in physical geology. From the top of the Alps to the bottom of Death Valley, the series examines the forces that have shaped, and continue to shape, our Earth. The telecourse begins with a historical look through the eyes of one of the pioneers of modern geological thought, Sir James Hutton, and concludes with an examination of specific natural resources. Throughout the series, noted experts on physical geology, aerial photography, and animation provide students with new insights into Earth's physical processes. Produced by BBC Open University and KRMA/Denver. 14 classes. One half-hour television class per week.

History

The American Adventure
The American Adventure covers the first semester of American history. The series focuses on the human story as well as the political and economic stories of early American history to 1877. 26 classes. Two half-hour classes per week.

The Western Tradition I

Part I of a two-semester television course built around the classroom lectures of Eugene Weber, internationally renowned author, historian, and professor at the University of California, Los Angeles. Weber spins thousands of years into a seamless story, making the abstract more concrete and developing the ability of students to analyze and appreciate history. By weaving together history, art, literature, religion, geography, government, and economics, *The Western Tradition* helps students recognize the pendulum swings of history, identify parallels in the modern world, and gain a sense of their own place in the evolution of human institutions. Produced by WGBH/Boston and part of the Annenberg/CPB Collection. 26 classes. Two half-hour television programs per week.

Psychology

Discovering Psychology

This telecourse covers the fundamental principles and major concepts of psychology, including brain and behavior, sensation and perception, conditioning and learning, cognitive processes, motivation and emotion, life-span development, the self and identity, sex and gender, testing and intelligence, social influences, psychopathology and therapy, stress and health issues, methodology, and new directories in the field. *Discovering Psychology* was produced by WGBH/Boston in association with the American Psychological Association and is part of the Annenberg/CPB Collection. 26 classes. Two half-hour television classes per week.

Sociology

Sociology

Social change, with all of its conflicts and problems, has been the great driving force in sociology from its beginnings. The goal of *The Sociological Imagination* is to give students the perspective and intellectual tools needed to think critically about social change and the social structures in which it takes place. The 26 video programs use a straightforward documentary style to engage the viewer on an emotional level. Each program tells a story, showing people in their family settings and at work, school, church, and play. These documentaries are thought-provoking illustrations of sociological issues and ideas. Produced by Dallas Telecourses and the Dal-

las County Community College District. 26 classes. Two half-hour television programs per week.

Spanish

Destinos I

This Spanish language telecourse introduces students to basic structures and language groups for listening, speaking, reading, writing, and cultural awareness of Spanish. *Destinos* uses a uniquely Hispanic genre, the "telenovela," to combine a dramatic story line with instruction. In this marriage of television drama and language instruction, the natural context of the situations in which the characters find themselves provides the basis for the grammar, vocabulary, and language functions studied. 26 classes. Two half-hour television classes per week.

Lees College
See **Kentucky Telecommunications Consortium**

Lexington Community College
See **Kentucky Telecommunications Consortium**

Madisonville Community College
See **Kentucky Telecommunications Consortium**

Midway College
See **Kentucky Telecommunications Consortium**

Morehead State University
See **Kentucky Telecommunications Consortium**

Murray State University
Academic Outreach
Continuing Education
1 Murray Street
Murray, KY   42071-3308

(800) 669-7654

Geographic Access: Kentucky

DELIVERY SYSTEMS

Broadcast Television
Telecourses may be viewed on WKMU Channel 38 in the Murray-Mayfield area.

INSTITUTION DESCRIPTION

Murray State University was established in 1922 as Murray Normal School. After several name changes, the present name was adopted in 1966. The Academic Outreach Program offers a variety of courses enabling students to complete work for degrees, to acquire new skills, and to pursue special interests for professional and cultural enhancement. In addition to traditional correspondence courses, broadcast television is utilized to offer distance learners the opportunity to study without leaving their home.

Telecourses are offered through broadcasts of Kentucky Educational Television (The Kentucky Network).

Accreditation: SACS

Official/Contact: Gerald M. Dinh, Coordinator

Admission Requirements: Open enrollment. Registration does not constitute admission to Murray State University.

Tuition: Undergraduate Kentucky resident $201 per 3-credit course, nonresident undergraduate $579. Graduate Kentucky resident $297 per 3-credit course, nonresident graduate $846. Textbooks must be purchased by the student.

Degree Credit: Credit earned through successful completion of a telecourse may be applied toward a degree at Murray State University.

Grading: Examinations must be proctored. The proctor must make a signed statement to Academic Outreach to the effect that the examination was taken under normal conditions and without the student's receiving assistance from any source. The grading system is A, B, C, D, F. The minimum passing grade is D. Credit is awarded in semester hour units.

Library: Officially registered students have access to the University Library.

COURSES OFFERED

Business

The Business File
This telecourse is an introduction to business for everyone who wants to expand their understanding of the contemporary business environment. It exposes students to the internal and external functions of businesses and to the challenges of business on an international scale. The programs feature many of the nation's academic and professional leaders commenting on their experiences with the business world. Mini-documentaries, computer graphics, and close-up looks at successful businesses in operation further enhance the academic content of *The Business File*. 28 half-hour telecasts (2 per week). An undergraduate course. (3 credits)

Economics

Economics U$A
This course is a comprehensive television course in macro- and microeconomics designed to address the sharply increasing demand for quality college courses in this critical field of study. The series is being offered at the graduate level for teacher educators. The video series is a documentary examination of major historic and contemporary events that have shaped 20th-century American economics. Through interviews, commentary, and analysis, the series establishes clear relationships between abstract economic principles and concrete human experiences. Produced by the Educational Film Center in cooperation with Wharton Econometric Forecasting Associates and the Southern California Consortium. The series is part of the Annenberg/CPB collection. 28 half-hour telecasts (2 per week). (3 credits)

Geoscience

The Earth Explored
The Earth Explored provides students with an international field trip in physical geology. From the top of the Alps to the bottom of Death Valley, the series examines the forces that have shaped, and continue to shape, our Earth. The telecourse begins with a historical look through the eyes of one of the pioneers of modern geologic thought, Sir James Hutton, and concludes with an examination of specific natural resources. Throughout the series, noted experts

on physical geology, aerial photography, and animation provide students with new insights into Earth's physical processes. Produced by BBC Open University and KRMA/Denver. 14 one-half hour television classes. (4 credits)

History

The American Adventure

This telecourse covers the first semester of American history. The series focuses on the human story as well as the political and economic stories of early American history to 1877. Taped on location in 23 states and Mexico, *The American Adventure* brings to life the conflicts and consequences of our nation's early history and illustrates how wars and treaties, elections, and legislation affected the people of the United States and helped develop America's democratic spirit. 26 half-hour telecasts (2 per week). An undergraduate course. (3 credits)

Psychology

Discovering Psychology

This telecourse covers the fundamental principles and major concepts of psychology, including brain and behavior, sensation and perception, conditioning and learning, cognitive processes, motivation and emotion, life-span development, the self and identify, sex and gender, testing and intelligence, social influences, psychopathology and therapy, stress and health issues, methodology, and new directions in the field. The video series was produced by WGBH/Boston in association with the American Psychological Association and is part of the Annenberg/CPB Collection. 26 half-hour telecasts (2 per week). An undergraduate course. (3 credits)

Sociology

The Sociological Imagination

The goal of *The Sociological Imagination* is to give students the perspective and intellectual tools needed to think critically about social change and the social structures in which it takes place. The video series uses a straightforward documentary style to engage the viewer on an emotional level. Each program tells a story, showing people in their family settings and at work, school, church, and play. These documentaries are thought-provoking illustrations of sociological issues and ideas. Produced by Dallas Telecourses and the Dallas County Community College District. 26 half-hour telecasts (2 per week). An undergraduate course. (3 credits)

Northern Kentucky University
Credit Continuing Education

Administrative Center 111
Highland Heights, KY 41099

(606) 572-5601

Geographic Access: Kentucky

DELIVERY SYSTEMS

Broadcast Television
Telecourses are broadcast by KET, The Kentucky Network over local television channels.

INSTITUTION DESCRIPTION

Northern Kentucky University was established in 1968. It is a member of the Kentucky Telecommunications Consortium which was created in 1978 for the purpose of providing college credit television courses throughout the state. KET, The Kentucky Network, provides major support by managing, promoting, and broadcasting the telecourses.

Accreditation: SACS

Official/Contact: Susan Kemper, Administrator

Admission Requirements: Open enrollment. Registration does not constitute formal admission to Northern Kentucky University.

Tuition: Undergraduate Kentucky resident $219 per 3-credit course, nonresident $594. Graduate Kentucky resident $309 per 3-credit course. Textbooks and supplementary materials must be purchased by the student.

Degree Credit: Credit earned through successful completion of a telecourse may be applied to a degree program.

Grading: Examinations must be proctored. Letter grades, A-F, are assigned. Credit is awarded in semester hour units.

Library: Officially registered students have access to the library facilities of the university.

COURSES OFFERED

Business

The Business File

This telecourse is an introduction to business for everyone who wants to expand their understanding of the contemporary business environment. Students are exposed to the internal and external functions of businesses and to the challenges of business on an international scale. The programs feature many of the nation's academic and professional leaders commenting on their experiences with the business world. Minidocumentaries, computer graphics, and close-up looks at successful businesses in operation further enhance the academic content. Produced by Dallas Telecourses and Dallas County Community College District. 28 half-hour telecasts (2 per week). An undergraduate course. (3 credits)

Something Ventured: Small Business Management

A telecourse designed to provide aspiring entrepreneurs and those already involved in a small business venture with the tools needed to enhance their potential for success. Students are given a unique opportunity to observe a variety of small businesses in operation in both rural and suburban communities as well as large metropolitan areas for an over-the-shoulder look at what it is like to start and operate a small business. The documentary footage is then analyzed by a council of leading experts in the small business arena. Developed and produced by IN-TELECOM (Southern California Consortium). 26 half-hour telecasts (2 per week). An undergraduate course. (3 credits)

Economics

Economics U$A

This is a comprehensive television course in macro- and microeconomics designed to address the sharply increasing demand for quality college courses in this critical field of study. The series is offered at the graduate level for teacher educators. The video series is a documentary examination of major historic and contemporary events that have shaped 20th-century American economics. Through interviews, commentary, and analysis, the series establishes clear relationships between abstract economic principles and concrete human experiences. Produced by the Educational Film Center in cooperation with Wharton Econometric Forecasting Associates and the Southern California Consortium. The series is part of the Annenberg/CPB Collection. Closed captioned for the hearing-impaired. 28 half-hour telecasts. (3 credits)

English

Literary Visions

This telecourse brings literature to life with dramatizations of individual works and readings of literary passages. Selections from contemporary and traditional works are presented with a strong emphasis on writing about literature so students can learn and use advanced compositional techniques. Organized around three major genres of literature—short fiction, poetry, and drama—the television programs examine literary elements such as character, plot, and symbolism. Developed by the Southern California Consortium in association with the Instructional Television Consortium and produced by Maryland Public Television. Closed captioned for the hearing-impaired. 26 half-hour telecasts (2 per week). An undergraduate course. (3 credits)

Geology

Physical Geology

The Earth Explored provides students with an international field trip in physical geology. The telecourse begins with a historical look through the eyes of one of the pioneers of modern geologic thought, Sir James Hutton, and concludes with an examination of specific natural resources. Produced by BBC Open University and KRMA/Denver. 14 half-hour telecasts (1 per week). An undergraduate course. (3 credits)

History

The American Adventure

This telecourse covers the first semester of American history. The series focuses on the human story as well as the political and economic stories of early American history to 1877. Produced by Dallas Telecourses and Dallas Community College District. 26 half-hour telecasts (2 per week). An undergraduate course. (3 credits)

The Western Tradition I

This telecourse is built around the classroom lectures of Eugen Weber, internationally renowned author, historian, and professor at the University of California, Los Angeles. Weber spins thousands of years into a seamless story, making the abstract more concrete and developing the ability of students to analyze and appreciate history. Produced by WGBH/Boston and part of the Annenberg/CPB Collection. Closed captioned for the hearing-impaired. 26 half-hour telecasts (2 per week). An undergraduate course. (3 credits)

Psychology

Discovering Psychology

Covers the fundamental principles and major concepts of psychology, including brain and behavior, sensation and perception, conditioning and learning, cognitive processes, motivation and emotion, lifespan development, the self and identity, sex and gender, testing and intelligence, social influences, psychopathology, therapy, stress and health issues, methodology, and new directions in the field. Produced by WGBH/Boston in association with the American Psychological Association. The video series is part of the Annenberg/CPB Collection. Closed captioned for the hearing-impaired. 26 half-hour telecasts (2 per week). An undergraduate course. (3 credits)

Sociology

The Sociological Imagination

The goal of this telecourse is to give students the perspective and intellectual tools needed to think critically about social change and the social structures in which it takes place. The video programs use a documentary style to engage the viewer on an emotional level. Each program tells a story, showing people in their family settings and at work, school, church and play. Produced by Dallas Telecourses and the Dallas County Community College District. 26 half-hour telecasts (2 per week). An undergraduate course. (3 credits)

Spanish

Destinos I

This language telecourse introduces students to basic structures and language groups for listening, speaking, reading, writing, and cultural awareness of Spanish. *Destinos* uses a uniquely Hispanic genre, the "telenovela," to combine a dramatic story line with instruction. In this marriage of television drama and language instruction, the natural context of the situations in which the characters find them-

selves provides the basis for the grammar, vocabulary, and language functions studied. Produced by WGBH/Boston and is part of the Annenberg/CPB Collection. Closed captioned for the hearing-impaired. An undergraduate course. (3 credits)

Owensboro Community College
See **Kentucky Telecommunications Consortium**

Paducah Community College
Telecourses
Registrar's Office
P.O. Box 7380
Paducah, KY 42002-7380

(502) 554-9200

Geographic Access: Kentucky

DELIVERY SYSTEMS

Broadcast Television
Telecourses are broadcast by WKPD/TV Channel 9 in Paducah.

INSTITUTION DESCRIPTION

Paducah Community College is located in the city of Paducah in the far western part of Kentucky, bordering southern Illinois and the boot-heel of Missouri. The college was founded in 1932.

Telecourses are offered via KET, The Kentucky Network.

Accreditation: SACS

Official/Contact: Sherry Cope, Telecourse Coordinator

Admission Requirements: Open enrollment for telecourses. Degree-seeking students must apply with high school transcripts, previous college transcripts, and health questionnaire.

Tuition: Undergraduate Kentucky resident $105 per 3-credit course, nonresident $315. Textbooks, course study guide, and other supplementary materials must be purchased by the student.

Degree Credit: Credit awarded upon successful completion of a telecourse may be applied toward an associate degree.

Grading: Examinations must be proctored by an officially approved supervisor (librarian, educator, school principal). Letter grades are assigned. Credit is awarded in semester hour units.

Library: Officially registered students have access to the Learning Resources Center on the campus.

COURSES OFFERED

English

Literary Visions
Brings literature to life with dramatizations of individual works and readings of literary passages. Selections from contemporary and traditional works are presented with a strong emphasis on writing about literature so students can learn and use advanced compositional techniques. Organized around three major genres of literature—short fiction, poetry, and drama—the television programs examine literary elements such as character, plot, and symbolism. Developed by the Southern California Consortium in association with the Instructional Television Consortium and produced by Maryland Public Television. 26 half-hour telecasts (2 per week). Closed captioned for the hearing-impaired. (3 credits)

History

The American Adventure
This telecourse covers the first semester of American history. The series focuses on the human story as well as the political and economic stories of early American history to 1877. Produced by Dallas Telecourses and Dallas County Community College District. 26 half-hour telecasts (2 per week). An undergraduate course. (3 credits)

Psychology

Discovering Psychology
Covers the fundamental principles and major concepts of psychology, including brain and behavior, sensation and perception, conditioning and learning, cognitive processes, motivation and emotion, life-span development, the self and identity, sex and gender, testing and intelligence, social influences, psychopathology and therapy, stress and health issues, methodology, and new directions in the field. Produced by WBGH/Boston in association with the American Psychological Association. The series is part of the Annenberg/CPB Collection. 26 half-hour telecasts (2 per week). Closed captioned for the hearing-impaired. (3 credits)

Sociology

The Sociological Imagination
The goal of this telecourse is to give students the perspective and intellectual tools needed to think critically about social change and the social structures in which it takes place. Each program in the series tells a story, showing people in their family settings and at work, school, church, and play. Produced by Dallas Telecourses and the Dallas County Community College District. 26 half-hour telecasts (2 per week). (3 credits)

Saint Catherine College
See **Kentucky Telecommunications Consortium**

Somerset Community College
See **Kentucky Telecommunications Consortium**

Southeast Community College
See **Kentucky Telecommunications Consortium**

Thomas More College
See **Kentucky Telecommunications Consortium**

Union College
See **Kentucky Telecommunications Consortium**

University of Kentucky
See **Kentucky Telecommunications Consortium**

University of Louisville
See **Kentucky Telecommunications Consortium**

Western Kentucky University
See **Kentucky Telecommunications Consortium**

Louisiana

Louisiana State University
Division of Continuing Education
Office of Independent Study

Room E106
Pleasant Hall
Baton Rouge, LA   70803

(504) 388-3171

Geographic Access: Worldwide

DELIVERY SYSTEMS

Audiocassette
Used primarily in foreign language courses.

Videocassette
Videocassettes supplement course materials.

INSTITUTION DESCRIPTION

Louisiana State University offers audio/video enhanced courses as part of the traditional correspondence courses offered through Independent Study. Most courses are taught by members of the university faculty. All courses contain a specific number of written assignments which are necessary to prepare a student for the final examination. These assignments are submitted consecutively by mail or in person to the Office of Independent Study for correction by the instructor. The instructor corrects the assignments, makes comments, and grades lessons so that they may be returned to the student to serve as progress reports. For the audio-enhanced courses, access to an audiocassette tape player/recorder is required. For video-enhanced courses, access to a videocassette player (VCR) is required.

In addition to college-level courses listed below, LSU Independent Study offers several high school-level courses that are audio- and video-enhanced. These include English I and II, Fine Arts Survey—Music and Arts, Fine Arts Survey—Art and Drama, French, and Spanish. Carnegie units are awarded upon completion of high school courses. See below for course descriptions.

Accreditation: SACS

Official/Contact: Donald W. Hammons, Director, Independent Study

Admission Requirements: Admission to college-level courses does not constitute admission to a degree program at the university.

Tuition: $50 per semester hour. Audio-enhanced courses require an additional payment of a $5 tape purchase fee. Video-enhanced courses require a $10 rental fee plus a $25 deposit (refunded in full when the video is returned). Textbooks must be purchased by the student and can be obtained locally or from the LSU Bookstore, 101 Union Building, Baton Rouge, LA 70803 (504) 388-5500. High school courses are $70 per 1/2 unit. Audio and video rental fees are the same as for college-level courses as cited above.

Degree Credit: The Office of Independent Study does not offer an external degree program. Credit earned may be accepted toward a degree by LSU. Students who wish to use credit earned at LSU to fulfill degree requirements at another university should obtain approval from the appropriate authority at the institution to which credit is to be transferred and should make certain that the courses selected will be accepted by the institution from which a degree is sought.

Grading: Grades of A, B, and C are given for satisfactory work. D is passing but unsatisfactory. An F indicates work failed. The minimum passing grade varies according to course/instructor. Exams must be proctored. Credit is awarded in semester hour units.

Library: The LSU library is available if the student is in the vicinity. No mailing of materials can be done.

COURSES OFFERED

English

Introduction to Drama and Poetry
Study and appreciation of these types of literature. (3 credits)

English—II, 2nd Semester
Essays, plays, poetry, and Shakespeare's *Julius Caesar*. Video-enhanced. 12 assignments, 2 exams. High school level. (1/2 unit)

Fine Arts

Fine Arts Survey—Music and Dance
A nontechnical introduction to various facets of music and dance as art forms, basic terms and concepts, personalities and history of music and dance. Audio- and video-enhanced. 12 assignments, 2 exams. High school level. (1/2 unit)

Fine Arts Survey—Art and Drama
Introduction to visual and dramatic arts, including the development, history, philosophy, and principles of art. Production of art work in various media, elements of drama and their interrelationships. 12 assignments, 2 exams. High school level. (1/2 unit)

French

Elementary French (1001)
Basic lexicon and structure of French with emphasis on communicative language use. Supplementary work in language lab. Audio-enhanced. 21 assignments, 3 exams. (4 credits)

Elementary French (1002)
For students with no previous study of French. Basic lexicon and structure of French. Emphasis on communicative language use. Supplementary work in language lab. Audio-enhanced. 21 assignments, 3 exams. (4 credits)

Intermediate French (2101)
Structures and lexicon of French. Additional emphasis on reading and writing. Audio-enhanced. 17 assignments, 2 exams. (3 credits)

French—I, 1st Semester
A high-school-level course. Beginning French with emphasis on development of pronunciation, listening comprehension, reading, and writing skills. Recorded exercises used for drill in pronunciation and listening comprehension. 12 assignments, 2 exams. (1/2 unit)

French—I, 2nd Semester
A continuation of the 1st Semester, high-school-level course. Audio-enhanced. 12 assignments, 2 exams. (1/2 unit)

French—II, 1st Semester
A continuation of high-school-level French I. Audio-enhanced. 12 assignments, 2 exams. (1/2 unit)

French—II, 2nd Semester
A continuation of the 1st Semester course. Audio-enhanced. 12 assignments, 2 exams. (1/2 unit)

German

Elementary German (1101)
Basic lexicon and structures of German. Emphasis on communicative language use. Audio-enhanced. 25 assignments, 2 exams. (4 credits)

Elementary German (1102)
A continuation of 1101. Audio-enhanced. 25 assignments, 2 exams. (4 credits)

Intermediate German (2101)
Reading, conversation, review of lexicon and structure. Audio-enhanced. 17 assignments, 2 exams. (3 credits)

Intermediate German (2102)
A continuation of 2101. Audio-enhanced. (3 credits)

Readings in German Literature
Analysis of literary text. Expansion of lexicon, comprehension, composition skills. Audio-enhanced. 15 assignments, 2 exams. (3 credits)

Music

Music Appreciation (1751)
The art of music, with emphasis on listening skills. A nontechnical approach to understanding vocabulary and materials of music. Correlation of musical literature with other disciplines in the humanities. Audio-enhanced. 12 assignments, 1 exam. (3 credits)

Music Appreciation (1752)

The varied facets of the musical arts: folk music, symphony, opera, ballet, vocal, and chamber music. Audio-enhanced. 12 assignments, 1 exam. (3 credits)

Music of the Baroque and Classic Eras

History of music from circa 1600 to 1815. Audio-enhanced. 11 assignments, 1 exam. (2 credits)

Music of Romantic and Modern Eras

History of music from circa 1815 to the present. Audio-enhanced. 11 assignments, 1 exam. (2 credits)

Music Appreciation (117)

A nontechnical, high-school-level introduction to music with emphasis on history and humanities. Audio-enhanced. 12 assignments, 2 exams. (1/2 unit)

Spanish

Elementary Spanish (1101)

For students with no preparation in Spanish. Basic lexicon and structures of Spanish. Emphasis on communicative language use. Audio-enhanced. 25 assignments, 2 exams. (4 credits)

Elementary Spanish (1102)

A continuation of 1101. Audio-enhanced. 25 assignments, 1 exam. (4 credits)

Spanish—I, 1st Semester

A high-school-level course. Beginning course in Spanish with emphasis on development of pronunciation, listening comprehension, and reading and writing skills. Cassette tape recorded exercises used for drills in pronunciation and listening comprehension. Audio-enhanced. 15 assignments, 2 exams. (1/2 unit)

Spanish—I, 2nd Semester

A continuation of the 1st Semester, high-school-level course. Audio-enhanced. 12 assignments, 2 exams. (1/2 unit)

Spanish—II, 1st Semester

A continuation of high-school-level Spanish I. Audio-enhanced. 12 assignments, 2 exams. (1/2 unit)

Spanish—II, 2nd Semester

A continuation of high-school-level Spanish II, 1st Semester. Audio-enhanced. 12 assignments, 2 exams. (1/2 unit)

Speech

Interpersonal Communication

Theories and research in human communication. One-to-one interaction. 17 assignments, 2 exams. (3 credits)

Argumentation and Debate

Principles of argumentation and debate, including analysis, briefing, evidence, reasoning, and refutation. Audio- and video-enhanced. 17 assignments, 1 exam. (3 credits)

Zoology

Human Physiology

Elements of human physiology. Controls and functions of the various organ systems. Video-enhanced. 16 assignments, 2 exams. (3 credits)

Maine

University of Maine at Augusta
Office of Distance Education
University Heights
Augusta, ME   04330-9410

(207) 621-3404 *Fax:* (207) 621-3405

Geographic Access: Maine

DELIVERY SYSTEMS

Interactive Audio/Video
Courses are offered to students over the Education Network of Maine from 7:00 a.m. until 10:00 p.m. on weekdays and from 7:00 a.m. until noon on Saturdays. Students in the remote ITV classrooms are taught by a professor who is simultaneously teaching to a classroom of students on campus. In the electronic classroom, one camera focuses on the instructor while another scans charts, diagrams, or other visual materials. The instructor and visual images are electronically transmitted to the remote sites where the students can see and hear the instructor on television monitors. An audio talk-back system permits students in the distant locations to interact with the instructor and with other students.

INSTITUTION DESCRIPTION

As the community college of the University of Maine System, the University of Maine (UMA) at Augusta has primary responsibility for off-campus associate degree education. As such, UMA selects and schedules the courses and faculty for associate-level degree programs offered on the network. Because of the statewide enrollment possibilities, network-delivered courses are not canceled for lack of sufficient enrollment, allowing small communities to offer the populations a full-range of college courses.

The extended off-campus network of courses and services are offered via the Education Network of Maine. The interactive television system (ITV) was designed and built for UMA by the Maine Public Broadcasting System in 1988. A three-channel audio and video fiber optic spine, leased from New England Telephone, connects electronic classrooms located at each of the University of Maine System campuses. At each of these seven campuses, the classroom signal is broadcast from one transmitter to the multiple receive antennae at the various receive sites. The signal can be transmitted from each campus throughout its own geographic region or throughout the entire state.

Accreditation: NEASC

Official/Contact: Jane Russo, Assistant Director, Distance Education

Admission Requirements: High school graduation or GED. Undergraduate degree candidates from University of Maine System who enroll in classes through UMA should complete a transcript request form from the Admissions and Records Office to aid in the transfer of credit to the appropriate campus.

Tuition: In-state undergraduate $82 per credit hour, graduate $116; out-of-state undergraduate $200 per credit hour, graduate $328. On-campus cost for an ITV course may vary from campus to campus. MasterCard and VISA accepted. Textbooks may be ordered from the UMA Bookstore (800) 621-0083. All syllabi for ITV courses are distributed through the Bookstore.

Degree Credit: Four degree programs are offered statewide, on a part-time basis, over the Education Network of Maine: (1) Associate of Science in General Studies; (2)Associate of Arts in Liberal Arts (comparable to the first half of most traditional bachelor of arts programs); (3) Associate of Arts in Social Services; (4) Associate of Science in Business Administration.

Grading: Letter grades (A-F) area assigned. Examinations must be proctored. Credit is awarded in semester hour units.

Library: Students have access to URSUS, the university's computerized public access catalog. This database lists the book holdings, periodicals, and state and federal documents of the University of Maine System. Journal articles may be searched through the Colorado Alliance of Research Libraries (CARL) or through INFOTRAC which includes an expanded index of academic, business, and health journals. Students may order materials from their computer terminal and have them sent directly to a specified location.

COURSES OFFERED

Architecture

Introductory Design Theory and Architecture Application and Expression

An introduction to basic design theory, and its application in architecture and daily living. Design process will be explored as a critical thinking, problem-solving activity. The course will include creativity, architectural space and its creation, scale relatedness, the effect of natural light on mood, and the architecture/behavior relationship. The course is not intended as a design-your-own-home or drafting or CAD course. For non-architecture majors only. (3 credits)

Art History

Art Appreciation and History I

Techniques and trends in architecture, sculpture, and painting as related to the history of art from prehistoric times through the Gothic period. Lectures, text, slides, and discussion. (3 credits)

Business

Introduction to Business

A survey of the business and management functions found in modern organizational environs. Course objectives are to provide a career orientation for students and a content foundation for future courses. (3 credits)

Principles of Accounting I

An introductory course in accounting. Emphasis is on the basic accounting cycle, management use of accounting data, construction and analysis of financial statements, asset valuation, and elementary cost analysis. (3 credits)

Principles of Accounting II

Books of original entry, analysis of assets and liabilities, negotiable instruments, and an introduction to partnership and corporation. (3 credits)

Intermediate Accounting I

A study of accounting theory including the conceptual framework, financial statements, the accounting for cash, temporary investments, receivables, and inventories. (3 credits)

Principles of Management

A comprehensive study of management in public and private sectors. The influence of human, social, and political factors are integrated with treatment of managers' structural and technical processes. Analyses focus on such theories as planning, controlling, decision making, organizational design, administrative skills, communications and information systems. (3 credits)

Business Ethics

A discussion of the principles and norms that guide responsible and ethical decision making within the business context. Course focuses on the development of value systems in organizational cultures along with methods of analysis of personal standards of behavior within the same context. (3 credits)

Business Finance

The use of data to reach business financial decisions. The concepts of projecting data for decision purposes is emphasized. Short and long term sources of financing, ratio analysis, leverage, break-even, capital budgeting, working-capital management, investments and dividend policy are examined. (3 credits)

Cost Accounting I

The principles of job order costs, including control and pricing, labor and analysis, and allocation of factory overhead. Principles and practices of process accounting. (3 credits)

Organizational Behavior

An analysis of the interaction between individual and work group behavior, leadership styles, and organizational cultures. Applications of behavioral sciences are made in areas of motivation and influence, structure of work, leader group relations, organizational design and change. Emphasis is on application of theory in case studies and simulations. (3 credits)

Communications

Interpersonal Communications

Concerned with verbal and nonverbal communication that takes place among individuals during interpersonal interaction. Typical areas of concern are perceiving others, presenting one's self, conversation and barriers to communication. Activities include games, exercises, and role playing. (3 credits)

Criminal Justice

Foundations of Justice II

This course is designed to provide a broad perspective of the structure and interrelationships of the criminal justice system, its personnel, and their functions, with emphasis placed on the investigation of issues that determine policy and decision making. (3 credits)

Economics

Principles of Economics I (Macroeconomics)

Deals with the economy as a whole, including a study of different economic organizations, income and employment theory, government fiscal and monetary policies, problems of price stability and economic growth. (3 credits)

Education

Management of Adult/Continuing Education Organizations

An introduction to the concept, functions, and tasks of management in relation to adult/continuing education organizations. Also examines managerial behavior and style. A graduate-level education course. (3 credits)

Preventing Early School Literacy Failure

This course will prepare teams of K-2 teachers and administrators, across two semesters, to implement research-based school practices to prevent early school literacy failure. *Prerequisite:* Participants must be in districts that are implementing Reading Recovery through a certified Teacher Training Center linked with the University of Maine College of Education. A graduate-level course. (3 credits)

Legal Responsibilities in Early Childhood Education

Focus on legal responsibilities relating to licensing of facilities and on the requirements of the state departments responsible for preschool programs, including basic information about laws governing child care services and legal and ethical considerations in dealing with individual parents and children. (2 credits)

English

College Writing

Intensive practice in expository writing with reading of illustrative materials. (3 credits)

Introduction to Literature

A general introduction to literary genres: the essay, short story, novel, drama, and poetry—including a study of critical terminology, close textual reading, and practice in writing. (3 credits)

Environmental Science

Understanding the Global Environment

A broad view of today's environmental problems, including human population, dynamics, pollution, energy, and basic ecological concepts. Problems are examined from the scientific, sociological and political points of view. Course is designed to acquaint students of varied backgrounds and interests with the urgency of environmental problems and the need for citizen participation in helping to solve these problems. (3 credits)

Government

American Government

Introduces principles and practices of American government. Studies the institution, the politics of democracy, and briefly considers the three branches of government. (3 credits)

History

Foundations of Western Civilization I

A survey of western civilization from its beginnings to the sixteenth century. Examines such topics as the special role of the Greeks in defining and shaping the civilization, the grandeur of Rome, the rise of Christianity, the evolution of western institutions during the Middle Ages, and the rebirth of the West in the Renaissance. (3 credits)

United States History I

From the exploration of America to 1877. The development of democracy, growth of the West, slavery and sectionalism, the Civil War, and Reconstruction. (3 credits)

Topics: Life Along the Kennebec River

An intensive study of life along the Kennebec River from prehistoric times to the present. Leading scholars, experts and authors will make presentations. Topics will include early native culture, Fort Western, area geology, and midwifery and the Franco experience. (3 credits)

Marketing

Marketing

Problems of distribution for representative industrial and consumer goods, including merchandising policies, selection of distribution channels, price policies, and advertising and sales promotion methods. (3 credits)

Mathematics

Foundations of Mathematics

This course emphasizes arithmetic computations and an introduction to algebra. Some of the topics included are elementary number theory, operations with fractions, decimals, integers and rational numbers, ratios, proportions, percents, algebraic equations, and the use of equations in problem solving. (3 credits)

Algebra I

Topics include real numbers, algebraic expressions, first degree equations in one variable, polynomials, factoring, rational expressions, graphing and exponents. Problem solving and informal geometry will be integrated throughout the course. (3 credits)

Mathematics for Business and Economics I

This course is designed to provide mathematical concepts and relevant application required by undergraduate students in business administration and related areas. Topics include applications of algebra, linear systems, matrix algebra, and linear programming. (3 credits)

Medical Laboratory Science

Medical Laboratory Techniques I

Orientation to the clinical laboratory stressing care and use of basic equipment, basic terminology, microscopy of urine, gastric contents and feces, and parasitology. (4 credits)

Meteorology

Meteorology

An introduction to the study of weather and weather-related phenomena including solar radiation, temperature, moisture, winds, air pressure, air masses, weather patterns, weather analysis, weather forecasting, climate, weather instruments, and computers. Upon completion of this course the student should have a qualitative understanding of how many of the basic principles of physics, chemistry, and mathematics are applied in meteorology, and ability to relate personal weather observations to data received from weather instruments and analyzed on standard weather charts. (4 credits)

Music

Understanding Music

A study of the basic elements of music necessary for intelligent listening, with emphasis on various historical movements, together with a study of the great composers and their contrasting styles as exemplified by their most important compositions. For the non-music major. (3 credits)

Nursing

Fundamentals of Nursing

This course enables the student to identify and explore concepts that form the basis for the practice of holistic nursing. Emphasis is placed on the unifying concepts of basic human needs and the nursing process. The focus is on an individual's state of health with attention to common stressors that can create interruptions in need attainment. The nursing process is introduced as the methodology that provides the basic structure for nursing practice. Students must pay an additional $30 nursing fee. (6 credits)

Nutrition

Human Nutrition

This course examines the basic concepts of human nutrition and their application to the needs of human beings throughout the life cycle. Discussion of factors affecting food practices and attitudes is included. (3 credits)

Philosophy

Introduction to Philosophy

Critical examination of philosophical writings on traditional philosophical problems, such as the existence of God, freedom and determinism, the mind-body problem, the nature of knowledge, the meaning of life. (3 credits)

Psychology

Introduction to Psychology

This is a basic course in the psychology sequence. Topics covered include background and methods, learning theories, brain and nervous system, personality, perception, intelligence, motivation, emotions, thinking and problem solving, human development, abnormal behavior, and social interaction. (3 credits)

Introduction to Community Health Care

An overview of the community health care movement. Emphasis will be on contemporary community mental health care, particularly services offered in the state of Maine. Course format primarily consists of a series of prominent speakers, panel discussions, and dialogues. (3 credits)

Psychosocial Rehabilitation I

Examines the basic principles of psychosocial rehabilitation with focus on client assessment, planning, intervention, and rehabilitation service strategies. Psychosocial rehabilitation approaches are applied to mental health and social service systems. (3 credits)

Crisis Identification and Intervention

A study of the areas of behavior that typically bring intervention, with particular focus on abuse of children, spouses, and the elderly and on severe depression. Students will learn to identify behaviors that indicate such crises, personal skills and modes of intervention, and appropriate referral tactics. Issues of personal, social, and legal relevance will be covered. (3 credits)

Topics: Models of Addiction

A comprehensive overview of the process of addiction, identifying characteristics including physical, psychological/emotional and behavioral mechanisms and symptoms will be examined. The model will be applied to identification of, strategies for, intervening in, and treatment of the disorder in general and special populations. (3 credits)

Human Development

Introduces the student to principles of human development. Human development provides a life span approach focusing on the physical, mental, emotional, social, and spiritual characteristics of individuals. Emphasis will be placed on psychological stages and needs. (3 credits)

Psychology of Childhood

A systematic study of the child's behavior and psychological development. Emphasis upon principles underlying development, methods of child study, and practical implications. (3 credits)

Real Estate

Real Estate Practice

Content will focus on ethics, financing, negotiations, real estate as an investment, fundamental elements of commercial transactions, listing and sales of condominiums, and other real estate functions. (3 credits)

Social Services

Introduction to Social Service Systems

An introduction to social welfare systems and their functions as they relate to social needs and problems within the political, social, and economic context. An overview of the history and development of social welfare systems, the range of current social services and the knowledge and skills necessary for responding to human needs are presented. (3 credits)

Chemical Dependency Counseling

The course is designed for those with experience or training in chemical dependency counseling. Areas covered include treatment process with emphasis on group process, behavioral counseling techniques and theory, human development with emphasis on adolescence and adulthood. (3 credits)

Case Management

Building upon an understanding of the social systems model, this course examines the various approaches to case management in mental health and social service settings. Content areas address history and concept, stages of engagement, assessment, planning, linkage, coordination, advocacy, disengagement, and organization supports. (3 credits)

Public Policy in the Chemical Dependency Field

This course provides an overview of public policy definition, its development, implementation, and its effect on the social services professional. Past alcohol and drug policy in the United States is reviewed. Focus will include current Maine alcohol and drug policies and how Maine citizens can influence policy. (3 credits)

Sociology

Introduction to Sociology

A general study of people in society, with emphasis on the nature of culture, social institutions, social interaction, social units, and the influence on the individual. An overview of sociological concepts and perspectives is also presented. (3 credits)

Sociology of Aging

Analysis of the demographic and sociocultural factors in aging, the aging individual as a person, older people as groups and aggregates within the culture and structure of a changing society, the manner in which society attempts to meet the needs of aging people. (3 credits)

Social Gerontology

Emphasizes the social aspects of the aging process, focusing upon the aging individual as a person and older people as groups within a changing society. In particular, the impact of aging upon the individual and society, and the reactions of the individual and society to aging are examined. (3 credits)

Special Education

Curriculum and Instructional Programming for Exceptional Children

Study of curricula and general teaching strategies appropriate for pupils with mild to moderate handicapping conditions. Topics include learning characteristics of pupils, direct instruction strategies, behavioral objectives and task analysis, data-based reinforcement strategies, and developing lesson plans. (3 credits)

Pre-Vocational Instructions for Students with Disabilities or at Risk

This course is intended to help students understand the process of transitions from the years of early intervention through the worlds of work and independent living. It will also help students identify and understand ways of teaching skills that lead to success in community and work environments as well as the school environment, identifying which skills are necessary and appropriate for students with different ability levels and different handicapping conditions. The academic areas focused on in this course are mathematics and oral and written communication. (3 credits)

Maryland

Allegany Community College
See **College of the Air**

Anne Arundel Community College
See **College of the Air**

Baltimore City Community College
See **College of the Air**

Bowie State University
See **College of the Air**

Carroll Community College
See **College of the Air**

Catonsville Community College
See **College of the Air**

Cecil Community College
See **College of the Air**

Charles County Community College
See **College of the Air**

Chesapeake College
See **College of the Air**

College of the Air
Maryland Public Television
11767 Owings Mills Boulevard
Owings Mills, MD   21117

(410) 356-5600

Geographic Access: Maryland, Pennsylvania, Virginia

DELIVERY SYSTEMS

Broadcast Television
Telecourses are broadcast over local PBS stations and in some cases over local cable networks.

INSTITUTION DESCRIPTION

College of the Air was organized in 1970 by Maryland Public Television with the cooperation of the Community College of Baltimore, Essex Community College, and Catonsville Community College. The initial effort was centered on the Baltimore area because at that time, MPT operated only a single transmitter in the Baltimore area. As MPT expanded its network to six stations across the state, additional colleges were added to the Consortium. Today, College of the Air is a regional consortium. Twenty-eight colleges and universities in Maryland, northern Virginia, and Pennsylvania work cooperatively with Maryland Public Television to provide telecourses to students who cannot take the traditional on-campus courses.

There is no formal contract between Maryland Public Television and the participating colleges, and there are no membership or initiation fees. The project is run essentially on a gentleman's agreement with the colleges free to use all or a portion of the courses selected. It is not unusual for an institution to decide to offer all of the courses in one semester, and the following semester choose just a few.

Courses are selected twice a year by the representative of the Consortium members. They choose the courses that are televised by Maryland Public Television and another group of courses that are broadcast only on local cable systems. A few of the colleges that do not have access to a cable system make the cable courses available to their students by placing videocassette copies of the TV lessons in the Learning Center where the student can check out the tapes just like a book. The selection of courses is accomplished a year in advance.

MPT's College of the Air staff is the administrative arm of the Consortium. MPT is responsible for providing preview tapes and course materials, leasing the courses, and paying all of the telecourse fees to the producers or distributors.

The students belong to the individual institution that registers them. Therefore, the students must meet the registration, examination, attendance, and prerequisite requirements of that college. The requirements may differ from one institution to another. Participating institutions and representatives to contact are:

- Allegany Community College (Cumberland MD), Gloria Stafford, (301) 724-7700, x209
- Anne Arundel Community College (Arnold MD), Mary Barnes, (410) 541-2464
- Baltimore City Community College (Baltimore MD), Synethia Jones, (410) 333-5585
- Bowie State University (Bowie MD), Dr. Ida Brandon, (301) 464-6586
- Carroll Community College (Westminster MD), Paul McAdam, (410) 876-9615
- Catonsville Community College (Catonsville MD), John Sneed, (410) 455-4179
- Cecil Community College (North East MD), Charles Hockersmith, (410) 287-6060
- Charles County Community College (La Plata MD), Jean Fuller, (301) 934-2251, x615
- Chesapeake College (Wye Mills MD), John Bronson, (410) 822-5400, x379
- Dundalk Community College (Dundalk MD), Chuck Kisner, (410) 285-9785
- Essex Community College (Baltimore MD), Rosalie Russell, (410) 780-6749
- Frederick Community College (Frederick MD), Kathy Wood, (301) 846-2400, x2557
- Garrett Community College (McHenry MD), Lillian Mitchell, (301) 387-6666

- Hagerstown Junior College (Hagerstown MD), Dr. Michael H. Parsons, (301) 790-2800, x231
- Harford Community College (Bel Air MD), Norman Tracy, (410) 879-8920, x282
- Harrisburg Area Community College (Harrisburg PA), Dr. Larry Adams, (717) 780-2306
- Howard Community College (Columbia MD), JoAnn Hawkins, (410) 992-4824
- Lehigh County Community College (Schnecksville PA), David Voros, (215) 799-1196
- Montgomery College (Rockville MD), Connie L. Cox, (301) 279-5254
- Montgomery County Community College (Blue Bell PA), Dr. Allan Carlson, (215) 641-6300
- Reading Area Community College (Reading PA), Carol Alspach, (215) 372-4721, x240
- Towson State University (Towson MD), Frank Mullen, (410) 830-2032
- Westmoreland County Community College (Youngwood PA), Dr. Mary Stubbs, (412) 925-4097
- Wor-Wic Tech Community College (Salisbury MD), Dr. Diane Lesser, (410) 749-6030.

Accreditation: MSA (member institutions)

Official/Contact: Mary Ann Spangler, Coordinator

Admission Requirements: Enrollment requirements may vary among the institutional members of the Consortium.

Tuition: Varies by institution.

Degree Credit: In most cases, credit awarded for successful completion of a telecourse is acceptable toward an associate degree.

Grading: Grade system and examination policy is set by the participating institutions. Credit is awarded according to the standards of the college/university, usually three credits per course.

Library: Students have access to the learning resource centers of the various institutions in which they are enrolled.

COURSES OFFERED

Art

Art of the Western World

This course examines the works of art that have come to define the Western visual tradition from ancient Greece to the present day.

Astronomy

Project Universe

This introductory astronomy course acquaints students with the origin, characteristics, and evolution of the solar system, the stars, the galaxies, and the universe.

Business

Business File

An introductory business course providing an overview of the contemporary business environment. The course presents leading scholars and corporate executives discussing business theory and its practical application. Topics covered include types of businesses, marketing, managing, accounting, business law, productivity, and technology.

Business and the Law

This introductory level course in business law emphasizes contracts and the legal system.

By the Numbers

This course explores business math from mathematical foundations to basic business concepts, and the role it plays in our professional and personal lives.

Something Ventured: Small Business Management

This small business management course provides entrepreneurs with the tools they need to compete effectively in the world of business.

Chemistry

The World of Chemistry

An introductory-level course developed for non-science majors. Stresses a humanistic approach to chemistry and de-emphasizes mathematical problem solving.

Child Development

A Time to Grow

This child development course is not only an integral part of study for psychology, education, and health-care students, it is also a basic component of child-care certificate programs and the foundation for parenting classes.

Computer Literacy

The New Literacy

An introductory course on data processing that prepares students to use computers in their personal and professional lives. It introduces students to terminology and examines how the computer can be applied to a range of organizational settings.

Computer Science

ComputerWorks

This course gives students the chance to gain familiarity with different types of computers, use and evaluate word processing, spreadsheet, graphics, database, accounting, communications, and publishing software programs.

Economics

Economics U$A

A comprehensive course in macro- and microeconomics covering basic principles: supply and demand, competition, efficiency, the business cycle, fiscal policy, inflation, deficits, and more.

English

Literary Visions

This introduction to literature brings literature to life with dramatizations, readings, and commentary from scholars and writers. By placing a strong emphasis on writing about literature, the course also teaches advanced compositional skills.

English Literature I

This first semester literature course stresses the interpretation of the individual literary works of authors from Beowulf to Henry Fielding.

English Literature II

This second semester literature course examines and interprets the works of authors from Wordsworth to Eliot.

The Write Course

An introductory English composition and rhetoric course taught from a "process" point of view. It presents deliberate strategies for pre-writing and revision as well as developing basic writing skills including composing effective sentences, paragraphs, and essays.

Environmental Science

Race to Save the Planet

This environmental science course explores the relationships between human society and the earth's natural resources.

Family Life

Portrait of a Family

An interdisciplinary course that takes a look at marriage, family, and alternative life styles in the closing decade of the twentieth century.

Finance

Personal Finance and Money Management

A personal finance course that covers basic skills students need to manage their money, e.g., budgeting, income tax and investments, and the wise use of insurance, wills, and trusts.

Gerontology

Growing Old in a New Age

This gerontology and health sciences course helps students understand the process of aging and its impact on the lives of the individual and society.

Health

Living with Health

This introductory health course encourages students to take a proactive stance toward maintaining health, with focus on the lifestyle components that encourage wellness. It encompasses all areas of health: the physical, emotional, social, intellectual, and spiritual.

History

American Adventure

The first semester of American history, covering the period from the discovery of the new world through the Civil War and Reconstruction. The course vividly illustrates how wars and treaties, elections and legislation affected the people of the United States and helped develop America's democratic spirit.

Western Tradition I

The first semester of a two-semester course in Western civilizations. Covers the Middle Ages to the Renaissance. It weaves together history, art, literature, religion, geography, government and economics to help students recognize the pendulum swings of history, identify parallels in the modern world, and gain a sense of their own place in the evolution of human institutions.

America in Perspective: U.S. History Since 1877

This second-semester history course provides an analytical frame of reference for U.S. events after the Civil War, including Native Americans, immigrants, minorities, Spanish-American War, World Wars I and II, the Vietnam War, and the end of the Cold War.

Civil War

Interweaving primary sources such as dramatic archival photos, period music, and rare news reel footage, this course provides students with an intimate understanding of the Civil War and its aftermath.

Humanities

Humanities Through the Arts

The humanities are approached through a study of nine major arts: film, dance, music, literature, photography, painting, theatre, sculpture, and architecture.

Mathematics

Introduction to Mathematics

A course for nonscience or math majors introducing students to the concepts and skills of linear equations, quadratic functions, systems of equations, matrices, and the mathematics of personal finance.

Management

Principles of Management

This course provides an introduction to the theories of management and business. Especially designed for managers without formal business training and undergraduates interested in a business career, the course provides essential information on planning, staffing, directing, decision making, motivating, and communicating.

Marketing

Marketing
This course provides an introduction to marketing as it relates to contemporary living and society's changing needs. Students learn how a marketing manager interacts with diverse areas of business, as well as basic marketing principles, including product, promotion, price and distribution, and their interrelationships.

Oceanography

Oceanus: The Marine Environment
This course focuses on the marine environment as a unique feature of the planet earth and investigates areas of intense scientific and public concern: the pervasiveness of the ocean and its effect on earth's weather, its stunning physical size and diversity of contained life forms, its contributions to the physical and historical development of man, the impact of oceanic pollutants and the potential exploitation of marine resources.

Political Science

Pacific Century
A survey of the modern history, economics, politics, and cultures of the Pacific Basin region.

Psychology

The World of Abnormal Psychology
This course examines the complex factors that cause behavioral disorders and demonstrates the psychological, biological, and social approaches to treatment and discusses current research.

Sociology

Sociological Imagination
This introductory-level sociology course is designed to give students an in-depth look at groups, communities, institutions, and social situations that illustrate major sociological concepts. The lessons, structured as documentaries, are thought provoking, emotionally strong illustrations of issues such as socialization, social control, sex and gender, aging, education, collective behavior, and social change.

Rural Communities: Legacy and Change
Visits fifteen diverse rural regions across the country, exploring the social problems faced by individuals, communities, and families.

Spanish

Destinos
This Spanish language course provides communicative proficiency in Spanish—listening, speaking, reading, and writing.

Statistics

Against All Odds
With this innovative introductory statistics course, students learn key statistical processes from the perspective of real people doing real statistical work.

Dundalk Community College
See **College of the Air**

Emergency Management Institute
Home Study Program
16825 South Seton Avenue
Emmitsburg, MD   21727-8998

(301) 447-1172

Geographic Access: Nationwide

DELIVERY SYSTEMS

Computer Tutorials
Computer-based training requires access to an IBM compatible personal computer with 640K memory and 5.25" diskette drive. This computer-based format is an option for course HS-3 and HS-6. The other courses listed are traditional correspondence-type courses whereby students study a textbook and mail in assignments.

INSTITUTION DESCRIPTION

The mission of the Emergency Management Institute is to serve as a national focal point for the development and delivery of emergency management technical training and professional education in order to enhance the mitigation, preparedness, response, and recovery capabilities of federal, state, and local government emergency managers and others in the public and private sectors who have responsibility for serving the public in time of disaster or emergency.

Lewis and Clark Community College (Illinois) is a Federal Emergency Management Agency (FEMA) contractor and administers the program. Upon completion of home study courses listed below, applicants may submit an application for one semester credit hour. Requests for credit must be in writing to the Emergency Management Institute.

Accreditation: The FEMA contractor, Lewis and Clark Community College (Godfrey, IL) is accredited by NCA.

Official/Contact: Gary L. Chase, Home Study Program Administrator

Admission Requirements: Courses HS1 through HS-5 and HS-7 are designed for both the general public and persons who have responsibility for emergency management. These courses require no prerequisites for enrollment. HS-6 is an emergency radio communications course and applicants must have responsibility for emergency radio communications to enroll.

Tuition: None. A $20 fee will be charged if the student applies for one semester hour of credit for each course completed.

Degree Credit: Credit awarded by Lewis and Clark Community College may be applied to a degree program if accepted by the student's home institution.

Grading: Examinations are open book. Pass/Fail grades are assigned. Minimum passing grade is 75%. Credit may be awarded in semester hour units.

Library: Students are encouraged to utilize the library facilities of their local communities.

COURSES OFFERED

Emergency Management

Emergency Program Manager (HS-1)

This first course in the study sequence covers the tasks and responsibilities of the Emergency Program Manager, emergency management functions, and the role of the emergency manager in mitigation, preparedness, response, and recovery. 8-12 hours of study required for completion.

Emergency Preparedness, USA (HS-2)

The topics in this course include natural and technological hazard risk analysis, application of the four phases of comprehensive emergency management, national security emergency, and the development of personal and community emergency plans. 10-12 hours of study required for completion.

Radiological Emergency Management (HS-3)

This course covers the fundamental principles of radiation, radiological transportation accidents, nuclear power plants, and nuclear attack and protective measures. 8-12 hours of study required for completion. This course is available in textbook and computer-based training formats.

Hazardous Materials: A Citizen's Orientation (HS-5)

The topics covered include hazardous materials and human health, hazardous materials regulation, identifying hazardous materials, preparing for hazardous materials incidents, and hazardous materials in the home. 10-14 hours of study required for completion.

Portable Emergency Data System (PEDS) (HS-6)

This course offers hands-on training with the Portable Emergency Data System (PEDS) and explains how PEDS can be utilized as an operational tool. Also covered are the identification of emergency response system frequencies: public safety, Civil Air Patrol, fire, police, and emergency management. Planning methods that support specific emergency communications are also included. 4 hours of study required for completion. This course requires an IBM compatible computer with 640K memory and a 5.25" diskette. Credit cannot be awarded for this course.

A Citizen's Guide to Disaster Assistance (HS-7)

The course gives an overview of disaster assistance, local and state response and recovery activities, federal disaster assistance, and the citizen's role in preparedness. 10-24 hours of study required for completion.

Essex Community College
See **College of the Air**

Frederick Community College
See **College of the Air**

Garrett Community College
See **College of the Air**

Hagerstown Junior College
See **College of the Air**

Harford Community College
See **College of the Air**

Home Study International
Collegiate Studies Program
12501 Old Columbia Pike
Silver Spring, MD   20904-4437

(301) 680-6570

Geographic Access: Worldwide

DELIVERY SYSTEMS

Audiocassette
All courses listed below require the use of audiocassettes for course enhancement and instruction.

INSTITUTION DESCRIPTION

Home Study International (HSI) was established in 1909. It has an enrollment of over 2,000 students, maintains six overseas branches, and provides traditional correspondence education for kindergarten, elementary, secondary, and college levels. Although designed to serve the needs of the Seventh-day Adventist school system, HSI has always welcomed anyone who wished to study whether for self-improvement or for upgrading in education.

The courses listed and described below are audio-enhanced correspondence courses. Students must have access to an audiocassette player.

Accreditation: DETC

Official/Contact: Alayne D. Thorpe, Education Director

Admission Requirements: For college courses, graduation from high school or equivalency certificate is required. At the discretion of HSI, students over 21 may be permitted to take college courses without a high school diploma.

Tuition: Enrollment fee of $60 for each application (which may include more than one course) plus $125 per semester hour. Textbooks, learning guides, and audiocassettes must be purchased by the student. Charges for cassettes are listed below with the course descriptions. MasterCard, VISA, and Discover Card accepted.

Degree Credit: HSI does not grant the baccalaureate degree, but its courses may be used as transfer credits to many colleges which do grant degrees. HSI courses may be used as transfer credits or as part of the external degree program at Columbia Union College.

Grading: Midterm and final examinations must be supervised by a school official or a responsible adult who is not a member of the student's family. Letter grades (A, B, C, D, F) are assigned. Minimum passing grade is D-. Credit is awarded in semester hour units.

Library: Students are encouraged to utilize the library facilities of their local communities.

COURSES OFFERED

Biology

A Scientific Study of Creation
A study of the evidences supporting a creative origin of the earth. The approach is scientific, rather than biblical. 2 audiocassettes: $8. (2 credits)

Business

Typing
A skill-building course for the development of speed and accuracy. An introduction to typing letters, reports, tables, and forms. 4 audiocassettes: $16. (4 credits)

Fine Arts

Music Appreciation
The development of a basic understanding of music and a training for sensitivity in music listening. 6 audiocassettes: $40. (3 credits)

French

French I
An introduction to written and spoken French through a study of basic vocabulary and grammar. Listening and speaking skills developed with audio-

cassette tapes and notes on phonetics. Includes information about French culture. 1st semester requires 4 audiocassettes: $14. 2nd semester requires 5 audiocassettes: $18. (4 credits)

Religious Studies

Prophetic Guidance

This is a study of one of the principal means by which God communicates with people. The work of His prophets in Old Testament times is explained. The tests and functions of a true prophet are examined. The works and life of Mrs. E.G. White and God's influence on His remnant church through her are stressed. 6 audiocassettes: $24. (2 credits)

Spanish

Spanish I

A study of simple spoken and written Spanish with a small amount of practice in writing and speaking. Audiocassette tapes build accurate pronunciation and provide listening exercises. 1st semester requires 7 audiocassettes: $28. 2nd semester requires 5 audiocassettes: $24. (4 credits)

Spanish II

The reading, grammar, and composition needed for a better knowledge of the language. Continued practice with spoken Spanish. 14 audiocassettes: $42. (4 credits)

Howard Community College
See **College of the Air**

Montgomery College
See **College of the Air**

Prince George's Community College

Office of Telecommunications

301 Largo Road
Largo, MD   20772-2199

(301) 322-0785

Geographic Access: Maryland

DELIVERY SYSTEMS

Broadcast Television

Access to campus channel PGCC-TV, MetroVision, Multivision, or public television station WMPT-22 is required. The components of a telecourse include a series of television programs, a comprehensive study guide, an academic textbook, and an on-campus instructor.

Videocassette

Students can rent videocassettes from the College Video Corporation, an educational video distributor responsible for the mail distribution of tapes to students. Under this option, students pay an additional $57.50 fee to have the tapes sent directly to their homes.

INSTITUTION DESCRIPTION

Prince George's Community College was founded in 1958 and began as an evening college with classes at Suitland High School. It has occupied the Largo campus since 1967. The college offers two-year programs in business administration, liberal arts, engineering, teacher education, engineering technology, health technologies, computer sciences, and public service technology. The college operates on the semester system and offers two summer sessions.

In 1993, 560 students enrolled in telecourse sections. The college's cable access channel PGCC-TV, MetroVision (A-24), MultiVision (B-25), and Maryland Public Television station WMPT-22 bring college credit telecourses to the home or workplace for students who need or desire this convenience. Students also have the opportunity to study at home by viewing telecourses on videocassettes.

Accreditation: MSA

Official/Contact: Robert I. Bickford, President

Admission Requirements: High school graduation or GED. Other students must be 16 years of age and have officially withdrawn from elementary or secondary school. For a degree-seeking student, an official transcript should be sent to the Office of Admissions and Records. Other students may register through the Largo campus or any extension center. Telecredit courses usually have registration deadlines and some courses require the completion of prerequisites.

Tuition: County residents $55 per credit hour; out-of-county residents $118 per credit hour; out-of-state residents $199 per credit hour. Registration fee $20; instructional services fee $15, $20, or $25, depending on course level (I, II, or III). MasterCard and VISA accepted.

Degree Credit: The PGCC's Telecredit Program has made it possible for nontraditional students to complete, through telecourses, almost all of the requirements for an associate of arts degree in general studies or in business management. Any telecredit course may also be taken for noncredit (regular tuition applies).

Grading: The letter grade system is used (A-F). Examinations must be taken at the PGCC Testing Center during specified hours. Credit is awarded in semester hour units.

Library: Telelessons are kept on videocassettes in the Learning Media Center (LMC). Missed lessons can be obtained on a rental basis or can be viewed in the LMC.

COURSES OFFERED

Accounting

Principles of Accounting I
Presents the process of accounting, the theory and principles of the language of business, and application of accounting practices to everyday business. TV title: *Accounting I.* (3 credits)

Anthropology

Introduction to Cultural Anthropology
Introduces cultural anthropology and highlights major lifestyles from around the world. Human adaptation to the environment and the balance between individual rights and public safety are presented. TV title: *Faces of Culture.* (3 credits)

Astronomy

Introduction to Astronomy
Introduces astronomy. Examines the origin, characteristics, and evolution of the solar system, the stars, the galaxies, and the universe. Includes speculative theories. TV title: *Project Universe.* (3 credits)

Business Administration

Introduction to Business
Provides a comprehensive view of the contemporary business environment, from internal functions to the

challenges of conducting international business. TV title: *The Business File.* (3 credits)

Principles of Management
An introductory course on the concept of management and business. Describes essential managerial skills and how to apply them. TV title: *Business of Management.* (3 credits)

Small Business Management
Presents documentaries of a variety of small businesses in operation and shows firsthand what it is like to start and operate a small business. Experts analyze and assess the documentary footage. TV title: *Something Ventured.* (3 credits)

Business Law
An introductory law course. Emphasizes contracts and the legal system and gives a comprehensive overview of law and the world of business. TV title: *Business and the Law.* (3 credits)

Computer Science

Computer Literacy
A comprehensive overview of the computer: what it can and cannot do, how it operates. Introduces terminology of data processing and examines computer applications. TV title: *The New Literacy.* (3 credits)

Microcomputer Applications
Surveys and analyzes the use of microcomputers in the business environment and describes and shows the capabilities of commonly available microcomputer applications and programs. TV title: *ComputerWorks.* (3 credits)

Ecology

Human Ecology
Describes the threats that different natural systems face in the global environment. Explains the sciences involved and dissects the connections that bind humans to the environment. TV title: *The Race to Save the Planet.* (3 credits)

Economics

Introduction to Economics
A comprehensive course in micro- and macroeconomics. Establishes the relationship between abstract economic principles and concrete human ex-

perience through documentaries. TV title: *Economics U$A*. (3 credits)

English

Composition I: Expository Writing
Teaches English composition and rhetoric from a process point of view. Emphasizes audience awareness and purpose for writing and presents deliberate strategies for prewriting and revision. TV title: *The Write Course*. (3 credits)

Composition II: Introduction to Literature
Introductory literature course that incorporates contemporary and traditional works of short fiction, poetry, and drama. Examines literary elements, including character, plot, and symbolism. TV title: *Literary Visions*. (3 credits)

English Literature I
TV title: *English Literature I*. (3 credits)

Introduction to Creative Writing
TV title: *Writer's Workshop*. (3 credits)

Finance

Financial Planning
Teaches the basics of budgeting and buying, home ownership, income tax and investments, insurance, wills, and trusts. TV title: *Personal Finance*. (3 credits)

Geology

Introduction to Physical Geology
Studies the Earth's physical processes and properties and emphasizes the scientific theories behind geological principles. Presents dramatic forces as well as more subtle, ever-present ones. TV title: *Earth Revealed*. (3 credits)

Health

Personal and Community Health
TV title: *Living with Health*. (3 credits)

History

Ancient and Medieval History
Weaves together the history, art, literature, religion, geography, government, and economics from pre-Western civilization through the Renaissance and

the Wars of Religion to the present. TV title: *The Western Tradition*. (3 credits)

United States History I
Illustrates how wars and treaties, elections, and legislation have affected the people of the U.S. from Columbian contact to the Civil War and Reconstruction. TV title: *The American Adventure*. (3 credits)

United States History II
Historians and eyewitnesses use an analytical frame of reference to judge past and present events. Explains how and why the U.S. is what it is today. Connects history to ordinary people. TV title: *America in Perspective*. (3 credits)

History of the American Civil War
Uses archival photographs to present the entire sweep of the Civil War from the battlefields to the homefronts and from the cause of the war to Lincoln's assassination. TV title: *The Civil War*. (3 credits)

History of the Vietnam War
Examines the historical and political context of the Vietnam era—its causes, record, and influence. Provides background on Vietnam and its people from 1945 to 1975. TV title: *Vietnam: A TV History*. (3 credits)

Management

Principles of Management
TV title: *Taking the Lead*. (3 credits)

Marketing

Introduction to Marketing
Presents basic principles of marketing as they apply to small businesses and large corporations. Uses real-world case histories. TV title: *Marketing*. (3 credits)

Mathematics

Algebra for Business and Social Science
TV title: *Introduction to Math*. (3 credits)

Oceanography

Introduction to Oceanography
Introduces the knowledge, theories, and predictions of North America's leading oceanographers. Fo-

cuses on the marine environment as a unique feature of the planet Earth. TV title: *Oceanus*. (3 credits)

Philosophy

Introduction to Philosophy
TV title: *From Socrates to Sartre*. (3 credits)

Contemporary Moral Values
Uses a case study approach to examine contemporary personal and professional ethical conflicts. Provides a grounding in the language, concepts, and traditions of ethics. TV title: *Ethics in America*. (3 credits)

Political Science

American National Government
Surveys United States government. Focuses on teaching students how to access their government. Combines political science with examples of how students involve themselves in government. TV title: *Government by Consent*. (3 credits)

Psychology

General Psychology
Introduces the fundamental principles and major concepts of psychology. Includes brain and behavior, life-span development, psychopathology and therapy, and methodology. TV title: *Discovering Psychology*. (3 credits)

Abnormal Psychology
Explores the complex causes, manifestations, and treatment of common behavior disorders. Shows abnormal behaviors along a continuum from functional to dysfunctional. TV title: *The World of Abnormal Psychology*. (3 credits)

Child Psychology
Addresses all aspects of children's physical, cognitive, and psychosocial development. Includes recent theoretical and applied perspectives on caring for and working with children. TV title: *Time to Grow*. (3 credits)

Religious Studies

Thinking About Religion
TV title: *Transformation of Myth*. (3 credits)

Science

Science and Society
Stresses a humanistic approach to chemistry that de-emphasizes mathematical problem solving. Presents chemical principles, facts, and theories. Includes the historical foundations of chemistry. TV title: *The World of Chemistry*. (3 credits)

Sociology

Introduction to Sociology
Introduces groups, communities, institutions, and social situations that illustrate major sociological concepts. Documentary structure covers such issues as social control and education. TV title: *Sociological Imagination*. (3 credits)

Human Growth and Development
Introduces life-span psychology. Examines significant events from infancy and early childhood to adolescence, early and middle adulthood, and late adulthood. TV title: *Seasons of Life*. (3 credits)

Marriage and the Family
Looks closely at marriage, family, and alternative lifestyles at the close of the twentieth century. Balances research and theory and examines personal choice. TV title: *Portrait of a Family*. (3 credits)

Towson State University
See **College of the Air**

University of Maryland University College
Open Learning Program
University Boulevard at Adelphi Road
College Park, MD   20742-1660

(301) 985-7722 *Fax:* (301) 985-4615

Geographic Access: Worldwide; Maryland for Interactive Television courses.

DELIVERY SYSTEMS

Computer Conferencing
Students may participate in online conferencing if access to a computer and a modem is available. After registration, students electing this option will be sent

an enrollment package that includes a syllabus, the *Computer Conferencing and Electronic-Mail User's Guide*, and other materials needed for the course.

Videocassette

These courses allow maximum flexibility. A syllabus is mailed at the beginning of the semester and faculty members are available by phone and mail. Video components are required. These courses are identified below where *Video* appears after the course title. Tapes for most courses are shown on University College cable stations, Channel 31B in Prince George's County and Channel 61 in Montgomery County. Video lessons are also available from University College on videocassette for home use. The Video Home Use Service permits use of the tapes for the entire semester ($50 fee of which $20 is refundable).

Interactive Audio/Video

In cooperation with the University of Maryland College Park, live broadcasts of courses are available at selected campuses. Students take advantage of state-of-the-art equipment and participate in discussions with the class and teacher in College Park. Participating campuses include Aberdeen Proving Ground, Annapolis, Fort Richie, Shady Grove Center, and Patuxent River Naval Air Warfare Center. Courses are identified below with *ITV* following the course title.

INSTITUTION DESCRIPTION

University College, one of the eleven degree-granting institutions of the University of Maryland System, extends its resources to part-time students at convenient sites across the state, nation, and around the world. Innovative curricula and state-of-the art instructional technology are combined to provide professional undergraduate and graduate programs, professional development courses, and special training seminars.

The Open Learning Program offers the opportunity to enroll in a baccalaureate degree program even if attending class is difficult. Open Learning is composed of carefully structured courses that enable the student to succeed independently, without classroom attendance. By integrating comprehensive course guides with other learning materials, including detailed syllabi, textbooks, articles, and audio and video materials, Open Learning courses are designed to accommodate the special needs of distance learners.

Many of the courses require or recommend video programs, available through the College's Home Use Service. Further, many of the video programs are shown on the University's cable channels in Montgomery and Prince George's counties.

Open Learning courses are offered in blocks of three or six credits, depending on the scope of the course. Courses offered for six credits provide greater depth and wider perspective than the three-credit courses.

Accreditation: MSA

Official/Contact: Ruthann Fagan, Assistant Dean, Open Learning Program

Admission Requirements: Graduation from high school or successful completion of the GED exams with a total score of 225 and no score below 40 on any of the five tests. Cumulative GPA of 2.0 or better on all college-level work attempted at other regionally accredited colleges and universities.

Tuition: Maryland resident $145 per semester hour, nonresident $155 per semester hour. $25 application for admission fee, registration fee $5 per course. MasterCard and VISA accepted. Courses may be audited for noncredit with tuition and fees the same as for credit courses. Students must purchase textbooks required. These can be ordered from the University Book Center (301) 314-7853, Maryland Book Exchange (301) 927-3510, Anne Arundel Community College Bookstore (410) 541-2220, Harford Community College Bookstore (410) 836-4209, or the Lerner Law Book Company (202) 842-4334.

Degree Credit: The baccalaureate degree may be earned through Open Learning courses. If a resident of Maryland, the student may be able to take lower-level credits through a local community college as a distance student. Students outside Maryland may also complete degrees through Open Learning, but should check with their local community colleges concerning completion of lower-level credits. Courses may also be taken by nondegree-seeking students.

Grading: Examinations may be taken at regional locations in College Park, Annapolis, Shady Grove, Waldorf, Aberdeen Proving Ground, and Fort Meade. Exams may also be taken with an approved proctor near the student's home or workplace. Letter grades are assigned. Credit is awarded in semester hour units.

Library: Currently enrolled students have borrowing privileges at all four-year, state-supported academic libraries in Maryland. A state-of-the-art system (VICTOR) provides access to the 13 library systems within the University of Maryland System as well as to article citations in over 10,000 journals.

COURSES OFFERED

Behavioral Science

Introduction to Behavioral and Social Sciences (Video)

An interdisciplinary introduction to the behavioral and social sciences with special attention to the interrelationships of anthropology, sociology, psychology, and political science. Basic concepts, major schools of thought, and the findings of scientific research are examined. Social phenomena are analyzed from an interdisciplinary perspective. (6 credits)

Race to Save the Planet (Video)

An exploration of global environmental problems: overpopulation, deforestation, pollution of air and water, waste and misuse of dwindling energy resources, the effects of industrialization, loss of species and the habitats that support the world's biodiversity, unsustainable agricultural practices, and changes in humankind's values and actions that can arrest the deterioration of our environment. The course examines the scientific basis underlying environmental deterioration and the means by which it can be halted. Environmental problems are placed within the context of personal and societal values. The value of sustainability is introduced and emphasized. The global extent of the problems and solutions is underscored by video segments filmed in 29 nations and all settled continents. Materials from the telecourse *Race to Save the Planet* are integrated into the presentation. (3 credits)

Business Administration

Business Finance (ITV)

An overview of the principles and practices of organizing, financing, and rehabilitating a business enterprise. Topics include the various types of securities and their usefulness in raising funds, methods of apportioning income/risk/control, intercorporate relations, and new developments. Emphasis is on solving problems of financial policy that managers face. (3 credits)

Hotel and Restaurant Management

Hotel Management and Operations (ITV)

A study of supervision and employee relations, with emphasis on human-relations organization and manpower planning and development. Employee compensation benefits in the hospitality industry are covered, along with ethics and policies. (3 credits)

Humanities

Cosmos (ITV)

An interdisciplinary study of space, time, and the universe. Topics of consideration include astronomy, interstellar communications, Egyptian hieroglyphics, comparative religion, biology, and genetics. Historical expeditions on this planet are compared and contrasted with the Voyager missions through the solar system. Materials from the telecourse *Cosmos*, created by Carl Sagan, are integrated into the course. (3 credits)

Myth and Culture (Video)

A presentation of reflections on the interrelations of myth, religion, and culture in which myths are evaluated as embodiments of ethnic and universal ideas. Religion is analyzed within American and non-American cultures. Students are introduced to ideas and symbols from mythology that provide background for literature, music, and art. Materials from the telecourse *Joseph Campbell: Transformations of Myth through Time* are integrated into the presentation. (3 credits)

Shakespeare: Power and Justice (ITV)

An intensive study of eight of Shakespeare's dramatic masterpieces as they illuminate the concepts of power and justice in a social and cultural context. The exercise of power, the nature of kingship, and the responsibilities of those who judge others are traced throughout *Henry IV, King Lear, Macbeth, Hamlet, the Merchant of Venice, A Midsummer Night's Dream, Much Ado About Nothing*, and *The Tempest*. Primary considerations are the analysis of text, the development of character, and the constraints that performance imposes on the writing of plays. (3 credits)

Information Science

Introduction to Computer-Based Systems (Video)

An overview of computer information systems. Hardware, software, procedures, systems, and human resources are introduced, and their integration and applications in business and in other segments of society are assessed. The fundamentals of solving problems by computer are discussed. Introductory exposure to software packages includes educational versions of word processing and database packages provided in MS-DOS format. (3 credits)

Data Structure (ITV)

A study of data structures (including lists and trees) in terms of their descriptions, properties, and storage allocations. Algorithms are used to manipulate structures. Applications are drawn from the areas of information retrieval, symbolic manipulation, and operating systems. (3 credits)

Marketing

Principles of Marketing (Video)

An overview of the field of marketing with special attention to marketing research, consumer behavior, and strategies of marketing. Areas covered include services and nonprofit marketing as well as international marketing. Strategies for selecting target markets are presented and appraised. Methods of developing, pricing, distributing, and promoting products are explained. Discussion also covers social and ethical issues in marketing. (6 credits)

Mathematics

Mathematics: Contemporary Topics and Applications (ITV)

A survey of contemporary topics in mathematics centering on applications and projects. Topics in-clude measurements, rates of growth, basic statistics, the mathematics of political power, the geometry of the solar system, and computer arithmetic. (3 credits)

Science

Oceanus: The Marine Environment (Video)

An introductory study of the marine environment as a unique feature of this planet. Presentation includes theories of the leading North American oceanographers concerning forces that shaped the continents and oceans, as well as predictions of the effects of pollution on life in the oceans. Topics include intertidal zones, continental margins, plate tectonics, islands, marine meteorology, ocean currents, wind waves and water dynamics, tides, plankton, nektons, reptiles and birds, mammals of sea and land, polar and tropical seas, biological and mineral resources, and pollution. (3 credits)

Sociology

The Sociology of Gender (ITV)

An inquiry into the institutional bases of gender roles and gender inequality, cultural perspectives on gender, gender socialization, feminism, and gender-role change. Emphasis is on contemporary American society. (3 credits)

Wor-Wic Tech Community College
See **College of the Air**

Massachusetts

Bridgewater State College
See **WGBH/Boston**

Bristol Community College
See **WGBH/Boston**

Bunker Hill Community College
See **WGBH/Boston**

Dean Junior College
See **WGBH/Boston**

Fitchburg State College
See **WGBH/Boston**

Massasoit Community College
See **WGBH/Boston**

North Shore Community College
See **WGBH/Boston**

WGBH/Boston
Community Programming
WGBH Educational Foundation

125 Western Avenue
Boston, MA   02134

(617) 492-2777 *Fax:* (617) 787-0714

Geographic Access: Massachusetts

DELIVERY SYSTEMS

Broadcast Television
Programs are broadcast on WGBH/Channel 2 or WGBX/Channel 44 as indicated below with the course description.

INSTITUTION DESCRIPTION

WGBH/Boston is one of the leading producers of telecourses for educational television stations around the nation. It has created a number of outstanding presentations in association with other organizations such as the British Broadcasting Corporation. WGBH/Channel 2 and WGBX/Channel 44 broadcast telecourses that fit a busy schedule. The telecourse productions are developed by academic and media professionals who often spend two years or longer producing a course that offers both quality learning and viewing enjoyment. Because the student can attend most classes at home, telecourses have proven to be a popular option for people who find it impossible or inconvenient to travel to a campus for regularly scheduled classes. WGBH works with seven colleges in Boston and the surrounding area to make courses available for college credit. The Courses Offered section indicates the institutions that offer credit for successful completion of each course. The participating colleges and contact people are:

- Bridgewater State College (Bridgewater MA), Dennis Bicknell, (508) 697-1261
- Bristol Community College (Fall River MA), John Gregory, (508) 678-2811
- Bunker Hill Community College (Boston MA), Mildred Wigon, (617) 241-8600
- Dean Junior College (Franklin MA), Joy Evans, (508 528-9100
- Fitchburg State College (Fitchburg MA), Dr. Michele M. Zide, (508) 345-2151

- Massasoit Community College (Brockton MA), Donna Briggs, (617) 821-2222
- North Shore Community College (Danvers MA), Philip Sbaratta, (617) 593-6722

Accreditation: All member institutions are accredited by NEASC.

Official/Contact: Margaret M. Yamamoto, Director, WGBH Public Affairs

Admission Requirements: Each college has different prerequisites and on-campus attendance requirements. Contact the college of choice for specific information.

Tuition: Tuition fees vary from campus to campus. Contact the college of choice for current information regarding tuition, fees, and other materials costs. Course materials include a study guide and textbook and these can be purchased at campus bookstores.

Degree Credit: The amount and type of college credit varies from campus to campus. Generally, three semester hours of credit are awarded for successful completion of a course.

Grading: Examinations must be proctored. Grades are assigned according to the policy of the institution. Credit is generally awarded in semester hour units.

Library: If the student misses a broadcast, many of the colleges have videotapes available at their Learning Resource Centers or libraries.

COURSES OFFERED

Archaeology

Out of the Past

A telecourse that uses visually dramatic on-site filming to explore how archaeologists reconstruct ancient societies and explain how and why they evolved. Research at the spectacular Classic Maya center of Copan, Honduras, forms the core of the series, but a broad comparative perspective includes many other cultures, past and present. Broadcast over WGBX, Channel 44. One hour program each week for 8 weeks. Closed captioned for the hearing impaired. Credit offered by Bunker Hill Community College, Massasoit Community College, and North Shore Community College.

Anthropology

Faces of Culture

An introductory course in anthropology featuring dramatic and unique film footage from around the world. It illustrates human adaptation to environment and embraces cultures from all continents, from the beginnings of the human species to the present. Broadcast over WGBX, Channel 44. Two half-hour programs each week for 13 weeks. Credit offered by Bunker Hill Community College.

Biology

The Secret of Life

This introductory biology telecourse for nonmajors provides students with the information they need to understand the rapidly changing world of molecular biology. Vivid narratives and personal case histories chronicle scientific findings. The unseen world of DNA, genes, proteins and receptors is revealed through three-dimensional animation and special photographic techniques. The telecourse units explore life at the cellular level, animal systems, how genes determine traits, and how we fit in the larger picture of our planet. Broadcast by WGBX, Channel 44. Closed captioned for the hearing impaired. One hour program each week for 8 weeks. Credit offered by Bunker Hill Community College and Fitchburg State College.

Business

Business and the Law

This introductory law course emphasizes contracts and the legal system. It includes modules on the law of sales, commercial paper, agency and property— and examines government regulation, employment practices, and consumer and environmental protection. Students will gain a comprehensive overview of law and business which can enhance their career potential. Broadcast over WGBX, Channel 44. Two half-hour programs each week for 15 weeks. Credit offered by Bristol Community College.

Gerontology

Growing Old in a New Age

This introductory-level gerontology course provides an understanding of the process of aging, old age as a stage of life, and the impact of aging on society. Journalist Susan Stamberg hosts this study of a growing segment of our society, the elderly. Conversations with 75 older adults reveal their triumphs, losses, health, and personal views on aging. Broadcast over WGBX, Channel 44. One hour program each week for 13 weeks. Closed captioned for the hearing impaired. Credit offered by Bridgewater State College, Fitchburg State College, and North Shore Community College.

Health

Living with Health

This introductory health course is an encouraging guide to healthy living. It uses case studies and commentaries to promote a lifestyle of wellness: physical, emotional, social, intellectual, and spiritual. It also examines current health issues such as AIDS, pollution, and other threats to public health. Broadcast over WGBX, Channel 44. Two half-hour programs each week for 13 weeks. Credit offered by Bristol Community College, Bunker Hill Community College, and North Shore Community College.

History

Americas

An introductory course on the 20th-century political, economic, social, and cultural history of Latin America and the Caribbean. Students will become familiar with key issues and events that are influencing the development of the modern-day Americas. Closed captioned for the hearing impaired. Broadcast over WGBX, Channel 44. One-hour program each week for 10 weeks. Credit offered by Bridgewater State College, Bunker Hill Community College, and Fitchburg State College.

Management

Taking the Lead: The Management Revolution

This new business management course gives an overview of management in the nineties, with an emphasis on the competencies that are essential for success. Noted authorities provide an inside view of businesses including General Dynamics, Hybritech, Patagonia, and the Four Seasons Hotel. We see how they are planned, organized, staffed, directed, and controlled. Broadcast over WGBX, Channel 44. Two half-hour programs each week for 13 weeks. Credit offered by Bristol Community College, Bunker Hill Community College, Massasoit Community College, and North Shore Community College.

Psychology

Discovering Psychology

This course covers the fundamental principles and major concepts of psychology and includes original footage of classic experiments, interviews with renowned psychologists, and documentaries on emerging research. Professor Philip G. Zimbardo of Stanford University is the host. Broadcast over WGBX, Channel 44. Two half-hour programs each week for 13 weeks. Closed captioned for the hearing impaired. Credit offered by Bristol Community College and Bunker Hill Community College.

Rural Sociology

Rural Communities

America's cultural, political, and economic roots can be traced back to rural beginnings, and a rural setting is presently home to almost a quarter of the population. This new course addresses the challenges facing rural America by traveling to 15 rural regions to learn how they maintain their vitality and character. Broadcast over WGBX, Channel 44. One hour program each week for 13 weeks. Closed captioned for the hearing impaired. Credit offered by Bunker Hill Community College and Fitchburg State College.

Small Business Management

Something Ventured: Small Business Management

A business telecourse designed to provide aspiring entrepreneurs an opportunity to observe a variety of small businesses in operation—in both rural and suburban communities, and in large metropolitan areas. Documentary footage is analyzed by a council of leading experts in the small business arena. Broadcast over WGBX, Channel 44. Two half-hour programs each week for 13 weeks. Credit offered by Bristol Community College and North Shore Community College.

Sociology

The Sociological Imagination

An introductory course designed to give students an in-depth look at groups, communities, institutions, and social situations. Each program is structured as a documentary, featuring interviews with people at home, work, school, worship, and play. Issues such as socialization, social control, sex and gender, aging, education, collective behavior, and social change are explored. Expert commentary from leading sociologists. Broadcast over WGBX, Channel 44. Two half-hour programs each week for 13 weeks. Credit offered by Bunker Hill Community College and North Shore Community College.

Spanish

Destinos: An Introduction to Spanish, Part 1

The first semester of a Spanish language course designed to give students full communicative proficiency in Spanish. *Destinos* combines a dramatic story with instruction. The situation and context of each episode introduces students to the basic structures, language functions, and vocabulary groups that are presented in the programs and resource materials. Closed captioned for the hearing impaired. Broadcast over WGBX, Channel 44. Two half-hour programs each week for 13 weeks. Credit offered by Bunker Hill Community College and Fitchburg State College.

Destinos: An Introduction to Spanish, Part 2

This is the second half of a two-semester Spanish language course designed to give students full communicative proficiency in Spanish. *Destinos* uses a uniquely Hispanic genre, the "telenovela," to combine a dramatic story with instruction. The situation and context of each episode introduces students to the basic structures, language functions, and vocabulary groups that are presented in the programs and resource materials. Closed captioned for the hearing impaired. Broadcast over WGBH, Channel 2. Two half-hour programs each week for 13 weeks. Credit offered by Bunker Hill Community College.

Michigan

Marygrove College
Graduate Studies

8425 West McNichols Road
Detroit, MI   48221-2599

(313) 862-8000 *Fax:* (313) 864-6670

Geographic Access: Nationwide

DELIVERY SYSTEMS

Videocassette
Telecourses are supplied on videocassettes, viewed by the student or group, and returned to the vendor, Lee Canter and Associates.

INSTITUTION DESCRIPTION

Founded in 1905, Marygrove College offers a variety of graduate education programs. The three graduate-level video courses are products of Lee Canter & Associates of Santa Monica, California. Upon successful completion of course requirements, the student will receive three semester hours of graduate credit per course.

Accreditation: NCA

Official/Contact: Edward F. Haggerty, Director

Admission Requirements: Open enrollment. Registration should be directed to Video Course, Lee Canter & Associates, P.O. Box 2113, Santa Monica, CA 90407-2113.

Tuition: $295 per course plus $10 processing fee. MasterCard, VISA, and Discover Card accepted. Tuition includes graduate credit, all course books, and the use of the videos. Tuition does not include the return of the videos or the cost of having your graded coursework returned to you.

Degree Credit: Credit may be applicable for recertification and salary advancement if the student holds a teaching certificate in Michigan. Total coursework for each course is equivalent to a 45-hour, 3-semester credit course.

Grading: Student must view 15 half-hour video segments, complete the group activities, complete the course workbook, and complete the final written assignment.

Library: It is recommended that students utilize libraries in their local communities.

COURSES OFFERED

Education

How to Get Parents on Your Side
Skills taught in this course will help: reduce behavior and homework problems by enlisting parent support, conduct all parent conferences with confidence and achieve results, stay calm and self-assured when parents challenge you, transform defensive parents into committed partners, team-up with parents to increase student motivation, lead the most motivational back-to-school night of your career. (3 credits)

Succeeding with Difficult Students
With this course, you will learn how to prevent disruptions and avoid student manipulation, reach students with a history of failure, stay calm and focused when students openly defy you/verbally abuse you or other students/ignore your directions/or are constantly off-task and out of their seats, and see improvement week after week throughout the year. (3 credits)

Assertive Discipline and Beyond
This results-oriented course will help you create a safe, positive learning environment where your stu-

dents behave responsibly and feel good about themselves. Reduce disruptions and manage student behavior by using a behavior management plan. Teach your students to behave responsibly during all classroom activities. Increase students' time on-task and raise their self-esteem using positive reinforcement skills and feel less stress when disciplining students who do not follow directions. Increase your confidence by using special communication skills to obtain parental and administrator support. (3 credits)

North Central Michigan College
Telecourse Program
Admissions Office

1515 Howard Street
Petoskey, MI   49770

(616) 347-3973

Geographic Access: Michigan

DELIVERY SYSTEMS

Broadcast Television
Telecourse broadcast schedules are announced prior to the fall/spring semesters.

INSTITUTION DESCRIPTION

North Central Michigan College is a two-year community college that was established in 1958. It is supported by the state and the county of Emmett. The college is located on Little Traverse Bay in northern Michigan, a resort and health center.

Telecourses are broadcast by CMU Public Broadcasting Network over the local PBS television station.

Accreditation: NCA

Official/Contact: Robert B. Graham, President

Admission Requirements: Students desiring to enroll in a telecourse should apply to the Admissions Office.

Tuition: Contact the Dean of Admissions for current tuition and fees.

Degree Credit: Credit earned by successful completion of a telecourse may be applied toward an associate degree. Students from other colleges should contact

their institutions to ascertain the transfer-acceptance policy.

Grading: Examinations must be taken on campus and supervised by a proctor. Letter grades are assigned. Credit is awarded in semester hour units.

Library: Students living in the vicinity of Petoskey have access to the Learning Resource Center of the college. Other students are encouraged to use the resources of their local community libraries.

COURSES OFFERED

Business

The Business File
This series provides a comprehensive overview of the contemporary business environment. Using a news interview format, the programs present leading scholars and corporate executives discussing business theory and its practical application. The series encompasses five general areas: (1) American business, foundation, and forms, (2) organizing and managing a business, (3) the internal workings of a business, (4) the environment of business, and (5) the challenge of business. Topics include marketing, finance, accounting, and management. Produced by Dallas Telecourses. 28 half-hour telecasts.

Political Science

Government By Consent
This American government survey provides students with an understanding of democracy, the U.S. Constitution, political parties, the three branches of government, and due process. The series marries political science instruction with examples of how students can involve themselves in government. Program topics include federalism, PACs, congress, the legislative process, domestic policy, foreign policy, the judiciary, first amendment freedoms, and rights of the accused. Produced by Dallas Telecourses.

Psychology

Discovering Psychology
This introductory psychology series covers the fundamental principles of psychology including: brain and behavior, sensation and perception, conditioning and learning, cognitive processes, psychopathol-

ogy, social influences, and therapy. The host for the series, Philip Zimbardo of Stanford University, weaves the thread of each topic through original footage of classic experiments, interviews with renowned psychologists, and segments on emerging research. He takes students into working laboratories and introduces leading scholars and researchers who seek to improve the quality of human life and our understanding of the mind. Produced by WGBH/Boston. 26 half-hour telecasts.

Sociology

The Sociological Imagination: Introduction to Sociology

This introductory sociology series features minidocumentaries that are emotionally strong illustrations of issues such as socialization, social control, sex and gender, aging, collective behavior, and social change. Expert commentary from noted sociologists provides an academic framework for sociological issues such as group dynamics, deviance, social class, religion, and family. Produced by Dallas Telecourses. 26 half-hour telecasts.

Northwestern Michigan College
Telecourse Program

1701 East Front Street
Traverse City, MI   49684

(616) 922-0650

Geographic Access: Michigan

DELIVERY SYSTEMS

Broadcast Television
Courses are broadcast over the CMU Public Broadcasting Network, headquartered in Mt. Pleasant, Michigan.

INSTITUTION DESCRIPTION

Northwestern Michigan College is located in a major tourist center. It was founded in 1951 and offered classes during the first three years in Coast Guard barracks located next to airport runways. The college moved to a permanent campus in 1954.

Telecourses are offered on a rotating basis and are

broadcast over the CMU Public Broadcasting Network.

Accreditation: NCA

Official/Contact: Timothy G. Quinn, President

Admission Requirements: Students should apply through the Dean of Admissions Office. Courses may be taken for noncredit.

Tuition: Contact the Admissions Office for current tuition and other fees. Textbooks must be purchased by the student.

Degree Credit: Credit earned through successful completion of a course may be applied toward an associate degree. Credit may be accepted in transfer by another institution, depending on that institution's acceptance policy.

Grading: Examinations must be proctored. The letter system of grading is followed. Credit is awarded in quarter hour units.

Library: Students living in the vicinity of the campus have access to the Learning Resources Center. Other students are encouraged to utilize local community libraries.

COURSES OFFERED

Business

The Business File
This series provides a comprehensive overview of the contemporary business environment. Using a news interview format, the programs present leading scholars and corporate executives discussing business theory and its practical application. The series encompasses five general areas: American business, foundation, and forms. Organizing and managing a business, the internal workings of a business, the environment of business, and the challenge of business. Topics include marketing, finance, accounting, and management. Produced by Dallas Telecourses. 28 half-hour lessons.

Political Science

Government by Consent
This American government survey provides students with an understanding of democracy, the U.S. Constitution, political parties, the three branches of

government, and due process. The series marries political science instruction with examples of how students can involve themselves in government. Program topics include federalism, PACs, congress, the legislative process, domestic policy, foreign policy, the judiciary, first amendment freedoms, and rights of the accused. Produced by Dallas Telecourses. 26 half-hour lessons.

Psychology

Discovering Psychology

This introductory psychology series covers the fundamental principles of psychology including: brain and behavior, sensation and perception, conditioning and learning, cognitive processes, psychopathology, social influences, and therapy. The host for the series, Philip Zimbardo of Stanford University, weaves the thread of each topic through original footage of classic experiments, interviews with renowned psychologists, and segments on emerging research. He takes students into working laboratories and introduces leading scholars and researchers who seek to improve the quality of human life and our understanding of the mind. Produced by WGBH/Boston. 26 half-hour lessons.

Sociology

The Sociological Imagination: Introduction to Sociology

This introductory sociology series features minidocumentaries that are emotionally strong illustrations of issues such as socialization, social control, sex and gender, aging, collective behavior, and social change. Expert commentary from noted sociologists provides an academic framework for sociological issues such as group dynamics, deviance, social class, religion, and family. Produced by Dallas Telecourses. 26 half-hour lessons.

Wayne County Community College

Telecourse Office

801 West Fort Street
Detroit, MI   48226

(313) 496-2500

Geographic Access: Michigan

DELIVERY SYSTEMS

Broadcast Television
In most cases, there is one showing on WTVS/Channel 56 and four showings on the College Cable Channel carried by participating cable companies.

INSTITUTION DESCRIPTION

Wayne County Community College was founded in 1969. It has five campuses: Downriver, Western, Downtown, Eastern, and Northwest.

Telecourse orientation is required for all students taking their first telecourse at WCCC. These sessions are designed to provide students with necessary information for the successful completion of course requirements. During these sessions, students will learn successful study techniques and be provided with the additional programmatic information necessary. Most telecourses utilize a textbook and study guide which provide students with reading materials in the subject area being studied. During the semester, should students encounter any problems relative to a course, the instructor can be reached by contacting the Telecourse Hotline (313) 496-2744.

Accreditation: NCA

Official/Contact: Deborah Fiedler, Manager

Admission Requirements: Open enrollment. High school graduation or equivalent for degree-seeking students.

Tuition: In-district $54 per credit hour. Out-of-district $70 per credit hour. Out-of-state $89 per credit hour. Registration fee $25 plus $2 activity fee per credit. Textbooks and study guides must be purchased by the student.

Degree Credit: Credit awarded for successful completion of a course may be applied toward a degree program.

Grading: Examinations must be proctored. Standard letter grades are assigned. Credit is awarded in semester hour units.

Library: The courses listed below are supported by tapes available at the Downriver and Downtown Learning Resources Centers. To make arrangements to view any of the tapes, students should contact the LRC directly and make an appointment.

COURSES OFFERED

Anthropology

Introduction to Cultural Anthropology
TV series title: *Faces of Culture.* 2 half-hour programs per week. (3 credits)

Business

Business Law I
TV series title: *Business and the Law.* 2 half-hour programs per week. This course aired on College Cable Channel only. (3 credits)

Introduction to Business
TV series title: *The Business File.* 2 half-hour programs per week. (3 credits)

Computer Applications in Business
TV series title: *ComputerWorks.* This course aired on College Cable Channel only. 1 half-hour program per week. (3 credits)

Economics

Principles of Economics I
TV series title: *Economics U$A.* 1 half-hour program per week. (3 credits)

Principles of Economics II
TV series title: *Economics U$A.* 1 half-hour program per week. (3 credits)

English

English I
TV series title: *The Write Course.* 2 half-hour programs per week. This course aired on College Cable Channel only. (3 credits)

English II
TV series title: *Read, Write, Research.* 2 half-hour programs per week. (3 credit hours)

Introduction to Poetry
TV series title: *Voices and Visions.* Attendance at 5 class sessions is mandatory. One 60-minute program per week. This course aired on the College Cable Channel only. (3 credits)

Finance

Personal Money Management
TV series title: *Personal Finance and Money Management.* Review tapes are not available for this course. 2 half-hour programs per week. (3 credits)

History

World Civilization II
TV series title: *The World: A Television Series.* 1 half-hour program per week. This course aired on College Cable Channel only. (3 credits)

History of the U.S. II
TV series title: *America in Perspective.* 2 half-hour programs per week. (3 credits)

Humanities

The Art of Humanities
TV series title: *Humanities Through the Arts.* 2 half-hour programs per week. (3 credits)

Marketing

Marketing Principles
TV series title: *Marketing.* 2 half-hour programs per week. (3 credits)

Mathematics

Business Mathematics
TV series title: *By the Numbers.* 2 half-hour programs per week. (3 credits)

College Algebra
TV series title: *College Algebra: In Simplest Terms.* 2 half-hour programs per week. This course aired on College Cable Channel only. (3 credits)

Philosophy

Comparative Religions II
TV series title: *Beliefs and Believers*. This course aired on the College Cable Channel only. Two 60-minute programs per week. (3 credits)

Political Science

Introduction to Political Science
TV series title: *Government by Consent*. Two 60-minute programs per week. (3 credits)

Psychology

Introductory Psychology
TV series title: *The Study of Human Behavior*. Two 60-minute programs per week. (3 credits)

Small Business Management

Small Business Management
TV series title: *Something Ventured*. This course aired on the College Cable Channel only. 2 half-hour programs per week. (3 credits)

Sociology

Sociology
TV series title: *Sociological Imagination*. 2 half-hour programs per week. (3 credits)

Western Michigan University
Department of Distance Education
Office of Self-Instructional Programs
Ellsworth Hall B-102
Kalamazoo, MI   49008-4105

(616) 387-4195

Geographic Access: Worldwide

DELIVERY SYSTEMS

Audio Conferencing
Courses are enhanced by telephone conferencing, allowing instructor response. A $10 fee is assessed for unlimited use of the 800 number.

Videocassette
Videotapes are mailed to the student upon registration. Return postage costs are the responsibility of the student.

INSTITUTION DESCRIPTION

Western Michigan University (WMU) is a large comprehensive university with a Carnegie Doctoral I University classification. WMU has been in existence since 1903 and currently enrolls 28,000 students.

Audio- and videocassette tapes are utilized in the courses described below. WMU's EduCABLE cablecasts many tapes used in self-instructional courses. All self-instructional courses must be completed within one year from the date of enrollment.

Accreditation: NCA

Official/Contact: Geraldine A. Schma, Director

Admission Requirements: Formal admission to the University is not required unless the student intends to graduate from WMU.

Tuition: $107.25 per credit. Additional fees assessed according to the number of videotapes required for the course (fees listed below with the course description). MasterCard and VISA accepted. Students must purchase textbooks. Additional postage fees for overseas students. Because of the complexity of monetary exchange, Canadian and and other international students should pay tuition and fees with a bank card or money order.

Degree Credit: WMU students in the General University Studies program may transfer up to 30 credit hours toward their degree.

Grading: Most classes require at least one written exam. Examinations vary in form with each course. Some examinations do not require a proctor. The grading system is the 4.0 scale. Credit is awarded in semester hour units.

Library: Officially registered students have access to all libraries on the WMU campus.

COURSES OFFERED

Archaeology

Introduction to Archaeology

The science of archaeology is explored in terms of the methods and concepts used to discover and interpret past human behavior. Select portions of the Old and New World prehistoric cultural sequences provide the frame of reference. 8 lessons, 1 short written assignment, final examination. 3 videotapes: $9. (3 credits)

Anthropology

Topics in World Culture Areas: Indians and Eskimos

This course will survey American cultures, from the initial peopling of the New World by immigrants from Asia to the Age of Exploration and colonization of North America by Europeans. Emphasis will be placed on adaptive requirements of varying environments and the nature of human responses. 8 lessons, 1 short written assignment, final examination. 3 videotapes: $9. (3 credits)

General Studies

Non-Western Societies in the Modern World: Sub-Saharan Africa

An analysis of the distinctive cultural configuration of Sub-Saharan Africa. Types of transitions being made in the particular region from traditional to modern society will be explored through an examination of interrelationship between technology, social structure, and ideology. 9 lessons, paper or final exam. 9 videotapes: $20. (4 credits)

Critical Times: Depression and War

This course will be an interdisciplinary examination of the period between 1929 and 1945, focusing on the American people and their society during the Great Depression and the Second World War. Students will study the so-called high and low culture of the era, including historical monographs, novels, biographies, autobiographies, movies, radio, and music. 10 lessons. 1 videotape: $5. (4 credits)

Critical Times: The Civil Rights Movement

The course proposes that the Civil Rights movement dramatically changed the course of American history. It forces the student to assess our democratic values. 10 lessons. 6 videotapes. $20. (4 credits)

Philosophy

Philosophy and Public Affairs: Ethics in America

A study of contemporary ethical problems based on the PBS television series, *Ethics in America*. Case studies in the series draw examples from business, government, law, journalism, medicine, and scientific research. Altruism, confidentiality, privacy, public service versus private interest, autonomy versus paternalism, and loyalty are among the issues considered. The issues are discussed by panels of leaders in government, business, law, the media, and the military. Readings especially prepared for the TV series will supplement the videos. 11 lessons, journal, term paper, 2 exams. 9 videotapes: $20. (4 credits)

Physical Education

Beginning Bowling

This course develops an enjoyment of the game while learning the basic skills and requirements. Skill levels will vary with individual students. 8 lessons, written exam, skill exam. 1 videotape: $5. (1 credit)

Intermediate Bowling

Designed to improve existing skills and teach some new ones. The student will become aware of faults and be assisted in correction/improvement of the game. Skill levels will vary with individual students. 9 lessons, written exam, skill exam. 1 videotape: $5. (1 credit)

Beginning Golf

Beginning Golf develops an enjoyment of the game. Skills are developed at the student's own pace by following step-by-step lessons. 8 lessons, written exam, skill exam. 1 videotape: $5. (1 credit)

Beginning Racquetball

This course develops an enjoyment of the game while learning the basic skills and requirements. Attained skill levels will vary with individual students. 8 lessons, written exam, skill exam. 1 videotape: $5. (1 credit)

Intermediate Racquetball

Designed to guide the student through improvement of present racquetball play. Attained skill levels will vary with individual students. 14 lessons, written exam, skill exam. 1 videotape: $5. (1 credit)

Beginning Tennis

Beginning Tennis develops an enjoyment of the game. Skills are developed at the student's own pace by following step-by-step lessons. At the end of the lessons, the student will develop a good forehand, backhand, drive, and a good tennis serve. 8 lessons, written exam, skill exam. 1 videotape: $5. (1 credit)

Intermediate Tennis

Designed to guide the student through improvement of present tennis play. Attained skill levels will vary with individual students. 14 lessons, written exam, skill exam. 1 videotape: $5. (1 credit)

Psychology

Brain, Mind, and Behavior

Designed to provide a comprehensive understanding of the human brain, this course presents current findings of a neuropsychological nature. 8 lessons. 8 videotapes: $20. (3 credits)

Social Work

The Black Struggle for Justice, 1965-Present

This course centers around the PBS television series, *Eyes on the Prize II*. It explores the ideals and strategies of such leaders as Dr. Martin Luther King Jr. and Malcolm X. The struggle for justice in the streets and the legislative and political arenas are also covered. 7 lessons. 8 videotapes: $20. (3 credits)

Sociology

Death, Dying, and Bereavement

Social structures, attitudes, beliefs and values about death, dying, and bereavement in contemporary American society as well as in other societies and other time periods will be considered. Medical, legal, religious, and psychological issues in relation to death, dying, and bereavement will be discussed. Not recommended for persons recently bereaved. An audio conferencing course. Additional fee: $10. (3 credits)

Western Michigan University - MITN

Office of Telecourse Programs
Department of Distance Education

Ellsworth, Room B-103
Kalamazoo, MI   49008-5161

(616) 387-4216 *Fax:* (616) 387-4222

Geographic Access: Nationwide

DELIVERY SYSTEMS

Broadcast Television
A student must become a subscriber of the Michigan Information Technology Network (MITN). MITN's two-way interactive key pad system allows students at remote locations to ask questions and share information. The university has reserved Tuesday and Thursday evenings from 6 to 9 PM for broadcasting its courses via satellite.

INSTITUTION DESCRIPTION

The Haworth College of Business of Western Michigan University offers a Master of Business Administration (MBA) degree by means of the Michigan Information Technology Network (MITN). MITN was formed by the state of Michigan through a partnership of education, government, and business. MITN's two-way interactive key pad system allows students at remote locations to ask questions and share information.

The University offers five courses per year through MITN. Two courses are offered in the fall and winter sessions and one in the spring and summer sessions. Thus, students who take the full cycle of courses can complete the graduate program in less than four years. Students must complete the degree in six years. Some courses, critically needed by students, are redistributed in an interactive videotape format. This is in addition to the usual MITN offerings.

"Common body of knowledge" courses available through MITN (identified below in the course descriptions) will precede the graduate course for which it is a prerequisite. Thus, all students may progress through the complete cycle of courses. Students with an undergraduate degree may only have to complete core and elective courses, thus shortening the time needed to complete the MBA degree. In addition to the University's regional accreditation, the program is accredited by the American Assembly of Collegiate Schools of Business.

Accreditation: NCA

Official/Contact: Geraldine Schma, Director

Admission Requirements: Official final transcript from the college or university where the baccalaureate degree was earned. The MBA program requires submission of test scores for the Graduate Management Admission Test (GMAT). $25 application fee.

Tuition: $256.50 per graduate credit hour, $232.25 per undergraduate credit hour (for "common body of knowledge courses" at the undergraduate level). Textbooks and $100 MITN fee per course are additional.

Degree Credit: The MBA degree at WMU is a 63-hour program. "Common body of knowledge" (prerequisites) comprise 30 hours of the program. Graduate level work is 33 hours. "Common body of knowledge" courses may be fulfilled in one of several ways: previously completed coursework with grade of C or better, coursework can be taken at an accredited two-year institution, or by waiver examination. Work experience is not a valid substitute for any course equivalency. Required core courses are listed under the subject heading Business Administration in the Courses Offered section.

Grading: Examinations must be proctored. Standard letter grading system is used. Credit is awarded in semester hour units.

Library: Students have access to the library facilities of Western Michigan University.

COURSES OFFERED

Accounting

Principles of Accounting 210

An introductory course in accounting which includes the recording and reporting of business transactions, and the measuring, planning, and controlling of business income, assets, and equities. An undergraduate prerequisite course. (3 credits)

Principles of Accounting 211

A continuation of course 210 with emphasis on managerial and cost accounting concepts. An undergraduate prerequisite course. (3 credits)

Business Administration

Accounting Control and Analysis

A study of management systems and techniques used for profit planning and control of a business firm. Organizational relationships and implications are examined in the development of operations controls, management controls, and strategic planning. (3 credits)

Computer Information Systems

The design, implementation, and use of computer information systems for decision making. Included are recent hardware and software developments, systems architecture, and systems procedure techniques. Hands-on experience with mainframe and microcomputers using a variety of statistical routines, PERT/CPM, VISICALC, word processing, and other software packages. (3 credits)

Legal Controls of the Business Enterprise

Reviews major legal problems encountered by business managers. The manager's role in dispute resolution, and the factors affecting the organization of business firms are reviewed. Problems in drafting and negotiating controls are examined. The administrative regulating process is discussed and various facets of product liability, antitrust, and employment laws are studied. (3 credits)

Financial Management

Study of the principles and problems underlying the management of capital in the business firm. Stresses the financial officer's responsibilities. Skills are developed in the marshaling and interpreting of data for use in making and implementing capital expenditure policies, solving short-term and long-term financing problems, establishing dividend policies, effecting mergers and consolidations, and adapting to trends in financial markets. Techniques used include case analysis and problem solving. Demonstrates financial management's role in the total management effort. (3 credits)

Applied Economics for Management

The course examines the relationship between the theory of the firm and recent developments in the area of operations research. Among the concepts and tools discussed are game theory, linear programming, capital budgeting, inventory theory, input-output analysis, price policy, and cost analysis. (3 credits)

Policy Formulation and Administration

This course focuses on the job of the general manager in formulating short and long run strategy. Using cases drawn from actual situations, the course develops ways of perceiving specific opportunities from an analysis of evolving environmental trends, understanding company strengths, and integrating strengths and opportunities in setting strategy and detailed operating plans. This is an integrative capstone course in that the tools and skills learned in other core courses are needed to develop practical, company-wide general management decisions. (3 credits)

Marketing Management

Analysis of marketing activities from management point of view. Includes study of decision making relative to competition, demand analysis, cost analysis, product analysis, product design, promotion, pricing, and channels of distribution. (3 credits)

Business Law

Legal Environment

An introduction to the legal environment in society. An examination of the role of law in society, the structure of the American legal system and the basic legal principles governing individual conduct. An undergraduate prerequisite course in an interactive videotape format. (3 credits)

Information Systems

Introduction to Information Processing

An introductory survey of the needs for and roles of computer information systems within business organizations which will prepare students to be relatively sophisticated computer users. Emphasis is on management information systems (MIS) including a focus on information management and information processing, microcomputer application, and the development of elementary level programs in BASIC language. An undergraduate prerequisite course. (3 credits)

Economics

Principles of Economics 201

An introduction to microeconomics, the study of the price system and resource allocation, problems of monopoly, and the role of government in regulating and supplementing the price system. An undergraduate prerequisite course. (3 credits)

Principles of Economics 202

An introduction to macroeconomics, the study of total output and employment, inflation, economics growth, and introduction to international trade and development. An undergraduate prerequisite course. (3 credit hours)

Finance

Business Finance

Presents a basis for understanding the financial management function of the business enterprise. Considers financial principles and techniques essential for planning and controlling profitability and liquidity of assets, planning capital structure and cost of capital, and utilizing financial instruments and institutions for capital raising. An undergraduate prerequisite course. (3 credits)

Management

Management Fundamentals

An introduction to the concepts, theories, models, and techniques central to the practice of management. Historical and contemporary thought are presented in the context of the behavioral, structural, functional, quantitative, and ethical aspects of managing organizations. Cross-cultural aspects of management are also explored. Expected outcomes for the student are a general familiarity with the management process and limited situational application of course content. An undergraduate prerequisite course. (3 credits)

Marketing

Principles of Marketing

Functions, institutions, and problems of marketing examined from the viewpoint of their effect on distribution of goods. An undergraduate prerequisite course. (3 credits)

Mathematics

Business Statistics

An applications-oriented study of statistical concepts and techniques. The course focuses on the student as a user of statistics who needs a minimal understanding of mathematical theory and formula derivation. Major topics of study are statistical description, central tendency, dispersion. distributional shapes, sampling, confidence levels, probability, comparison tests, association tests, regression and time series. The objectives of the course are to develop the skill to apply these concepts in conjunction with computer usage and make appropriate decisions regarding actual business problems. An undergraduate prerequisite course. (3 credits)

Personnel Administration

Economic Analysis for Administrators
This required technical core course will focus on those basic principles of applied economics which illuminate policy analysis and problems of resource allocation encountered by administrators. It is intended to provide participants with those tools of economic analysis required to address resource allocation and similar issues. Those who enroll in this course will be expected to apply the economic tools presented to policy analysis and policy implementation questions facing agencies by which they are employed. A graduate level course. (3 credits)

Minnesota

University of Minnesota
Department of Independent Study

Wesbrook Hall
77 Pleasant Street, Southeast
Minneapolis, MN 55455

(612) 624-0000 *Fax:* (612) 626-7900

Geographic Access: Nationwide

DELIVERY SYSTEMS

Audiocassette

Many courses described below use audiocassettes as part of the course learning materials. Some audiocassette courses were originally radio courses broadcast over the University's public radio station, KUOM. Other courses (in foreign language or music) use taped exercises.

Broadcast Television

Telecourses are broadcast over stations KTCI, KWCM, KSMQ, and WDSE.

Computer Tutorials

Students in computer-oriented courses must have access to an IBM PC or combatible or be able to use the microcomputers in one of the University's computer labs.

Radio Broadcast

Courses offered on weekdays over KUOM radio (770 AM) take advantage of KUOM's call-in format. Students and other listeners are able to telephone the station and ask questions of the instructor and receive prompt and personal feedback. The call-in feature is not available for Saturday repeats and other Saturday courses.

Videocassette

The videotapes for many courses are available for home rental.

INSTITUTION DESCRIPTION

The University of Minnesota was established and chartered in 1851. Independent Study was initiated in 1909.

Several kinds of media-assisted courses are offered: radio, television, audiocassette, and videocassette. The radio and television courses are offered with the cooperation of University Media Resources, public radio stations, and public television stations. The courses are broadcast each quarter of the academic year. After one of these degree-credit courses has been broadcast, it is converted to an audiocassette or a videocassette course so that students may continue to enroll in it.

Each media-assisted course consists of the media component, a course study guide, and texts. The study guide integrates all of the course components—it details the reading assignments from the required texts, gives the viewing or listening assignments, and contains study notes, written assignments, and/or exam information. Those courses which are available for graduate credit are indicated below with the course description.

Accreditation: NCA

Official/Contact: Deborah L. Hillengass, Director

Admission Requirements: There are no admission requirements to enroll in a course. Enrollment does not constitute admission to the University of Minnesota. Credit to be applied to a degree must meet the requirements of the institution in which the student may be formally enrolled.

Tuition: Varies with department and level of instruction. Tuition and fees are listed below with the course descriptions. Students must purchase textbooks and other supplementary materials. MasterCard and VISA accepted.

Degree Credit: Credit earned through Independent Study may be applied to a degree program at the University of Minnesota. Students should check with their local institution for acceptability of transfer credits.

Grading: Examinations must be proctored. Grading system is A-F. Satisfactory/Unsatisfactory is an alternate method of grading. Credit is awarded in quarter hour units.

Library: The University of Minnesota Libraries are available to officially enrolled students. The Learning Resources Center on the Minneapolis campus has copies of the audiocassettes and videocassettes that are required in the various courses described below. Any interested person can use its listening and viewing facilities or can make copies of its audiocassettes. Many Minnesota colleges and universities will extend library privileges to Independent Study students who show a fee statement/confirmation of registration form. Most Minnesota libraries are participants of the Minnesota Interlibrary Telecommunications Exchange (MINITEX), a legislatively funded program that shares library resources.

COURSES OFFERED

African Studies

Introduction to African Literature
An audiocassette course. A survey of 19th- and 20th-century African literature, including oral narratives, written poetry, short stories, novels, and plays. All readings in English. 11 assignments, 2 exams. Tuition and fees $284, text price $60, study guide and supplement $20, 11 audiocassettes $29. (4 credits)

American Studies

Topics in American Studies: Ellery Queen and the American Detective Story
An audiocassette course. Surveys American detective fiction, both classic and hard-boiled, to suggest reasons for its continued popularity. Novels and stories by the major writers (Poe, Hammett, Ellery Queen, Rex Stout, and others) will be assigned for reading and discussion. Audiocassettes focus on Ellery Queen as an example of the changing style of the genre. 7 assignments, no exams. Tuition and fees

$274, text $48, study guide $10, 10 audiocassettes $26.50. (4 credits)

Topics in American Studies: The Meaning of Place
A videocassette course. This course provides direct experiences in analyzing the cultural and psychological messages of our surroundings. With guidance from a cultural historian and a landscape architect, students will observe and explore various settings to discover what present day environments can reveal about the past and to gain a better understanding of the connections between sense of place and feelings of well-being. Places picked for analysis include the Minneapolis and St. Paul neighborhoods, village and small town settings inside and outside Minnesota, and various landscapes of the open countryside. 6 assignments, no exams. Tuition and fees $284, text $56, study guide $20, video rental $50 ($25 refund). (4 credits)

Anthropology

Introduction to Social and Cultural Anthropology
A videocassette course. An introduction to the ways in which the cross-cultural, comparative, and holistic study of contemporary societies and cultures across the world and of their social, political, economic, technological, and religious institutions can provide an understanding of human diversity, adaptation, and condition. 2 assignments, 1 exam. Tuition and fees $342.50, text $57, study guide $20, video rental $50 ($25 refund). (5 credits)

Antiques and Collectibles

Principles of Antique Collecting
An audiocassette course. This course is designed to increase a student's visual literacy and ability to assess quality, condition, and authenticity of antiques and collectibles. Students gain insight into the importance and meaning of objects in the material culture and the significance of collecting as a human endeavor. Also contains useful information on differentiating the various practices and procedures of the business of antique buying and selling. 5 assignments, no exams. Tuition and fees $322, text $27, study guide $10, 10 audiocassettes $26.50. (4 credits)

Architecture

The Meanings and Messages of Place, City, Town, and Countryside

A videocassette course. This course provides direct experiences in analyzing the cultural and psychological messages of our surroundings. 6 assignments, no exams. Tuition and fees $308, text $56, study guide $20, video rental $50 ($25 refund). (4 credits)

Art

Introduction to Visual Arts

A videocassette course. Basic problems of art. Examples of painting and sculpture analyzed to illustrate the roles of art in society, problems of design, materials, and techniques, presented topically rather than chronologically. 2 assignments, 2 exams. Tuition and fees $274, text $40, study guide $10, video rental $50 ($25 refund). (4 credits)

Classical Studies

Magic, Witchcraft, and the Occult in Greece and Rome

An audiocassette course. Magic and witchcraft in classical literature and mythology, the practice of magic as observed from papyri, epigraphical and literary evidence, and beliefs and practices concerning prophecy and the interpretation of dreams are considered. The course also explores the changing role of witchcraft and divine possession from early to later antiquity, and the relation of these phenomena to changes in economic and social conditions. 3 assignments, 1 exam. Tuition and fees $274, text $20, study guide $10, 10 audiocassettes $26.50. (4 credits)

Roman Realities: Life and Thought in the Roman Empire

An audiocassette course. The eruption of Vesuvius buried and preserved the Italian cities of Pompeii and Herculaneum so quickly and completely that excavations now enable us to construct a vivid picture of life at that time. Using this evidence and other research, this course focuses on social history through the study of art, archaeology, literature, dream interpretation, medical writing, and magic. 11 assignments, no exams. Tuition and fees $284, text $64, study guide $10, 10 audiocassettes $26.50. (4 credits)

Eroticism and Family Life in the Graeco-Roman World

An audiocassette course. Analysis of Greek and Roman family life in the shaping of personality, diachronic change in modes of erotic expression, narcissism and homosexuality, the status and roles of women, evolving views of sexual morality in the ancient world compared to present trends. Representative views taken for analysis and discussion from art and literature. Development of early Christian attitudes toward sexuality. 10 assignments, no exams. Tuition and fees $284, text $79, study guide and supplement $20, 10 audiocassettes $26.50. (4 credits)

Madness and Deviant Behavior in Ancient Greece and Rome

Definitions of madness in Greece and Rome and theories of its etiology. Assessment of predisposing factors in Greece and Rome. Examples of madness from mythology, legend, and history. Cross-cultural comparison with contemporary United States. 15 assignments, no exam. Tuition and fees $284, text $26, study guide $20, 15 audiocassettes $39.50. (4 credits)

Communications

Introduction to Technical and Business Communication

A videocassette course. Introduction to the processes used to define a topic, draft, and edit texts for business, government, and technical fields. 8 assignments, no exams. Tuition and fees $137, text $30, study guide $10, video rental $50 ($25 refund). (2 credits)

Computer Science

Introduction to Microcomputer Applications

Introduction to IBM microcomputer applications, including microcomputer components, operating system (DOS), word processing, spreadsheet, and database management software. All assignments done on computers. Access to an IBM PC is required. 9 assignments, 1 exam. Tuition and fees $342.50 plus text fee. (5 credits)

Introduction to Computer Programming

Experience in using the microcomputer as a problem-solving tool. Students design, write, code, and run computer programs written in the BASIC computer language. Topics include problem-solving techniques as applied to computing, elements of BASIC, external data file manipulation, writing structured programs, and integration of programming with data created by other applications. Gives background for further programming courses. Students must have access to an IBM PC or compatible computer with a BASIC interpreter. 9 assignments, 3 exams. Tuition and fees $342.50, text $37. (5 credits)

Education

Inventing the Future—Living, Learning, and Working in the 1990s

A videocassette course. This field-based course is for managers, human services and health services workers, counselors, teachers, and upper division or graduate students in many different fields. Topics include trends in work, leisure, education, technology, health, spirituality, homelife, and more. 3 assignments, no exams. Tuition and fees $308, study guide $20, video rental $50 ($25 refund). (4 credits)

Inventing the Future—Living, Learning, and Working in the 1990s

A broadcast television course. See description above. May be taken for graduate credit. 3 assignments, no exams. Tuition and fees undergraduate $308, graduate $376, study guide $20. (4 credits)

Second Language Programs for Young Children: Like Child's Play

A videocassette course. Examines current approaches to teaching second languages to young children, with emphasis on innovative curricular models. Provides information about the way young children acquire language and the effects of bilingualism on child development, and presents rationales, advantages, and pedagogical theories of various program models, from full immersion to programs that emphasize cultural understanding. 7 assignments, no exams. Tuition and fees $308, text $31, study guide and supplement $20, video rental $50 ($25 refund). (4 credits)

Second Language Programs for Young Children: Like Child's Play

A broadcast television course. See description above. May be taken for graduate credit. 7 assignments, no exams. Tuition and fees Undergraduate $308, graduate $376, text $31, study guide and supplement $20. (4 credits)

Counseling Psychology: Career Development and Planning

A videocassette course. This course is designed primarily for counselors, teachers, and human resource personnel who want to update their knowledge and skills in the field of career development and the career planning process. Topics include life span career development, the career planning process, labor market data and trends, sex-role socialization and stereotyping, career decision making, dual careers, and career change and transitions. 1 assignment, 1 exam. Tuition and fees $308, text $14, study guide $20, video rental $50 ($25 refund). (4 credits)

Education of the Gifted and Talented

A videocassette course. Origin and development of terms such as giftedness, creativity, genius, talent, and intelligence. Implications for educational practice, current issues and trends. 4 assignments. Tuition and fees $231, text $49, study guide $10, video rental $50 ($25 refund). (3 credits)

Education of the Gifted and Talented

A broadcast television course. See description above. May be taken for graduate credit. Tuition and fees undergraduate $231, graduate $282, text $49, study guide $10. (3 credits)

English

Introduction to American Literature: Some Major Figures and Themes

An audiocassette course. Introduction to some major themes and writers in American literature. Readings from Faulkner, Malamud, Melville, Fitzgerald, Chopin, Ellison, Henry James, and Dickey are complemented by audiocassette programs. 9 assignments, 1 exam. Tuition and fees $274, text $62, study guide $10, 10 audiocassettes $26.50. (4 credits)

Introduction to Literature: Modern Science Fiction

An audiocassette course. Deals with the evolution of modern science fiction and fantasy from their 19th-century roots to the popular literature of today. Considers such major themes as the future of technology, religion, and sexuality in the works of Le Guin, Huxley, and Sturgeon, among others, and also the contributions of such eminent fantasists as Tolkien, C.S. Lewis, and Richard Adams. No assignments, 2 exams. Tuition and fees $274, text $53, study guide $10, 10 audiocassettes $26.50. (4 credits)

Introduction to Modern Poetry

A broadcast television course. A study of modern British and American poetry organized around themes (war, the city, nature, death, love, etc.) and including such writers as Yeats, Thomas, Auden, Eliot, Frost, cummings, and Stevens. 5 assignments, 1 exam. Tuition and fees $274, text $29, study guide $10. (4 credits)

Literature of American Minorities

A radio broadcast course. Representative works by Afro-American, American Indian, Asian American, and Chicano/Chicana writers. Examination of relevant social factors. Tuition and fees $274 plus texts and study guide. (4 credits)

Shakespeare I

An audiocassette course. Study of Shakespeare's early and middle plays, with attention to history, literary values, and theatrical performance. Students will read *A Midsummer Night's Dream, Romeo and Juliet, Richard II, Henry IV Part I, Henry V, Much Ado About Nothing, Julius Caesar, Comedy of Errors, Othello*, and *Hamlet*. 12 assignments, 2 exams. Tuition and fees $284, text $37, study guide $10, 10 audiocassettes $26.50. (4 credits)

Shakespeare II

An audiocassette course. Study of Shakespeare's middle and late periods. Students will read *As You Like It, Macbeth, King Lear, Antony and Cleopatra, Coriolanus, The Winter's Tale*, and *The Tempest*. Special attention is given to imagining theatrical performance. 12 assignments, 2 exams. Tuition and fees $284, text $28, study guide $10, 10 audiocassettes $26.50. (4 credits)

Survey of American Literature, 1900-1960

An audiocassette course. American literature from the end of the 19th century to the 1960s. Authors studied include Frost, Eliot, Fitzgerald, Hurston, Wright, Olsen, and Rich, as well as a selection of contemporary poets. 15 assignments, no exams. Tuition and fees $284, text $58, study guide $10, 10 audiocassettes $26.50. (4 credits)

The English Language

A videocassette course. An introduction to the English language, including historical changes, syntax, phonetics and phonology, semantics, pragmatics, British and American dialects, and the acquisition of English as a first language. 10 assignments, no exams. Tuition and fees $284, text $34, study guide $10, video rental $50 ($25 refund). (4 credits)

Topics in English and American Literature: The Celtic World

An audiocassette course. A wide-ranging introductory survey of the history, music, folkways, and traditional oral culture of the six Celtic countries (Brittany, Cornwall, Ireland, Isle of Man, Scotland, and Wales). Topics considered are ancient culture, tribal society, saints/druids/bards/poets, the age of King Arthur, languages, and the future of Celtic culture. 1 assignment, 1 exam. Tuition and fees $284, text $48, study guide $10, 10 audiocassettes $26.50. (4 credits)

Topics in English and American Literature: D.H. Lawrence and Freud

An audiocassette course. An intensive reading of the prose fiction and poetry of D.H. Lawrence alongside key texts by Freud. The course will examine modern culture and its discontents as interpreted by these two writers. 6 assignments, 1 exam. Tuition and fees $284, text $66, study guide $10, 10 audiocassettes $26.50. (4 credits)

James Joyce

An audiocassette course. An introduction to the life and works of Joyce, including the epiphanies, the poems, the play *The Dubliners, A Portrait of the Artist as a Young Man, Ulysses*, and bits of *Finnegan's Wake*. 3 assignments, 1 exam. Tuition and fees $284, text $73, study guide $10, 10 audiocassettes $26.50. (4 credits)

European Folk Tales

An audiocassette course. The course is devoted to the folk tales of Germany, Scandinavia, France, Russia, and England. It discusses the structure, message for adults and children, origins of folk tales as a genre, and compares the tales of different nations and states the differences and similarities among them. Folk tales will be analyzed within the broader context of oral literature and folklore. 1 assignment, 2 exams. Tuition and fees $284, text $53, study guide $10, 10 audiocassettes $26.50. (4 credits)

Intermediate Fiction Writing

An audiocassette course. An examination of the essential elements in creative writing. Discussion of the creative process in writing fiction and intensive practice in the genre. Readings, discussion, and practice will include such topics as diction, structure, plotting, and dialogue. 5 assignments, no exams. Tuition and fees $284, text $19, study guide $10, 10 audiocassettes $26.50. (4 credits)

Intermediate Poetry Writing

An audiocassette course. This course is intended to help students develop new ways of using language to explore the world around them and in them. There are numerous writing assignments, readings in contemporary poetry, and consideration of such topics as rhythm, image, structure, diction, voice, and tone. 5 assignments, no exams. Tuition and fees $284, text $45, study guide $10, 10 audiocassettes $26.50. (4 credits)

Topics in Creative Writing: Journaling into Fiction

An audiocassette course. An exploration of the links between private and public writing. Students will build on the strengths and skills already present in their private writing as they move more fully into the world of the imagination to create fiction, poems, or song. The writing assignments illustrate the ways private journaling may be turned into fiction, using techniques such as dreams, prose poems, stream of consciousness, found art, and many others. 7 assignments, no exams. Tuition and fees $284, text $17, study guide $10, 10 audiocassettes $26.50. (4 credits)

Journal and Memoir Writing

Students will read selected journals and memoirs as well as completing exercises based on the readings. The journal writing process—informal and fragmentary—will be the basis of all writing suggestions. Students will be encouraged to work from memory and personal experience. The student course project will be to write a memoir or autobiographical work. 3 assignments, no exam. Tuition and fees $284, text $43, study guide $10, 10 audiocassettes $26.50. (4 credits)

Family Life

Family Relationships

A videocassette course. This course will examine the family as an institution and system of relationships. It surveys current developments in the study of family, changes in American society and their influence on family life. Course will be offered in an innovative format, including lectures, simulated family interaction, and participation of a studio audience. 1 assignment, 2 exams. Tuition and fees $402.50, text $72, study guide $10, video rental $50 ($25 refund). (5 credits)

Family Relationships

A broadcast television course. See description above. May also be taken for graduate credit. 1 assignment, 2 exams. Tuition and fees Undergraduate $402.50, graduate $800, text $72, study guide $10. (5 credits)

American Families in Transition

An audiocassette course. The course will present a comprehensive view of family life and examine historical and contemporary family issues. Focus will be on helpful information related to adjustment to rapid changes in family. No assignments, 2 exams. Tuition and fees $322, text $47, study guide $10, 10 audiocassettes $26.50. (4 credits)

American Families in Transition

A radio broadcast course. See description above. No assignments, 2 exams. Tuition and fees $322, text $47, study guide $10. (4 credits)

French

Beginning French I

An audiolingual approach to elementary French, adapted for home use. 10 assignments, 1 exam. Tuition and fees $342.50, text $70, 8 audiocassettes $21.50. (5 credits)

Beginning French II

A continuation of Beginning French I. 7 assignments, 1 exam. Tuition and fees $342.50, text $70, 5 audiocassettes $13.75. (5 credits)

Beginning French III

A continuation of Beginning French II. 7 assignments, 1 exam. Tuition and fees $342.50, text $70, 5 audiocassettes $13.75. (5 credits)

Geography

Geography of Minnesota (Videocassette Course)

The changing geography of Minnesota and the Upper Midwest. Explores the legacy from the railroad era, transformation in the auto-air age, and the emerging future. 10 assignments, 2 exams. Tuition and fees $284, text $38, study guide $10, video rental $50 ($25 refund). (4 credits)

Geography of Minnesota (Broadcast Television Course)

See description of Geography of Minnesota (Videocassette Course). 10 assignments, 2 exams. Tuition and fees $284, text $38, study guide $10. (4 credits)

Hebrew

Introduction to Classical Hebrew

Hebrew alphabet, basic grammar, and vocabulary needed to read narratives and legal portions of the Hebrew Bible and of the middle Hebrew texts of Mishnah, Tosefta, Midrash, and the Talmud. Also introduces the civilization and religion of classical Hebrew culture. For students without previous knowledge of Hebrew. 12 lessons, 2 exams. Tuition and fees $342.50, text $63, 1 audiocassette $11. (5 credits)

History

American History I

A videocassette course. United States history from colonial times to Reconstruction. A survey course emphasizing political, economic, social, and diplomatic history of the U.S. to 1880. 12 assignments, no exams. Tuition and fees $274, text $83, video rental $50 ($25 refund). (4 credits)

American History II

A videocassette course. United States history survey course from 1880 to the present. 11 assignments, 1 exam. Tuition and fees $274, text $83, video rental $50 ($25 refund). (4 credits)

Cultural Pluralism in American History

A videocassette course. A survey of the development of American society focusing on the roles of African-Americans, Native Americans, Asian-Americans, and Hispanic-Americans. Issues of cultural pluralism, empowerment, racism, and inter-group relations are explored within a comparative historical framework. 7 assignments, 3 exams. Tuition and fees $274, text $70, study guide $10, 10 audiocassettes $26.50. (4 credits)

Cultural Pluralism in American History

A radio broadcast course. See description above. 7 assignments, 3 exams. Tuition and fees $274, text $70, study guide $10. (4 credits)

The United States in the 20th Century: 1932-1960

A videocassette course. The Great Depression and the New Deal, the challenge of fascism and the coming of World War II, the origins of the Cold War, the great red scare, the politics and culture of the Eisenhower era, the origins of the civil rights movement, labor relations. 10 assignments, 2 exams. Tuition and fees $284, text $54, study guide $10, video rental $50 ($25 refund). (4 credits)

American Business History

A videocassette course. Explores the role of business leaders such as James J. Hill, Carnegie, Rockefeller, Morgan, and Ford. The development of business institutions, the interaction of business with economic developments, social values, and government economic policies. 3 assignments, 2 exams. Tuition and fees $284, text $39, study guide $20, video rental $50 ($25 refund). (4 credits)

History of American Foreign Relations

A videocassette course. American foreign policy from Franklin D. Roosevelt to Reagan. Deals with issues such as American isolationism, economic diplomacy, World War II, the Cold War, and Vietnam. 12 assignments, 2 exams. Tuition and fees $284, text $63, video rental $50 ($25 refund). (4 credits)

Horticulture

Home Horticulture: Landscape Gardening and Design

An audiocassette course. Working knowledge of propagation and culture of common landscape materials: turf, flowers, trees, and shrubs. Principles and practices of gardening. Prepared for beginners but also valuable for advanced or experienced gardeners. Topics include planting, transplanting, seeds, soils, fertilizers, preparing beds and planting areas, selecting a good garden site, controlling garden pests, weeding, watering, cultivating, vegetable gardening, and landscape maintenance. Also discusses annuals, perennials, bulbs, and roses for northern gardens. 14 assignments, no exams. Tuition and fees $274, text $40, study guide $10, 10 audiocassettes $26.50. (4 credits)

Humanities

Discourse and Society

A videocassette course. Nature of the humanities explored through interpretation of major works from literature, rhetoric, history, philosophy, the visual arts, music, and film. Humanities knowledge and its place in a liberal education. Tuition and fees $274 plus texts, video rental $50 ($25 refund). (4 credits)

Text and Context

A videocassette course. Examination of varied historically grounded case studies—early 18th century art, two novels, a historical work, an anthropological work, an opera, examples of mass culture, and analysis of advertising. Ways social and political conflicts of particular moments and specific locations are represented in the discourse of these case studies. Students relate the cultural discourses represented in the case studies to the larger socio-historical conditions out of which they arise by learning to apply Marxist critical theory, discourse theory, ideological critique, and theories of gender and race. 9 assignments, 2 exams. Tuition and fees $274, text $81, video rental $50 ($25 refund). (4 credits)

Italian

Beginning Italian I

Speaking, reading, and cultural objectives based on an audiolingual approach. Students learn to understand and express fundamental ideas, to write anything they can say, and to master the fundamental structures of Italian. Tuition and fees $342.50, text $86, 5 audiocassettes $13.75. (5 credits)

Jewish Studies

Introduction to Judaism

A videocassette course. Concepts, movements, and institutions in the development of classical Judaism, as manifested in the literature and festivals of the Jewish people from Second Commonwealth times to the present. 10 assignments, 2 exams. Tuition and fees $284, text $77, video rental $50 ($25 refund). (4 credits)

The Holocaust

An audiocassette course. Nazi destruction of Jewish life in Europe 1933-1945. Historical and social background of European communities. Anti-Semitism and Nazism. Ghettoes under Nazi rule, social and cultural organization, and government. Nazi terror and destruction, Jewish resistance, historical consequences. 4 assignments, no exams. Tuition and fees $284, text $36, 10 audiocassettes $26.50. (4 credits)

Journalism

Magazine Writing (Audiocassette Course)

Writing nonfiction feature articles for adult consumer and trade publications is covered, as is a study of market free lance methods, including query letters. 20 assignments, no exams. Tuition and fees $284, text $38, 10 audiocassettes $26.50. (4 credits)

Magazine Writing (Radio Broadcast Course)

See description for Magazine Writing (Audiocassette Course). 20 assignments, no exams. Tuition and fees $284, text $38, study guide $10. (4 credits)

Latin

Latin Poetry: Catullus

A computer-assisted course. Selected poetry of C. Valerius Catullus, lyric genius of the late Roman Republic. Students must have access to an Apple computer (not an Apple II) with Hypercard or be able to use the computers in the University's computer labs to use the word-by-word dictionary and grammar analysis, line-by-line metrical analysis, and online reference grammar and text-search facilities. 10 assignments, 1 exam. Tuition and fees $355 plus texts and computer software. (5 credits)

Linguistics

The Nature of Human Language

A videocassette course. This introductory course presents a survey of the nature of human language, its properties, its possible origins, and how it differs from animal communication. Methods of describing the sounds, structures, and meanings of language are also examined, along with a consideration of the relationship between language and the brain, how children acquire language, and the different roles of language in society. 4 assignments, 1 exam. Tuition and fees $274, text $19, video rental $50 ($25 refund). (4 credits)

Mathematics

Calculus I

A videocassette course. Analytical geometry and calculus of functions of one variable, applications. 10 assignments, 2 exams. Tuition and fees $342.50, text $55, study guide $10, video rental $50 ($25 refund). (5 credits)

Music

Music Appreciation

An audiocassette course. Analyzes music in the repertory of our culture—forms and styles from the 17th century to the present. Discusses the basic musical elements of rhythm, tonality, melody, and texture. The course is intended to increase the listener's musical vocabulary and skills in analyzing and appreciating musical forms such as symphonies, concertos, chamber, keyboard, and choral music, opera, and song. 6 assignments, 1 exam. Tuition and fees $284 (no text required), study guide $10, 14 audiocassettes $37. (4 credits)

American Music: Twentieth-Century American Music

An audiocassette course. Analysis of American music during this century: folk, popular and classical, black and Chicano, opera and symphony, contemporary music. 6 assignments, 1 exam. Tuition and fees $284, text $35, study guide $10, 10 audiocassettes $26.50. (4 credits)

Nursing

Life Span Growth and Development I

A videocassette/audiocassette course. Introductory course that incorporates biological, sociological, and psychological perspectives of human life span development from conception through adolescence. May be taken for graduate credit. 5 assignments, 1 exam. Tuition and fees undergraduate $161, graduate $320, study guide $10, 8 audiocassettes $21.50, video rental $50 ($25 refund). (2 credits)

Life Span Growth and Development II

A videocassette/audiocassette course. Introductory course that incorporates biological, sociological, and psychological perspectives of human life span development from young adulthood through aging and the death experience. May be taken for graduate credit. Tuition and fees undergraduate $161, graduate $320, plus texts, 5 audiocassettes $13.75, video rental $50 ($25 refund). (2 credits)

Physics

The Changing Physical World

A videocassette course. Introduces the nonscientist to the changing world of 20th-century physics. Against a background of history and philosophy, the course will highlight the new ideas and discoveries of relativity, cosmology, and quantum theory as seen from the vast scale of stars and galaxies, through the everyday realm of matter and energy, to the submicroscopic level of atoms and nuclei. No assignments, 4 exams. Tuition and fees $274, text $24, study guide $10, video rental $50 ($25 refund). (4 credits)

Political Science

Contemporary Political Ideologies

A videocassette course. A systematic survey of the major competing ideologies of the 20th century, including communism, conservatism, liberalism, fascism, "liberation" and "green" ideologies, and others. Special emphasis is placed on the historical sources, philosophical foundations, and argumentative structure of these influential ideologies. 4 assignments, 2 exams. Tuition and fees $274, text $51, study guide $10, video rental $50 ($25 refund). (4 credits)

Portuguese

The Everpresent Past in Spanish and Portuguese Culture

An audiocassette course. Most readings will be in the original language. Student must be Portuguese major. No assignments, 2 exams. Tuition and fees $284, study guide $10, 11 audiocassettes $29. (4 credits)

Public Health

Toward an Understanding of Child Sexual Abuse

A videocassette course. The ten programs of this course deal with a historical understanding of child sexual abuse, including definitions, dynamics, effects on the victim, how society intervenes, and prevention methods. This course is aimed at the professional in public health, health sciences, social work, education, and law. 11 assignments, no exams. Tuition and fees $360, text $39, study guide $10, video rental $50 ($25 refund). (4 credits)

Child Abuse and Neglect

A videocassette course. This course is a survey of the basic concepts and knowledge of child abuse and neglect. It includes a historical overview and the issue of balance of rights between children and their parents. Examples of child abuse and neglect, understanding why it occurs, its consequences, and how society can intervene and prevent it is presented. 11 assignments, no exams. Tuition and fees $270, text $19, study guide $10, video rental $50 ($25 refund). (3 credits)

Religious Studies

Religions of South Asia

A videocassette course. Introduction to Hinduism, Buddhism, and Jainism. 11 assignments, 2 exams. Tuition and fees $274, text $48, study guide supplement $10, video rental $50 ($25 refund). (4 credits)

Russian

Beginning Russian I

An audiocassette/computer-assisted course. A multipurpose program of instruction in the fundamentals of the Russian language. Acquaints students with all four basic language skills: listening, reading, speaking, and writing. Use of computer materials in IBM or Macintosh format. 9 assignments, 2 exams. Tuition and fees $342.50, text $20, 15 audiocassettes $39.50. (5 credits)

Beginning Russian II

A continuation of Beginning Russian I. 17 assignments, 2 exams. Tuition and fees $342.50, text $20, 16 audiocassettes $42. (5 credits)

Beginning Russian III

A continuation of Beginning Russian II. 17 assignments, 2 exams. Tuition and fees $342.50, text $20, 20 audiocassettes $53.50. (5 credits)

Spanish

Beginning Spanish I

Fundamentals of Spanish. Students develop listening and speaking skills by means of tapes, and learn to read and write basic Spanish in the cultural context of Spain and Spanish America. 14 assignments, 6 exams. Tuition and fees $342.50, text $80, 8 audiocassettes $21.50. (5 credits)

Beginning Spanish II

A continuation of Beginning Spanish I. 15 assignments, 2 exams. Tuition and fees $342.50, text $80, 7 audiocassettes $19. (5 credits)

Beginning Spanish III

A continuation of Beginning Spanish II. 15 assignments, 2 exams. Tuition and fees $342.50, text $80, 7 audiocassettes $19. (5 credits)

Intermediate Spanish I

Speaking and comprehension, development of reading and writing skills based on materials from Spain and Spanish America. Grammar review and compositions. 10 assignments, 2 exams. Tuition and fees $342.50, text $89, 5 audiocassettes $13.75. (5 credits)

Intermediate Spanish II

A continuation of Intermediate Spanish I. 10 assignments, 2 exams. Tuition and fees $342.50, text $89, 5 audiocassettes $13.75. (5 credits)

Topics in Spanish-Portuguese Civilization and Culture

An audiocassette course. Investigates how the concept of "regenerationism" has retained and exerted cultural force in the Iberian nations, forming a part of their cultural systems—and how it continues to exert that force today. The survey begins with the Portuguese poet Luis de Camoes' epic poem of 1578 and ends with documents about the Spanish "nationalities" of the post-Franco era. Readings in translation. No assignments, 2 exams. Tuition and fees $284, text $35, study guide $10, 11 audiocassettes $29. (4 credits)

The Everpresent Past in Spanish and Portuguese Culture

An audiocassette course. Most readings will be in the original language. Must be Spanish major. No assignments, 2 exams. Tuition and fees $284, study guide $10, 11 audiocassettes $29. (4 credits)

Statistics

Introduction to the Ideas of Statistics

A computer-assisted course. Learning under uncertainty, using probabilities to describe uncertainty, making inferences about causality using sample information, comparing treatments, correlation, estimating, predicting, testing hypotheses. Applications in business decision making, sports, medicine, and in the physical and social sciences. Students must have access to a Macintosh computer or be able to use the microcomputers in the University's computer labs. 9 assignments, no exams. Tuition and fees $274 (plus computer software), no required texts. (4 credits)

Swedish

Beginning Swedish I

An introduction to written and spoken Swedish through basic grammar, workbook exercises, and easy composition. Vocabulary useful to everyday situations is covered. 17 assignments, no exams.

Tuition and fees $342.50, text $73, 4 audiocassettes $11.50. (5 credits)

Beginning Swedish II

Continued development of basic skills in reading, writing, and speaking. Exercises also include grammar and oral assignments. 22 assignments, no exams. Tuition and fees $342.50, text $73, 2 audiocassettes $6.75. (5 credits)

Beginning Swedish III

A continuation of foundation skills in reading, writing, and listening. 20 assignments, no exams. Tuition and fees $342.50, text $73, 1 audiocassette $3.75. (5 credits)

Intermediate Swedish I

Further development of reading, writing, and listening skills. Grammar review, composition. 22 assignments, no exams. Tuition and fees $342.50, text $73, 1 audiocassette $3.75. (5 credits)

Intermediate Swedish II

Intended to allow the student to gradually begin to master Swedish in advanced contexts. Texts by various Swedish writers. Grammar exercises cover a systematic overview of prepositions, word order, and sentence structure. Texts include two dictionaries. 8 assignments, no exams. Tuition and fees $342.50, text $127, 4 audiocassettes $11.50. (5 credits)

Technical Writing

Technical Writing for Engineers

The course deals with the problem of writing for a multiple audience (expert, executive, and lay), the writing process iteself, and ways to master apprehension about writing. It also provides information about the appropriate format for technical writing, whether instruction manual, memo, or formal report.

Students must have access to an Apple Macintosh with HyperCard or be able to use the microcomputers in one of the University's computer labs. 8 assignments, no exams. Tuition: $284. (4 credits)

Theatre

Introduction to the Theatre

A videocassette course. History and theory of plays and playwrights. 3 assignments, 1 exam. Tuition and fees $274, text $66, video rental $50 ($25 refund). (4 credits)

Playwriting

An audiocassette course. Techniques of playwriting are explored in detail by students with some playwriting competence. The craft of writing a well-made play and experimentation in more modern styles are examined in the context of each student working toward the completion of a one-act or full-length play. 2 assignments, no exams. Tuition and fees $284, text $35, study guide $10, 10 audiocassettes $26.50. (4 credits)

History of the American Theatre

Examines the theatre from colonial days to the present as a mirror of our society. Playwrights, performers, and productions are seen in the context of our cultural, social, and political life. No assignments, 1 exam. Tuition and fees $284, text $65, study guide $10, 11 audiocassettes $29. (4 credits)

Women's Studies

Northern Minnesota Women: Myths and Realities

An audiocassette course. Examines the stereotypes and realities of life for Northern Minnesota Indian, Yankee, and immigrant women from the times of early settlement to the present day. 9 assignments, 1 exam. Tuition and fees $205.50, text $28, study guide $20, 10 audiocassettes $26.50. (3 credits)

Missouri

University of Missouri
Center for Independent Study
University Extension

136 Clark Hall
Columbia, MO   65211

(314) 882-2491 *Fax:* (314) 882-6808

Geographic Access: Worldwide

DELIVERY SYSTEMS

Audiocassette
Used primarily in foreign language courses.

Broadcast Television
Some courses may be viewed over cable broadcast television.

Videocassette
Students enrolling in video courses must indicate how they wish to view tapes (home use, viewing center, or group enrollment).

INSTITUTION DESCRIPTION

The University of Missouri was established in 1839 and includes campuses in Columbia, Kansas City, Rolla, and St. Louis.

The Independent Study program was established in 1911. Students enrolled in the program come from every county in Missouri, every state in the nation, and from more than a dozen foreign countries.

The Center for Independent Study pioneered the use of the Computer-Assisted Lesson Service (CALS) in 1974. CALS courses are processed by computer, which speeds up the lesson response time and provides computer-generated feedback that helps students review lessons and study for exams. There are three types of CALS courses: CALS Mail-In requires completed lesson assignments on answer sheets that are provided with the course study guide to be mailed to the Center. The answer sheet is scanned by a computer, which generates a lesson report containing the student's score, general comments on performance, and feedback on all incorrect answers. CALS-Online requires access to a computer terminal with a modem and a printer. Lessons are submitted directly to a University computer and the student's lesson report prints out as soon as the lesson is completed. PC-Based CALS is particularly suited to military personnel stationed overseas or on ships at sea. It operates much like CALS-Online except that no phone line or modem is needed. The lesson report is generated via computer software provided by the University of Missouri. Because of technical limitations, some courses cannot be taken using CALS-Online or PC-Based CALS.

Accreditation: NCA

Official/Contact: Roger G. Young, Director

Admission Requirements: Students may enroll at anytime. Enrollment in a course does not constitute admission to the University of Missouri.

Tuition: Undergraduate, $81.40 per credit hour; graduate $103 per credit hour. Textbooks must be purchased by the student. Additional fees for audio- and videocassette rental are listed below with the course descriptions. A refund of 70% of the rental fee is made upon return of the tapes in good condition.

Degree Credit: A degree cannot be earned entirely through Independent Study.

Grading: The A, B, C, D, F system of grading is used. Some courses may be taken on a satisfactory/unsatisfactory basis. Examinations must be proctored. Credit is awarded in semester hour units.

Library: University of Missouri Video Viewing Centers are located throughout the state.

COURSES OFFERED

Accounting

Introduction to Accounting

An introduction to financial accounting theory and practice, this course emphasizes the accounting cycle and the preparation of general-purpose financial statements for proprietary, partnership, and corporate entities. Topics include the nature of financial reporting, income recognition concepts, the accounting accumulation process, and accounting for selected balance sheet accounts. 7 half-hour video lessons, 5 exams (3 hours each). Videotape rental: $54. (3 credits)

Astronomy

Cosmic Evolution/Introductory Astronomy

Planets: A brief survey of their motions and properties. Stars: Observations, including stellar spectra and colors, stellar evolution, and star clusters. Galaxies: Structure and content of the Milky Way Galaxy, its relationship to other galaxies. Cosmology: The origin and evolution of the universe. 19 lessons, 17 submitted. 2 exams (2 hours each). 30 half-hour video lessons. Videotape rental: $110. (3 credits)

Business Administration

Entrepreneurship/Small Business Management

An integrative general management course designed to communicate the academic principles of business management applicable to the solving of problems of small- and medium-sized businesses and to assist in their development. Provides a background in the forms of business, the development of business plans and systems integration, venture capital, accounting procurement, promotion, financing, distribution and negotiations for initial organization, and operation and expansion of the firm. 11 lessons, 10 submitted plus 1 project for undergraduate students, 2 for graduate students. 10 half-hour video lessons. 2 exams (2 hours each). Videotape rental: $75. (3 credits)

Computer Science

Introduction to BASIC

An introduction to Microsoft and IBM PC BASIC. Emphasis on language syntax, structured programming, and problem solving. For teachers and persons in related occupations. Students may use any computer capable of running BASIC but the lessons will focus on IBM DOS. 14 lessons, 4 submitted. 8 half-hour video lessons. 3 exams (1 hour each). Videotape rental: $85. (3 credits)

Software Applications on the PC

An introduction to operating systems, word processing, spreadsheets, and database manipulation. A postbaccalaureate course designed for teachers and persons in related occupations. 15 lessons, 4 submitted. 8 video lessons. 3 exams (1 hour each). Videotape rental: $100. (3 credits)

Economics

Introduction to the American Economy

Introduction to economic analysis and problems through an examination of the development and operations of the American economy. Study of its evolutions, institutions, and principal problems. 12 lessons, 12 submitted. 28 half-hour video lessons. 4 exams (2 hours each). Videotape rental: $115. (3 credits)

Education

Microcomputers: Applications for Teachers

Provides the student with an in-depth analysis of computer applications. Classroom applications have been added in response to the needs of teachers who have had introductory coursework in computers. The application phase focuses not only on location, evaluation, and use of software, but also on computer-assisted instruction, including development of classroom teaching materials with database and/or word processing programs. A microcomputer is required to do the coursework. A one-day seminar is also required (usually held in St. Louis or at group enrollment sites). 10 lessons, 2 written assignments or 1 project. 10 half-hour video lessons. 1 exam (2 hours). The PBS videotape *Making the Most of the Micro* is not available for home use. (3 credits)

Photography for Teachers

Basic 35mm photography techniques and processes, photo publications, and basic slide/tape production as they apply to educational settings. Student will need access to a 35mm single-lens reflex (SLR) camera, flash, tripod, and filters. 16 lessons, 8 submitted (includes 6 photo assignments and 2 projects). 16 half-hour video lessons. 3 exams (2 hours each). Videotape rental: $115. (3 credits)

Teaching of Reading Comprehension

This course reviews the most current research on reading comprehension. Particular emphasis is given to classroom applications and the role of the teacher. Specific techniques for the improvement of reading comprehension are discussed and illustrated in the context of the typical classroom setting. 14 lessons, term paper. 14 half-hour videos. 2 exams (2 hours each). Videotape rental: $95. (3 credits)

The Role of the Mentor Teacher

Development of the role of the mentor teacher with emphasis on the elements necessary for a successful relationship between the mentor teacher and the beginning teacher. Topics include the nature and purpose of induction programs, establishing the mentor relationship, how to begin the school year, time management, how to develop student motivation, dealing with stress, and meeting the needs of at-risk students. 12 lessons, 12 submitted. Journal and analysis paper required. 12 half-hour video lessons. No exams. Videotape rental: $55. (3 credits)

Introduction to the Gifted

Surveys the history and philosophy of gifted education and examines characteristics of gifted learners and teachers of the gifted. Program models and curricular/instructional design are also discussed. 10 lessons, 10 submitted. 10 half-hour videos. No exams. Videotape rental: $80. (3 credits)

A Changing World—A Changing Classroom:
Dealing with Critical Situations in the School

Examines a range of current social problems, such as drug abuse, school violence, divorce, suicide, and illiteracy, and their effect on classroom management and school curriculum. Coping strategies are suggested through exemplary presentations in the area of class management and person-to-person interactions. A two-day seminar is required (held in Kansas City and at group enrollment sites). 7 lessons, one to three papers and application notebook submitted. 6 half-hour video lessons. Videotape rental: $57. (3 credits)

Coping with Student Problems in the Classroom:
Dealing in Discipline

Designed to help teachers deal more effectively with interpersonal conflicts and disruptive behavior in the classroom. This course examines behavioristic methods, humanistic methods, and methods designed to foster self-control and responsibility in students. Each method is applied to simulated classroom situations at both the elementary and secondary levels. Ways of dealing with drug problems and special situations in urban schools are examined, and basic information on an educator's legal rights and responsibilities is provided. A two-day seminar is required (held in Kansas City and at group enrollment sites). 9 lessons, one to three papers and applications notebook submitted. No exams. 8 half-hour video lessons. Videotape rental: $65. (3 credits)

Engineering

Management for Engineers

The transition of the engineer to manager, planning and organizing technical activities, selecting and managing projects, team building and motivation, techniques of control and communications, and time management. 28 lessons. 3 exams (1 hour 15 minutes each). 25 one-hour video lessons. Videotape rental: $135. (3 credits)

English

Themes and Forms in Literature (Shakespeare)

Designed to lead students to a better understanding of Shakespearean drama in performance. Using the BBC-TV video series, this course examines the following plays: *A Midsummer Night's Dream, Richard III, Romeo and Juliet, The Merchant of Venice, Julius Caesar, Hamlet, Othello, King Lear, Measure for Measure,* and *The Winter's Tale.* The video productions will play a central role in the course. In assignments and examinations, students will be asked to consider various aspects of these productions: director's interpretations, actors' realizations of major roles, the effect of camera work, lighting, etc. 10 lessons, 10 submitted. Book report, paper. 10 video lessons varying in length from 2 to 4 hours each. 2 exams (1 hour each). Videotape rental: $130. (3 credits)

French

Elementary French I

Introduction to French grammar and composition. Practice in hearing and speaking French through the use of audiocassette tapes. 13 lessons, 13 submitted. 4 exams (first three 1-1/2 hours each, final 2-1/2 hours). Audiotape rental: $10. (5 credits)

Elementary French II

A continuation of French grammar and composition. Practice in hearing and speaking through the use of audiocassette tapes. 19 lessons, 19 submitted. 4 exams (first three 1-1/2 hours each, final 2-1/2 hours). Audiotape rental: $10. (5 credits)

Elementary French III

A multiskill course centering on cultural/literary readings and including a grammar review, practice in the spoken language, as well as some practice in written expressions. Practice in hearing and speaking French through the use of audiocassette tapes. 11 lessons, 11 submitted. 2 exams (1-hour midterm, 2-hour final). Audiotape rental: $10. (3 credits)

Geology

Earth Science

A broad and general study of the earth, its origin, the development of its crustal features and the processes which shape them, its oceans, climates, and neighbors in the solar system. 13 lessons, 6 submitted. 2 exams (1-1/2 hours each). 14 half-hour video lessons. Videotape rental: $75. (3 credits)

German

Elementary German I

Covers the basics of speaking, reading, and writing German. 14 lessons, 14 submitted. 2 exams (2 hours each). Audiotape rental: $15. (5 credits)

Elementary German II

A continuation of Elementary German I. 13 lessons, 13 submitted. 2 exams (2 hours each). Audiotape rental: $15. (5 credits)

History

The War in Vietnam and the U.S.

Understanding the political experience and the lessons and legacies of the war in Vietnam and the United States. 12 lessons, 6 submitted. 3 exams (2 hours each). 15 one-hour video lessons. Videotape rental: $105. (3 credits)

History of Science

A survey of science from ancient times to the twentieth century focusing on the leading conceptual developments within science, the scientific revolution, and sciences' role in society. 10 lessons, 2 submitted. 2 exams (1-1/2 hours each). 10 one-hour video lessons. Videotape rental: $100. (3 credits)

Latin

Elementary Latin

Forms, grammar, syntax. 20 lessons, 10 submitted. 2 exams (2 hours each). Audiotape rental: $2. (5 credits)

Intensive Beginning Latin

Forms, grammar, syntax. 20 lessons, 10 submitted. 2 exams (2 hours each). Audiotape rental: $2. (3 credits)

Mathematics

Fundamentals of Algebra III

Topics covered include operations on fractions, exponents, radicals, and quadratic equations. 8 lessons, 8 submitted. 2 exams (2-hour midterm, 3-hour final). 8 one-hour video lessons. Videotape rental: $66. (2 credits)

Philosophy

Ethics and the Professions

Examination of ethical issues confronted by members of different professions such as medicine, law, business, journalism, and engineering. 10 lessons, 6 submitted. 2 exams (2 hours each). Annenberg/CPB *Ethics in America* videotape rental: $100. (3 credits)

Physics

The Mechanical Universe

Includes the basic elements of differential and integral calculus. Emphasis on astronomical applications and on historical development. 26 lessons, 26 submitted. 3 exams (2 hours each). 26 half-hour video lessons. Videotape rental: $110. (3 credits)

Political Science

Congressional Politics
A study of legislative institutions, procedures, and behavior. 11 lessons, 7 submitted (including term paper). 3 exams (1 hour each). 26 half-hour video lessons. Videotape rental: $110. (3 credits)

The American Constitution
Leading American constitutional principles as they have evolved through important decisions of the United States Supreme Court. 15 lessons. 3 exams (2-1/2 hours each). 15 one-hour video lessons. Videotape rental: $75. (3 credits)

Psychology

Brain, Mind, and Behavior
Explains what science knows—and does not know—about the human brain to date. Grounded in psychology and neurobiology and structured in terms of human brain function, the course draws on important research and a selection of international case studies to present the most current findings, theories, and applications of brain science. 8 lessons. 3 exams (2 hours each). 8 one-hour video lessons. Videotape rental: $65. (3 credits)

Sociology

Criminology
Sociology of law. Constitutional, psychological, sociological theories of criminal behavior. Process of criminal justice, treatment of corrections, control of crime. 15 lessons, none submitted. 3 exams (first and second are 1 hour each, 2-hour final). 13 half-hour video lessons. Videotape rental: $86. (3 credits)

Spanish

Elementary Spanish I
Introduction to the Spanish language. Practice in hearing and speaking Spanish through the use of audiocassette tapes. 11 lessons, 10 submitted. 2 exams (1-hour midterm, final of 2-1/2 hours). Audiotape purchase price: $26.70. (5 credits)

Elementary Spanish II
A continuation of Elementary Spanish I. Practice in hearing and speaking Spanish through the use of audiocassettes. 10 lessons, 10 submitted. 2 exams (1-hour midterm, final of 1-1/2 hours). Audiotape purchase price: $16.50. (5 credits)

Elementary Spanish III
A multiskill course following the above course centering on cultural/literary readings, and including a grammar review, practice in the spoken language, as well as some practice in written expression. 14 lessons, 8 submitted. 2 exams (2 hours each). Audiotape purchase price: $5. Six-part videotape program purchase price: $40. (3 credits)

Special Education

The Psychology and Education of Exceptional Individuals
The psychology and education of individuals with special problems and/or abilities. Survey of theories and strategies for the learning-teaching process and sources of assistance to educators and parents. Required for many certification programs. A seminar is required for a grade of A or B (held in St. Louis or at group enrollment sites. 12 lessons, 0-12 submitted depending on grade contracted for. 2 exams (1 hour each). 12 half-hour video lessons. Videotape rental: $108. (3 credits)

Theatre

The Theatre in Society
Examines the role and scope of the theatre in the modern world community. 11 lessons, 11 submitted. 2 exams (2 hours each). Videotapes: *Oedipus Rex, Romeo and Juliet, School for Scandal, The Wild Duck, The Dumb Waiter, True West, Sweeney Todd, Death of a Salesman, The Merchant of Venice.* Videotape rental: $100. (2 credits)

Nebraska

University of Nebraska at Kearney
Office of Continuing Education

Kearney, NE 68849

(308) 234-8840

Geographic Access: Nebraska

DELIVERY SYSTEMS

Broadcast Television

Access to the telecourses is obtained through Nebraska Educational Television Network (NETV) or through local or regional cable distribution systems. In Kearney, access is through Channel 3 (without cable) or Channel 12 (with cable).

INSTITUTION DESCRIPTION

The University of Nebraska at Kearney, formerly Kearney State College, was established in 1903. It became part of the University of Nebraska system in 1991.

Telecast requirements for each course will vary from 9 to 15 one-hour sessions. Students will be provided a course outline from the coordinating instructor detailing the specific activities and course expectations. Additional coursework will be required and completed at the direction of the coordinating instructor as listed with each course. Textbook, study guide, and other course materials developed by the instructor will be an integral part of the course.

Accreditation: NCA

Official/Contact: Doyle Howitt, Dean

Admission Requirements: Open enrollment. Special advising sessions are scheduled for persons interested in pursuing a program of study at the University of Nebraska at Kearney. The sessions are informal and Deans and/or representatives of the various colleges will be available to discuss individual interests and assist in planning a program or advising and consulting on matters of personal concern.

Tuition: $55 per credit hour for undergraduate credit; $62.25 for graduate credit.

Degree Credit: Credit awarded is applicable to degree programs at the University.

Grading: Three grading options are available, unless otherwise exempted in the course description: traditional (A, B, C, D, F), credit/no credit, and audit.

Library: The Calvin R. Ryan Library provides materials and services to support all faculty and students participating in off-campus classes at both the graduate and undergraduate level.

COURSES OFFERED

Art

Art Appreciation

An introductory-level telecourse that examines the works of art that have come to define the Western visual tradition from ancient Greece to the present day. The course helps students to appreciate the formal qualities, iconography, and technical achievements of these extraordinary monuments. It will also show how they closely reflect the prevailing attitudes of the society in which they were created, as well as the goals of the artists and partrons responsible for their creation. Telecourse title: *Art of the Western World*. 9 one-hour programs. (3 credits)

Business

Introduction to Business

This introduction to business is for everyone who wants to expand their understanding of business. The course provides a comprehensive view of the contemporary environment from the internal functions of a business to the challenges of business on an international scale. It delves into the complex functions of a business, exposing a student to the detailed internal and external operations affecting both large and small businesses. Telecourse title: *The Business File*. 28 half-hour programs. (3 credits)

Economics

Principles of Economics - Micro

A comprehensive course in microeconomics that is an absorbing documentary examination of major historic and contemporary events that have shaped twentieth-century American economics. Through the use of interviews, commentary and analysis, the course establishes a clear relationship between abstract economic principles and concrete human relationships. In addition to the video programs, participants utilize audio modules to provide further analysis and information. The 14 half-hour audio programs provide expanded interviews with economists who appear in the video portion of the lesson. Audiocassettes are required for the course and will be furnished through the Antelope Bookstore at a cost of $11.66 for the 14 audiotapes. Telecourse title: *Economics U$A*. 14 half-hour programs. (3 credits)

English

Expository Writing

English composition and rhetoric taught from a "process" point of view is the focus of a challenging telecourse in basic expository writing. It is appropriate for the beginning student in English and for those wishing to improve and expand their writing skills. Dramatization and mini-documentaries are used throughout the series. Most of the nation's leading authorities on the teaching of composition are interviewed along with many interviews with such well-known writers as Irving Stone, Irving Wallace, Larry Gelbart, and Melville Shavelson. Telecourse title: *The Write Course*. 30 half-hour programs. (3 credits)

Psychology

General Psychology

Covers the fundamental principles and major concepts of psychology, including brain and behavior, sensation and perception, conditioning and learning, cognitive processes, motivation and emotion, lifespan development, the self and identity, sex and gender, testing and intelligence, social influences, psychopathology and therapy, stress and health issues, methodology, and new directions. The host for the video programs is Philip Zimbardo who has taught introductory psychology for more than 30 years. Telecourse title: *Discovering Psychology*. 26 half-hour programs. (3 credits)

Abnormal Psychology

This telecourse explores the complex causes, manifestations, and treatment of common behavior disorders. Interviews with patients give students an invaluable perspective on the emotional toll paid by those who suffer from behavior disorders. In addition, commentary by therapists and other mental health professionals presents the multiple approaches to treatment. The course introduces abnormal behavior along a continuum from functional to dysfunctional. 13 one-hour programs. (3 credits)

Sociology

Marriage and Family

This telecourse takes a close look at marriage and family in the closing decade of the twentieth century. Documentary footage, combined with expert commentary, brings into focus the fascinating mosaic of family forms that exist today: traditional families, single-parent families, stepfamilies, families without children, dual-worker marriages, cohabiting couples. Telecourse title: *Portrait of a Family*. 26 half-hour programs. (3 credit hours)

Introduction to Sociology

An introductory-level college telecourse designed to give students an in-depth look at groups, communities, institutions, and social situations that illustrate major sociological concepts. Each lesson is structured as a documentary, featuring interviews with people in their family settings, at work, school, worship, and play. These documentaries are thought provoking, emotionally strong illustrations of issues such as socialization, social control, sex and gender, aging, education, collective behavior, and social change. Telecourse title: *Sociological Imagination.* 26 half-hour programs. (3 credits)

Spanish

Beginning Spanish

A two-semester Spanish language telecourse designed to give students full communicative proficiency in Spanish—listening, speaking, reading, and writing. In addition to the video programs via NETV, participants utilize audio modules to provide further learning instruction. The videos use a uniquely Hispanic genre, the "telenovela," to combine a dramatic storyline with instruction. The situation and context of each episode introduce students to the basic structures, language functions, and vocabulary groups that are presented in the programs and resource materials. 52 half-hour programs. (8 credits)

Statistics

Elementary Statistics

An introductory statistics telecourse that provides an extraordinary exploration of statistical processes, stressing data-centered topics rather than the more traditional path from probability to formal inference. Telecourse title: *Against All Odds: Inside Statistics.* 26 half-hour programs. (3 credits)

University of Nebraska at Lincoln
Department of Independent Study
Division of Continuing Studies

269 Nebraska Center for Continuing Education
Lincoln, NE   68583-0900

(402) 472-1926 *Fax:* (402) 472-8220

Geographic Access: Nationwide

DELIVERY SYSTEMS

Audiocassette
Used extensively in the high school TeleLanguage Program.

Computer Tutorials
Requires access to an IBM PC or compatible.

INSTITUTION DESCRIPTION

The University of Nebraska is a state university established as a land-grant college in 1871. The Department of Independent Study, in addition to offering traditional correspondence courses (college and high school) offers TeleLanguage courses at the high school level. This program combines traditional independent study with telephone conferencing to give students a sound base in French, German, Spanish, or Latin. Teachers work with the students on the telephone and evaluate assignments and examinations.

Accreditation: NCA

Official/Contact: Monty McMahon, Director

Admission Requirements: Students may enroll in any course provided they have met all prerequisites. Enrollment in a course does not constitute admission to the University of Nebraska.

Tuition: College courses $69.75 per credit. High school language courses $79 per half-unit. Additional fees are listed below with the course description. Students must purchase textbooks. American Express, MasterCard, and VISA accepted.

Degree Credit: Students should contact an academic adviser to make sure the course to be taken will meet the requirements of the degree.

Grading: Examinations must be proctored. Students living within a 35-mile radius of Lincoln or Scottsbluff must take their examinations at one of the University's test sites. Other students may have their examinations proctored by an individual active in the educational field as a teacher, counselor, or an administrator. Credit is awarded in semester hour units for college courses and 1/2 Carnegie unit per high school course.

Library: Officially enrolled students have access to the campus library. Students are encouraged to utilize their local community libraries.

COURSES OFFERED

French

French 1

A TeleLanguage course, high school level. Students are introduced to the basic grammatical concepts necessary to develop reading and writing skills in French. They become acquainted with French culture through a variety of readings in both French and English. Students also have the opportunity to develop speaking and listening skills as they hear French and speak it themselves. This course covers the basic sentence structure of positive and negative statements, commands and questions, and the present and future tenses. Audiocassette tapes: $8. (1/2 unit)

French 2

A TeleLanguage course, high school level. This course reinforces and augments the grammatical concepts presented in French 1. Students build new vocabulary, learn more advanced grammar concepts, increase their reading comprehension skills, and develop their knowledge of several essential parts of speech and a number of commonly used French idioms and expressions. Audiocassette tapes: $8. (1/2 unit)

French 3

A TeleLanguage course, high school level. In this course, students look at the United States from the French perspective and take an imaginary tour of Paris. After reviewing the grammar and rules presented in French 1 and 2, students study indirect objects, emphatic/interrogative/reflexive pronouns. Also studied are verbs in the reflexive voice, the imperfect tense, and the conditional mood. Audiocassette tapes: $8. (1/2 unit)

French 4

A TeleLanguage course, high school level. This course presents a historical survey of French civilization. Students are introduced to famous people and events and study the broad social, economic, and political forces that shaped French culture. Students study the *subjonctif* and are introduced to the *passé simple*. In addition, they increase their awareness of the subtleties of the language as they learn specific strategies and helpful techniques for reading and listening. Audiocassette tapes: $8. (1/2 unit)

Second-Year French

A TeleLanguage course, high school level. The reading selections in this course describe French and Parisian life. Students are introduced to new concepts about reflexive pronouns and verbs, the *imparfait* and *plus-que-parfait* tenses, the *conditional* mood, and other topics. Audiocassette tapes: $8. (1/2 unit)

German

German 1

A TeleLanguage course, high school level. The reading selections are designed to familiarize students with German as it is written and spoken. Students study nouns, articles, personal pronouns, possessive adjectives, and prepositions. Also studied are the uses of nominative, accusative, genitive, and dative cases plus agreement and positions of direct and indirect objects. The analysis of verbs is confined to the present tense of regular, irregular, and reflexive verbs. Audiocassette tape: $3. (1/2 unit)

German 2

A TeleLanguage course, high school level. Students learn about the legends, customs, and daily lives of the German people. Idiomatic expressions receive considerable attention in the course, while periodic reviews reinforce points that students may have forgotten. Among the topics emphasized are plurals of nouns and articles in the genitive and dative cases, declension of nouns and articles, uses of der- and ein- words, "doubtful" prepositions, and uses of da- and wo- compounds. The forms and uses of the past, perfect, past perfect, and future tenses of regular, irregular, and reflexive verbs in the active voice are introduced. Audiocassette tape: $3. (1/2 unit)

German 3

A TeleLanguage course, high school level. The reading selections included in this course help students develop an understanding of German culture and its contributions to Western civilization. A concise review of the principles studied in German 1 and 2 lays the foundation for more advanced study of German grammar and sentence structure. Students consider expressions of time, declension of adjectives, degrees of adjectives and adverbs, past tense of modal auxiliaries, modal auxiliaries with dependent infinitives, principal parts of separable/inseparable/mixed verbs, and intransitive verbs with dative subjects. Audiocassette tape: $3. (1/2 unit)

German 4

A TeleLanguage course, high school level. In this course, students not only further their appreciation of German history and culture but also practice and extend their skills in reading, writing, and speaking German. Because mastery of verbs is essential to mastery of the German language, much of the grammar pertains directly or indirectly to the forms and uses of verbs, infinitives, and modal auxiliaries. By the end of this course, students should have a German vocabulary of approximately 1300 words, know the meaning of approximately 150 idioms, and have a firm grasp of German sentence structure. Audiocassette tape: $3. (1/2 unit)

History

Nebraska History

A survey of the political, economic, and social development of Nebraska from the earliest exploration to the present. Audiocassette tapes: $10. (3 credits)

Latin

Latin 1

A TeleLanguage course, high school level. The Latin readings for this introductory course are adapted from Roman mythology and history. As they translate the readings into English, students become familiar with the structure of Latin sentences. They work most intensively with nouns, adjectives, and verbs. Students examine the common uses of first- and second-declension nouns in the nominative, genitive, dative, accusative, and ablative cases and the formation and meaning of the present, imperfect, future, and perfect tenses of active-voice verbs of the first, second, third, and fourth conjugations. (1/2 unit)

Latin 2

A TeleLanguage course, high school level. The philosophy that studying grammar is an aid to reading Latin underlies this course. Students increase their appreciation of Roman culture and its contributions to Western civilization as they read Latin selections based on Roman history, mythology, and literature. They study pronouns, infinitives, participles, ablative absolutes, and adverbial expressions. Students should have a Latin vocabulary of approximately 800 words and a good grasp of common grammatical constructions by the end of this course. (1/2 unit)

Latin 3

A TeleLanguage course. high school level. The Latin readings for this course are adaptations of Livy's account of Hannibal's exploits during the Second Punic War. Considerable attention is given to verbs in the subjunctive mood. In addition, students become familiar with tense sequences and the construction of dependent clauses. (1/2 unit)

Latin 4

A TeleLanguage course, high school level. Selections from Caesar's *Gallic Wars* that are appropriate to students' growth and depth in the language are presented. Students also read selections from Suetonius and Apuleius, and they identify the characteristic and unusual aspects of syntax and grammar found in these readings. (1/2 unit)

Latin 5

A TeleLanguage course, high school level. The Roman writer Cicero had a powerful influence on the writing and philosophy of his own contemporaries as well as on that of succeeding generations. Students come to understand Cicero's contributions as they study his life and read selections from his orations, philosophical works, and letters. Reading selections by Quintilian and Seneca give students the opportunity to see how writing styles varied from writer to writer and changed through time. (1/2 unit)

Latin 6

A TeleLanguage course, high school level. Students broaden their understanding of the variety of Latin literature and Roman thought as they read selections written during the Classical Period of Rome. Included among the readings are lyrical poems of Catullus, selections from epic poetry of Virgil, satiric epigrams of Marital, letters of Pliny, and an adaptation of a comedy by Plautus. Students gain further insight into the Latin language as they read a story and a poem written during the Middle Ages. (1/2 unit)

Marketing

Marketing

Examination of the marketing system, its relations with the socioeconomic system, and the influences of each upon the other. Study of the evolution and present structure of marketing institutions and processes. Consideration of customer attributes and behavioral characteristics, and how a marketing manager responds to these in the design of marketing strategies, using research, product development, pricing, distribution structure, and promotion. To take this course, students must have access to an IBM PC or XT (minimum 64K and one disk drive) with color card and color monitor. 12 diskettes: $25. (3 credits)

Spanish

Spanish 1

A TeleLanguage course, high school level. Students develop a good grasp of fundamental Spanish grammar that enables them to read simple stories and to compose simple paragraphs. In addition, they develop an understanding of the culture and geography of the Spanish-speaking world. Basic sentence structure, parts of speech, regular and irregular verbs in the present tense are covered. Students develop vocabulary related to clothing, the house, time, weather, the calendar, numbers, and family relationships. Audiocassette tapes: $8. (1/2 unit)

Spanish 2

A TeleLanguage course, high school level. Against a cultural backdrop that includes discussion of such diverse topics as jobs and entertainment, traditional Hispanic foods, and Spanish history and travel, students increase their vocabulary, their understanding of grammatical constructions, and their ability to read and write Spanish. Students focus on the study of stem-changing and irregular verbs, possessive adjectives, comparison of adjectives, and the preterite tense. Audiocassette tapes: $8. (1/2 unit)

Spanish 3

A TeleLanguage course, high school level. Students increase their ability to read, write, and speak Spanish as they systematically study more advanced language concepts. A thorough review of regular, irregular, and stem-changing verbs in the present and preterite tenses leads smoothly and naturally into a study of reflexive and spelling-change verbs and the imperfect, present progressive, and present perfect tenses. Students expand their ability to write complex sentences in Spanish using reflexive, direct object, and indirect object pronouns and increase their knowledge of Spanish culture as they read and hear about special occasions, holidays, and practices observed by the Spanish people. Audiocassette tapes: $8. (1/2 unit)

Spanish 4

A TeleLanguage course, high school level. Students thoroughly review regular, irregular, and stem-changing verbs in the present, preterite, and imperfect tenses before beginning a study of the future, conditional, and present subjunctive tenses. (1/2 unit)

University of Nebraska - CorpNet
Nebraska CorpNet
Academic Telecommunications

157 Nebraska Center for Continuing Education
P.O. Box 830900
Lincoln, NE   68583-0900

(402) 472-1924 *Fax:* (402) 472-1901

Geographic Access: Nebraska

DELIVERY SYSTEMS

Interactive Audio/Video

The staff at Educational Television schedule satellite time, provide technical support for instructors, and help site coordinators and students troubleshoot equipment and transmission problems. Technical engineers add sites to the audio bridge at the beginning of each class, and operate three cameras in the CorpNet classroom. Support staff in the University Television office act as a contact point for students and site coordinators for technical assistance.

INSTITUTION DESCRIPTION

The University of Nebraska was established and chartered in 1869 and offered first instruction at the postsecondary level in 1871.

Nebraska CorpNet is a corporate training network for the onsite delivery of University of Nebraska college courses and workshops. The CorpNet system utilizes one-way video and two-way audio connections that allow participants in the workplace to interact with the instructors, as well as with their on-campus and off-campus classmates, in a live exchange of information and ideas. The interactive capability provides an opportunity to ask questions, offer comments, and take an active role in the teaching/learning process. CorpNet is a cooperative effort of several operating units at the University of Nebraska: academic departments and colleges, University of Nebraska—Lincoln Division of Continuing Studies, and the University of Nebraska—Lincoln Television Department and Station KUON-TV.

CorpNet makes it possible for students to earn master's degrees in mechanical engineering, industrial and management systems engineering, manufacturing systems engineering, and computer science. Students interested in taking engineering classes but whose place of employment is not a member of Nebraska CorpNet may attend classes at any one of the following open sites: Central Community College, Platte Campus, Columbus, NE; College Park at Grand Island; University of Nebraska at Kearney; or University of Nebraska Panhandle Education Center, Scottsbluff.

Accreditation: NCA

Official/Contact: Marv Van Kekerix, Director

Admission Requirements: Students can be admitted to Graduate Studies at UNL as either degree-seeking or unclassified (nondegree). Application can be made at any time. Most CorpNet students choose to complete an unclassified admission to Graduate Studies at the time of first enrollment through CorpNet.

Tuition: Graduate courses $414.75; undergraduate $348.75. An additional fee of $40 is required. All materials used in the course must be purchased by the student from UNL Division of Continuing Studies. American Express, MasterCard, and VISA accepted.

Degree Credit: The master's program in Manufacturing Systems Engineering is an interdisciplinary program designed to give the student the necessary background and knowledge to design, install, operate, and alter manufacturing systems composed of people, material, machines, information, and technology. To earn this degree, students must complete 30 hours of graduate courses including a six-hour thesis (optional nonthesis degree requires 36 hours of graduate work). The Master's Program in Industrial and Management Systems Engineering designed for middle management people is available to students who have experience in industry and possess a baccalaureate degree in engineering or the hard sciences. The degree requires 30 hours of graduate courses including a six-hour thesis (non-thesis degree requires 36 hours of graduate work). The Master's Degree Program in Mechanical Engineering is designed to dovetail with other graduate engineering courses so students can also get backgrounds in management, decision science, and manufacturing. Three areas of emphasis are available: thermal-fluid sciences, systems and design, and metallurgy. The program requires the completion of 30 hours of graduate courses including a six-hour thesis (non-thesis degree requires the completion of 36 hours of graduate courses). The Master's Program in Computer Science is designed for people who want to learn and keep abreast with the frontiers in the computer field. The degree requires the completion of 30 hours of

graduate courses including a six-hour thesis (non-thesis degree program requires the completion of 36 hours of graduate courses). Courses are announced prior to each semester. The courses listed below represent a partial number of those that are available. The student should consult the announcements for new course availability as well as the rescheduling of previously offered courses.

Grading: Examinations are taken at the student's work site according to the schedule established by the instructor. All closed-book examinations will be proctored by a representative of the student's company or by a learning center coordinator. Grades are issued by the UNL Office of Registration and Records. Credit is awarded in semester hour units.

Library: Students have access to a number of library services from the University Libraries of University of Nebraska—Lincoln. A major resource available to students is IRIS (Innovative Research Information System), the automated catalog for the University Libraries. If the student has a personal computer, modem, and telecommunications software, it is possible to dial into HuskerNet and then access IRIS from home or office. Reference assistance is also available.

COURSES OFFERED

Civil Engineering

Theoretical Soil Mechanics II
A comprehensive study of both analytical and approximate solutions to seepage problems encountered in the analysis of earth structures that impound water. Problems dealing with estimating the quantity of seepage, definition of the flow domain, uplift pressure, piping, and slope stability are considered. (3 credits)

Computer Science

Combinatorial Methods for Computer Science
Models of computation, generating functions, recurrence relations, graphs and algorithms on graphs, Ramsey Theory, applications of planar graphs to VLSI. (3 credits)

Automata, Computation, and Formal Languages
Introduction to the classical theory of computer science. Finite state automata and regular languages, minimization of automata, context free languages and pushdown automata, Turing machines and other

models of computation, undecidable problems, introduction to computational complexity. (3 credits)

Industrial and Management Systems Engineering

Ergonomics I

Human factors affecting work. Focus on man: energy requirements, lighting, noise, monotony and fatigue, learning, simultaneous versus sequential tasks. (3 credits)

Packaging Engineering

Investigation of packaging processes, materials, equipment, and design. Container design, material handling, storage, packaging and environmental regulations, and material selection. (3 credits)

Theory and Practice of Materials Processing

Theory, practice, and application of conventional machining, forming, and nontraditional machining processes with emphasis on tool life, dynamics of machine tools, and adaptive control. (3 credits)

Industrial Systems Analysis I

The analysis of technologically based systems and problems using digital simulation with an emphasis on the construction of simulation models and on the use of special purpose simulation languages with applications for industrial systems. (3 credits)

Mechanical Engineering

Finite Element Methods for Fluid Mechanics

Application of the finite element method to nonlinear fluid flows for both viscous and inviscid fluids. Compressible flow Euler equations and incompressible flows will be considered. (3 credits)

Advanced Combustion Theory

Detailed analysis of modern combustion wave theory, particularly chain reaction calculations and flame temperature determination. Gas dynamics of flames. Advanced mass transfer as applied to combustion. Aerodynamics of flame stabilization by vortices. Critical examination of present experimental techniques and results. (3 credits)

Nevada

University of Nevada - Reno
Independent Study Department
Division of Continuing Education

Midby-Byron Center, Room 225
1041 North Virginia Street
Reno, NV   89557

(702) 784-4652

Geographic Access: Worldwide

DELIVERY SYSTEMS

Audiocassette
Audio-enhanced courses are used primarily in the teaching of foreign languages.

Videocassette
Videotapes accompany the course in hotel administration.

INSTITUTION DESCRIPTION

The University of Nevada - Reno is a land-grant institution that was established by the Nevada State Constitution of 1864. Through the Independent Study Department, college-level courses are offered for both credit and noncredit. In addition to the traditional correspondence courses, video- and audio-enhanced courses are available and described below. The Hotel Administration course described below is offered by the University of Nevada - Las Vegas and credit will be from that institution. Registration, however, should be made to the Division of Continuing Education in Reno at the address above.

Accreditation: NASC

Official/Contact: Catharine D. Sanders, Director

Admission Requirements: Formal admission to the University of Nevada is not required. Admission to distance learning courses does not constitute admission to the University.

Tuition: $52 per credit. Additional fees for tape rental are listed below with the course descriptions. Other fees for stationery and handling. Discover, Master-Card, and VISA accepted.

Degree Credit: A degree cannot be earned through independent study courses, although credit may be applied to the student's degree program. Students from other universities/colleges should check with their institutions for transfer-in eligibility.

Grading: The letter system, A-F, is applied. Students may select a Pass/Fail option. Examinations must be proctored. Credit is awarded in semester hour units.

Library: Students have access to the Getchell Library at the University of Nevada - Reno and Library Resource Centers at Truckee Meadows Community College and Western Nevada Community College.

COURSES OFFERED

Education

Special Problems in Curriculum and Instruction (Five Teaching Skills)
Five teaching skills practiced in microteaching situations and coding from an audiotape. A method of self-analysis of classroom interactions. 18 lessons, final exam. Audiotape deposit: $10.00 ($7.50 refundable). (1 credit)

English

Oral English for Non-Native Speakers
Individualized practice in the oral properties of English for persons who need to improve their fluency

(requires access to a learning laboratory or cassette recorder). 15 lessons, final exam. Set of 6 audiocassettes to accompany texts. Audiotape fee: $7.50 (refundable). (3 credits)

Introduction to Language

Nature and function of language, including an introduction to the linguistic subsystems of modern English and the development of the English language. 15 lessons, midterm and final exams. Audiotape fee: $7.50 (refundable).

Descriptive Grammar

Modern English grammar and usage. 20 lessons, midterm and final exams. Audiotape fee: $7.50 (refundable). (3 credits)

French

Elementary French I

Introduction to the language through the development of language skills and through structural analysis. Includes an introduction to French culture. 20 lessons, 4 progress tests, final exam. Audiotape fee: $7.50 (refundable). (4 credits)

Elementary French II

A continuation of Elementary French I. 20 lessons, 4 progress tests, final exam. Audiotape fee: $7.50 (refundable). (4 credits)

German

Elementary German I

Introduction to the language through the development of language skills and through structural analysis. Includes an introduction to German culture. 27 lessons, 2 progress tests, final exam. Videotape fee: $15 (refundable). Audiotape fee: $30 ($15 refundable). (4 credits)

Elementary German II

A continuation of Elementary German I. 27 lessons, 2 progress tests, final exam. Videotape fee: $15 (refundable). Audiotape fee: $30 ($15 refundable). (4 credits)

Hotel Administration

Hotel Advertising and Sales Promotions

A practical approach to contemporary advertising for hotels, restaurants, and tourist destinations. Fo-cuses on the distinctive aspects of hospitality, advertising, principles, strategies, techniques, and their application to industry situations. Emphasis on providing the hospitality manager with a working knowledge in the areas of planning, developing, and implementing effective advertising campaigns. 18 lessons, 2 progress tests, final exam. Videotape fee: $15 (refundable). (3 credits)

Italian

Elementary Italian I

Introduction to the language through the development of language skills and through structural analysis. Includes an introduction to Italian culture. 50 lessons, 2 progress tests, final exam. Audiotape fee: $7.50 (refundable). (4 credits)

Elementary Italian II

A continuation of Elementary Italian I. 50 lessons, 2 progress tests, final exam. Audiotape fee: $7.50 (refundable). (4 credits)

Second Year Italian

Structural review, conversation and writing, readings in modern literature. 48 lessons, midterm and final exams. Audiotape fee: $22.50 ($7.50 refundable). (3 credits)

Spanish

Elementary Spanish I

Introduction to the language through the development of language skills and through structural analysis. Includes an introduction to Spanish and Latin American culture. 27 lessons, 2 progress tests, final exam. Videotape fee: $15 (refundable). Audiotape fee: $30 ($15 refundable). (4 credits)

Elementary Spanish II

A continuation of Elementary Spanish I. 27 lessons, 2 progress tests, final exam. Videotape fee: $15 (refundable). Audiotape fee: $30 ($15 refundable). (4 credits)

Women's Studies

Introduction to Women's Studies

Interdisciplinary analysis of women in culture and society from historical and cross-cultural perspectives. 15 lessons, midterm and final exams. Videotape fee: $30 ($15 refundable). (3 credits)

New Hampshire

University of New Hampshire
School for Lifelong Learning
Office of the Dean

Dunlap Center
Durham, NH   03824

(800) 582-7248

Geographic Access: New Hampshire

DELIVERY SYSTEMS

Broadcast Television
Telecourses are broadcast over NHPTV Channel 11 in one-hour time blocks, resulting in 13 weeks of televised programming during a semester. In addition to the video component, SLL schedules several seminar meetings to provide student/faculty interaction. Loanable videotapes and/or audiocassettes containing all programs are also available.

Interactive Audio/Video
Special studio classrooms have been designed at the University of New Hampshire campuses in Durham and Manchester and at Plymouth State College and Keene State College. These studio classrooms are able to transmit and receive live televised instruction with interactive capabilities. Students and instructor can interact with one another using closed circuit television and audio/visual equipment located at each of the sites.

INSTITUTION DESCRIPTION

The School for Lifelong Learning of the University of New Hampshire is the nonresidential state college for adults offering individualized degree study in eleven regional offices of the state. It is one of four institutions in the University System of New Hampshire (USNH). Over the past ten years, the School for Lifelong Learning (SLL), Public Broadcasting Service (PBS), and New Hampshire Public Television (NHPT) have collaborated in the offering of telecourses for individuals throughout New Hampshire. Telecourses are geared mainly for individuals who because of distance or tight work schedules cannot attend weekly traditional class meetings. SLL's newest endeavor is Interactive Television (ITV), a cooperative USNH venture that dramatically widens the door of opportunity to New Hampshire residents who wish to pursue higher education. This new project allows students at four different sites (Plymouth, Keene, Durham, and Manchester) to interact with each other and the instructor using closed circuit television and audiovisual equipment at each of the sites.

Accreditation: NEASC

Official/Contact: Fran Mahoney, Associate Dean for Academic Affairs

Admission Requirements: Registration may be made with the School for Lifelong Learning. For degree programs, students must have high school graduation, GED, or other demonstrated ability to do college work. All courses are credit courses, therefore students pursuing degree programs should be formally admitted to an institution of higher learning in order for credit to be applied.

Tuition: Tuition rates vary by course. See listings below with course descriptions. Textbooks must be purchased by the student.

Degree Credit: Credit for courses successfully completed may be applied to a degree program.

Grading: Letter grades (A-F) are assigned. Examinations must be proctored. Credit is awarded in semester hour units.

Library: Regional public and private libraries are used in conjunction with institutional libraries of the university system.

COURSES OFFERED

Anthropology

Faces of Culture

An introductory telecourse that examines how societies are based on an integrative culture which satisfies human needs and facilitates survival. Among the concepts explained are the nature of culture, how cultures are studied, language and communication, social strategies, religion and magic, patterns of subsistence, and kinship and dissent. Tuition: $424 plus $15 registration fee. (4 credits)

Biology

The Human Brain

An Interactive Television (ITV) course that explores the relationship between the brain and characteristics of the mind. The human brain is the only biological organ capable of systematic self-awareness and self-exploration. The underlying theme is that the mind is actually a function of the brain. Topics include basic anatomy and physiology of the nervous system, language and consciousness, emotion, sleep and dreams, learning and memory, development and aging, gender differences, motivation, aggression and violence, mental disorders, addiction, and more. Tuition: $424 plus $15 registration fee. (4 credits)

Business

Something Ventured: Small Business Management

This telecourse provides aspiring entrepreneurs and those already involved in small business ventures with the tools needed to enhance potential for success. Observes small businesses in day-to-day operations and presents over-the-shoulder first-hand case studies of successful small business ventures. Tuition: $424 plus $15 registration fee. (4 credits)

Criminal Justice

Criminal Justice: Organization/Administration

An Interactive Television (ITV) course that is an introduction to the criminal justice system and to the administrative practices. The course focuses on an overview of the field, the efficient use of personnel, facilities, and equipment, as well as planning, budgeting, decision making, and internal and external communications. Additional in-depth focus will be placed on subsystems: law enforcement, courts, and corrections. Included are various management styles and organizational structures based on size, locale, and roles. Tuition: $424 plus $15 registration fee. (4 credits)

Education

Assessment of Prior Learning

An Interactive Television (ITV) course is designed for adults who have gained knowledge and related skills from life/work experiences that may be equivalent to college-level learning. Emphasis is placed on preparing a written portfolio which documents and demonstrates the knowledge they have gained and how it relates to the student's own degree plan of study. Tuition: $424 plus $15 registration fee. (4 credits)

Educating for Adult Literacy

An Interactive Television (ITV) course that examines current theory and practice related to effective service delivery in the field of adult basic skills instruction. Topics will include various approaches to defining literacy, barriers to learning, motivational and instructional techniques to promote retention and effective classroom learning, commonly used basic skills tests, as well as informal assessment techniques. The course will also explore recent government policy and funding amendments related to adult literacy. Tuition: $424 plus $15 registration fee. (4 credits)

English

Literary Visions

This telecourse focuses on major genres of literature—fiction, poetry, and drama—with individual lessons on the elements of these genres: plot and structure, character, setting, style, symbolism and myth, and theme. The programs bring literature to life with dramatizations of individual works, readings of literary passages, and interviews with authors. Tuition: $424 plus $15 registration fee. (4 credits)

Fine Arts

Art of the Western World
An introductory telecourse that examines the works of art that have come to define the Western visual tradition from ancient Greece to the present day. The course examines the formal qualities and technical achievements of important works from each of the major periods in Western art, as well as the prevailing attitudes of the society in which they were created. Tuition: $424 plus $15 registration fee. (4 credits)

History

The American Adventure
A telecourse focusing on American history from its prehistoric beginnings to the centennial celebration in 1876. Examines important national events and times of crisis as well as the contributions of political leaders, reformers, explorers, immigrants, industrialists, and other shapers of American life. Tuition: $424 plus $15 registration fee. (4 credits)

Humanities

Campbell: Transformations of Myth Through Time
An interdisciplinary telecourse that presents a scholarly perspective on the interaction of myth, religion, and culture. This course explores the ties between ancient religions and modern day culture, revealing the similarities and the differences of Eastern and Western religions. Tuition: $424 plus $15 registration fee. (4 credits)

Library Science

Fundamentals of Library Programming
An Interactive Television (ITV) course that details the basics for successful programming: planning, preparation, publicity, production, and evaluation as well as grant writing. Learners will become familiar with the selection of audiovisual equipment and the techniques of using it for programming. Tuition: $318 plus $15 registration fee. (3 credits)

Management

The Business of Management
A telecourse for the individual who has decided upon a career in business, government, or educational management. This introductory course explores management and business concepts. It is intended to provide essential skills in organizing and planning, directing, decision making, motivating, communicating, and applying managerial skills to a business organization. Tuition: $424 plus $15 registration fee. (4 credits)

Philosophy

Critical Thinking
An Interactive Television (ITV) course that focuses on developing the ability to think clearly, logically, and analytically in a wide range of problem solving situations. Emphasizes the relationship between reading and critical thinking and gives learners a structured way of interpreting the content and organization of written materials. Involves frequent, active participation in increasingly more complex individual and small group exercises requiring the use of appropriate intellectual strategies. Tuition $424 plus $15 registration fee. (4 credits)

Political Science

The Pacific Century
This telecourse is an overview of the political and economic powerful developments of the past 150 years of the Pacific Basin. Rather than focusing on individual countries, this course highlights the significant themes and trends that have affected the entire region, primarily focusing on modernity versus tradition, conflict between East and West, democracy/political authority/economic growth, and the United States in the Pacific. Tuition: $424 plus $15 registration fee. (4 credits)

Psychology

Abnormal Psychology
This telecourse explores complex factors that contribute to abnormal behavior and examines various treatment and therapy approaches. Examples of behaviors are shown along a continuum from functional to dysfunctional and are examined by teachers, clinicians, and researchers to highlight, analyze, and interpret what has been shown. Different perspectives from multiple approaches will be used, including the psychological, biological, environmental, and social, to provide a broad understanding of the issues involved. Tuition: $424 plus $15 registration fee. (4 credits)

The Mind

An introductory telecourse exploring the relationship between neuroscience and psychology. This course examines both the mind and its corollary—behavior. The course also explores topics in basic and applied psychology such as addiction, depression, and violence. Tuition: $424 plus $15 registration fee. (4 credits)

Spanish

Destinos: An Introduction to Spanish: Part I

This introductory Spanish language telecourse uses the appeal of a uniquely Hispanic genre—the telenovela—to make language and culture come alive. Basic Spanish language skills in listening, speaking, reading, and writing are developed. Learners experience both the variety as well as the commonalities that exist in the language and culture of the Spanish-speaking world through the many locations where the series was filmed. Tuition: $424 plus $15 registration fee. (4 credits)

Destinos: An Introduction to Spanish: Part II

A continuation of Destinos I described above. Tuition: $424 plus $15 registration fee. (4 credits)

Statistics

Against All Odds: Inside Statistics

An introductory telecourse covering basic statistical topics through a focus on real world applications. Major sections include analysis of data in distributions and in relationships, sampling techniques, and design mechanisms. Also covered are concepts of probability as the basis for inference, statistical tests and methods. Tuition: $424 plus $15 registration fee. (4 credits)

New Jersey

Bergen County Community College
See **WNET/New York City**

County College of Morris
See **WNET/New York City**

New Jersey Institute of Technology
ACCESS NJIT Telecourses
Center for Distance Learning
University Heights
Newark, NJ   07102-1982

(201) 596-3177 *Fax:* (201) 596-3203

Geographic Access: Worldwide

DELIVERY SYSTEMS

Broadcast Television
Students may receive video lessons on the Cable Television Network (CTN), NJN, or WNET-13 transmission. Specific delivery schedules are published in the NJIT Registrar's bulletin.

Videocassette
Tape circulation is limited to students with a bonafide need (where TV programming has been preempted). The cost for tape leasing is $55 per set. Several VHS sets can be leased from an outside video service.

INSTITUTION DESCRIPTION

Since its founding in 1881 at the urging of the Newark Board of Trade, New Jersey Institute of Technology has maintained close ties with industry by preparing successive generations of students to assume leadership roles in an increasingly technological society. The university, located on a 40-acre campus in the University Heights section of Newark, offers programs in engineering, technology, architecture, computer science and other applied sciences, management, mathematics, and policy studies.

The availability of credit-bearing telecourses via ACCESS NJIT provides an additional educational option to remote learners, nontraditional students, or those needing more flexible scheduling. Students can view material through closed-circuit television, through circulating VHS tapes, or through cable television. While faculty experts are actually in the process of teaching traditional students, telecourses are captured on tape and/or transmitted live to remote sites. Thus, the growing inventory of courses available have the same course content and quality as on-campus courses.

Accreditation: MSA

Official/Contact: Ann Lippel, Director, Distance Learning

Admission Requirements: Undergraduate credit courses are open to students with the appropriate background and are supervised by an NJIT mentor and to high school students supervised by school personnel and an NJIT mentor. Certificate credit courses are open to K-12 teachers and/or high school students under the supervision of an NJIT mentor. Courses taken for program enhancement are limited to K-12 institutions and civic groups and are by special arrangement with the Office of Distance Learning.

Tuition: $141 per credit for in-state undergraduate student; $293 per credit for out-of-state undergraduate student. In addition, all students pay a $34 fee per credit per course. A nonmatriculated student must pay a registration fee of $30. Any course may be taken for noncredit but the same tuition applies as for a credit course. Books must be purchased by the student and can be obtained from the NJIT Book Store.

Degree Credit: The curriculum for the B.A. in Computer and Information Science provides the student with a solid foundation in applying the principles of computing and information systems to business and industrial problems and managerial decision making in areas such as accounting, finance, marketing, environmental science, and manufacturing science. At least 24 of the total 125 hours must be earned through courses in the NJIT Computer and Information Science Department in order to guarantee a degree. Fourteen-week courses are available three times a year (fall, spring, and summer semesters). A course learning package includes video material, textbook, workbook, detailed syllabus, and assignments. Homework assignments, quizzes, and computer projects are submitted online where possible.

Grading: Letter grades (A-F) are awarded. Examinations must be proctored. If the student cannot attend the in-person administration of a midterm or a final examination, an arrangement can be made to take the exams at a site near home upon approval of the nominated proctor. Credit is awarded in semester hour units.

Library: Missed lessons can be viewed at the University Learning Center in Weston Hall.

COURSES OFFERED

Chemistry

College Chemistry for Advanced Placement or College Credit (Course 108)

The first half of a one-year course in college chemistry. Topics include matter and measurements, atoms/molecules/ions, chemical formulas and equations, gases, electronic structure, the periodic table, main group metals, thermochemistry, covalent bonding, molecular structure, liquids and solids, solutions, and reactions in aqueous solutions. 28 television lessons of 30 minutes each. (3 credits)

College Chemistry for Advanced Placement or College Credit (Course 109)

A continuation of the above course. Topics include gaseous equilibrium, acids and bases, acid-base and precipitation equilibria, complex ions, rate of reaction, the atmosphere, spontaneity of reactions, elec-

trochemistry, chemistry of transition metals, nonmetals, nuclear reactions, organic chemistry, polymers. 28 lessons of 30 minutes each. (3 credits)

Computer Science

Introduction to Computer Progamming and Problem Solving

This is a course in FORTRAN programming and its use in solving engineering and scientific problems. The emphasis is on logical analysis of a problem and the formulation of a computer program leading to its solution. Topics include programming and problem solving using FORTRAN and an overview of computer science. A personal computer with a FORTRAN 77 compiler is required. 32 television lessons of 30 minutes each. (2 credits)

Computer Science with Problem Solving

This course in computer science covers applications in engineering and technology problems with emphasis on programming and methodology using the FORTRAN language as the vehicle to illustrate concepts. Topics include basic concepts of a computer system, software engineering, algorithm design, programming languages, and data abstractions with applications. A personal computer with a FORTRAN 77 compiler is required. 32 television lessons of 30 minutes each. (3 credits)

Introduction to Computer Science

Fundamentals of computer science are introduced with emphasis on programming methodology and problem solving. Topics include concepts of computer systems, software engineering, algorithm design, programming, languages and data abstraction, with applications. The Pascal language is fully discussed and serves as the vehicle to illustrate many of the concepts. A computer with a compiler and Pascal software is required. 15 television lessons of 30 minutes each. (3 credits)

Principles of Operating Systems

This course covers the organization of operating systems, including structure, process management and scheduling, interaction of concurrent processes, interrupts, I/O, device handling, memory and virtual memory management and file management. Laboratory work will require that the student have access to a computer. 26 television lessons of 90 minutes each. (3 credits)

Economics

Managerial Economics

A course combining traditional economic analysis with the tools and techniques of statistical analyses and decision sciences. Topics include optimization techniques, demand theory, estimating demand functions, production theory, technological change, analysis of costs, linear programming, market structure, pricing techniques, and risk analysis. Access to NJIT's VAX computer required. 14 television lessons of 60 minutes each. (3 credits)

Humanities

Culture and History I: The Western Tradition

Peoples changing view of themselves and their world as seen in the history, literature, arts, and philosophy of past eras, from ancient time through the Renaissance. An interdisciplinary approach. Topics include Ancient Egypt, the rise of Greek civilization, Hellenistic Age, Roman Empire, Byzantine Empire, Middle Ages, and the Renaissance. 26 television lessons of 30 minutes each. (3 credits)

Culture and History II: From the Reformation to the Present

Peoples changing view of themselves and their world as seen in the history, literature, arts and philosophy of past eras, from the 17th century through the contemporary world. An interdisciplinary approach. Topics include the Reformation, Age of Absolutism, Enlightenment, American Revolution, French Revolution, Industrial Revolution, Age of the Nation-States, First World War and the Rise of Fascisim, Second World War, and the Cold War. 26 television lessons of 30 minutes each. (3 credits)

Management

The Business of Management

This course provides a valuable introduction to the concept of management and business. It is designed for the managerial candidate who has not had formal training in business management as well as for the undergraduate student. The course is intended to provide essential skills in planning and organizing, staffing and directing, controlling, decision making, motivating, communicating, and applying managerial skills to business and other types of organizations. 26 lessons of 30 minutes each. (3 credits)

Marketing

Principles of Marketing

This course examines the factors relating to the marketing process within the organization and its environments. The nature and significance of consumer and organization buying behavior, competition, government regulations, consumerism, and social responsibility are analyzed. The methods of decision making in the areas of marketing research, product development, pricing, etc. 26 television lessons of 30 minutes each. (3 credits)

Mathematics

Introduction to Calculus I

This course is the first in a series of calculus for students in non-science, business, education, or liberal arts curricula. Topics include functions, limits, differentiation, continuity, maxima/minima, curve sketching, and related rates. 48 television lessons of 30 minutes each. (3 credits)

Introduction to Calculus II

The second in a series of calculus for students in non-quantitative sciences, business, education, or liberal arts curricula. Topics include integration, area under a curve, volumes of revolution, lengths of curve, surface areas, centroids, and transcendental functions. 46 television lessons of 60 and 30 minutes length. (3 credits)

Calculus I

This course is the first in a series of calculus for students in mathematics, quantitative sciences, or engineering curricula. Considers the theory and techniques of differentiation and integration with applications of both processes to engineering and science. Topics include functions, differentiation, integration, and applications. 44 television lessons of 60 and 30 minutes length. (4 credits)

Calculus II

The second in a series of calculus for students in mathematics, quantitative sciences, or engineering curricula. Topics considered include the differentiation and integration of inverse trigonometric, exponential, and logarithmic functions. Further methods of integration, infinite series, Taylor series, and applications of the definite integral to physical problems. Includes transcendental functions, methods of integration, analytic geometry, hyperbolic functions, polar coordinates, infinite series, and power series. 66 television lessons of 30 minutes each. (4 credits)

Introduction to Mathematical Modeling

This course will review algebra, trigonometry, analytic geometry, precalculus and calculus, with a wide range of examples from engineering applications. Students will develop decision-making skills and will become comfortable with quantitative methodologies, graphs, and spatial relations. They will have a better understanding of natural laws and how scientific principles can be applied to engineering and other quantitative disciplines. Topics include proportionality, linear functions, quadratic functions, graphs, vectors, conic sections, and rates of change. 33 lessons of 30 minutes each. (3 credits)

Differential Equations

Methods of solving ordinary differential equations are studied together with physical and geometrical applications. Topics include differential equations, initial and boundary value problems, first order differential equations, Laplace transforms, linear differential equations, direction fields, numerical solutions, series solutions. 60 television lessons of 30 minutes each. (4 credits)

Survey of Probability and Statistics

A first-level course in probability and statistics. Topics include basic ideas of data analysis, least squares approximations, elementary probability, random variables, and special distributions and sampling. 15 television lessons of 30 minutes each. (1 credit)

Probability and Statistics

A course in modern probability, statistics, and statistical inference. Topics include discrete and continuous distributions on random variables, probability models in science, statistical inference, regression and correlation, analysis of variance, and ANOVA and correlation. 41 television lessons of 30 minutes each. (3 credits)

Physics

Physics I

This course is the first in a two-course introductory physics sequence. It deals with the study of elementary mechanics. Emphasis is placed on the fundamental concepts and laws of mechanics, scalar and vector quantities of mechanics, rectilinear and circular motion, equilibrium and Newton's laws of motion, work/energy/momentum, the conservation laws. Topics include vectors, kinematics, projectile motion, circular motion, Newton's Laws, friction, dynamics of circular motion, gravitational attraction, work and energy, conservation of energy, impulse and momentum, rotational motion, torque, rotational form of Newton's Second Law, angular momentum, and rotational motion problem solving. 15 television lessons of 90 minutes each. (3 credits)

Psychology

Discovering Psychology

Covers the fundamental principles and major concepts of psychology including brain and behavior, sensation and perception, conditioning and learning, cognitive processes, motivation and emotion, life-span development, the self and identity, sex and gender, testing and intelligence, social influences, psychopathology and therapy, stress and health issues, methodology and new direction. 26 television lessons of 30 minutes each. (3 credits)

Sociology

The Sociological Imagination: Introduction to Sociology

This course is an examination of modern society and culture and an analysis of the forces for stability and change. Each of the 26 half-hour programs centers around a documentary presentation of a major concept in sociology, such as socialization, social control, sex and gender, aging, education, collective behavior, social change, among many others. The programs are very personal and emotionally strong in that footage endeavors to find individuals and groups whose experiences best illustrate the sociological concepts being examined in each lesson. Tapes show people in their family settings, at work, school, church, and play. 26 lessons of 30 minutes each. (3 credits)

New York

College of New Rochelle - Rosa Parks Campus

See WNET/New York City

Empire State College
State University of New York
Center for Distance Learning

Two Union Avenue
Saratoga Springs, NY   12866-4390

(518) 587-5404

Geographic Access: Nationwide

DELIVERY SYSTEMS

Telephone Contact

Students work through CDL courses under the guidance of a faculty tutor who maintains regular contact with them by telephone. A regular schedule for telephone communication is set up early in each term.

Videocassette

CDL offers several courses that require or recommend video components. Although these components are not generally available through Empire State College, most are easily accessible from a variety of sources: tape rental from The College Video Corporation (800) 852-5277, local cable television station, Public Broadcasting System, and satellite broadcasts via Jones Intercable (Mind Extension University).

Computer Conferencing

Several CDL courses offer optional (and required) computer components. This may be in the form of completing assignments utilizing the computer or a required computer conference.

Electronic Mail

Students may be able to communicate with their tutors via the college's e-mail system. Students must have access to a computer with a modem and obtain a VAX account with CDL.

INSTITUTION DESCRIPTION

The Center for Distance Learning (CDL) is a unit of SUNY Empire State College, especially designed for students needing a program free of time and space limitations. It offers adults a college program that requires no classroom attendance. It is designed for adults who, because of work or home circumstances, prefer a program that requires no classes or travel. Degrees from the Center are fully accredited by the State University of New York.

CDL offers three areas of concentration: Business, Human Services, and Interdisciplinary Studies. Within the business area, a baccalaureate in Fire Service Administration is available to residents of New York, Rhode Island, Pennsylvania, Vermont, New Hampshire, Massachusetts, Connecticut, Maine, and eastern Canada. The Center also offers a wide range of courses in general studies. Students can study with CDL from any location in the continental United States where telephone and postal services are available.

The Center has three 15-week terms per year: fall, spring, summer. Course registration opens approximately eight weeks before the beginning of each term. Courses listed below are representative of the curriculum at CDL. Under the subject heading, courses are listed beginning with the most basic and ending with the most advanced.

Accreditation: MSA

Official/Contact: Daniel Granger, Director

Admission Requirements: Students who wish to earn a degree through the Center for Distance Learning must complete an application to the College which is included in the College Admissions Packet. Those students who wish to take single courses only and who do not intend to earn a degree with the College may enroll on a nonmatriculated basis.

Tuition: $90.35 per credit hour for matriculated students; $107.35 per hour for nonmatriculated students. Textbooks must be purchased by the student. Additional fees for a VAX account, audio- and videotapes may apply. Course materials average $15 to $25 per credit.

Degree Credit: Associate and baccalaureate degrees can be earned in Business, Human Services, and Interdisciplinary studies.

Grading: Empire State College does not ordinarily award letter grades for work successfully completed. Rather, a written, individualized narrative evaluation is prepared by the tutor.

Library: Libraries and some Empire State College centers and units have videotape libraries from which the student may borrow videos. A Library Access Package enables students, using a computer and modem, to dial into over 30 online card catalogs at academic libraries across New York State. This resource assists the student in developing extensive bibliographies, enhancing research skills, and gaining valuable practice in searching online systems.

COURSES OFFERED

Accounting

Accounting for Decision Makers
Designed for students who do not aspire to a career as an accountant or CPA but who do desire a working knowledge of accounting terms and practices. This survey course provides managers with an understanding of fundamentals of accounting, transformation of accounting information into financial statements for use in making decisions, role and implementation of internal controls, effective use of financial information, and communication of management needs to accounting professionals. (6 credits)

Accounting I
In this introductory accounting course, students will employ fundamental accounting principles, recog-

nize and understand accounting systems and reporting cycles, and design and utilize accounting statements. The scope of the course includes analyzing business transactions, general journals, general ledgers, worksheets, adjusting and closing entries, and accounting for sole proprietorships. (4 credits)

Accounting II
A continuation of the above course. Pursues further intensive study of the terms, concepts, and principles of accounting as they apply to a partnership, a corporation, and a manufacturing entity. (4 credits)

Intermediate Accounting I
The major thrust of this course is the application of financial accounting principles in a corporate setting to topics such as revenue and expense recognition, income statement and balance sheet analysis, stockholders' equity and present value, working capital management including cash management, receivables, inventories, and liabilities. (4 credits)

Intermediate Accounting II
This course applies accounting principles in a corporation setting to topics such as long-term liabilities, capital stock, earnings per share, securities and funds investment, revenue recognition, leases, pension funds, financial reporting, and basic financial statements analysis. (4 credits)

Cost Accounting
During this course, students will develop an understanding of the attributes of cost behavior, cost accumulation systems and techniques, management planning and control systems, relevant cost information for short term decision making, and accounting data in long-term budgeting decisions. A 6-credit option requires completion of assignments using a computerized accounting program. An IBM-PC or compatible with 512K, DOS 2.0 or higher, double disk drive or hard and single disk drives, monitor, and a printer are the hardware requirements. (4 or 6 credits)

Anthropology

Faces of Culture
This introduction to anthropology examines cultures throughout the world such as the Aymara Indians of the Bolivian Andes and the Asmats of New Guinea. There is a required video component which consists of 26 half-hour programs. The videos are available by rental from College Video Corporation. (4 credits)

Competition and Cooperation: Cultural Anthropology

This course uses a comparative approach to examine assumptions about the bases of human competitiveness. It also examines why differences in competitive and cooperative behavior exist and delves into theories concerning the origins of human competitiveness. (4 credits)

Biology

Topics in Biology

This course uses a topical approach to introduce students to three important areas of study within the field of biology: genetics, evolution, and ecology. (4 credits)

Business

Business Mathematics

A lower level course designed for students intending to study business and management who need to refine and refresh their mathematical skills. This course is divided into several units based on the type of business concept being introduced. These units include the mathematics of trade, operating a business, financial decisions, owning or investing in a business, summarizing and analyzing data. (4 credits)

Statistics

A comprehensive introductory course covering the fundamental concepts and methods of descriptive and inferential statistics. (4 credits)

Legal Environment of Business I

This course provides an exposure to the dynamic nature of law, the American legal processes and specific areas of law that guide business decisions. Areas of emphasis are an introduction to the legal system, tort and criminal law, contract and sales law, negotiable instruments, secured transactions, and bankruptcy. (4 credits)

Legal Environment of Business II

Course topics include agency, partnerships, corporations, and selected aspects of regulatory law. An environmental approach both reaffirms the law's goal for stability in guiding business relationships and gives recognition to the dynamic nature of law in responding to our changing social, political, regulatory, and economic development. (4 credits)

Economics - Macro

This foundation course focuses primarily on inflation, unemployment, and economic growth. It is designed to provide students with an understanding of the broad and general aspects of the economy as a whole. (4 credits)

Economics - Micro

This foundation course assists students to develop an understanding of the micro aspects of economics by examining a wide range of problems from prices to monopolies and from urban decay to industrial pollution. Topics include microeconomics, the anatomy of the market system, prices and allocation of resources, the market, competition and the firm, big business, market imperfections, income distribution, trade, the underdeveloped world, and economic planning. (4 credits)

Management Principles

Introduces the student to the concepts through which a modern business organization can be studied as a system. The functions of management are discussed with an emphasis on guiding the student towards practical applications of management concepts in the work environment. (4 credits)

Marketing Principles

A survey course designed to develop a strong conceptual framework for understanding and application of principles of marketing. Major topics include modern marketing, markets, products, price systems, distribution structures, promotional activities, marketing arithmetic, and planning and evaluating the marketing effort. (4 credits)

Economic Policy Analysis

This course is a study in the use of economic analysis undergirding the determination of public policy in the allocation of scarce resources, distribution of income, and general functioning of the economy. Topics include government and the market, public versus private goods, externalities and inefficiencies, cost-benefit analysis, market failure and antitrust, market failure and regulation of natural monopolies, dynamic efficiency, consumer and worker protection. (4 credits)

International Business

An introduction to the essential elements and emerging theories of international business through an exploration of the complex interrelations among business, government, and society. (4 credits)

Marketing and Sales Promotion

This course is designed to expand the student's knowledge of marketing by an in-depth study of the various aspects of promotion. Topics include personal selling, advertising, public relations, publicity and other promotional efforts of organizations. Assignments include case studies and experiential exercises as well as an application paper focused on the development of a promotional program for an actual firm. (4 credits)

Human Resource Management and Development

Topical material will emphasize the theory and problems associated with the recruiting, forecasting, selecting, developing, utilizing, allocating, motivating, compensating, and retaining of human resources. Also covers newly emerging issues and techniques involving the environmental setting: equal employment, occupational safety and health, work restructuring, and employee involvement. (4 credits)

Corporate Finance

Major topics include the financial environment, techniques of financial analysis and planning, management of working capital, capital structure, dividend policies, and sources of long-term financing. (4 credits)

Investing

This course surveys the theory and practice of investment decision making under uncertainty. Topics include financial markets, tax structure and the laws governing securities trading, sources of investment information and advice, measuring investment return and risk, common stock analysis, pricing and efficient markets, bonds and other fixed-income securities, options, convertible securities and commodity futures contracts, mutual funds and real estate investments, portfolio management and performance evaluation. (4 credits)

Income Tax I

The course objective is to provide theoretical discussion and overview of the Federal Income Tax structure and its legislative history with emphasis on taxation for the individual. Topics include tax computation, gross income, itemized deductions, business income and deduction, depreciation and amortization, determination of gain or loss on property transactions, and alternative minimum taxes. (4 credits)

Income Tax II

This course aims to provide an understanding of the theory and regulation of federal taxation of corporations and partnerships. Topics include estate and gift taxes, taxation of corporations, corporate liquidations, reorganizations and distributions, and limited and general partnerships. (4 credits)

Income Tax Practicum

The focus of this course is the participation in the Volunteer Income Tax Assistance (VITA) IRS program during the tax filing season. In order to participate, students must successfully complete the IRS exam for the VITA program, have accessibility to a Volunteer Center in the local area, and be approved by the IRS. Students work with real taxpayers to complete actual tax returns. (2 credits)

Auditing

An upper level study that focuses on the process by which financial statements are analyzed and certified for general accuracy and fairness. Topics for study include generally accepted auditing standards and the appropriate methods used to write and understand audit reports. Guidelines for general audit planning and specific audits of of internal business functions will also be presented. In addition, a review of professional ethics and legal liability of the auditor will be performed. (4 credits)

Advanced Quantitative Methods in Management

This course explores quantitative methods and techniques for decision-support in a management environment, including applications of the computer in this important area. Major topics include formal project management tools and techniques, use of time series analysis for forecasting, applications of regression analysis in management, and aspects of decision theory and simple modeling. (4 credits)

Labor-Management Relations

A survey course designed to explore the nature, determinants, and socioeconomic impact of collective bargaining and labor-management relations in the United States. Considerable attention will be devoted to the procedural and substantive aspects of the collective bargaining process and the settlement of labor-management disputes. (4 credits)

International Marketing

This course examines the issues and problems of global marketing from a strategic and managerial perspective. It will focus on the choice of marketing mix in an international setting. In addition, export trade procedures and the coordination and controlling of international marketing will be explored. (4 credits)

Money and Banking

Presents the conceptual framework for the study, understanding, and application of the theories of money and banking, especially as they concern the changing aspects of modern society. (4 credits)

Organizational Behavior

This course focuses on the study and understanding of human behavior in organizations, especially those organizations where human behaviors cause problems for managers. Topics include a background to organization behavior, a micro-perspective of organizational behavior, cognitive processes and personality, motivation and learning, dynamics of organizational behavior, management process and organizational theory, management applications and personal organizational development. (4 credits)

Business Policy

The course deals with the formulating, implementing, and evaluating of organizational strategy and policy in a complex business environment. (4 credits)

Marketing Management

This course is designed to develop the conceptual framework for the understanding and application of the principles, skills, and techniques of the field. Topics include strategic planning, situation analysis and implementation, and the corporate perspective in a marketing context. (4 credits)

Marketing Research

Integrating the areas of marketing and research design, the focus of this course is to develop a conceptual framework for the understanding and application of the principles, skills, and techniques used in marketing research. Topics include marketing problem identification, sources of secondary data, marketing decision making and research planning, sampling, experimentation, measurement concepts, data collection, analysis, and report preparation. (4 credits)

Communications

Communications for Professionals

Students study the various roles a communicator must play: a writer, a creator, a motivator, a representative of an organization, and a speaker who must convey an oral message clearly and directly. The goal is to develop an organized portfolio of materials that students can use in their own work or career. (4 credits)

Communications Decisions

Students can acquire the knowledge and understanding of basic rhetorical and communications theories so that they can apply those theories to communications in real-world settings. The course is concerned with interpersonal, group, organization, and societal communications. Students will communicate with the course tutor and other students through the Empire State College VAX system. Students must have access to a computer with a modem. (4 credits)

Communications Analysis

This advanced-level course gives students the opportunity to develop skills in comprehending underlying meanings in public communications. Students work with basic principles of argumentation and debate, rhetorical criticism, the narrative paradigm, social influence, and propaganda analysis. The goal is to develop critical skills for responding competently to the multimediated, corporately managed communications of the late twentieth century. (4 credits)

The Television Environment

Students in this course will have an opportunity to acquire skill in making detailed and accurate observations of what is available to hear and see, to discover some key editing and programming conventions, to read and critically evaluate articles, including several that use statistics to support assertions about supposed effect, and in general to become a more knowledgeable and selective viewer. Students will need to have full access to a television set and VCR and be prepared to purchase their own blank videotapes. (4 credits)

Computer Science

Introduction to Computer Programming: BASIC

This course is for students who have little or no experience with computer programming. The major portion of the course is devoted to programming in BASIC, the most common high-level language for personal computers. Topics include fundamental statements and commands, expressions and functions, interactive I/O, decision structures/branching/control loops, string variables and character manipulation, subroutines, and an introduction to arrays and to files. (4 credits)

Computer Information Systems

The course provides an overview of both hardware and software development, an overview of computer languages, and types and applications of commercial utility software. Topics include systems analysis and design, data and file organization, decision-support systems and applications, telecommunications, and computers in society. (4 credits)

Systems Analysis and Design

This course begins with an overview of the elements that comprise an information system, moves to a discussion of project goals and project management, and then explores in detail the major stages of systems development using the REDI model. Strategies, techniques, and tools for each stage are illustrated, and there is considerable emphasis on microcomputer systems environment. (4 credits)

Education

Thinking about Education

This course focuses on the learning process. It offers students an opportunity to begin to develop the intellectual skills of analysis, synthesis, evaluation, and application. (4 or 6 credits)

English

Introduction to Literature

A survey of different types of written works including drama, short story, essay, poetry, and the novel. The central objectives of this course are (1) to enable students to establish meaningful connections between literature and their own lives, (2) to develop the techniques of critical thinking, reading and analytical writing that are key elements in life as well as in literature, and (3) in a step-by-step fashion, to acquire a general understanding of the major types of literature. (4 credits)

College Writing

The course prepares students to write competently within any academic discipline by focusing on and fostering the underlying processes of academic writing: researching and analyzing data and synthesizing and presenting evidence in a logical and effective manner. (4 credits)

Literature of the Americas

Students will investigate three important literary traditions of North and South America: Spanish-American, African-American, and Canadian fiction. Students will first study each group of works separately to get a sense of the uniqueness of each culture. (6 credits)

Fire Service Administration

Fire Prevention, Organization, and Management

This course provides an extensive review of the agencies, procedures, programs, and strategies involved with fire prevention. Topics include background and concepts, nongovernmental fire prevention functions, government fire prevention efforts, preparation of fire prevention personnel, fire prevention through building and fire safety codes, effective fire prevention inspection, human reaction to fire emergencies, public fire education, research in fire prevention, international fire prevention practices, evaluation of fire safety efforts, cause determination, and arson suppression. (4 credits)

Advanced Fire Administration

The course addresses such issues as personnel administration, goalsetting, control/coordination/direction/organization of a fire department, and the matching of human and physical resources. (4 credits)

Personnel Management for the Fire Service

This course seeks to develop an understanding of basic personnel management concepts, their legal foundations, and their application to the fire service. (4 credits)

Analytic Approaches to Public Fire Protection

This course has its foundation in systems analysis, exploring both fire prevention and suppression systems. Significant application of mathematics to the fire service is required, including formulas for resolving such issues as response time and resource utilization. (4 credits)

Fire-Related Human Behavior

The purpose of this course is to explore the interaction of traditional fire service concerns with a range of social sciences, relating theory to practice. It focuses on the dynamics of human behavior during fire incidents and explores how these are related to fire prevention practices, programs, codes, and ordinances. (4 credits)

Disaster and Fire Defense Planning

This course is designed to help students develop an understanding of "disaster," its impact on human populations, the control of its consequences, the modes of preparation and planning for disaster contingencies, and the institutional context of disaster and fire defense planning. (4 credits)

Fire Protection Structures and Systems Design

An examination of the impact of building construction and materials on fire development and the impact of uncontrolled fire on structural integrity as measured by the fire's effect on structural members, materials, and assemblies. (4 credits)

Political and Legal Foundations of Fire Protection

A major purpose of this course is to provide students with an understanding of the implications of and relationships among the fire service, politics, and law. (4 credits)

History

American History, 1492-1865: The Origin and Growth of the United States

An audio-enhanced course. This first course in a sequential survey of American history examines the social, economic, and political development of the United States through the Civil War. The course materials include 13 half-hour audiocassette programs. (4 credits)

American History, 1865 to the Present: The Origin and Growth of the United States

An audio-enhanced course. This second half of a sequential survey of American history traces the social, economic, and political development of the United States from Reconstruction of the South after the Civil War to the present. Topics of America's transformation from an agrarian nation and minor member of the international community to an industrial world power are examined to help students understand the nature of current national issues. Course materials include 15 half-hour audiocassette programs. (4 credits)

The Western Tradition I

A video-enhanced course. The first half of a sequential survey of Western civilization will range from the pre-Western civilizations through the classical period to the high middle ages and will introduce students to the great events, forces, and personalities that have shaped Western civilization. The study guide integrates print materials with 26 half-hour video programs. Videos are available by rental from College Video Corporation. (4 credits)

The Western Tradition II

A video-enhanced course. This second half of the sequential survey of Western civilization will carry through the Renaissance and the industrial modernization to the present era. The course continues to explore the great events, forces, and personalities that have shaped Western civilization and brings students to the doorstep of the future as we confront the challenges of the 21st century. The study guide integrates the print materials with 26 half-hour video programs which can be rented from College Video Corporation. (4 credits)

Eyes on the Prize

A video-enhanced course. A comprehensive history of the people, the stories, the events, and the issues of the civil rights struggle in America. The course focuses on the period of American history from World War II to the present and includes print, video, and audio instructional material. Videos are available by rental from College Video Corporation. (4 credits)

Legacies: An Introduction to the History of Women and the Family in America 1607-1870

An audio-enhanced course. A coherent introduction to one of the most vital areas of recent historical scholarship. The course materials include 18 half-hour audio programs, a companion volume written expressly for the course which provides background reading, learning objectives, program reviews, and reading assignments. (4 credits)

Human Services

Introduction to Human Services

This is the basic course for all those interested in exploring the field of community and human services. It provides an overview of the types of work available in the field and gives a preview of the topics of study that can be undertaken in the area of community and human services. The course focuses on the organized system through which aid and assistance are given and on understanding the human factors involved in meeting human needs. (4 credits)

Human Services Delivery: New Perspectives on Cultural Diversity

This course is intended to provide students with the opportunity to acquire a new perspective on the historical development of cultural diversity in the United States. Students will learn of demographic trends, past and present, that have changed and are changing the characteristics of many clients of the human service worker. (6 credits)

Human Service Management

This course examines human service management from three perspectives. The writings of major contributors to the field of management are considered, major theoretical orientations are examined, and the applications of different management theories and models are explored. (4 or 6 credits)

Issues in Human Services

This course considers some of the wider ramifications of human service work and should be taken toward the end of the student's studies in the concentration. The course is organized around the exploration of four sets of issues: social policy in an aging society, continuing racial misunderstanding in American society, ethical issues in the human services, and professional roles and stresses in human service work. (4 or 6 credits)

Humanities

The Middle East

Students will explore such fundamental questions as the origins of the current political conditions and what links its disparate ethnic, religious, and political groups. Topics include the land and its people, Islam, conquest and civilization, Western expansion, nationalism and modernization, the consequences of World War I, the assault on tradition, oil, independence, change and revolution, Israel and the Palestinians, Lebanon, and fundamentalism and sectarianism. Additionally, the crisis in the Persian Gulf and the war with Iraq and the aftermath will be studied. Learning materials include a study guide, texts, and video programs. Videos are available by rental from College Video Corporation. (4 credits)

Science and Culture in the Western Tradition

Beginning with the ancient Greeks, this course surveys the history of Western civilization from the perspective of developments in science and scientific thinking. The study guide integrates the print materials with 10 one-hour video programs. The videos are available by rental from College Video Corporation. (4 credits)

The News in Historical Perspective

This course is designed to make each day of the term connect with newsworthy events at home and abroad. Students will become more informed about contemporary issues, problems, controversies, questions, and topics of national and international significance. (4 credits)

Ancient Greece

This course uses an interdisciplinary approach that includes history, sociology, philosophy, the history of art and architecture, and drama and literature to help students understand the particular qualities of this high civilization. (8 credits)

Humanities through the Arts

Stresses an awareness of self and society as it can be encouraged through a study of Western art. Each of the arts is considered from the perspectives of historical development, the elements used in creating works of art, meaning and form expressed, and criticism or critical evaluation. The study guide integrates the print materials with 30 half-hour video programs. Videos are available by rental from College Video Corporation. (4 credits)

War and American Society

This course draws material from selected disciplines within the humanities to explore how and why America has gone to war and to examine how war has shaped the homefront and had a lasting effect on peacetime society. Seven half-hour video programs are optional and available by rental from College Video Corporation. (6 credits)

Mathematics

Algebra

This introductory college-level course should provide or enhance facility in basic algebra concepts and problem-solving techniques. (4 credits)

Contemporary Mathematics

This course, based on the video series *For All Practical Purposes* and its companion text and study guide, illustrates the power and importance of mathematics and quantitative thinking in our contemporary world. By exploring applications in many different settings in business, government, industry, and everyday life, it provides an understanding of the tools and language of mathematics and an increased appreciation for its use in modern problem solving and decision making. The video programs use computer graphics, animation sequences, and location shooting to enrich the presentation of mathematical concepts and methods in a real-world context. The course is organized around five major topics: management science, statistics, decision making, size/shape/patterns of growth, and computers. Areas of mathematics covered include algebra, geometry, diagrams and graphs, and algorithms, in addition to statistics. Videos are available by rental from College Video Corporation. (4 credits)

Music

Concepts of Music Listening

In this introductory course, focused on listening skills, students become familiar with the fundamentals of musical composition, together with stylistic and historical contexts of the works selected for exemplification. Although reading music is not a primary outcome expected, students do begin to understand some elements of traditional, Western notation. (4 credits)

Nutrition

Human Nutrition

The major objectives of this course are to provide an understanding of the scientific basis of human nutrition and to develop a critical approach to nutrition information. The course provides a systematic study of micro- and macro-nutrients necessary for human health. It includes discussion of the digestion, absorption, metabolism, and dietary sources of these nutrients. It also explores the social, psychological, and economic forces which affect nutrition and food choice. (4 credits)

Political Science

The American Political System: An Introduction to American Government

An introductory study of the basic principles, institutions, and processes of the national government of the United States. The interrelationships of institutions and processes, politics and public policy as well as their impacts on American society are examined. (4 credits).

Theories of the Labor Movement

Addresses the origins, purposes, methods, and future of the labor movement. The first part of the course covers the development of American labor ideology. The second part explores how prominent labor theorists have attempted to explain the development of labor movements, how and why such movements function, and what the goals and methods of a labor movement are and should be. (4 credits)

The Constitution: The Judiciary and Public Policy

A course about public policy examined through judicial decisions involving selected clauses and articles of the Constitution. This course has required video and computer/modem components. Students will be required to view a series of 13 video seminars entitled *The Constitution: That Delicate Balance* in which constitutional experts and public officials discuss issues covered in the course. Students will participate in a seminar via computer conferencing. (4 credits)

Citizen Participation in the Political Process

An in-depth examination of the major ways in which citizens participate in setting the public policy agenda and influence policy making. (4 credits)

Politics and Leadership in the Bureaucracy

An advanced-level study of bureaucratic power and managerial leadership in public administration and public policy contexts. (4 credits)

Psychology

Introduction to Psychology

This course is a general overview of the field of psychology. Students have the opportunity to become sufficiently familiar with the subject matter of psychology to decide if they wish to pursue further study. (4 credits)

Seasons of Life

The intent of this course is to encourage students to think about the life cycle as a whole, to understand that it has a history, both collective and individual, while introducing students to some of the most useful theoretical perspectives for understanding their own and others' lives. (4 credits)

Social Psychology

The objective of this course is the understanding of social behavior and experience. A number of perspectives on the interacting individual are considered, including the social context of behavior, socialization, moral development, the genesis and modification of the concept of the self, social perception, and the formation and change of attitudes. (8 credits)

The Abnormal Personality

This course is intended to provide students opportunities to learn some basic information about and understanding of a typical behavior from several theoretical perspectives. (6 credits)

Public Administration

Introduction to Public Administration

A survey of the organization, management, and growing influence of public bureaucracies at the federal, state, and local levels of government. The course evaluates initiatives designed to make public organizations more accountable, rational, cost-effective, and creative. Particular attention is given to case studies which illustrate theories and concepts from the perspective of the practicing administrator. (4 credits)

Introduction to Public Policy

Examines the various stages of the public policy process in terms of the structures and processes of American government. The study places special emphasis on understanding how public policy is made at the national level and of important recent domestic and foreign policy decisions. It is, therefore, an excellent preparation for advanced studies in specific areas of public policy, such as health, social welfare, education, energy, and environment. (4 credits)

Religious Studies

Islam: Religion and Culture

This course provides the student with an understanding of how Islam originated, developed, and spread over the centuries. It covers how it has responded to the challenges originating both internally and externally and how its main characteristics have changed over time. Also, how Islamic culture contributed to the Western world. (4 credits)

Religious Perspectives I

This course begins with a study of religious meaning which describes different study approaches and examines several modes and structures of religious awareness. It then proceeds to acquaint the student with religious concepts, forms of worship, spiritual practices, and institutions of Native American religion, African religions, Hinduism, and Buddhism. (4 credits)

Religious Perspectives II

This course aims to acquaint the student with religious concepts, forms of worship, spiritual practices, and institutions of Chinese and Japanese religions, Judaism, Christianity, and Islam. (4 credits)

Social Science

Societies in Transition

The course explores societies that have been profoundly altered by the Industrial Revolution. Students gain historical and cultural perspectives about the transformation of England, the United States, and the Third World which draw from works in history, literature, geography, and anthropology. (4 credits)

Hispanic America

This course focuses on two major Spanish-speaking minorities in the United States: Puerto Ricans and Mexicans. They are studied in relation to push/pull factors (immigration, patterns of settlement, forces of assimilation). The entry of minorities into the political arena is also covered. (4 credits)

Iona College
See **WNET/New York City**

New School for Social Research
New School Media Studies - Online Program
2 West 13th Street
New York, NY   10011

(914) 428-8766 *Fax:* (914) 428-8775

Geographic Access: Worldwide

DELIVERY SYSTEMS

Computer Conferencing

Any type of telecommunications and word processing software can be used. The courses are conducted entirely in an electronic computer conferencing environment in which faculty and students enter comments and messages electronically in a continuing exchange throughout the course. During the two months in which the courses are conducted, students can read and retrieve material entered by faculty and other students, as well as ask questions of their own at any time of their choosing. Students can also communicate with faculty through private message systems, and there are facilities for live, real-time exchanges between faculty and students. Courses offered vary every two months. Courses below are representative of those offered.

INSTITUTION DESCRIPTION

The New School for Social Research is a privately supported institution and is chartered by the Regents of the State of New York. It was established in 1919 as an informal center for the exchange of ideas and in 1934 offered instruction at the postsecondary level. The undergraduate program began in 1944 and the Media Studies Program was added in 1975.

The New School Online Program utilizes the latest computer communications technology to enable students to take courses from their offices or homes anywhere in the world. Students receive lectures and recitations, interact with faculty and other students, ask and respond to questions, read assigned and optional papers, submit assignments, and are given grades and comments entirely via personal computer and modem. An important feature of the program is that any microcomputer or terminal and modem can be used to participate. The program is offered in cooperation with Connected Education, Inc., a not-for-profit organization that specializes in online education, computer conferencing services, and electronic publishing.

Accreditation: MSA

Official/Contact: Paul Levinson, Director

Admission Requirements: Formal admission to the New School for Social Research is required of all degree-seeking candidates. Graduate status assumes possession of a baccalaureate degree. Other students may take courses on a nonmatriculated basis.

Tuition: $393 per undergraduate credit; $416 per graduate credit. Tuition is inclusive of all necessary connect costs except local telephone call to hook into the conferencing network. New School registration fees of $60 for graduate course work and $20 for undergraduate. Noncredit fees are the same as undergraduate. Special half-tuition rates are available for some courses. Tuition and fees subject to change at any time.

Degree Credit: Credits earned may be applied toward a degree at a student's local institution (assuming they agree to accept the credits in transfer). The Master of Arts in Media Studies can be pursued entirely via online courses.

Grading: The grading system is A-F. Examinations are submitted online. Credit is awarded in semester hour units.

Library: Students have access to the Connect-Ed Library that contains hundreds of papers pertinent to the courses and computer conferencing.

COURSES OFFERED

Cognitive Science

Brain, Mind, Computer
This course surveys the accomplishments of cognitive science. It draws facts and ideas from psychology, anthropology, computer science, neuroscience, and several other fields. The course delves into such activities as perception and language, develops a unifying theory of cognition and its expression in media. The course concludes with a critique of the mind-body problem. (3 credits)

Computer Conferencing

Computer Conferencing in Business and Education
This course focuses on the electronic transmission of text and numbers through computers and telephone/carrier wave media, and the impact of these forms of transmission on American and international business and education. Topics include electronic fund transfer and home banking, commercial consensus via computer conferencing, electronic libraries and 24-hour databases, comparisons of major computer conferencing systems available today, relationship between speed and permanence of information and decision making, bulletin boards, commercial and public service information systems. Attention is given to psychological as well as practical consequences of these developments. (3 credits)

Desktop Publishing

Desktop Publishing
This course explores the growing potential of low-cost desktop publishing systems for both large organizations and smaller enterprises. Emphasis is on the use of personal computing and printing equipment for production of finished hard copy, inter-

changeable with the products of traditional printing houses. Major hardware and software options and costs are explored for IBM, Macintosh, and Atari St-based systems along with relative ease of use and the suitability of each for different kinds of applications, including the preparation and publication of reports, pamphlets, in-house newsletters and catalogs, and government materials. (3 credits)

Journalism

Online Journalism

This course examines the growing field of online journalism and its similarities to and differences from traditional print journalism. Available markets and other outlets for electronic journalists and writers are explored. Such markets include electronic publishing, videotext publications, and electronic magazines. Techniques for writing for the videotext market, including digesting techniques and writing to fit the format of an electronic publication, are studied. The course is intended to give students a working knowledge of the field. (3 credits)

Management

Managing in the Postmodern World

A survey of new developments in cognitive science, philosophy, psychology, anthropology, literature, history, and popular culture. Examines how these factors relate to management styles, problems, and strategies in business, social relations, and personal concerns. Issues include postmodern feminism, personal identity and morality, informational ethics and the politically correct controversy. Students develop scenarios for future threads of Western and global culture, based on the issues addressed in the course. (3 credits)

Marketing

Electronic Marketing

An exploration of new marketing/promotion opportunities available to retailers/corporations and entrepreneurs in electronic text media. Issues include history of marketing in print and broadcast media, new opportunities opened by online services, and strategies of print/electronic synergy. Case studies are employed and a marketing plan for a major electronic retail operation is developed. (3 credits)

Online Retrieval Systems

Introduction to Online Retrieval Systems

This course explores the characteristics of commercial and scholarly online, interactive databases, including Dialog, CompuServe, VuText, and Social Science Citation Index. Students discuss and implement strategies for effective online searching, methods of keeping search costs low, and choosing the best database for a search. Direct hands-on experience in online searching is provided via connection to Dialog's Ontap training base at no extra charge. Practical work is complemented with reading and discussion of texts in information theory and computer networks. (3 credits)

Political Science

Democracy and the 21st Century

This course begins by examining weaknesses in current American political, economic, and social decision-making processes. Innovations needed to improve these processes are explored with special attention to the potential roles of new interactive media and personal computers in the flow of information and the resolution of disputes. The development of electronic democracy is considered as a central case study. Linkages between decision making via computers and processes of democratic government are explored. (3 credits)

Science Fiction

Science Fiction and Space Age Mythology

An examination of the emerging mythology of the Space Age, with emphasis on its expression in science fiction films and other mass audience genres. Taking off from the acclaimed video series and book, *The Power of Myth* by Joseph Campbell, the course considers the positive role of myths in individual lives and societies. This concept is applied to the worldwide technological society that is emerging in our era. Traditional myths are compared and contrasted with the myths represented in popular science fiction. (3 credits)

Telecommunications

Telecommunication Applications

A practical survey of new electronic communication media and their social impact on the world today, including computer networks, satellite communications, teleconferencing, databases, and electronic banking. (3 credits)

New School for Social Research - DIAL
Distance Instruction for Adult Learners
Office of Educational Advising and Admissions
66 West 12th Street
New York, NY   10011

(212) 229-5630; *Fax:* (212) 645-0661

Geographic Access: Nationwide

DELIVERY SYSTEMS

Computer Conferencing
Class members will be connected via computer and modem. Students must have access to an IBM PC or compatible.

INSTITUTION DESCRIPTION

The New School for Social Research is offering a new way to complete courses toward a bachelor of Arts degree. Using electronic communication, the student will be able to come to the New School by turning on a computer at home or at work. Prior computer experience is not necessary.

Beginning in the Spring 1994 term, the courses listed below will be offered. The DIAL courses have been developed under a grant from the U.S. Department of Education, Fund for the Improvement of Postsecondary Education. The New School is collaborating with the University of Michigan on the assessment and evaluation of the distance learning curriculum.

Accreditation: MSA

Official/Contact: Elizabeth Dickey, Dean

Admission Requirements: Students may register by telephone. Permission to enroll must be obtained for the courses listed below.

Tuition: Students enrolled in the Spring 1994 pilot DIAL courses will receive a tuition reduction. General tuition is $420 per credit. Textbooks and other study materials must be purchased by the student.

Degree Credit: Credit earned by successful completion of a course is applicable toward a baccalaureate degree and may be used in transfer to other institutions upon their acceptance.

Grading: Examinations must be proctored. Grading system is the option of the instructor. Credit is awarded in semester hour units.

Library: Officially registered students have access to all library facilities of the New School.

COURSES OFFERED

Humanities

The Making of Americans
The title of this course comes from Gertrude Stein's astonishing novel *The Making of Americans*. Students study some provocative works of 20th-century American literature, music, art, photography, and film, and explore some exemplary modern artistic lives. The course is interdisciplinary and multimedia. Individual works are explored intensively but also are placed within the broadest cultural and historical context. (3 credits)

Philosophy

Philosophical Dilemmas of Technological Society
Some unique and epistemological and ethical issues have emerged in an increasingly technological society. This cross-disciplinary study of these issues consists of a theoretical introduction and conclusion in which students are encouraged to examine them in the light of such abstractions as technological versus cultural determinism and critiques of Western technology such as Marxism, feminism, and Afro-centrism. The central part of the course is devoted to case studies and simulations of exemplary "dilemmas," for which students are given individual and collaborative assignments to complete and discuss. (3 credits)

Sociology

Identity: The Modular Construction of Personality
The debate over the cultural versus universal categories of human nature go back to Plato. Re-invent-

ing the debate in a contemporary setting, students examine the nature of personal identity and how it is formed in present-day society. (3 credits)

New York Institute of Technology
On-Line Campus

P.O. Box 8000
Old Westbury, NY   11568-8000

(800) 222-6948 *Fax:* (516) 484-8327

Geographic Access: Nationwide

DELIVERY SYSTEMS

Computer Conferencing

To log-on to CoSy computer conferencing at NYIT a student will need either a Macintosh or MS-DOS IBM or IBM-compatible computer, preferably with a hard disk drive to provide large storage and rapid access to data. Also needed is any Hayes-compatible modem operating at 1200 or 2400 BPS, Procomm or PC Plus (or Microphone for Macintosh) communication software, and any compatible printer. CoSy computer conferencing organizes users by course and instructor. A student does not need prior computer experience to join CoSy conferences because new students take a special 1-credit course (Introduction to Computer Conferencing) that demonstrates how to get the most out of taking courses online.

INSTITUTION DESCRIPTION

New York Institute of Technology (NYIT) is an independent senior institution operating year-round. Traditional and accelerated formats in day, evening, and weekend sessions are available, in addition to noncredit and personal enrichment programs and off-campus independent study. Campuses are maintained in Old Westbury and Central Islip on Long Island. An urban location, the Manhattan Campus, is situated near Lincoln Center in New York City.

NYIT's On-Line Campus (formerly known as the American Open University) allows a student to acquire a college degree from start to finish without entering a traditional classroom. The distance learning program is tailored for students who cannot attend conventional classes on a traditional campus because of obstacles such as time, geography, dependent children, or work conflicts.

Students study independently and in organized groups using a wide-area computer network. Interaction with instructors and classmates is accomplished by sending test files back and forth through NYIT's VAX 750 mainframe computer.

Accreditation: MSA

Official/Contact: Marshall Kremers, Director

Admission Requirements: High school graduation or GED. Official transcripts required for degree-seeking students. Students may register for courses anytime during the year in any of the six fixed terms, each approximately five months in length.

Tuition: $243 per credit. Telecommunications fee of $75 for first course; $11 per hour for system time after the first term. Textbooks must be purchased by the student.

Degree Credit: Baccalaureate degrees in Interdisciplinary Studies, Business Administration, and Behavioral Sciences.

Grading: The letter system is used (A-F). Examinations are submitted to the instructor via electronic mail. Credit is awarded in semester hour units.

Library: Students have direct access to NYIT's library staff on the CoSy system.

COURSES OFFERED

Accounting

Accounting I

A study of accounting fundamentals. Topics include the accounting cycle, statement preparation, systems, asset valuations, accounting concepts, and principles for the sole proprietorship. (3 credits)

Accounting II

Continues the study of accounting fundamentals. Topics include partnerships, corporations, liabilities, manufacturing, accounting, and statement analysis. (3 credits)

Anthropology

Anthropology

An introduction to the study of ancient man and primitive cultures. Major topics include the origins and evolution of man, the evolution of different cultural forms in terms of craft and technology, magic, religion, and government. (3 credits)

Business Administration

Introduction to Marketing

Study of the process by which goods are transferred from place of origin to place of consumption. The role of marketing institutions in the economy and the channels through which goods flow from producer to consumer. (3 credits)

Sales Management

Problems involved in recruiting and supervising the sales force. Methods of evaluating prospective salespersons. Budgeting and control as they apply to the sales function. Incentive programs to stimulate sales activity. (3 credits)

Retailing Management

An investigation of the organization of the retail function. Consideration of managerial problems in the operation of large and small retailing organizations, control of retail operations, design of retailing facilities, retailing strategies, and current developments in the field. (3 credits)

Management of Promotion

A consideration of cost factors and budgeting for promotion activities including, but not limited to, media advertising. The relationship of the firm with advertising agencies. Choice of promotion methods and measurement of results therefrom. (3 credits)

Business Law I

An introductory course with emphasis on the law of contracts. Designed to give a basic understanding of the legal aspects of contractual obligations. (3 credits)

Business Law II

Law of property, bailments, agency, and related subjects. An analysis of the Uniform Commercial Code as it applies to the law of sales. Designed to give a basic understanding of legal problems in the marketing and transportation of goods. (3 credits)

Business Law III

A study of the forms of business organization with emphasis on the law of partnership and corporations.

An analysis of the Uniform Commercial Code with respect to commercial paper. (3 credits)

Corporate Finance

Consideration of the sources and uses of corporate funds, techniques employed in the financing of assets, capital structure, debt and equity instruments, cash management, and dividend policies. (3 credits)

Principles of Investments

An analysis of the types of securities available in the market, measurements of performance for stock and bond investment, interpretation of financial statement data as an aid in decision making, operation and regulation of securities markets. (3 credits)

Introduction to EDP in Business

Designed for business students with emphasis in the following areas: A survey of the methods and trends in EDP as applied to business organizations. Introduction to computer architecture, systems, and application techniques. Introduction to programming and systems development. Includes a survey of implementation techniques. (3 credits)

Statistical Sampling Theory

Introduction and application of various techniques of sampling theory, terminating with simple regression analysis. (3 credits)

Quantitative Applications to Making Managerial Decisions

An expansion of the work of Statistical Sampling Theory and as an aid in managerial decision making. Elementary concepts in linear programming, simulation, PERT, inventory management, and related areas. (3 credits)

Personnel Administration

This course is designed to familiarize personnel executives and students with modern personnel policies, techniques, and methods successfully adopted in progressive industrial and commercial organizations. (3 credits)

Introduction to Management Information Systems

The concept of management information systems is introduced and examined. The systems approach will be used to identify management requirements in relation to computerization. Capabilities and limitations of management information systems will be discussed. Case studies and experimental exercises will be used in this course. (3 credits)

Business Cycles and Forecasting

A study of the aggregate fluctuation in business, tracing its main stages of development from upswing through prosperity to downswing, and the leading theories on the causes of business cycles. The study will also cover methods of measuring business cycles and how to forecast the cyclical behavior with the aid of indicators. (3 credits)

Business Organization and Administration

A study of organizations and of the activities of the manager in an organization. The course follows a functional approach, analyzing such management concepts as organizing decentralization, use of staff human relations, conflict, decision making, planning, supervision, communication, and financial and production control systems such as budgeting and PERT. (3 credits)

Collective Bargaining and Labor Relations

The course is designed to introduce the student to the background and relationships between economics, public policy, unionism, and business management. Also, the course seeks to provide a basic orientation to the framework, processes, and strategies involved in collective bargaining plus the resolution of labor grievances and arbitration in management-labor relations. (3 credits)

New Product Management

Techniques and practices applied to conceiving, developing, launching, and managing new products. An in-depth evaluation of the life cycle concept will analyze various stages and how careful planning and managing can extend it. The product management concept and its effectiveness as a management tool will also be studied. (3 credits)

Small Business Management

An examination of required skills, resources, and techniques which transform an idea into a viable business. Entrepreneurial decision making will be stressed and the role it plays in idea generation, conception, opportunity analysis, marshalling of resources, implementation of plans, management of ongoing operations, and providing for growth. (3 credits)

Criminal Justice

Criminal Law and Proceedings

A study of the elements of the Penal Law (New York) particularly relevant to police officers, including a review and analysis of major criminal offenses with consideration given to the available defense and judicial interpretations. (3 credits)

Police Administration

An introduction to the organization and structure of a police department. Topics include an overview of police departments, an analysis of the police function, tables of organization, chains of command and lines of authority, division of labor, and the informal police organization. Attention centers on typical problems of police administration and the coordination of police services. (3 credits)

Introduction to Criminal Investigation and Forensic Science

This course surveys the fundamentals of criminal investigation and forensic science. The focus includes scientific crime detection, elements of proof, and criminalistics. A balanced perspective is provided on methods of investigation, crime-scene search, preservation of evidence, methods of obtaining information, and the functions of the police crime laboratory. (3 credits)

Police and Community Relations

This course analyzes the complex relationship between police and community attitudes toward police, the efforts of the police organization to create a more favorable public image, the emergence of a civil rights and civil liberties movement, and the contribution of the individual police officer to police-community relations. (3 credits)

Crisis Intervention for Public Safety Personnel

Examines the concepts and techniques used by criminal justice practitioners in handling crisis situations. The focus of the course will be the development of skills to intervene effectively with specific types of crises, thereby diffusing the immediate conflict situation. Topics to be covered include landlord/tenant disputes, family fights, suicide attempts, civil disorder and demonstrations, labor/management relations, and common crises occurring at institutional and corporate sites. (3 credits)

Crime Prevention: The Systems Approach

Examines the role of the criminal justice system, the private-protection field, and the general community in reducing crime, and describes the actual program models used to accomplish this goal. Areas to be covered include the development of crime-specific approaches, hardware versus software concepts, productivity issues, citizen participation programs, systematic approaches to crime prevention, and the evaluation of these programs. (3 credits)

Physical Security Strategies

Introduces students to contemporary physical security strategies, and prepares them to conduct a comprehensive physical security audit. Students will be able to identify and assess security risks or hazards and propose pragmatic crime prevention recommendations. Topics to be covered include new concepts in protective lighting and alarm technology, the development of executive protection programs, external and internal security considerations, and an overview of the special physical security problems confronted by commercial establishments, hospitals, educational institutions, and high-rise office buildings. (3 credits)

Security and Protection Management

Examines security and protection management principles. Topics to be covered include the development of risk-management strategies, the use of organizational development techniques in planning/organizing/directing/staffing/controlling/budgeting the security operation. Additionally, the course will address management information systems and electronic data processing programs, the topic of cybernetics, and conflict management strategies. (3 credits)

Probation and Parole

An examination of organization and management in probation and parole systems. Topics include distinctions between probation and parole in terms of organizational function and types of clients served. Client relationships and interactions with other social control agencies. Case loads, case work methods, and case supervision. Problems in pre-sentence investigation. Job requirements and performance standards for probation and parole officers with particular emphasis on recruitment, training, and assignment. (3 credits)

Correction Administration

An analysis of the organization of various types of correction agencies. Topics include theories of prison administration, interagency and public relations, planning and budgeting, laws governing the treatment of inmates, and security considerations. (3 credits)

Principles of Correction

The development of modern correction ideology. Topics include the growth of humanitarianism in treatment of the offender, the concept of resocializing the offender as a productive member of society, principles and procedures for reintroducing the offender to society, and systems and practices employed by other nations. (3 credits)

The American Court System

Provides for an understanding of a variety of court structures and the emerging trends in court administration on both the state and federal levels. Examines the environment in which the judicial system operates and analyzes the roles played by the various actors employed in this element of the justice system. (3 credits)

Contemporary Corrections

Examines the development and organization of correctional systems at the local, state, and federal levels. An analysis of the major issues confronting corrections will be made, with particular emphasis placed on examining the problems of custody and rehabilitation. Topics to be covered include community-based programs, the future of parole, the "Justice Model," and the relationship of corrections to the other elements of the criminal justice system. (3 credits)

Private Security: Concepts and Strategies

Examines the fourth component of the American justice system—the private security industry. Some of the topics to be covered include the history and development of private security, the development and enforcement of standards and goals, security personnel issues, alarm technology, and environmental design concepts, and the issue of government regulation of the security industry. (3 credits)

Criminology

Criminology

An examination of crime and theories of crime causation. Topics include the white collar criminal, the professional criminal, and the structure of organized crime. The criminal-justice process is analyzed, including the role of the police, the criminal courts, the probation officer, correctional services, and the reentry of the offender into society. (3 credits)

Economics

Principles of Economics I

A study of basic economic concepts emphasizing analysis of the aggregate economy. This course covers the fundamental concepts of national income and its determination, economic fluctuations, monetary and fiscal policies, and economic growth. (3 credits)

Principles of Economics II

An examination of the processes of price determination, output, and resource allocation in perfect and imperfect competition. The course also covers labor economics, international trade and finance, and alternative economic systems. (3 credits)

Basic Economics

A basic introduction to economic analysis with emphasis on the problems and issues of a modern economy. (3 credits)

Money and Banking

The structure and function of the banking system in the United States. The use of monetary policy in the regulation of the national economy. The role of the Federal Reserve System. (3 credits)

Monetary Theory and Policy

An advanced course in monetary theory and policy making. The role of monetary theory in regulation of the economy, agencies responsible for policy making, the structure and role of the Federal Reserve Bank. (3 credits)

Commercial Banking

The operation of banking institutions, regulation of banking activities, the role of commercial banks in credit and monetary expansion. (3 credits)

English

College Composition I

Instruction in and application of the principles and skills involved in effective expository writing, with most readings from nonfiction prose. (3 credits)

College Composition II

Continuation and expansion of the above course. Development of library skills leading to a documented term paper. Introduction to literature and criticism. (3 credits)

Basic Speech Communication

Study of the fundamentals of verbal communication, including public speaking, interpersonal communication, and small group interaction. Training in methods of obtaining and organizing materials and ideas for effective verbal communication. (3 credits)

Business Writing

An intermediate-level course for students in business. Instruction and practice in all phases of business communications, such as reports, memoranda, and correspondence, as well as in-depth study of research methods. (3 credits)

Technical Writing

An intermediate-level writing course for those studying the physical and life sciences and technology. Emphasis on style in technical writing, modes of technical discourse (definition, description, analysis, interpretation), and strategies for effective business communication, including resume writing and technical reports. Methods and procedures of research are explored in depth. (3 credits)

Report Writing

An intermediate-level writing course for students of the behavioral and social sciences. Methods and procedures of research with emphasis on reports and advanced research papers. Strategies for effective business communication, including resume writing. (3 credits)

History

American History I

The political, social, cultural, and economic factors pertaining to American history and civilization up to the year 1865. Two major areas of study are the colonial era through the American Revolution and the nineteenth century. (3 credits)

American History II

A survey of American history from 1865 to the present. Particular attention is given to the various political movements and the four major wars. The American position as a world power and its role in international affairs. Effects of the growth of labor unions and corporations as integrated into merging historical patterns. (3 credits)

World History I

A survey of history from the beginning to about 1650 A.D., including Ancient Egypt, Mesopotamia and the Persian Empires, the Indus Valley civilization, early Greek developments, the first Chinese dynasties, the flowering of Greece, the spread of Hellenistic culture, and Rome. The course proceeds to the expansion of the Indian and Chinese civilizations, the Barbarian invasion, Islam, Medieval Europe, and the Turkish and Mongol conquests. Japan,

Southeast Asia, Africa, and the Americas. Finally, the Period of Discovery, the Renaissance, Reformation, and Counter-Reformation are examined. (3 credits)

World History II

This course covers the emergence of Russia and the Americas starting about 1650, the events in Islam and the Far East to 1700, the enlightenment and the French Revolution, attendant events in the Western Hemisphere, Russia, and Asia. The Industrial and French Revolutions are studied with their consequences on Europe, Africa, Asia, and the Americas. Both world wars and their worldwide repercussions are analyzed with due emphasis on the non-Western world. The approach stresses broad sociocultural factors. (3 credits)

Management

Operations Management

Provides the student with insight into how production of goods and services is brought about with emphasis on the management decision process. A survey of basic economic techniques will precede the development of a variety of techniques for improving the operating efficiency in the manufacturing and service sectors. (3 credits)

Philosophy

Problems of Philosophy

An introduction to philosophy by way of selected problems from various areas of philosophy. Topics include the nature of *a priori* knowledge and of scientific explanation, the existence of God, whether or not there can be moral knowledge, and the problem of free will. The course objective is to acquaint students with these philosophical issues and, through detailed discussion, to teach them how to analyze ideas critically. (3 credits)

Ethics and Social Philosophy

An examination of some of the most critical issues of moral and social philosophy. These include subjects such as the linguistic analysis of terms such as good, evil, duty, right, and others. The basis of different moral systems will be studied, and selections from ethical and social philosophers will be read. (3 credits)

Political Science

American Government and Politics

An introduction to the processes of the American form of government. The nature and structure of government, its characteristics and functions. The intimate relation of government to other interests. (3 credits)

Government and Business

A consideration of relationships between business enterprise and the societal and political milieu in which these enterprises operate. New concepts in business ethics and corporate responsibility. Government regulation of business activity. (3 credits)

Comparative Government

An introduction to comparative political structures and institutions covering the major European governments as well as non-Western political systems. (3 credits)

Basic Legal Concepts and Administration of Justice

This course covers the judicial process and its evolution, the rights of accused persons, and the administration of justice in the light of the elementary foundations and functions of substantive and adjective law. The theoretical aspects of basic concepts will be examined, but the stress will be on the practical aspects. (3 credits)

Politics of Technical Assistance

A discussion on the derivative sociopolitical problems of giving and receiving technical assistance. The political basis of economic development and development of a modernizing public service, a bilateral and multilateral technical assistance program, exchange of information between the U.S. and the U.S.S.R., prospects of world economic development and political stability. (3 credits)

Psychology

Introductory Psychology

An introduction to selected concepts, methods, and vocabulary of psychology. Focus of study will be on the individual and the conditions that influence behavior. Topics that will be covered include growth and development, learning and thinking, emotions and motivations, personality and assessment, maladjustment and mental health, groups and social interaction, and social influence and society. (3 credits)

Physiological Basis of Behavior

A basic course to familiarize students with the bodily processes involved in various aspects of human behavior. Physiological psychology studies the biological basis of psychological functions such as sleeping, emotions, motivations, perceptions, learning, memory, and problem solving. Two major biological systems most relevant to psychology are the nervous system and the glandular system. (3 credits)

Learning Theory

A fundamental science course. The student is asked to trace the emergence of modern cognitive learning theory (neobehaviorism) from the original works of Pavlov, Thorndike, and Watson through the "black box" Skinnerian school of thought. The course emphasizes theoretical rather than methodological issues and, as such, is designed to give the student a firm grasp of the conditions under which permanent behavior change occurs. (3 credits)

Social Psychology

An analysis of the structures and properties of human groups. Topics include group formation, development of role relationships, intragroup and intergroup conflict, factors influencing group effectiveness, the role of motivation, and attitudes in group processes. (3 credits)

Measurement Concepts

The construction, validation, and interpretation of test results. Group and individual tests of aptitude, intelligence, and personality are analyzed. (3 credits)

Educational Psychology

Emphasis on human learning. Consideration of concepts of readiness, individual tests of aptitude, individual differences, motivation, retention, transfer, concept development, reasoning, mental health, and measurement as related to learning. Psychological principles of teaching-learning technology are examined. (3 credits)

Marriage and the Family

The course covers historical changes in family patterns, contemporary family life in different cultures and subcultures, evolution of the American family pattern, functions of the family, the family as a primary group, kinship patterns, and nuclear and extended families. (3 credits)

Quantitative Methods for the Behavioral Sciences

Designed to provide the behavioral science student with an appreciation for basic quantitative tools developed to communicate research findings in the disciplines of psychology, sociology, criminal justice, and community health. (3 credits)

American Urban Minorities

An in-depth analysis of the diverse ethnic structure of the urban community. Major attention is given to Black, Puerto Rican, and Mexican groups. Topics include a survey of each group's social and economic structure, an examination of ghetto conditions and their effects, the impact of urban conditions on the new arrival, a comparison with the adaptation and treatment accorded earlier migrants, the validity of the melting pot concept, and a comparison of the life styles of various minority groups. (3 credits)

Social Stratification

The nature of caste and class in societies. Topics include theories of social differentiation and stratification, comparison of caste, estate-class, and class systems, social mobility, and structural change. Emphasis is given to local national stratification systems in the United States. (3 credits)

Child Psychology

The study of human growth and development. Emphasis is placed on physical, emotional, and personality development with an aim toward understanding the period of human growth on which adulthood is founded. Special topics include identification of conditions in childhood leading to normal psychological development. (3 credits)

Adolescent Psychology

An introduction to the study of that portion of human development called adolescence. Some of the topics treated include the significance of puberty, biological and social sex roles, adolescence image, the emergence of new figures such as peers and idols, society at large as agents of socialization in place of parents and family, the extinction of old habits and practices and their replacement with new behavioral patterns. Theoretical consideration will be supplemented with observational experience. (3 credits)

Psychology of Adulthood and Aging

The study of human aging and changes during adulthood. This course is designed to give the student an understanding of early, middle, and later adulthood. (3 credits)

Theories of Personality

A survey of the major theoretical approaches to understanding the development, structure, and dynamics of personality. (3 credits)

Introduction to Sociological Theory

The development of sociological theory in Europe and the United States during the 19th and 20th centuries from Comte to the present day. Emphasis is given to comparing and contrasting various schools of theoretical thought. (3 credits)

Behavioral Sciences in Marketing

An investigation of the behavioral sciences disciplines as they affect marketing decisions. Consideration of such fields as psychology, sociology, and anthropology as the basis for studying consumer motivation and behavior. (3 credits)

Occupational Psychology

Stresses the process of entry into the realm of work both from the standpoint of the individual and the organization. (3 credits)

The Institutional Community

The study of an institution as a functional community. Special emphasis is placed on closed institutions such as prisons and mental hospitals. The course treats the problems of adjusting to the institutional environment, the development of inmate culture, systems of social stratification, normative order, and systems of conformity. (3 credits)

Community Mental Health

An analysis of the current status of the community mental health movements which attempts to define and anticipate future trends. (3 credits)

Urban Society

A sociological analysis of modern urban ways of life. Major emphasis is on the New York metropolitan area as compared with other major cities. (3 credits)

Job Satisfaction and Job Stress

Theories of motivation, techniques of motivating workers, the components of job satisfaction, meaning of job stress, sources of job stress, effects of job stress on the worker, and techniques of stress measurement and management. All aspects of job design and organizational structure are examined as they relate to job satisfaction and worker stress. (3 credits)

Organizational Behavior

A detailed survey of organizational development permitting students to explore the organizational contexts in which managers are influenced and, in turn, influence change. A broad overview of literature in organization theory provides a perspective from which students may develop personally useful concepts and skills in managing organization change. (3 credits)

Communication and Interviewing Techniques

The examination of communication from various standpoints, as illustrated by different types of interviews. Interviewing techniques employed for personnel selection are compared with those used in interrogation and those used for therapeutic purposes. Practice in interviewing. (3 credits)

Introduction to Effective Communication

In-depth training in the concepts and skills needed for effective oral and written communication between individuals and in groups. Interpersonal effectiveness in listening, responding, and presenting. Methods of effective communication are examined, and attention is given to the impact of language on behavior, particularly on personal decision making. (3 credits)

Abnormal Psychology

Topics covered include definitions of mental health, mental illness, problems of adjustment, the causes/diagnosis/treatment/prevention of mental disorders. Case studies supplement and illustrate the theoretical parts of the course material. (3 credits)

Psychology of Salesmanship

Major topics include developing new customers, preparing and presenting proposals (both written and verbal), delivering and installing equipment, satisfying existing customers. Individual sales skills will be stressed. (3 credits)

Introductory Research Methods for Behavior Sciences

This course stresses the classical approach to experimental research on human behavior. Students conduct and report on experiments in the fields of psychophysics, psychomotor learning, memory, and perception. (4 credits)

Juvenile Delinquency

An inquiry into the causes of juvenile delinquency and the social and psychological factors involved in the predictive studies and theories concerning the development of delinquency. Topics also include formation of youth gangs, methods of coping with gang activity, the types of crime committed by children and youths, narcotics problems, neglected and retarded children, the youthful offender and wayward minor, the operation of the Children's Court, and crime prevention programs. (3 credits)

Environmental Psychology

An analysis of the relationship between human behavior and experience and the physical environment. Topics include the built environment, buildings and social institutions, cities, social behavior as it relates to the physical environment, the natural environment and its effects on behavior. (3 credits)

Occupations

A study of the world of work for the student's own vocational guidance and for use in such fields as teaching, counseling, personnel administration, employment interviewing, social work, and probation and parole. Topics include sources of information about jobs, vocational choice and development, necessary qualifications and preparation, and the effective classification of over 20,000 occupations. (3 credits)

Introduction to Counseling

Theories and practical techniques of counseling, including advisement, guidance, and supportive psychotherapy, by both directive and nondirective methods. Counseling is considered both as a career in itself and as a component of one's job in such fields as teaching, business and personnel management, health occupations, social work, and the law. (3 credits)

Rehabilitation Psychology

Review of contemporary theories, practices, and research in rehabilitation of the emotionally, mentally, and physically handicapped. Selected topics will include various addictions, mental retardation, learning disabilities, emotional disorders, and physical incapacities. (3 credits)

Science

Introduction to the Life and Health Sciences

An introductory course in the life and health sciences emphasizing practical human applications. Physiological and psychological factors affecting human health are integrated and provide an understanding of the individual's role in health care. Prevention, healing, and curing as approaches to major

disease control are discussed. A project emphasizing constructive behavior to minimize adverse health practices is required. (3 credits)

Environmental Sciences

A multidisciplinary approach to the environmental and ecological sciences emphasizing principles, problems, and alternative approaches to solutions. The issues are treated in sufficient depth to permit quantitative reasoning and assessment, especially in such vital topics as the demographic trends of humanity in a resource-limited biosphere. Human physiological and behavioral requisites are interwoven with the fabric of culture and technology in modern society. In addition to lectures and seminars, students are required to become involved in a term activity, project, or paper which may integrate several disciplines. (3 credits)

Philosophy and History of Science

An examination of the principal moments in the development of scientific thought, with special emphasis on the analysis of the principles of scientific methodology. The contributions of individuals like Aristotle, Ptolemy, Copernicus, Galileo, Kepler, Newton, Kant, Darwin, and Einstein will be carefully explored. Notions such as induction, deduction, proof, explanation, and truth will be subjected to extensive criticism. (3 credits)

Social Work

Introduction to Social Work

A survey of the various approaches and orientations to the general field of social work. Consideration is given to case work, group work, and community organization as well as to the interrelationship of psychology, sociology, and anthropology with the social work profession. (3 credits)

Community Psychology

The broad range of activities of psychologists and counselors in community settings will be examined. An intensive study will be made of between twenty and twenty-five special areas of community involvement, including hospitals, rehabilitation services, halfway houses and outreach clinics, crisis intervention centers, and correctional institutions. Emphasis is on the prevention, recognition, and remediation of problems, including field experience. The social, professional, and personal rationales for community psychology as a separate academic and professional entity will be considered. (3 credits)

Social Work II

This is the second social work course open to students who have completed *Introduction to Social Work*. It is designed to meet the dual purpose of providing students with a framework for assessing and understanding the range of policy issues and delivery of social services in the United States, and for evaluating proposals being made in the arenas of public policy for more comprehensive systems of social service. Emerging models of social service delivery systems will be reviewed. (3 credits)

Sociology

Introduction to Sociology

An analysis of the social and cultural forces which govern human behavior. The principle topics include social interaction and organization, socialization processes, primary groups and the family (association, bureaucracy, and other social institutions), collective behavior, population, and ecology. (3 credits)

Social Problems

A sociological analysis of social problems in American society. All social problems will be viewed from a structural perspective, i.e., the root cause of a social problem lies in the institutional arrangements of a given society. Various institutional arrangements of American society that give rise to social problems will be evaluated in terms of value-conflicts, power structures, and economic institutions. Major topics include inequality, poverty, environmental destruction, ageism, educational institutions, social deviance, employment, problems of the city. (3 credits)

Medical Sociology

This course examines the social structure of health care service and the interplay of the various health-related professions. Special attention will be given to the institutional pattern of health care, including the social aspects of health, sickness, dying, types of practitioners, and the social organization of therapeutic settings. (3 credits)

Political Sociology

This course will discuss the nature and various dimensions of power in society, with emphasis on some of the ideas of Karl Marx and Max Weber. It will survey the theoretical and empirical material dealing with power structures on a national and community level. (3 credits)

Social Policy

A theoretical and empirical analysis of the development and implementation of social policies relating to health, education, and welfare. Examination of the socioeconomic, legal, and political contexts within which social policy is formed. Analysis and evaluation of the present social service system and possible changes for the future. (3 credits)

New York University
The Virtual College
Information Technologies Institute

NYU School of Continuing Education
48 Cooper Square, Room 104
New York, NY   10003

(212) 998-7190

Geographic Access: Worldwide

DELIVERY SYSTEMS

Online Services

Using their personal computers and the Lotus Notes group communications package, teleprogram students collaborate at long-distance during a six-week online workshop and actively participate in the development of a major systems project. Students must have a 386 or 486 IBM-compatible PC with Microsoft Windows 3.1, 2M memory, 10M available hard disk space, 1.4M 3.5-inch diskette drive, VGA monitor, and a 9600 baud or faster Hayes or Hayes-compatible modem.

INSTITUTION DESCRIPTION

New York University is a private, independent, nonprofit institution. It was established and chartered in 1831. The many resources of New York City are blended into the many programs offered by the NYU School of Continuing Education.

The Virtual College offers a teleprogram designed for business generalists faced with the need to analyze and redesign existing business data and communications flows, develop and operate online virtual workplaces for their own organizations, and manage projects and lead multidisciplinary teams working within networked environments.

The teleprogram provides students with a working knowledge of the techniques and technologies of information analysis, systems development, project management, and virtual work group communications. As the physical infrastructure of international business is changing from concrete and steel to computers and communications, this interactive teleprogram gives students those collaborative and technical skills necessary for working within (as well as on) today's decentralized and networked workplaces—in effect, a virtual college preparing employees for tomorrow's virtual organizations.

Accreditation: MSA

Official/Contact: Richard Vigilante, Director

Admission Requirements: The graduate course requires a basic knowledge of Microsoft Windows 3.1. Degree or credit students currently matriculated at NYU should register for the teleprogram through their school or division. All others should register through the Information Technologies Institute.

Tuition: $1,933 total fee.

Degree Credit: Credit earned may be applied toward a degree at NYU or be accepted in transfer by other institutions.

Grading: Examination projects occur online. A letter grade is assigned. Credit is awarded in semester hour units.

COURSES OFFERED

Virtual Work Group Communications

The Virtual College
During the teleprogram, students receive instruction, interview clients, conduct analyses, resolve problems, and build systems—all largely at their own convenience. The Lotus Notes data network provides an electronic workplace for students and faculty, allowing them to go from talking about projects to actually completing them. All teleprogram work is conducted from the home or office PC—there are no on-campus sessions. Online sessions involve the systems request, preliminary analysis, alternatives analysis, output design, input design, and systems implementation. Each teleprogram student receives a fully-licensed copy of Lotus Notes, a powerful new group communications pro-

gram giving people who work together an electronic environment within which to create, access, and share text, data, graphics, and video, using networked personal computers. Lotus Notes supports such business applications as computer conferencing, information distribution, status reporting, project management, and electronic mail. (4 credits)

Rochester Institute of Technology
Office of Distance Learning
P.O. Box 9887
Rochester, NY   14623-0887

(716) 475-5089 *Fax:* (716) 475-5077

Geographic Access: Nationwide

DELIVERY SYSTEMS

Computer Conferencing
Students may communicate with teachers and classmates via electronic mail and an electronic bulletin board.

Audiographic Conferencing
At selected sites, students may use a computer blackboard and ask audio questions of their professors.

Audio Conferencing
Used for question and answer sessions and test reviews.

Online Services
Includes open discussion forums, library services, and 24-hour electronic messaging services to campus departments.

Videocassette
Videotapes are an integral part of the instruction.

INSTITUTION DESCRIPTION

The Rochester Institute of Technology (RIT) is a private, independent, nonprofit institution. It was established in 1829 as the Rochester Athenaeum and introduced instruction at the postsecondary level in 1912. The present name was adopted in 1944.

Distance learning courses have been offered by RIT since 1980. The program offers phone-in registration, 24-hour fax numbers, 800-numbers to call professors, mail-order for textbooks, and telephone advising services. The program also ensures that the quality of classes is the same as that on campus. Over 1,600 students nationwide take distance learning courses from RIT each year.

Credit programs in Distance Learning include the Bachelor of Science in Arts and Science, Master of Science in Telecommunications Software Technology, and Master of Science in Software Development and Management. Certificate programs are offered in Applied Computing and Communications, Data Communications, Voice Communications, Health Systems Administration, and Emergency Management.

Equipment needed includes a telephone, VHS videocassette player, a VT200-300 series terminal with a modem (or an IBM PC or compatible, or Apple Macintosh Plus or better, with communications software obtainable from the RIT bookstore).

Accreditation: MSA

Official/Contact: Joseph T. Nairn, Director

Admission Requirements: Students pursuing a baccalaureate degree must have an associate degree or equivalent. Official transcripts required of all degree-seeking students. Students pursuing courses for professional development, or a certificate program, need not meet the associate degree or equivalent requirement. If desiring to register only for courses, registration as a nonmatriculated student is all that is required.

Tuition: Undergraduate $298 per credit hour; graduate $380 per credit hour.

Degree Credit: The Bachelor of Science in Applied Arts and Science is a multidisciplinary degree requiring the completion of 23 courses for a total of 90 quarter hours (an associate degree or equivalent is required for admittance to the program).

Grading: RIT uses a single letter grading system (A-F). The minimum passing grade is D. Exams are taken online or proctored at RIT. Exams may be taken locally with an approved proctor.

Library: Distance learning students have access to the Wallace Library EINSTEIN computer-based library menu system. Access is available to the Dow Jones news retrieval service, INTERNET, and CARL (an index of over 10,000 current journal articles).

COURSES OFFERED

Accounting

Financial Accounting

Emphasis is placed on analyzing and recording business transactions, and understanding the results of these transactions. Preparation of basic financial statements required by any business is included. (4 credits)

The Role of Accounting in the Organization

The objective of this course is to provide students with an understanding of how accounting is used to help organizations achieve their goals. Students will learn both how to account and the reasons why we account as we do. Special emphasis will be placed on the resolution of the firm's goals. Positive accounting theory and agency theory will be discussed throughout. (4 credits)

Communications

Technical Writing

This course develops those skills necessary for completing technical writing tasks, such as instructional memos, letters of inquiry, reports (trip, progress/status, accident, research, feasibility), problem analyses, specifications, flow charts, technical manuals. (4 credits)

Communication

Focuses on refining writing skills. Emphasized are organization, support, and effective expression of ideas in multiparagraph papers. (4 credits)

Communication in Business

Covers the development of those communication skills essential to functioning effectively in the business world. Students learn the process of analyzing communication situations and responding to them appropriately. (4 credits)

Organizational Communication

This course examines both interpersonal and small-group communication in organizational settings. Topics include information flow and networks, organizational theory, managerial decision making, interviewing, organizational development, and conflict resolution. (4 credits)

Human Communication

An overview of the field of communication, including the contexts of interpersonal, group, mass, and public communication. (4 credits)

Mass Communication

An introduction to the study of the mass media. The focus of the course is on the history, development, law, and regulation of the mass media in the United States. (4 credits)

Computer Science

Introduction to Computers and Programming

Basic concepts and overview of computer science. The topics include historical development, algorithms, flowcharting, and programming in BASIC. Exposure to assembler language, hardware concepts, software concepts, binary and hex numbers, and logic. (4 credits)

Introduction to Programming

A first course in programming using PASCAL in writing modular, well-documented programs. Topics include an overview of problem-solving methods. (4 credits)

Program Design and Validation

A second course in programming and data structures, where students use PASCAL to implement moderately large programs (4 credits)

Computer Concepts and Software Systems

An introduction to the overall organization of digital computers and operating systems for nonmajors. (4 credits)

Data Communications and Computer Networks

An introduction to data communications hardware and software, and the use of these components, communications software, packet switching, network control, common carrier issues, long-hall versus local area networks, and performance considerations. (4 credits)

Applied Database Management

An introduction to issues in data management in organizations, and the role of database management systems in addressing these issues. Topics include the uses and needs for data in organizations, review of simple data structures, the influence of computer architecture and I/O devices on the management of data, basic file organizations supporting data management (sequential, direct access, indexed sequen-

tial), logical data models and their physical implementation, database administration, and DBMS selection. (4 credits)

Economics

Principles of Economics I

This course will focus on basic economic concepts and macroeconomics. Topics of primary interest include economic methodology, the economizing problem, capitalist ideology, supply and demand, national income accounting, income determination, inflation, money, and the role of government in the economy. (4 credits)

Principles of Economics II

This course will focus on microeconomics. Topics of primary interest include market structure, supply and demand analysis involving elasticity, the theory of cost in the short and long run, perfect competition, monopoly, monopolistic competition oligopoly, marginalist distribution theory, the labor market, and general equilibrium analysis. (4 credits)

Emergency Management

Earth Science for the Emergency Manager

Introduction to applied meteorology and crustal dynamics, and the forecast capabilities of the National Weather Service and private forecasters. (4 credits)

Manmade Hazards

This course focuses on the potential threats associated with chemical and radioactive accidents. The course surveys the chemistry of hazardous materials and the effect of toxins, caustics, flammables, and reactives on humans. Also referenced is the physics of radiation, the design of commercial power reactors, and reactor crisis situations. (4 credits)

Emergency Preparedness Laws and Regulation

An examination of the principal statutes, regulations, and court cases governing emergency preparedness in New York. (4 credits)

Emergency Planning and Methodology

The scope of a comprehensive emergency plan and quantitative methods of risk and hazard analysis. Also, turf problems with multiagency plans, command structures, and the role of new technologies in disaster response. Preparation of hazard analyses and sections of plans for actual communities. (4 credits)

Emergency Operations

A study of the roles of fire, police, EMS, and volunteer agencies such as the Red Cross on disaster sites. Also, command posts and off-site operations centers, the Incident Command System, and how to critique incidents. Role playing on an incident simulator. (4 credits)

English

Introduction to Literature

A study of some of the great literary works of our culture to enrich lives and reinforce analytical abilities. The students read representative poems, dramas, and narratives drawn from the Ancient, Medieval-Renaissance, and Modern Periods. (4 credits)

Finance

Personal Financial Management

The course deals with personal budgeting, protection of personal assets, consumer credit, investments, and estate planning. (4 credits)

Theory and Application of Basic Financial Concepts

This course develops some of the basic principles of finance, and shows some of the ways in which they may be applied to business decisions and problems. Concepts and applications include time value of money, ratio analysis, cash budgeting and pro forma forecasting, credit decisions, capital budgeting techniques, forms of borrowing, and capital structure decisions. (4 credits)

Health Systems Administration

Survey of Health Care Systems

An overview of the current forces transforming health care, including physician practice and payment, private and government health insurance. The impact of medical technology, manpower issues, hospital services and reimbursement systems, ambulatory and long-term care, alternate delivery systems. (4 credits)

Health Systems Administration

A survey of administration in health care facilities focusing on organizational structures and practices and on the application of basic management principles in the health care setting. (4 credits)

Health Care Economics and Finance

An examination of the efficiency effectiveness and equity of the new economics of health care. A conceptual and practical look at health care finance. Sources of funding, the accounting and reporting process, and the influence of third-party payers. (4 credits)

Legal Aspects of Health Care Administration

Federal, state, and local legislation applying to the health care industry. Medicare and Medicaid, New York State Health Code, labor regulations, tort liability of health care providers, patients' rights, accreditation. (4 credits)

Health Care Quality Assurance

An introduction to quality assurance in health care, including past and present definitions of quality and competing concepts of quality assurance. A review of quality assurance requirements and accrediting organizations, federal and state agencies, and third-party payers. (4 credits)

Health Planning and Program Development

The methodology of planning effectively for health care services, including the use of data systems, forecasting, and identifying and analyzing problems. Students will develop sample applications to new programs to submit to regulatory agencies. (4 credits)

Humanities

Black Civil Rights in the 20th Century

This course examines the social and legal history of civil rights in the U.S. with particular attention to the demonstrations of the 1950s and 1960s and the philosophy of Dr. Martin Luther King, Jr. The course will compare his views with those of the recent Black Power Movement. (4 credits)

Modern America

The political, social, cultural, and economic development of the American people in the modern period are examined in this course. A study of the United States and its foreign relations. (4 credits)

Management

Introduction to Work Organizations

This course introduces students to the concept of work organizations and how they function. Students learn of the different types of industries in which work organizations fall, and how to become and help others to be effective members of the organization through motivation, leadership, interpersonal conflict management, and handling stress. (4 credits)

Management Concepts

The student is introduced to the four functions of management: planning, organizing, staffing, and controlling. In addition, topics such as organizational change, stress, productivity, and decision making are covered. (4 credits)

Tools for Quality Management

An examination of the concepts of quality and total quality. The course addresses, as a theme, the tools and techniques that may be used, and in what manner. (4 credits)

Marketing

Marketing for Total Customer Satisfaction

This course will review the fundamentals of marketing: formulating marketing strategy (segmentation and positioning) and the marketing mix (price, product, promotion, and distribution decisions). The mechanisms of delivering total customer satisfaction throughout the marketing mix will be emphasized via applying quality management principles to the marketing function. (4 credits)

Mathematics

Elementary Statistics I

An introduction to elementary techniques of statistical description and inference. Topics include descriptive statistics, probability, estimation of parameters, hypothesis testing, and simple linear regression. The statistical software package MINITAB will be used to introduce students to the use of computers in statistical analysis. (4 credits)

Technical Mathematics I

An introduction to college algebra and trigonometry covering basic algebraic concepts and operations, algebraic and transcendental functions. (4 credits)

Technical Mathematics II

A continuation of the above course. (4 credits)

Political Science

American Politics

A study of the national political system, its theoretical foundations and institutions, and the contemporary issues that confront it. (4 credits)

Government and Politics of Russia and the CIS

This course provides an analysis of the politics and governmental systems in Russia and the former republics of the Soviet Union that now comprise the Commonwealth of Independent States (CIS). Emphasis will be on the dynamics of political, economic, and social change, as well as political leadership and contemporary issues. (4 credits)

Psychology

Introduction to Psychology

Introduces the student to the scope and methodology of psychology. Topics include aims and methods, sensation and perception, learning and memory, emotion and motivation, normal and abnormal personality, and social psychology. (4 credits)

Abnormal Psychology

This course examines the major categories of mental disorder not only from the descriptive point of view, but also in terms of the major theoretical explanations of the causes of disorder. The major treatment modalities also are covered. (4 credits)

Science

Contemporary Science: Mechanical Universe

Topics covered include units and dimensional analysis, motion, force, energy, heat, waves, light, relativity, atoms, and quantum mechanics. (4 credits)

Contemporary Science: Oceanus

The marine environment will be investigated in terms of basic scientific concepts. Topics to be discussed will include plate tectonics and earthquake prediction, the impact of ocean pollutants, climate fluctuations, cetacean intelligence, and resources from the sea. (4 credits)

Modern Warfare Technology and Arms Control

The study of the importance of science and technology to defense matters. An investigation of how modern weapons, both nuclear and conventional, their delivery systems, and reconnaissance and surveillance methods have seriously affected the character of armed conflict and of preventing wars. (4 credits)

Philosophy of Science

An examination of the nature of the scientific enterprises. Possible discussion topics include the presuppositions of science, its logic, its claims to reliability, and its relationships to society and to problems of human values. (4 credits)

Sociology

Foundations of Sociology

This course introduces students to the way sociologists interpret social reality, the major elements of the field, and the most important research findings. Included are such topics as cultural differences and ethnocentrism, socialization, social statuses and roles, group dynamics, social institutions, stratification, collective behavior. (4 credits)

Sociology of Health

A survey of the sociological aspects of health and illness. Some areas of study will be the definition, causes, and cure of disease in various societies and social groups. Also included will be a discussion of the epidemiology of disease, access to and delivery of health care in contemporary U.S. society, problems of patient care, and the study of mental illness and death and/or dying. (4 credits)

Solid Waste Management

Principles of Municipal Solid Waste Systems

Introduction to municipal solid waste systems. The topics include an overview of the relationship of municipal solid waste, environmental protection, protection of public health, and public service. Solid waste generation and natural resources. The unit operations of municipal solid waste collection, transfer, resource recovery, and disposal. (4 credits)

Solid Waste Management I: Recycling

A survey of recycling technology and its relationship to the general problem of municipal solid waste management that explores both the mechanics and the economics of the problem. Topics include the separation and collection of recyclable materials, recycling as a manufacturing process, the development of markets, and public education issues. (4 credits)

Telecommunications

Data Communications and Computer Networks

An introduction to data communications hardware and software, and use of these components in computer networks. Topics include communication system components, communications software, packet switching, network control, common carrier issues, long-haul versus local area networks, and performance considerations. (4 credits)

Telecommunication Fundamentals

A survey and an introduction to the structure and regulation of the telecommunications industry is provided. The basics of data communications, telephony, switching systems, integrated service digital networks (ISDN), multiplexing, and networks are introduced. (4 credits)

Voice Communications: Principles and Technology

Provides an understanding of basic telephony concepts and associated voice-based applications. Various telephone architectures are studied. Topic highlights include audiotext, ISDN, and voice mail. (4 credits)

Switching Technologies

This course familiarizes the student with the various switching methods and equipment used in the telephone network. Voice and data switching methods such as matrix, circuit, message packet, burst, and LAN are studied and compared. (4 credits)

Data Communications Technology

Provides a practical overview of data communications environment, historical evolution, technology, and applications. Topic highlights include networking concepts, cellular/mobile communications, fiber distributed data interface (FDDI), digital-fiber networks and applications. (4 credits)

Telecommunications Policy and Issues

This course provides an introductory overview of domestic and global information/telecommunications policy, standards, and regulation. (4 credits)

Network Management

Provides an intensive practical experience in network management. The technical and management issues associated with the administration of complex, highly integrated networks are examined using various hardware and software tools. (4 credits)

Rockland Community College
Special Programs Office

145 College Road
Suffern, NY   10901

(914) 574-4300

Geographic Access: New Jersey, New York

DELIVERY SYSTEMS

Audiocassette
Audiotapes supplement the text and course guide.

Broadcast Television
Some courses may be viewed on Channel 13 (WNET), Channel 6 (WNJN), or TKR Cable Channel 30.

Videocassette
Tapes enhance textual material that is utilized in the courses. Selected courses are on videocassettes for home viewing by students who have their own VCRs. All telecourses may be viewed in the Library Media Center.

INSTITUTION DESCRIPTION

Rockland Community College is an institution of the State University of New York. It was founded in 1969. Courses are planned to benefit the community in diversified areas which include agreement with major institutions to maximize academic benefits for transfer students, one- and two-year programs for technical expertise, an honors program whose graduates have been admitted to upper division colleges, a College Skills Program, an English-as-a-Second-Language program, low cost study abroad programs, and a large selection of noncredit courses of general and specialized interest to the community.

Distance Learning at Rockland is one of the Special Programs offered. Each course is accompanied by a course guide written by the course developer. Courses are accompanied by audio- or videotapes. Distance learning physical education courses are designed to meet the needs of students for whom work or personal schedules or religious practices make attendance at on-campus physical education courses impossible. These distance learning courses are identified as such in the Courses Offered section.

Telecourses listed below are those courses in which one learning activity consists of watching a series of instructional video programs at home or at Rockland Community College. Along with the viewing, there are other learning activities involving the reading of textbooks, study guides, and other material that may be assigned. Telecourses are distinct from the Distance Learning Program courses.

Accreditation: MSA

Official/Contact: Sue Commanday, Coordinator of Special Programs

Admission Requirements: Open enrollment. Special application form required for admission to the physical education courses.

Tuition: Contact the college for current tuition rates. Students must purchase textbooks required for the course. Videotapes require a refundable deposit of $50; audiotapes $25.

Degree Credit: Credit earned may be applied to an associate degree program.

Grading: Letter grades are awarded. Credit earned for the Wellness for Life series meets the Rockland Community College requirement in physical education. Exams may be taken at the RCC Testing Center in the Library Media Center.

Library: The Learning Materials Center contains 50 audio/video carrels that can be used by students without access to an audiocassette player or VCR.

COURSES OFFERED

Accounting

Principles of Accounting I and II
A Distance Learning Program course. Theory and practice of proprietorships, partnerships, and corporations. *First Semester*: Worksheet, closing process, and financial statements, payroll accounting, cash control procedures, inventory and asset valuation, accounting for notes. *Second Semester*: Partnership and corporation accounting procedure, financial statement analysis, statement of changes in financial position, introduction to cost accounting, budgeting and managerial concepts. Meets degree requirements in business or as an unrestricted elective in other degree programs. Audio tapes, course guide, and text. (3 credits each semester)

Allied Health

Here's to Your Health

This telecourse presents contemporary approaches to maintaining good health. The series helps students define a healthy life style and make knowledgeable decisions about health issues. The course focuses on such topics as stress, hypertension, nutrition, depression, smoking, and sexually transmitted diseases. There is an up-to-date discussion of such problems as herpes and AIDS. 26 half-hour videotapes. (3 credits)

Anthropology

Cultural Anthropology

An introductory study of the basic concepts of culture, including subsistence patterns, ways of transmitting culture, economics, political organizations, social control, and culture change. Methods of anthropological research and major theoretical orientations are described. Examples of primitive as well as modern societies provide many examples of cultural variation. Includes such topics as psychological anthropology, patterns of marriage and family relationships, and religion and magic. 20 half-hour videotapes. (3 credits)

Culture and Language

The video series, *The Story of English*, shows how language and culture interact. It traces the development of the English language, from its conception and use by only one small tribe, into the most widely used language in the world. Some topics include the effects of the Anglo-Saxon invasion, the influence of the Christian church's Latin/Greek/Hebrew, the role played by Shakespeare, the use of English in America, and language as an instrument of political control. Many societies which contributed to the development of English are examined and their influence analyzed. 9 one-hour videotapes. (3 credits)

Art

Art of the Western World

This telecourse examines art in the western tradition, beginning with ancient Greece and moving chronologically to the present. The course takes a social and historical perspective examining the connection between the great works and the social and cultural environments in which they were created. Topics include the art of classical Greece and Rome, Gothic art and architecture, the Renaissance, Baroque and naturalistic styles of the 17th century, Rembrandt, Romanticism, Realism, Impressionism and Post-Impressionism, Cubism, Surrealism, Abstract Expressionism, and Pop Art. 9 one-hour videotapes. (3 credits)

History of Art I

A Distance Learning Program course. The history of Western art from prehistoric times through the Middle Ages presented through a series of videocassettes dealing with each stylistic period, an illustrated text, and an accompanying study guide. (3 credits)

History of Art II

A Distance Learning Program course. This course is the second half of an Art History survey course. It covers art from the Renaissance to the 20th century as well as the art of Islam, China, Japan, and India. Videos, text, and course guide. (3 credits)

History of American Art

A Distance Learning Program course. With the aid of a short text, a specially created course guide, and a series of videos, the student will be introduced to American painting, sculpture and architecture from the Colonial period to the present. 20 videotapes, course guide, and text. (3 credits)

Business

An Introduction to Business

A telecourse that provides a comprehensive view of the contemporary business environment. Delves into the complex functions of a business, showing the student the detailed internal and external operations affecting large and small businesses, on a local and international scale. Includes discussions related to creation of a business, management, marketing, and the relationship between business and government, law and the economy. 28 half-hour videotapes. (3 credits)

Business Law I

This course examines the system and concepts of business law in the United States. The topics include bailments, wills and trusts, landlord-tenant, contracts, agency, real and personal property. 30 half-hour videotapes. (3 credits)

Economics

Fundamentals of Economics: Microeconomics
This course looks at the structure and function of the market system with emphasis on the role of supply and demand, the individual firm, the competition and monopoly, and distribution of income. Related problems such as government intervention, pollution, minimum wages, and farm income are examined. 14 half-hour videotapes and 14 audiotapes. (3 credits)

Fundamentals of Economics: Macroeconomics
A study of factors that influence the level of national income. Topics include resources and scarcity, market and prices, gross national product, causes of business cycles, lessons of the Great Depression, fiscal policy and economic control, inflation, the banking system, the Federal Reserve, federal deficits. 14 half-hour videotapes and 14 audiotapes. (3 credits)

English

English Composition I: The Write Course
An opportunity to achieve the competencies of Freshman English reading and writing by watching a series of videotapes, reading the assigned texts, and writing the required number of papers. 30 half-hour videotapes. (3 credits)

English Composition II
A Distance Learning Program course. Continues the goals and objectives of the above course. Students study various forms of imaginative literature to develop perception and critical insight and to exercise these skills in writing assignments. Course guide and text. (3 credits)

On Poets and Poetry
A Distance Learning Program course. This course explores work by selected poets, including William Carlos Williams, Anne Sexton, James Dickey, Richard Wilbur, John Allman, and others. Individual works are analyzed in detail, exploring issues of form, style, and theme. The audiotapes include readings and some discussion of poetry in America, poetry by survivors of the Beat Generation, war poetry, and love poetry. 18 audiotapes and a course guide. (3 credits)

Nobel Prize Literature
A Distance Learning Program course. This course focuses on the works of authors who have won the highest international literary award, the Nobel Prize. Poetry, fiction, and drama by writers from all over the world will be studied to see how they reflect their times and their cultures, and why they represent the summit of literary achievement. Course guide and texts. (3 credits)

Finance

Personal Financial Management
How to manage one's finances by learning some of the skills of the experts. Discusses the basics of budgeting and buying, the intricacies of home ownership, income tax and investments, and the wise use of insurance, wills, and trusts. 26 half-hour videotapes. (3 credits)

History

World History I
Taking a global view of the last 200 years, this course uses live action footage of the central personalities and events of the times, and reveals often exotic and remote geographic growth of imperialism, the advance of modern science and technology, the World Wars, Perestroika, the continuing development of the Third World, and new geopolitical alignments. Opportunities and hazards for the future will be projected from a review of the past and present. 12 half-hour videotapes. (3 credits)

American History to 1877
The video series, *The American Adventure*, begins with the Colonial period and continues through the Civil War and Reconstruction. Topics include the Colonial contribution to American democracy, the struggle for independence, the formation of a national government, Jacksonian democracy, western expansion, the controversy over slavery, the Civil War, and Reconstruction. The course vividly illustrates how wars and treaties, elections, and legislation affected the people of the United States and helped develop America's democratic spirit. 26 half-hour videotapes. (3 credits)

American History 1877 to Present
The video series, *America: The Second Century*, begins with the Centennial and continues to the present. Topics considered include industrial growth, the labor movement, the Depression, the New Deal, America as a world power, and the emergence of an urban and suburban society in America. The telecourse takes a topical rather than

chronological approach, examining this dynamic century of change on-location across the country. 30 half-hour videotapes. (3 credits)

Vietnam: An Historical Study

This course provides a full record of the conflict—from background on Vietnam and its people, through the French presence, to a chronology of the period from 1945-1975, with an examination of the impact of the war on American society in the years that followed. 13 one-hour videotapes. (3 credits)

War and Peace in the Nuclear Age

This course explores the major events of the period and the underlying issues of nuclear policy, strategy, and technology. It covers topics as current as the present battle over the "Star Wars" defense system and the halting steps towards a U.S.-Soviet Arms agreement. 13 one-hour videotapes. (3 credits)

History of the Civil War

The elements of this course are interwoven to convey the passions of the period and underscore the relevance of these events to the present. Students will come to learn of the sacrifices of everyday soldiers and citizens and come to understand the difficulties faced by the African-Americans who were the focal point of the struggle. The social, political, and economic changes that took place during the Civil War years left an indelible mark on our society. 9 one-hour to ninety-minute videotapes. (3 credits)

Humanities

Humanities through the Arts

This course takes the viewpoint that, while science and technology provide us with objective information about the world around us, we must look to the humanities for the insights necessary to an understanding of ourselves and our society. This course stresses an awareness of self and society as it can be developed through a study of seven major arts: film, drama, music, literature, painting, sculpture, and architecture. 30 half-hour videotapes. (3 credits)

Management

Principles of Management

For those who wish to enter or move ahead in business, the course discusses planning and organization, staffing and directing, decision making, mo-

tivating, communicating, and the application of managerial skills. 26 half-hour videotapes. (3 credits)

Business Software Analysis

This course surveys and analyzes the capabilities of most commonly available microcomputer applications. The applications are concisely described and presented in real-life, case-study situations that allow students the opportunity to use and evaluate them in action. The uses of microcomputers are explored in many settings, from small-business applications to multidivisional organizations, showing students the variety of problems managers must solve. An introductory program presents background information and defines relevant terminology in computer science. 16 half-hour videotapes, 15 floppy disks, and 5 audiotapes. (3 credits)

Small Business Management

This telecourse will provide students with the tools that will enhance their potential business success. The video programs will allow students to observe a variety of small businesses in operation. Each of the major modules concludes with a program that profiles a single small business. 26 half-hour videotapes. (3 credits)

Marketing

Marketing

An introduction to marketing in which students learn theories and compare them to case studies. Topics include the contemporary marketing environment, identification of consumer needs, production/distribution/promotional/pricing strategies, international marketing. 26 half-hour videotapes. (3 credits)

The Sales Connection: Principles of Selling

This course is designed to provide aspiring salespeople and those already involved in sales, with the tools and insight they need to compete in the age of long-term, consultative-style selling. Real-life sales specialists will be videotaped "in the trenches" as they go through their normal routine of identifying prospects, setting sales appointments, preparing for presentations, meeting with clients, striving for closure, and servicing their sales. 26 half-hour videotapes. (3 credits)

Mathematics

Math Skills

A Distance Learning Program course. This course will give students an opportunity to learn or relearn topics in basic mathematics. Topics include whole numbers, multiplication and division, fractions, decimals, introduction to percents, finding the amount, finding the rate, finding the base, and miscellaneous problems. Text and course guide. (4 credits)

Elementary Algebra for College Students

A Distance Learning Program course. Designed for those who need to improve their skills in algebra. Topics include properties of real numbers, operations with signed numbers, ordering on the number line, solution of linear equalities and inequalities, graphing of linear equations, exponents and radicals, operations with polynomials, factoring, solution of quadratic equations. 9 one-hour videotapes, course guide and text/workbook. (3 credits)

Intermediate Algebra for College Students

A Distance Learning Program course. An intermediate course designed for students who wish to improve their skills in algebra. 8 one-hour videotapes, course guide, and text/workbook. (3 credits)

Philosophy

Six Great Thinkers

This course covers the development of philosophy in western civilization through the writings of six major philosophers: Plato, Descartes, Hume, Hegel, Marx, and Sartre. The influence of each author is considered in relation to his culture as well as our own. 30 half-hour videotapes. (3 credits)

Ethics in America

Contemporary ethical conflicts are examined through highly charged case studies which invite the student to struggle with real ethical dilemmas and to learn to understand the process for ethical decision making. 10 one-hour videotapes. (3 credits)

Physical Education

Wellness for Life: Aerobics

A Distance Learning Program course. The first course in a series that will allow the distance learner to engage in guided physical exercise and development, and to monitor his/her own progress. Exercises will include aerobic activities appropriate to

individuals without access to professional facilities and/or with physical handicaps. Course guide and text. (1 credit)

Wellness for Life: Strength Building

A Distance Learning Program course. The second course in a series of courses that allow the distance learner to gain insight into starting a general strength conditioning program by learning the facts about getting started, how to lift, body building, strength training for sports, fitness for life, and fitness for work. Course guide and text. (1 credit)

Wellness for Life: Diet and Exercise

A Distance Learning Program course. The third course in a series of courses that will allow the distance learner to develop understanding of the relationship between diet and exercise and a sense of healthy well being. Course guide and text. (1 credit)

Political Science

American Government

This telecourse explores the process, the politics, the people being governed and the people governing in the United States. Each program explores its main theme while creating the excitement, drama, and immediacy typical of network newscasts. The student is led to inquire how the citizen is affected by and can become involved in the governmental process while seeking solutions to political, social, and economic problems. 13 one-hour videotapes. (3 credits)

The Constitution

This course is an introduction to constitutional rights and public policy. It considers in depth such contemporary constitutional issues as the conflict between freedom of the press and national security, criminal justice versus a defendant's right to a fair trial, congressional limits on presidential control of foreign policy, the insanity defense and the death penalty, individual privacy versus state intervention in life and death decisions. 13 one-hour videotapes. (3 credits)

Psychology

General Psychology

This introductory course in psychology encourages an understanding of the scientific approach to the study of human behavior. Topics which will be covered include sensation and perception, motivation, learning and memory, maturation and development, social psychology, personality theory, and psychotherapy. 26 half-hour videotapes. (3 credits)

Life Span and Psycho-Social Development

This telecourse presents the provocative insights emerging from current research in psychology, biology, anthropology, and sociology. Documentary footage introduces real stories from each "season" of life: infancy and early childhood, childhood and adolescence, early adulthood, and late adulthood. The stories, and the experts who interpret them, give a rich picture of the entire human life span. 5 one-hour videotapes and 26 half-hour audiotapes. (3 credits)

Psychology of Childhood

A presentation of the interplay of the biological factors, social structure, cultural forces, and human interaction that shape the growing child. The course spans the development from the womb through adolescence. 26 half-hour videotapes. (3 credits)

Abnormal Psychology

An exploration of the biological, psychological, and sociological approaches to abnormal disorders, and of the methodologies of the field. Topics include anxiety disorders, psychological approaches in the treatment of headaches/heart disease/cancer, personality disorders, substance abuse and addiction, sexual disorders, mood disorders, the schizophrenias, organic mental disorders, and behavior disorders of childhood. 13 one-hour videos. (3 credits)

Social Science

Interdisciplinary Study of the Middle East

This course will examine the recent economic, political, and social history of the Middle East, particularly focusing on the emergence of independent states, the significance of religious and ethnic diversity, the critical changes affecting family and community life, as well as major contemporary developments shaping international relations within that region. 26 half-hour videotapes. (3 credits)

The Pacific Century

This interdisciplinary Asian studies telecourse explores how the Pacific Basin has evolved to emerge as a principal political and economic center of the coming century. The video series, *The Pacific Century*, is built around classroom lectures by Japanese and Asian affairs expert Frank Gibney. Throughout

the series, four major themes emerge: modernity versus tradition, the conflict between East and West, democracy/political authority/economic growth, and the United States in the Pacific. This course also draws upon the experiences and insights of an international panel of scholars and journalists to bring the important people, events, and trends of modern Asia-Pacific history to life. 13 one-hour videotapes. (3 credits)

Latin America and the Caribbean

The video series, *Americas*, is an examination of the contemporary history, politics, economics, religion, culture, and social structures of the countries of Latin America and the Caribbean. From Mexico to the Malvinas, the series and course explore the stories behind the limited images and incomplete information that capture public attention in newspapers and popular magazines. 10 one-hour videotapes. (3 credits)

Sociology

Marriage and the Family

The women's movement, skyrocketing divorce rates, increasing acceptability of alternative lifestyles, urbanization, economic uncertainty and AIDS have all had dramatic implications for the forms and functions of marriage and family. *The Portrait of a Family* video series examines these and a wide range of other sensitive and controversial topics, and provides a framework for students to better understand their own relationships. The family is explored in the multiplicity of its modern forms: traditional families, single-parent families, step families, families without children, dual-worker marriages, and cohabiting couples. 26 half-hour videotapes. (3 credits)

The Civil Rights Movement: A Socio-Historical Perspective

This course is a comprehensive history of the people, stories, events, and issues of the civil rights struggle in America. The focus is from World War II to the present. The course includes reading as well as video and audio segments. 6 one-hour videotapes and 5 one-hour audiotapes. (3 credits)

Principles of Sociology

A Distance Learning Course. An introduction to a study of American society: the home, the family, the workplace, marriage. The discipline of sociology helps students understand social change and its meaning in relation to their own personal experience. 7 audiotapes containing a total of 13 half-hour lessons, course guide, study guide, and text. (3 credits)

Legacies of Women in America

A Distance Learning Course. A course for learning about the early experience of ordinary American women: Indians and immigrants, slaves, and free Blacks, indentured servants, and pioneer women. It examines changes in both the ideals and the reality of family life and recognizes the resilience of the family in response to ongoing social and economic change. Students will have the opportunity to develop a new kind of awareness of the struggles and triumphs, and the diversity and commonality for women in the early years of this century. 18 one-hour audiotapes, course guide, and texts. (3 credits)

Suffolk County Community College

See **WNET/New York City**

Westchester Community College

See **WNET/New York City**

WNET/New York City
Educational Services

356 West 58th Street
New York, NY   10019

(212) 560-6613

Geographic Access: New York

DELIVERY SYSTEMS

Broadcast Television
Telecourses are broadcast over WNET/Channel 13 which is available throughout the New York City metropolitan area.

INSTITUTION DESCRIPTION

WNET/Channel 13 of New York City collaborates with the Public Broadcasting Service (PBS) and colleges and universities in Channel 13's viewing area to broadcast a special selection of telecourses each semester. The portfolio of telecourses includes many disciplines in undergraduate and graduate curricula such as computer and business skills, art, sociology, and psychology, American history, environmental studies, and much more. Usually nine courses are broadcast each semester.

Local colleges that offer credit for telecourses include the following:

- Bergen County Community College (Paramus NJ), (201) 447-7176
- College of New Rochelle, Rosa Parks Campus (New York NY), (212) 662-7500
- Iona College (New Rochelle NY), (914) 633-2470
- Suffolk County Community College (Selden NY), (516) 451-4196
- County College of Morris (Randolph NJ), (201) 328-5185
- Westchester Community College (Valhalla NY), (914) 285-6985

Accreditation: All participating institutions are accredited by MSA.

Official/Contact: Sandra Sheppard, Coordinator

Admission Requirements: Requirements vary among the college participants. Degree-seeking students are usually required to be formally admitted to the college while noncredit participation requires only following the enrollment procedure.

Tuition: Tuition and fees vary among the colleges. Contact the college of choice for current information regarding fees and other materials costs. Textbooks and study guides must be purchased by the student and can be obtained at the various college bookstores.

Degree Credit: Credit awarded for successful completion of a course may be applied toward a degree. The amount and type of credit depends upon the policy of the institution.

Grading: Examinations must be proctored. Letter grades are assigned. Credit is usually awarded in semester hour units.

Library: Students are encouraged to utilize their local libraries but as officially enrolled students, they have access to the library resources of their institution.

COURSES OFFERED

Archaeology

Out of the Past: An Introduction to Archaeology
Uses visually dramatic on-site film to allow students to explore how archaeologists reconstruct ancient societies and explain how and why they evolved. Research at the spectacular Classic Maya Center of Copan, Honduras, forms the core of the series, but a broadly comparative perspective includes many other civilizations and cultures from Central and North America, Africa, and the Middle East. Students will understand how archaeology and anthropology interact. This telecourse is part of the Annenberg/CPB Collection. Closed captioned for the hearing impaired. 26 half-hour programs.

Business

Business and the Law
An introductory law course which highlights contracts and the development of the legal system. This series includes modules on the law of sales, commercial paper, agency, and property. It also examines critical legal topics in government regulation, employment practices, and consumer and environment protection. The telecourse provides students with a comprehensive overview of law and the world of business. 30 half-hour programs.

English

Literary Visions
This telecourse brings literature to life with dramatizations of individual works and readings of literary passages. It incorporates both contemporary and traditional works from Shakespeare to Dickinson to Alice Walker. The course also places a strong emphasis on writing about literature as a way for students to learn and use advanced composition techniques. Five programs from this telecourse can also be used as professional development for English/Literature professors. 26 half-hour programs.

French

French in Action
Combines video, audio, and print to teach French based on an innovative method developed by Pierre Capretz of Yale University. This two-semester telecourse features an original romantic comedy filmed on location in France. Each program is composed of an episode of the story followed by a variety of images that illustrate and explain its content. Viewers see and hear native speakers interacting in familiar situations and learn to associate what they hear with the situations they see. This telecourse is part of the Annenberg/CPB Collection. 52 half-hour programs.

History

America in Perspective
An introductory course which chronologically analyzes the people, events, and forces that have shaped American history since 1877. This series combines historical film and photographs, interviews with leading historians, and eyewitness accounts of national developments in the United States. 26 half-hour programs.

Americas
A multidisciplinary study of the twentieth-century political, economic, social, and cultural history of Latin America and the Caribbean. This introductory level telecourse explores various Latin American issues such as the changing regional ethnic identities, the evolving role of women, national economics and political instability, reform movements and revolutions, and the impact of migration and urbanization. This telecourse is part of the Annenberg/CPB Collection. Closed captioned for the hearing impaired. 10 one-hour programs.

The Western Tradition, Part I
The first part of a two-semester course that features lectures from Eugene Weber, internationally renowned author, historian, and professor. Eugene Weber blends concepts of history, art, literature, religion, geography, government, and economics to help students identify the parallels in today's society. The first semester consists of 13 units that cover pre-Western civilizations, the Middle Ages, and the Renaissance period. This telecourse is part of the annenberg/CPB Collection. Closed captioned for the hearing impaired. 26 half-hour programs.

Marketing

Principles of Marketing Management
A business telecourse designed to provide students with the opportunity to learn about the world of marketing. This telecourse focuses on the fundamental principles of analysis, and provides a step-

by-step method for analyzing marketing situations. The telecourse includes interviews, film clips and on-site footage of major companies in action such as Walt Disney, Atlantic Richfield, Apple Computers, and Lawry/Lipton. 15 half-hour programs.

Spanish

Destinos

A two-semester telecourse that allows beginning Spanish language students to hear Spanish and ex-perience the cultural diversity of Hispanic society while following a compelling story. In each episode, students are exposed to conversational Spanish and are encouraged to use context to follow the story. The conclusion of each episode features a review of the significant points of the story to increase student comprehension. This telecourse is part of the Annenberg/CPB Collection. Closed captioned for the hearing impaired. 52 half-hour programs.

North Carolina

North Carolina State University
Instructional Telecommunications
Division of Continuing Studies
Campus Box 7401
Raleigh, NC   27695-7401

(919) 515-7730; *Fax:* (919) 515-5778

Geographic Access: North Carolina

DELIVERY SYSTEMS

Broadcast Television
Students may view their courses on The Education Channel (Cablevision of Raleigh, Channel 18). They are encouraged to videotape classes and view/review them at a convenient time. For those without access to cable, recordings of cable classes may be viewed in the NCSU D.H. Hill Library Media Center.

Videocassette
Students who choose to take courses via videocassette are loaned a complete set of tapes for the semester. Courses via videocassette registrants are limited to the number of tape sets available. The tape sets are assigned on a first-come-first-served basis.

INSTITUTION DESCRIPTION

North Carolina State University is a land-grant university and a constituent institution of The University of North Carolina.

Courses via telecommunications from NCSU are available to students everywhere. This program was introduced to satisfy students' needs for convenient and flexible course access by offering classes on cable television and by videocassette. Students who ordinarily would not be able to enroll in classes because of scheduling, distance, physical, or time limitations, may earn credit towards a degree without attending class on campus. Contact between the student and the faculty occurs by mail, telephone, and/or convenient meetings.

Courses described in the Courses Offered section represent those currently available. The courses offered depend on instructor availability and other logistics. New and different courses are offered each year.

Accreditation: SACS

Official/Contact: Thomas L. Russell, Director

Admission Requirements: Students currently enrolled in degree programs may apply to the Office of Instructional Telecommunications. Registration forms and "Telefacts" (in-depth course information) may be obtained from that office.

Tuition: Tuition for each course is included below with the course description and assumes North Carolina residency. Add $50 for each course for those U.S. residents outside of North Carolina. Non-U.S. registrants add $100. Textbooks must be purchased by the student. MasterCard and VISA accepted.

Degree Credit: A complete degree program is not offered, but credit for successful completion of any course may be applied toward a degree.

Grading: Letter grades are assigned. Examinations must be proctored. Credit is awarded in semester hour units.

Library: The D.H. Hill Library Media Center supports all students officially registered for courses via telecommunications.

COURSES OFFERED

Accounting

Accounting II: An Introduction to Managerial Accounting

Analysis of accounting data that are useful in managerial decision making and in the control and evaluation of the decisions made within business organizations. An introduction to basic models, financial statement analysis, cost behavior analysis, and cost control procedures. A videocassette course. Tuition: $260. (3 credits)

Adult Education

Organization and Operation of Training and Development Programs

An overview of the field of training and development including related fields such as organizational development, career development, and human resource management. The various roles that practitioners perform and the competencies required. The theoretical framework and origins of the field along with an introduction to adult learning theory, the critical importance of the learning environment, professional development and the code of ethics critical to the progression. Applications within human resource development (HRD) as they relate to the training and development practitioner, including sales, executive, management, supervisory, and technical training. The background and historical perspectives of the field are presented, along with implications for the future of training and development. Course is broadcast via cable. Tuition: $275. (3 credits)

Biology

Biology in the Modern World

Principles and concepts of biology including cellular structure and function, metabolism and energy transformation, homeostasis, reproduction, heredity, diversity of life, ecology, evolution and animal behavior. Emphasis on human affairs and human examples. Course is cable broadcast. Tuition: $290. (4 credits)

Chemistry

Organic Chemistry I

First half of a two semester sequence in the fundamentals of modern organic chemistry covering structure and bonding, stereochemistry, reactivity and synthesis of carbon compounds. Detailed coverage of aliphatic hydrocarbons, alcohols, and alkyl halides along with an introduction to spectral techniques will be provided. On-campus lab participation required. Course is broadcast via cable. Tuition: $290. (4 credits)

Communications

Interpersonal Communication

Interpersonal communication competence, self-concept, perception, emotions, self-disclosure, language, nonverbal communication, reflective listening, conflict management and relational communication. Interpersonal communication improvement project. Course is broadcast via cable. Tuition: $225. (3 credits)

English

English Literature

Survey of English literature from its beginning until 1660, including such figures as Chaucer, Spenser, Marlowe, Shakespeare, Jonson, Donne, and Milton. A videocassette course. Tuition: $260 (textbook provided). (3 credits)

American Literature

Survey of American literature from the Colonial beginnings until 1855, including such figures as John Smith, Anne Bradstreet, Mary Rowlandson, Benjamin Franklin, Phillis Wheatley, Washington Irving, Edgar Allan Poe, Nathaniel Hawthorne, Herman Melville, Henry David Thoreau, and Walt Whitman. Course is broadcast via cable. Tuition: $225. (3 credits)

History of the English Language

Development of the English language from its Indo-European origins to the present. Emphasis on historical and comparative and linguistic methodology and on detailed changes in sound, syntax, and meaning. A videocassette course. Tuition: $260. (3 credits)

History

History of the Republic of South Africa
Evolution of the Republic of South Africa's society, with emphasis on the interaction of diverse peoples and cultures. Particular attention is given to the period since 1870. A videocassette course. Tuition: $260. (3 credits)

Horticulture

Home Horticulture
Introduction and review of home horticulture as it relates to the horticultural enthusiast. A general understanding of plant structure and development, house plants, flower arranging, home greenhouses, growing trees, shrubs, and flowers in the home landscape. Vegetable and fruit gardening, pesticides for the home gardener, and other related topics. A videocassette course. Tuition: $260. (3 credits)

Mathematics

Topics in Contemporary Mathematics
Primarily for students in humanities and social sciences. Course presents a collection of topics illustrating contemporary uses of mathematics (may vary from one semester to another). Common offerings include selections from logic, counting procedures, probability, modular arithmetic, matrices, cryptography, mathematics of finance, and game theory. A videocassette course. Tuition: $260 (textbook provided). (3 credits)

Physical Education

Body Conditioning and Aerobics
Instruction in exercise prescription, safety precautions during exercise, and proper exercise techniques. This is a one hour elective physical education course that may be used to fulfill part of the university requirement of four semester hours of physical education for graduation. Students will be required to visit campus twice during the semester for pre-post-fitness testing. Each testing date will last 2 to 3 hours. A videocassette course. Tuition: $190. (1 credit)

Public Administration

Introduction to Public Administration
Administration in city, state, and national governments: effectiveness and responsiveness, involvement in policy areas, and issues of ethics and responsibilities. A videocassette course. Tuition: $260. (3 credits)

Religious Studies

Religious Traditions of the World
Major Eastern and Western religious traditions with attention to their basic teachings and practices as well as to the historical, geographical, social, and political settings in which they have arisen and developed. A videocassette course. Tuition: $260. (3 credits)

Spanish

Intermediate Spanish II
Last of four sequential courses, completing the learning of the foundations of the Spanish language. Writing receives greater attention as well as the cultural heritage of Spanish-speaking people. Course is broadcast via cable. Tuition: $225. (3 credits)

University of North Carolina
Independent Studies
CB 1020, The Friday Center
Chapel Hill, NC 27599-1020

(919) 962-1104

Geographic Access: Nationwide

DELIVERY SYSTEMS

Audiocassette
Students enrolled in audio-enhanced courses must have access to an audiocassette player/recorder.

Videocassette
Some courses are video-enhanced. In some cases, videos can be viewed at the option of the student.

INSTITUTION DESCRIPTION

The University of North Carolina opened its doors to students in 1795 and was the first state university in the United States to award university diplomas. Independent Studies is a joint effort by eight institutions of the university system.

In 1975 the Division of Continuing Education assumed management responsibility for the multi-institutional instruction program. In addition to the audio- and video-enhanced courses listed below, traditional correspondence courses and off-campus classes are also offered.

Accreditation: SACS

Official/Contact: Norman H. Lowenthal, Associate Director

Admission Requirements: Courses are open to anyone who wishes to enroll. However, if working toward an academic degree, special approvals from the student's degree-granting institution to transfer credit may be required.

Tuition: $55 per semester hour. Textbooks must be purchased by the student. MasterCard and VISA accepted.

Degree Credit: Most courses are offered for academic credit at the undergraduate college level. Credit earned may be applied toward a degree if the course is applicable to the requirements of the student's particular program. Any course may be taken for noncredit.

Grading: The following grading system is currently in effect: A, B, C, D, F. Examinations must be supervised at an accredited college, university, community college, or technical college. Persons serving in the military may have the examination supervised by an Education Officer on their base or ship. Credit is awarded in semester hour units.

Library: If the student does not have access to equipment (audiocassette player or VCR), the library or learning resource center of community and technical colleges may be able to assist the student in satisfying the listening/viewing requirement.

COURSES OFFERED

French

French 1

This course has been designed to follow the basic format of the first semester course in elementary French given at UNC—Chapel Hill. It has the same primary goals as the program upon which it is modeled: to give the beginning student a solid grasp of the underlying structures and vocabulary of modern French, and to systematically develop the four basic skills of listening, speaking, reading, and writing. Audiocassette tapes ($39.00) are required. 26 assignments. (4 credits)

Geography

Physical Geography

An assessment of the occurrence, characteristics and interrelationships of the earth's climates, landforms, natural vegetation and soils, especially as they influence man's attempt to utilize his environment. Course includes optional viewing of selected videocassette tapes. (3 credits)

German

Elementary German 1

The student will acquire some elementary communications skills and get a systematic introduction to the basic grammatical patterns of the German language. While reading and writing will get the major emphasis, tape recordings will make it possible to practice listening and speaking. This use of all four basic skills enables the student to approach the new language from every possible angle and thus to lay the foundation for future reading or conversation courses. Audiocassette tapes, *Deutsch Heute,* Part One ($23.55), are required. 27 assignments. (3 credits)

Elementary German 2

A continuation of the above course. Audiocassette tapes *Deutsch Heute,* Part Two audiocassette tapes ($23.55) required. (3 credits)

Interdisciplinary Studies

Technology and Change

Based on the BBC's telecourse *Connections,* this course examines the impact of technology on society and the individual. Topics treated include automation, bureaucracy, computerization, and the interrelationship of technological innovations. 5 assignments. (3 credits)

Italian

Elementary Italian 1

This course is designed to introduce students to the most essential elements of Italian structure and vocabulary, as well as some basic aspects of Italian culture. All four language skills are stressed: listening comprehension, speaking, reading, and writing (in that order). Audiocassette tapes ($5.50) are required. 22 assignments. (3 credits)

Elementary Italian 2

The emphasis of the course will still be placed on developing the four basic skills of listening, speaking, reading, and writing and all major grammatical points will be covered. Audiocassette tapes ($2.50) are required. 22 assignments. (3 credits)

Latin

Elementary Latin

The principles of Latin necessary for the translation of Latin into English are introduced. A pronunciation tape is required. 24 assignments. (3 credits)

Music

Fundamentals of Music I

This course is directed primarily at the student with little or no formal background in music. Musical notation, major and minor scales, key and time signatures, rhythms, simple keyboard chord progressions, and melody-writing are included. Optional material on the guitar. There is no textbook but students need music staff paper, blank audiocassette tapes, and access to a piano and to an audiocassette tape player. Audiocassette tapes ($2.00) required. (3 credits)

Masterworks of Music

This course is directed primarily to students with little or no formal background in music. A grounding in the fundamentals of music theory is given in the first two lessons. The main body of the course teaches music appreciation through a study of the main periods of music history and through detailed examination of representative works from each period. The course seeks to lay a foundation for the understanding and enjoyment of music of any period or genre. Recording of excerpts from *Carmen* ($10.00) and audiocassettes ($8.00) required. 16 assignments. (3 credits)

Psychology

General Psychology

This course is designed as an introduction to the basic methods, theories, and applications of psychology to a wide range of issues. Areas reviewed will include biological, developmental, cognitive, clinical, social, and personality psychology. Coverage of the course material will be supplemented by videotapes. 18 assignments. Tape series: *Discovering Psychology*, rental fee $50 plus a deposit of $10 which will be refunded when the tapes are returned. (3 credits)

North Dakota

Bismarck State College
See **North Dakota Interactive Video Network**

Dickinson State University
See **North Dakota Interactive Video Network**

Mayville State University
See **North Dakota Interactive Video Network**

Minot State University
See **North Dakota Interactive Video Network**

North Dakota Interactive Video Network

North Dakota University System
State Capitol

600 East Boulevard Avenue
Bismarck, ND   58505

(701) 224-2964

Geographic Access: North Dakota

DELIVERY SYSTEMS

Interactive Audio/Video

Two-way video systems transmit live, high quality audio and color video between several sites. The system is voice activated. Sound causes the camera to switch to different sites. The actual picture is controlled by the classroom presenter or technician. Although only one site is seen at a time, all sites can be heard.

INSTITUTION DESCRIPTION

The North Dakota Interactive Video Network (ND IVN) is a cooperative project of the North Dakota University System and the North Dakota Information Services Division. A main goal of the network's mission is to "deliver quality postsecondary programs and services to citizens who would not otherwise have access to those services." The ND IVN uses two-way video systems to transmit live audio and video between several sites. An instructor at the home site is able to see and hear the students in the remote sites. Students are able to see and hear the teacher and all other students.

Courses are offered by a host site (*see* Courses Offered) and transmitted to other sites. Locations and site coordinators are as follows:

- Bismarck State College (Bismarck ND), Pat Gross, (701) 224-5584
- Dickinson State University (Dickinson ND), Julie Schepp, (701) 227-2582
- Mayville State University (Mayville ND), Marjorie Fugleberg, (701) 786-4817
- Minot State University (Minot ND), Jim Croonquist, (701) 857-3822
- North Dakota State College of Science (Wahpeton ND), Larry Christensen, (701) 671-2524
- North Dakota State University (Fargo ND), Jan Flack, (701) 237-7017
- North Dakota State University (Bottineau, ND), Myron Faa, (701) 228-5466
- University of North Dakota (Grand Forks ND), Jean Johnson, (701) 777-3308
- University of North Dakota—Lake Region (Devils Lake ND), Doug Darling, (701) 662-1508
- University of North Dakota (Williston ND), Ken Quamme, (701) 774-4207

- Valley City State University (Valley City ND), Jan Drake, (701) 845-7302

- West River/Missouri Valley High Schools, Bill Strasser, (701) 442-3201

- Heart of the Valley High Schools, Jerry Bartholomay, (701) 436-4360

- North Dakota State Hospital, Joel Wilson, (701) 253-3604

Accreditation: NCA

Official/Contact: Russell Poulin, Director

Admission Requirements: Preregistration is required and can be accomplished through the site coordinator nearest the student.

Tuition: Current tuition rates of the host institution are applicable. Textbooks and study materials must be purchased by the student.

Degree Credit: Credits earned may be applied toward a degree and may be acceptable in transfer to another institution.

Grading: Examinations are taken at the classroom site. Grading system is according to the policy of the host site offering the course. Credit is awarded in semester hour units.

Library: Students are encouraged to use their local community libraries and may use the library facilities of any campus participating in the interactive system.

COURSES OFFERED

Agriculture

Farm and Ranch Management

Acquisition and organization of factors of production. Application of economic principles in decision making. Risk management and enterprise analysis. Host campus: UND-Lake Region. (3 credits)

Crop Production II

Topics to be covered include selection of varieties of crops, harvesting crops, and pasture improvements. Host campus: UND-Lake Region. (2 credits)

Business

Principles of Management

Basic objectives of this course include an introduction to the management discipline and its subdisciplines, to study basic management theories and principles, to understand relevant managerial terminology, to create an awareness of current issues in management, and to begin to develop problem-solving and decision-making skills in management through application of materials studies. Host campus: North Dakota State University. (3 credits)

Accounting Problems

Special problems in accounting, including consolidated statements, partnerships, estates, trusts, and receiverships. Host campus: Mayville State University. (3 credits)

Childhood Education

Young Children's Language and Thought

This course examines both typical and atypical development of language and thought in children 0-8 as a basis for understanding and working with young children in educational settings. Host campus: University of North Dakota. (3 credits)

Childhood Development Practice II

The objective of this course is to provide an in-depth examination of the thirteen functional areas identified as essential by the Council for Early Childhood Professional Recognition. Intensive preparation for the credentialing will be through the development of knowledge and expertise in developmentally appropriate practices and writing entries for the professional resource file. Host campus: North Dakota State University. (4 credits)

Dental Health

Periodontics

Etiology and classification of periodontal disease. Also includes the principles of periodontology and their clinical application. Host campus: North Dakota State College of Science. (1 credit)

Driver Education

Driver and Traffic Safety Education

Introduction to driver and traffic education. A review of various high school textbooks and other teaching tools. Host campus: Minot State University. (3 credits).

Education

Educational Law I

The initial survey course in educational law concerning building-level issues. Includes topics such as religion and the public schools, tort liability, students' rights, and the handling of student records. Some consideration is given to process of legal research in education. Host campus: University of North Dakota. (3 credits)

Staff and Program Evaluation

A study of the evaluation of staff, including teachers, administrators, support personnel, and boards. For the purposes of accreditation, the evaluation of components that support the curriculum. Procedures, processes, and instruments will be identified and analyzed. Host campus: University of North Dakota. (3 credits)

Introduction to Educational Leadership

An introduction to models of educational leadership including organizational structure, theory, and leadership styles. The course involves consideration of concepts, problems, and issues in administration. Host campus: North Dakota State University. (2 credits)

Secondary School Counseling

An overview of principles and functions of a secondary school counseling program and an examination of secondary school counseling materials. Host campus: North Dakota State University. (2 credits)

Guidance Administration and Consulting

The role of administrators, guidance personnel, and teachers in the management of and consulting in K-12 guidance programs. Host campus: North Dakota State University. (2 credits)

Instructional Models

Investigation of current practices and trends in instructional models. Emphasis will be placed on the relationship of current research to contemporary practice. Host campus: North Dakota State University. (2 credits)

Dynamics of Addiction

A study of the theories and scope of addiction from both the personal and social viewpoints with consideration given to the impact on the family. Host campus: North Dakota State University. (3 credits)

School Finance and Business Management

An overview of school fund revenues and expenditures pertaining to local, state, and federal funding. This includes an in-depth study of practices of school business administration pertaining to all activities in instruction and ancillary funds. Host campus: North Dakota State University. (4 credits)

Finance

Managerial Finance

The development of financial decision-making skills using the case-analysis method through application of financial theory to topical areas of analysis, planning control, asset management, financial instruments, markets, capital structure, dividend policy, cost of capital, etc. Host campus: University of North Dakota. (3 credits)

History

American Women in History

Reading, discussion, and analysis of the role of women in American history. Host campus: Valley City State University. (3 credits)

Management

Advanced Managerial Theory

Analysis of macro- and micro-behavioral approaches to the study of effective human resource management within the organization. Topics covered include the environment, the individual, the small group, leadership, motivation, job design, evaluation, rewards, and growth. Macro-behavioral topics such as organizational design, climate, and change, intervention strategies, methods, and assessments. Special emphasis will be given to the active research approach which underlies the philosophy of the organizational development process. Host campus: University of North Dakota. (3 credits)

Mathematics

Problem Solving and Applications

Investigation of the theory and techniques of problem solving. Examination of problems and mathematical applications at various levels of mathematics education. Host campus: Minot State University. (3 credits)

Nursing

Introduction to Adult Nursing

This course utilizes the medical systems model to introduce abnormal states and conditions resulting from disease in the developing biopsychosocial and spiritual adult client. Communication techniques, physical assessment, and skilled nursing procedures are taught in lecture, demonstrated and applied in the laboratory and clinical settings. Emphasis is placed on the disease process, assessments, and interventions utilizing the nursing process, thereby assisting the student to provide safe and effective nursing care by helping the client adapt to his/her environment. Nursing care of the client in the long-term care setting is emphasized. Host campus: North Dakota State College of Science. (6 credits)

Adult Nursing

This course builds on prior learning to gain knowledge in the methodology of diagnostic testing, medical-surgical interventions, and aspects of nutritional and pharmacological roles in the delivery of nursing care to the patient/client. Assessments will employ the systems approach with emphasis placed on nursing care utilizing the Nursing Process. The teaching-learning process will be emphasized in the care of the client. Problem-solving skills will be utilized in the identification of environmental risks in planning the care of the adult patient/client. Host campus: North Dakota State College of Science. (5 credits)

Adult Health Nursing

Focus is on selected theories and principles of adult nursing practice, education, and research with particular emphasis on the acute biological aspects. Lecture, discussion, and special assignments. Host campus: University of North Dakota. (4 credits)

Childbearing Nursing I

Focus is on nursing care for health maintenance and health promotion during childbearing. Host campus: University of North Dakota. (2 credits)

Child Health Nursing I

Focus is on nursing care for health maintenance and health promotion during childhood. Host campus: University of North Dakota. (2 credits)

Trends and Issues

The focus of this course is on the investigation and discussion of current issues and trends that affect the nursing profession and health care. Nursing as an autonomous, interdependent, and collaborative pro-fession is examined through utilization of the seminar format. Host campus: Dickinson State University. (2 credits)

Nursing in the Community

This is a theory course with a focus on health promotion, maintenance, and adaptation of the individual, family, group, and community throughout the life cycle. Content includes discussion of multicultural groups, the wellness-illness continuum, and community health nursing roles. Host campus: Dickinson State University. (3 credits)

Nursing in the Community Clinic

The focus of this clinical course is on promoting adaptation of the individual, family, group, and community. Clinical affiliations are in community health settings and include public health, home health, and community mental health. Roy's Adaptation Model is used in applying this nursing process. Satisfactory/unsatisfactory grade only. Host campus: Dickinson State University. (3 credits)

Nursing Research

Introduction to the research process and its application to nursing practice. Host campus: North Dakota State University. (2 credits)

Research Design and Methods in Nursing

The course focuses on the analysis and critique of published nursing research. The course also focuses on the development of research proposals, including application of a theoretical framework, selection of design and methodology. Host campus: University of North Dakota. (3 credits)

Epidemiology in Nursing

This course will focus on epidemiologic techniques and research for advanced nursing. Host campus: University of North Dakota. (3 credits)

Advanced Nursing Practice for Rural Cultures I

This practicum provides the graduate student opportunities to test nursing and related theories with families, groups, and communities. In addition, nursing roles in assessment, planning, and interventions within a rural community will be assumed and critiqued. Host campus: University of North Dakota. (3 credits)

Nutrition

Nutrition and Introduction to Diet Therapy
A study of the basic principles of nutrition including: nutrition in the community, the role of nutrients in the maintenance of normal health, and nutrition in the life cycle. Also included is the application of these principles to all age groups, and for diet modification during illness. Host campus: North Dakota College of Science. (3 credits)

Paralegal Studies

Legal System and Ethics
Function and ethics of the legal assistant in the law office and legal system. An introduction to the federal and state court systems and the historical development and nature of the law. Host campus: UND-Lake Region. (4 credits)

Pharmacy

Drugs Subject to Abuse
Biochemical, pharmacological, behavioral, and therapeutic aspects of substance abuse. Host campus: University of North Dakota. (2 credits)

Political Science

Problems in Political Science: Politics and Policy Making in North Dakota
Governor George Sinner, Former House Majority Leader Earl Strinden, and other political practitioners will discuss the various problems and facets of making and implementing policy and state government. The course will cover the importance of political culture, the media, interest groups, political parties, constituents, intergovernmental relations, the bureaucracy, the legislature and the executive branch—in development, consideration, adoption, and implementation of public policy in North Dakota. Host campus: University of North Dakota. (2 credits)

Research Methods
This course will first focus on various approaches to analyzing political phenomena with the goal of developing students' ability to think analytically and to distinguish between empirical and normative analysis. The course will then introduce techniques of empirical research including research design, measurement, data gathering, and data analysis.

Host campus: University of North Dakota. (3 credits)

Seminar: Problems in State and Local Government
Directed in-depth inquiry into the contemporary structural and policy problems of state and local governments. During the course, each student will prepare a research paper relevant to a current problem suitable for publication and distribution to an identifiable body of public officials and citizens for problem-solving purposes. Host campus: University of North Dakota. (3 credits)

Psychology

Psychological and Pathological Effects of Drugs
Emphasis will be placed on biological effects attributable to chemicals and the synergistic effect when drugs are combined. Host campus: Minot State University. (3 credits)

Introduction to Personality
Examination of basic concepts in the field of personality. Host campus: University of North Dakota. (3 credits)

Elementary Counseling
Application of counseling theory in working with young children in elementary schools. Host campus: Minot State University. (3 credits)

Social Work

Drugs: Addiction Dynamics
This course is an introduction to the dynamics of drug addiction and related drug abuse issues. Special emphasis will be placed on alcohol as the most frequently used and abused drug. Host campus: University of North Dakota. (2 credits)

Sociology

Drugs and Society
Social factors affecting use and control of self-administered psychoactive drugs, including alcohol, cigarettes, marijuana, and more illicit substances. Topics include social definitions, causes, controls, and consequences of drug problems. Host campus: University of North Dakota. (3 credits)

Special Education

Early Intervention for Children with Special Needs
An introduction to the field of early childhood special education, primarily for students interested in entering the field. Issues such as program design, parent involvement, identification, infant education, and effects of handicaps will be covered. Host campus: University of North Dakota. (2 credits)

North Dakota State College of Science
See **North Dakota Interactive Video Network**

North Dakota State University
See **North Dakota Interactive Video Network**

North Dakota State University - Bottineau
See **North Dakota Interactive Video Network**

University of North Dakota
Outreach Programs
Division of Continuing Education
P.O. Box 8277
University Station
Grand Forks, ND   58201

(701) 777-3044

Geographic Access: Worldwide

DELIVERY SYSTEMS

Audiocassette
Audiotapes supplement the text in foreign language courses.

Videocassette
Videotapes enhance the course in Visual Arts described below.

INSTITUTION DESCRIPTION

The University of North Dakota (UND) began its service of outreach programs in 1910. Traditional correspondence courses are offered as well as audio- and video-enhanced courses. *See* Courses Offered.

UND is also a host site for the North Dakota Interactive Video Network that uses two-way video systems to transmit live audio and video between several sites. An instructor at the home site is able to see and hear the students in remote sites. Students are able to see and hear the teacher and all other students. For these interactive audio/video courses hosted by UND, *see* North Dakota Interactive Video Network.

Accreditation: NCA

Official/Contact: Karen Berthold, Director

Admission Requirements: There are no institutional admission requirements but enrollment does not constitute admission to the University of North Dakota. Enrollment can be made at any time.

Tuition: $53 per semester hour. An administrative fee of $10 per course plus additional fees for rental of audio or video materials (listed below with course description).

Degree Credit: Credit earned through distance learning may be applied to a degree program at the University of North Dakota. Students from other institutions should check for transfer-in acceptability.

Grading: Letter grades are awarded. Students have the option of satisfactory/unsatisfactory grading. Credit is awarded in semester hour units.

Library: Students in the vicinity of the campus have access to the University's libraries.

COURSES OFFERED

French

Beginning French 101
Fundamentals of French grammar, oral use of the language and reading of easy French. The audio-oral approach through tapes is required. 18 lessons, 2 exams. Audiotape fee: $21. (4 credits)

Beginning French 102
Continued study of fundamentals of French grammar, oral use of the language and reading of easy French. 18 lessons, 2 exams. Audiotape fee: $27. (4 credits)

German

Beginning German 101
Fundamentals of German grammar, oral use of the language and reading of easy German. 28 lessons, 6 exams. Audiotape fee: $30. (4 credits)

Beginning German 102
Continuing study of fundamentals of German grammar, oral use of the language and reading of easy German. 29 lessons, 5 exams. Audiotape fee: $21. (4 credits)

Latin

First-Year College Latin 101
Introduction to Latin grammar and syntax, followed by Latin prose and poetry selections. The audio-oral approach through tapes is required. 20 lessons, 1 exam. Audiotape fee: $3. (4 credits)

First-Year College Latin 102
Continued study of Latin grammar and syntax, reading of Latin prose and poetry selections. 20 lessons, 1 exam. Audiotape fee: $3. (4 credits)

Medical Terminology

Medical Terminology
Knowledge of medical terminology. 5 exams. Audiotape fee: $8. (1 credit)

Music

Introduction to the Understanding of Music
Music appreciation for students without an extensive background in music. 10 lessons, 2 exams. Audiotape fee: $6. (3 credits)

Norwegian

Beginning Norwegian 101
Grammar, pronunciation, reading and translation, oral and written exercises. 22 lessons, 2 exams. Audiotape fee: $9. (4 credits)

Spanish

Beginning Spanish 101
Pronunciation and fundamental grammatical principles introduced through the development of skill in listening, comprehension, and speaking, followed by practice in reading and writing. 12 lessons, 2 exams. Audiotape fee: $24. (4 credits)

Beginning Spanish 102
A continuation of Beginning Spanish 101. 12 lessons, 2 exams. Audiotape fee: $24. (4 credits)

Second-Year Spanish 201
Review of the structure of the language, readings in Spanish, practice in oral and written expression. 12 lessons, 2 exams. Audiotape fee: $9. (4 credits)

Second-Year Spanish 202
A continuation of Second-Year Spanish 201. 12 lessons, 2 exams. Audiotape fee: $9. (4 credits)

Visual Arts

Introduction to Drawing and Color Materials
Introduction for nonmajors to drawing and color media and techniques. Includes working from still lifes, models, and landscapes. 7 lessons, no exams. Videotape fee: $30 ($15 refundable). (3 credits)

University of North Dakota - Lake Region
See **North Dakota Interactive Video Network**

University of North Dakota - Williston
See **North Dakota Interactive Video Network**

Valley City State University
See **North Dakota Interactive Video Network**

Ohio

Edison State Community College
College by Cassette
Division of Outreach Services
413 Walnut Street
Greenville, OH   45331

(513) 548-5546

Geographic Access: Ohio

DELIVERY SYSTEMS

Videocassette
The course orientation meeting informs students about course assignments and requirements. Videocassettes in VHS format only are distributed at this session.

INSTITUTION DESCRIPTION

Edison State Community College is located in rural southwestern Ohio. It serves three counties. Chartered in 1973 as Edison State General and Technical College, the present name was adopted in 1977.

The College by Cassette program at Edison State is a distance learning program whereby the student reads the textbook and views televised instruction on VHS videotape cassettes. This allows students to control when and where they will view the class materials as opposed to being tied to a weekly class session that may conflict with work or family obligations. The other components of a college course—reading textbooks, completing workbooks, writing papers, and taking tests—are more rigorous for the College by Cassette courses than for traditional courses. More preparation time, self-discipline, and motivation is required from the student to complete the assignments.

Accreditation: NCA

Official/Contact: Garry Heberer, Associate Dean

Admission Requirements: New students must be accepted for admission to Edison State Community College prior to registering for any classes. Edison State requires official copies of high school transcripts, and transcripts from all other colleges previously attended.

Tuition: Students pay the college's regular tuition and a lab fee composed of $40 telecourse fee and a refundable $3 deposit for each videocassette. (Lab fees are listed below with each course.) Textbooks must be purchased by the student.

Degree Credit: Credit earned for completion of courses is applicable toward the student's degree program.

Grading: Final examinations are conducted on campus by appointment and with the instructor's prior approval. Students must submit all remaining written assignments and return all videocassettes at the time of the examinations. Letter grades are assigned and credit is awarded in semester hour credits.

Library: The Learning Resource Center offers its services to officially registered students.

COURSES OFFERED

Art

Art History through the Renaissance
An introductory examination of works of art which define the western visual tradition. Instruction on formal qualities, iconography, and technical achievements. Lab fee: $49. (3 credits)

Economics

Fundamentals of Economics
A survey course which investigates causes and effects of major economic events in the 20th century. Interviews with Milton Friedman and Paul Samuelson. Lab fee: $61. (3 credits)

History

European History 1300-1715
History, art, literature, religion, geography, government, and economics presented to help students recognize pendulum swings of history and their parallels to modern history and the evolution of human institutions. Lab fee: $52. (3 credits)

European History 1715-1871
Europe in an age of revolutions—political, industrial, social, and intellectual. Lab fee: $55. (3 credits)

Management

Principles of Management
Introduction to the management skills of planning and organizing, staffing and directing, controlling, decision making, motivating, communicating, and applying managerial skills to business organizations. Lab fee: $61. (3 credits)

Psychology

Introduction to Psychology I
Presents major concepts including brain and behavior, sensation and perception, cognitive processes, life-span development. Lab fee: $61. (3 credits)

Introduction to Psychology II
Social psychology, neuroses and psychoses, psychotherapy, human sexuality, counseling, human intelligence, and states of consciousness are surveyed. Lab fee: $61. (3 credits)

Ohio State University
Department of Educational Policy and Leadership
College of Education
29 West Woodruff Avenue
Columbus, OH   43210-1177

(614) 292-1636

Geographic Access: Ohio

DELIVERY SYSTEMS

Broadcast Television
The course consists of 12 one-half hour programs broadcast by WOSU/WPBO-TV. Students are encouraged to tape the programs.

Interactive Audio/Video
Four interactive teleconferences are held during the course. These are conducted with the cooperation of Instructional Technology Services of Central Ohio, Inc.

INSTITUTION DESCRIPTION

The Ohio State University's College of Education offers a telecourse for K-12 educators. It is offered in conjunction with WOSU-TV Columbus and WPBO-TV Portsmouth with the cooperation of Instructional Technology Services of Central Ohio, Inc. The graduate-level course is intended for K-12 teachers and administrators who are interested in learning to integrate technology in the curriculum. No campus visits are necessary.

Accreditation: NCA

Official/Contact: Ms. Leslie Hall, Coordinator

Admission Requirements: If the prospective student has never been enrolled as a graduate student at OSU, he/she must be admitted to graduate nondegree status before registration. A bachelor's or higher degree is required.

Tuition: $265 for the 2-credit course. Tuition is subject to change. The course manual must be purchased by the student from Instructional Technology Services of Central Ohio, Inc.

Degree Credit: Credit earned may be applied to a master's degree program.

Grading: Satisfactory/Unsatisfactory is awarded upon completion of all course requirements. Credit is awarded in quarter hour units.

Library: None.

COURSES OFFERED

Education

Technology in the Curriculum: A Distance Learning Telecourse for K-12 Educators

The course includes practical examples for the integration of technology for teaching and learning, a framework for the strategic planning for the use of technology in the curriculum, opportunities for networking, and presentations by K-12 teachers. Teachers at all grade levels will be featured using technology in the areas of Reading/Language Arts, Science, Social Studies, Math, and the Arts. Most currently available technologies used in education will be discussed. Course requirements include viewing the 12 half-hour programs, participating in the 4 one-hour teleconferences, completing 5 reading assignments and corresponding written assignments, and completing a final technology integration project which may be done individually or as a group. The course text is a manual that includes instructions for accessing electronic mail, readings and assignments, a bibliography of suggested readings, classroom activities using technology, sources for free or inexpensive materials, and a glossary of technology terms. (2 credits)

Ohio University
Independent Study Program
Lifelong Learning Programs

302 Tupper Hall
Athens, OH   45701-2979

(614) 593-2910 *Fax:* (614) 593-2901

Geographic Access: Worldwide

DELIVERY SYSTEMS

Audiocassette
Audiotapes enhance and supplement the text and study guides in a variety of courses.

Computer Tutorials
Used particularly in computer science courses.

Videocassette
Videotapes supplement the text and study guide.

INSTITUTION DESCRIPTION

Ohio University is a coeducational, state-assisted institution that offers undergraduate study in 120 areas and numerous graduate programs. Chartered in 1804, the university currently has five regional campuses in addition to the main campus in Athens.

The Ohio University Independent Study Program was begun in 1924.

Accreditation: NCA

Official/Contact: Richard W. Moffitt, Director

Admission Requirements: Courses are open to anyone who can profitably pursue them. Formal admission to Ohio University is not required. Present Ohio University students must receive permission from their college to enroll in any course. Acceptance in a course does not constitute admission to Ohio University.

Tuition: $48 per quarter hour credit plus a $10 nonrefundable enrollment fee per course. Textbooks must be purchased by the student. Additional rental fees for video and/or audio tapes. MasterCard and VISA accepted.

Degree Credit: Credit earned may be applied toward a degree at Ohio University. Students from other institutions should verify the transferability of credit.

Grading: Final grades are generally determined by grades on written lessons and supervised examinations. These grades are reported on an A-F scale. Method of grading is explained in detail in each course guide. Examinations must be supervised by an approved proctor. Credit is awarded in quarter hour units.

Library: Students living in an area near an Ohio University campus may use the campus library, although borrowing privileges may be restricted. No other services are offered, although students are encouraged to use local library facilities and interlibrary loan services to obtain information and materials.

COURSES OFFERED

Business

Introduction to Business Computing

Computer applications used in business and industry. Students do computer assignments using DOS operating system, WordPerfect, Lotus 1-2-3, and Harvard Graphics. Students must have use of a computer system that meets the following requirements: IBM or compatible with DOS 2.0 or higher, hard disk, 640K RAM, 5-1/4 or 3-1/2 inch floppy disk drive, EGA or VGA graphics, letter-quality dot-matrix or laser printer, software for DOS operating system, WordPerfect 5.0 or 5.1, Lotus 1-2-3 V. 2.01 or higher, Harvard Graphics 2.1 or higher. (4 credits)

English

Women and Literature

Survey of work of significant women writers of past and present. Students may purchase optional audiotape of selections from some lessons. Audiotape fee: $7. (4 credits)

History

American History to 1828

Political, diplomatic, social, and economic development of American history. Covers 1607 to 1828: colonial America, founding of new nation, and early national period. Use of audiocassette tapes is essential in this course. Audiotape fee: $49 ($21 refundable). (4 credits)

History of the United States, 1828-1900

Political, diplomatic, social, and economic development of American history. Covers 1828 to 1900: Jacksonian democracy, territorial expansion, sectionalism and controversy, Civil War, reconstruction, and impact of expanded Industrial Revolution. Use of audiocassette tapes is essential in this course. Audiotape fee: $42 ($18 refundable). (4 credits)

History of the United States Since 1900

Political, diplomatic, social, and economic development of American history. Covers 1900 to present: progressive movement, WWI, prosperity and depression, WWII, and problems of the cold war era. Use of audiocassette tapes is essential in this course. Audiotape fee: $35 ($15 refundable). (4 credits)

History of Blacks in America Since 1865

Concerns emancipation and its continuing effects on the black person in America. Life in the South, migration to the North, and conservative and radical attempts by the black community to deal with these problems. Use of audiocassette tapes is essential in this course. Audiotape fee: $70 ($30 refundable). (4 credits)

Human Services

Deaf Language and Culture

This course is designed to teach basic sign language and to examine the problems faced by hearing-impaired persons, as well as their capabilities and contributions. Course is especially designed for persons in helping and service professions. Videotape purchase fee: $20. Not available for overseas enrollment except APO and FPO addresses. (3 credits)

Interpersonal Communication

Fundamentals of Human Communication

Introductory analysis of oral communication in human relationships with focus on a variety of contexts including: dyadic, small group, and public communication experiences. Serves as a survey of human communication processes. Audiotape purchase fee: $10 for 2 tapes. (4 credits)

Fundamentals of Public Speaking

Principles of public speaking, practice in presenting informative and persuasive speeches with emphasis on communicative process. Students must have use of VHS format color camera and videotape player (VCR) to videotape some lesson assignments. (4 credits)

Library Science

Basic Acquisitions of Media

Basic procedures in ordering, receiving, organizing, and processing of printed library materials. Visit to library required. Videotape fee: $35 ($15 refundable). Not available for overseas enrollment except APO and FPO addresses. (4 credits)

Music

History and Literature of Music I

History of music with survey of musical literature to 1600. Course requires use of audiocassette tapes. Audiotape purchase fee: $8. (3 credits)

History and Literature of Music II
History of music with survey of musical literature, 1600-1750. Audiotape purchase fee: $8. (3 credits)

Jazz History
Introduction to various musics collectively known as jazz, using textbook and recordings. Topics covered include background and history of various jazz styles, characteristics of various styles, identities of major composers, arrangers, and performers of jazz. Course is nontechnical. Audiotape purchase fee: $7. (3 credits)

Philosophy

Islam
Introduction to basic ideas, history, and background. Videotape fee: $35 ($15 refundable). Tapes cannot be sent to overseas students, except APO and FPO addresses. (4 credits)

Theatre

Theatre History I
Development of theatre and drama in prehistoric, Greek, and Roman periods. An optional videotape of one of the plays is available for a fee of $35 ($15 refundable). Tape cannot be sent to overseas students except APO and FPO addresses. (4 credits)

University of Cincinnati
Telecourse Enrollment
Clifton Avenue
Cincinnati, OH   45221

(513) 475-8000

Geographic Access: Ohio

DELIVERY SYSTEMS

Broadcast Television
Telecourses are broadcast over WCET, Channel 48 on Saturdays and Sundays from 7:00 AM to 8:00 AM.

INSTITUTION DESCRIPTION

The University of Cincinnati is a state institution that was established in 1819 as the Cincinnati College and Medical College of Ohio. The present name was adopted in 1870.

Telecourses are offered for credit and aired over WCET, Channel 48 in Cincinnati.

Accreditation: NCA

Official/Contact: Jean McGee Wilson, Coordinator

Admission Requirements: Open enrollment. For degree-seeking students, graduation from secondary school and formal admittance to the University of Cincinnati.

Tuition: Contact the Telecourse Coordinator at the University of Cincinnati or Manager, Instructional Television of WCET, Channel 48 at (513) 381-4033 for current information regarding tuition and fees.

Degree Credit: Credits earned for successful completion of a course may be applied to a degree program. Students should confer with their home university/college regarding eligibility of the transfer of credit.

Grading: Examinations must be proctored. Letter grades are assigned. Credit is awarded in quarter hour units.

Library: Students have access to the University of Cincinnati libraries.

COURSES OFFERED

Finance

Personal Finance and Money Management
The wise use of financial resources today requires more than an income-producing job and simple subtraction skills. In today's world, an individual must approach his/her financial needs with the savvy of an investment counselor managing the affairs of the company's most important client. With the guidance of finance author and lecturer Bob Rosefsky, students will learn the basics of budgeting and buying, the intricacies of home ownership, income tax and investments, and the wise use of insurance, wills, and trusts. 26 half-hour lessons, 2 per week.

Management

Taking the Lead: The Management Revolution
This vital and insightful new business management telecourse provides an overview of management in the nineties, with an emphasis on the competencies that are essential for success. The series features

such noted authorities as Warren Bennis, John Kotter, George Labovitz, and William Ouchi, and provides viewers with an inside view of management in a variety of businesses, including General Dynamics, Hybritech, Patagonia, and the Four Seasons Hotel. 26 half-hour broadcasts, 2 per week.

Oklahoma

Oklahoma State University
Independent Study
University Extension

001 Classroom Building
Stillwater, OK 74078

(405) 744-6390

Geographic Access: Nationwide

DELIVERY SYSTEMS

Audiocassette
Audiotapes are utilized in a variety of courses, particularly English, engineering, and foreign language.

Broadcast Television
Courses with a video-assisted format are broadcast over public television stations in Oklahoma (OETA).

Computer Tutorials
Computer-assisted courses will require access to a computer and, in some cases, a special modem connection.

Videocassette
Videotapes are available for a rental fee of $50, but $25 will be refunded if the set of tapes is returned undamaged. Rental fees are included with the materials costs listed below with the course description.

INSTITUTION DESCRIPTION

Oklahoma State University was founded in 1890 and has an enrollment of over 19,000 students. Its library houses over 1,700,000 volumes. The Independent Study program at OSU is designed to meet the needs of students both on and off campus. The courses are available to all qualified persons who are interested in academic, cultural, career, and professional advancement.

OSU is a member of the National Universities Degree Consortium (NUDC) which offers bachelor's degree completion programs with reduced residency requirements. Course enrollment is handled by Mind Extension University, a delivery system for cable television, satellite, and videocassettes. *See* Mind Extension University.

Accreditation: NCA

Official/Contact: Charles Feasely, Director

Admission Requirements: Any person who is a graduate of a high school or who is 21 years of age or older may enroll. Admission to the university is not a requirement for enrollment.

Tuition: $50 per semester hour credit. Additional materials fees, including tape rental, are given below with the course description. MasterCard and VISA accepted.

Degree Credit: Up to 30 credit hours of independent study may be applied toward at degree. Students from other institutions should verify the acceptability of transfer credits.

Grading: Final examinations or equivalent projects are required for all courses and comprise a substantial part of the final grade. Examinations must be proctored by approved education personnel. Credit is awarded in semester hour units.

Library: For on-campus students, a complete set of program videotapes are available for viewing in the Media and Microform Room of OSU's Edmon Low Library.

COURSES OFFERED

Art

Introduction to Art

An introduction to the analysis and interpretation of visual arts. Visual, emotional, and intellectual aspects of art in painting, sculpture, printmaking, and architecture. 9 assignments, 2 exams. A video-assisted course. Materials fee: $131. (3 credits)

Business Law

Law of Contracts and Property

General concepts of jurisprudence, judicial systems, substantive law of torts, contracts, and property as they relate to the business environment. 10 assignments, 3 exams. A video-assisted course. Materials fee: $112. (3 credits)

Computer Science

Computer Programming

Programming in a high-level programming language. Introduction to algorithms, problem-solving techniques, and structured programming. Examples of applications from various areas such as business, science, or engineering. Students should have passed college algebra and have use of a computer with a PASCAL compiler. 11 assignments, 4 exams. Materials fee: $52.55. (3 credits)

Introductory BASIC Programming

A beginning course in the art and science of computer programming. Requires having access to a computer with BASIC interpreter or compiler and printer. Programming examples are executed on DEC-SYSTEM 20, Apple, IBM-PC, TRS-80, and PET/Commodore 64, but computers with different versions of BASIC can be used. 8 assignments, 3 exams. Materials fee: $43.25. (2 credits)

Economics

Introduction to Microeconomics

Goals, incentives, and outcomes of economic behavior with applications and illustrations from current social issues. Operation of markets for goods, services, and factors of production. The behavior of firms and industries in different types of competition, income distribution, and international exchange. A video-assisted course. 8 assignments, 3 exams. Materials fee: $62. (3 credits)

Education

Psychological Foundations of Childhood

The child from conception to puberty focusing on educational implications of development in cognitive, affective, and psychomotor domains. 14 assignments, 2 exams. Materials fee: $118.90 (includes videotapes). (3 credits)

English

English Grammar

The traditional terminology and concepts of English grammar leading or evolving into the several current systems of descriptions. 16 assignments, 2 exams. An audio-enhanced course. Materials fee: $114.50. (3 credits)

American Poetry Post 1900

A video-assisted course that explores the lives and works of 13 American poets. 15 assignments, 2 exams. Materials fee: $114.50. (3 credits)

Engineering

Thermodynamics

Properties of substances and principles governing changes in form of energy. First and second laws. 11 assignments, 4 exams. An audio-enhanced course. Materials fee: $109.20. (3 credits)

Family Relations

Human Development Within the Family

Human development within the family system from a lifespan perspective. Principles of development and dynamics of behavior and relationships. Directed observation. 9 assignments, 4 exams. A video-assisted course. Materials fee: $137.19. (3 credits)

Marriage

Consideration of courtship and marriage with special emphasis on building a healthy paired relationship. Communication and decision making, and coping with such problems as money, sex, role taking, in-laws, and children. 12 assignments, 2 exams. A video-based course. Materials fee: $118.50. (3 credits)

French

Elementary French I

Main elements of grammar and pronunciation, with work on the four basic skills of listening comprehension, speaking, reading, and writing. 9 assignments, 5 exams. An audio-enhanced course. Materials fee: $91.25. (5 credits)

Elementary French II

A continuation of Elementary French I. 9 assignments, 4 exams. An audio-enhanced course. Materials fee: $91.25. (5 credits)

General Technology

Engineering Design Graphics with CAD

Sketching and using CAD system to generate engineering drawings to ANSI standards. Interpretation of typical industrial drawings: multiviews, sections, auxiliary views, dimensioning, tolerancing, design and working drawings. Assignments may be turned in by sketching or by mechanical drawing using drafting instruments or by using a CAD system such as AUTOCAD, CADKEY, DESIGNCAD, or SILVER SCREEN. 18 assignments, 3 exams. Materials fee: $89.25. (3 credits)

History

American History to 1865

From European background through the Civil War. 13 assignments, 2 exams. A video-assisted course. Materials fee: $90.25. (3 credits)

American History since 1865

Development of the United States including the growth of industry and its impact on society and foreign affairs. 8 assignments, 4 exams. A video-assisted course. Materials fee: $109.85. (3 credits)

Western Civilization to 1500

History of western civilization from the ancient world to the Reformation. A video-based course. Materials fee: $102.50. (3 credits)

Western Civilization after 1500

History of western civilization from the Reformation to the present. 12 assignments, 2 exams. A video-based course. Materials fee: $101.25. (3 credits)

Modern Japan

Modernization process in Japan since 1868. 8 assignments, 2 exams. A video-based course. Materials fee: $104.50. (3 credits)

Management

Introduction to Management

This video-assisted course explores management principles and decision making as applied to management systems, organizations, interpersonal relationships, and production. 9 assignments, 2 exams. Students must have access to a typewriter or a computer with a printer. Materials fee: $121.25. (3 credits)

Philosophy

Philosophies of Life

An introductory ethics course that utilizes video- and audiocassette tapes to examine a broad range of problems confronting persons who belong to various career groups and professions in our society. Materials fee: $111.50. (3 credits)

Political Science

American Government

Organization, processes, and functions of the national government of the United States. 14 assignments, 2 exams. A video-assisted course. Materials fee: $120.50. (3 credits)

Problems of Government, Politics, and Public Policy: War and Peace in the Nuclear Age

Complicated war and peace issues of the past 50 years are addressed, as well as some of the challenges of the future. 6 assignments, 2 exams. A video-based course. Materials fee: $102.50. (3 credits)

Sociology

Introductory Sociology

The science of human society. Emphasis on basic concepts. Assists the student in understanding the social influences of day-to-day life. 9 assignments, 3 exams. A video-assisted course. Materials fee: $111.50. (3 credits)

Spanish

Elementary Spanish I

Pronunciation, conversation, grammar, and reading. An audio-enhanced course. Materials fee: $90.50. (5 credits)

Elementary Spanish II

A continuation of Elementary Spanish I. 21 assignments, 3 exams. An audio-enhanced course. Materials fee: $90.50. (5 credits)

Rose State College
Telecourse Department
Developmental Studies

6240 Southeast 15th Street
Midwest City, OK   73110-2797

(405) 733-7344

Geographic Access: Oklahoma

DELIVERY SYSTEMS

Broadcast Television
All of the courses are available on cable in Midwest City, Del City, Spencer, and Tinker Air Force Base. Some of the courses are broadcast on OETA Channel 13.

INSTITUTION DESCRIPTION

Rose State College is located in Midwest City, a suburb of Oklahoma City. The college was originally named Oscar Rose Junior College and began operation in 1970. It became a member of the state higher education system and adopted its present name in 1973.

All students enrolling in telecourses at Rose State College are required to attend an orientation that lasts approximately one hour. The instructors give homework outlines, telephone numbers for obtaining help, and exam information.

Most of the telecourses have a study guide and/or textbook required. Generally, a telecourse is 26 to 30 lessons with 2 to 4 lessons broadcast per week.

Accreditation: NCA

Official/Contact: Larry Nutter, President

Admission Requirements: Any telecourse may be taken as independent study. Students working toward a degree should check with an adivsor to be sure of the acceptability of credit toward their degree program.

Tuition: The cost for telecourses is the same as for on-campus courses, $30.25 per credit. Students enrolling for the first time at Rose State College will also be charged a one-time application fee of $15. Textbooks and study guides must be purchased by the student.

Degree Credit: Credit earned upon successful completion of a telecourse is applicable toward a degree at Rose State College. Students from other institutions should inquire before enrollment of the transferability of credit to be earned.

Grading: Examinations must be proctored. Letter grades are assigned. Credit is awarded in semester hour units.

Library: All telecourse tapes are available for individual viewing in the Learning Resources Center.

COURSES OFFERED

Anthropology

General Anthropology

The study of the development of man as a species. Introduction to archaeology as a study of the material remains of ancient man and his activities. An analysis of cultural anthropology with emphasis placed on the social and cultural beliefs, particularly in small-scale or non-Western societies. Based on *Faces of Culture* produced by Coast Telecourses. (3 credits)

Business

Introduction to Business

An introductory course for students specializing in business fields. A survey of basic principles, forms, and practices involved in administration of the business firm in the American economy. Based on *The Business File* produced by the Dallas County Community College District. (3 credits)

Business Law I

A study of general principles of the law of contracts, agencies, torts, bailments, employer-employee relationships. Based on *Business and the Law* produced by the Southern California Consortium. (3 credits)

Business Law II

A study of the general principles of the law of negotiable instruments and sales. Based on *Business and the Law* produced by the Southern California Consortium. (3 credits)

Child Development

Child Growth and Development

Growth and development of the child from conception to the age of six years. Includes roles and responsibilities of parenthood, physical growth, intellectual growth, personality development, societal and family adjustment. Based on *A Time to Grow* produced by Coast Telecourses. (3 credits)

Economics

Principles of Microeconomics

A study of the concept of scarcity as it applies to consumer behavior, product markets, and resource markets with an emphasis on the application of these theories to current microeconomic problems. Based on *Economics U$A* produced by Adult Learning Service. (3 credits)

Principles of Macroeconomics

A study of the concept of scarcity as it applies to aggregate demand and aggregate supply. This study will investigate the problems of inflation, unemployment and economic growth through the presentation of Keynesian theory, monetary theory, and other concepts developed to deal with these issues. Based on *Economics U$A* produced by Adult Learning Service. (3 credits)

English

English Composition I

This course concentrates on principles of expository composition through the writing of paragraphs and essays. Grammar and the mechanics of writing will be emphasized. Based on *The Write Course* produced by the Dallas County Community College District. (3 credits)

English Composition II

A continuation of English I, this course includes extensive composition assignments of varying length with emphasis on expository writing. Also included are reading and analysis of selected models of literary types and an introduction to research techniques. Based on *Literary Visions* produced by the Southern California Consortium. (3 credits)

French

Conversational French I

An introduction to French for the beginning student, geared to help the student acquire a basic vocabulary and a command of everyday situations. Includes an audio component. Based on *French in Action* produced by the Annenberg/CPB project. (3 credits).

Conversational French II

A more advanced course in conversation for those students who have acquired a basic vocabulary and knowledge of grammatical points. Includes an audio component. Based on *French in Action* produced by the Annenberg/CPB project. (3 credits)

Health

Personal Health

Fundamentals of personal health and community health. Correction of physical defects and first aid. Based on *Here's to Your Health* produced by the Dallas County Community College District. (2 credits)

History

U.S. History to 1877

A survey course in American history from the colonial period to 1877. Based on *The American Adventure* produced by the Dallas County Community College District. (3 credits)

U.S. History since 1877

A survey course in American history since 1877. Based on *America in Perspective* produced by the Dallas County Community College District. (3 credits)

Ancient and Medieval Civilization

A survey of western civilization to about 1300 A.D. covering the early history of man, the civilization of the Ancient Near East, Greece, and Rome, and the Middle Ages. Based on *The Western Tradition* produced by WGBH/Boston. (3 credits)

History of Europe, 1815 to Present

A survey of Europe in the 19th and 20th centuries covering the significant political, economic, social, and intellectual developments. Based on *The Western Tradition* produced by WGBH/Boston. (3 credits)

Japan: The Living Tradition

This video series examines the premodern history and traditional culture of Japan. The programs are designed to introduce Americans to Japanese history and culture which is still tightly interwoven into the fabric of modern Japanese society. Based on *Japan: The Living Tradition* produced by Great Plains National. (2 credits)

Humanities

Art in Life

A course designed to develop an awareness and appreciation of art through the study of art terms, artists, techniques, and cultures. Based on *Art of the Western World* produced by WNET/New York. (3 credits)

General Humanities from 1400

A second course in general humanities covering the period from the Middle Ages to the present. Based on *Humanities Through the Arts* produced by Coast Telecourses. (3 credits)

Management

Principles of Management

Introduces the systematic approach to examine the functions of management: planning, organizing, directing, and controlling. Includes a study of the qualities necessary for managerial success. Based on *The Business of Management* produced by the Southern California Consortium. (3 credits)

Small Business Management

This course will include setting up simple accounting procedures, managing a small retail establishment, or running a small manufacturing plant. Basic principles of personnel merchandising and promotion, with possibly a small amount of quantitative analysis. Based on *Something Ventured* produced by the Southern California Consortium. (3 credits)

Marketing

Principles of Marketing

Study of the movement of goods and services from the producer to the consumer. Includes functions of marketing such as pricing, product promotion, distribution channels, market research, and an overview of legal ramifications. Based on *Marketing* produced by Coast Telecourses. (3 credits)

Mathematics

Business Math

This course is designed to give a brief review of the fundamental operations of arithmetic, common and decimal fractions, and percentages. Application of those fundamental operations to cash and trade discounts, merchandising, simple and compound interest, depreciation, taxes, and insurance is studied. Based on *By the Numbers* produced by the Southern California Consortium. (3 credits)

Music

Music in Life

A nontechnical course that develops the student's appreciation of a wide variety of musical types and styles and his or her ability to listen critically to a musical selection. Based on *Music in Time* produced by Films for the Humanities. (3 credits)

Philosophy

Introduction to Philosophy

A survey of perennial philosophic issues (the nature of man, our understanding of the world in which we live, the status of value judgments). Issues will be treated in their historical context and then in their living form as life-and-death issues for contemporary man. Based on *Ethics in America* produced by WNET/New York. (3 credits)

Political Science

American National Government

Study of the structures, constitutional powers, and political processes at work in the executive, legislative, and judicial branches of the national government. Includes parties and interest groups, political theory, civil rights, and political behavior. Based on *Government By Consent* produced by the Dallas Community College District. (3 credits)

Psychology

General Psychology

A general survey of the field of psychology as a behavioral science. Attention is given to the basic concepts and methods of psychological inquiry. Based on *Study of Human Behavior* produced by Coast Telecourses. (3 credits)

Sociology

Introduction to Sociology

A study of social structure and culture, the process of socialization, family and religious institutions, social stratification, and the nature and dynamics of social groups. Based on *Sociological Imagination* produced by the Dallas County Community College District. (3 credits)

Family in Society

This course is designed to provide a basic understanding of the family as a social institution by looking at family life in other societies and our own historical past, as well as the contemporary American family, from a sociological perspective. (3 credits)

Spanish

Conversational Spanish I

A course for those having no previous experience with the language. Emphasis is placed on acquiring good pronunciation, building basic vocabulary, understanding elementary constructs, and learning simple conversational patterns. Includes an audio component. Based on *Survival Spanish* produced by Miami Dade. (3 credits)

Conversational Spanish II

A continuation of the skill-building processes of Conversational Spanish I with an introduction to more difficult grammatical constructs and the practice of more complex conversational patterns. Includes an audio component. Based on *Survival Spanish* produced by Miami Dade. (3 credits)

University of Oklahoma
Division of Outreach Services
College of Continuing Education

1700 Asp Avenue
Norman, OK   73037-0001

(405) 325-1096 *Fax:* (405) 325-7679

Geographic Access: Oklahoma

DELIVERY SYSTEMS

Broadcast Television
Lectures are broadcast on public television channel OETA Channel 13 in Oklahoma City, The Literacy Channel 43 in Central Oklahoma, and Norman Cable Channel 30.

INSTITUTION DESCRIPTION

The University of Oklahoma is a state institution founded in 1890. It offers a full range of undergraduate, graduate, and professional programs on its campus. Telecourses are offered through the College of Continuing Education.

The Telecourse Office is committed to making its activities as accessible as possible. The College and the University provide a range of special services for those with disabilities.

Telecourses are residence credit courses taken through a modified independent study format in which students view lectures broadcast on public television channels. Students must visit the Norman campus only for orientation and examinations. The orientation sessions provide the student with written materials concerning dates, times, place of course examinations, review sessions, written assignments, how to contact the instructor, viewing lab information, and broadcast schedules.

Accreditation: NCA

Official/Contact: P. Susan Engh, Telecourse Coordinator

Admission Requirements: Students pursuing a degree must be admitted to the University of Oklahoma. Courses may also be taken for cultural enrichment.

Tuition: Lower division courses, resident $52.15 per credit hour, nonresident $152.15 per credit hour. Upper division courses, resident $55.15 per credit hour, nonresident $167.90 per credit hour. Students must purchase books and study materials. Telecourse students are subject to all deadlines, penalties, and fees.

Degree Credit: A degree cannot be earned through telecourse participation although credits may be applied toward a degree upon successful completion of the telecourse.

Grading: Examinations must be proctored and taken on the Norman campus. Letter grades (A, B, C, D, F) are assigned. Credit is awarded in semester hour units.

Library: Students registered for a telecourse have access to the libraries of the University of Oklahoma.

COURSES OFFERED

Anthropology

Introduction to Archaeology
This course explores how archaeologists reconstruct ancient societies and explains how and why they evolved. Using a broadly comparative perspective students will understand how archaeology and anthropology interact, with emphasis on how people behaved in the past with reconstruction of basic social, political, and economic institutions of their cultures. Television series title: *Out of the Past*, produced by WQED-TV Pittsburgh (part of the Annenberg/CPB Collection). (3 credits)

Economics

Principles of Economics-Macroeconomics
A documentary examination of major historic and contemporary events that have shaped 20th-century American economics. Through the use of interviews, commentary and analysis, the series establishes a clear relationship between abstract economic principles and concrete human experience. Television series title: *Economics U$A*, Lesson 1-14, and 28, produced by Educational Film Center. (3 credits)

Family Life

Contemporary Marriage
This course takes a close look at marriage, family and alternative life styles in the closing decade of the twentieth century. Several interrelated themes are developed. The first is the tension between the individual and the societal environment, and the existence of contradictory cultural values. Another is the shift in focus that is taking place from viewing marriage as an institution to viewing it as a relationship in which one expects to find companionship and intimacy. Television series title: *Portrait of a Family*, produced by Intelecom. (3 credits)

History

U.S. 1492-1865
A general survey of United States history from its colonial origins to the end of the Civil War, with emphasis on national, political, diplomatic, economic, constitutional, social, and intellectual developments. Television series title: *The American Adventure*, produced by Dallas Telecourses. (3 credits)

Western Civilization I
This course weaves together history, art, literature, religion, geography, government, and economics, helping students to recognize the pendulum swings of history, identify parallels in the modern world, and gain a sense of their own place in the evolution of human institutions. It begins with the influential pre-Western civilizations and continues through the Middle Ages to the Renaissance. Television series title: *The Western Tradition* Lessons 1-26, produced by WGBH Educational Foundation/Boston (part of the Annenberg/CPB Collection). (3 credits)

Topics in Asian History
Examines the premodern history and traditional culture of Japan. The course will introduce the student to Japanese history and culture which is still tightly interwoven into the fabric of modern Japanese society. Topics will include the typical Japanese family, Japan's location and physical/geographical resources, feudalism, visual arts, literature, performing arts and religion. Television series title: *Japan: The Living Tradition*, produced by University of Mid-America. (3 credits)

Information Skills for Academic Research

Information Skills for Academic Research
This course will teach students basic information skills, strategies, and concepts necessary for successful use of library and information resources in academic environments. The research process will be emphasized, as will the applicability of skills learned to a variety of information problems. (3 credits)

Political Science

Government of the U.S.
Focuses on the way individuals can impact the way they are governed and how to access the government. Emphasis is placed on an active contingency and provides examples of how students can involve themselves in government. Television series title: *Government By Consent*, produced by Dallas Telecourses. (3 credits)

Sociology

Introduction to Sociology

Examines major sociological principles and issues taking a documentary approach through interviews with people at work, play, and home as well as commentary from leading sociologists. Topics covered are social interaction, sociology as a social science, culture and its diversity, social structures, stratification by race/gender/age, social institutions/social control and deviance, collective behavior and social movements. Television series title: *The Sociological Imagination*, produced by Dallas Telecourses. (3 credits)

Oregon

Portland State University
Office of Extended Studies

P.O. Box 1491
Portland, OR   97207

(503) 725-4865 *Fax:* (503) 725-4840

Geographic Access: Nationwide.

DELIVERY SYSTEMS

Computer Tutorials
Students must have access to a personal computer according to the course descriptions below.

Videocassette
Several courses listed below require the use of a VHS videocassette player.

INSTITUTION DESCRIPTION

Portland State University, a unit of the Oregon System of Higher Education, was established in 1946 as the Vanport Extension Center. It was chartered as Portland State College in 1955 and adopted its present name in 1969.

The Oregon State System of Higher Education Office of Independent Study is administered by Portland State University School of Extended Studies. It provides university, college, and high school credit as well as noncredit learning opportunities through correspondence study for persons who seek education outside the traditional classroom setting. Students may begin courses at any time, proceed at their own pace, and study at convenient times and places. The courses listed below are offered for educators who are seeking to increase their knowledge of the use of computers and software in their field. See Courses Offered for descriptions and prerequisites.

Accreditation: NASC

Official/Contact: Paul A. Wurm, Director, Independent Study

Admission Requirements: There are no entrance requirements for enrollment but enrollment does not constitute admission to Portland State University.

Tuition: Course fees are listed below and are payable upon registration. Textbooks must be purchased by the student. MasterCard and VISA accepted.

Degree Credit: Credit is generally accepted in transfer for degree purposes. Students are responsible for determining the applicability of courses to degree programs at the institution where they plan on earning degrees.

Grading: The quality of student work is graded as follows: A, exceptional; B, superior; C, average; D, inferior; F, failure. Students may elect to enroll in courses on a Pass/No Pass basis, however, the election must be made at the time of registration. Examinations must be proctored. Credit is awarded in quarter hour units.

Library: Students residing in the university service area are allowed use of the University Library.

COURSES OFFERED

Education

AppleWorks for Educators: Introduction
The use of the AppleWorks program. Prerequisites: teaching experience, prior experience with software, access to an Apple IIe, IIc, or IIgs computer with printer. It is also helpful to have a colleague or local expert available who could be of assistance when necessary. 10 written assignments. Course fee: $382. (4 credits)

Software Sampler I

Select and evaluate educational software for use with students or as teacher tools. Design, teach, and evaluate lessons using software of potential interest. Alternately, students may use and evaluate personal productivity software in performing teacher tasks such as creating test or student reports. Course appropriate for K-8 educators, computer coordinators, and inservice providers. Prerequisites: K-8 teaching experience, some prior experience with computers, access to either an Apple IIe, IIc, IIgs, Macintosh or IBM PC, and access to students. 6 written lessons. Course fee: $437. (4 credits)

Introduction to Microsoft Works for Educators

A course for educators to learn to use the computer as a personal tool as well as a classroom tool. One part of each lesson is devoted to learning the Microsoft Works program. The other part is devoted to applying learning to the classroom. Includes hands-on guided workbook activities. Prerequisites: access to a Macintosh Plus or higher computer with two disk drives or a hard disk, experience with another Macintosh based computer program or access to a colleague who could be of assistance, experience with loading and saving programs. 9 written lessons. Course fee: $382. (4 credits)

PageMaker for Educators (Macintosh)

A course designed for educators in K-12 and higher education. Students learn effective graphic design and desk-top publishing concepts while learning capabilities and features of Aldus PageMaker. Includes assigned and self-selected projects. Provides a model for teaching PageMaker to others in a classroom or self-directed setting. Students version of PageMaker supplied with course materials. Prerequisites: in-depth experience with at least one Macintosh application, access to a Macintosh Plus or higher computer with minimum two megabytes of RAM, hard drive, and printer. 11 written assignments. Course fee: $287. (3 credits)

Learning HyperCard and HyperTalk Programming

Provides an introduction to HyperCard including creating HyperCard stacks and using HyperTalk programming language. The history, issues, and current research surrounding the use of hypermedia in education and examples of hypermedia on videotape. Assignments involve creating stacks of the student's choice that demonstrate mastery of new ideas about HyperCard and HyperTalk. Students also write a number of short papers based on reading

assignments. Prerequisites: access to a Macintosh computer that will run HyperCard and has a hard drive and 1 megabyte of RAM, access to HyperCard version 1.2.5 or version 2 or higher, access to a VHS videotape player, availability of a colleague or some students to use as "subjects" for one lesson, familiarity with the Macintosh interface. 8 written lessons. Course fee: $382. (4 credits)

Computers in Mathematics Education

Math modeling (preparing problems for machine solution), calculator and computer use, and math unmodeling (interpreting pure math solutions as they relate to real world problems). Prerequisites: student should be able to use a disk computer system, have a working knowledge of word processing, and have at least elementary experience in either BASIC or LOGO programming. Students must have access to elementary or secondary mathematics students, to several computers that can be used with students, to a large screen projection device (of any type) or large screen monitor, and to assorted mathematics, problem-solving and LOGO software for use with students. Any brand of computer is acceptable. 10 written lessons. Course fee: $382. (4 credits)

Computers in Education: Fundamentals

The use of microcomputers in the elementary and secondary curriculum. Includes an overview of software and readings on how computers impact schools. Prerequisites: teaching experience, basic familiarity with microcomputer operations and working knowledge of a word processing program, access to a computer system with a printer and word processing software, an assortment of current educational software, a commercial database program, one of the following model computers: Apple IIe, IIc or IIgs, IBM PC, IBM PCjr or IBM compatible, Commodore 64 or 128 and a printer capable of printing LOGO graphics, a standard VHS videocassette player, access to students and one or more computers so that it can be used with students. It is also helpful to have access to people who can give assistance if necessary. 10 written assignments. Course fee: $382. (4 credits)

LOGO for Educators: Introduction

Content includes the LOGO programming language, writing well-structured and readable programs, the history and philosophy of LOGO, and the application of LOGO to the classroom. Prerequisites: teaching experience, previous experience with computers equivalent to at least one computers-in-education course, access to students and one or more computers to use with students, access to a computer and printer capable of printing graphics with LogoWriter (e.g., Apple IIe, IIc, or IIgs, an IBM PC, PCjr or compatible, or Commodore 64 or 128) and to a video recorder for viewing assignments. 10 written lessons. Course fee: $352. (4 credits)

Telecommunications and Information Access

Explores electronic mail, conferencing, distance education, and information access using a computer information service and identifies ways in which these tools can be used in the classroom. Prerequisites: experience in teaching and a reasonable amount of knowledge in the field of instructional use of computers, access to a computer with two disk drives, a modem (minimum of 1200 baud), communication software and a reasonably private phone line, and a printer. This course requires "connect time" that will incur additional costs of approximately $42 to $66. 7 written lessons. Course fee: $382. (4 credits)

Computers in Composition

Integrates tool software such as word processors, spelling and grammar checkers, outlines, and graphics programs into the teaching of writing. Course content is based on recent writing theory and research, with particular emphasis on the writing process. Prerequisites: classroom teaching experience, access to a computer and word processing software, experience with word processing, access to students, one or more computers, and some writing-related software plus a colleague with whom ideas may be shared. 10 written assignments. Course fee: $382. (4 credits)

Effective Inservice for Instructional Use of Computers in Education

A course that helps students learn to design, conduct, and evaluate an inservice experience. The goal of this course is to improve the knowledge and skill of educators who do inservice staff development in the field of instructional uses of computers. Course is suited to precollege teachers at all levels and in all disciplines as well as computer coordinators, inservice providers, and teachers of teachers. Prerequisites: experience in teaching and reasonable amount of knowledge in the field of instructional use of computers, substantial training and experience in the field of instructional use of computers, access to educators in order to practice the ideas covered in the course, and access to a computer with word processing software. 7 written assignments. Course fee: $382. (4 credits)

Pennsylvania

Harrisburg Area Community College
See **College of the Air**

Lehigh County Community College
See **College of the Air**

Montgomery County Community College
See **College of the Air**

Pennsylvania State University
Department of Independent Learning
125 Mitchell Building
University Park, PA   16802-3693

(800) 458-3617

Geographic Access: Worldwide; Pennsylvania for broadcast television

DELIVERY SYSTEMS

Broadcast Television
Courses with televised lessons must be started at the beginning of a semester. Not all courses with televised lessons are offered every semester. Lessons are telecast in Pennsylvania at least once each academic year over WPSX-TV and the PENNARAMA Channel, Pennsylvania's network.

Videocassette
A variety of sources are used to obtain videos appropriate for the course. Telecourse packages and videos are reviewed and may be modified by a Penn State faculty member.

Audiocassette
Students must supply their own audiocassette player and recordable tapes where specified.

INSTITUTION DESCRIPTION

The Pennsylvania State University was chartered by the state legislature in 1855 as Farmers' High School. In 1862 it became the Agricultural College of Pennsylvania and was designated as the land-grant college of the state. In 1874 the college was renamed the Pennsylvania State College. The present name was adopted in 1953.

Correspondence courses were provided beginning in 1892. The present-day Department of Independent Learning traces its origin back to 1918 when the College of Engineering developed the first credit correspondence courses.

Accreditation: MSA

Official/Contact: David Mercer, Director, Independent Learning

Admission Requirements: High school diploma or equivalent. Degree-seeking students must be formally admitted by Penn State. Other students may enroll for college courses for either credit or noncredit (tuition is the same).

Tuition: $90 per credit. Materials costs are listed below with the course description. Costs are subject to change at any time. MasterCard and VISA accepted. Video courses require a nonrefundable rental fee and a deposit fee. All video materials are provided by College Video of Bethesda, Maryland.

Degree Credit: Three associate degrees can be earned through Independent Learning: Extended Letters, Arts, and Science; Extended Dietetic Food Systems Management; and Extended Business Administration.

Courses can also be applied to a baccalaureate degree at Penn State or at other educational institutions.

Grading: Course grades A-F are awarded. Examinations must be administered by a qualified proctor. Credit is awarded in semester hour units.

Library: Students may view videos for courses with a video component at the Sparks Building Learning Center on the University Park campus.

COURSES OFFERED

Accounting

Introductory Financial Accounting
Fundamentals of the collection, recording, summarization, and interpretation of accounting data. Course materials $73.50 includes a refundable deposit of $25. Video materials from the *Principles of Accounting* series. (3 credits)

Art

The Visual Arts and the Studio: An Introduction
An introduction to the visual arts including the practice of the visual arts and the social, cultural, and aesthetic implications of studio activity. Course materials $131.15 includes a refundable deposit of $25. Videos: *The Power of Myth 2* and *Paul Cézanne*. (3 credits)

Art History

Survey of Western Art I
Survey of the major monuments and trends in the history of art from prehistory through the late Gothic period. Course materials $130.15 includes a refundable deposit of $25. Video material from *The Art of the Western World* series. (3 credits)

Survey of Western Art II
Survey of the major monuments and trends in the history of art from the Renaissance to the modern era. Course materials $122.85 includes a refundable deposit of $25. Video material from *The Art of the Western World* series. (3 credits)

Special Topics: Africa
Examines the art of various African peoples in historical, religious, sociological, and geographic contexts. Contemporary African art, the influence of African art on European art, and Afro-American art.

Course materials $143 includes a refundable deposit of $25. Video materials: *Path of Ancestors/Dance of the Spirit* and *Since the Harlem Renaissance*. (3 credits)

The Arts
The student develops critical perception, knowledge, and judgments through an examination of the basic concepts common among the arts. Students must attend a live performance of a concert and a play of their choosing. Course materials $140.75 includes a refundable deposit of $25. Video: *Through the Arts* series and *Ballet with Edward Villella*. (3 credits)

Astronomy

Astronomical Universe
Nonmathematical description of the astronomical universe and the development of scientific thought. Audio: 4 cassettes (optional). Course materials $88.30. (3 credits)

Biological Science

Environmental Science
This course covers kinds of environments, past and present uses and abuses of natural resources, disposal of human wastes, prospect for the future. Contact the Department of Independent Learning for current costs. Video materials from the series *Race to Save the Planet*. (3 credits)

Business Administration

Problems of Small Business
Analysis of problems of the small firm, particularly for the student who wishes to venture into business. Course materials $89.25 includes a refundable deposit of $25. Video: *Three Buoys Houseboat Vacation* and *The Kettle Creek Canvas Co*. (3 credits)

Business Law

Legal Environment
Courts, basic policies underlying individual and contractual rights in everyday society, and social control through law. Course materials $108.35 includes a refundable deposit of $25. Video material from *Business and the Law* series. (3 credits)

Business Logistics

Business Logistics Management

Management of logistics function in the firm, including physical supply and distribution activities such as transportation, storage facility location, and materials handling. Course materials $162 includes a refundable deposit of $25. Video material from *Business Logistics Management* series. (3 credits)

Career Guidance

Job Placement Skills and Strategies

Strategies and skills designed to identify career/life goals and implement career decisions. Course materials $88.80 includes a refundable deposit of $25. Video: *The Interview: What to Expect.* (1 credit)

Comparative Literature

Masterpieces of Western Literature since the Renaissance

Universal themes and cultural values in works by such writers as Voltaire, Goethe, Ibsen, Flaubert, Doestoevsky, Dickinson, Mann, Duras, Borges, and Rich. Course materials $98.10 includes a refundable deposit of $25. Videos: *Tartuffe* and *Grand Illusion.* (3 credits)

Computer Science

Introduction to Computers with Applications

Introduction to computers and computer applications such as word processing, spreadsheets, database management, business graphics, and communications. Students must have access to an IBM-compatible computer as well as an audiocassette player. Software runs on IBM PC, XT, AT, and true compatibles that have at least 256 kilobytes of memory, a graphics display adapter, and one floppy disk drive. Course materials $107.35. Video materials from *ComputerWorks* series. (3 credits)

Dietetics

The Profession of Dietetics

Introduction to the profession and exploration of the roles and responsibilities of dietetic professionals. Call the Department of Independent Learning for current cost of materials. Audio: "The Dietetic Technician Completes the Team." (1 credit)

Sanitation Practices in Food Service Operations

Practical applications related to the management of the sanitation subsystem within a food service operation. Course materials $66.45. Audio: 30-minute cassette tape. (3 credits)

Earth Science

Out of the Fiery Furnace

A history of materials, energy, and humans, with emphasis on their interrelationships. Contact the Department of Independent Learning for current cost of course materials. Video materials from *Out of the Fiery Furnace* series. (3 credits)

Ecology

Wildlife Ecology and Management

This course covers the general principles of wildlife management. Population dynamics, managing wildlife for harvest, endangered and extinct species, refuges, parks, and reserves. $50 fee, course materials $39.50, media fee $15.50. Refundable video deposit $40. Videos: *Bird Brain: Mystery of Bird Navigation* and *The White-Tailed Deer: Pennsylvania's Most Controversial Animal.* (4.4 CEUs)

Engineering

Statics

Covered in this course are the equilibrium of coplanar force systems, analysis of frames and trusses, noncoplanar force systems, friction, centroids and moments of inertia. Course materials $157.75 includes a refundable deposit of $25. Video material from the *Statics* series. (3 credits)

English

History of the English Language

Historical and structural study of developments in English sounds, forms, inflections, syntax, derivations, and meanings. Course materials $58.90. Video: *The Story of English* series. (3 credits)

Finance

Introduction to Finance

The nature, scope, and interdependence of the institutional and individual participants in the financial system. Course materials $136.20 includes a refundable deposit of $25. Videos: *Anatomy of a Hostile*

Takeover from the *Ethics in America* series and *The Wall Street Guide to Money and Markets*. (3 credits)

French

Elementary French I

Grammar, with reading and writing of simple French. Oral and aural work stressed. Audio component. Course materials $120.90 includes a refundable deposit of $15. (4 credits)

Elementary French II

Grammar and reading continued. Oral and aural phases progressively increased. Audio component. Course materials $120.90 includes a refundable deposit of $15. (4 credits)

Intermediate French

Grammar, reading, composition, oral and aural exercises. Audio component. Course materials $73.30. (4 credits)

Geoscience

Planet Earth

Nontechnical presentation of earth processes, materials, and landscape. Practicum includes field trips, study of maps, rocks, dynamic models, and introduction to geologic experimentation. Course materials $196.90 includes a refundable deposit of $25. Video material from *The Earth Explored* series. (3 credits)

History

American Civilization since 1877

A historical survey of the American experience from the emergence of urban-industrial society in the late nineteenth century to the present. Course materials $104.10 includes a refundable deposit of $25. Video material from *Walk through the Twentieth Century with Bill Moyers, TR and His Times—the Twenties* and *The Helping Hand*. (3 credits)

History of Communism

Marxism, Leninism, and evolution of the Soviet Union. Formation and development of the Communist bloc. The impact of Chinese Communism. Course materials $98.30 includes a refundable deposit of $25. Video material from *All Under Heaven: Life in a Chinese Village and Russia* and *The People Speak*. (3 credits)

History of Fascism and Nazism

The study of right-wing totalitarianism in the twentieth century, with special emphasis on Fascist Italy and Nazi Germany. Course materials $156.25 includes a refundable deposit of $25. 65 slides $22 ($10 refunded). Video: *Triumph of the Will*. Audiocassette of Hitler's speeches and music plus a recording by a Holocaust survivor. (3 credits)

Vietnam at War

This course covers the rise of nationalism and communism, origin of conflict, United States involvement, impact on postwar regional and international politics, and contemporary Vietnam. Course materials $133.25 includes a refundable deposit of $25. Video materials from the series *Vietnam: A Television History*. (3 credits)

Horticulture

Plant Propagation

Principles and practices of asexual plant propagation. Course materials $129.80 includes a refundable deposit of $25. Videos: *Cycles of Beauty and Grafting* and *Plant Propagation*. (3 credits)

Industrial Relations

Industrial Relations

Introductory analysis of the employment relationship and of the interrelated interests of management, workers, unions, and the public. Audio component. Course materials $101.65 includes a refundable deposit of $10. (3 credits)

Justice Administration

Introduction to the American Criminal Justice System

Criminal justice system, including a formulation of laws, extent of crime, processing and correction of offenders, victims. Call the Department of Independent Learning for cost of course materials. Videos: *Crime Files I* and *II*, *Short Eyes*, and *The Unquiet Death of Julius and Ethel Rosenberg*. (3 credits)

Policing in America

This course will focus on the current status of law enforcement in the United States. Course materials $146.30 includes a refundable deposit of $25. Video: *Prince of the City and Police Tapes*. (3 credits)

Linguistics

The Study of Language

A nontechnical introduction to the study of human language and its role in human interaction. Course materials $136.30 includes a refundable deposit of $25. Videos: *Out of the Mouths of Babes* and *Teaching Sign Language to the Chimpanzee Washoe*. (3 credits)

Management

Survey of Management

Introduction to organizational factors relevant to management processes, including leadership, motivation, job design, technology, organizational design and environments, systems, change. Course materials $128.15 includes a refundable deposit of $25. Video: *Managing in Organizations*. (3 credits)

Mathematics

Basic Mathematics

Operations with whole numbers, fractions, decimals, and integers. Ratio, proportion, percents, unit conversions, estimates, graph and table reading. Emphasis on applications. Course materials $101.70 includes a refundable deposit of $25. Media fee $40.50. Video: *Essential Arithmetic*. (Noncredit)

General View of Mathematics

Survey of mathematical thought in logic, geometry, combinatorics, and chance. Course materials $69.50. Video: *For All Practical Purposes* series. (3 credits)

Insights into Mathematics

Examples of mathematical thought in number theory, topology, theory of symmetry, and chance. Course materials $62.50. Video: *For All Practical Purposes* series. (3 credits)

Music

An Introduction to Western Music

A general survey of art music in Western society highlighting important composers and stylistic developments. Course materials $97.70 for CDs, $90.50 for cassettes. Audio: *Musical Involvement* text and 2 audiocassettes recorded by Stephen Stace. (3 credits)

Evolution of Jazz

A study of the origins and development of jazz as an art form. Course materials $127.40 (cost varies depending on whether student orders cassettes or compact disks). Audiocassette tape rental fee $18 includes a refundable deposit of $10. Audio: Smithsonian Collection of Classic Jazz (5 CDs or 5 cassettes). Two audiocassettes recorded by the author. Audiocassette included with textbook, *Jazz Styles: History and Analysis*. (3 credits)

Rudiments of Music

Introduction to the elements of music, notation, scales, meter, rhythm, intervals, basic chord structure. Course materials $56.95. Audio: 45-minute audiocassette tape recorded by Burt Fenner (instructor). (3 credits)

Nutrition

Diet Therapy and Nutrition Care in Disease

Principles of nutrition care to meet therapeutic needs, inpatient care, and rehabilitation. Course materials $71.85. Audio: one prerecorded cassette (nonreturnable). (4 credits)

Independent Studies: Nutrition in Action

Nutrition instruction for elementary school teachers to use in the classroom. Course materials $138.40 includes a refundable deposit of $25. Video materials from the *Nutrition in Action* series. (3 credits)

Philosophy

Major Figures in Philosophy

Introduction to philosophy through the study of the writings of representative thinkers in the history of philosophy. Course materials $149.50 includes a refundable deposit of $25. Video materials from the series *From Socrates to Sartre*. (3 credits)

Ethics and Social Issues

Ethical issues such as war, privacy, crime and punishment, racism and sexism, civil liberties, affirmative action, abortion, and euthanasia. Course materials $133.20 includes a refundable deposit of $25. Video materials from the series *Ethics in America*. (3 credits)

Physics

Introduction to Quantum Physics
Relativity and quantum theory applied to selected topics in atomic, molecular, solid state, and nuclear physics. Course materials $126.80 includes a refundable deposit of $25. Video materials from the series *The Mechanical Universe and Beyond*. (3 credits)

Polish

Beginning Polish
An elementary course to enable the student to achieve a measure of proficiency in reading and speaking Polish. Audio component. Course materials $47.80. (4 credits)

Political Science

The Constitution: That Delicate Balance
Examination of all facets of a number of constitutional rights. Course materials $121.20 includes a refundable deposit of $25. Video: *The Constitution: That Delicate Balance* series. (3 credits)

Psychology

Psychology
Introduction to general psychology. Includes the principles of human behavior and their applications. Course materials $169.10 includes a refundable deposit of $25. Video materials from the series *Discovering Psychology*. (3 credits)

Religious Studies

An Introduction to the Religions of the East
Religious experience, thought, patterns of worship, morals, and institutions in relation to culture in Eastern religions. Course materials $155.95 includes a refundable deposit of $25. Video materials from the series *The Religious Quest*. (3 credits)

Social Science

Science, Technology, and Society
An overview of the interactions of science, technology, and society from perspectives of humanities and social sciences, and their integration in addressing social policy issues. Course materials $123.90 includes a refundable deposit of $25. Video materials in 25 segments. (3 credits)

Spanish

Intermediate Spanish
An audiolingual review of structure, writing, reading. Audio: 3 cassettes with the textbook *Spanish in Review*, 2nd edition. Course materials $103.80. (4 credits)

Sport Science

The Modern Olympic Games
An analysis of the modern Olympic Games from their inception to modern times. Course materials $77.80 includes a refundable deposit of $25. Videos: *Olympia I, Olympia II, Jesse Owens Returns to Berlin, For the Honor of Their Country, American at the Olympics, 16 Days of Glory: The 1984 Summer Olympics/Part I, Seoul '88: 16 Days of Glory*. (3 credits)

Reading Area Community College
See **College of the Air**

Westmoreland County Community College
See **College of the Air**

Rhode Island

Community College of Rhode Island
Telecourse Instruction
Off-Campus Credit Programs
1762 Louisquisset Pike
Lincoln, RI   02865-7146

(401) 333-7146

Geographic Access: Rhode Island

DELIVERY SYSTEMS

Broadcast Television
Courses are broadcast over Channel 36, WSBE-TV, and various cable channels. Channel 36 is carried on all cable TV systems in Rhode Island. In most cases, two 30-minute programs will be broadcast back-to-back. Schedules are announced prior to each semester.

Telephone Contact
Once enrolled in a course, the student will receive a telephone number for reaching the instructor who will be available to answer questions and to discuss matters related to the course.

INSTITUTION DESCRIPTION

Established in 1960 by an Act of the Rhode Island General Assembly, Rhode Island Junior College opened its doors in 1964 with 325 students. In 1981 the college adopted its present name.

The Community College of Rhode Island offers courses by television that are different from on-campus courses only in the delivery method. Course content, requirements, assignments, evaluation, and testing procedures are the same. Delivery of basic course content by television offers accessibility and flexibility to adult learners who may have personal or professional responsibilities that prohibit travel to a campus every week for traditional classes.

Accreditation: NEASC

Official/Contact: Jack Sousa, Dean

Admission Requirements: Open enrollment.

Tuition: $204 per 3-credit course (subject to increase at any time). Senior citizens will not be charged tuition for telecourses. Textbooks must be purchased by the student.

Degree Credit: Credits earned through the completion of telecourses may be applied to degree programs.

Grading: Tests, papers (critiques, research, etc.), and a final examination will be administered by the instructor. The student's final grade will be based on these factors.

Library: Videotapes of all courses are available for viewing at the Learning Resources Center at each campus (Lincoln, Warwick, and Providence).

COURSES OFFERED

Accounting

Survey of Accounting
An overview of the processes of accounting introducing the theory and principles of the language of business activities. Topics covered include basic financial statements from the recording of transactions to the closing process, cash, payroll, and merchandising. Telecourse: *Principles of Accounting*. (3 credits)

Biology

Man and Environment
Provides a dynamic report of the current outlook for the global environment, describing the threats that different natural systems face and dissecting the complex web of interconnections that bind human society to the environment. The course will help develop a set of intellectual tools, an understanding of the sciences involved, and ways of thinking about people and the environment that will enable students to evaluate for themselves how serious a given environmental problem might be. Telecourse: *Race to Save the Planet*. (3 credits)

Business Administration

Introduction to Business
The course provides a comprehensive view of the contemporary business environment from the internal functions of a business to the challenges of business on an international scale. It delves into the complex functions of a business, exposing a student to the detailed internal and external operations affecting both large and small business. The lesson series encompasses five general areas: American business—foundation and forms, organizing and managing a business, the internal workings of a business, the environment of business, and the challenges of business. Telecourse: *The Business File*. (3 credits)

Small Business Administration
This course affords students an opportunity to observe a variety of small businesses in operation—in both rural and suburban communities, as well as large metropolitan areas—to get an "over-the-shoulder," first-hand look of what it is like to start and operate a small business. Telecourse: *Something Ventured: Small Business Management*. (3 credits)

Business Law

Law of Contracts
Emphasizes contracts and the legal system. By including modules on the law and sales, commercial paper, agency, and property—and examining such critical legal environment topics as government regulation, employment practices, and consumer and environment protection—students will gain a comprehensive overview of law and the world of business. Telecourse: *Business and the Law*. (3 credits)

Business Management

Principles of Management
This course provides a valuable introduction to the concepts of management and business. It is designed for the managerial candidate who has not had formal training in business management as well as for the undergraduate student. The course is intended to provide essential skills in planning and organizing, staffing and directing, controlling, decision making, motivating, communicating, and applying managerial skills to business and other types of organization. Telecourse: *The Business of Management*. (3 credits)

Computer Science

Introduction to Computers
An up-to-date survey of electronic data processing, computer hardware and software systems, and developments that will provide the basis for further advancements in information processing. The course is designed to provide a comprehensive overview of the computer—what it is, what it can and cannot do, how it operates, how it may be instructed to solve problems. It introduces learners to the terminology of data processing, examines the application of the computer to a broad range of organizational settings and social environments, prepares students to understand and utilize computers in both their personal and professional lives. Telecourse: *The New Literacy*. (3 credits)

Economics

Principles of Economics
This course aspires students to think analytically and thereby understand and also come to informed conclusions about the myriad of economic facts. It is a macroeconomics course dealing with money, GNP, unemployment, inflation, productivity and economic growth, the role of the government and related topics. Telecourse: *Economics U$A*. (3 credits)

English

Composition I
English composition and rhetoric taught from a "process" point of view is the focus of this course for freshman English students. With emphasis on audience awareness and purpose for writing, the course presents deliberate strategies for prewriting

and revision. Dramatizations and mini-documentaries are used throughout the series. Most of the nation's leading authorities on the teaching of composition are interviewed along with many interviews with such well-known writers as Irving Wallace, Larry Gelbart, and Melville Shavelson. Students will be encouraged to develop individual writing processes with particular emphasis on skills needed for academic and business writing. Telecourse: *The Write Course*. (3 credits)

Introduction to Literature

This course brings literature to life with dramatizations of individual works and readings of literary passages. This introduction to literature incorporates both contemporary and traditional works in its selection of literary texts. It also places a strong emphasis on writing about literature as a way for students to learn and use advanced compositional techniques. Telecourse: *Literary Visions*. (3 credits)

Finance

Personal Finance

With the guidance of author and lecturer Bob Rosefsky, students will learn the basics of budgeting and buying, the intricacies of home ownership, income tax and investments, and the wise use of insurance, wills, and trusts. Telecourse: *Personal Finance*. (3 credits)

Health

The Human in Health and Disease

A basic health course dealing with the many health problems self-inflicted. Topics include cardiovascular and infectious diseases, cancer, genetic disorders, drug abuse, diet and fitness problems. Film clips factually document the issues. Research findings and emerging theories are explored. Points of controversy are debated by leading scholars. Telecourse: *Here's to Your Health*. (3 credits)

History

Survey of Western Civilization I

The course is built around the classroom lectures of Eugene Weber, internationally renowned author, historian, and professor at the University of California at Los Angeles. Professor Weber spins thousands of years into a seamless story, making the abstract more concrete and developing the ability of students to analyze and appreciate history. By weaving together history, art, literature, religion, geography, government and economics, this course helps students recognize the pendulum swings of history, identify parallels in the modern world, and gain a sense of their place in the evolution of human institutions. Telecourse: *The Western Tradition*. (3 credits)

Survey of Western Civilization II

This course narrates the fascinating story of America from its pre-historic beginnings to the Centennial celebration in 1876. Taking a balanced view of each important national event and crisis, the telecourse portrays the political leaders, reformers, artisans, explorers, farmers, soldiers, immigrants, industrialists, artists, and "good ole boys" who contributed to the panorama of American life. Telecourse: *The American Adventure*. (3 credits)

History of the U.S. from 1877

The course begins with the Centennial and ends with today. The course examines and interprets the economic, political, diplomatic/military, and social developments which have shaped and continue to shape the United States in the twentieth century. Telecourse: *America: The Second Century*. (3 credits)

Marketing

Principles of Marketing

This course explores introductory marketing concepts in the context of over 20 different "real world" profit and nonprofit organizations. Students learn trends and concepts of marketing including the contemporary marketing environment, identifying consumer needs and targeting markets, product safety distribution strategy, promotional strategy, pricing strategy, and international marketing. Telecourse: *Marketing*. (3 credits)

Mathematics

Topics in Mathematics

This course introduces the concepts of statistics by focusing on techniques of data analysis used by practicing statisticians to solve problems in a wide variety of applied fields. Among the topics introduced will be probability distributions, models and designs of experiments, estimation, and hypothesis testing. Telecourse: *Against All Odds: Inside Statistics*. (3 credits)

Business Mathematics

An innovative business mathematics telecourse. The content evolves from mathematical foundations, to basic business concepts, and then incorporates mathematics of retailing, mathematics of finance, business accounting concepts, and communication with numbers. These concepts are interwoven with practical applications: constructing a building, investing money, setting prices of products. Telecourse: *By the Numbers*. (3 credits)

Psychology

General Psychology

Covers the fundamental principles and major concepts of psychology including: brain and behavior, sensation and perception, conditioning and learning, cognitive processes, motivation and emotion, life-span development, the self and identity, sex and gender, testing and intelligence, social influences, psychopathology and therapy, stress and health issues, methodology and new directions. Telecourse: *Discovering Psychology*. (3 credits)

Developmental Psychology

The principal theme of this course is the interplay of biological factors, individual personality, social structure, and other environmental forces in shaping the growing child. In scope, the course treats the influences of the development from conception to adulthood. Further, the course explores the major philosophical approaches to studying children. Telecourse: *The Growing Years*. (3 credits)

Abnormal Psychology

This course explores the complex causes, manifestations, and treatment of common behavior disorders. Interviews with patients give students an invaluable perspective on the emotional toll paid by those who suffer from behavior disorders. In addition, commentary by therapists and other mental health professionals presents the multiple approaches to treatment. The course introduces abnormal behavior along a continuum from functional to dysfunctional. Telecourse: *The World of Abnormal Psychology*. (3 credits)

Sociology

General Sociology

This course offers the student clues to understanding the myriad of sociological events of our time. Through interviews with renowned social scientists and close examination of the portions of society experiencing changes, this telecourse explores the intersection of history and biography in our society where the social conditions of the present relate to the attitude of the recent past. Telecourse: *The Sociological Imagination*. (3 credits)

Marriage and the Family

A survey of the basic factors of courtship, mate selection, engagement, marriage, and rearing children in preparation for successful marriage and parenthood. Marital values and problems are discussed. The course studies the family as the basic unit in society and its relationship to society as a whole. Current changes in family life and their causes are examined. Telecourse: *Portrait of a Family*. (3 credits)

South Carolina

Columbia Bible College and Seminary
Columbia Extension

7435 Monticello Drive
Columbia, SC   29230

(803) 754-4100

Geographic Access: Worldwide

DELIVERY SYSTEMS

Videocassette
Available for all courses except where noted in the course description. *See* Courses Offered. Tapes can be either rented or purchased.

Audiocassette
Available for all courses except where noted in the course description. *See* Courses Offered. Tapes can be either rented or purchased.

INSTITUTION DESCRIPTION

Columbia Bible College was founded in 1923 as Columbia Bible School, offering a two-year program in biblical studies. In 1927, the college occupied its former campus in downtown Columbia, then moved to its present 400-acre location in 1960. At that time it became Columbia Bible College and Seminary. Columbia Extension offers courses for graduate and undergraduate credit, verified audit, or continuing education units.

Accreditation: SACS

Official/Contact: Shirl Schiffman, Director

Admission Requirements: High school graduation or GED, English fluency, testimony of Christian conversion experience and commitment to the Christian faith and lifestyle. Enrollment in a course does not constitute enrollment in a degree program.

Tuition: Undergraduate $85 per quarter hour; graduate $93 per quarter hour. Additional materials charges plus purchase or rental of audiotapes or videotapes.

Degree Credit: Up to 50 quarter hour credits may be applied to an undergraduate degree at Columbia Bible School and Seminary. Transfer of credits to other institutions subject to their acceptance.

Grading: All grading is done by a numerical system (0-100). The minimum passing grade for undergraduate courses is 70; for graduate courses, 65. All examinations for a course must be taken in the presence of a proctor (pastor, chaplain, church leader, school faculty member, administrator, or other nonrelative). The name of the proctor must be registered with the independent study office before acceptance of the completed examination. Proctor Arrangement forms are in the course study guide. Transfer credits must have been awarded by accredited institutions. Credit is awarded in semester hour units. Graduate courses are so indicated after the course title.

Library: Students may apply for interlibrary loan of materials from the CBC Library.

COURSES OFFERED

Apologetics

Christian Evidences
    A survey of the principles involved in the science of apologetics, examining the reasonableness of the evidence for Christian faith, with emphasis on the major approaches taken in apologetics and the basic considerations of each. 18 sessions, 60 minutes each. (2 quarter hours)

Bible

Old Testament Survey: Genesis—Song of Solomon

An introduction to the scope and content of the historical and poetical books of the Old Testament and to the importance of the main people and events of the period. Audiotape version only. (5 quarter hours)

New Testament Survey: Gospels/Life of Christ

A chronological, synthetic study of the four Gospel records, emphasizing the time, place, circumstances, and persons involved in the events of the Lord's ministry, with a view to a fuller understanding of the significance of his words and works. 20 sessions, 45-50 minutes each. (5 quarter hours)

New Testament Survey: Acts to Revelation

Acts is used as an historical framework for study of the earlier New Testament letters as well as an introduction to its later letters and to the culmination in the apocalypse. Sustained application of the New Testament teachings to individual and corporate lives as believers is integrated into the course. Audiotape version only. (5 quarter hours)

Bible Studies in Prayer

A scriptural study of the place, power, principles, and practice of prayer. Examples are noted from textbooks and personal experiences as well as from the Scriptures. The goal is the deepening of the student's prayer life. Audiotape version only. (2 quarter hours)

Galations

A detailed study of one of Paul's greatest and most influential letters set in the context of the life and times of the Apostle and the early church. Emphasis is on Paul's vindication of his apostleship and message to call early Christians back from legalism to grace. Audiotape version only. (2 quarter hours)

Philippians

An inductive study that involves both chapter-by-chapter overview and analysis with expository commentary on one of Paul's most practical epistles. Major emphases include the development of inductive study skills and the transformation of personal attitudes towards people and circumstances by application of biblical principles. Audiotape version only. (2 quarter hours)

James

An in-depth study of the book of James, including the themes of trials in the Christian life, temptation, respect of persons, the tongue, true wisdom, and humility. Audiotape version only. (2 quarter hours)

Old Testament Survey: Prophetic Books

A survey of the Old Testament prophetic books in their chronological order, historical background, theme, and plan of each book. Enough study of detailed content is offered to make the message of each book applicable to personal life. Audiotape version only. (5 quarter hours)

Principles of Bible Interpretation

Basic principles that are essential for the correct interpretation of the Scriptures. Attention is given to faulty approaches to the Bible, but the emphasis is on those laws of the Spirit and of human language which are necessary to understand the meaning of the Word of God. Audiotape version only. (5 quarter hours)

Living Your Faith: Studies in Amos

A thorough study of God's Word in the book of Amos through lectures and independent study. The course also presents methods for discovering and teaching biblical principles so that students are challenged to live the Christian faith they profess. 5 sessions, 40-45 minutes each. (2 quarter hours)

I John

An inductive study of I John carefully examining each verse. The basic focus is on understanding the biblical principle of fellowship with God with all of its implications and provisions for maintaining that fellowship in daily living. 18 sessions, 45-50 minutes each. (2 quarter hours)

Judges

An inductive chapter-by-chapter study of the book of Judges. This Old Testament historical book describes an age of apathy, apostasy, and anarchy during which God raised up key leaders to rule His people. Practical application consistently follows through from the observation and interpretational steps done in this study. Audiotape version only. (2 quarter hours)

I Peter

An in-depth study emphasizing the historical background plan and purpose of this book. The course examines key words and phrases in the text and guides the student to apply these truths to his life. Audiotape version only. (2 quarter hours)

II Peter

An inductive study of this brief epistle which focuses on how to live when surrounded by the problems and perplexities of the end time. Style and questions of authenticity are considered. Audiotape version only. (2 quarter hours)

The Gospel of Mark: the Cross in Our Lives

A combination of lectures and independent study on the Gospel of Mark with emphasis on analyzing the content and purposes of the book, inductive Bible study methods, and applying and teaching biblical truths. Audiotape version only. (2 quarter hours)

Colossians/Philemon

A study in the New Testament letters of Colossians and Philemon, using the English Bible and with particular emphasis on applied sanctification. The course combines five lectures with directed independent study projects. 5 sessions, 45 minutes each. (2 quarter hours)

Philippians: How to Study and Teach a Bible Book

A "how-to" course demonstrating biblical learning and teaching techniques through a study of Philippians. Lectures and independent study projects encourage teachers and their students to actively explore the pressures, problems, and principles that contemporary Christians share with the Philippian church. 5 sessions, 55 minutes each. (2 quarter hours)

I Corinthians

This course outlines and overviews Paul's first letter to the Corinthian Church with its variety of problems. Exposure is given to a summary of the historical treatment of controversial passages and to suggested interpretations based upon sound hermeneutical principles. Audiotape version only. (3 quarter hours)

Ephesians

A verse-by-verse exposition of Ephesians against the background of the life and times of Paul and the Ephesian church. Emphasis is on the interaction of believers within the body of Christ and their relation to the lost world. Audiotape version only. (3 quarter hours)

Daniel and Revelation

This course builds from the survey of the Bible and the study of the principles of interpreting the Bible, and is designed to be the beginning of the detailed study of the two books of "prophecy," Daniel and

Revelation. The student will do some exegesis and application as part of the course development. Audiotape version only. (3 quarter hours)

Progress of Redemption

This study traces God's redemptive plan as it unfolds chronologically throughout the entire Bible. This involves an examination of what God is doing in the world and the methods He uses. 20 sessions, 50-55 minutes each. (3 quarter hours)

The Epistle to the Hebrews

An academic in-depth study of the epistle to the Hebrews. Focus is on the person and work of Christ, His availability and adequacy for the Christian. Audiotape version only. (3 quarter hours)

The Sermon on the Mount

A detailed study of Matthew 5-7 in light of the context, its relationships to Jewish thought and custom, its use in the rest of the New Testament, and its application to today. Audiotape version only. (3 quarter hours)

The Upper Room Experience

An in-depth study of Jesus' last recorded teaching of the disciples in John 13-17. The passage is examined in light of its historical context and as the foundation for truth revealed in the epistles to the Church. Emphasis is on a thorough knowledge of the facts, the significance of the content, and the interpretive problems. 13 sessions, 35 minutes each. (2 quarter hours)

Old Testament Survey: Genesis—Poetical Books (Graduate Level)

A survey of the Old Testament including geographical, cultural, and historical backgrounds, and introductory matters. Emphasis is upon the theme, structure, general content, and significance of each book. Audiotape version only. (4 quarter hours)

Old Testament Survey: Prophetic Books (Graduate Level)

A general overview of the prophets, noting for each book the author, date of writing, and the times in which the events took place. The occasion, theme, structure, and general content of each book are emphasized. Relevant contemporary applications are given special attention. Audiotape version only. (4 quarter hours)

New Testament Survey: Gospels/Life of Christ (Graduate Level)

A harmonization of the four gospel accounts of the life of the Lord Jesus with special attention given to the historical/grammatical context in which the words and works of Christ are placed. Special studies of words and key events highlight this thorough study. 20 sessions, 45-50 minutes each. (4 quarter hours)

New Testament Survey: Acts to Revelation (Graduate Level)

A study of the introductory background, structure, and content of the New Testament books from Acts to Revelation. Focus is on understanding these books in their first-century life setting, as well as synthesizing the epistles into the historical backdrop of Acts. Audiotape version only. (4 quarter hours)

Basic Biblical Hermeneutics (Graduate Level)

The purpose of this course is to assist the student in gaining the knowledge and skill necessary to determine the meaning of any passage of Scripture and to apply it appropriately. The student will be able to use all the guidelines which have been studied, identify the meaning of any passage of Scripture, and exegete confidently. Access to reference materials is needed for some assignments. Audiotape version only. (4 quarter hours)

The Gospel of Mark: The Cross in Our Lives (Graduate Level)

A combination of lectures and independent study on the Gospel of Mark with emphasis on analyzing the content and purposes of the book, inductive Bible study methods, and applying and teaching biblical truths. 5 sessions, 45 minutes each. (2 quarter hours)

Understanding the Old Testament (Graduate Level)

A survey of the history of salvation in the Old Testament especially as it relates to the whole of Old Testament theology, i.e., the rule of God or the establishment of God's kingdom upon the earth. Audiotape version only. (4 quarter hours)

The Pentateuch (Graduate Level)

A study of the contents of the Pentateuch against its archaeological background together with consideration of the particular Pentateuchal problems of evolution and higher criticism. The laws which form the basis of Israel's theocracy are examined with regard to their content, meaning, and applicability today. Audiotape version only. (4 quarter hours)

Conquest and Settlement (Graduate Level)

A study of the conquest and settlement period in Israel's history from the standpoint of archaeology, theological truths, and history. The books included in the study are Joshua, Judges, and Ruth. Special consideration is given to Late Bronze Age materials from Palestine which provide the cultural background for this era. Audiotape version only. (3 quarter hours)

The Sermon on the Mount (Graduate Level)

A detailed study of Matthew 5, 6, and 7, with particular attention given to the cultural setting and the target audience. This centerpiece of Christian theology is harmonized with other fundamental passages. Audiotape version only. (3 quarter hours)

The Upper Room Experience (Graduate Level)

An in-depth study of Jesus' last recorded teaching of the disciples in John 13-17. The passage is examined in light of its historical context and as the foundation for truth revealed in the epistles to the Church. Lectures with some research assignments. 13 sessions, 35 minutes each. (2 quarter hours)

Living Your Faith: Studies in Amos (Graduate Level)

A thorough study of God's Word in the book of Amos through lectures and independent study. The course also presents methods for discovering and teaching biblical principles so that students are challenged to live the Christian faith they profess. 5 sessions, 45 minutes each. (2 quarter hours)

Psalms (Graduate Level)

An introduction to the book of Psalms with emphasis on the principles involved in the exegesis of the hymnic literature and the application of these principles in select portions. Special attention is given to the various forms of the Psalms and their setting within the historical experience of Israel. Audiotape version only. (3 quarter hours)

I Corinthians (Graduate Level)

This course is designed to assist the student in developing a thorough understanding of the thought and presentation of the message of I Corinthians. The student is exposed to a summary of the historical treatment of controversial passages and to suggested interpretations based upon sound hermeneutical principles. Audiotape version only. (3 quarter hours)

Philippians: How to Study and Teach a Bible Book (Graduate Level)

A "how-to" course demonstrating biblical learning and teaching techniques through a study of Philippians. Lectures and independent study projects encourage teachers and their students to actively explore the pressures, problems, and principles that contemporary Christians share with the Philippian church. 5 sessions, 55 minutes each. (2 quarter hours)

Colossians/Philemon (Graduate Level)

A study in the New Testament letters of Colossians and Philemon using the English Bible with particular emphasis on applied sanctification. The course combines five lectures with directed independent study projects. 5 sessions, 45 minutes each. (2 quarter hours)

Ephesians (Graduate Level)

A careful examination of this cyclical letter and its development of the salvation of the believer, the unity of the church, the Body of Christ, the practice of the Christian life in various relationships, and spiritual warfare in the body of New Testament theology. Audiotape version only. (3 quarter hours)

The Epistle to the Hebrews (Graduate Level)

An in-depth study of the Epistle to the Hebrews. Emphasis is on the person and work of Christ. His availability and adequacy for the Christian is carefully studied as uniquely set forth in this landmark epistle. Audiotape version only. (3 quarter hours)

Acts in Historical, Theological, and Missiological Perspective (Graduate Level)

This course is a study of the historical sequence of events in Acts, in light of Luke's theological themes. It helps one to develop the ability to soundly draw out timeless principles from the Acts narrative and then use them to develop and evaluate modern missions strategy. Audiotape version only. (4 quarter hours)

Romans (Graduate Level)

A rigorous study of the book of Romans which seeks to understand its message in the light of the original first century situation. Consideration is also given to the significance of the epistle's message for today. Special emphasis is placed on the development of exegetical skills. Audiotape version only. (4 quarter hours)

Progress of Redemption (Graduate Level)

A study of God's plan of redemption as it progressively unfolds in the Bible. The basic historical revelation is traced to see what God is doing over time and how God's words and works are interrelated, and the progressive development of doctrine is observed. 20 sessions, 50-55 minutes each. (2 quarter hours)

Messianic Prophecy (Graduate Level)

A study of Old Testament messianic themes and how they are fulfilled in Jesus Christ. This course emphasizes how to correctly interpret Bible prophecy, identifies Old Testament messianic themes, and covers Old Testament passages which teach these themes. Audiotape version only. (3 quarter hours)

Daniel and Revelation (Graduate Level)

Building upon a foundation of biblical survey and principles of Bible interpretation, this course presents a detailed study of Daniel and Revelation. Audiotape version only. (3 quarter hours)

The Pastoral Epistles (Graduate Level)

An expository and exegetical study of I and II Timothy and Titus, with emphasis on their special exegetical and interpretive problems and on their relevance for society, church, and especially church leadership. Audiotape version only. (4 quarter hours)

The Christian and Old Testament Theology (Graduate Level)

A study of the foundational theology applied by the Old Testament for the New Testament Church. This study identifies the doctrinal focal point of both the Old and New Testaments. It also deals with the question of continuity and discontinuity between the Old and New Testament. Included are the topics of faith, the people of God, the doctrine of atonement, relationship between the law and wisdom theology, kingdom of God, the Messiah, the place of the Gentiles, the theology of the Holy Spirit, and the preparation for the New Covenant. Audiotape version only. (4 quarter hours)

Christian Education

Leadership and Administration

A study designed to develop leadership potential in students and to give them a familiarity with various elements of the administrative process, including goal setting and achieving, organization, delegation, human relations, group dynamics, supervision, and the training of other leaders. Though the principles are universal, the focus of the course is the Christian organization, particularly the local church. Audiotape version only. (4 quarter hours)

The Philosophy of Christian School Education

An introduction to traditional and contemporary philosophies of education with the intent of developing an educationally sound, thoroughly biblical approach to Christian education. Through lectures, readings, and independent study, students will learn to distinguish educational thought and methods that are compatible with biblical teaching. 3 sessions, 40 minutes each. (2 quarter hours)

Christian Ministries

Introduction to Missions

This course in Christian missions surveys the biblical foundation of world evangelism for all Christians, its progress from Pentecost until the present, the political challenges to the Gospel, traditional and innovative methods, and current prospects for church growth. Audiotape version only. (4 quarter hours)

History of Missions (Graduate Level)

A survey of Christianity through the ages with emphasis on a cultural and structural analysis of its growth. The influence of personalities, political developments, cultural factors, and methods and strategies will be highlighted. Attention is given to the post-Reformation era emphasizing the causative factors that led to the present development of world missions. Audiotape version only. (4 quarter hours)

Principles of Community Development (Graduate Level)

This study includes approaches to development and change, the biblical basis for community development, mobilizing people to change, promoting grassroots participation, the literature of community development, and integrates lessons from field experience. Audiotape version only. (3 quarter hours)

Cultural Anthropology (Graduate Level)

An introduction to missionary anthropology. Application of anthropological principles is made to case studies, seeking to understand similarities and differences in human behavior patterns with a view to contextualizing the Christian message. The study also undertakes an ethnographical study. Audiotape version only. (4 quarter hours)

Traditional Religions

A study of the basic features of animistic societies, witchcraft, sorcery, shamanism, and prophetic movements are considered with reference to the planting of indigenous churches. Audiotape version only. (4 quarter hours)

China and Chinese Ministry (Graduate Level)

An overview of the Chinese world for those exploring options for service to the Chinese. The Chinese world view, contemporary Chinese politics, the history of the Chinese missions and the Chinese Church, as well as ways to become involved in ministry to the Chinese are all investigated. Audiotape version only. (3 quarter hours)

Urban Missions

A course that focuses on Christian mission and ministry in the world's growing cities. The biblical basis for urban ministry is presented and case studies of effective urban strategies worldwide are examined. Attention is given to urban issues such as ministry to the poor and homeless, pastoring and raising a family in the city, and planting urban churches. Audiotape version only. (4 quarter hours)

Church History

Modern Pseudo-Christian Cults

Survey of the more important pseudo-Christian cults, those groups claiming to be Christian but deviating in one or more major doctrines from historic orthodox biblical Christianity. The history, beliefs, practices, refutation of cultic errors, and methods of witnessing to cultists will be studied. Audiotape version only. (2 quarter hours)

Greek

The Pastoral Epistles (Graduate Level)

An expository and exegetical study of I and II Timothy and Titus, from the original Greek text, with emphasis on their special exegetical and interpretive problems and on their relevance for society, church, and especially church leadership. Audiotape version only. (4 quarter hours)

History

The Ancient Church, 95 A.D.-600 A.D. (Graduate Level)

Following a historical progression, this course covers the development of doctrine and introduces the main figures in the Patristic age. Audiotape version only. (4 quarter hours)

Pastoral Studies

Biblical Counseling by Encouragement

This course is based on the concept and belief that caring, mature Christians in local churches can and should learn to develop an encouragement/counseling ministry through the use of a well-timed word to stimulate one another to love and good deeds. Counseling by encouragement is the most basic form of counseling. This course is designed to help one understand the importance and techniques of this ministry in the local church. 13 sessions, 30 minutes each. (2 quarter hours)

Principles of Personal Discipling

This course is designed to challenge Christians, irrespective of their stage of maturity, to develop a lifestyle which implements the basic principles of Christian growth. The philosophy of Christian growth in its theological framework is presented together with a workable methodology emphasizing (1) biblical concepts of conversion and Christian growth, (2) how conversion and Christian growth relate to each other, and (3) how to train others in these concepts. Audiotape version only. (2 quarter hours)

Marriage and Family Counseling (Graduate Level)

A variety of issues are considered along with biblical evaluation and solutions. The course is recommended for the student or church leader who has a good understanding of Scripture and is seeking more specific information about the subject. Audiotape version only. (4 quarter hours)

Management of Christian Organizations (Graduate Level)

This course will enhance one's knowledge in the strategic areas of: the concept of management, strategic thinking, organizing for innovation, team building for effective ministry, the process of control, the management of change and more. Audiotape version only. (3 quarter hours)

Biblical Marriage (Graduate Level)

A treatment of the major factors leading up to marriage and the problems faced in a marital relationship. Marriage must be built according to God's "blueprint" if it is to be truly Christian. This biblical blueprint for marriage is contrasted at several points with predominant patterns in contemporary American culture. 10 sessions, 30 minutes each. (2 quarter hours)

Biblical Parenting (Graduate Level)

This course examines the nature of the parenting process and the biblical framework for parenting and then treats the parenting process in relation to the child, the home, the marriage, relationships, training, and the child's spiritual life. 12 sessions, 30 minutes each. (3 quarter hours)

Principles of Personal Discipling (Graduate Level)

A course which challenges Christians to develop a lifestyle which is founded upon the basic principles of Christian growth. The philosophy of Christian growth is presented with a theological framework and a working methodology. It emphasizes biblical precepts on conversion, and how conversion and growth interrelate. Audiotape version only. (2 quarter hours)

Social Studies

Family Life I: Courtship and Marriage

This course seeks to present an overview of marriage, including courtship and partner selection, the nature of marriage, and the problems faced in a marital relationship. The approach emphasizes the availability and applicability of the plan and principles established by God upon which a marriage must be founded if it is to be truly "Christian." 10 sessions, 30 minutes each. (2 quarter hours)

Family Life II: Parenting

This course covers the biblical and natural principles of parenting on which individuals can develop and evaluate their own techniques and style of parenting. Important topics include the goal of parenting, the place of understanding the child, relating to children, training, and the work of God in the child. 12 sessions, 30 minutes each. (3 quarter hours)

Theology

Principles of the Christian Life

An introduction to the ethical/spiritual life and its implications for personal and social ethics. The course includes a detailed study of God's standard for Christian living, God's provision for man to meet that standard, and man's responsibility toward God's provision. It also incorporates a practical study of 20th-century ethical problems. Audiotape version only. (4 quarter hours)

The Doctrine of the Church

A study of the biblical doctrine of the Church including its purposes, structure and life, leadership, basic nature and functions, and its significance in the world today. 15 sessions, 45-50 minutes each. (2 quarter hours)

Bibliology: Inerrancy and Authority of the Scriptures

The historical development of the Church's attitude concerning the nature of the Bible is presented. Topics include the evangelical position regarding revelation, inspiration and phenomena, and inspiration and hermeneutics. Audiotape version only. (2 quarter hours)

Christian Theology I

An overview study of the doctrines of revelation and inspiration, the being and works of God, angels, man and sin, the Person and work of Christ, and the atonement. Thirty-one study units with practical and personal interaction with biblical and historical perspectives framed against the contemporary scene. Audiotape version only. (4 quarter hours)

Christian Theology II

A continuation of the above course including the doctrines of the person and work of the Holy Spirit, the work of redemption and the Christian life (sanctification applied), the Church, and Eschatology. Audiotape version only. (4 quarter hours)

The Theology of Jonathan Edwards (Graduate Level)

Taking a topical approach, this course covers Edwards' teachings regarding all the major points of systematic theology with particular emphasis on Edwards' unique theological contributions. Audiotape version only. (4 quarter hours)

University of South Carolina
Distance Learning
Office of Independent Learning

915 Gregg Street
Columbia, SC   29208

(800) 922-2577

Geographic Access: Worldwide

DELIVERY SYSTEMS

Audiocassette

Students must have access to an audiocassette player. Used specifically in foreign language courses.

Videocassette

Students must have a VHS player using the American Standard VHS format. These tapes will not play on a VCR that is European format VHS or VHS from another country.

INSTITUTION DESCRIPTION

The University of South Carolina, chartered in 1801 as South Carolina College, is among the oldest state universities. It has emerged as a leading educational institution of 16 academic units and enrolls over 35,000 students on all campuses.

Independent Learning is a part of the University of South Carolina's undergraduate program. It is designed for students who desire some freedom in the selection of courses, who cannot schedule classes on campus, or who need to supplement their schedules, and who desire to learn independently. Independent learning allows students with time or distance restraints to take college-level courses for credit or for pleasure. As much as possible, the content of an independent learning course is the same as that of its corresponding campus-based course.

Courses by videocassette permit the student to view course lectures at a time that fits his/her schedule. A student can review a lecture or any portion of one as many times as desired. The combination of course lectures on videocassette, the course syllabus, text(s), and feedback from the instructor on assignments provides a well-designed and effective learning experience.

Accreditation: SACS

Official/Contact: Sylvia A. Brazell, Director of Student Support Services

Admission Requirements: Formal admission to the University of South Carolina is not required to enroll and earn credits in independent learning courses. However, established admission requirements must be met at the time of formal enrollment in any academic program. It is the students responsibility to determine if a course will meet an institution's requirements if credits are to transfer.

Tuition: $107 per semester hour for all videocassette courses. A nonrefundable tape rental fee of $25 is required. MasterCard and VISA accepted. Textbooks must be purchased by the student. Students must sign a Video/Audiocassette Usage Agreement.

Degree Credit: An external degree is not available through Independent Learning. Credits may be used to supplement the resident curriculum.

Grading: Letter grades are awarded (A-F). The final examination is generally the only supervised component of an independent learning course. A passing grade on the final examination is required in order to earn credit for a course. Credit is awarded in semester hour units.

Library: Distance learning students are encouraged to use their local community library resources.

COURSES OFFERED

English

Modern American Literature
The Eminent Scholar/Teacher Series provides the opportunity to study with the most respected authorities on their subjects. This course treats the main currents of literary activity, major authors, and key works in America between 1900 and World War II. The thirteen experts include Walton Litz (on T.S. Eliot), Louis Rubin (on Thomas Wolfe), Cleanth Brooks (on William Faulkner), and Matthew Bruccoli (on F. Scott Fitzgerald). (3 credits)

Writer's Workshop
An insightful course featuring interviews with contemporary fiction and nonfiction writers. Kurt Vonnegut, Nora Ephron, Tom Wolfe, William Price Fox, James Dickey, and nine other writers whose specialties range from poetry to film criticism relate their impressions of writing as a profession and as a form of artistic expression. Experienced or aspiring writers, book lovers, and anyone interested in the writing process will gain perspective on the world of writing through this course. (3 credits)

French

Introductory French (C-109)
Introduction to grammar and practical vocabulary necessary for fundamental communication skills. Restricted to those who have never studied French previously. Audiocassette rental fee: $10. (3 credits)

Introductory French (C-110)
A continuation of Introductory French (C-109). Audiocassette rental fee: $10. (3 credits)

History

The American South Comes of Age
In the three decades that followed the beginning of World War II, the American South underwent remarkable changes in its economy, its politics, and its race relations. Occuring in an unusually short period of time, those changes represent one of the great transformations in American history. The purposes of this course are to develop an understanding of this transformation and to place it in historical perspective. (3 credits)

International Studies

The Vietnam War
Built around the outstanding PBS television series *Vietnam: A Television History*, this course provides in-depth knowledge of the Vietnam War, from its historical origins to its eventual resolution. The course also provides a firmer understanding of America's role in the war and familiarizes students with different perspectives and interpretations of the Vietnam War. (3 credits)

Latin

Beginning Latin I
Introduction to grammar and practical vocabulary necessary for fundamental skills. Admission restricted to those who have never studied Latin previously. Audiocassette rental fee: $10. (3 credits)

Beginning Latin II
A continuation of Beginning Latin I. Audiocassette rental fee: $10. (3 credits)

Library Science

Jump Over the Moon

Provides an introduction to the selection and sharing of literature for and with young children (birth through age 10). Hundreds of children's books, including concept books, Mother Goose stories, and fairy tales, are presented for the viewer's examination through excellent use of the television camera. The course is designed for anyone interested in children's literature, especially media specialists, nursery school and elementary teachers, and parents. (3 credits)

Nursing

Geriatric Nutrition

Provides an in-depth study of the nutritional requirements of older people with emphasis on the preventative and therapeutic nutrition principles related to health problems of the elderly. (3 credits)

Social Work

Foundations of Social Welfare

Social welfare agencies, the education and ethical code of social workers, principles/theories/research underlying social work practice and methods. (3 credits)

Spanish

Beginning Spanish I

Introduction to grammar and practical vocabulary necessary for fundamental communication skills. Admission restricted to those who have never studied Spanish previously. Audiocassette rental fee: $10. (3 credits)

Beginning Spanish II

A continuation of Beginning Spanish I. Audiocassette rental fee: $10. (3 credits)

South Dakota

University of South Dakota
University Telecourses
State-Wide Educational Services
414 East Clark Street
Vermillion, SD 57069-2390

(605) 677-5651 *Fax:* (605) 677-5073

Geographic Access: Iowa, Minnesota, Nebraska, North Dakota, South Dakota

DELIVERY SYSTEMS

Broadcast Television
University Telecourses programs are available to all qualified South Dakota Public Television (SDPTV) viewers.

INSTITUTION DESCRIPTION

The University of South Dakota was founded in 1882. The Extension Division was formally established in 1918. In 1967, the Extension Division was designated as State-Wide Educational Services. It provides a variety of services including high school and college independent study, off-campus extension classes, workshops, institutes, and short courses for credit and noncredit.

The professional staff of University Telecourses constantly monitor professional telecourse literature, searching for telecourses that will meet certain needs of area students. Telecourses are developed by a wide variety of organizations, including colleges and universities, public television stations, academic organizations, and independent producers.

Accreditation: NCA

Official/Contact: Jane Bromert, Dean

Admission Requirements: Formal admission to the University of South Dakota is not required. If pursuing graduate credit, a baccalaureate degree is required. Enrollment in a telecourse does not constitute admission to the University of South Dakota.

Tuition: In-state tuition $68.25 per undergraduate credit hour, $89.25 per graduate credit. Out-of-state tuition $99.75 per undergraduate credit, $115.50 per graduate credit. Processing fee $20 per course. Textbooks must be purchased by the student. MasterCard and VISA accepted.

Degree Credit: Credit earned by successful completion of a telecourse may be applied toward a degree at the University of South Dakota. Students from neighboring states should consult with their institution to determine the policy for transfer of credit.

Grading: All telecourse students are required to select and have a person proctor or supervise their course exams (librarian, minister, principal, school superintendent). Letter grades are assigned. Credit is awarded in semester hour units.

Library: Many libraries across the state of South Dakota are online with the South Dakota Library Network through the Project for Automated Library Systems (PALS). This service allows access to books from across the state.

COURSES OFFERED

Archaeology

Introduction to Archaeology
Utilizing dramatic on-site filming at the spectacular Classic Maya center of Copan, Honduras, as well as at other archaeological sites worldwide, *Out of the Past* allows the student to join archaeologists as they

reconstruct ancient societies and explain how and why they evolved. 8 one-hour telecasts. (3 credits)

Education

The Effective Teacher

By combining current and past research and practice in teaching and learning, and applying it to such topics as classroom organization, individual differences, methodologies for teaching, and assessment, *The Effective Teacher* offers the student the opportunity to learn from a variety of national figures and practicing classroom teachers. A combination of theory, research, and practical examples is designed to help the student become a better classroom teacher. 13 one-hour telecasts. This course may be taken for graduate credit. (3 credits)

Workshop

In a classroom setting, *Calico Pie* offers valuable discussions between an early childhood specialist and teachers about activities and materials that can make learning meaningful for young children. Topics covered include science and math, language, arts, music, social studies, and outdoor learning. 8 one-hour telecasts. May be taken for undergraduate or graduate credit. (3 credits)

Restructuring America's Schools

This topical program provides the student with a coherent and systematic examination of the goals, purpose, and structure of schools and schooling. Through reading and interviews with national experts, the telecourse offers a comprehensive professional development activity and provides a wide variety of activities that can be used as the basis for planning and initiating changes in the students' own schools and communities. Nine 90-minute telecasts. For graduate credit only. (3 credits)

Teaching for Thinking: Creativity in the Classroom

This telecourse is designed to help teachers help their students to learn to think for themselves. It effectively presents useful classroom techniques and strategies used to help students feel free in classroom situations without the fear of rejection. Although the ideas and examples in this telecourse are presented in language arts, social studies, and science, they are applicable to teachers of all subjects. May be taken for undergraduate or graduate credit. 6 one-hour telecasts. (3 credits)

English

Introduction to Literature

Shakespearean actress Fran Dorn brings both contemporary and traditional literature alive through dramatizations of individual works and readings of literary passages in *Literary Visions*. Organized around three major genres of literature—short fiction, poetry, and drama—the programs examine literary elements such as character, plot, and symbolism. A strong emphasis is placed on writing about literature as a way for the student to learn and use advanced compositional techniques. Contemporary authors James Dickey, August Wilson, Maxine Hong Kingston, and Tillie Olson, among others, also share their inspirations and discuss the craft of creative writing. 13 one-hour telecasts. (3 credits)

Professional Writing

This telecourse is for anyone whose work requires effective written communication. The goal of this course is to improve individual written communication skills and includes situations on rhetorical strategies, methods of organizing technical information, and precise use of the language. Exercises guide students through the entire writing process. Information gathering, organizing, drafting, revising, and polishing. 10 half-hour telecasts. May be taken for undergraduate or graduate credit. (3 credits)

Family Relations

Family Practice Seminar

This course will provide the student with information needed to build/maintain effective relationships with team members (including parents). *Early Intervention Teams* will explore models of service coordination/case management, negotiated decision making, and emphasize interdisciplinary/interagency collaboration with an appreciation of cultural issues. 9 one-hour telecasts. This course may be taken for graduate credit. (2 credits)

Health

Current Problems in Health Education

The purpose of this course is to help the student to become a more responsible and healthier individual by placing emphasis on preventing problems before they occur. By focusing on such topics as stress, hypertension, nutrition, depression, smoking, and sexually transmitted diseases, *Here's to Your Health* offers the opportunity to draw upon the advice of experts in managing one's own health. 13 one-hour telecasts. This course may be taken for graduate credit. (3 credits)

History

American History
America in Perspective takes the student on an exciting voyage from 1877 to the end of the recent cold war. Video programs combine interviews, historical film and photographs to provide an analytical frame of reference through which the events of the past and present can be understood. 13 one-hour telecasts. (3 credits)

Latin America
Americas presents a multidisciplinary study of the twentieth-century political, economic, and cultural history of Latin America and the Caribbean. The video program focuses on the key issues and events that are crucial to understanding the development of the modern-day Americas, from the relationship of this region to the rest of the world to the region's changing ethnic identities. This course will help the student understand the political history of Latin America and the Caribbean by giving a solid foundation for studying and evaluating this complex region's future issues and concerns. 10 one-hour telecasts. (3 credits)

Marketing

Personal Selling
The Sales Connection: Principles of Selling offers the tips, tools, and tactics needed to successfully compete in today's long-term, consultative-style sales environment. In each of the video programs, several of the nation's top sales experts offer valuable information and advice about identifying sales prospects, as well as developing and maintaining good sales relationships. At the same time, the student will be taken "into the trenches"—into retail, wholesale, manufacturing, and service industries—to see theories put to practical use through the first-hand stories of professional sales people. 13 one-hour telecasts. (3 credits)

Mathematics

Introduction to Finite Mathematics
For All Practical Purposes is an entry-level college mathematics course divided into five topics: man-

agement science, statistics, social choices, size and shape, and computer science. By demonstrating the practical applications of mathematics to a wide variety of topics, the course allows the student to examine how mathematics is used as the modern language of problem solving in the world around us. 26 half-hour telecasts. (4 credits)

Political Science

Government
Government By Consent, an introduction to American Government, is a blending of traditional political science instruction with examples of how to get involved in government. 13 one-hour telecasts. (3 credits)

Psychology

Psychology of Abnormal Behavior
The World of Abnormal Psychology presents interviews with patients and their families, clinicians, and researchers to offer a thoughtful look at real people with emotional problems ranging from simple stress to paranoid schizophrenia. Hour-long episodes are devoted to specific sets of disorders, the exploration of newer research in the field, methods of assessment, forms of psychotherapy, and attempts to prevent psychological disorders. 13 one-hour telecasts. (3 credits)

Human Development Through the Life Span
Seasons of Life is an introductory life-span psychology telecourse that examines significant events and major developmental changes across the life-span. This course explores the fascinating biological, social, and psychological changes that occur from the beginning of life to its end. Illustrated with dramatic documentary footage and interviews with over 100 people, the course offers students the opportunity to understand the seasons of people's lives. 13 one-hour audio programs and 5 one-hour telecasts. May be taken for undergraduate or graduate credit. (3 credits)

Sociology

Sociology of the Family
Portrait of a Family lets the student examine the increased population, urbanization, and economic uncertainty that have left deep imprints of dissatisfaction on personal and family interactions. The video segments in this course offer a balance be-

tween a theoretical and practical examination of personal choice and decision making within families. 13 one-hour telecasts. This course may be taken for graduate credit. (3 credits)

Rural Sociology

Rural Communities: Legacy and Change addresses the challenges facing rural America by traveling to 15 rural regions and examining various facets of community life. Visits are made to rural dwellers including the workers in a rural manufacturing plant in Georgia, Laotian immigrants in rural Kansas, and entrepreneurs planning a world-class ski resort in California's Sierra Nevada mountains. The student will learn how rural communities such as these inevitably confront decisions about how much change is acceptable and necessary, and what tools and techniques are most effective in assuring the vitality and maintaining the character of their community. 13 one-hour telecasts. This course may be taken for graduate credit. (3 credits)

Spanish

Introductory Spanish

By following Raquel Rodriguez, a Mexican lawyer, on her quest to solve a family mystery, *Destinos: An Introduction to Spanish* takes the student to Spain, Argentina, Puerto Rico, and Mexico to study the rich and diversified cultural context in which Spanish is spoken worldwide. 13 one-hour telecasts. (4 credits)

Special Education

Educating Able Learners

This telecourse helps teachers, administrators, and parents play a key role in nurturing gifted and talented students to reach their full potential. Offering practical, hands-on advice from national teaching experts, this telecourse describes and models how the student can enhance the potential of gifted students in the regular classroom, in pull-out settings, and in individualized development programs. May be taken for undergraduate or graduate credit. 12 half-hour telecasts. (3 credits)

Statistics

Introduction to Statistics

Against All Odds: Inside Statistics is an introductory statistics course that provides an extraordinary explanation of statistical processes, stressing data-centered topics rather than the more traditional path from probability to formal inference. By emphasizing the importance of collection and description of data, the student will experience a blend of exposition and entertainment, and will have the opportunity to examine the applicability of statistics to a variety of training settings. 26 half-hour telecasts. (3 credit hours)

Tennessee

East Tennessee State University
School of Continuing Studies

Johnson City, TN 37614

(615) 929-4112

Geographic Access: Tennessee

DELIVERY SYSTEMS

Broadcast Television
Telecourses are broadcast over WSJK, Channel 2, an eastern Tennessee PBS affiliated station.

INSTITUTION DESCRIPTION

East Tennessee State University was established in 1909 and has been offering instruction at the postsecondary level since 1911. The university offers varied programs at the undergraduate and graduate levels.

In 1991, ETSU licensed more programming from the Adult Learning Satellite Service than any other four-year college or university. In cooperation with WSJK-Channel 2, courses are offered each semester and summer. Telecourses are intended for students who have past college experience and who can learn in a more independent way than is required in regular classes. Although the televised programs eliminate the requirement to attend weekly in-classroom lectures, the other academic requirements remain, e.g., textbooks, tests, and research papers. Students are supervised by a faculty member and attend scheduled meetings during the semester. An orientation before each course is held before the first broadcast.

Contact the official listed for current course offerings.

Accreditation: SACS

Official/Contact: Darcey M. Cuffman, Video Resource Coordinator

Admission Requirements: Students who are degree-seeking candidates must fulfill the regular admission requirements of the university.

Tuition: $69 per semester hour for state residents. $157 per semester hour for out-of-state residents. Students must purchase textbooks required.

Degree Credit: Credit awarded is applicable to a degree program.

Grading: Letter grades are awarded with credit in semester hour units.

Library: Videotapes are also available for viewing at the Instructional Media Center on the university campus as well as at the Kingsport University Library.

University of Tennessee
Division of Continuing Education
Department of Independent Study

420 Communications Building
Knoxville, TN 37996

(615) 974-5134

Geographic Access: Nationwide

DELIVERY SYSTEMS

Audiocassette
Audiotapes are utilized as supplementary materials in foreign language courses.

Videocassette
Optional use of videotapes is available with some courses. Students must have access to a VHS video recorder/player.

INSTITUTION DESCRIPTION

The University of Tennessee, the land-grant institution of the state, is dedicated to providing research, instruction, and public service to the citizens of Tennessee and the nation. The goal of independent study by correspondence is to make many of the University's instructional resources available to any qualified student at any location. To achieve this goal, correspondence courses are open for enrollment throughout the year. Students work at their own location and pace. The University of Tennessee has offered this service since 1923. The courses listed below are media-assisted by use of audio- or videocassettes.

Accreditation: SACS

Official/Contact: David F. Holden, Director

Admission Requirements: Courses may be taken for credit or noncredit by anyone who wishes to enroll. There are no admission requirements. However, enrollment does not constitute admission to a degree program at the University of Tennessee.

Tuition: The fee for each course is listed under Courses Offered with the course description. Textbooks and special instructional materials are not included in this fee. Some supplementary materials may be required.

Degree Credit: The University of Tennessee does not offer an external degree program, that is, a program for earning an entire degree away from campus. The courses below do count toward graduation and credit may be accepted in transfer by other institutions.

Grading: An instructor may use letter grades, numerical grades, or S (satisfactory) and U (unsatisfactory) to indicate the quality of work on assignments. All examinations in courses for college credit must be supervised by properly authorized testing personnel. Credit is awarded in semester hour units.

Library: Students in the vicinity of a University of Tennessee campus have access to the library facilities.

COURSES OFFERED

English

Advanced Grammar
Study of system and pattern implicit in the English language. Basic sentence patterns, inflections, determiners, parts of speech, expansions, complementa-

tion, and usage. 20 assignments. Fee: $207. Text: $31.60. Audiotape: $5. (3 credits)

French

Elementary French, First Semester
Introduction to French. 24 assignments. Fee: $207. Text: $44.45. Workbook: $24.30. Audiotapes: $30 of which $20 will be refunded if the tapes are returned in good condition. (3 credits)

German

Elementary German, First Semester
23 assignments. Fee: $207. Text: $75.90. Audiotapes: $25 of which $15 will be refunded if tapes are returned in good condition. (3 credits)

Elementary German, Second Semester
22 assignments. Fee: $207. Text: $86.10. Two texts the same as for Elementary German, First Semester, other two texts $13.92. Audiotapes: $30 of which $20 will be refunded if tapes are returned in good condition. (3 credits)

Medical Terminology

Medical and Scientific Vocabulary
An introduction to the immediate constituents of medical and scientific vocabulary building and recognition through study and analysis of the most common technical prefixes, combining forms, and suffixes. 15 assignments. Fee: $207. Text: $41. Required audiotapes: $30 of which $20 is refunded if tapes are returned in good condition. (3 credits)

Pharmacy

Environmental Monitoring for Aseptic Processing Areas in Pharmacies
This course consists of a 45-minute videotape and accompanying independent study manual that explores the use of several commonly used environmental monitoring devices, illustrates the collection, recording, and interpretation of environmental monitoring data, and discusses the application of these factors in maintaining environmental quality in an intravenous admixture program. 1 assignment. Fee: $22. Videotape rental: $45 of which $30 is refunded if tape is returned in good condition. (Noncredit)

Sociology

The City

The revolutionary impact of cities and city life as seen from an ecological perspective. The organization of life in cities into communities, neighborhoods, and other territories. Urban planning and problems. 17 assignments. Fee: $207. Text $14.25. Optional videotapes: $75 for the set of which $50 will be refunded when returned in good condition. $15 rental fee for a single cassette of which $10 will be refunded. (3 credits)

Spanish

Elementary Spanish, First Semester

Introduction to Spanish. 17 assignments. Fee: $207. Text: $77.10. Audiotapes: $30 of which $20 will be refunded if tapes are returned in good condition. (3 credits)

Elementary Spanish, Second Semester

17 assignments. Text same as for Elementary Spanish, First Semester. Audiotapes: $30 of which $20 will be refunded if tapes are returned in good condition. (3 credits)

Intermediate Spanish, First Semester

Reading, writing, listening, and speaking of Spanish to prepare for upper division courses in the language. 19 assignments. Fee: $207. Test: $58.30. Audiotapes: $30 of which $20 will be refunded if tapes are returned in good condition. (3 credits)

Intermediate Spanish, Second Semester

Text same as for Intermediate Spanish, First Semester. 16 assignments. Fee: $207. Audiotapes: $30 of which $20 will be refunded if tapes are returned in good condition. (3 credits)

Texas

Brookhaven College
See **Dallas County Community College District**

Cedar Valley College
See **Dallas County Community College District**

Dallas County Community College District
R. Jan LeCroy Center for Educational Telecommunications
9596 Walnut Street
Dallas, TX   75243-2112

(214) 952-0333

Geographic Access: Texas

DELIVERY SYSTEMS

Broadcast Television
Telecourses are aired over the PBS television stations in the Dallas area.

INSTITUTION DESCRIPTION

The Dallas County Community College District (DCCCD) produced and offered its first telecourse in the fall of 1972. Dallas Telecourses is a major producer of transferable college-credit telecourses in North America, and a principal supplier of telecourses to the PBS Adult Learning Service. From the R. Jan LeCroy Center for Educational Communications, Dallas Telecourses serves educational institutions not only in the Dallas County Community College District, but nationally and internationally as well. More than 160,000 students have enrolled in telecourses in the DCCCD's seven colleges. The courses listed below are offered at varying semesters by the participating DCCCD colleges which are:

- Brookhaven College (Farmers Branch TX), (214) 620-4700
- Cedar Valley College (Lancaster TX), (214) 372-8200
- Eastfield College (Mesquite TX), (214) 838-6514
- El Centro College (Dallas TX), (214) 746-2037
- Mountain View College (Dallas TX), (214) 333-8700
- North Lake College (Irving TX), (214) 572-1911
- Richland College (Dallas TX), (214) 238-6200

Accreditation: All participating colleges are accredited by SACS.

Official/Contact: J. William Wenrich, Chancellor

Admission Requirements: Open enrollment for credit or noncredit. Prospective students should contact the college campus (telephone number listed above) for enrollment procedure.

Tuition: Contact the college of choice for up-to-date tuition, fees, and other materials costs. Students must purchase textbooks which can be obtained at the various college bookstores.

Degree Credit: Credit awarded for successful completion of a course may be applied toward a degree program at any of the DCCCD campuses. Students desiring to transfer earned credit to a four-year college/university should determine beforehand the transfer-in policy of that institution.

Grading: Examinations must be supervised by an approved proctor or taken at a testing site on the campus. Letter grades are assigned. Credit is awarded in semester hour units. Each course described is generally for 3 semester hours of credit. However, the amount of credit awarded is the option of the college offering the telecourse.

Library: Students officially registered for a telecourse have access to the library resources of the college in which they are enrolled.

COURSES OFFERED

Business

Introduction to Business

The Business File provides a comprehensive view of contemporary business environment and introduces business fundamentals. Using a format similar to ABC's "Nightline," the series host conducts interviews with some of the nation's academic and professional leaders in business, encompassing general areas such as the foundation and form of American business, organizing and managing a business, and the internal works of business. 28 half-hour programs. (3 credits)

Principles of Accounting

Financial accounting practices are linked with everyday business activities in this one-semester financial accounting telecourse. Electronic graphics, animation, and on-location footage motivate and pace the student through this step-by-step presentation of the accounting process, covering: balance sheets, financial statements, cost accounting, organizational forms, and much more. 30 half-hour programs. (3 credits)

Earth Science

Earth, Sea, and Sky

The science of survival, as earth science might be called, is the focus of this complete introductory telecourse. Astronomy, meteorology, climatology, oceanography, and a major concentration on geology are all addressed in this series. The course introduces students to the tools of scientific investigation, observation, and interpretation. 30 half-hour programs. (3 credits)

Environmental Science

The Living Environment

By asking crucial questions about human survival in the face of advancing technology and a declining environment, this telecourse provides a survey of critical ecological issues facing mankind today. Physical, biological, and social preservation of planet Earth is the focus of this course. On-location footage, interviews and scientific demonstrations feature such issues as population growth, food resources, air and water pollution, waste disposal, natural resource conservation, and alternative sources of energy. 23 half-hour programs. (3 credits)

Health

Living With Health

This telecourse is presented from an individual point of view, bringing the many important issues relating to health and wellness into a personal perspective for each student. The course is wellness oriented, building on the foundation of teaching lifestyle components that promote the five dimensions of health: emotional, physical, social, intellectual, and spiritual. Students are motivated to explore their own health values and beliefs, and to challenge their superstitions and biases in order to make behavior changes that will improve their own health and that of their loved ones. 26 half-hour programs. (3 credits)

History

The American Adventure

This series takes the student to many historical sites and focuses on the human story. It explores the political and economic stories of America, from its beginning to the Civil War and Reconstruction. Renowned historians are interviewed throughout the video lessons. Illustrated narratives, oral histories, paintings, and artifacts provide students with a better understanding of America's past. 26 half-hour programs. (3 credits)

America in Perspective: U.S. History Since 1877

The primary goal of this series is to increase students' knowledge and understanding of how and why the United States came to be what it is today and to develop in the students a sense of healthy skepticism. The series seeks to instill in them habits of historical thinking that will allow them to live more competent and interesting lives in their local communities and in the nation at large. The video programs provide a new visual representation of American history since 1877 and connect us with the past. Each program emphasizes analysis from leading historians to help students understand the material presented. 26 half-hour programs. (3 credits)

Humanities

In Our Own Image

This telecourse introduces students to the study of art. It combines information from the major arts areas: painting and sculpture, music, dance, theatre, and film. On-location videos and in-depth interviews are featured. Among the interviewees offering advice and opinions for the series are: Thomas Hoving of the Metropolitan Museum of Art, Arthur Mitchell of the Dance Theatre of Harlem, Willie Nelson (the country/western music star), Fernando Bujones of the American Ballet Theatre, Mervyn LeRoy (film director), and Warren Beatty (movie actor and director). 30 half-hour programs. (3 credits)

Political Science

Government By Consent: A National Perspective

All aspects of government—the process, the politics, the institutions, the people governing and the people being governed—are explored in a "news broadcast" format. Each program builds around a major theme, using the on-camera host, minidocumentaries, interviews, and graphics. Students are guided through the traditional political science content of a survey course, seeing and hearing actual views and works of nationally known journalists, politicians, and academic experts. 26 half-hour programs. (3 credits)

Government By Consent: A Texas Perspective

This telecourse explains the mechanics of Texas politics and introduces students to participants in the process to ensure that government is no longer viewed as remote and larger than life, but as an essential and important part of our lives. 26 half-hour programs. (3 credits)

Sociology

The Sociological Imagination: Introduction to Sociology

All facets of this telecourse are focused on the overarching vision which engages the viewer on an emotional level, utilizing a straightforward documentary style and approach that provides thought-provoking illustrations of sociological issues and ideas. More than 40 sociologists reveal the multifaceted nature

and depth of sociology and provide sociological interpretation for every program. 26 half-hour programs. (3 credits)

Writing

The Write Course

Taught from a "process" point of view, this telecourse helps students develop writing skills useful in both the academic environment and the business world. The traditional host is replaced by an instructional drama which presents strategies for pre-writing and revision, as well as emphasizing the basic writing skills such as composing effective sentences, paragraphs, essays, and research papers. Assisting the team in their decision making are 30 leading experts and visits to such places as the Document Design Center in Washington, D.C. 30 half-hour programs. (3 credits)

Communicating Through Literature

Dramatized segments and examples of the works of many writers make this a unique introduction to writing composition. Anthony Burgess, Judith Crist, Nikki Giovanni, Richard Adams, William Safire, Joseph Heller, Charles Kuralt, and Jean Marsh discuss their writing techniques and artistic concerns. Poetry, drama, fiction, the essay, and film are all explored to combine instruction in composition with an introduction to literature. Literature is seen not only as a source of pleasure, but as a means of strengthening the student's ability to communicate thoughts about one's self and the world in which we live. 30 half-hour programs. (3 credits)

Eastfield College
See **Dallas County Community College District**

El Centro College
See **Dallas County Community College District**

Mountain View College
See **Dallas County Community College District**

North Lake College
See **Dallas County Community College District**

Richland College
See **Dallas County Community College District**

San Antonio College

Telecourse Office

1300 San Pedro Avenue
San Antonio, TX   78212-4299

(210) 733-2181

Geographic Access: San Antonio, TX

DELIVERY SYSTEMS

Broadcast Television
Lessons are telecast on KLRN Channel 19 and Paragon Cable 19.

INSTITUTION DESCRIPTION

San Antonio College attracts most of its students from San Antonio. Students are nearly evenly divided between college transfer and those pursuing technical programs which lead to employment. The college was founded in 1925. In 1946, it became part of the San Antonio Union Junior College District. The district's name was changed to Alamo Community College District in 1981.

The college enrolls approximately 1500 students in telecourses per semester. Telecourses are of the same academic quality and carry the same credit and transferability as classes taken on campus. Each course requires one hour of television each week, reading a textbook and/or study guide, and a mandatory orientation on campus at the beginning of the semester.

Accreditation: SACS

Official/Contact: Robert Ziegler, Telecourse Coordinator

Admission Requirements: Open enrollment.

Tuition: Because the television courses are offered by the community colleges, the same tuition and fees as for other courses of the Alamo Community College District apply. For current tuition and fees, contact the Telecourse Office.

Degree Credit: A student may earn only one-third of the hours required for a degree or certification through telecourse participation.

Grading: Exams, approximately one per month, are administered on campus at convenient and flexible hours to accommodate varied work and personal schedules.

Library: Officially registered students have access to the holdings of the San Antonio College Learning Resource Center.

COURSES OFFERED

Child Development

Child Growth and Development
Deals with normal growth and development, conception through adolescence. The student learns to observe and recognize different stages of cognitive, emotional/social, physical, and language development. (3 credits)

Computer Science

Introduction to Computers
Provides a comprehensive overview of the computer, what it is, what it can do, how it operates, and how it affects our society. (3 credits)

Government

American Government: State
Combines study of U.S. and Texas government and meets requirements for Texas teacher certification and Texas Constitution requirement for 4-year degree programs. (3 credits)

American Government: National
Study of U.S. government processes and public policy. (3 credits)

History

History of U.S. - Part I
A general survey of United States history from the discovery of America through the Civil War era. Satisfies one-half of the legislative requirement for six semester hours in American history. (3 credits)

History of U.S. - Part II
A general survey of U.S. history from the Civil War era to the present. Satisfies one-half of the legislative requirement for six semester hours in American history. (3 credits)

History of Civilization - Part I
Based on the dynamic lectures of Eugene Weber, the Joan Palevsky Professor of History at the University

of California, Los Angeles. The course spans the influential pre-western civilizations through the classical period of Greece, Rome, and Byzantium to the high Middle Ages. (3 credits)

History of Civilization - Part II

Continues the above course, beginning with the Renaissance and continuing through the industrial revolution, modernization, and the key events of the 20th century into our present era. (3 credits)

Humanities

Western Culture

A nontraditional, interdisciplinary course in the humanities which presents in understandable terms the major humanistic disciplines as resources through which all people can enhance the quality of their lives. (3 credits)

Psychology

Child Psychology

Examines major phases of growth, physical and motor development, social relations, perception, emotion, and self awareness. (3 credits)

General Psychology

Surveys the various aspects of human thought and behavior. Examines motivation, learning, maturation, social interaction, and the effects of environmental influences on human development. (3 credits)

Spanish

Beginning Conversational Spanish I

Development of the ability to speak the language with concentration on every day situations developed in dialogues. (3 credits)

Sociology

Introduction to Sociology

Provides an analysis of culture, social groups, socialization, stratification, social institutions, social change, and social issues. (3 credits)

Marriage and the Family

Provides an analysis of human sexuality, sex roles, mate selection, marital adjustment, family patterns in the middle and later years, and family disruption. (3 credits)

Tarrant County Junior College
Instructional Television Center
TJC South Campus

5301 Campus Drive
Fort Worth, TX   76119

(817) 531-4532

Geographic Access: Tarrant County (Texas)

DELIVERY SYSTEMS

Broadcast Television

In addition to cable broadcasts, several courses are scheduled to be broadcast over KDTN, Channel 2 (programs are broadcast on Saturday and/or Sunday). Cable broadcasts occur Monday through Friday on a published schedule.

Videocassette

A full set of videocassettes for all courses is maintained in the library on each campus. A student may view a videocassette by presenting their TCJC ID card and identifying the course and program to the staff at the tape center.

INSTITUTION DESCRIPTION

Tarrant County Junior College is a comprehensive community college and an open-door institution providing a wide range of programs including development, general academic, and technical-vocational. The college was formed in 1965 and currently comprises four campuses in the Fort Worth area.

A variety of credit courses are available through the Instructional Television Center. Most telecourses are broadcast over KDTN, Channel 2, and/or various cable stations in Tarrant County. Other courses utilize on-campus viewing/and or audio lessons only. In addition to the television broadcasts (telelessons) which serve as the lecture portion of the course, telecourses combine on-campus sessions (orientation, seminars, and examinations) with related reading and assignments.

The Instructional Television Center serves as the district operating center for all courses offered through Instructional Television, Interactive Television, and Computer Delivered Instruction. The Center provides support services for faculty and students involved in these modes of instruction.

Accreditation: SACS

Official/Contact: Jack Pirkey, Associate Dean

Admission Requirements: Open enrollment. A student must attend an orientation session for each ITV course in which they are enrolled.

Tuition: Contact the Instructional Television Center for current tuition and fees. A lease tape kit containing extended play VHS video- and/or audiotapes is available in selected courses for students to check-out for the semester. The nonrefundable fee is $10. Textbooks must be purchased by the student.

Degree Credit: Upon successful completion of a course, a student will receive full college credit. The courses and credit hours are equivalent to those offered on campus. All courses apply toward associate degree requirements and many fulfill certificate program requirements and/or requirements for bachelor degrees.

Grading: Most courses have three to four examinations covering information contained in the telelessons, textbooks, and study guide. Exams are usually objective in nature, although some may involve essay questions. English courses also require on-campus compositions during scheduled testing weeks. Examinations for all courses are administered by special testing centers on each campus. Objective test grades are awarded. Credit is awarded in semester hour units.

Library: The Jenkins Garrett Library offers support to officially registered students.

COURSES OFFERED

Anthropology

Introduction to Anthropology
  Telecourse: *Faces of Culture.* 26 half-hour programs. (3 credits)

Biology

General Biology II
  Telecourse: *Introducing Biology.* Students develop an understanding of the basic concepts of biology, the characteristic elements, processes, and features common to all life forms, the nature and workings of the human body, and the vital role humans play in the total ecology of the earth. 36 half-hour programs/lessons. (3 credits)

Environmental Biology
  Telecourse: *Race to Save the Planet.* Covers recycling projects, environmental conservation based on economic development, alternative fuels development, industrial economies, and pollution. 10 one-hour programs. (3 credits)

Business

Introduction to Business
  Telecourse: *The Business File.* Provides a comprehensive overview of the contemporary business environment. 28 half-hour programs. (3 credits)

Business Mathematics
  Telecourse: *By the Numbers.* Explores the role business math plays in professional and personal lives. Students learn about the business applications of math concepts such as fractions and percents and learn how to figure interest, cash flow, cost allocations, and financial statements. 26 half-hour programs. (3 credits)

Business Law I
  Telecourse: *Business and the Law.* Emphasizes contracts and the legal system. Students will learn from modules on the law of sales, commercial paper, agency, and property as well as such critical legal topics as government regulation, employment, and consumer and environmental protection. 30 half-hour programs. (3 credits)

English

English Composition I
  Telecourse: *The Write Course: An Introduction to College Composition.* 30 half-hour programs. (3 credits)

English Composition II
  Telecourse: *Literary Visions.* An introduction to literature and literary analysis. 26 half-hour programs. (3 credits)

Finance

Personal Money Management
  Telecourse: *Personal Finance and Money Management.* Covers basic skills students need to manage their money. Students learn the basics of budgeting and buying, the intricacies of home ownership, income tax and investments, and the wise use of insurance, wills, and trusts. 26 half-hour programs. (3 credits)

Government

United States Government
Telecourse: *Government by Consent: A National Perspective.* A survey course providing students with an understanding of democracy, the Constitution, political parties, the branches of government, due process. 26 half-hour programs. (3 credits)

Texas State and Local Government
Telecourse: *Government by Consent: A National Perspective.* 26 half-hour programs. (3 credits)

Health

Personal and Community Health
Telecourse: *Here's to Your Health.* 26 half-hour programs. (3 credits)

History

U.S. History to 1877
Telecourse: *American Adventure: Beginnings to 1877.* 26 half-hour programs. (3 credits)

U.S. History Since 1877
Telecourse: *America in Perspective: U.S. History Since 1877.* Provides an analytical frame of reference for U.S. events after the Civil War. 26 half-hour programs. (3 credits)

Management

Principles of Management
Telecourse: *The Business of Management.* An introduction to the theories of management and business. Provides essential information on planning, staffing, directing, decision making, motivating, and communicating. 26 half-hour programs. (3 credits)

Small Business Management
Telecourse: *Something Ventured.* Provides entrepreneurs with the tools needed to compete effectively in the world of business. 26 half-hour programs. (3 credits)

Marketing

Salesmanship
Telecourse: *The Sales Connection: Principles of Selling.* Designed to provide aspiring sales people and those already involved in sales with the tools and insight needed to compete in the age of long-term,

consultative type of selling. 26 half-hour programs. (3 credits)

Music

Music Appreciation
Text required is *Music: An Appreciation* (Kamien, McGraw-Hill, 1990). The textbook and two cassette tapes will be packaged and sold as a set. (3 credits)

Philosophy

Ethics in America
Telecourse: *Ethics in America.* Produced by Columbia University Seminars on Media and Society. 10 one-hour programs. (3 credits)

Psychology

Introduction to Psychology
Telecourse: *Psychology: The Study of Human Behavior.* 26 half-hour programs. (3 credits)

Child Growth and Development
Telecourse: *Time to Grow.* 26 half-hour programs. (3 credits)

Life Span Growth and Development
Telecourse: *Seasons of Life.* This study of what makes human beings "tick" provides provocative insights from current research in psychology, biology, anthropology, and sociology. 5 one-hour programs. (3 credits)

Religious Studies

Great Religions of the World
Telecourse: *The Long Search: A Study of Religions.* 26 half-hour programs. (3 credits)

Sociology

Introduction to Sociology
Telecourse: *Sociological Imagination: Introduction to Sociology.* Features minidocumentaries that are emotionally strong illustrations of issues such as socialization, social control, sex and gender, aging, collective behavior, and social change. 26 half-hour programs. (3 credits)

Texas Tech University
Independent Study
Division of Continuing Education

Box 42191

Lubbock, TX   79409-2191

(800) 692-6877 *Fax:* (806) 742-2318

Geographic Access: Nationwide

DELIVERY SYSTEMS

Audiocassette
Used primarily in foreign language courses. Access to an audiocassette player is required.

Computer Tutorials
Access to an IBM PC or compatible is required in some courses (mathematics, computer science).

Videocassette
Access to television and a VCR are required.

INSTITUTION DESCRIPTION

Texas Tech University is a multipurpose state university that provides the opportunity for a liberal education for all students and for professional training at the undergraduate and graduate levels. The Division of Continuing Education recognizes continuing education as one of the University's major functions.

The Independent Study department offers distance learning instruction at the high school and college levels as well as courses for which continuing education units can be earned. The level of study for each course is listed below at the beginning of the course description.

Accreditation: SACS

Official/Contact: Suzanne Logan, Director

Admission Requirements: Current enrollment in a college or university is not required to take college courses. Texas Tech students must secure their academic dean's approval for enrollment. High school students must have their principal's or superintendent's signature of approval to enroll in a course. Any continuing education or college course may be taken on a noncredit basis.

Tuition: College courses $40 per credit hour. High School courses $74 per one-half unit. Continuing Edu-

cation courses $22 per Continuing Education Unit (CEU). Students must purchase textbooks.

Degree Credit: Up to 18 hours of Independent Study coursework may be applied toward a baccalaureate degree. Out-of-state students should check the transfer-in policy of the home institution to determine the acceptability of completed coursework.

Grading: The grading system for college courses is A, B, C, D, F; the minimum passing grade is D. Number grades are given for high school courses; the minimum passing grade is 70. Courses for which academic credit is awarded require proctored examinations. Credit is awarded in semester hour units.

Library: Distance learning students are encouraged to utilize the library resources of their local communities.

COURSES OFFERED

Business

Business Computer Progamming

High school level. An introduction to computers, computer-related terminology, history and development of computers, use of the computer, communicating instructions to the computer, and problems and issues of computer use in society. Using BASIC computer language, students are introduced to problem-solving skills, algorithm development, and syntax. Access to a computer with BASIC helpful but not required. (1/2 unit)

Business Computer Applications

High school level. An introductory course for the use of computers in the business world. The course covers basic system components, ways computers improve decision-making, applications software, and hands-on experience with word processing, database, and spreadsheets. Students must have access to a computer printer, word processing, database, and spreadsheet software. (1/2 unit)

Business Writing

A continuing education credit course. The student learns how to write clearly, accurately, and fast. How to express valuable and complicated ideas in a way that pleases the reader and creates a pleasant, dignified image. How to organize for the busy reader's needs without fumbling over false starts and rewrites. There is a $35 materials fee of which $20 will be refunded when all materials have been returned in good condition. (2 CEUs)

Keyboarding

A continuing education credit course. Keyboard mastery technique, speed and accuracy in keyboarding, copy arrangement skills, communication skills, problem typing skills, production competencies, electronic information processes. Student must have access to either an Apple, IBM compatible, or Tandy computer. Diskettes ($43.78) required: Alphabetic keyboarding numeric keypad operation. (3 CEUs)

Introduction to Information Systems in the Automated Office

A continuing education credit course. New technology, concepts, and skills needed by today's office worker. Student must have access to an IBM PC or compatible computer. (3 CEUs)

Computer Science

Introduction to Computers in Business

A college level course that surveys computer principles, procedures, concepts, hardware, information systems, and business oriented computer use. Students must have access to an IBM computer, MS DOS, Lotus 1-2-3, WordPerfect 4.2 or 5.0, and dBase III+ or IV software. (3 credits)

Education

Changing Attitudes—The Beginnings

This course will give teachers hands-on activities and lessons that can be put to use immediately. The teacher will view actual classroom demonstrations involving positive self-concept, goal setting, and accepting responsibility in learning. Video: *Changing Attitudes—The Beginnings* ($9.10). (1 CEU)

English

English as a Second Language

High school level. Listening, speaking, reading, and writing concepts and skills for speakers of other languages. Students must be able to speak English and will need access to a cassette tape recorder. (1/2 unit)

Fine Arts

Music History and Literature

High school level. Works from major historical periods, composers, musical style, musical form, and relationship of music to history. 8 cassette tapes ($45.90) required. (1/2 unit)

Music Theory

High school level. A study of basic pitch and rhythmic notation, scale structures, intervals, chord structure and movement, simple partwriting, and ear training. 2 cassette tapes ($6.20) required. (1/2 unit)

French

French Level I (1A)

A beginning high school course in French. 14 audiocassette tapes ($27.50) required. (1/2 unit)

French Level I (1B)

A continuation of French Level I (1A). 14 audiocassette tapes ($27.50) required. (1/2 unit)

French Level II (2A)

An intermediate high school course in French. 1 audiocassette tape ($3.50) required. (1/2 unit)

French Level II (2B)

A continuation of French Level II (2A). 1 audiocassette tape ($3.10) required. (1/2 unit)

Journalism

Journalism

High school level. Explores the essential elements of journalism from its history to its contemporary role through its basic features: journalistic writing, graphics, design and layout, and advertising. One cassette tape ($3.10) and one video tape ($9.82) required. (1/2 unit)

Latin

Latin Level I (1A)

A high school course in reading and writing in Latin. Learning Roman history and culture and understanding how Latin has influenced languages. 1 audiocassette tape ($3.10) required. (1/2 unit)

Latin Level I (1B)

A continuation of Latin Level I (1A). (1/2 unit)

Latin Level II (2A)

A continuation of Latin Level I (1B). 1 audiocassette tape ($3.10) required. (1/2 unit)

Latin Level II (2B)

A continuation of Latin Level II (2A). (1/2 unit)

Mathematics

Computer Mathematics I

High school level. Access to a computer helpful but not required. An introductory programming course using the BASIC language with applications in algebra, geometry, and consumer math. Skills will be developed using IF-THEN, FOR-NEXT, GOTO, and sequential programming. (1/2 unit)

Computer Mathematics II

High school level. A continuation of Computer Mathematics I. Covers functions, subroutines, nested loops, and arrays with applications in algebra and geometry. (1/2 unit)

Music

Elementary Theory (1403)

A college level course. Melody, rhythm, and diatonic harmony in four voices, together with dictation, sight-singing, and keyboard skills. Student must have access to Apple II computer and a DAC board synthesizer with proper interface. The student will need to provide the instructor with a blank diskette. (4 credits)

Elementary Theory (1404)

A continuation of Elementary Theory (1403). The student will need to provide the instructor with a blank diskette. (4 credits)

Intermediate Theory (2403)

A college level course. Analysis, written work, keyboard and dictation in four-voice texture including diatonic and altered triads, sevenths, augmented sixth, small contrapuntal forms, sight-singing. The student will need to provide the instructor with a blank diskette. Student must have access to an Apple II computer and a DAC board synthesizer with computer interface. (4 credits)

Intermediate Theory (2404)

A continuation of Intermediate Theory (2403) with same equipment requirements. (4 credits)

Paralegal Studies

Introduction to the Legal Assistant Profession

A continuing education credit course. Presents a brief overview of the growing need for legal assistants, the birth and evolution of the profession, benefits and drawbacks of the profession, and what the future of legal assistants holds. Videotape produced by the National Association of Legal Assistants ($7.54) required. (1 CEU)

Psychology

General Psychology

A college level course. Introduction to fundamental concepts in psychology. Emphasis on the physiological, social, and environmental determinants of behavior. Students who have access to an IBM compatible computer may choose to do all their lessons on a tutorial disk. This disk, which includes the chapter tests and sample final, gives students immediate feedback. (3 credits)

Spanish

Spanish Level I (1A)

Begins the high school student's study of Spanish through listening, speaking, reading, writing, and learning about the culture while incorporating other essential elements for Spanish. 5 audiocassette tapes ($15.50) required. (1/2 unit)

Spanish Level I (1B)

A continuation of Spanish Level I (1A). 5 audiocassette tapes ($15.50) required. (1/2 unit)

Spanish Level II (2A)

Continues the high school student's study of Spanish through listening, speaking, reading, writing, and learning about the culture while incorporating other essential elements for Spanish. 3 audiocassette tapes ($9.30) required. (1/2 unit)

University of Texas at Austin
TeleLearning Center

P.O. Box 7700
Austin, TX   78713-7700

(512) 471-7716 *Fax:* (512) 471-7716

Geographic Access: Texas

DELIVERY SYSTEMS

Audio Conferencing

During classes, students and teachers talk with each other via telephone equipment that uses multiple source input and reception, connecting all participants in a manner similar to a typical conference call.

INSTITUTION DESCRIPTION

The TeleLearning Center at the University of Texas at Austin was established in 1989 and has been recognized by small rural school districts as an organization devoted to providing quality education for students who are separated from their teacher by distance. Unlike many other distance learning programs, the TeleLearning Center utilizes an audio-based system that helps maintain the low cost of the courses it offers. The Center provides: instruction from certified teachers; classroom materials, including lesson plans and handouts; course and program administration; telephone bridging service and operator; teleconference training session for site facilitators. Participating school districts must provide: a site facilitator for each class; a telephone line to the classroom; long distance service (pass-through billing available through the University of Texas at reduced rates); textbooks; audio reception equipment such as a speaker phone or convener; fax machine; access to electronic bulletin boards.

Accreditation: SACS

Official/Contact: Darcy Walsh Hardy, Manager

Admission Requirements: There are no general enrollment requirements.

Tuition: Contact the TeleLearning Center for the costs for organizing a local class.

Degree Credit: Credits earned may be applied to a degree program at any of the University of Texas campuses.

Grading: Letter grades (A-F) are awarded. Exams are proctored by the local instructor. Credit is awarded in semester hour units.

Library: Access to the University of Texas library system is available through an electronic bulletin board (TENET).

COURSES OFFERED

Economics

Introduction to Macroeconomics

This course focuses on an analysis of the economic behavior of individual consumers, firms, and workers. Special attention is given to the role of markets. (3 credits)

English

Technical Writing

Designed to meet the technical writing needs of students or practitioners in engineering, business, accounting, and the health professions (includes a review of basic writing skills). This course is also suitable for liberal arts majors who wish to develop or enhance technical writing skills. (3 credits)

Mathematics

Mathematics of Investment

The scope of this course includes topics, formulas, and procedures for applications of mathematics to finance and investment. Emphasis is on rationales rather than proofs. Topics covered include simple interest and simple discount, compound interest (with special attention given to the concepts of compound interest, discounting with compound interest equivalent rates, and equations of value, which are the foundation for the remainder of the course), simple annuities, amortization and sinking funds, and bonds. (3 credits)

Nursing

Concepts of Professional Nursing

Designed for the Registered Nurse who is considering reentry into a formal education program to earn a B.S.N. degree. The course will give an overview of contemporary issues facing the nursing professional. (3 credits)

Nutrition

Introductory Nutrition

This course, required or recommended for many B.S.N. degrees, examines the basic components of diet, digestion, and metabolism and emphasizes the importance of good diet to good health. Students will use learning objectives and the text as the source of instruction. (3 credits)

Political Science

American Foreign Relations

This course addresses the aims, methods, and accomplishments of U.S. foreign policy since World War II, by geographic areas and by special problems. (3 credits)

Psychology

Abnormal Psychology

This course explores the biological and social factors in the development and treatment of psychopathology. (3 credits)

Statistics

Statistical Methods in Psychology

Introductory descriptive and inferential statistics is designed for the student who knows relatively little mathematics. Measures of central tendency and variability, statistical inference, correlation, and regression. (3 credits)

Utah

Brigham Young University
Department of Independent Study
Division of Continuing Education

206 Harman Continuing Education Building
Provo, UT   84602

(801) 378-2868

Geographic Access: Nationwide

DELIVERY SYSTEMS

Audiocassette
Audio-enhanced courses are primarily in foreign languages.

Computer Tutorials
Computer science courses require access to an IBM-PC or compatible.

Videocassette
Videotapes accompany various courses.

INSTITUTION DESCRIPTION

Brigham Young University is a private institution affiliated with the Church of Jesus Christ of Latter-day Saints. It was established in 1875 as Brigham Young Academy and adopted its present name in 1903.

The Department of Independent Study was created in 1921 as a part of the Division of Continuing Education. Media-assisted courses are among the many traditional correspondence courses offered by BYU.

Accreditation: NASC

Official/Contact: Ralph A. Rowley, Director

Admission Requirements: The only requirement is that students have a working knowledge of the English language. Enrollment in a course does not constitute admission to Brigham Young University.

Tuition: $66 per credit hour. Textbooks must be purchased by the student. Additional fees for computer disks, audio- and videocassettes are listed with the course description. *See* Courses Offered.

Degree Credit: BYU undergraduates may use up to 36 semester hours of independent study toward a baccalaureate degree or 18 hours toward an associate degree.

Grading: Examinations must be proctored. Students not residing in Utah County or near one of the BYU Centers of Continuing Education must take examinations under the supervision of an approved proctor. The grading system is A through E (failing). The minimum passing grade is D-. Credit is awarded in semester hour units.

Library: Students in the campus vicinity may use the BYU Library after obtaining a library card from the Independent Study Office. Other students are encouraged to utilize their local community libraries.

COURSES OFFERED

Computer Science

Elementary Computer Science
Computer organization, problem solving, and information systems, emphasizing use of the computer for problem solving and developing programming skills. Required minimum equipment includes an IBM-PC or compatible with 256K memory, DOS 2.1 or later, monochrome monitor with graphics card, one printer port, two disk drives, standard Pascal compiler, and one blank diskette and mailer for lesson submission. Twenty 5.25 inch double density instructional diskettes ($9.50). 27 lessons (including 7 programming assignments), 2 midcourse exams, final exam. (2 credits)

Dance

Aerobic Dance

Dance and other rigorous activities performed to music to attain cardiovascular fitness. Student must engage in the program for at least thirteen weeks to receive credit for the course. 6 lessons, final exam. Videotape: $25. (.5 credit)

Social Dance, Beginning

Traditional and popular ballroom dance and social skills. 7 lessons, final exam. Required: A person who already knows the dances to evaluate progress. Videotape $8, or 4 audiotapes $12. (.5 credit)

Education

Microcomputers in the Schools

Applying computer technology in public schools, evaluating educational software programs, using computer tools, computer programming in LogoWriter. Requires access to a microcomputer (Apple IIe or Apple IIGS preferred), a printer, and Appleworks or some other word processing program. 5 lessons, final exam. Computer disk rental fee for 14 computer disks: $25. Students must sign a computer software loan agreement certifying that they will not copy the software and will return it upon completion of the course. (1 credit)

Improving Discipline in the Schools

Principles and strategies to enhance teacher-student rapport, help the teacher understand and change student behavior, and help students make long-term behavioral improvements. 6 lessons, final exam. 1 audiotape: $3. (1 credit)

Educational Psychology

Introduction to the Education of Children with Visual Handicaps

Major issues in the education of those with visual handicaps, their characteristics and needs, and research gaps needing attention. 10 lessons, final exam. 11 audiocassette tapes: $33. (2 credits)

English

English at Home, Part 1

Introduction to the English language. Specifically for speakers of Spanish. Simple vocabulary and grammar using written and oral activities. 15 les-sons, 8 submitted. Fee: $58. 8 audiotapes: $24. (Noncredit)

English at Home, Part 2

Continuation of Part 1, also written specifically for speakers of Spanish. Reinforces and builds on materials learned in Part 1. 15 lessons, 8 submitted. Fee: $58. 8 tapes: $24. (Noncredit)

English at Home, Part 3

Continuation of Part 2 for any non-English speaker. Assumes some knowledge of English since all instructions are given in English. 20 lessons, 5 submitted. Fee: $58. 10 tapes: $30. (Noncredit)

Family Life

Nurturing Your Child's Natural Curiosity

Helping parents teach their own children through inquiry and discovery. Reinforcing the child's natural desire for discovery and learning. Recognizing when children want answers and when they want help. 6 lessons, no submissions. Fee: $30. 1 audiotape: $3. (Noncredit)

French

Intermediate French, Part 1

Reading, writing, conversation, vocabulary building, and review of grammar. 15 lessons, midterm and final exams. Audiotapes: $26.85. (4 credits)

Music

Guitar for Everyone, Part 1

A beginning course in guitar using tapes and extensive step-by-step instruction in folk and contemporary music. Logical progression in chords and technique. Skills, theory, elementary transposition, and arrangement are covered in a pleasant way as you learn to play forty-four songs. 8 lessons, 4 submitted. Fee: $58. 4 audiotapes, guitar pick, and capo: $13.25. (Noncredit)

Guitar for Everyone, Part 2

A continuation of Part 1. 8 lessons, 4 submitted. Fee: $58. 4 audiotapes, guitar pick, and capo: $13.25. (Noncredit)

Personal Development

How to Handle Conflict at Home and Other Places

A practical course in human relationships, emphasizing application to all aspects of life. Topics and skills include creating safe and trusting condition, accepting and liking self, developing equal relationships with others, breaking the cycle of hostility, placing responsibility properly, exploring consequences, and the commitment process. 9 lessons, 8 submitted. Fee: $58. 5 tapes: $15. (Noncredit)

Spiritual Roots of Human Relations
Uses Stephen R. Covey's books on human relations to apply gospel principles to human interactions and communications. Self-understanding, emphasizing commitment to self-improvement. 8 lessons. Fee: $58. 2 audiotapes: $6. (Noncredit)

Ancient Documents and the Pearl of Great Price
Based on videotapes of Hugh Nibley teaching. Fee: $73. 13 videotapes: $130. (Noncredit)

Spanish

Introductory Spanish
For those who have had no Spanish and desire maximum time for assimilation. Fundamental Spanish, emphasizing communication. 5 lessons, midterm and final exams. 5 audiotapes: $15. (2 credits)

Second-Year Spanish
Review of grammar, reading, writing, and conversation. 25 lessons (19 submitted), midterm and final exams. 9 audiotapes: $27. (4 credits)

University of Utah
Center for Independent Study
Division of Continuing Education
2180 Annex Building
Salt Lake City, UT 84112

(801) 581-6472 *Fax:* (801) 581-3165

Geographic Access: Worldwide

DELIVERY SYSTEMS

Computer Tutorials
These tutorials provide a self-paced program to help students master course material. Students are provided a disk with software that contains complete definitions of key concepts, terms, and theories from the assigned text. Following the guide in the course manual, the student studies the text and reviews the key concepts on the computer. The computer programs include a number of different models such as multiple choice, matching, recall, and a practice midterm and final examination. The "Computer Tutor" software requires an MS DOS computer with a 286 or higher processor, 540K RAM and either a 3.5 or 5.25 inch disk drive with a hard drive.

Videocassette
Videotapes are utilized in a variety of subjects.

INSTITUTION DESCRIPTION

The University of Utah was founded in 1850, two and one-half years after the arrival of the pioneers in the valley of the Great Salt Lake. The university has grown from a few classes held in a private parlor to a comprehensive institution of widely varied services.

The Center for Independent Study celebrated its 75th year in 1992. Video-enhanced courses are available in a variety of subjects.

Accreditation: NASC

Official/Contact: Cynthia White, Program Manager

Admission Requirements: Admission to an independent study course does not constitute admission to the University of Utah. The only requirement for enrollment is to have a working knowledge of English.

Tuition: Course fees are given with the course descriptions and include royalty fees for use of videotapes. See Courses Offered. Additional partially refundable deposit fees are required. Textbooks must be purchased by the student. MasterCard and VISA accepted. Fees for "Computer Tutor" courses in Sociology are given with the course descriptions.

Degree Credit: Independent Study does not offer external degrees and the program does not offer graduate credit courses.

Grading: Examinations must be proctored. Students unable to visit the campus office may take exams under the supervision of an official proctor, high school principal, school superintendent, college testing center, or independent testing center. Military students may contact their Education Officer for proctoring. Letter grades A-F are assigned. Credit is awarded in quarter hour units.

Library: An independent study student may obtain a student library card to use the facilities of the Marriott

Library. Students outside the continental United States are not able to borrow materials, but photocopies are available through interlibrary loan.

COURSES OFFERED

Art History

Art History

Masterpieces of the western world are presented in their cultural and historical settings. From elegant classical tradition to energetic and spontaneous modern art, each artistic movement is interpreted through its major paintings, sculptures, and works of architecture. Internationally known art experts and critics evaluate each work and help us understand why and how it was created. Course fee: $208 plus $10 for course manual. A $100 deposit ($75 refunded upon return of tapes rewound and in good condition) is required for the PBS video series, *Art of the Western World*. Midterm and final examination. (4 credits)

Communication Disorders

Beginning Sign Language

This course offers the student a basic communicative vocabulary in beginning sign language, the third most used language in the United States. Information on American Sign Language (ASL) and the deaf community will give the student a greater appreciation and understanding of this unique culture. Sign language involves finger spelling, the body, and face. Course fee: $126 plus $10 for course manual. Two videotapes: $45. Open captioned videotapes are available for the hearing impaired. Midterm and final examination. (3 credits)

English

Introduction to Creative Writing

Students will learn the basic principles involved in developing ideas and in using words to create settings and moods, to draw believable characters, to write dialogue, and to begin to create both poetry and fiction. A $100 videotape deposit ($75 refunded upon return of tapes rewound and in good condition) is required. 20 lessons, final portfolio. (4 credits)

Geography

Geography of Utah

Examines the state's physical, historical, cultural, economic, recreational, and political geography. The course is a learning package of 22 video programs and a comprehensive publication of program notes, maps, charts, and statistical materials. The course articulates major issues and problems that concern the citizens of Utah. All programs were shot on location in various parts of the state to simulate a field-trip experience. More than 150 experts appear in interviews to provide facts and feelings about Utah. The course presents Utah in a manner that is not possible in any other way. Course fee: $220 plus $10 for course manual. A $100 deposit ($75 refundable upon return of tapes rewound and in good condition) is required. 22 lessons, final examination. (5 credits)

Music

Basic Concepts of Music

The goal of this course is to improve students' ability to listen to music. The first part of the course breaks music down into its individual component parts such as rhythm, melody, harmony, and form. Students examine how these component parts interact in texture, meaning and emotion, words, movement, and style. Musical perception will be developed through active listening, increased ability to understand and apply musical terminology, expanded musical boundaries, increased awareness of the interaction of music with its social, cultural, and historical contexts. The student may then apply all this to making personal musical choices from a new level with new awareness. Course fee: $126 plus $10 for course manual. PBS audiotapes: $92.50 for 12 half-hour audio programs plus audio glossary and notation tutorial on 8 cassettes and core repertory of 4 one-hour cassettes containing 29 repertory pieces. 15 lessons, final examination. (3 credits)

Persian

Persian

Designed primarily to teach practical language skills—understanding, speaking, reading, and writing. The two styles of Persian, spoken and written, will be presented from the beginning. Systematic practice will be given on sound patterns of Persian and basic sentence structures. Useful vocabulary items will be used and practiced in the context of dialogues, reading lessons, and written assignments. The writing system and the correspondence of letters to sound segments is introduced. Reading, translating from and into Persian, and copying models of simple handwriting will be utilized to reinforce the mastery of the materials introduced in the textbooks. Offered in a three-course sequence: Persian 101, 102, and 103. Course fee: $210 for each course plus $10 for course manual. Album of 4 audiocassettes: $40.31. (5 credits)

Political Science

Political Science

The focus in this course is on the great issues that confront policy makers and citizens in America today. Achievement of a good working acquaintance with the U.S. Constitution is an important course goal. Course is based on the PBS video series entitled *The Constitution, That Delicate Balance.* Course fee: $208 plus $20 for course manual. 13 lessons, final examination. (4 credits)

Psychology

Psychology of Infancy and Childhood

The major focus of this course, based on the video series *The Growing Years*, is the interplay of biological factors, individual personality, social structure, and other environmental factors that shape the growing child. Topics of contemporary social significance include the effects of divorce, single parenthood, and parents' work and changing sexual attitudes and behavior. Course fee: $208 plus $10 for course manual. A $100 deposit ($75 refundable upon return of tapes rewound and in good condition) for the use of the video series. 20 lessons, midterm and final examination. (4 credits)

Sociology

Introduction to Sociology

By focusing sociological analysis on the great social changes from the past up to the present as well as on the enduring personal issues of the individual in society, this course expands the frontiers of sociological inquiry and integrates them with the basic concerns of an introductory level course. Course fee: $210 plus $10 for course manual. Computer disk: $25. 24 lessons, written project, midterm and final examination. (5 credits)

Introduction to Research Methods

Presents the application of measurements and research methodology to sociological data. Course fee: $210 plus $10 for course manual. Computer disk: $25. 19 lessons, written project, midterm and final examination. (5 credits)

Introduction to Social Statistics

This course is designed to provide an introduction to statistics for students in the social sciences—sociology and related fields such as criminal justice, political science, social work, psychology, public administration, and education. It is designed to fill the perceived need for an understandable treatment of the rationale and use of statistical methods. Course fee: $210 plus $10 for course manual. Computer disk: $25. 16 lessons, written project, midterm and final examination. (5 credits)

Sociology of Marriage and Family

This course provides an assessment of the nature of marriage and family life in contemporary American society. Topics discussed include a discussion of today's aftermath of the sexual revolution and why much that was believed true of sexual attitudes before and during the revolution is now obsolete. Also discussed is the recent and unprecedented "value shift" of men toward greater involvement in the family, the way the move has benefited both sexes and the new problems it has created. The rise in egalitarian marriage, husbands' more androgynous attitude toward sex roles, and the mass movement of wives and mothers into the job market are also discussed. Course fee: $210 plus $10 for course manual. Computer disk: $25. 20 lessons, written project, midterm and final examination. (4 credits)

Current Social Problems in America

This course provides an assessment of the social problems of particular concern in contemporary society. Discussion covers crime and social deviance, family and generational problems, conflicts of religion and education, health care issues, population trends and problems associated with modernization and industrialization, discrimination, prejudice, poverty, civil liberty, mass communication and environment as influenced by society. Course fee: $210 plus $10 for course manual. Computer disk: $25. 19 lessons, term project, midterm and final examination. (5 credits)

Introduction to Criminology

Provides a basic overview of the field of criminology. The traditional emphasis of sociologists on the causes of crime are discussed along with the functioning of the courts and correctional systems. The course covers how law relates to traditional topics in criminology and the role of the courts in the reformation of the criminal justice system. The course concludes with an assessment of society's response to criminal behavior. Course fee: $168 plus $10 for course manual. Computer disk: $25. 16 lessons, written project, midterm and final examination. (4 credits)

Juvenile Delinquency

The study of delinquency focuses on the rights of children, their needs, care and treatment. The focus of the course is on contemporary issues in law, theory, policy, and practice in delinquency control and treatment. Course fee: $168 plus $10 for course manual. Computer disk: $25. 20 lessons, written project, midterm and final examination. (4 credits)

The Criminal Justice System

The focus of the course is on the major issues confronting the criminal justice system. The course is also concerned with the future of criminal justice, including an emphasis on high-tech crime, computer crime, technology, international terrorism, and changes in individual rights in the face of burgeoning crime fighting technologies. Course fee: $126 plus $10 for course manual. Computer disk: $25. 15 lessons, written project, midterm and final examination. (3 credits)

Law Enforcement in Society

Provides a basic overview of the entire field of law enforcement: its role in society, the relationship between police and community, the history of law enforcement, the nature and importance of civil rights and civil liberties, crime in the U.S. and the role of the police in its control, organization of police departments, and training of police officers including content and orientation. Course fee: $168 plus $10 for course manual. Computer disk: $25. 21 lessons, written project, midterm and final examination. (4 credits)

Statistics

Elementary Statistics

Introduces the student to the basic concepts of probability and statistics, emphasizing the practical applicability of these ideas in everyday decision making. Topics include describing data, finding data relationships, collecting useful data, understanding probability models and distributions, estimating population values from sample data, and testing hypotheses. Course fee: $208 plus $10 for course manual. A deposit of $100 ($75 refundable upon return of tapes rewound and in good condition) is required. 20 lessons, midterm and final examination. (4 credits)

Utah State University
Independent Study Programs

Logan, UT   84322-5000

(801) 750-2014

Geographic Access: Nationwide

DELIVERY SYSTEMS

Audiocassette

Many courses require the use of audiotapes for which the student must supply an audiocassette player.

Interactive Audio/Video

Courses utilizing this technology are transmitted via Com-Net, USU's statewide telecommunications system. For courses in this media, contact Com-Net, Utah State University, Logan, UT 84322-3720 or telephone (801) 750-1698.

Videocassette

Videotapes are included with course materials requirements in various courses described below. Students must have access to a VHS player/recorder.

INSTITUTION DESCRIPTION

Utah State University (USU), founded in 1888, is a member of the American Land-Grant Association of Colleges and State Universities. A rich curriculum is offered for technical, scientific, and professional training at both the undergraduate and graduate levels.

Through the services of University Extension, USU provides a liberal program of educational offerings for individuals who cannot come to the campus for organized coursework. This program includes off-campus resident classes organized in selected centers, correspondence courses, educational conferences and institutes, and a number of other services.

Media-assisted courses are described below. In addition to these courses, USU offers a statewide telecommunications system called Com-Net. Com-Net courses are credit courses offered during day and evening hours. Electronic writing boards and slow-scan (freeze frame) TVs are used to transmit class lectures to center locations throughout Utah. In addition to the writing board and slow scan, each center location has a public address system for two-way communication with the faculty and other students throughout the state.

Accreditation: NASC

Official/Contact: Gary S. Poppleton, Director

Admission Requirements: Admission to Utah State University is not required for enrollment in a course. Registration may be accomplished at any time during the year.

Tuition: $35 per credit plus any audiovisual materials fee (tapes, slides, videos).

Degree Credit: Students of USU may apply up to 45 credits earned through distance learning courses to a degree.

Grading: Examinations must be proctored. Students who do not live in Logan and are unable to come to the Independent Study Office to take the final examination should send the name and address of one of the following who would be willing to administer the examination: a college dean, superintendent, principal, county agent, librarian, or military educational director. Relatives are not eligible to proctor exams. The grading system is A, B, C, D, F with D being the minimum passing grade. A pass/fail option is also available. Credit is awarded in quarter hour units.

Library: If local facilities cannot supply the student with necessary resource materials, the USU Merrill Library can be contacted for assistance through its Distance Education Library Services.

COURSES OFFERED

Art

Basic Typography Design

Typography is the art and process of working with type. The student will study, organize, and communicate the technical concepts of type through a series of projects. Conveying specific ideas and creating aesthetic designs with type will be emphasized. This is not a course in calligraphy or brush lettering. 15 assignments. Slides optional: $10 rental fee, $7 refunded when materials are returned in good condition. (3 credits)

Biology

Human Physiology

A survey of human physiology that deals with the functioning of the human body. It provides an understanding of various body functions and provides the student with a vocabulary that will permit him/her to understand better and appreciate the values of scientific investigation. 32 assignments. Audiocassette tapes required: $25. (5 credits)

Communication Disorders

Listening Problems in the Classroom

Identification of children with hearing and auditory perceptual problems, management of classroom acoustics, hearing aids, and FM radio equipment. 16 assignments. Videotape required: $20 rental fee, $15 refunded when materials are returned in good condition. (3 credits)

Listening and Speech Training for the Hearing Impaired

Basic considerations, programs, materials, and methods for providing listening and speech testing and training for children and adults with hearing impairments. 4 cassettes and 1 video will be included with the textbook (no used books or materials will be refunded by the bookstore). 16 assignments. (3 credits)

Family Life

Child Abuse and Neglect: A Multidisciplinary Approach

This course is designed to provide a comprehensive overview of a significant social problem. Audiocassette tapes and slides are required: $20 rental fee, $15 refunded when all materials are returned in good condition. 14 assignments. (3 credits)

Update on Family Issues

This course is designed to provide the student with an awareness of the current issues that have a direct impact on marriages and families. 1 paper, 3 exams. Videotapes are required: $20 rental fee, $15 refunded when materials are returned in good condition. (3 credits)

Update on Children's Issues

This course consists of videotaped information, assigned readings from the text, and three exams. The exams cover both video and written materials. Videotape rental: $20, $15 refunded when materials are returned in good condition. (3 credits)

French

Elementary French 101

A beginning course using the "Natural Approach." Work through the textbook with the instructor guiding step-by-step on audiocassette. 25 assignments. Audiocassette tapes are required: $15 rental fee, $10 refunded when materials are returned in good condition. (5 credits)

Elementary French 102

Again, using the "Natural Approach," the instructor guides the student step-by-step on audiocassette. 25 assignments. Audiocassette tapes are required: $15 rental fee, $10 refunded when materials are returned in good condition. (5 credits)

Landscape Architecture

Introduction to Landscape Architecture

This course endeavors to acquaint the student with the landscape in his/her environment, as a practical approach to the pleasure that comes from appreciation and understanding of subject. Emphasis is placed on design and arrangement of outdoor space as it relates to home living, however, public buildings and areas are discussed because of their interrelationship to each other and because all of these areas are the concern of the landscape architect. 11 assignments. Audiocassette tapes and slides are required: $10 rental fee, $7 refunded when materials are returned in good condition. (3 credits)

Music

Enjoying Music

A nontechnical course designed to bring about a better understanding and enjoyment of music serving a wide range of musical styles and forms. The course is complete with taped listening exercises and examples. 15 assignments. Audiocassette tapes are required: $15 rental fee, $10 refunded when materials are returned in good condition. (3 credits)

Fundamentals of Music

Musicians and laymen, at all levels of talent and perception, are fascinated by the sound of music through a systematic study of the basic characteristics of sound and the vocabulary of the musician. The purpose of this course is to familiarize the layman with the language of music and to suggest prerequisite skills for continued understanding, utilization, and enjoyment. Audiocassette tape is required: $5 fee. (3 credits)

Oceanography

Oceanography

A multidisciplinary subject that draws upon and integrates many fields of science. A combination of information from geology, physics, chemistry, and biology provides an overview of ocean processes. Includes discussion of man's interrelationship with the oceans historically and some of the social, economic, and political ramifications thereof. Videotapes are required: $20 rental fee, $15 refunded when materials are returned in good condition. 25 assignments. (4 credits)

Spanish

Elementary Spanish 101

A beginning course not open to students having had more than one year of Spanish in high school or the equivalent. Audiocassette tapes are required: $15 rental fee, $10 refunded when materials are returned in good condition. (5 credits)

Elementary Spanish 102

A beginning course open to students having had Spanish 101 or at least one, but not more than two years of Spanish in high school. Audiocassette tapes are required: $15 rental fee, $10 refunded when all materials are returned in good condition. (5 credits)

Elementary Spanish 103

A beginning course open to students having completed Spanish 102 or at least one, but not more than three, years of Spanish in high school. Audiocassette tapes are required: $15 rental fee, $10 refunded when all materials are returned in good condition. (5 credits)

Intermediate Spanish 201

An intermediate course open to students having completed Spanish 103 or at least two, but not more than three, years of Spanish in high school. Audiocassette tapes are required: $15 rental fee, $10 refunded when all materials are returned in good condition. (5 credits)

Intermediate Spanish 202

An intermediate course open to students having completed Spanish 201 or at least three, but not more than four years of Spanish in an integrated high school program. Audiocassette tapes are required: $15 rental fee, $10 refunded when materials are returned in good condition. (5 credits)

Weber State University
Continuing Education
Independent Study
Ogden, UT   84408-4007

(800) 848-7770

Geographic Access: Worldwide

DELIVERY SYSTEMS

Audiocassette
Several of the courses listed utilize audiotapes as supplemental materials.

Computer Tutorials
A series of courses in Gerontology is available in a computer-assisted tutorial format for an additional nominal fee (inquire to the Independent Study Office).

Interactive Audio/Video
Courses in Computer Information Systems are conducted on interactive video disk equipment in the Wattis Business Building on the campus. Lab assistants are always on duty to answer questions, and an instructor is available for further information.

Videocassette
The course in Human Development utilizes both videotapes and audiotapes.

INSTITUTION DESCRIPTION

Weber State University is a member of the American Council on Education and the American Association of State Colleges and Universities. Through Independent Study, students are offered a self-paced, individualized mode of study in courses that meet degree requirements, enhance professional skills, or achieve personal goals. In addition to the traditional correspondence courses, Weber State offers audio-enhanced courses, interactive video classes, and a computer-tutorial sequence of courses in gerontology. These specialized courses are described. *See* Courses Offered.

Accreditation: NASC

Official/Contact: Tamara Aird, Program Administrator

Admission Requirements: Anyone may enroll in an independent study course. These courses may be taken for university credit or noncredit. If credit is desired, the applicant must fulfill university admission requirements prior to completing the course.

Tuition: $40 per credit hour. Textbooks can be ordered by mail directly from the Independent Study Office. A course may include tapes, kits, or additional materials. These materials will be checked out to the student upon payment of a materials deposit. Upon return to the Independent Study Office, a refund will be made. VISA and MasterCard accepted.

Degree Credit: A full degree cannot be earned through independent study, although Weber State University students may apply 45 credits of independent study toward a bachelor's degree. Students desiring to transfer credit earned to another institution should consult their colleges/universities for regulations governing the transfer of credit.

Grading: Examinations must be taken at the WSU Testing Center if the student resides within 50 miles of the campus. Otherwise, examinations must be supervised by a qualified person approved by the Independent Study Office. Letter grades (A, B, C, D, or E) are assigned. Credit is awarded in quarter hour units.

Library: Students living near the campus have the use of all library facilities of WSU. Students are encouraged to utilize the resources of their local community libraries.

COURSES OFFERED

Computer Information Systems

Hardware/DOS

An exploration of the personal computer system, the functions of each component, and how to use DOS, the disk operating system. An interactive video course. Fee: $60. (1 credit)

Introduction to Word Processing

An understanding of the concept of word processing and how it differs from the typewriter. WordPerfect is the software used for instruction. An interactive video course. Fee: $60. (1 credit)

Introduction to Spreadsheets

The student learns spreadsheet functions, manipulations, and applications using Lotus 1, 2, 3. An interactive video course. (1 credit)

Introduction to Database Management Systems

Examines the basic components and applications of dBase IV Plus. An interactive video course. (1 credit)

English

Fiction Writing

Techniques of narration and description involving character in conflict. Basic, simplified approaches to the short story. Audiotape (optional) deposit $10. (3 credits)

Poetry Writing

This course is designed for those who want to learn to write poetry or who are already writing it and would like to learn more about the techniques of poetry writing. Audiotape (optional) deposit $10. (3 credits)

Gerontology

Gerontological Development and Policy

National awareness, historical growth and policy development in response to gerontology in the United States will be covered. Specific examples will include social and health insurances, White House conferences, legislation, Administration on Aging, National Institute on Aging, scientific and applied groups, and the financing of programs. A computer-assisted tutorial. (3 credits)

Aging: Adaptation and Behavior

An examination of the physical and psychological processes of aging. The emphasis is on behavioral and social adaptation to these processes. A computer-assisted tutorial. (3 credits)

Ethnicity and the Aging

A study of the importance of ethnicity and social policy on the social functioning of older people. A computer-assisted tutorial. (3 credits)

Societal Response to Aging

A study of how aging, as a dimension of social reorganization, touches every life, every home, every community, and every relationship. A computer-assisted tutorial. (3 credits)

Retirement: Adjustment/Planning

This course is designed to cover aspects of retirement relating to job change or discontinuance. The processes, events, social roles, and phases of life will be presented. A computer-assisted tutorial. (3 credits)

Human Development

Human Development

Fundamentals of growth and development relating to effective human relationships within the family and a study of behavior and cultural influences from infancy through adolescence. Videotapes include *Drama of Life, Roots of Happiness, Terrible Two's, Frustration Four's, Cipher in the Snow*, and *What do You Think?* Audiotapes are *Drama of Life*, parts 1 and 2. Deposit for all tapes needed for this class is $35. (5 credits)

Marketing

Fundamental Selling Techniques

A retail, wholesale, and direct selling course. Emphasis on mastering and applying the fundamentals of selling. Preparation for and execution of sales demonstrations required. Sales demonstration videotape (optional) deposit: $25. (4 credits)

Music

Evolution of Jazz

A history of the evolution of jazz, important jazz musicians, and various eras or changes in jazz since 1900. Audiotapes from each era enhance the course. Audiotape deposit $10. Student will also need to listen to a set of record albums for which a deposit of $50 is required. (3 credits)

Virginia

Northern Virginia Community College
Extended Learning Institute

8333 Little River Turnpike
Annandale, VA 22003-3796

(703) 323-3379 *Fax:* (703) 323-3392

Geographic Access: District of Columbia, Maryland, Virginia

DELIVERY SYSTEMS

Broadcast Television

These courses employ videotaped televised instruction, with some using up to 15 hours of TV and others as little as 2 hours. ELI leases some telecourses through PBS and produces some locally in NVCC's fully-equipped TV studio. The NVCC Telecommunications Center has remote and studio production capabilities, satellite uplink and downlink capabilities, its own cable TV channel, air time on other cable companies, and teleconference facilities. A limited number of videotapes are kept on reserve at campus library resource centers. Rental tapes are available for $50 each from College Video Corporation. Details are provided with the course guide.

Computer Conferencing

Students use either their own computer and modem or a campus terminal to dial in to the college's mainframe computer to submit assignments, comment on each other's work, and to enter into a dialogue with the instructor and other students.

Interactive Audio/Video

NVCC offered its first nine courses via this delivery method in 1990. Each campus participates in live instruction with two-way audio and video communication.

INSTITUTION DESCRIPTION

Northern Virginia Community College (NVCC) is one of the two largest multicampus community colleges in the United States and is the largest educational institution in Virginia. NVCC was founded in 1964 and has grown to an enrollment of over 35,000 students. The college serves Arlington, Fairfax, Loudoun, and Prince William counties. It is a member of the Virginia Community College System of 23 colleges. NVCC offers courses and degrees in more than 65 disciplines. The college operates on the semester system with a summer session.

The Extended Learning Institute (ELI) was established in 1975 as the distance learning administrative unit of NVCC. It has enrolled over 100,000 students and currently offers 75 college credit courses delivered by mixtures of cable and broadcast television, video- and audiotapes, print-based media, and computer conferencing. ELI has a director, four instructional designers, registration staff, course specialists, and support staff. Over 30 full-time faculty from all five campuses teach part of their load at ELI.

Accreditation: SACS

Official/Contact: Randal A. Lemke, Director

Admission Requirements: High school graduation or GED. For most courses, registration is continuous throughout the year. Television courses usually have registration deadlines. Courses allow four- or six-months for completion, but a student may finish any time within those time periods. Some courses require completion of prerequisites. A course may be audited rather than pursued for credit (regular tuition rate applies).

Tuition: State resident $44 per credit hour; out-of-state student $145 per credit hour.

Degree Credit: ELI offers a means for students to take all, or some, of their courses toward an associate degree in either Business Administration or General Studies. Prospective degree students should contact a campus counselor or an academic advisor to plan their program of study.

Grading: The letter system is used (A-F). Examinations must be taken on campus in a Learning Lab. Typically, there are four exams in a course. In limited situations, a proctor from outside the college may be permitted to give a student the exam.

Library: ELI maintains a library workstation that can be accessed from the student's home via computer/modem/communication software. Searches can be made through the college catalog or periodical abstracts. Reference librarians are also available to help.

COURSES OFFERED

Accounting

Principles of Accounting I

A six-month course that requires some computer use. (3 credits)

Principles of Accounting II

A six-month course that requires some computer use. (3 credits)

Art

Art in World Culture

A telecourse entitled *Art in the Western World* is viewed. Includes nine one-hour programs. Cable broadcast. (3 credits)

Biology

General Biology I

This course requires one trip to the Alexandria campus science lab and two trips to the Smithsonian Institution. Requires viewing 13 half-hour television lessons on cable TV. (4 credits)

General Biology II

Same requirements as General Biology I. (4 credits)

Business Administration

Principles of Management

The telecourse entitled *Business of Management* is viewed in this six-month course. Twenty-six 30-minute programs are broadcast via local cable television channel. (3 credits)

Business Law I

This sixteen-week course requires the viewing of a telecourse entitled *Business and the Law*. Twenty-four 30-minute programs are broadcast via local cable channel. (3 credits)

Computer Information Systems

Introduction to Information Systems

This six-month course requires the use of a personal computer for short word processing and BASIC programming assignments. An online computer conference is optional. (3 credits)

Economics

Principles of Economics I

The first part of a six-month course. Requires viewing *Economics U$A* that includes fourteen 30-minute programs. Cable broadcast. (3 credits)

Principles of Economics II

A continuation of Principles of Economics I. A six-month course includes fourteen 30-minute programs. Cable broadcast. (3 credits)

Survey of Economics

This six-month course utilizes the telecourse *Economics U$A* that includes eighteen 30-minute programs. (3 credits)

English

Technical Writing

An online computer conference is optional for this sixteen-week course. (3 credits)

Survey of American Literature II

Covers literature from Reconstruction to the present. An online computer conference is optional for this six-month course. (3 credits)

World Literature I

This six-month course requires viewing 10 televised lessons. Cable broadcast. (3 credits)

Women in Literature I

A six-month course covering the 17th to 19th centuries. An online computer conference is optional. (3 credits)

Women in Literature II

This six-month course covers the 20th century. An online computer conference is optional. (3 credits)

Film and Literature (Section 90)

Focuses on mysteries in film and fiction. Requires watching a number of films available for home viewing from local libraries or video stores. A six-month course. (3 credits)

Film and Literature (Section 93)

Focuses on critical viewing of films through the study of major elements of cinematic meaning. Requires watching a number of films available for home viewing from local libraries or video stores. A six-month course. (3 credits)

Finance

Personal Finance

The telecourse entitled *Personal Finance and Money Management* is viewed. Thirteen 1-hour programs are cable broadcast. (3 credits)

History

History of Western Civilization I

This sixteen-week course utilizes the telecourse entitled *The Western Tradition I*. It covers history through the 17th century. Cable broadcast. (3 credits)

History of Western Civilization II

The telecourse entitled *The Western Tradition II* covers history from the 17th century to the present in sixteen 1-hour programs. A sixteen-week course. Cable broadcast. (3 credits)

United States History I

This sixteen-week course covers from the pre-Columbian times through the Civil War. Requires either viewing seven 1-hour televised lectures broadcast locally or regular participation in a computer conference. Also requires 4 projects involving visits to local historical sites or libraries. (3 credits)

United States History II

Covers from Reconstruction to the present. Requires either viewing seven 1-hour televised lectures (cable broadcast) or regular participation in a computer conference. During the sixteen-week course, the student is required to complete 4 projects involving visits to local historical sites or libraries. (3 credits)

Marketing

Principles of Marketing

This six-month telecourse includes twelve 1-hour programs. Cable broadcast. (3 credits)

Mathematics

Technical Mathematics I

An eighteen-week course with televised lectures. Cable broadcast. (3 credits)

Technical Mathematics II

Also an eighteen-week course with televised lectures. Cable broadcast. (3 credits)

Music

Music Appreciation I

Covers elements of music from the Middle Ages through Classical Periods. Requires listening to 7 half-hour instructional audiotapes. Musical selections from an additional 12 cassettes or CDs available in the college bookstore (at significant extra cost) or at a campus library resource center. A six-month course. (3 credits)

Music Appreciation II

Covers the Romantic Period through modern times. Requires listening to 9 half-hour instructional audiotapes. Musical selections from an additional 12 cassettes or CDs available in the college bookstore (at significant extra cost) or at a campus library resource center. A sixteen-week course. (3 credits)

Office Systems Technology

Word Processing I: Introduction to WordPerfect

Requires access to WordPerfect version 5.1 on an IBM compatible computer with printer. A six-month course. (3 credits)

Word Processing II: Advanced WordPerfect

Requires access to WordPerfect version 5.1 on an IBM compatible computer with printer. A six-month course. (3 credits)

Philosophy

Introduction to Philosophy I

A telecourse entitled *From Socrates to Sartre* requires the viewing of twenty-four 30-minute programs. A six-month course. Cable broadcast. (3 credits)

Introduction to Philosophy II

This course includes five 1-hour televised lectures. A six-month course. Cable broadcast. (3 credits)

Logic I

This course includes five 1-hour televised programs. Cable broadcast. A six-month course. (3 credits)

Logic II

Videotaped lectures are utilized in this course (no broadcast). Tapes are available only in library resource centers. A six-month course. (3 credits)

Political Science

U.S. Government I

Part 1 of a telecourse entitled *Government by Consent*. Thirteen 30-minute programs. Cable broadcast. A six-month course. (3 credits)

U.S. Government II

Part 2 of a telecourse entitled *Government by Consent*. Includes thirteen 30-minute programs. Cable broadcast. A six-month course. (3 credits)

Psychology

Introduction to Psychology I

Includes the viewing of one videotape broadcast locally or viewed at the campus library resource center. A sixteen-week course. (3 credits)

Washington

City University
Distance Learning Program

335 116th Avenue Southeast
Bellevue, WA   98004

(800) 426-5596 *Fax:* (206) 746-2567

Geographic Access: Worldwide

DELIVERY SYSTEMS

Videocassette
Videotapes supplement the textbook and study guide for the courses listed and described. *See* Courses Offered.

INSTITUTION DESCRIPTION

City University is a private, independent, decentralized nonprofit institution established in 1973. It provides instruction in communities throughout the state of Washington as well as sites in Oregon, California, British Columbia, and Switzerland.

The Distance Learning Program offers courses to students around the world who are interested in taking one class or earning an entire degree. Courses begin on the first day of each month throughout the year and are 10 weeks in duration unless you are stationed outside of North America or are an incarcerated student, in which case the courses are 20 weeks in duration. The deadline for enrollment in a course is the 20th of the month preceding the month in which the course begins.

Accreditation: NASC

Official/Contact: Michael A. Pastore, President

Admission Requirements: High school graduation or equivalent. Formal application must be made to Admissions, 14506 NE 20th, Bellevue, WA 98007 with a nonrefundable $50 application fee.

Tuition: General Education courses and all lower division courses are $53 per credit hour plus books and materials. Upper division undergraduate courses are $152 per credit hour plus books and materials. Graduate courses are $210 per credit hour plus books and materials. VISA, MasterCard, Discover, and American Express accepted.

Degree Credit: Up to 65 lower division credits from approved sources may be transferred and applied to the Associate of Science in General Studies degree, and up to 90 lower division and 45 upper division credits may be transferred and applied to the Bachelor's degree programs if such credits are approved and applicable.

Grading: Examinations must be proctored. Letter grades are assigned. Credit is awarded in quarter hour units.

Library: Students are encouraged to use the library facilities in their local communities.

COURSES OFFERED

English

English Composition
A writing course designed to teach students the arts of style, organization, and thoughtful content. Students are encouraged to think critically so that their writing style will reflect their ability to isolate crucial issues, reason logically, analyze problems effectively, and make sound decisions. A series of supplemental videotapes illustrate how practical writing methods should be applied. A lower division course. (5 credits)

Environmental Science

Environmental Science
A course that explores environmental change on a global scale, emphasizing the fundamental concepts of matter, energy, and ecology as applied to contemporary concerns. Environmental issues impacting twenty-nine countries are illustrated in an accompanying video series in order to develop an international perspective on the environmental challenges facing the planet. A lower division course. (5 credits)

Geoscience

An Introduction to Geoscience: The Planet Earth
A survey of earth science. Topics emphasized are recent developments in atomspheric chemistry, geology, and astrophysics. The course will also explore the impact humans will continue to have on the fate of the earth. Supplemental video lectures narrated by world famous atmospheric chemists, geologists, and astrophysicists expose the student to recent discoveries in the field of earth science. A lower division course. (5 credits)

History

History of Western Tradition I
An analysis of the ideas, events, and institutions that shaped life in the Western world from prehistory to the Renaissance. A series of video lectures expose the student to works illustrating the development of Western civilization exhibited at the Metropolitan Museum of Art in New York City. A lower division course. (5 credits)

History of Western Tradition II
An analysis of the ideas, events, and institutions that shaped life in the Western world from the Reformation to the present day. A series of supplemental video lectures exposes the student to works illustrating the development of Western civilization exhibited at the Metropolitan Museum of Art in New York City. A lower division course. (5 credits)

The Nuclear Age: World War II to the Present
An examination of nuclear strategy in the context of international and domestic politics since the development of atomic and hydrogen weapons. A series of videotapes details the development of contemporary nuclear politics. The impact of the collapse of the Soviet Union and formation of a Russian confederation will also be explored in the course. A lower division course. (5 credits)

Humanities

Art of the Western World
A survey of major paintings, sculptures, and works of architecture of the Western world. Each masterpiece will be examined in terms of artistic technique and value as well as the historical trends reflected in these works. Supplemental video instruction exposes students to great works of art located throughout the Western world. A lower division course. (5 credits)

History and Culture of the African Continent
An example of the complexities of the African continent. Special attention will be devoted to the impact of nineteenth-century colonialism, the slave trade, twentieth-century political instability, and the role of Africa as an international economic and political power. A series of supplemental video lectures filmed on location in sixteen African countries expose the student to African geography and culture. A lower division course. (5 credits)

Great American Poets
This course utilizes the videotape series, *Voices and Visions*, and text materials to provide a lively overview of thirteen major American poets and their poetry. Through the work of these poets the student is introduced to basic elements of poetry, such as voice, rhythm, structure, and sound. The student is also introduced to the unique factors which have combined to produce this diverse, distinctive body of original American poetry. A lower division course. (5 credits)

Neuroscience

An Introduction to Neuroscience: Brain, Mind, and Behavior
A course designed to expose students to the latest neuroscientific understanding of the brain and its relation to behavior. Emphasis will be placed on the theme that all the normal functions of the brain and the disorders of the diseased brain, no matter how complex, will ultimately be explained in terms of basic components of the brain and the ways in which they interact. A supplemental series of videotapes narrated by world famous brain scientists expose the students to the brain's operating principles. A lower division course. (5 credits)

Political Science

Interpreting the American Constitution
An examination of the evolution of the Constitution with an emphasis upon contemporary constitutional issues such as executive privilege, executive war powers and covert action, the death penalty, freedom of the press, the right to live and the right to die, and debates surrounding affirmative action and reverse discrimination. Supplemental videotapes expose the student to the opinions of Gerald Ford, Gloria Steinem, Bill Moyers, and Archibald Cox, among others. A lower division course. (5 credits)

University of Washington
Distance Learning
University of Washington Extension

5001 25th Avenue, Northeast
Seattle, WA 98195

(800) 543-2320 *Fax:* (206) 685-9359

Geographic Access: Worldwide

DELIVERY SYSTEMS

Audiocassette
Audiocassettes are used as supplementary material in all language courses.

Computer Tutorials
Interactive tutorial package accompanies course materials and requires that the student have access to an IBM-PC.

Videocassette
Supplementary videotapes enhance the course content.

INSTITUTION DESCRIPTION

The University of Washington, founded in 1861, is located in the metropolitan Seattle area. Its 680-acre main campus is one of the largest in the western United States. The UW community consists of approximately 33,000 students, 3,500 faculty, and 12,000 staff.

Each registrant for a Distance Learning course receives a study guide containing the course outline, a list of required texts and materials, study instructions, supplementary information, and specific lesson assignments. Audio- and videotapes expand the scope of a distance learning course.

Accreditation: NASC

Official/Contact: Muriel Dance, Coordinator

Admission Requirements: Distance Learning Courses are open to any high school graduate or person 18 or older. Enrollment does not constitute admission to the University of Washington.

Tuition: $55 per credit. $15 registration fee. Master-Card and VISA accepted. Students must purchase textbooks which can be obtained from the University Book Store. Additional fees for audio- and/or videocassette tapes are given with the course description. *See* Courses Offered.

Degree Credit: Students who have an associate degree can accumulate as many as 45 additional credits via distance learning courses before applying to the University of Washington to earn a four-year degree.

Grading: Letter grades are assigned. Students have the option of taking courses on a satisfactory/nonsatisfactory basis. Examinations must be proctored. Credit is awarded in quarter hour units.

Library: The Odegaard Undergraduate Library supports all officially registered students. Distance Learning students living outside the Seattle area may request specific library materials through Resource Sharing Services located in the Suzallo Library on the UW campus. Local students have full access to the Language Center and the Micro Computer Lab on the UW campus.

COURSES OFFERED

Anthropology

Principles of Sociocultural Anthropology
Comparison of lifeways of various non-Western and Western peoples. Introduction to basic theories and methods used in the field. 4 lessons, 1 examination. Videotape: $15. (5 credits)

Chemistry

General Chemistry C140
For science, engineering, and other majors who plan to take a year or more of chemistry courses. Atomic nature of matter, nuclear chemistry, stoichiometry,

periodic table, quantum concepts, chemical bonding, gas laws. 7 lessons, 3 examinations. Videotape: $10. (4 credits)

General Chemistry C150

Introduction to inorganic chemistry, solids, solutions, acid-base, chemical equilibrium. 7 lessons, 3 examinations. Videotape: $10. (4 credits)

Danish

Elementary Danish C101

Fundamentals of written and oral Danish. 12 lessons, 2 examinations. 2 audiocassettes: $8. (5 credits)

Elementary Danish C102

A continuation of Danish C101. 13 lessons, 2 examinations. 2 audiocassettes: $8. (5 credits)

Economics

Introduction to Microeconomics

Introduction to analysis of markets: consumer demand, production, exchange, the price system, resource allocation, government intervention. 5 lessons, 2 examinations. Optional interactive tutorial package available for IBM-PC: $10. (5 credits)

Introduction to Macroeconomics

Analysis of the aggregate economy: national income, inflation, business fluctuations, unemployment, monetary system, federal budget, international trade and finance. 5 lessons, 2 examinations. Optional interactive tutorial package available for IBM-PC: $10. (5 credits)

French

Elementary French C101

Essentials of French grammar. Although all assignments are written, oral practice is provided through the use of tape recordings. 12 lessons, 3 examinations. 5 audiocassettes: $20. (5 credits)

Elementary French C102

A continuation of Elementary French C101. 9 lessons, 3 examinations. 4 audiocassettes: $20. (5 credits)

Elementary French C103

A continuation of Elementary French C102. 8 lessons, 3 examinations. 4 audiocassettes: $20. (5 credits)

German

First-Year German (C101)

For persons who have had no previous instruction in German. Acquisition of a fairly large vocabulary. Grammar practice in reading and writing. 28 lessons, 2 examinations. 5 audiocassettes: $20. (5 credits)

First-Year German C102

A continuation of First-Year German C101. 28 lessons, 2 examinations. 6 audiocassettes: $20. (5 credits)

First-Year German C103

A continuation of First-Year German C102. 28 lessons, 2 examinations. 3 audiocassettes: $12. (5 credits)

Italian

Elementary Italian C101

Basic study of Italian grammar and idiomatic usage of the language. All assignments and examinations are written, but oral practice is provided by the use of required tape recordings. 27 lessons, 3 examinations. 6 audiocassettes: $25. (5 credits)

Elementary Italian C102

A continuation of Elementary Italian C101. 28 lessons, 2 examinations. One audiocassette: $4. (5 credits)

Elementary Italian C103

A continuation of Elementary Italian C102. 28 lessons, 2 examinations. One cassette: $4. Supplemental readings: $20. (5 credits)

Mathematics

Intermediate Algebra

Similar to the third term of high school algebra. 10 lessons, 3 examinations. Course fee: $165. Optional videotapes: $80, refund of $45 on return. (Noncredit)

Political Science

Introduction to American Politics

Introduction to people, institutions, and politics in the American political system. Provides various ways of thinking about how significant problems, crises, and conflicts of American society are resolved politically. 5 lessons, 1 examination. 6 audiocassettes: $24. Supplemental reading: $4.50. (5 credits)

The Politics of Mass Communication in America

Role of mass audiences in politics from the standpoint of the communication strategies used to shape their political involvement. Topics include social structure and political participation, political propaganda and persuasion, the political uses of public opinion, and the mass media and politics. 4 lessons, 1 examination. Videotape: $15. Supplemental reading: $30. (5 credits)

Russian

First-Year Russian C101

Introduction to Russian. Emphasis on oral communication with limited vocabulary. Basic grammatical features and some reading. Student must purchase a blank cassette tape for oral exercises. 12 lessons, 3 examinations. 4 audiocassettes: $20. (5 credits)

First-Year Russian C102

A continuation of First-Year Russian C101. 12 lessons, 3 examinations. 4 audiocassettes: $20. (5 credits)

First-Year Russian C103

A continuation of First-Year Russian C102. 12 lessons, 3 examinations. 4 audiocassettes: $20. (5 credits)

Sociology

Survey of Sociology

Human interaction, social institutions, social stratification, socialization, deviance, social control, social and cultural change. Course content may change depending upon instructor. 10 lessons, 2 examinations. Optional interactive tutorial simulations available for IBM-PC: $15. Supplemental reading: $6. (5 credits)

Spanish

Elementary Spanish C101

Recommended for those who wish to work primarily toward a reading knowledge of the language. 13 lessons, 2 examinations. 6 audiocassettes: $24. (5 credits)

Elementary Spanish C102

A continuation of Elementary Spanish C101. 13 lessons, 2 examinations. 6 audiocassettes: $24. (5 credits)

Elementary Spanish C102

A continuation of Elementary Spanish C102. 16 lessons, 2 examinations. 8 audiocassettes: $32. (5 credits)

Intermediate Spanish C201

Intensive practice in reading and writing. Functional review in grammar. All assignments and examinations are written, but oral practice is provided through purchase and use of tape recordings. 15 lessons, 2 examinations. 6 audiocassettes $25. (5 credits)

Intermediate Spanish C202

A continuation of Intermediate Spanish C201. 15 lessons, 2 examinations. 6 audiocassettes: $25. (5 credits)

Washington State University
Independent Study
Extended University Services

Van Doren Hall, Room 106
Pullman, WA   99164-5220

(800) 422-4978 *Fax:* (509) 335-0945

Geographic Access: Worldwide

DELIVERY SYSTEMS

Audiocassette
Used primarily in foreign language courses.

Videocassette
Videotapes enhance and supplement the text and study guide.

INSTITUTION DESCRIPTION

As the land-grant university of the state of Washington, WSU is located in Pullman in the southeastern part of the state. The University enrolls approximately 18,000 students, more than 1,600 of whom attend courses at branch campuses and extended centers.

The Independent Study Program has been in existence for over fifty years. While on-campus classes follow a standard semester schedule, independent study courses can begin at any time and students have a full year to complete the work, set their own pace and schedule. Several courses listed are offered on a semester basis only and are so indicated in the course description. *See* Courses Offered.

Accreditation: NASC

Official/Contact: Ellen Krieger, Coordinator

Admission Requirements: Any adult may register for WSU's independent study courses. Transcripts, entrance examinations, and Washington residency are not necessary. Enrollment does not constitute admission to Washington State University.

Tuition: $60 per semester hour for both credit and noncredit courses. Some courses have additional fees for instructional materials such as slides, audio- and/or videocassettes. These additional fees are listed below with the course description. A refund of two-thirds of the purchase price is made upon the return of tapes in good condition. Textbooks must be purchased by the student. Discover, MasterCard, and VISA accepted.

Degree Credit: Credit earned is applicable to a degree program at WSU and may be accepted by other institutions. Students are advised to consult their institution for transfer-of-credit information.

Grading: Standard letter grades are awarded. Examinations must be proctored. Credit is awarded in semester hour units.

Library: Students enrolled in independent study courses may use the WSU libraries upon presentation of course receipts. Materials not available in the student's local community may be requested through Interlibrary Loan Services.

COURSES OFFERED

Arabic

First Semester Arabic

Fundamentals of speaking, listening to, reading, and writing Arabic. Not open to native speakers. Contact the Independent Study Office for additional charges for audiotapes and written material. (4 credits)

Second Semester Arabic

Continued development of basic skills. Not open to native speakers. Contact the Independent Study Office for details on additional charges for audiotapes and written material. (4 credits)

Third Semester Arabic

A continuation of Arabic instruction. Not open to native speakers. Contact the Independent Study Office for details on additional charges for audiotapes and written materials. (4 credits)

Criminal Justice

Criminal Law

Substantive criminal law. Principles, functions, and limits. Basic crime categories, state and national legal research materials. (3 credits)

French

First Semester French

Fundamentals of speaking, reading and writing. This course combines video, audio, and print to teach French in the context of French-speaking cultures. Students learn to associate what they hear with the familiar situations they see, while learning to understand and use authentic French from the French perspective. Audiotapes: $22.75. Videotapes: $50. (4 credits)

Second Semester French

Continued development of basic skills in speaking, reading, and writing. Audiotapes: $22.75. Videotapes: $50. (4 credits)

Third Semester French

Grammar review and further development of speaking, reading, and writing skills. Audiotapes: $22.75. Videotapes: $50. (4 credits)

Fourth Semester French

Continued practice in spoken and written language. Selected texts in a cultural context. Audiotapes: $22.75. Videotapes: $50. (4 credits)

German

First Semester German

Fundamentals of speaking, reading, and writing. Audiotapes provide exposure to verbal skills. Audiotapes: $7. (4 credits)

Second Semester German

Continued development of basic skills in speaking, reading, and writing. Audiotapes: $7. (4 credits)

History

World Civilizations I

Integrated study of social, political, and philosophical religious systems in early civilizations, with an introduction to distinctive art forms. An additional charge for an audio- and/or videotape is payable upon registration. Contact the Independent Study Office for details. (3 credits)

World Civilizations II

A continuation of World Civilizations I. An additional charge for an audio- and/or videotape is payable upon registration. Contact the Independent Study Office for details. (4 credits)

American History Since 1877

Social, economic, cultural history of the United States, 1877 to present. Audiotape: $28. (3 credits)

Nursing

Profession of Nursing

Theoretical/historical aspects of professional nursing. Development of nursing roles, scopes of practice, problem solving, and ethical decision making. 2 written assignments, 2 course evaluations, 2 papers. Communication with instructor by telephone is required. Videotape rental: $150. (2 credits)

Physics

General Physics

Fundamental principles and applications of mechanics, heat, and sound. Videotape rental: $150. (3 credits)

Spanish

First Semester Spanish

Fundamentals of speaking, reading, and writing. Cassette tapes provide exposure to correct Spanish pronunciation, accent, and intonation, and a model for student imitation. Audiotapes: $17.50. (4 credits)

Second Semester Spanish

Continued development of basic skills in speaking, reading, and writing. Audiotapes: $17.50. (4 credits)

Western Washington University
Independent Study
University Extended Programs

Old Main 400
Bellingham, WA   98225

(206) 676-3650

Geographic Access: Worldwide

DELIVERY SYSTEMS

Audiocassette
Audiotapes supplement the text in the history course. *See* Courses Offered.

Videocassette
PBS video series are utilized in the courses described under Courses Offered.

INSTITUTION DESCRIPTION

Western Washington University is a state institution founded in 1893 as the New Whatcom State Normal School. After several name changes, the present name was adopted in 1977.

In addition to traditional correspondence courses, three video-enhanced courses are offered and described under Courses Offered.

Accreditation: NASC

Official/Contact: Janet Howard, Program Manager

Admission Requirements: WWU's independent study programs are open to anyone with a desire to learn. Enrollment does not constitute admission to the University.

Tuition: $49 per credit. Nonrefundable registration fee $15. Additional fees for PBS royalty and syllabus fee (both given below with the course descriptions). Textbooks must be purchased by the student. MasterCard and VISA accepted.

Degree Credit: Courses through Independent Study do not qualify for master's credit. A maximum of 45 independent study credits may apply to a baccalaureate degree at WWU.

Grading: Examinations must be proctored. Arrangements to have examinations proctored by an education official or librarian in the student's local community may be arranged. The standard system of grading (A, B, C, D, F) is used at WWU. Credit is awarded in quarter hour units.

Library: To accommodate independent study students who have difficulty locating supplemental library materials through their local sources, WWU's Wilson Library has initiated a borrow-by-mail service.

COURSES OFFERED

Anthropology

Joseph Campbell: Transformations of Myth Through Time

Explores primal mythologies, American Indian myths, the mythological and historical roots of the Exodus story in Egypt. Noted author, scholar, teacher, and storyteller Joseph Campbell shows how myth answers fundamental questions about our origins, our life, and our death. The student will view 14 videotapes in addition to assigned readings. Thirteen papers. PBS fee: $29. Refundable videotape fee: $25. (5 credits)

History

Introduction to East Asian Civilization

The origins and evolution of the political, economic, and social aspects of East Asian civilization to the present. Student may listen to taped lectures in addition to readings. Ten quizzes. Syllabus fee: $3. Mailing fee for tapes: $15. (5 credits)

Philosophy

Ethics in America

Examines contemporary ethical conflicts and teaches the language, concepts, and traditions of ethics. This course will equip students with the intellectual and analytic tools needed to cope with ethical and moral dilemmas in nearly every occupation. Students will view 10 videocassettes and listen to 3 audiocassettes in addition to readings. PBS fee: $29. Refundable videotape fee: $25. (3 credits)

Ethics in America, Advanced

Based on the same materials as the Ethics in America course. Will require greater depth in student assignments. Students will view 10 videocassettes and listen to 3 audiocassettes in addition to readings. Four papers. PBS fee: $29. Refundable videotape fee: $25. (3 credits)

West Virginia

Bluefield State College
See **West Virginia Higher Education Instructional Television Consortium**

Concord College
See **West Virginia Higher Education Instructional Television Consortium**

Fairmont State College
See **West Virginia Higher Education Instructional Television Consortium**

Glenville State College
See **West Virginia Higher Education Instructional Television Consortium**

Marshall University
See **West Virginia Higher Education Instructional Television Consortium**

Shepherd College
See **West Virginia Higher Education Television Consortium**

Southern West Virginia Community College
See **West Virginia Higher Education Instructional Television Consortium**

University of West Virginia - College of Graduate Studies
See **West Virginia Higher Education Instructional Television Consortium**

West Liberty State College
See **West Virginia Higher Education Instructional Television Consortium**

West Virginia Higher Education Instructional Television Consortium
West Virginia Public Broadcasting
191 Scott Avenue
Morgantown, WV   26507-1316

(304) 293-6511

Geographic Access: West Virginia

DELIVERY SYSTEMS

Broadcast Television
Telecourses are aired over three stations of West Virginia Public Television: WSWP, WNPB, and WPBY. These three stations cover the entire viewing area of West Virginia.

INSTITUTION DESCRIPTION

The West Virginia Higher Education Instructional Television Consortium is made up of 14 public colleges and universities. About 3,000 students take telecourses for credit each year and three public television stations in the state broadcast about nine courses each term. While all courses under Courses Offered will be broadcast by West Virginia Public Television, the number of courses offered for credit by each institution varies. For specific details, contact the school of choice or call Anne Selinger, WNPB-TV Adult Learning Supervisor at (304) 293-6511. The member institutions and contact persons are:

- Bluefield State College (Bluefield WV), Dr. Thomas Blevins, (304) 327-4059
- Concord College (Athens WV), Dr. Dean Turner, (304) 384-3115
- Fairmont State College (Fairmont WV), Roger Rousseau, (304) 367-4692
- Glenville State College (Glenville WV), Kevin Cain, (304) 462-7361
- Marshall University (Huntington WV), Dr. H. Keith Spears, (304) 696-2965
- Shepherd College (Shepherdstown WV), Dr. David Eldridge, (304) 876-2511
- Southern West Virginia Community College (Logan WV), (304) 792-4300
- University of West Virginia, College of Graduate Studies (Institute WV), Dr. Bobbi Nicholson, (304) 766-2000
- West Liberty State College (West Liberty WV), Laurence Williams, (304) 336-8124
- West Virginia Institute of Technology (Montgomery WV), Rodney Stewart, (304) 442-3200
- West Virginia Northern College (New Martinsville WV), Garnet Persinger, (304) 455-4684
- West Virginia State College (Institute WV), Mami Blaylock, (304) 766-3000
- West Virginia University (Morgantown WV), Anne Selinger, (304) 293-6511
- West Virginia University at Parkersburg, David Winger, (304) 485-7587

Accreditation: All participating colleges are accredited by NCA.

Official/Contact: Anne Selinger, Adult Learning Supervisor

Admission Requirements: Open enrollment. Requirements for degree-seeking students may vary from campus to campus. Contact the instructional television coordinator at the school of choice for pertinent information.

Tuition: Contact the instructional television coordinator for current tuition, fees, and materials costs. These may vary among the campuses. Textbooks, study guide, and materials cost are the responsibility of the student and may be purchased at any of the college bookstores.

Degree Credit: Credit earned at the successful completion of a telecourse may be applied to a degree program. Each course listed below is for three semester hours of credit.

Grading: General course requirements include viewing a series of television programs on West Virginia Public Television, reading assignments in a textbook and/or study guide, and other class activities determined by the instructor. Examinations must be proctored. Letter grades are assigned. Credit is awarded in semester hour units.

Library: Students officially enrolled are granted access to the library resources of the member institutions upon presentation of registration credentials.

COURSES OFFERED

Business

The Business File

An introduction to business, this telecourse is for everyone who wants to expand their understanding of business. The course provides a comprehensive view of the contemporary business environment from the internal functions of a business to the challenges of business on an international scale. (3 credits)

The Sales Connection: Principles of Selling

A business telecourse designed to provide aspiring salespeople, and those already involved in sales, with the tools and insight they need to compete in the age of long-term, consultative-style selling. (3 credits)

Child Development

Time to Grow

This telecourse covers all aspects of children's physical, cognitive, and psychosocial growth and development from birth through adolescence, including the most recent theoretical and applied perspectives about effective ways of caring for and working with children. (3 credits)

Chinese Studies

The Chinese

This telecourse helps students understand the heritage that the Chinese bring with them as they face the problems of modernization. The telecourse examines Chinese culture from both historical and contemporary perspectives. (3 credits)

Earth Science

Planet Earth

An introductory study of the state of our planet—its interior, oceans, continents, mountains and volcanoes, energy and mineral resources, climate, sun and atmosphere. This interdisciplinary approach to the earth sciences gives students a detailed update on our "new earth" and on the scientific advances that are helping us to rediscover it. (3 credits)

Family Life

Portrait of a Family

A course that takes a close look at marriage, family, and alternative lifestyles in the closing decade of the twentieth century. Although the in-depth study of male and female interaction is a relatively new development in sociological scholarship, *Portrait of a Family* provides a balance between the solid research and theoretical base students need and the practical examination of personal choice and decision making students want. (3 credits)

Economics

Economics U$A

This course enables students to learn the principles of economics through examination of recent historic events interpreted by prominent economists and leaders in the public and private sectors. (3 credits)

Health

Living with Health

A user-friendly guide to healthy living. This health telecourse encourages students to take a proactive stance toward maintaining health, with focus on the lifestyle components that encourage wellness. Encompasses all areas of health: the physical, emotional, social, intellectual, and spiritual. (3 credits)

History

Americas

Presents a multidisciplinary study of the twentieth-century political, economic, social, and cultural history of Latin America and the Caribbean. This telecourse focuses on the key issues and events that are crucial to understanding the development of the modern-day Americas. (3 credits)

The Civil War

This telecourse presents the entire sweep of the war, from the battlefields to the homefronts, from the politicians and generals to the enlisted men and their families, from the causes of the war to Lincoln's assassination and beyond. (3 credits)

Humanities

Joseph Campbell: Transformations of Myth Through Time

Joseph Campbell, as author, scholar, teacher, and storyteller, is an inspiration to people of all walks of life the world over. In this telecourse, students will gain a deeper understanding of mythology's role in human history. (3 credits)

Eyes on the Prize

This course takes the point of view that the period of the contemporary civil rights movement is one of the most significant in our history. It made America a more democratic society, gave rise to a host of other movements which transformed the face of American culture, changed those who participated in it, and influenced and created a new generation of American leadership. (3 credits)

Management

Taking the Lead: The Management Revolution

A business management telecourse that provides an overview of management in the nineties, with an emphasis on the competencies that are essential for success. It explains how managers and organizations can reinvent themselves for today's new economy. (3 credits)

Philosophy

Ethics in America

Examines contemporary ethical conflicts and provides a grounding in the language, concepts, and traditions of ethics. Experts grapple with moral concerns that arise in both personal and professional life. Students are provided with the intellectual tools to analyze moral dilemmas in the fields they choose to pursue. (3 credits)

Political Science

The Pacific Century
This telecourse offers a survey of the modern history, economics, politics, and cultures of the Pacific Basin region. It explores how the Pacific Basin has evolved to emerge as a principal political and economic center of the upcoming century. (3 credits)

Rural Sociology

Rural Communities: Legacy and Change
America's cultural, political, and economic roots can be traced back to rural beginnings, and a rural setting is presently home to almost a quarter of the population. Addresses the challenges facing rural America by traveling to 15 rural regions and examining various facets of community life. (3 credits)

Small Business Management

Something Ventured: An Entrepreneurial Approach to Small Business Management
A business telecourse designed to provide aspiring entrepreneurs, and those already involved in a small business venture, with the tools needed to enhance their potential for success. (3 credits)

Spanish

Destinos: An Introduction to Spanish
A Spanish language telecourse designed to give students full communicative proficiency in Spanish—listening, speaking, reading, and writing. (3 credits)

West Virginia Institute of Technology
See **West Virginia Higher Education Instructional Television Consortium**

West Virginia Northern College
See **West Virginia Higher Education Instructional Television Consortium**

West Virginia State College
See **West Virginia Higher Education Instructional Television Consortium**

West Virginia University
See **West Virginia Higher Education Instructional Television Consortium**

West Virginia University at Parkersburg
See **West Virginia Higher Education Instructional Television Consortium**

Wisconsin

Milwaukee Area Technical College
College of the Air

700 West State Street
Milwaukee, WI   53233-1443

(414) 278-6940

Geographic Access: Wisconsin

DELIVERY SYSTEMS

Broadcast Television
Telecourses are broadcast on WMVT-TV, Channel 36. Class schedules are announced prior to the beginning of each semester.

INSTITUTION DESCRIPTION

Milwaukee Area Technical College was founded in 1912 and serves the greater Milwaukee metropolitan area on four campuses.

The College of the Air offers telecourses at the college and high school levels. It is also possible to pursue an Associate in Arts degree entirely through video-based instruction.

Accreditation: NCA

Official/Contact: Barbara D. Holmes, President

Admission Requirements: Open enrollment. Formal application required for degree-seeking students.

Tuition: See the course descriptions under Courses Offered for current fees. Textbooks must be purchased by the student.

Degree Credit: The Associate of Arts (Liberal Arts) degree may be earned entirely through video-based courses.

Grading: Examinations are proctored and may be taken at any of the four campus locations. Credit is awarded in semester hour units.

Library: The Library Resources Center offers support to officially enrolled students. Videotapes are available for viewing at any campus library.

COURSES OFFERED

Accounting

Financial Accounting
"Accounting for nonaccountants"—stresses a user's approach to basic financial statements. Telecourse title: *Principles of Accounting*. 30 half-hour lessons, two lessons (back-to-back) per week. Fee: $132.05. (3 credits)

Business

Microcomputers in Business
Survey and analyze the use of microcomputer hardware and software in the business environment. In this course the student will compare and contrast applications in a way that teaches one to evaluate what is best for a particular situation. The investigation of software options and hardware peripherals exposes the student to the task of evaluating the components individually and within the context of the entire system, and to selecting the combination of hardware and software to meet specific business needs. 16 half-hour lessons, two lessons per week. Fee: $132.05. (3 credits)

Business Organization and Management
Gives a comprehensive view of the contemporary business environment—from internal functions of a business to challenges of business on an international scale. Delves into the complex functions of

business and expands understanding of the detailed internal and external operations affecting both large and small businesses in five general areas: American business foundation and forms, organizing and managing a business, the internal working of a business, the environment of business, and the challenges of business. Telecourse title: *The Business File.* 28 half-hour lessons, two lessons per week. Fee: $132.05. (3 credits)

Business Law I

A comprehensive overview of law and the world of business. Telecourse title: *Business and the Law.* 26 half-hour lessons, two back-to-back lessons per week. Fee: $124.95. (3 credits)

Chemistry

The World of Chemistry

Basic chemistry involving everyday circumstances covering the principles and fundamentals of chemistry relative to medical, environmental, and industrial applications. Telecourse title: *The World of Chemistry.* 26 half-hour lessons, two lessons (back-to-back) per week. Fee: $173.45. (3 credits)

Communications

Communication Skills

Emphasis in this introductory course in communications skills is on developing the four basic skills: writing, reading, speaking, and listening. Activities are designed to help the student understand the course material and develop valuable skills for school, job, or personal use. A speech is required as part of this course. 30 half-hour lessons, two lessons per week. Fee: $132.05. (3 credits)

Economics

Economics

An exploration of the principles underlying the American economy. Topics include alternate economic systems, consumer/resource/international economics, demand and supply, allocation of scarce resources, efficiency, business operation, money and banking, inflation and recession, the government's role in the country's economy, economic growth, national output and employment. Telecourse title: *Economics U$A.* 30 half-hour lessons, two lessons per week. Fee: $132.05. (3 credits)

Principles of Macroeconomics

National income and product analysis, financial institutions and the federal reserve system, and macroeconomic models as applied to inflation, unemployment, and business are covered. Telecourse title: *Principles of Macroeconomics.* 24 one-hour lessons, two lessons per week. Fee: $173.45. (3 credits)

English

English I

With an emphasis on thinking processes and practices in organizing and developing clear expository and persuasive writing, this course examines the content and structure of essays to provide background for student writing assignments. Telecourse title: *Read, Write, and Research: The Story of English.* 26 half-hour lessons, two lessons per week. Fee: $173.45. (3 credits)

English Composition II

An exploration of the literary genre of short story, novel, play, and poem with emphasis on literary analysis and the research paper. A diagnostic writing sample is required. Telecourse title: *Literary Visions.* 26 half-hour lessons, two lessons (back-to-back) per week. Fee: $173.45. (3 credits)

General Education Development Test (GED)

Preparation for the GED Test

The five subjects of the GED test—math, science, social studies, reading, and writing skills—are covered in the program. Telecourse title: *TV High School for Adults.* 43 half-hour lessons, two lessons per week. No tuition fee. (Noncredit)

Geology

General Geology

This course travels the globe, studying forces that shape Earth's features. Topics studied include place tectonics, Earth history, and the rock cycle. Practical laboratory experience through hands-on experience coordinated with the video, *Earth Revealed.* 26 half-hour lessons, two lessons per week. Fee: $254.60. (4 credits)

History

Contemporary Civil Rights

The people, the stories, the events, and the issues of the civil rights struggle that cover the period of American history from World War II to the present. Telecourse title: *Eyes on the Prize 1 and 2.* 14 one-hour lessons, one lesson per week. Fee: $173.45. (3 credits)

Marketing

Principles of Marketing

The study of the marketing process as it relates to the problems and policies of the profitable operation of a business enterprise. Telecourse title: *Marketing.* 26 half-hour lessons, two lessons (back-to-back) per week. Fee: $132.05. (3 credits)

Mathematics

College Algebra

Designed for highly motivated individuals with above average reading skills. This comprehensive course is intended for undergraduates at two- and four-year institutions. Step-by-step progression to a thorough understanding and working knowledge of the concepts and practical real-life applications of algebra. The graphing component of the course can be enhanced by optional use of a graphing calculator. Telecourse title: *College Algebra: In Simplest Terms.* 26 half-hour lessons, two lessons per week. Fee: $230.10. (4 credits)

Psychology

Introductory Psychology

In a format designed to encourage an understanding and appreciation of the scientific approach to the study of human behavior, the student will survey the psychological, interpsychic, and social-behavioral perspectives on human thought and behavior, sensation and perception, motivation, learning and memory, maturation and development, personality theory and psychotherapy, and social psychology. Telecourse title: *Psychology: The Study of Human Behavior.* 30 half-hour lessons, two lessons per week. Fee: $173.45. (3 credits)

Abnormal Psychology

A course that surveys the features, causes, assessment, and treatment of various types of abnormal behavior from major theoretical perspectives in the field. Telecourse title: *The World of Abnormal Psychology.* 13 one-hour lessons, one lesson per week. Fee: $173.45. (3 credits)

Sociology

Introduction to Sociology

Designed to give the student an enriched understanding of the social world, this course provides a scientific study of interpersonal relationships with particular emphasis on groups and the consequent structure of society. Detailed in the course are the various social processes and concepts that shape human behavior and an analysis of such phenomena as culture, social roles, groups, collectives, social class, deviance, sexuality, race and ethnic relationships, and populations and ecology. Telecourse title: *The Sociological Imagination.* 30 half-hour lessons, two lessons per week. Fee: $173.45. (3 credits)

University of Wisconsin (UW)
Extension Independent Study

432 North Lake Street
Madison, WI   53706-1498

(800) 442-6460 *Fax:* (608) 262-4096

Geographic Access: Wisconsin

DELIVERY SYSTEMS

Audiocassette
Audiotapes are utilized in language courses.

Broadcast Television
Telecourses are offered at various times throughout the year. Off-air taping rights are automatically granted to students enrolled in the telecourses. University of Wisconsin Extension cannot send videotapes to students enrolled in the courses as they are broadcast via cable TV stations in Wisconsin.

Videocassette
A video-enhanced course utilizes videocassettes that can be purchased.

INSTITUTION DESCRIPTION

The University of Wisconsin was chartered and established in 1848. It is part of the state-wide system of public higher education comprised of 13 universities and 13 associate degree-granting centers.

The Extension arm of the university has been offering correspondence courses since 1891. The courses described under Courses Offered are audio- and/or video-enhanced. The television-related courses are available only to students in Wisconsin.

Accreditation: NCA

Official/Contact: Sylvia N. Rose, Director, Independent Study

Admission Requirements: Open enrollment. Applicants must have met any prerequisites prior to enrolling in the course.

Tuition: $50 per semester hour credit. Textbooks are not included in the tuition and must be purchased by the student. Audiocassettes may be obtained by the student for the fee listed with the course description. *See* Courses Offered. The fee for a continuing education course (noncredit) is listed where appropriate.

Degree Credit: UW Extension does not grant degrees. Credit earned can be transferred and applied toward an associate or baccalaureate degree from any of the degree-granting institutions in the University of Wisconsin System. Students from other institutions should check with an adviser to make sure the chosen course is appropriate for the degree program being pursued.

Grading: Examinations must be taken under the direct supervision of an approved proctor. Standard letter grades (A-F) are assigned. Credit is awarded in semester hour units. Completion of a continuing education course results in the awarding of Continuing Education Units (CEUs).

Library: An officially registered student may use materials on the premises of any UW System library. Proper identification is required.

COURSES OFFERED

Arabic

First Semester Arabic

For those with no previous instruction in the language. Elements of reading, writing, and pronouncing Arabic, as well as essential facts about Arabic. 32 assignments, 1 exam. Audiocassette: $4.20. (4 credits)

Second Semester Arabic

A continuation of First Semester Arabic, beginning with a review. Emphasis is on reading and writing, with a final lesson on calligraphy. 32 assignments, 2 exams. Audiocassette: $4.20. (4 credits)

Childhood Education

Caring for Children: An Introduction to the Child-Care Profession

A television-based course designed to provide an introduction to the child-care profession for both assistant child care teachers and family day care providers. The course is built around 12 half-hour videotapes that present examples of teaching practices for teachers of young children in child-care homes and centers. The topics include an overview of child care, caring for infants/toddlers/preschoolers/school-age children in child-care homes and centers, child growth and development from birth through age eight, environments for children, health/safety/nutrition, enhancing children's self-esteem and respecting diversity, developing effective teaching techniques, building partnerships with parents, and professional development. 12 assignments, 2 exams. (3 credits)

Counseling

Human Resource Development: Communications Skill-Building Study of Self as a Communicator

An audio-enhanced course. Taught from a counseling perspective, this is a course for preschool and K-12 teachers and administrators, for parents, and for other persons who want to sharpen their abilities to make and maintain friendships. The assignments focus on exploring fresh choices in relating, including initiating communication, resolving disagreements, saying what you mean, and developing higher quality relationships. Specific topics include freeing ourselves from self-defeating habits, alternate ways of communicating, nonverbal communication, and building quality relationships. 7 assignments, 1 exam. Audiocassette: $3.50. (1 credit)

Educational Psychology

Educational Psychology of the Gifted, Talented, and Creative: Educating Able Learners

A television-based course that deals with programming for able learners in terms of Wisconsin's new law which states that each school board shall provide access to an appropriate program for pupils identified as gifted and talented. Students will focus on able learners—people who learn rapidly and well in both breadth and depth and address the different levels and needs of gifted learners. Topics include giftedness, intellectual gifts, regular classroom programs, pull-out programs, individual programs, counseling, under-represented gifted, and mentoring. There is a required project instead of an examination. 12 assignments, 1 project. (2 credits)

Programming for the Gifted: Models and Methods

A telecourse that focuses on five general models of educational programs for gifted students: acceleration, enrichment, counseling, curriculum modifications, and instructional strategy changes. Students who take the course should develop a sufficient knowledge base to make reasoned judgments between and among the five models. There is a required project instead of an examination. 12 assignments, 1 project. (2 credits)

Teachers Tackle Thinking

A television-based course that is an introduction to teaching critical thinking skills in the classroom. It focuses on developing effective thinking, classroom climate, questioning, deductive reasoning, inductive thinking, problem solving, decision making, computers, and critical thinking in specific content areas such as science, language arts, and social studies. There is a required project instead of an examination. 12 assignments, 1 project. (3 credits)

Engineering

Statics

A video-enhanced course. Force systems, moments, couples, resultants, rigid body equilibrium, frames and machines, truss analysis, friction, centroids, distributed loads, moment of inertia. Students must have access to a VHS videotape player. Videotapes: $25. (3 credits)

English

Introduction to Modern English and American Literature I: The Nineteenth Century

An audio-enhanced course. Introduces students to English and American works from the period between the publication of Blake's *Songs of Innocence* (1789) and the death of Queen Victoria (1901), a time that laid the foundation for modernism in art. Twelve audio programs developed with funds from

the Annenberg/Corporation for Public Broadcasting (CPB) Project add a dimension to the study of literature by drawing on the expertise and enthusiasm of a nationwide faculty and the skill of professional actors and readers. 12 assignments, 1 exam. Audiocassettes: $32.50. (3 credits)

Introduction to Modern English and American Literature: The Twentieth Century

An audio-enhanced course. Introduces students to English and American poetry, fiction, and nonfiction of the twentieth century. Twelve audio programs developed with funds from the Annenberg/CPB Project enable students to hear professional readings of the literature as well as commentary by scholars and writers throughout the country. 12 assignments, 2 exams. Audiocassettes: $32.50. (3 credits)

Finance

Stocks, Bonds, and the Beginning Investor

Six half-hour taped discussions explore what successful investment is about and different types of investments, such as money market funds, stocks, bonds, treasury notes. How they are bought and sold, their advantages and risks, returns on investments, and the importance of financial planning. Explains Wall Street terms and how to read the financial pages. No text required. 6 assignments, 1 exam. Fee: $60. 3 audiocassettes: $9. (6 CEUs)

History

American History, 1492-1865: The Origin and Growth of the United States

An audio-enhanced course. A general survey of American history from the era of exploration to the close of the Civil War. The 13 units of study are well balanced between political history and social and revolutionary origins in the first four units, the next nine carry national development through the shaping of the new nation, territorial expansion, the rise and transformation of political parties, the age of reform, the diverging economies and societies of North and South, the crises of the 1850s, and the Civil War. Thirteen audiotapes developed through the Annenberg/CPB Project add new content dimensions to the readings. 13 assignments, 2 exams. Audiocassettes: $30.50. (4 credits)

American History, 1865 to the Present: The Origin and Growth of the United States

An audio-enhanced course. This general survey of the American experience from reconstruction of the South after the Civil War through 1990 examines major changes in America's role in international affairs. Political developments, social change, especially in the status of blacks and women, and the transformation of the national economy. The course is designed to illustrate patterns of continuity and discontinuity over the past 125 years. Fifteen audiotapes developed with a grant from the Annenberg/CPB Project add to the content dimensions of the readings. 15 assignments, 2 exams. Audiocassettes: $32.50. (4 credits)

Italian

First Semester Italian

Presents the vocabulary of Italian pronunciation, vocabulary, and grammatical principles and introduces the student to Italian culture. 20 assignments, 2 exams. 7 audiocassettes: $25.65. (4 credits)

Second Semester Italian

A continuation of First Semester Italian. 20 assignments, 2 exams. 7 audiocassettes: $23.65. (4 credits)

Music

Appreciation and History of Music I

The purposes of this course are to increase a student's enjoyment of music by proceeding gradually from simple to more advanced levels and to expand the student's horizons by developing new tastes. The intent is to arouse an interest and curiosity in music while imparting a knowledge of composers and their works and the periods of history in which they lived that will help the student respond to this musical heritage. The course begins with the nineteenth-century Romantic period and then turns to the eighteenth-century Classical period and covers the materials of music. 12 assignments, 2 exams. Standard version of 8 twelve-inch records 33-1/3rpm, $47.20 or basic set of 8 CDs, vol. 1, $42.00 and vol. 2, $42.00. (2 credits)

Appreciation and History of Music II

A continuation of Appreciation and History of Music I covering the second half of the text. It begins with a consideration of the Middle Ages and Renaissance and proceeds to the main currents in baroque music. The course concludes with the music of the twentieth century and a special look at the American scene. 12 assignments, 2 exams. Recordings: same as for the above course. (2 credits)

Basic Concepts of Music

Designed to teach basic skills and understanding of music concepts to help students become "empowered listeners" who are able to make informed choices about what they will listen to and so have a greater enjoyment of music. Each of the twelve units is accompanied by a half-hour audio program on cassette, and "core repertory" tapes present other music throughout the course. There is also an optional unit (again accompanied by audio materials) on music notation. Topics of study include rhythm, melody, harmony, form, style, meaning and emotion, and making choices to become an empowered listener. Audiotapes developed through the Annenberg/CPB Project. 12 assignments, no exams. Audiocassette album (8 cassettes): $18.40. Core repertory album (4 cassettes): $31.60. (3 credits)

Norwegian

Beginning Norwegian I

For those who have had no previous instruction in the language. Also recommended for students who can speak the language but have never learned to read it or to analyze its grammatical structure. 23 assignments, 2 exams. 7 audiocassettes: $24.50. (4 credits)

Beginning Norwegian II

A continuation of Beginning Norwegian I. 28 assignments, 2 exams. 6 audiocassettes: $21.00. (4 credits)

Nursing

Adult Patient Assessment: Subjective and Objective Data Base

For nurses who are not familiar with the components of the history and physical examination. This course offers an introduction in a unique format. Using taped presentations, printed materials, exercises, self-guided practice, pre- and posttests, illustrations, and suggested references, the learner is guided through the process of physical assessment. The subjective data base (Health History) and the objective data base (Physical Assessment) are included. No assignments, 1 exam. Fee: $60 with audiocassettes. (4 CEUs)

Interpersonal Relations—Utilizing the Basics: Effective and Therapeutic Communications in Nursing

This audiocassette course has been specifically designed to help nurses augment their ability to utilize effective communications as part of a therapeutic relationship. The course assists nurses in evaluating effective communications and in providing information and emotional support to others. The problem-solving process and crisis intervention are presented, with theories and techniques to facilitate communications. No assignments, 1 exam. Fee: $60 with cassettes. (3 CEUs)

Writing for Nursing Publications

This course will guide nurses through the writing process from becoming aware of publishing opportunities to developing a topic and understanding the procedure for submitting an article to a nursing publication. Nurses will learn to identify what editors look for and how to avoid problems and pitfalls relating to copyrights. No assignments, 1 exam. Fee: $60 with cassettes. (4 CEUs)

Philosophy

Ethics in Business

Examining the difference between legal and moral issues from a philosophic perspective, the course uses actual cases to motivate interest in this timely subject. Twelve audiocassettes developed with funds from the Annenberg/CPB Project add discussions and dramatic vignettes on real-life applications of philosophic principles. 12 assignments, 3 exams. Audiocassettes: $15.75. (4 credits)

Sociology

Marriage and the Family

The course looks at definitions and varieties of families, explores the family life cycle, and considers some of the problems facing the contemporary family. Twelve audiotapes developed through the Annenberg/CPB Project add new dimensions to the discussion of the American family. 12 assignments, 3 exams. Audiocassettes: $15.75. (3 credits)

Sociological Foundations

The course examines a broad range of human social relationships and social structures and the many forces—historical, cultural, and environmental—that shape them. Thirteen audiotapes developed through the Annenberg/CPB Project add new dimensions to the content. The audiotapes take an in-depth look at such topics as the sociology of violence, the consequences of divorce, and the influence of media. 13 assignments, 2 exams. Audiocassettes: $29.00. (3 credits)

Spanish

First Semester College Spanish

Teaches the fundamentals of Spanish, providing basic vocabulary, grammar and pronunciation, training in translation and elementary composition, and practical reading knowledge. Also introduces the student to Hispanic culture. The optional cassette tapes offer the opportunity for oral practice. 22 or 24 assignments, 2 exams. 6 audiocassettes (optional): $20.05. (4 credits)

Second Semester College Spanish

Begins with a review of First Semester College Spanish and continues to develop skills in reading, writing, and understanding Spanish. Also continues introducing the student to Hispanic culture. The optional cassette tapes provide the opportunity for oral practice. 22 or 24 assignments, 2 exams. 5 audiocassettes (optional): $17.50. (4 credits)

Statistics

Principles of Statistics

Introduces students with limited mathematical background to the key concepts of experimentation, inference from data sets, and decision making. Examines the main issues and methods of modern statistics and illustrates them by examples from the world around us. Stresses the importance of knowing the field in which statistical research is being done so that improper application of the raw data can be avoided. Twelve audio programs developed with funds from the Annenberg/CPB Project present the practical experiences of several leading statisticians. 12 assignments, 2 exams. Audiocassettes: $30.60. (3 credits)

University of Wisconsin - Eau Claire
See **Wisconsin Educational Communications Board**

University of Wisconsin - Green Bay
See **Wisconsin Educational Communications Board**

University of Wisconsin - La Crosse
See **Wisconsin Educational Communications Board**

University of Wisconsin - River Falls
See **Wisconsin Educational Communications Board**

University of Wisconsin - Stout
See **Wisconsin Educational Communications Board**

University of Wisconsin - Whitewater
See **Wisconsin Educational Communications Board**

Wisconsin Educational Communications Board
Telecourses
Educational Programming
3319 West Beltline Highway
Madison, WI 53713-4296

(608) 264-9600; *Fax:* (608) 264-9622

Geographic Access: Wisconsin

DELIVERY SYSTEMS

Broadcast Television
Telecourses are broadcast over Wisconsin Public Television and are available for viewing throughout Wisconsin on local PBS stations and various cable networks.

INSTITUTION DESCRIPTION

The Wisconsin Educational Communications Board is the coordinating agency for distance education throughout Wisconsin. Telecourses are offered by the University of Wisconsin (UW) and the Vocational, Technical, and Adult Education (VTAE) systems for credit, recertification, or continuing education units. The telecourses are available statewide through broadcasts over Wisconsin Public Television. Sponsoring institutions for the courses listed are noted with the course description. *See* Courses Offered. Sponsoring UW campuses and VTAE technical colleges include:

- UW-Eau Claire (Eau Claire WI), (715) 836-2326
- UW-Extension (Madison WI), (608) 262-1234
- UW-Green Bay (Green Bay WI), (414)465-2207
- UW-La Crosse (La Crosse WI), (608) 785-8000
- UW-River Falls (River Falls WI), (715) 346-2123
- UW-Stout (Menomonie WI), (715) 232-2441
- UW-Whitewater (Whitewater WI), (414) 472-1918

Accreditation: NCA

Official/Contact: Charlotte Bell, Director of Educational Planning

Admission Requirements: Students can register for credit or noncredit courses by mail and meet with instructors either in person or by phone. Information regarding the VTAE-sponsored courses can be obtained by calling (800) 472-0024.

Tuition: Contact the institution sponsoring the course for current tuition and fees. Students must purchase textbooks required.

Degree Credit: Credit earned through successful completion of a course may be applied toward a degree.

Grading: Coursework and exams are graded by mail. The grading system is the option of the sponsoring institution. Credit is awarded in semester hour units.

Library: Students officially registered for a telecourse have access to the library facilities of the University of Wisconsin and the learning resource centers of the VTAE technical colleges.

COURSES OFFERED

Archaeology

Out of the Past: An Introduction to Archaeology
This archaeology telecourse illustrates, using dramatic footage, how archaeology and anthropology interact and how archaeologists reconstruct ancient societies. Research at the Classic Maya Center of Copan, Honduras, forms the core of the course, which also compares civilizations and cultures, past and present, from all over the world. May also be taken for graduate credit. Offered through UW-River Falls. (3 credits)

Business

Business and the Law

Contracts and the legal system—including government regulation, employment practices, and consumer and environmental protection—are the emphasis in this introductory business course. A VTAE course. (3 credits)

Child Care

Caring for Infants and Toddlers

Topics include an overview of quality infant and toddler caregiving, identify characteristics of quality programs, and define the skills needed to be a competent infant/toddler caregiver. Offered by UW-Extension. (1 credit)

Caring for Children: An Introduction to the Child Care Profession

Developed for family living specialists as well as individuals interested in providing child care services. Topics include development, need, regulations, time management, and licensing. Offered through UW-Extension. (3 credits)

Economics

Economics U$A

This comprehensive course in macro- and microeconomics examines major historical and contemporary events that have shaped 20th-century economics in the United States. The series uses a documentary-style format. A VTAE course. (3 credits)

Education

Educating Able Learners

This telecourse is designed to help educators develop curriculum that complies with Wisconsin's law regarding instruction for able learners. The course focuses on students gifted academically, intellectually, creatively, and artistically. Offered through UW-Extension. (3 credits)

Restructuring America's Schools

Educators in both rural and urban settings will benefit from this telecourse, which provides a research-based framework for new visions of learning and strategies for restructuring schools. Offered for graduate credit through University of Wisconsin—River Falls and University of Wisconsin—Stout. (3 credits)

General Education Development Test (GED)

GED Español

This telecourse will help prepare adults whose principal language skills are in Spanish for the General Education Development (GED) exams required to earn a high school equivalency certificate. Lessons address five areas covered by the GED tests: reading, writing, science, social studies, and math. All instructional materials, both video and print, are in Spanish. A VTAE course.

GED Preparation

Adults can prepare for the General Education Development (GED) exams required to earn a high school equivalency certificate. Lessons address five skill areas covered by the GED tests: reading, writing, science, social studies, and math. A VTAE course.

Marketing

Marketing

In addition to teaching basic marketing concepts and principles, this course goes behind the scenes at more than 20 companies, both large and small, to show marketing managers handling a range of contemporary problems. Topics include time- and money-saving marketing techniques, new product promotion, distribution channels, and identifying customer needs. A VTAE course. (3 credits)

The Sales Connection: Principles of Selling

This course offers both prospective and experienced sales professionals valuable insight into the world of consultative-style selling and provides tips, tools, and tactics to help ensure success in contemporary sales. Sales specialists from successful companies provide useful insights, and discussions with customers illuminate the sales process from the buyer's point of view. The course explores new ways to identify sales prospects, develop and maintain good sales relationships, put sales theories and processes into practice, and provide service after the sale. A VTAE course. (3 credits)

Mathematics

By the Numbers

This telecourse translates basic business mathematical concepts—including communication with numbers and the mathematics of retail and finance—into practical applications, such as constructing a building, investing money, and setting prices. A VTAE course. (3 credits)

Political Science

Americas

The contemporary history, politics, culture, economics, religion, and social structures of the countries in Latin America and the Caribbean. The introductory course focuses on the key issues and events that are crucial to understanding the development of the modern-day Americas. Offered through UW-River Falls. May also be taken for graduate credit. (3 credits)

Psychology

Discovering Psychology

A mix of classic experiments, simulations, cutting-edge research, documentary footage and computer animation combine to introduce students to the fundamental principles and major concepts of psychology. A VTAE course. (3 credits)

Small Business Management

Something Ventured: An Entrepreneurial Approach to Small Business Management

Prospective entrepreneurs learn how to investigate and evaluate business opportunities, market products and services, manage human business demands,

and deal with community relations. A VTAE course. (3 credits)

Sociology

Seasons of Life

From the "terrible twos" through the twilight years, this course studies life-span psychology and the influences of heredity and environment on an individual's successful adaptation to each stage of life. Human development is examined through the influences of three distinct "clocks"—physical, social, and psychological. May also be taken for graduate credit. Offered through UW-Stout. (3 credits)

Sociological Imagination

This introductory sociology course takes a documentary-style look at groups, communities, institutions, and social situations that illustrate major sociological concepts. By interweaving expert commentary and interviews with people at work, play, and home, the course examines issues such as social control, aging, sex and gender, and collective behavior. A VTAE course. (3 credits)

Spanish

Destinos: An Introduction to Spanish

Using a Hispanic serial drama format known as "telenovela," this telecourse helps motivate beginning Spanish language students to develop basic language skills—listening, speaking, reading, and writing. Offered by UW-Whitewater. (Noncredit)

Wyoming

Central Wyoming College
Nontraditional Programs

2660 Peck Avenue
Riverton, WY   82501

(307) 856-9291

Geographic Access: Wyoming

DELIVERY SYSTEMS

Broadcast Television
Lessons are broadcast on KCWC-TV Channel 4 in the Lander-Riverton area, and may be carried by the local cable channel in the students area. If living outside the broadcast area of KCWC-TV or if the local cable company does not carry the feed from KCWC-TV, the student may borrow a set of tapes.

INSTITUTION DESCRIPTION

Founded in 1966, Central Wyoming College is a two-year community college offering a variety of education, vocational, and enrichment programs. The college opens its doors to all serious students regardless of their educational or personal background. The campus is located in Fremont County on the outskirts of Riverton, a city of about 12,000 on the banks of the Wind River.

The telelessons offered are highly concentrated and equate to about an hour and a half of traditional lecture. Certain courses rotate in and out of the broadcast schedule.

Accreditation: NCA

Official/Contact: Jon P. Cobes, Director

Admission Requirements: Open enrollment. Students from other colleges/universities should ensure that credit awarded is transferable to their institution.

Tuition: All Central Wyoming College registration procedures and fees apply to telecourses, except for an additional nonrefundable $5 telecourse fee. Textbooks and study guides must be purchased by the student. MasterCard and VISA accepted.

Degree Credit: Credit may be applied toward a degree at Central Wyoming College and may be accepted in transfer by other institutions. Students should check with their advisor to be sure a course will transfer if planning to attend a four-year college to pursue a baccalaureate degree.

Grading: Examinations are administered in certain off-campus locations as well as on-campus. Letter grades are assigned. Credit is awarded in semester hour units.

Library: The campus library has a set of tapes for all current courses offered. These are noncirculating, but VCRs are available at all times for in-house viewing.

COURSES OFFERED

Anthropology

Introduction to Archaeology
This telecourse is entitled *Out of the Past*. The course uses on-site filming to enable the student to explore how archaeologists reconstruct ancient societies and how and why they evolved. A focus of the series is research at the Maya Center of Copan. (3 credits)

Business

Introduction to Business
This course is for anyone who wants to expand their understanding of business. It investigates the complex functions of a business, exposing the student to

the detailed internal and external operations and forces affecting both large and small business. Telecourse title: *The Business File*. (3 credits)

English

Composition I

English composition and rhetoric taught from a "process" point of view. The course emphasizes audience awareness and purpose as fundamental to writing, and uses dramatizations and minidocumentaries to underscore major points in the writing process. Telecourse title: *The Write Course*. (3 credits)

English II

This course features dramatizations of individual works and readings of literary passages, including both contemporary and traditional works. The course emphasizes writing about literature as a way for students to learn about advanced compositional techniques. Telecourse title: *Literary Visions*. (3 credits)

Geology

Physical Geology

Through the use of on-location footage shot at major geologic sites around the world, the student is exposed to the dramatic forces as well as the more subtle but ever-present elements of the geologic process. Telecourse title: *Earth Revealed*. (4 credits)

History

U.S. History I

This course is the first half of a two-semester history series. It illustrates American history from Columbian contact to the Civil War and Reconstruction. Taped in 23 states and Mexico, the course is vivid and real in its depiction and illustration of the emergence of the American nation and people. Telecourse title: *American Adventure*. (3 credits)

U.S. History II

The second semester of CWC's televised history series. The course combines historical film and photography with interviews of leading historians and living eyewitnesses to the unfolding of modern America. Telecourse title: *America in Perspective, U.S. History Since 1877*. (3 credits)

Humanities

Art of Being Human

A humanities course which is not quite an introduction to philosophy, but one in which philosophy is used as a key to understanding the wondrous differences between just being alive and really living. Telecourse title: *The Art of Being Human*. (3 credits)

Management

Business Management

This course features such notables as Warren Bennis, John Kotter, George Labovitz, and William Ouchi, and gives an inside look at General Dynamics, Hybritech, Patagonia, and the Four Seasons Hotel. Telecourse title: *Taking the Lead*. (3 credits)

Mathematics

Problem Solving

This course is an introduction to contemporary mathematics, showing mathematics as the language of modern problem solving. Computer graphics, animation sequences, and location shooting enliven the course and help make mathematics contemporary and useful. Telecourse title: *For All Practical Purposes*. (3 credits)

Political Science

American and Wyoming Government

This course focuses on teaching students how to access their own government. The course weds political science instruction with examples of how to be involved with government and make it work, in fact, by consent. Telecourse title: *Government By Consent*. (3 credits)

Psychology

General Psychology

The telecourse host, Phillip Zimbardo, illustrates each program topic through original film footage of classical experiments, interviews with renowned psychologists, and documentaries on emerging research. Telecourse title: *Discovering Psychology*. (4 credits)

Sociology

Introduction to Sociology

This introductory course in sociology is designed to give students an in-depth look at groups, communities, institutions, and social situations that illustrate major sociological concepts. Telecourse title: *Sociological Imagination.* (3 credits)

Spanish

First-Year Spanish

This is the first of a two-semester telecourse in Spanish. The course is set in the form of a "telenovela," a continuing drama played and largely explained in conversational Spanish. The drama is set in Mexico, Spain, Argentina, and Puerto Rico. Reviews conducted in English and Spanish make this a first-rate experience in Spanish language and cultures. Telecourse title: *Destinos.* (4 credits)

Spanish II

The second semester of *Destinos.* The student will continue to travel and learn with Rachel Rodriguez and to further be immersed in the Spanish language and the many exciting customs of the Spanish-speaking peoples of the world. (4 credits)

Eastern Wyoming College
See **KRMA/Denver**

Laramie County Community College
See **KRMA/Denver**

University of Wyoming
School of Extended Studies

P.O. Box 3294
Laramie, WY   82071-3294

(307) 766-5631 *Fax:* (307) 766-3445

Geographic Access: Nationwide

DELIVERY SYSTEMS

Audiocassette
Audio-enhanced courses are offered in a variety of subjects.

Videocassette
Videotapes accompany courses in English, geography, geology, psychology, range management, sociology, and other subject areas.

INSTITUTION DESCRIPTION

The University of Wyoming is a state institution and land-grant college. It was established and chartered in 1886 and awarded its first degree in 1891.

The School of Extended Studies offers a variety of traditional correspondence courses as well as the media-assisted courses described. *See* Courses Offered.

Accreditation: NCA

Official/Contact: Heikki I. Leskinen, Coordinator

Admission Requirements: Anyone whose educational background in a subject qualifies him/her to do the required work is eligible to enroll in any course. Enrollment does not constitute admission to the University of Wyoming.

Tuition: $64 per semester hour. Textbooks must be purchased by the student. Audiovisual materials require a refundable deposit. Deposit fees are given with the course description. *See* Courses Offered. Master-Card and VISA accepted.

Degree Credit: Up to 24 semester hours of credit earned by the successful completion of distance learning courses may be applied toward a baccalaureate degree at the University of Wyoming. Students from other institutions should check with their registrar to determine acceptability of credits in transfer.

Grading: Examinations must be proctored. Students not in the campus vicinity should obtain the services of an administrator to act as the examination proctor. The letter grading system (A-D, F) is used in most courses. Credit is awarded in semester hour units.

Library: Officially registered students have access to the University of Wyoming libraries. Students in other areas are encouraged to use their local community libraries.

COURSES OFFERED

Agriculture

Current Topics in Seeded Forages: Production and Utilization

Description, adaptation, establishment, management, diseases, insects, weeds, economics, and utilization of forage crops. 3 exams. Videocassette deposit: $60. (2 credits)

Anthropology

Introduction to Physical Anthropology

Basic concepts relating to the origin, evolution and biological nature of the human species. 11 lessons, 2 exams. Videocassette deposit: $20. (3 credits)

Communications

Introduction to Mass Media

An overview of mass media, newspapers, magazines, books, radio, television, and films, and a study of their historical development with emphasis on understanding the techniques of expression and impact on American culture. A survey of the content of mass media. Consideration of contemporary problems and trends. No lessons, 3 exams. Videocassette deposit: $50. (3 credits)

Introduction to Human Communication

Introduction to theories and research investigated by social and behavioral scientists on the process of communication. Orients beginning students of communication by focusing on concepts and issues central to human communication. Videocassette deposit: $30. (3 credits)

Education

Reading Disabilities

Designed to provide the student with the theories, concepts, and practical methods of diagnosing reading disabilities. The student will be taken from an intensive discussion of current theories of reading disabilities to the practical application of these theories in diagnosing actual cases of reading disability. The student will be expected to administer tests of reading ability to at least four individuals. Then, the student will be responsible for diagnosing the reading disabilities of each individual. This will give the student practical experience in diagnosing reading disabilities when he/she enters the classroom to teach. The course is intended for students who have had at least one course in the foundation of reading instruction. 12 lessons, 2 exams. Audio- and videocassette deposit: $40. (3 credits)

Engineering

Statics

Vector statics of particles, rigid bodies, and distributive loads. 7 lessons, 3 exams. Videocassette deposit: $50. (3 credits)

Dynamics

Vector dynamics of particles and rigid bodies, impulse-momentum and work-energy. 6 lessons, 3 exams. Audiocassette deposit: $30. (3 credits)

English

American Literature II

A survey of major figures and literary movements from Whitman to Faulkner. 10 lessons, 2 exams. Audio- and videocassette deposit: $60. (3 credits)

Regional U.S. Literature: The West

Major themes and writers in Western American literature: frontiersman, Native Indians, trails, mining, cattlemen, settlers, etc. Audio- and videocassette deposit: $25. (3 credits)

Geography

Introduction to World Regional Geography

Introduction to the world's major geographic regions highlighting political, economic, and social systems of selected newsworthy countries. 11 lessons, 3 exams. Videocassette deposit: $20. (3 credits)

Health

Standard First Aid and Personal Safety

Study of accident prevention, examination procedures, and first aid care for victims of accidents or sudden illness before medical assistance is available. New Red Cross content is presented. CPR is presented. 15 lessons, 2 exams. Audio- and videocassette deposit: $20. (2 credits)

History

Western Civilization I

A basic survey of western European civilization from the decline of the Roman Empire to 1700. 8 lessons, 2 exams. Videocassette deposit: $50. (3 credits)

Western Civilization II

A broad survey of European history in the Western tradition from 1700 to the present. 8 lessons, 2 exams. Videocassette deposit: $50. (3 credits)

History of Wyoming

A study of Wyoming from its beginning to the present. 3 lessons, 1 exam. Videocassette deposit: $50. (2 credits)

History of the U.S. West

An introductory survey of the American West, with consideration of developments in both the 19th and 20th centuries. 9 lessons, 2 exams. Audiocassette deposit: $30. (2 credits)

History of United States Indians

A study of American Indian history, with emphasis on Indians of the American West. Consideration is given to Indian political, social, and economic continuity and change. Developments in the 19th and 20th centuries are featured in the course. 2 lessons, 2 term papers, 2 exams. Audiocassette deposit: $20. (3 credits)

French

First Year French I

Fundamentals of grammar, composition, conversation, and reading. 17 lessons, 2 exams. Audiocassette deposit: $10. (4 credits)

Second Year French

Reading simple novels, short stories, and dramas. Grammar review, conversation. 16 lessons, 2 exams. Audiocassette deposit: $10. (4 credits)

Mathematics

Business Calculus I

First semester course in business calculus. Topics include review of functions, their graphs and their algebra, derivatives and their applications, techniques of differentiation, the calculus for the exponential and logarithmic functions with applications to business, integration and applications, the trigonometric functions and their calculus, differential equations and applications. 17 lessons, 3 exams. Videocassette deposit: $30. (4 credits)

Music

Introduction to Music

A course in music appreciation designed for the student who has had little or no musical training. Emphasis is on developing listening skills. 14 lessons, 2 exams. Audiocassette deposit: $30. (3 credits)

United States Ethnic Music

A survey of American folk music, American Indian music, work music, and other music indigenous to various ethnic groups. 12 lessons, 1 exam. Audiocassette deposit: $30. (2 credits)

The Classical Period

Concentrated survey and style analysis of music of the classical period. 12 lessons, 2 exams. Audiocassette deposit: $30. (2 credits)

The Romantic Period

Survey of romantic musical literature. 12 lessons, 2 exams. Audiocassette deposit: $30. (2 credits)

Nursing

Development Influences on Health

This survey course provides the opportunity for students to explore the interaction between development and health. Human development of physiological, psychological, cognitive, sociocultural lines of defense are discussed across the life span. Selected theories associated with development over the life span and implications for nursing are identified. The course provides a foundation for more in-depth consideration of developmental factors related to health maintenance. 11 lessons, 4 exams. Videocassette deposit: $30. (3 credits)

Psychology

General Psychology

A basic introductory course covering a general survey of psychology through lecture notes, audiotapes, and assigned readings. Topics treated include the development of behavior, the physiological mechanisms of behavior, perception, motivation and emotion, learning, intelligence, individuality and personality, and mental health. 16 lessons, 2 exams. Audiocassette deposit: $20. (4 credits)

Child Psychology

The development and behavior of children from conception to adolescence is treated with emphasis on the major roles played by maturation and learning. The purpose of the course is to acquaint the student with the area of child study in terms of research findings, and theories of child development. 12 lessons, 2 exams. Audiocassette deposit: $20. (3 credits)

Cognitive Psychology

This course deals with those higher mental processes that are primarily unique to human beings from both a theoretical and a research orientation. Emphasis is placed upon the interrelationships between the various cognitive processes, and upon the continuity of those processes with perceptual and noncognitive activities. It is concerned with how information is processed and remembered. 12 lessons, 2 exams. Audiocassette deposit: $20. (2 credits)

The Adolescent

This course emphasizes a descriptive view of adolescent development. Consideration is given to physical and physiological growth, intellectual/cognitive/academic/vocational development, changes in attitudes/interests/activities, and development of interpersonal relationships. 9 lessons, 4 exams. Audio- and videocassette deposit: $50. (3 credits)

Abnormal Psychology

This course provides a general overview of abnormal behavior with emphasis on types, etiology, and treatment methods. No lessons, 4 exams. Audiocassette deposit: $20. (3 credits)

Theories of Personality

This is an extensive study of the major theoretical approaches to the explanation of personality as well as the historical trends that culminated in the theories. No lessons, 4 exams. Audiocassette deposit: $20. (3 credits)

Sociology

Introductory Sociology

An introductory course providing both a survey of the discipline and a foundation for other sociology courses. Major areas of interest—ranging from small groups to families to bureaucracies and movements—are explored. Significant concepts and theories are introduced, along with the tools of social research. Though much attention is given to contemporary American society, comparative and historical material is included. 16 lessons, 4 exams. Videocassette deposit: $20. (3 credits)

Spanish

First Year Spanish I

Fundamentals of grammar, composition, conversation, and reading. 15 lessons, 2 exams. Audiocassette deposit: $10. (4 credits)

First Year Spanish II

Fundamentals of grammar, composition, conversation, and reading. 15 lessons, 2 exams. Audiocassette deposit: $10. (4 credits)

Statistics

Fundamentals of Statistics

The goal of this course is to present the central ideas and applications of statistical inference. Topics include probability, probability models, inferences for means, variances and parameters of discrete distributions. 13 lessons, 3 exams. Videocassette deposit: $25. (3 credits)

Indexes

Subject Index

This index is arranged alphabetically by subject, by state, by institution. Courses are in order by level of difficulty and are listed for each subject under the institution names.

Accounting

* University of Alaska, Fairbanks, **AK**
   Elementary Accounting I
   Elementary Accounting II

* Colorado SURGE, Fort Collins, **CO**
   Managerial Accounting

* Mind Extension University, Englewood, **CO**
   Introductory Financial Accounting

Governors State University, University Park, **IL**
   Financial Accounting
   Managerial Accounting for Health Care Organizations

Prince George's Community College, Largo, **MD**
   Principles of Accounting I

* Western Michigan University - MITN, Office of Telecourse Programs, Kalamazoo, **MI**
   Principles of Accounting 210
   Principles of Accounting 211

* University of Missouri, Columbia, **MO**
   Introduction to Accounting

* Empire State College, Saratoga Springs, **NY**
   Accounting for Decision Makers
   Accounting I
   Accounting II
   Intermediate Accounting I
   Intermediate Accounting II
   Cost Accounting

* New York Institute of Technology, Old Westbury, **NY**
   Accounting I
   Accounting II

* Rochester Institute of Technology, Rochester, **NY**
   Financial Accounting
   The Role of Accounting in the Organization

Rockland Community College, Suffern, **NY**
   Principles of Accounting I and II

North Carolina State University, Raleigh, **NC**
   Accounting II: An Introduction to Managerial Accounting

* Pennsylvania State University, University Park, **PA**
   Introductory Financial Accounting

Community College of Rhode Island, Lincoln, **RI**
   Survey of Accounting

Northern Virginia Community College, Annandale, **VA**
   Principles of Accounting I
   Principles of Accounting II

Milwaukee Area Technical College, Milwaukee, **WI**
   Financial Accounting

Adult Education

* Colorado SURGE, Fort Collins, **CO**
   Processes and Methods
   Adult Teaching and Learning I

North Carolina State University, Raleigh, **NC**
   Organization and Operation of Training and Development Programs

Advanced Technology and Management

National Technological University, Fort Collins, **CO**
   Advanced Technology and Management

Aerospace and Mechanical Engineering

* University of Arizona, Tucson, **AZ**
   Reliability Engineering
   Probabilistic Mechanical Design

African Studies

Governors State University, University Park, **IL**
   African Civilizations

* University of Minnesota, Minneapolis, **MN**
   Introduction to African Literature

*Institute provides nationwide or worldwide course access

Agricultural Economics

* Western Illinois University, Macomb, **IL**
  Marketing Grain and Livestock Products
  Commodity Markets and Futures Trading
  Options on Futures
  Market Logic

Agricultural Engineering

* Colorado SURGE, Fort Collins, **CO**
  Soil-Water Engineering
  Environmental Law
  Drainage Engineering
  Hydraulic Design of Farm Irrigation
  Groundwater Quality and Contaminant Transport
  Flow in Porous Media

Agriculture

* Colorado SURGE, Fort Collins, **CO**
  Agricultural and Resource Economics

  North Dakota Interactive Video Network, Bismarck, **ND**
  Farm and Ranch Management
  Crop Production II

* University of Wyoming, Laramie, **WY**
  Current Topics in Seeded Forages: Production and Utilization

Agronomy

* Colorado SURGE, Fort Collins, **CO**
  Agricultural Experimental Design

Alaska Native Studies

* University of Alaska, Fairbanks, **AK**
  Alaska Native Claims Settlement Act

Allied Health

Rockland Community College, Suffern, **NY**
Here's to Your Health

American Studies

* Indiana University, Bloomington, **IN**
  Representative Americans—Special Topic: People with Disabilities

* University of Minnesota, Minneapolis, **MN**
  Topics in American Studies: Ellery Queen and the American Detective Story
  Topics in American Studies: The Meaning of Place

Animal Science

* Mind Extension University, Englewood, **CO**
  Animal Products Option Completion Program

Anthropology

* University of Alaska, Fairbanks, **AK**
  Introduction to Anthropology
  Native Cultures of Alaska
  World Ethnography: Indian Sikhs

* University of Arizona, Tucson, **AZ**
  Culture and the Individual

  INTELECOM, Pasadena, **CA**
  Faces of Culture

  Northern California Telecommunications Consortium, Sacramento, **CA**
  Faces of Culture

  KRMA/Denver, Denver, **CO**
  Faces of Culture

  Belleville Area College, Belleville, **IL**
  Cultural Anthropology

  North Iowa Area Community College, Mason City, **IA**
  Faces of Culture

* University of Iowa, Iowa City, **IA**
  Faces of Culture
  Out of the Past: An Introduction to Archaeology

* University of Kansas, Lawrence, **KS**
  Introduction to Cultural Anthropology
  Myth, Legend, and Folk Belief in East Asia

  Prince George's Community College, Largo, **MD**
  Introduction to Cultural Anthropology

  WGBH/Boston, Boston, **MA**
  Faces of Culture

  Wayne County Community College, Detroit, **MI**
  Introduction to Cultural Anthropology

* Western Michigan University, Department of Distance Education, Kalamazoo, **MI**
  Topics in World Culture Areas: Indians and Eskimos

* University of Minnesota, Minneapolis, **MN**
  Introduction to Social and Cultural Anthropology

  University of New Hampshire, Durham, **NH**
  Faces of Culture

* Empire State College, Saratoga Springs, **NY**
  Faces of Culture
  Competition and Cooperation: Cultural Anthropology

* New York Institute of Technology, Old Westbury, **NY**
  Anthropology

  Rockland Community College, Suffern, **NY**
  Cultural Anthropology
  Culture and Language

  Rose State College, Midwest City, **OK**
  General Anthropology

  University of Oklahoma, Norman, **OK**
  Introduction to Archaeology

  Tarrant County Junior College, Fort Worth, **TX**
  Introduction to Anthropology

*Institute provides nationwide or worldwide course access

* University of Washington, Seattle, **WA**
  Principles of Sociocultural Anthropology

* Western Washington University, Bellingham, **WA**
  Joseph Campbell: Transformations of Myth Through Time

Central Wyoming College, Riverton, **WY**
  Introduction to Archaeology

* University of Wyoming, Laramie, **WY**
  Introduction to Physical Anthropology

Antiques and Collectibles

* University of Minnesota, Minneapolis, **MN**
  Principles of Antique Collecting

Apologetics

* Columbia Bible College and Seminary, Columbia, **SC**
  Christian Evidences

Arabic

* Washington State University, Pullman, **WA**
  First Semester Arabic
  Second Semester Arabic
  Third Semester Arabic

University of Wisconsin (UW), Madison, **WI**
  First Semester Arabic
  Second Semester Arabic

Archaeology

Metropolitan State College of Denver, Englewood, **CO**
  Archaeology

WGBH/Boston, Boston, **MA**
  Out of the Past

* Western Michigan University, Department of Distance Education, Kalamazoo, **MI**
  Introduction to Archaeology

WNET/New York City, New York, **NY**
  Out of the Past: An Introduction to Archaeology

University of South Dakota, Vermillion, **SD**
  Introduction to Archaeology

Wisconsin Educational Communications Board, Madison, **WI**
  Out of the Past: An Introduction to Archaeology

Architecture

University of Maine at Augusta, Augusta, **ME**
  Introductory Design Theory and Architecture Application and Expression

* University of Minnesota, Minneapolis, **MN**
  The Meanings and Messages of Place, City, Town, and Countryside

Art

* University of Alaska, Fairbanks, **AK**
  Two-Dimensional Design

* Rio Salado Community College, Phoenix, **AZ**
  Art History: Prehistory to Gothic

Harold Washington College, Chicago, **IL**
  The Photographic Vision: All About Photography

Teikyo Marycrest University, Davenport, **IA**
  Art of the Western World

* University of Iowa, Iowa City, **IA**
  Calligraphy I
  Calligraphy II

* University of Kansas, Lawrence, **KS**
  Introduction to Art History

College of the Air, Owings Mills, **MD**
  Art of the Western World

* University of Minnesota, Minneapolis, **MN**
  Introduction to Visual Arts

University of Nebraska at Kearney, Kearney, **NE**
  Art Appreciation

Rockland Community College, Suffern, **NY**
  Art of the Western World
  History of Art I
  History of Art II
  History of American Art

Edison State Community College, Greenville, **OH**
  Art History through the Renaissance

* Oklahoma State University, Stillwater, **OK**
  Introduction to Art

* Pennsylvania State University, University Park, **PA**
  The Visual Arts and the Studio: An Introduction

* Utah State University, Logan, **UT**
  Basic Typography Design

Northern Virginia Community College, Annandale, **VA**
  Art in World Culture

Art History

Northern California Telecommunications Consortium, Sacramento, **CA**
  Art of the Western World

University of Maine at Augusta, Augusta, **ME**
  Art Appreciation and History I

* Pennsylvania State University, University Park, **PA**
  Survey of Western Art I
  Survey of Western Art II
  Special Topics: Africa
  The Arts

* University of Utah, Salt Lake City, **UT**
  Art History

*Institute provides nationwide or worldwide course access

Astronomy

INTELECOM, Pasadena, **CA**
Project Universe

Northern California Telecommunications Consortium, Sacramento, **CA**
Project Universe

* University of California, Berkeley, **CA**
Introduction to General Astronomy

* Southeastern College, Lakeland, **FL**
Astronomy

Harold Washington College, Chicago, **IL**
Descriptive Astronomy

College of the Air, Owings Mills, **MD**
Project Universe

Prince George's Community College, Largo, **MD**
Introduction to Astronomy

* University of Missouri, Columbia, **MO**
Cosmic Evolution/Introductory Astronomy

* Pennsylvania State University, University Park, **PA**
Astronomical Universe

Aviation Technology

* University of Alaska, Fairbanks, **AK**
Private Pilot Ground School

Belleville Area College, Belleville, **IL**
Private Pilot Ground School

Baccalaureate Degree Completion

* Mind Extension University, Englewood, **CO**
Bachelor's Completion Degrees from NUDC

Behavioral Science

* University of Maryland University College, College Park, **MD**
Introduction to Behavioral and Social Sciences (*Video*)
Race to Save the Planet (*Video*)

Bible

* Taylor University, Fort Wayne, **IN**
Romans

* Columbia Bible College and Seminary, Columbia, **SC**
Old Testament Survey: Genesis—Song of Solomon
New Testament Survey: Gospels/Life of Christ
New Testament Survey: Acts to Revelation
Bible Studies in Prayer
Galations
Philippians
James
Old Testament Survey: Prophetic Books
Principles of Bible Interpretation

Living Your Faith: Studies in Amos
I John
Judges
I Peter
II Peter
The Gospel of Mark: the Cross in Our Lives
Colossians/Philemon
Philippians: How to Study and Teach a Bible Book
I Corinthians
Ephesians
Daniel and Revelation
Progress of Redemption
The Epistle to the Hebrews
The Sermon on the Mount
The Upper Room Experience
Old Testament Survey: Genesis—Poetical Books (*Graduate Level*)
Old Testament Survey: Prophetic Books (*Graduate Level*)
New Testament Survey: Gospels/Life of Christ (*Graduate Level*)
New Testament Survey: Acts to Revelation (*Graduate Level*)
Basic Biblical Hermeneutics (*Graduate Level*)
The Gospel of Mark: The Cross in Our Lives (*Graduate Level*)
Understanding the Old Testament (*Graduate Level*)
The Pentateuch (*Graduate Level*)
Conquest and Settlement (*Graduate Level*)
The Sermon on the Mount (*Graduate Level*)
The Upper Room Experience (*Graduate Level*)
Living Your Faith: Studies in Amos (*Graduate Level*)
Psalms (*Graduate Level*)
I Corinthians (*Graduate Level*)
Philippians: How to Study and Teach a Bible Book (*Graduate Level*)
Colossians/Philemon (*Graduate Level*)
Ephesians (*Graduate Level*)
The Epistle to the Hebrews (*Graduate Level*)
Acts in Historical, Theological, and Missiological Perspective (*Graduate Level*)
Romans (*Graduate Level*)
Progress of Redemption (*Graduate Level*)
Messianic Prophecy (*Graduate Level*)
Daniel and Revelation (*Graduate Level*)
The Pastoral Epistles (*Graduate Level*)
The Christian and Old Testament Theology (*Graduate Level*)

Biblical Languages

* Taylor University, Fort Wayne, **IN**
Introduction to Biblical Hebrew

Bilingual Reading and Writing

* University of Arizona, Tucson, **AZ**
Bilingual Reading and Writing

Biological Science

* Pennsylvania State University, University Park, **PA**
Environmental Science

*Institute provides nationwide or worldwide course access

Biology

* University of Alaska, Fairbanks, **AK**
    Natural History of Alaska
    Introduction to Marine Biology

Northern California Telecommunications Consortium, Sacramento, **CA**
    Introduction to Biology

* University of California, Berkeley, **CA**
    Modern Biology
    Plants and Civilization
    Plant Life in California

* Mind Extension University, Englewood, **CO**
    Introduction to Biology

Pikes Peak Community College, Colorado Springs, **CO**
    Environmental Biology

Belleville Area College, Belleville, **IL**
    Introduction to Marine Biology

Harold Washington College, Chicago, **IL**
    General Biology I and II

* Indiana State University, Terre Haute, **IN**
    Conversational Biology: Reproduction, Growth, and Development
    Conversational Biology: Human Genetics

* Indiana University, Bloomington, **IN**
    Biology of Women

Indiana Vocational Technical College, South Bend, **IN**
    Biology
    Biology Lab

* University of Kansas, Lawrence, **KS**
    Principles of Biology

* Home Study International, Silver Spring, **MD**
    A Scientific Study of Creation

WGBH/Boston, Boston, **MA**
    The Secret of Life

University of New Hampshire, Durham, **NH**
    The Human Brain

* Empire State College, Saratoga Springs, **NY**
    Topics in Biology

North Carolina State University, Raleigh, **NC**
    Biology in the Modern World

Community College of Rhode Island, Lincoln, **RI**
    Man and Environment

Tarrant County Junior College, Fort Worth, **TX**
    General Biology II
    Environmental Biology

* Utah State University, Logan, **UT**
    Human Physiology

Northern Virginia Community College, Annandale, **VA**
    General Biology I
    General Biology II

Business

University of Alabama, Tuscaloosa, **AL**
    Labor Law

* University of Alaska, Fairbanks, **AK**
    Basics of Investing
    Real Estate Law
    Applied Business Law I
    Applied Business Law II

* Rio Salado Community College, Phoenix, **AZ**
    Import/Export Business

INTELECOM, Pasadena, **CA**
    Business and the Law
    The Business File

Northern California Telecommunications Consortium, Sacramento, **CA**
    Business and the Law
    The Business File

* Colorado SURGE, Fort Collins, **CO**
    Managerial Economics
    Business Policy
    Production Administration

KRMA/Denver, Denver, **CO**
    The Business File
    Business and the Law

Connecticut Community-Technical College System, Hartford, **CT**
    Something Ventured

Florida West Coast Public Broadcasting, Inc., Tampa, **FL**
    The Business File

Belleville Area College, Belleville, **IL**
    Introduction to Business

Harold Washington College, Chicago, **IL**
    Fundamentals of Accounting
    Introduction to Business
    Business Mathematics
    Business Law I and II

Indiana Vocational Technical College, South Bend, **IN**
    Introduction to Business: The Business File

North Iowa Area Community College, Mason City, **IA**
    The Business File

Elizabethtown Community College, Elizabethtown, **KY**
    The Business File

Kentucky Telecommunications Consortium, Lexington, **KY**
    The Business File
    Something Ventured: Small Business Management

Murray State University, Murray, **KY**
    The Business File

Northern Kentucky University, Highland Heights, **KY**
    The Business File
    Something Ventured: Small Business Management

University of Maine at Augusta, Augusta, **ME**
    Introduction to Business
    Principles of Accounting I

*Institute provides nationwide or worldwide course access

Principles of Accounting II
Intermediate Accounting I
Principles of Management
Business Ethics
Business Finance
Cost Accounting I
Organizational Behavior

College of the Air, Owings Mills, **MD**
Business File
Business and the Law
By the Numbers
Something Ventured: Small Business Management

* Home Study International, Silver Spring, **MD**
Typing

WGBH/Boston, Boston, **MA**
Business and the Law

North Central Michigan College, Petoskey, **MI**
The Business File

Northwestern Michigan College, Traverse City, **MI**
The Business File

Wayne County Community College, Detroit, **MI**
Business Law I
Introduction to Business
Computer Applications in Business

University of Nebraska at Kearney, Kearney, **NE**
Introduction to Business

University of New Hampshire, Durham, **NH**
Something Ventured: Small Business Management

* Empire State College, Saratoga Springs, **NY**
Business Mathematics
Statistics
Legal Environment of Business I
Legal Environment of Business II
Economics - Macro
Economics - Micro
Management Principles
Marketing Principles
Economic Policy Analysis
International Business
Marketing and Sales Promotion
Human Resource Management and Development
Corporate Finance
Investing
Income Tax I
Income Tax II
Income Tax Practicum
Auditing
Advanced Quantitative Methods in Management
Labor-Management Relations
International Marketing
Money and Banking
Organizational Behavior
Business Policy
Marketing Management
Marketing Research

Rockland Community College, Suffern, **NY**
An Introduction to Business

Business Law I
WNET/New York City, New York, **NY**
Business and the Law

North Dakota Interactive Video Network, Bismarck, **ND**
Principles of Management
Accounting Problems

* Ohio University, Athens, **OH**
Introduction to Business Computing

Rose State College, Midwest City, **OK**
Introduction to Business
Business Law I
Business Law II

Dallas County Community College District, Dallas, **TX**
Introduction to Business
Principles of Accounting

Tarrant County Junior College, Fort Worth, **TX**
Introduction to Business
Business Mathematics
Business Law I

* Texas Tech University, Lubbock, **TX**
Business Computer Progamming
Business Computer Applications
Business Writing
Keyboarding
Introduction to Information Systems in the Automated Office

West Virginia Higher Education Instructional Television
Consortium, Morgantown, **WV**
The Business File
The Sales Connection: Principles of Selling

Milwaukee Area Technical College, Milwaukee, **WI**
Microcomputers in Business
Business Organization and Management
Business Law I

Wisconsin Educational Communications Board, Madison,
WI
Business and the Law

Central Wyoming College, Riverton, **WY**
Introduction to Business

Business Administration

* University of Phoenix - San Francisco, San Francisco, **CA**
Management and Leadership
Business Communications
Business Law
Computers and Information Processing
Business Research Project
Statistics in Business
Economics for Business
Financial Accounting
Managerial Finance
Marketing
Quantitative Analysis in Business

*Institute provides nationwide or worldwide course access

* International School of Information Management, Inc., Denver, **CO**
    Management
    Accounting
    Quantitative Analysis
    Finance
    Marketing Management
    Managerial Economics
    Strategic Planning
    Strategies for Change
    Emerging Technologies
    Capstone Project
    Specialization

* Mind Extension University, Englewood, **CO**
    MBA Program

Prince George's Community College, Largo, **MD**
    Introduction to Business
    Principles of Management
    Small Business Management
    Business Law

* University of Maryland University College, College Park, **MD**
    Business Finance (*ITV*)

* Western Michigan University - MITN, Office of Telecourse Programs, Kalamazoo, **MI**
    Accounting Control and Analysis
    Computer Information Systems
    Legal Controls of the Business Enterprise
    Financial Management
    Applied Economics for Management
    Policy Formulation and Administration
    Marketing Management

* University of Missouri, Columbia, **MO**
    Entrepreneurship/Small Business Management

* New York Institute of Technology, Old Westbury, **NY**
    Introduction to Marketing
    Sales Management
    Retailing Management
    Management of Promotion
    Business Law I
    Business Law II
    Business Law III
    Corporate Finance
    Principles of Investments
    Introduction to EDP in Business
    Statistical Sampling Theory
    Quantitative Applications to Making Managerial Decisions
    Personnel Administration
    Introduction to Management Information Systems
    Business Cycles and Forecasting
    Business Organization and Administration
    Collective Bargaining and Labor Relations
    New Product Management
    Small Business Management

* Pennsylvania State University, University Park, **PA**
    Problems of Small Business

Community College of Rhode Island, Lincoln, **RI**
    Introduction to Business

*Institute provides nationwide or worldwide course access

Small Business Administration

Northern Virginia Community College, Annandale, **VA**
    Principles of Management
    Business Law I

Business Information Systems

* Colorado SURGE, Fort Collins, **CO**
    Computer Applications in Decision Making
    Advanced Systems Design

Business Law

* Western Michigan University - MITN, Office of Telecourse Programs, Kalamazoo, **MI**
    Legal Environment

* Oklahoma State University, Stillwater, **OK**
    Law of Contracts and Property

* Pennsylvania State University, University Park, **PA**
    Legal Environment

Community College of Rhode Island, Lincoln, **RI**
    Law of Contracts

Business Logistics

* Pennsylvania State University, University Park, **PA**
    Business Logistics Management

Business Management

* Mind Extension University, Englewood, **CO**
    Legal and Regulatory Environment of Business
    World Economic Development
    International Business
    Industrial and Labor Relations
    Leadership and Management in an Age of Diversity
    Accounting for Managers
    The Global Business Environment
    Organizational Communication
    Principles of Marketing
    Marketing for Managers
    Total Quality Management
    Managerial Planning and Competitive Strategies

Community College of Rhode Island, Lincoln, **RI**
    Principles of Management

Career Guidance

Northern California Telecommunications Consortium, Sacramento, **CA**
    Voyage: Challenge and Change in Career/Life Planning

* Pennsylvania State University, University Park, **PA**
    Job Placement Skills and Strategies

Chemical Engineering

* Colorado SURGE, Fort Collins, **CO**
  Unit Operations and Transport Phenomena II
  Chemical Engineering Thermodynamic Fundamentals
  Process Control and Instrumentation
  Advanced Reactor Design

Chemistry

Northern California Telecommunications Consortium, Sacramento, **CA**
  The World of Chemistry

Metropolitan State College of Denver, Englewood, **CO**
  Chemistry and Society

College of the Air, Owings Mills, **MD**
  The World of Chemistry

* New Jersey Institute of Technology, Newark, **NJ**
  College Chemistry for Advanced Placement or College Credit
    (Course 108)
  College Chemistry for Advanced Placement or College Credit
    (Course 109)

North Carolina State University, Raleigh, **NC**
  Organic Chemistry I

* University of Washington, Seattle, **WA**
  General Chemistry C140
  General Chemistry C150

Milwaukee Area Technical College, Milwaukee, **WI**
  The World of Chemistry

Child Care

Wisconsin Educational Communications Board, Madison, **WI**
  Caring for Infants and Toddlers
  Caring for Children: An Introduction to the Child Care Profession

Child Development

* University of Alaska, Fairbanks, **AK**
  Child Development

INTELECOM, Pasadena, **CA**
  Time to Grow

* Mind Extension University, Englewood, **CO**
  Psychological Foundations of Childhood

Governors State University, University Park, **IL**
  Child Development

Harold Washington College, Chicago, **IL**
  Human Growth and Development

College of the Air, Owings Mills, **MD**
  A Time to Grow

Rose State College, Midwest City, **OK**
  Child Growth and Development

San Antonio College, San Antonio, **TX**
  Child Growth and Development

West Virginia Higher Education Instructional Television Consortium, Morgantown, **WV**
  Time to Grow

Childhood Education

North Dakota Interactive Video Network, Bismarck, **ND**
  Young Children's Language and Thought
  Childhood Development Practice II

University of Wisconsin (UW), Madison, **WI**
  Caring for Children: An Introduction to the Child-Care Profession

Chinese

* University of California, Berkeley, **CA**
  Elementary Chinese: Course I

* University of Iowa, Iowa City, **IA**
  Chinese I
  Chinese II

Chinese Studies

West Virginia Higher Education Instructional Television Consortium, Morgantown, **WV**
  The Chinese

Christian Education

* Southeastern College, Lakeland, **FL**
  Children's Ministries
  Family Ministries

* Taylor University, Fort Wayne, **IN**
  Christian Education of Children
  Perspectives on the World Christian Movement

* Columbia Bible College and Seminary, Columbia, **SC**
  Leadership and Administration
  The Philosophy of Christian School Education

Christian Leadership Development

* Southeastern College, Lakeland, **FL**
  Leadership Development
  Organizational Behavior and Leadership Styles
  Conflict Management
  Counseling and Contemporary Issues

Christian Ministries

* Columbia Bible College and Seminary, Columbia, **SC**
  Introduction to Missions
  History of Missions (*Graduate Level*)
  Principles of Community Development (*Graduate Level*)
  Cultural Anthropology (*Graduate Level*)
  Traditional Religions

*Institute provides nationwide or worldwide course access

China and Chinese Ministry (*Graduate Level*)
Urban Missions

Christian Missions

* Southeastern College, Lakeland, **FL**
Missionary Field Work
Theology of Missions
Area Study: Latin America
History of Missions
Modern Missions Survey
Anthropology
Missionary Methods
Area Study: Europe
The Urban Context for Ministry
Area Study: Middle East
Area Study: Far East
Area Study: Africa
Contemporary Issues in Missions
Cross-Cultural Communications

Church History

* Columbia Bible College and Seminary, Columbia, **SC**
Modern Pseudo-Christian Cults

Civil Engineering

* Colorado SURGE, Fort Collins, **CO**
Basic Hydrology
Engineering Hydrology
Modeling Watershed Hydrology
Residuals Management
Aqueous Chemistry
Unit Processes of Environmental Engineering
Water Resource Systems Analysis
Earth and Earth-Retaining Structures
Fundamentals of Vibrations
Advanced Design of Wood Structures
Urban Water Management
Infrastructure Engineering and Management
Wind Effects on Structures
Computational Fluid Dynamics
Open Channel Flow
Hydraulics of Closed Conduits
Water Quality Hydrology
Solutions to Groundwater Problems
Design of Dams
Foundations of Solid Mechanics
Finite Element Method
Advanced Structural Analysis
Advanced Design of Metal Structures
River Mechanics
Stochastic Analysis in Water Resources

University of Nebraska - CorpNet, Nebraska CorpNet, Lincoln, **NE**
Theoretical Soil Mechanics II

Classical Studies

* Indiana University, Bloomington, **IN**
Medical Terms from Greek and Latin

* University of Minnesota, Minneapolis, **MN**
Magic, Witchcraft, and the Occult in Greece and Rome
Roman Realities: Life and Thought in the Roman Empire
Eroticism and Family Life in the Graeco-Roman World
Madness and Deviant Behavior in Ancient Greece and Rome

Cognitive Science

* New School for Social Research, New York, **NY**
Brain, Mind, Computer

Communication Disorders

* University of Kansas, Lawrence, **KS**
Survey of Communication Disorders
Communication Disorders

* University of Utah, Salt Lake City, **UT**
Beginning Sign Language

* Utah State University, Logan, **UT**
Listening Problems in the Classroom
Listening and Speech Training for the Hearing Impaired

Communications

* Rio Salado Community College, Phoenix, **AZ**
Introduction to Human Communication

University of Maine at Augusta, Augusta, **ME**
Interpersonal Communications

* University of Minnesota, Minneapolis, **MN**
Introduction to Technical and Business Communication

* Empire State College, Saratoga Springs, **NY**
Communications for Professionals
Communications Decisions
Communications Analysis
The Television Environment

* Rochester Institute of Technology, Rochester, **NY**
Technical Writing
Communication
Communication in Business
Organizational Communication
Human Communication
Mass Communication

North Carolina State University, Raleigh, **NC**
Interpersonal Communication

Milwaukee Area Technical College, Milwaukee, **WI**
Communication Skills

* University of Wyoming, Laramie, **WY**
Introduction to Mass Media
Introduction to Human Communication

Comparative Literature

* Pennsylvania State University, University Park, **PA**
    Masterpieces of Western Literature since the Renaissance

Computer Conferencing

* New School for Social Research, New York, **NY**
    Computer Conferencing in Business and Education

Computer Education

* Nova University, Fort Lauderdale, **FL**
    Practicum Proposal in Computer Education (Part I)
    Practicum Report in Computer Education (Part II)
    Introduction to Structured Programming in Pascal
    Advanced Computer Programming in Pascal

Computer Information Systems

* Weber State University, Ogden, **UT**
    Hardware/DOS
    Introduction to Word Processing
    Introduction to Spreadsheets
    Introduction to Database Management Systems

Northern Virginia Community College, Annandale, **VA**
    Introduction to Information Systems

Computer Literacy

INTELECOM, Pasadena, **CA**
    The New Literacy

Northern California Telecommunications Consortium, Sacramento, **CA**
    The New Literacy

College of the Air, Owings Mills, **MD**
    The New Literacy

Computer Science

* University of Alaska, Fairbanks, **AK**
    Introduction to Computer Programming

Northern California Telecommunications Consortium, Sacramento, **CA**
    ComputerWorks

* University of California, Berkeley, **CA**
    Concepts of Data Processing
    Introduction to Progamming with BASIC

* Colorado SURGE, Fort Collins, **CO**
    Computer Organization
    Algorithms and Data Structures
    Discrete Structures
    C Programming Module
    Comparative Programming Languages
    Foundations of Computer Science
    Software Development Methods
    System Architecture and Software

    Introduction to Computer Graphics
    Introduction to Artificial Intelligence
    Data Communications
    Computer Graphics
    Artificial Intelligence
    Algorithmic Language Compilers
    Advanced Computer Architecture
    Parallel Processing
    Performance Evaluation and Modeling
    Architecture of Advanced Systems (Optical Communication Networks)

Belleville Area College, Belleville, **IL**
    Introduction to Data Processing

Harold Washington College, Chicago, **IL**
    Introduction to Data Processing
    Introduction to Microcomputers

* Indiana University, Bloomington, **IN**
    Introduction to Microcomputers and Computing
    Advanced Microcomputing: Programming with Applications
    Introduction to Programming
    COBOL and File Processing
    Introduction to Computer Science
    COBOL Programming

Indiana Vocational Technical College, South Bend, **IN**
    Electronic Spreadsheets: Lotus 1-2-3, V. 2.3
    Microcomputer Database Management: dBASE IV, V. 1.1
    Word Processing: WordPerfect, V. 5.1
    Advanced Word Processing: Advanced WordPerfect 5.1

* University of Iowa, Iowa City, **IA**
    The New Literacy

College of the Air, Owings Mills, **MD**
    ComputerWorks

Prince George's Community College, Largo, **MD**
    Computer Literacy
    Microcomputer Applications

* University of Minnesota, Minneapolis, **MN**
    Introduction to Microcomputer Applications
    Introduction to Computer Programming

* University of Missouri, Columbia, **MO**
    Introduction to BASIC
    Software Applications on the PC

University of Nebraska - CorpNet, Nebraska CorpNet, Lincoln, **NE**
    Combinatorial Methods for Computer Science
    Automata, Computation, and Formal Languages

* New Jersey Institute of Technology, Newark, **NJ**
    Introduction to Computer Progamming and Problem Solving
    Computer Science with Problem Solving
    Introduction to Computer Science
    Principles of Operating Systems

* Empire State College, Saratoga Springs, **NY**
    Introduction to Computer Programming: BASIC
    Computer Information Systems
    Systems Analysis and Design

* Rochester Institute of Technology, Rochester, **NY**
    Introduction to Computers and Programming

*Institute provides nationwide or worldwide course access

Introduction to Programming
Program Design and Validation
Computer Concepts and Software Systems
Data Communications and Computer Networks
Applied Database Management

* Oklahoma State University, Stillwater, **OK**
Computer Programming
Introductory BASIC Programming

* Pennsylvania State University, University Park, **PA**
Introduction to Computers with Applications

Community College of Rhode Island, Lincoln, **RI**
Introduction to Computers

San Antonio College, San Antonio, **TX**
Introduction to Computers

* Texas Tech University, Lubbock, **TX**
Introduction to Computers in Business

* Brigham Young University, Provo, **UT**
Elementary Computer Science

Computer-based Learning

* Nova University, Fort Lauderdale, **FL**
Online Information Systems
Statistics, Measurement, and Quality Control
Database Management Systems
The Theory of Human Factors
Systems Analysis and Design
Strategic Management, Leadership, and Finance
Case Analysis
Special Topics in Computer-Based Learning

Counseling

* Southeastern Bible College, Birmingham, **AL**
Counseling

University of Wisconsin (UW), Madison, **WI**
Human Resource Development: Communications Skill-Building Study of Self as a Communicator

Criminal Justice

* Mind Extension University, Englewood, **CO**
Strategies of Crime Control

University of Maine at Augusta, Augusta, **ME**
Foundations of Justice II

University of New Hampshire, Durham, **NH**
Criminal Justice: Organization/Administration

* New York Institute of Technology, Old Westbury, **NY**
Criminal Law and Proceedings
Police Administration
Introduction to Criminal Investigation and Forensic Science
Police and Community Relations
Crisis Intervention for Public Safety Personnel
Crime Prevention: The Systems Approach
Physical Security Strategies
Security and Protection Management

Probation and Parole
Correction Administration
Principles of Correction
The American Court System
Contemporary Corrections
Private Security: Concepts and Strategies

* Washington State University, Pullman, **WA**
Criminal Law

Criminal Law

* Mind Extension University, Englewood, **CO**
Criminal Law

Criminology

* New York Institute of Technology, Old Westbury, **NY**
Criminology

Dance

* Brigham Young University, Provo, **UT**
Aerobic Dance
Social Dance, Beginning

Danish

* University of Washington, Seattle, **WA**
Elementary Danish C101
Elementary Danish C102

Dental Health

North Dakota Interactive Video Network, Bismarck, **ND**
Periodontics

Desktop Publishing

* New School for Social Research, New York, **NY**
Desktop Publishing

Dietetics

* Pennsylvania State University, University Park, **PA**
The Profession of Dietetics
Sanitation Practices in Food Service Operations

Driver Education

North Dakota Interactive Video Network, Bismarck, **ND**
Driver and Traffic Safety Education

Earth Resources

* Colorado SURGE, Fort Collins, **CO**
Modeling Watershed Hydrology

*Institute provides nationwide or worldwide course access

Earth Science

Northern California Telecommunications Consortium, Sacramento, **CA**
 The Earth Revealed: Introductory Geology
 Planet Earth

Miami-Dade Community College, Miami, **FL**
 Introduction to Earth Science

* Pennsylvania State University, University Park, **PA**
 Out of the Fiery Furnace

Dallas County Community College District, Dallas, **TX**
 Earth, Sea, and Sky

West Virginia Higher Education Instructional Television Consortium, Morgantown, **WV**
 Planet Earth

East Asian Languages and Cultures

* University of Kansas, Lawrence, **KS**
 Myth, Legend, and Folk Belief in East Asia

Ecology

Prince George's Community College, Largo, **MD**
 Human Ecology

* Pennsylvania State University, University Park, **PA**
 Wildlife Ecology and Management

Economics

* University of Alaska, Fairbanks, **AK**
 The Alaskan Economy
 Principles of Economics I: Microeconomics
 Principles of Economics II: Macroeconomics

* Rio Salado Community College, Phoenix, **AZ**
 Macroeconomic Principles

INTELECOM, Pasadena, **CA**
 Economics U$A

Northern California Telecommunications Consortium, Sacramento, **CA**
 Economics U$A

KRMA/Denver, Denver, **CO**
 Economics U$A

* Mind Extension University, Englewood, **CO**
 Survey of Economic Issues
 Introduction to Microeconomics

* University of Florida, Gainesville, **FL**
 Principles of Macroeconomics

* University of Idaho, Moscow, **ID**
 Principles of Economics (Macro)
 Principles of Economics (Micro)
 Money and Banking

Belleville Area College, Belleville, **IL**
 Introduction to Economics

Governors State University, University Park, **IL**
 Principles of Macroeconomics

Harold Washington College, Chicago, **IL**
 Principles of Economics I and II

Kentucky Telecommunications Consortium, Lexington, **KY**
 Economics U$A

Murray State University, Murray, **KY**
 Economics U$A

Northern Kentucky University, Highland Heights, **KY**
 Economics U$A

University of Maine at Augusta, Augusta, **ME**
 Principles of Economics I (Macroeconomics)

College of the Air, Owings Mills, **MD**
 Economics U$A

Prince George's Community College, Largo, **MD**
 Introduction to Economics

Wayne County Community College, Detroit, **MI**
 Principles of Economics I
 Principles of Economics II

* Western Michigan University - MITN, Office of Telecourse Programs, Kalamazoo, **MI**
 Principles of Economics 201
 Principles of Economics 202

* University of Missouri, Columbia, **MO**
 Introduction to the American Economy

University of Nebraska at Kearney, Kearney, **NE**
 Principles of Economics - Micro

* New Jersey Institute of Technology, Newark, **NJ**
 Managerial Economics

* New York Institute of Technology, Old Westbury, **NY**
 Principles of Economics I
 Principles of Economics II
 Basic Economics
 Money and Banking
 Monetary Theory and Policy
 Commercial Banking

* Rochester Institute of Technology, Rochester, **NY**
 Principles of Economics I
 Principles of Economics II

Rockland Community College, Suffern, **NY**
 Fundamentals of Economics: Microeconomics
 Fundamentals of Economics: Macroeconomics

Edison State Community College, Greenville, **OH**
 Fundamentals of Economics

* Oklahoma State University, Stillwater, **OK**
 Introduction to Microeconomics

Rose State College, Midwest City, **OK**
 Principles of Microeconomics
 Principles of Macroeconomics

University of Oklahoma, Norman, **OK**
 Principles of Economics-Macroeconomics

*Institute provides nationwide or worldwide course access

Community College of Rhode Island, Lincoln, **RI**
Principles of Economics

University of Texas at Austin, Austin, **TX**
Introduction to Macroeconomics

Northern Virginia Community College, Annandale, **VA**
Principles of Economics I
Principles of Economics II
Survey of Economics

* University of Washington, Seattle, **WA**
Introduction to Microeconomics
Introduction to Macroeconomics

West Virginia Higher Education Instructional Television
Consortium, Morgantown, **WV**
Economics U\$A

Milwaukee Area Technical College, Milwaukee, **WI**
Economics
Principles of Macroeconomics

Wisconsin Educational Communications Board, Madison,
WI
Economics U\$A

Education

* University of Alaska, Fairbanks, **AK**
Literature for Children
Diagnosis and Evaluation of Learning
The Exceptional Learner
Building a Practical Philosophy of Education

* Rio Salado Community College, Phoenix, **AZ**
MCCCD Certification Course

KRMA/Denver, Denver, **CO**
Education of the Gifted and Talented
Teaching Problem Solving in Mathematics

* Mind Extension University, Englewood, **CO**
Educational Technology Leadership

* Southeastern College, Lakeland, **FL**
Exceptional Student Education
Teaching Language Art Skills
Teaching Health and Physical Education
Instructional Media for Education
Media Practicum
Teaching Reading in the Content Areas
Teaching English in the Secondary School
Early Childhood Education I
Early Childhood Education II
Special Methods of Teaching Secondary Subjects
Teaching Social Studies in the Elementary School
Teaching Social Studies in the Secondary School
Introduction to Reading
Diagnosis and Remediation of Reading
Teaching Art for the Elementary Teacher
Teaching Science in the Elementary School
Music for the Elementary Teacher
Curriculum Design K-12
Organization and Administration of Christian Schools

* University of Idaho, Moscow, **ID**
Microcomputer Applications

Governors State University, University Park, **IL**
Foundations of Education

* University of Iowa, Iowa City, **IA**
Time to Grow

University of Maine at Augusta, Augusta, **ME**
Management of Adult/Continuing Education Organizations
Preventing Early School Literacy Failure
Legal Responsibilities in Early Childhood Education

* Marygrove College, Detroit, **MI**
How to Get Parents on Your Side
Succeeding with Difficult Students
Assertive Discipline and Beyond

* University of Minnesota, Minneapolis, **MN**
Inventing the Future—Living, Learning, and Working in the
1990s
Inventing the Future—Living, Learning, and Working in the
1990s
Second Language Programs for Young Children: Like Child's
Play
Second Language Programs for Young Children: Like Child's
Play
Counseling Psychology: Career Development and Planning
Education of the Gifted and Talented
Education of the Gifted and Talented

* University of Missouri, Columbia, **MO**
Microcomputers: Applications for Teachers
Photography for Teachers
Teaching of Reading Comprehension
The Role of the Mentor Teacher
Introduction to the Gifted
A Changing World—A Changing Classroom: Dealing with
Critical Situations in the School
Coping with Student Problems in the Classroom: Dealing in
Discipline

* University of Nevada - Reno, Reno, **NV**
Special Problems in Curriculum and Instruction (Five Teaching Skills)

University of New Hampshire, Durham, **NH**
Assessment of Prior Learning
Educating for Adult Literacy

* Empire State College, Saratoga Springs, **NY**
Thinking about Education

North Dakota Interactive Video Network, Bismarck, **ND**
Educational Law I
Staff and Program Evaluation
Introduction to Educational Leadership
Secondary School Counseling
Guidance Administration and Consulting
Instructional Models
Dynamics of Addiction
School Finance and Business Management

Ohio State University, Columbus, **OH**
Technology in the Curriculum: A Distance Learning Telecourse for K-12 Educators

*Institute provides nationwide or worldwide course access

* Oklahoma State University, Stillwater, **OK**
  Psychological Foundations of Childhood

* Portland State University, Portland, **OR**
  AppleWorks for Educators: Introduction
  Software Sampler I
  Introduction to Microsoft Works for Educators
  PageMaker for Educators (Macintosh)
  Learning HyperCard and HyperTalk Programming
  Computers in Mathematics Education
  Computers in Education: Fundamentals
  LOGO for Educators: Introduction
  Telecommunications and Information Access
  Computers in Composition
  Effective Inservice for Instructional Use of Computers in Education

University of South Dakota, Vermillion, **SD**
  The Effective Teacher
  Workshop
  Restructuring America's Schools
  Teaching for Thinking: Creativity in the Classroom

* Texas Tech University, Lubbock, **TX**
  Changing Attitudes—The Beginnings

* Brigham Young University, Provo, **UT**
  Microcomputers in the Schools
  Improving Discipline in the Schools

Wisconsin Educational Communications Board, Madison, **WI**
  Educating Able Learners
  Restructuring America's Schools

* University of Wyoming, Laramie, **WY**
  Reading Disabilities

Educational Psychology

* Brigham Young University, Provo, **UT**
  Introduction to the Education of Children with Visual Handicaps

University of Wisconsin (UW), Madison, **WI**
  Educational Psychology of the Gifted, Talented, and Creative: Educating Able Learners
  Programming for the Gifted: Models and Methods
  Teachers Tackle Thinking

Electrical Engineering

* University of Arizona, Tucson, **AZ**
  Active and Passive Filter Design
  Digital Signal Processing
  Fundamentals of Device Electronics
  Solid State Circuits
  Energy Conversion
  Random Processes for Engineering Applications
  Digital Image Processing
  Synthesis of Control Systems
  Analog Integrated Circuits
  Electronic Packaging Principles
  Power Electronics
  Engineering Applications of Graph Theory

  Modern Computer Architecture
  Fundamentals of Computer Networks

* Colorado SURGE, Fort Collins, **CO**
  Introduction to Microprocessors
  Digital Control and Digital Filters
  Communications Systems
  MOS Integrated Circuits
  Operational Amplifier Circuits
  Microwave Theory and Component Design
  Digital Optical Computing
  Optical Materials and Devices
  Testing of Digital Systems
  Estimation and Filtering Theory
  Design Automation
  Multidimensional Digital Signal Processing
  Performance Evaluation and Modeling
  Architecture of AVLSI System Design II
  Topics in Electromagnetics
  Topics in Solid State Electronics

Emergency Management

* Emergency Management Institute, Emmitsburg, **MD**
  Emergency Program Manager (HS-1)
  Emergency Preparedness, USA (HS-2)
  Radiological Emergency Management (HS-3)
  Hazardous Materials: A Citizen's Orientation (HS-5)
  Portable Emergency Data System (PEDS) (HS-6)
  A Citizen's Guide to Disaster Assistance (HS-7)

* Rochester Institute of Technology, Rochester, **NY**
  Earth Science for the Emergency Manager
  Manmade Hazards
  Emergency Preparedness Laws and Regulation
  Emergency Planning and Methodology
  Emergency Operations

Engineering

University of Alabama, Tuscaloosa, **AL**
  FORTRAN Programming
  Computer Management Information Systems
  Microcomputer Applications
  Engineering Statistics
  Engineering Materials I - Structure and Properties
  Finite Element Analysis
  Optimal Control
  Statistical Applications in Civil Engineering
  Structural Analysis
  Process Calculations
  Analysis of Operating Systems
  Control Systems Analysis
  Engineering Economics
  Integer Programming
  Manufacturing Systems Design Computer-Aided Manufacturing
  Introduction to Computing
  Production Planning and Control
  Statistical Quality Control
  Work Design and Human Performance
  Operations Research

*Institute provides nationwide or worldwide course access

Human Information Processing
Network Optimization
Advanced Dynamics of Machinery
Advanced Analytical Methods in Heat Transfer
Statics
Mechanics of Materials I
Dynamics
Fluid Mechanics
Genetic Algorithms in Optimization and Machine Learning
Neural Networks
Metallurgical Process Calculations

* Colorado SURGE, Fort Collins, **CO**
Linear Programming and Network Flows
Nonlinear Programming
Engineering Decision Support and Expert Systems

* University of Idaho, Moscow, **ID**
Statics

* University of Missouri, Columbia, **MO**
Management for Engineers

* Oklahoma State University, Stillwater, **OK**
Thermodynamics

* Pennsylvania State University, University Park, **PA**
Statics

University of Wisconsin (UW), Madison, **WI**
Statics

* University of Wyoming, Laramie, **WY**
Statics
Dynamics

English

* Southeastern Bible College, Birmingham, **AL**
English Grammar and Composition
English Composition

* University of Alaska, Fairbanks, **AK**
Methods of Written Communication
Intermediate Exposition with Modes of Literature
Introduction to Creative Writing: Poetry
Frontier Literature of Alaska

* Rio Salado Community College, Phoenix, **AZ**
Fundamentals of Writing
19th Century American Fiction
Creative Writing

INTELECOM, Pasadena, **CA**
Literary Visions

Northern California Telecommunications Consortium, Sacramento, **CA**
Literary Visions
Voices and Visions

KRMA/Denver, Denver, **CO**
Literary Visions

Pikes Peak Community College, Colorado Springs, **CO**
College Spelling Skills
Review of Writing

Miami-Dade Community College, Miami, **FL**
English Composition 1
English Composition 2
Advanced English Composition 1

* Southeastern College, Lakeland, **FL**
Major British Authors
Advanced Grammar
Contemporary Literature
Contemporary Christian Writers
Introduction to Shakespeare
The American Novel

* University of Idaho, Moscow, **ID**
World Literature

Governors State University, University Park, **IL**
Literature for Children and Adolescents
Shakespeare's Plays

Harold Washington College, Chicago, **IL**
Composition I and II
Literature and Film

* Western Illinois University, Macomb, **IL**
Literature of the Americas

Indiana Vocational Technical College, South Bend, **IN**
English Composition I: The Write Course

* University of Kansas, Lawrence, **KS**
Introduction to Poetry

Elizabethtown Community College, Elizabethtown, **KY**
Literary Visions

Kentucky Telecommunications Consortium, Lexington, **KY**
Literature

Northern Kentucky University, Highland Heights, **KY**
Literary Visions

Paducah Community College, Paducah, **KY**
Literary Visions

* Louisiana State University, Baton Rouge, **LA**
Introduction to Drama and Poetry
English—II, 2nd Semester

University of Maine at Augusta, Augusta, **ME**
College Writing
Introduction to Literature

College of the Air, Owings Mills, **MD**
Literary Visions
English Literature I
English Literature II
The Write Course

Prince George's Community College, Largo, **MD**
Composition I: Expository Writing
Composition II: Introduction to Literature
English Literature I
Introduction to Creative Writing

Wayne County Community College, Detroit, **MI**
English I
English II
Introduction to Poetry

*Institute provides nationwide or worldwide course access

* University of Minnesota, Minneapolis, **MN**
    Introduction to American Literature: Some Major Figures and
        Themes
    Introduction to Literature: Modern Science Fiction
    Introduction to Modern Poetry
    Literature of American Minorities
    Shakespeare I
    Shakespeare II
    Survey of American Literature, 1900-1960
    The English Language
    Topics in English and American Literature: The Celtic World
    Topics in English and American Literature: D.H. Lawrence
        and Freud
    James Joyce
    European Folk Tales
    Intermediate Fiction Writing
    Intermediate Poetry Writing
    Topics in Creative Writing: Journaling into Fiction
    Journal and Memoir Writing

* University of Missouri, Columbia, **MO**
    Themes and Forms in Literature (Shakespeare)

University of Nebraska at Kearney, Kearney, **NE**
    Expository Writing

* University of Nevada - Reno, Reno, **NV**
    Oral English for Non-Native Speakers
    Introduction to Language
    Descriptive Grammar

University of New Hampshire, Durham, **NH**
    Literary Visions

* Empire State College, Saratoga Springs, **NY**
    Introduction to Literature
    College Writing
    Literature of the Americas

* New York Institute of Technology, Old Westbury, **NY**
    College Composition I
    College Composition II
    Basic Speech Communication
    Business Writing
    Technical Writing
    Report Writing

* Rochester Institute of Technology, Rochester, **NY**
    Introduction to Literature

Rockland Community College, Suffern, **NY**
    English Composition I: The Write Course
    English Composition II
    On Poets and Poetry
    Nobel Prize Literature

WNET/New York City, New York, **NY**
    Literary Visions

North Carolina State University, Raleigh, **NC**
    English Literature
    American Literature
    History of the English Language

* Ohio University, Athens, **OH**
    Women and Literature

* Oklahoma State University, Stillwater, **OK**
    English Grammar
    American Poetry Post 1900

Rose State College, Midwest City, **OK**
    English Composition I
    English Composition II

* Pennsylvania State University, University Park, **PA**
    History of the English Language

Community College of Rhode Island, Lincoln, **RI**
    Composition I
    Introduction to Literature

* University of South Carolina, Columbia, **SC**
    Modern American Literature
    Writer's Workshop

University of South Dakota, Vermillion, **SD**
    Introduction to Literature
    Professional Writing

* University of Tennessee, Knoxville, **TN**
    Advanced Grammar

Tarrant County Junior College, Fort Worth, **TX**
    English Composition I
    English Composition II

* Texas Tech University, Lubbock, **TX**
    English as a Second Language

University of Texas at Austin, Austin, **TX**
    Technical Writing

* Brigham Young University, Provo, **UT**
    English at Home, Part 1
    English at Home, Part 2
    English at Home, Part 3

* University of Utah, Salt Lake City, **UT**
    Introduction to Creative Writing

* Weber State University, Ogden, **UT**
    Fiction Writing
    Poetry Writing

Northern Virginia Community College, Annandale, **VA**
    Technical Writing
    Survey of American Literature II
    World Literature I
    Women in Literature I
    Women in Literature II
    Film and Literature (Section 90)
    Film and Literature (Section 93)

* City University, Bellevue, **WA**
    English Composition

Milwaukee Area Technical College, Milwaukee, **WI**
    English I
    English Composition II

University of Wisconsin (UW), Madison, **WI**
    Introduction to Modern English and American Literature I:
        The Nineteenth Century
    Introduction to Modern English and American Literature: The
        Twentieth Century

*Institute provides nationwide or worldwide course access

Central Wyoming College, Riverton, **WY**
Composition I
English II

* University of Wyoming, Laramie, **WY**
American Literature II
Regional U.S. Literature: The West

Environmental Science

Northern California Telecommunications Consortium, Sacramento, **CA**
Race to Save the Planet

KRMA/Denver, Denver, **CO**
Race to Save the Planet

Miami-Dade Community College, Miami, **FL**
Energy in the Natural Environment

Boise State University, Boise, **ID**
Race to Save the Planet

University of Maine at Augusta, Augusta, **ME**
Understanding the Global Environment

College of the Air, Owings Mills, **MD**
Race to Save the Planet

Dallas County Community College District, Dallas, **TX**
The Living Environment

* City University, Bellevue, **WA**
Environmental Science

Environmental Studies

Harold Washington College, Chicago, **IL**
Man and Environment

Evangelism

* Southeastern College, Lakeland, **FL**
Healing: A Ministry of the Holy Spirit
Evangelism and the Gifts of the Holy Spirit
Modern Cults
Royal Ranger Leadership Training
Worship and the Gifts of the Holy Spirit

Family Life

* Rio Salado Community College, Phoenix, **AZ**
The Modern Family

INTELECOM, Pasadena, **CA**
Portrait of a Family

* Mind Extension University, Englewood, **CO**
Marriage

College of the Air, Owings Mills, **MD**
Portrait of a Family

* University of Minnesota, Minneapolis, **MN**
Family Relationships
Family Relationships

American Families in Transition
American Families in Transition

University of Oklahoma, Norman, **OK**
Contemporary Marriage

* Brigham Young University, Provo, **UT**
Nurturing Your Child's Natural Curiosity

* Utah State University, Logan, **UT**
Child Abuse and Neglect: A Multidisciplinary Approach
Update on Family Issues
Update on Children's Issues

West Virginia Higher Education Instructional Television Consortium, Morgantown, **WV**
Portrait of a Family

Family Relations

* Southeastern Bible College, Birmingham, **AL**
Marriage and Family Counseling
Marriage and Family

* University of Georgia, Athens, **GA**
Development within the Family

* Oklahoma State University, Stillwater, **OK**
Human Development Within the Family
Marriage

University of South Dakota, Vermillion, **SD**
Family Practice Seminar

Finance

INTELECOM, Pasadena, **CA**
Personal Finance and Money Management

Northern California Telecommunications Consortium, Sacramento, **CA**
Personal Finance and Money Management

* Colorado SURGE, Fort Collins, **CO**
Financial Environment and Operations
Financial Markets

College of the Air, Owings Mills, **MD**
Personal Finance and Money Management

Prince George's Community College, Largo, **MD**
Financial Planning

Wayne County Community College, Detroit, **MI**
Personal Money Management

* Western Michigan University - MITN, Office of Telecourse Programs, Kalamazoo, **MI**
Business Finance

* Rochester Institute of Technology, Rochester, **NY**
Personal Financial Management
Theory and Application of Basic Financial Concepts

Rockland Community College, Suffern, **NY**
Personal Financial Management

North Dakota Interactive Video Network, Bismarck, **ND**
Managerial Finance

*Institute provides nationwide or worldwide course access

University of Cincinnati, Cincinnati, **OH**
Personal Finance and Money Management

* Pennsylvania State University, University Park, **PA**
Introduction to Finance

Community College of Rhode Island, Lincoln, **RI**
Personal Finance

Tarrant County Junior College, Fort Worth, **TX**
Personal Money Management

Northern Virginia Community College, Annandale, **VA**
Personal Finance

University of Wisconsin (UW), Madison, **WI**
Stocks, Bonds, and the Beginning Investor

Fine Arts

Harold Washington College, Chicago, **IL**
History of Painting, Sculpture, and Architecture

* Indiana State University, Terre Haute, **IN**
Visual Arts in Civilization

* Taylor University, Fort Wayne, **IN**
Introduction to Art

* Louisiana State University, Baton Rouge, **LA**
Fine Arts Survey—Music and Dance
Fine Arts Survey—Art and Drama

* Home Study International, Silver Spring, **MD**
Music Appreciation

University of New Hampshire, Durham, **NH**
Art of the Western World

* Texas Tech University, Lubbock, **TX**
Music History and Literature
Music Theory

Fire Service Administration

* Empire State College, Saratoga Springs, **NY**
Fire Prevention, Organization, and Management
Advanced Fire Administration
Personnel Management for the Fire Service
Analytic Approaches to Public Fire Protection
Fire-Related Human Behavior
Disaster and Fire Defense Planning
Fire Protection Structures and Systems Design
Political and Legal Foundations of Fire Protection

Folklore

* Indiana University, Bloomington, **IN**
Introduction to Folklore
Introduction to American Folklore

Forest Sciences

* Colorado SURGE, Fort Collins, **CO**
Advanced Design of Wood Structures

French

Northern California Telecommunications Consortium, Sacramento, **CA**
French in Action

* University of California, Berkeley, **CA**
French: Elementary Course I
French: Elementary Course II

* University of Georgia, Athens, **GA**
Elementary French (FR 101)
Elementary French (FR 102)
Elementary French (FR 103)
Intermediate French

* Indiana University, Bloomington, **IN**
Elementary French I
Elementary French II: Language and Culture

* University of Iowa, Iowa City, **IA**
Elementary French (9:1)
Elementary French (9:2)

* University of Kansas, Lawrence, **KS**
Elementary French I
Elementary French II

* Louisiana State University, Baton Rouge, **LA**
Elementary French (1001)
Elementary French (1002)
Intermediate French (2101)
French—I, 1st Semester
French—I, 2nd Semester
French—II, 1st Semester
French—II, 2nd Semester

* Home Study International, Silver Spring, **MD**
French I

* University of Minnesota, Minneapolis, **MN**
Beginning French I
Beginning French II
Beginning French III

* University of Missouri, Columbia, **MO**
Elementary French I
Elementary French II
Elementary French III

* University of Nebraska at Lincoln, Department of Independent Study, Lincoln, **NE**
French 1
French 2
French 3
French 4
Second-Year French

* University of Nevada - Reno, Reno, **NV**
Elementary French I
Elementary French II

WNET/New York City, New York, **NY**
French in Action

* University of North Carolina, Chapel Hill, **NC**
French 1

*Institute provides nationwide or worldwide course access

* University of North Dakota, Grand Forks, **ND**
  Beginning French 101
  Beginning French 102

* Oklahoma State University, Stillwater, **OK**
  Elementary French I
  Elementary French II

  Rose State College, Midwest City, **OK**
  Conversational French I
  Conversational French II

* Pennsylvania State University, University Park, **PA**
  Elementary French I
  Elementary French II
  Intermediate French

* University of South Carolina, Columbia, **SC**
  Introductory French (C-109)
  Introductory French (C-110)

* University of Tennessee, Knoxville, **TN**
  Elementary French, First Semester

* Texas Tech University, Lubbock, **TX**
  French Level I (1A)
  French Level I (1B)
  French Level II (2A)
  French Level II (2B)

* Brigham Young University, Provo, **UT**
  Intermediate French, Part 1

* Utah State University, Logan, **UT**
  Elementary French 101
  Elementary French 102

* University of Washington, Seattle, **WA**
  Elementary French C101
  Elementary French C102
  Elementary French C103

* Washington State University, Pullman, **WA**
  First Semester French
  Second Semester French
  Third Semester French
  Fourth Semester French

* University of Wyoming, Laramie, **WY**
  First Year French I
  Second Year French

Gardening

  Belleville Area College, Belleville, **IL**
  Home Gardening

General Education Development Test (GED)

  Milwaukee Area Technical College, Milwaukee, **WI**
  Preparation for the GED Test

  Wisconsin Educational Communications Board, Madison, **WI**
  GED Español
  GED Preparation

General Studies

* Western Michigan University, Department of Distance Education, Kalamazoo, **MI**
  Non-Western Societies in the Modern World: Sub-Saharan Africa
  Critical Times: Depression and War
  Critical Times: The Civil Rights Movement

General Technology

* Oklahoma State University, Stillwater, **OK**
  Engineering Design Graphics with CAD

Geography

* University of Alaska, Fairbanks, **AK**
  Introductory Geography
  Elements of Physical Geography
  Geography of Alaska

* Mind Extension University, Englewood, **CO**
  Environment and Culture

* University of Minnesota, Minneapolis, **MN**
  Geography of Minnesota (Videocassette Course)
  Geography of Minnesota (Broadcast Television Course)

* University of North Carolina, Chapel Hill, **NC**
  Physical Geography

* University of Utah, Salt Lake City, **UT**
  Geography of Utah

* University of Wyoming, Laramie, **WY**
  Introduction to World Regional Geography

Geology

* University of Alaska, Fairbanks, **AK**
  Principles of Geology

* Rio Salado Community College, Phoenix, **AZ**
  Introduction to Physical Geology I: Physical Lecture

  INTELECOM, Pasadena, **CA**
  Earth Revealed

* University of California, Berkeley, **CA**
  Introduction to Physical Geology
  Geology of California

* Colorado State University, Fort Collins, **CO**
  Introduction to Geology: The Earth Explored

  KRMA/Denver, Denver, **CO**
  Earth Revealed
  Planet Earth

  Metropolitan State College of Denver, Englewood, **CO**
  General Geology

  Pikes Peak Community College, Colorado Springs, **CO**
  Earth Science

*Institute provides nationwide or worldwide course access

Connecticut Community-Technical College System, Hartford, **CT**
Introductory Geology

* Southeastern College, Lakeland, **FL**
Geology

* Western Illinois University, Macomb, **IL**
Planet Earth

* University of Iowa, Iowa City, **IA**
The Earth Revealed

Kentucky Telecommunications Consortium, Lexington, **KY**
Physical Geology

Northern Kentucky University, Highland Heights, **KY**
Physical Geology

Prince George's Community College, Largo, **MD**
Introduction to Physical Geology

* University of Missouri, Columbia, **MO**
Earth Science

Milwaukee Area Technical College, Milwaukee, **WI**
General Geology

Central Wyoming College, Riverton, **WY**
Physical Geology

Geophysics

* Southeastern College, Lakeland, **FL**
Planet Earth

Geoscience

Murray State University, Murray, **KY**
The Earth Explored

* Pennsylvania State University, University Park, **PA**
Planet Earth

* City University, Bellevue, **WA**
An Introduction to Geoscience: The Planet Earth

German

* University of California, Berkeley, **CA**
German: Elementary Course I
German: Elementary Course II
German: Elementary Course III

* University of Florida, Gainesville, **FL**
Beginning German 1
Beginning German 2
Beginning German 3

* University of Georgia, Athens, **GA**
Elementary German I
Elementary German II
Elementary German III

* Indiana University, Bloomington, **IN**
Beginning German I
Beginning German II

* University of Iowa, Iowa City, **IA**
Elementary German

* University of Kansas, Lawrence, **KS**
Elementary German I
Elementary German II

* Louisiana State University, Baton Rouge, **LA**
Elementary German (1101)
Elementary German (1102)
Intermediate German (2101)
Intermediate German (2102)
Readings in German Literature

* University of Missouri, Columbia, **MO**
Elementary German I
Elementary German II

* University of Nebraska at Lincoln, Department of Independent Study, Lincoln, **NE**
German 1
German 2
German 3
German 4

* University of Nevada - Reno, Reno, **NV**
Elementary German I
Elementary German II

* University of North Carolina, Chapel Hill, **NC**
Elementary German 1
Elementary German 2

* University of North Dakota, Grand Forks, **ND**
Beginning German 101
Beginning German 102

* University of Tennessee, Knoxville, **TN**
Elementary German, First Semester
Elementary German, Second Semester

* University of Washington, Seattle, **WA**
First-Year German (C101)
First-Year German C102
First-Year German C103

* Washington State University, Pullman, **WA**
First Semester German
Second Semester German

Gerontology

Arkansas Telecommunications Consortium, Russellville, **AR**
Growing Old in a New Age

Connecticut Community-Technical College System, Hartford, **CT**
Social Gerontology

College of the Air, Owings Mills, **MD**
Growing Old in a New Age

WGBH/Boston, Boston, **MA**
Growing Old in a New Age

* Weber State University, Ogden, **UT**
Gerontological Development and Policy

Aging: Adaptation and Behavior
Ethnicity and the Aging
Societal Response to Aging
Retirement: Adjustment/Planning

Government

INTELECOM, Pasadena, **CA**
Government By Consent

North Iowa Area Community College, Mason City, **IA**
Government by Consent

University of Maine at Augusta, Augusta, **ME**
American Government

San Antonio College, San Antonio, **TX**
American Government: State
American Government: National

Tarrant County Junior College, Fort Worth, **TX**
United States Government
Texas State and Local Government

Greek

* Southeastern Bible College, Birmingham, **AL**
Greek I
Greek II

* Columbia Bible College and Seminary, Columbia, **SC**
The Pastoral Epistles (*Graduate Level*)

Health

* University of Alaska, Fairbanks, **AK**
Science of Nutrition

* Rio Salado Community College, Phoenix, **AZ**
Healthful Living

Florida West Coast Public Broadcasting, Inc., Tampa, **FL**
Living with Health

Belleville Area College, Belleville, **IL**
Health

Governors State University, University Park, **IL**
Contemporary Health Issues
Nutrition

Harold Washington College, Chicago, **IL**
Health Education

* University of Kansas, Lawrence, **KS**
AIDS and STDs: Facts of Life

College of the Air, Owings Mills, **MD**
Living with Health

Prince George's Community College, Largo, **MD**
Personal and Community Health

WGBH/Boston, Boston, **MA**
Living with Health

Rose State College, Midwest City, **OK**
Personal Health

Community College of Rhode Island, Lincoln, **RI**
The Human in Health and Disease

University of South Dakota, Vermillion, **SD**
Current Problems in Health Education

Dallas County Community College District, Dallas, **TX**
Living With Health

Tarrant County Junior College, Fort Worth, **TX**
Personal and Community Health

West Virginia Higher Education Instructional Television Consortium, Morgantown, **WV**
Living with Health

* University of Wyoming, Laramie, **WY**
Standard First Aid and Personal Safety

Health Systems Administration

* Rochester Institute of Technology, Rochester, **NY**
Survey of Health Care Systems
Health Systems Administration
Health Care Economics and Finance
Legal Aspects of Health Care Administration
Health Care Quality Assurance
Health Planning and Program Development

Hebrew

* Southeastern Bible College, Birmingham, **AL**
Introduction to Biblical Hebrew

* University of Minnesota, Minneapolis, **MN**
Introduction to Classical Hebrew

History

* Southeastern Bible College, Birmingham, **AL**
History of Christianity

* University of Alaska, Fairbanks, **AK**
Western Civilization I
Western Civilization II
Alaska, Land and Its People
History of the U.S. I
History of the U.S. II
History of Alaska
Maritime History of Alaska
Polar Exploration and Its Literature
History of the American Military
History of U.S. Foreign Policy

Arkansas Telecommunications Consortium, Russellville, **AR**
Americas

INTELECOM, Pasadena, **CA**
America in Perspective
American Adventure

Northern California Telecommunications Consortium, Sacramento, **CA**
American Adventure

*Institute provides nationwide or worldwide course access

America in Perspective: U.S. History Since 1877
The Western Tradition
The Africans
The Chinese: Adapting the Past, Building the Future

* University of California, Berkeley, **CA**
While Soldiers Fought: War and American Society I
While Soldiers Fought: War and American Society II

KRMA/Denver, Denver, **CO**
The American Adventure
The Western Tradition

Metropolitan State College of Denver, Englewood, **CO**
Western Civilization Since 1715

* Mind Extension University, Englewood, **CO**
American South Comes of Age
History of Islam
History of Modern Japan Since 1800
Twentieth-Century Russia
The Presidents and the Cold War
Western Civilization to 1500
Western Civilization After 1500

Pikes Peak Community College, Colorado Springs, **CO**
The Civil War

Connecticut Community-Technical College System, Hartford, **CT**
Americas: Modern Latin American History
Pacific Century

Florida West Coast Public Broadcasting, Inc., Tampa, **FL**
American Adventure

* Southeastern College, Lakeland, **FL**
Western Civilization I
Western Civilization II
Modern European History to 1870
Modern European History Since 1870
The Ancient World
American Church History
History of Religious Renewal Movements

Belleville Area College, Belleville, **IL**
U.S. History to 1877

Governors State University, University Park, **IL**
History of Civil Rights

Harold Washington College, Chicago, **IL**
History of the American People to 1865
History of the American People from 1865

Sangamon State University, Springfield, **IL**
Eyes on the Prize
Vietnam
The Middle East
The Pacific Century

Teikyo Marycrest University, Davenport, **IA**
The American Adventure
Americas

Elizabethtown Community College, Elizabethtown, **KY**
The American Adventure

Kentucky Telecommunications Consortium, Lexington, **KY**
The American Adventure

The Western Tradition I

Murray State University, Murray, **KY**
The American Adventure

Northern Kentucky University, Highland Heights, **KY**
The American Adventure
The Western Tradition I

Paducah Community College, Paducah, **KY**
The American Adventure

University of Maine at Augusta, Augusta, **ME**
Foundations of Western Civilization I
United States History I
Topics: Life Along the Kennebec River

College of the Air, Owings Mills, **MD**
American Adventure
Western Tradition I
America in Perspective: U.S. History Since 1877
Civil War

Prince George's Community College, Largo, **MD**
Ancient and Medieval History
United States History I
United States History II
History of the American Civil War
History of the Vietnam War

WGBH/Boston, Boston, **MA**
Americas

Wayne County Community College, Detroit, **MI**
World Civilization II
History of the U.S. II

* University of Minnesota, Minneapolis, **MN**
American History I
American History II
Cultural Pluralism in American History
Cultural Pluralism in American History
The United States in the 20th Century: 1932-1960
American Business History
History of American Foreign Relations

* University of Missouri, Columbia, **MO**
The War in Vietnam and the U.S.
History of Science

* University of Nebraska at Lincoln, Department of Independent Study, Lincoln, **NE**
Nebraska History

University of New Hampshire, Durham, **NH**
The American Adventure

* Empire State College, Saratoga Springs, **NY**
American History, 1492-1865: The Origin and Growth of the
United States
American History, 1865 to the Present: The Origin and
Growth of the United States
The Western Tradition I
The Western Tradition II
Eyes on the Prize
Legacies: An Introduction to the History of Women and the
Family in America 1607-1870

*Institute provides nationwide or worldwide course access

* New York Institute of Technology, Old Westbury, **NY**
American History I
American History II
World History I
World History II

Rockland Community College, Suffern, **NY**
World History I
American History to 1877
American History 1877 to Present
Vietnam: An Historical Study
War and Peace in the Nuclear Age
History of the Civil War

WNET/New York City, New York, **NY**
America in Perspective
Americas
The Western Tradition, Part I

North Carolina State University, Raleigh, **NC**
History of the Republic of South Africa

North Dakota Interactive Video Network, Bismarck, **ND**
American Women in History

Edison State Community College, Greenville, **OH**
European History 1300-1715
European History 1715-1871

* Ohio University, Athens, **OH**
American History to 1828
History of the United States, 1828-1900
History of the United States Since 1900
History of Blacks in America Since 1865

* Oklahoma State University, Stillwater, **OK**
American History to 1865
American History since 1865
Western Civilization to 1500
Western Civilization after 1500
Modern Japan

Rose State College, Midwest City, **OK**
U.S. History to 1877
U.S. History since 1877
Ancient and Medieval Civilization
History of Europe, 1815 to Present
Japan: The Living Tradition

University of Oklahoma, Norman, **OK**
U.S. 1492-1865
Western Civilization I
Topics in Asian History

* Pennsylvania State University, University Park, **PA**
American Civilization since 1877
History of Communism
History of Fascism and Nazism
Vietnam at War

Community College of Rhode Island, Lincoln, **RI**
Survey of Western Civilization I
Survey of Western Civilization II
History of the U.S. from 1877

* Columbia Bible College and Seminary, Columbia, **SC**
The Ancient Church, 95 A.D.-600 A.D. (*Graduate Level*)

* University of South Carolina, Columbia, **SC**
The American South Comes of Age

University of South Dakota, Vermillion, **SD**
American History
Latin America

Dallas County Community College District, Dallas, **TX**
The American Adventure
America in Perspective: U.S. History Since 1877

San Antonio College, San Antonio, **TX**
History of U.S. - Part I
History of U.S. - Part II
History of Civilization - Part I
History of Civilization - Part II

Tarrant County Junior College, Fort Worth, **TX**
U.S. History to 1877
U.S. History Since 1877

Northern Virginia Community College, Annandale, **VA**
History of Western Civilization I
History of Western Civilization II
United States History I
United States History II

* City University, Bellevue, **WA**
History of Western Tradition I
History of Western Tradition II
The Nuclear Age: World War II to the Present

* Washington State University, Pullman, **WA**
World Civilizations I
World Civilizations II
American History Since 1877

* Western Washington University, Bellingham, **WA**
Introduction to East Asian Civilization

West Virginia Higher Education Instructional Television Consortium, Morgantown, **WV**
Americas
The Civil War

Milwaukee Area Technical College, Milwaukee, **WI**
Contemporary Civil Rights

University of Wisconsin (UW), Madison, **WI**
American History, 1492-1865: The Origin and Growth of the United States
American History, 1865 to the Present: The Origin and Growth of the United States

Central Wyoming College, Riverton, **WY**
U.S. History I
U.S. History II

* University of Wyoming, Laramie, **WY**
Western Civilization I
Western Civilization II
History of Wyoming
History of the U.S. West
History of United States Indians

Horticulture

Northern California Telecommunications Consortium, Sacramento, **CA**
    The Home Gardener

* University of Minnesota, Minneapolis, **MN**
    Home Horticulture: Landscape Gardening and Design

North Carolina State University, Raleigh, **NC**
    Home Horticulture

* Pennsylvania State University, University Park, **PA**
    Plant Propagation

Hotel Administration

* University of Nevada - Reno, Reno, **NV**
    Hotel Advertising and Sales Promotions

Hotel and Restaurant Management

* University of Maryland University College, College Park, **MD**
    Hotel Management and Operations (*ITV*)

Human Development

* Southeastern Bible College, Birmingham, **AL**
    Introduction to Human Development

* Weber State University, Ogden, **UT**
    Human Development

Human Development and Family Studies

* Colorado State University, Fort Collins, **CO**
    Marriage and Family Relationships

Human Resources Management

* Mind Extension University, Englewood, **CO**
    Management of Human Resources

Human Services

* Empire State College, Saratoga Springs, **NY**
    Introduction to Human Services
    Human Services Delivery: New Perspectives on Cultural Diversity
    Human Service Management
    Issues in Human Services

* Ohio University, Athens, **OH**
    Deaf Language and Culture

Humanities

* Rio Salado Community College, Phoenix, **AZ**
    Human Origins and the Development of Culture

Arkansas Telecommunications Consortium, Russellville, **AR**
    Humanities Through the Arts

INTELECOM, Pasadena, **CA**
    Humanities Through the Arts

Northern California Telecommunications Consortium, Sacramento, **CA**
    Humanities through the Arts

* Mind Extension University, Englewood, **CO**
    Introduction to Art
    The Humanities Through the Arts

Connecticut Community-Technical College System, Hartford, **CT**
    Eyes on the Prize

Miami-Dade Community College, Miami, **FL**
    Humanities

Harold Washington College, Chicago, **IL**
    General Course I
    General Course II

* Indiana University, Bloomington, **IN**
    Modern Literature and Other Arts: An Introduction

North Iowa Area Community College, Mason City, **IA**
    Ethics in America

College of the Air, Owings Mills, **MD**
    Humanities Through the Arts

* University of Maryland University College, College Park, **MD**
    Cosmos (*ITV*)
    Myth and Culture (*Video*)
    Shakespeare: Power and Justice (*ITV*)

Wayne County Community College, Detroit, **MI**
    The Art of Humanities

* University of Minnesota, Minneapolis, **MN**
    Discourse and Society
    Text and Context

University of New Hampshire, Durham, **NH**
    Campbell: Transformations of Myth Through Time

* New Jersey Institute of Technology, Newark, **NJ**
    Culture and History I: The Western Tradition
    Culture and History II: From the Reformation to the Present

* Empire State College, Saratoga Springs, **NY**
    The Middle East
    Science and Culture in the Western Tradition
    The News in Historical Perspective
    Ancient Greece
    Humanities through the Arts
    War and American Society

* New School for Social Research - DIAL, New York, **NY**
    The Making of Americans

* Rochester Institute of Technology, Rochester, **NY**
    Black Civil Rights in the 20th Century
    Modern America

*Institute provides nationwide or worldwide course access

Rockland Community College, Suffern, **NY**
Humanities through the Arts

Rose State College, Midwest City, **OK**
Art in Life
General Humanities from 1400

Dallas County Community College District, Dallas, **TX**
In Our Own Image

San Antonio College, San Antonio, **TX**
Western Culture

* City University, Bellevue, **WA**
Art of the Western World
History and Culture of the African Continent
Great American Poets

West Virginia Higher Education Instructional Television Consortium, Morgantown, **WV**
Joseph Campbell: Transformations of Myth Through Time
Eyes on the Prize

Central Wyoming College, Riverton, **WY**
Art of Being Human

Industrial and Management Systems Engineering

University of Nebraska - CorpNet, Nebraska CorpNet, Lincoln, **NE**
Ergonomics I
Packaging Engineering
Theory and Practice of Materials Processing
Industrial Systems Analysis I

Industrial Relations

* Pennsylvania State University, University Park, **PA**
Industrial Relations

Industrial Science

* Colorado SURGE, Fort Collins, **CO**
Cost, Productivity, and Financial Control
Research Methods

Information Management

* International School of Information Management, Inc., Denver, **CO**
Managing in a Rapidly Changing Environment
Management of Information Systems
Information Systems Strategic Planning
Technology Ethics and Social Responsibility
Telecommunications
Emerging Technologies
Capstone Project

* Nova University, Fort Lauderdale, **FL**
Practicum Proposal in Information Technology and Resource Management (Part I)
Practicum Report in Information Technology and Resource Management

Telecommunications in Information Technology and Resource Management
Emerging Technology in Information Technology and Resource Management

Information Science

* University of Maryland University College, College Park, **MD**
Introduction to Computer-Based Systems (*Video*)
Data Structure (*ITV*)

Information Skills for Academic Research

University of Oklahoma, Norman, **OK**
Information Skills for Academic Research

Information Systems

* Rio Salado Community College, Phoenix, **AZ**
Business Systems Analysis and Design

* Nova University, Fort Lauderdale, **FL**
Practicum Proposal in Information Systems (Part I)
Practicum Report in Information Systems (Part II)
Planning and Policy Formulation in Management Information Systems
Emerging Technologies in Information Systems
Operations Research
Information Systems in Organizations
Database Management Systems
Information and Systems Analysis
Data Communication Systems and Networks
Modeling and Decision Systems
Expert Systems
Information Systems Management
Survey of Fourth-Generation Languages
Office Automation Systems
Legal and Ethical Aspects of Computing
Computer Integrated Manufacturing
Computer Graphics for Information Managers
Distributed Database Management
Computer Security
Decision Support Systems
System Design Process
Computer-Aided Software Engineering
Human Factors in Computing Systems
Data Center Management

* Western Michigan University - MITN, Office of Telecourse Programs, Kalamazoo, **MI**
Introduction to Information Processing

Information Technology

* International School of Information Management, Inc., Denver, **CO**
Data Communications
Systems Design
Telecommunications Policy
Telephony

*Institute provides nationwide or worldwide course access

Interdisciplinary Social Science Degree Completion

* Mind Extension University, Englewood, **CO**
    Interdisciplinary Social Science Degree Completion Program

Interdisciplinary Studies

* University of North Carolina, Chapel Hill, **NC**
    Technology and Change

Interior Design

Northern California Telecommunications Consortium, Sacramento, **CA**
    Designing Home Interiors

International Studies

* University of South Carolina, Columbia, **SC**
    The Vietnam War

Interpersonal Communication

* Ohio University, Athens, **OH**
    Fundamentals of Human Communication
    Fundamentals of Public Speaking

Italian

* University of California, Berkeley, **CA**
    Elementary Italian I
    Elementary Italian II

* Indiana University, Bloomington, **IN**
    Elementary Italian I
    Elementary Italian II

* University of Minnesota, Minneapolis, **MN**
    Beginning Italian I

* University of Nevada - Reno, Reno, **NV**
    Elementary Italian I
    Elementary Italian II
    Second Year Italian

* University of North Carolina, Chapel Hill, **NC**
    Elementary Italian 1
    Elementary Italian 2

* University of Washington, Seattle, **WA**
    Elementary Italian C101
    Elementary Italian C102
    Elementary Italian C103

University of Wisconsin (UW), Madison, **WI**
    First Semester Italian
    Second Semester Italian

Jewish Studies

* University of Minnesota, Minneapolis, **MN**
    Introduction to Judaism
    The Holocaust

Journalism

* University of Alaska, Fairbanks, **AK**
    Introduction to Mass Communications
    Introduction to Broadcasting
    Journalism and Yearbook Production and Theory

* University of Minnesota, Minneapolis, **MN**
    Magazine Writing (Audiocassette Course)
    Magazine Writing (Radio Broadcast Course)

* New School for Social Research, New York, **NY**
    Online Journalism

* Texas Tech University, Lubbock, **TX**
    Journalism

Judaic Studies

* University of Arizona, Tucson, **AZ**
    Women in Judaism

Justice Administration

* Pennsylvania State University, University Park, **PA**
    Introduction to the American Criminal Justice System
    Policing in America

Landscape Architecture

* Utah State University, Logan, **UT**
    Introduction to Landscape Architecture

Latin

* University of Georgia, Athens, **GA**
    Elementary Latin
    Elementary Latin II
    Elementary Latin III

* University of Minnesota, Minneapolis, **MN**
    Latin Poetry: Catullus

* University of Missouri, Columbia, **MO**
    Elementary Latin
    Intensive Beginning Latin

* University of Nebraska at Lincoln, Department of Independent Study, Lincoln, **NE**
    Latin 1
    Latin 2
    Latin 3
    Latin 4
    Latin 5
    Latin 6

* University of North Carolina, Chapel Hill, **NC**
    Elementary Latin

*Institute provides nationwide or worldwide course access

* University of North Dakota, Grand Forks, **ND**
    First-Year College Latin 101
    First-Year College Latin 102

* University of South Carolina, Columbia, **SC**
    Beginning Latin I
    Beginning Latin II

* Texas Tech University, Lubbock, **TX**
    Latin Level I (1A)
    Latin Level I (1B)
    Latin Level II (2A)
    Latin Level II (2B)

Latin American Studies

* University of Iowa, Iowa City, **IA**
    Americas

Library Science

* University of Arizona, Tucson, **AZ**
    Literature for Children's Librarians
    Literature for Adolescents
    School Library Administration and Organization
    Library Collection Development
    Organization, Cataloging, and Classification of Materials
    Basic Reference

* Mind Extension University, Englewood, **CO**
    Master of Arts in Library Science
    Introduction to the Organization of Information
    Library Collection Development
    Foundations of Library and Information Services
    Basic Reference
    Research Methods
    Library Management
    Trends in Library Management
    Introduction to Information Science
    Information Storage and Retrieval
    Library Systems Analysis
    Public Librarianship
    Academic Librarianship
    Special Librarianship
    Human Factors in Information Systems
    Literature for Children's Librarians

* University of Idaho, Moscow, **ID**
    Computer Applications in Libraries

University of New Hampshire, Durham, **NH**
    Fundamentals of Library Programming

* Ohio University, Athens, **OH**
    Basic Acquisitions of Media

* University of South Carolina, Columbia, **SC**
    Jump Over the Moon

Linguistics

* University of Alaska, Fairbanks, **AK**
    Nature of Language

* University of Minnesota, Minneapolis, **MN**
    The Nature of Human Language

* Pennsylvania State University, University Park, **PA**
    The Study of Language

Management

University of Alabama, Tuscaloosa, **AL**
    Organizational Theory and Behavior
    Introduction to Human Resources Management

* Rio Salado Community College, Phoenix, **AZ**
    Owning and Operating a Small Business
    Human Relations in Business

INTELECOM, Pasadena, **CA**
    Taking the Lead: The Management Revolution

Northern California Telecommunications Consortium, Sacramento, **CA**
    The Business of Management

* University of Phoenix - San Francisco, San Francisco, **CA**
    Personnel Management
    Finance and Accounting for Managers
    Contemporary Issues in Management
    Strategic Planning
    Human Resource Management
    Managing Information
    Budgeting
    Advanced Budgeting
    Decision Making
    Project Management
    Applied Management Science Project
    Applied Managerial Statistics
    Marketing for Customer Satisfaction
    External Environment of Business
    Fundamentals of Executive Management
    Human Relations and Organizational Behavior
    Legal Environment of Business
    Information Management in Business
    Advanced Managerial Economics
    Advanced Managerial Accounting
    Advanced Managerial Finance
    Advanced Marketing Management
    Strategy Formulation and Implementation
    International Business Management
    Management of the Total Enterprise

* Colorado SURGE, Fort Collins, **CO**
    Management of Organization Development
    Management
    Managerial Planning and Control
    Basic Business Statistics

* International School of Information Management, Inc., Denver, **CO**
    Customers, Markets, and Technology in Technology-Intensive Organizations
    Information Systems Policy
    Planning for Information Networks
    Technology and the Global Environment

*Institute provides nationwide or worldwide course access

KRMA/Denver, Denver, **CO**
Taking the Lead

* Mind Extension University, Englewood, **CO**
Management

Governors State University, University Park, **IL**
Principles of Management

Harold Washington College, Chicago, **IL**
Principles of Management

Indiana Vocational Technical College, South Bend, **IN**
Techniques of Supervision

College of the Air, Owings Mills, **MD**
Principles of Management

Prince George's Community College, Largo, **MD**
Principles of Management

WGBH/Boston, Boston, **MA**
Taking the Lead: The Management Revolution

* Western Michigan University - MITN, Office of Telecourse Programs, Kalamazoo, **MI**
Management Fundamentals

University of New Hampshire, Durham, **NH**
The Business of Management

* New Jersey Institute of Technology, Newark, **NJ**
The Business of Management

* New School for Social Research, New York, **NY**
Managing in the Postmodern World

* New York Institute of Technology, Old Westbury, **NY**
Operations Management

* Rochester Institute of Technology, Rochester, **NY**
Introduction to Work Organizations
Management Concepts
Tools for Quality Management

Rockland Community College, Suffern, **NY**
Principles of Management
Business Software Analysis
Small Business Management

North Dakota Interactive Video Network, Bismarck, **ND**
Advanced Managerial Theory

Edison State Community College, Greenville, **OH**
Principles of Management

University of Cincinnati, Cincinnati, **OH**
Taking the Lead: The Management Revolution

* Oklahoma State University, Stillwater, **OK**
Introduction to Management

Rose State College, Midwest City, **OK**
Principles of Management
Small Business Management

* Pennsylvania State University, University Park, **PA**
Survey of Management

Tarrant County Junior College, Fort Worth, **TX**
Principles of Management
Small Business Management

West Virginia Higher Education Instructional Television
Consortium, Morgantown, **WV**
Taking the Lead: The Management Revolution

Central Wyoming College, Riverton, **WY**
Business Management

Management Degree Completion

* Mind Extension University, Englewood, **CO**
Management Degree Completion Program

Marketing

* University of Alaska, Fairbanks, **AK**
Principles of Advertising
Principles of Marketing

* Rio Salado Community College, Phoenix, **AZ**
Principles of Marketing

INTELECOM, Pasadena, **CA**
Marketing
The Sales Connection

Northern California Telecommunications Consortium, Sacramento, **CA**
Marketing

* University of California, Berkeley, **CA**
Principles of Marketing

* Colorado SURGE, Fort Collins, **CO**
Marketing Systems

KRMA/Denver, Denver, **CO**
Marketing
The Sales Connection

* Mind Extension University, Englewood, **CO**
Advertising and Promotion

Connecticut Community-Technical College System, Hartford, **CT**
The Sales Connection: Principles of Selling

University of Maine at Augusta, Augusta, **ME**
Marketing

College of the Air, Owings Mills, **MD**
Marketing

Prince George's Community College, Largo, **MD**
Introduction to Marketing

* University of Maryland University College, College Park,
MD
Principles of Marketing (*Video*)

Wayne County Community College, Detroit, **MI**
Marketing Principles

* Western Michigan University - MITN, Office of Telecourse Programs, Kalamazoo, **MI**
Principles of Marketing

* University of Nebraska at Lincoln, Department of Independent Study, Lincoln, **NE**
Marketing

* New Jersey Institute of Technology, Newark, **NJ**
  Principles of Marketing

* New School for Social Research, New York, **NY**
  Electronic Marketing

* Rochester Institute of Technology, Rochester, **NY**
  Marketing for Total Customer Satisfaction

Rockland Community College, Suffern, **NY**
  Marketing
  The Sales Connection: Principles of Selling

WNET/New York City, New York, **NY**
  Principles of Marketing Management

Rose State College, Midwest City, **OK**
  Principles of Marketing

Community College of Rhode Island, Lincoln, **RI**
  Principles of Marketing

University of South Dakota, Vermillion, **SD**
  Personal Selling

Tarrant County Junior College, Fort Worth, **TX**
  Salesmanship

* Weber State University, Ogden, **UT**
  Fundamental Selling Techniques

Northern Virginia Community College, Annandale, **VA**
  Principles of Marketing

Milwaukee Area Technical College, Milwaukee, **WI**
  Principles of Marketing

Wisconsin Educational Communications Board, Madison, **WI**
  Marketing
  The Sales Connection: Principles of Selling

Mathematics

* Southeastern Bible College, Birmingham, **AL**
  College Math

* University of Alaska, Fairbanks, **AK**
  Basic College Mathematics
  Elementary Algebra
  Review of Elementary Algebra
  Intermediate Algebra
  Review of Intermediate Algebra
  Review of Basic Geometry
  Elementary Functions
  Trigonometry
  Concepts and Contemporary Applications of Mathematics
  Concepts of Math
  Calculus I
  Calculus II
  Calculus III
  Mathematics for Elementary School Teachers I
  Mathematics for Elementary School Teachers II

* Rio Salado Community College, Phoenix, **AZ**
  Intermediate Algebra
  College Algebra

* Colorado SURGE, Fort Collins, **CO**
  Discrete Structures
  Linear Programming and Network Flows
  Nonlinear Programming
  Applied Mathematics II

KRMA/Denver, Denver, **CO**
  College Algebra: In Simplest Terms

Metropolitan State College of Denver, Englewood, **CO**
  College Algebra
  Introduction to Statistics

* Mind Extension University, Englewood, **CO**
  Statistical Methods for the Natural Scientist
  Mathematics in the Social Sciences

Pikes Peak Community College, Colorado Springs, **CO**
  Developmental Mathematics
  College Algebra

Miami-Dade Community College, Miami, **FL**
  General College Mathematics
  Intermediate Algebra

* University of Florida, Gainesville, **FL**
  Basic College Algebra

* University of Georgia, Athens, **GA**
  Finite Mathematics I

Harold Washington College, Chicago, **IL**
  College Algebra

University of Maine at Augusta, Augusta, **ME**
  Foundations of Mathematics
  Algebra I
  Mathematics for Business and Economics I

College of the Air, Owings Mills, **MD**
  Introduction to Mathematics

Prince George's Community College, Largo, **MD**
  Algebra for Business and Social Science

* University of Maryland University College, College Park, **MD**
  Mathematics: Contemporary Topics and Applications (*ITV*)

Wayne County Community College, Detroit, **MI**
  Business Mathematics
  College Algebra

* Western Michigan University - MITN, Office of Telecourse Programs, Kalamazoo, **MI**
  Business Statistics

* University of Minnesota, Minneapolis, **MN**
  Calculus I

* University of Missouri, Columbia, **MO**
  Fundamentals of Algebra III

* New Jersey Institute of Technology, Newark, **NJ**
  Introduction to Calculus I
  Introduction to Calculus II
  Calculus I
  Calculus II
  Introduction to Mathematical Modeling
  Differential Equations

*Institute provides nationwide or worldwide course access

Survey of Probability and Statistics
Probability and Statistics

* Empire State College, Saratoga Springs, **NY**
Algebra
Contemporary Mathematics

* Rochester Institute of Technology, Rochester, **NY**
Elementary Statistics I
Technical Mathematics I
Technical Mathematics II

Rockland Community College, Suffern, **NY**
Math Skills
Elementary Algebra for College Students
Intermediate Algebra for College Students

North Carolina State University, Raleigh, **NC**
Topics in Contemporary Mathematics

North Dakota Interactive Video Network, Bismarck, **ND**
Problem Solving and Applications

Rose State College, Midwest City, **OK**
Business Math

* Pennsylvania State University, University Park, **PA**
Basic Mathematics
General View of Mathematics
Insights into Mathematics

Community College of Rhode Island, Lincoln, **RI**
Topics in Mathematics
Business Mathematics

University of South Dakota, Vermillion, **SD**
Introduction to Finite Mathematics

* Texas Tech University, Lubbock, **TX**
Computer Mathematics I
Computer Mathematics II

University of Texas at Austin, Austin, **TX**
Mathematics of Investment

Northern Virginia Community College, Annandale, **VA**
Technical Mathematics I
Technical Mathematics II

* University of Washington, Seattle, **WA**
Intermediate Algebra

Milwaukee Area Technical College, Milwaukee, **WI**
College Algebra

Wisconsin Educational Communications Board, Madison, **WI**
By the Numbers

Central Wyoming College, Riverton, **WY**
Problem Solving

* University of Wyoming, Laramie, **WY**
Business Calculus I

Mechanical Engineering

* Colorado SURGE, Fort Collins, **CO**
Design of Models for Decision Making

Manufacturing Engineering
Materials Engineering

University of Nebraska - CorpNet, Nebraska CorpNet, Lincoln, **NE**
Finite Element Methods for Fluid Mechanics
Advanced Combustion Theory

Medical Laboratory Science

University of Maine at Augusta, Augusta, **ME**
Medical Laboratory Techniques I

Medical Terminology

* University of Florida, Gainesville, **FL**
Medical Terminology for the Health-Related Professions

Indiana Vocational Technical College, South Bend, **IN**
Medical Terminology

* University of North Dakota, Grand Forks, **ND**
Medical Terminology

* University of Tennessee, Knoxville, **TN**
Medical and Scientific Vocabulary

Meteorology

University of Maine at Augusta, Augusta, **ME**
Meteorology

Mineral Exploration

* University of Alaska, Fairbanks, **AK**
Mineral Exploration Techniques

Mineralogy

* University of Alaska, Fairbanks, **AK**
Minerals, Man, and the Environment

Music

* University of Alaska, Fairbanks, **AK**
Music Fundamentals
Appreciation of Music

* Southeastern College, Lakeland, **FL**
Church Music Organization and Administration

* University of Idaho, Moscow, **ID**
Survey of Music

* Indiana University, Bloomington, **IN**
Music for the Listener

* Taylor University, Fort Wayne, **IN**
Music Appreciation

* University of Kansas, Lawrence, **KS**
Introduction to Jazz

*Institute provides nationwide or worldwide course access

* Louisiana State University, Baton Rouge, **LA**
  Music Appreciation (1751)
  Music Appreciation (1752)
  Music of the Baroque and Classic Eras
  Music of Romantic and Modern Eras
  Music Appreciation (117)

University of Maine at Augusta, Augusta, **ME**
  Understanding Music

* University of Minnesota, Minneapolis, **MN**
  Music Appreciation
  American Music: Twentieth-Century American Music

* Empire State College, Saratoga Springs, **NY**
  Concepts of Music Listening

* University of North Carolina, Chapel Hill, **NC**
  Fundamentals of Music I
  Masterworks of Music

* University of North Dakota, Grand Forks, **ND**
  Introduction to the Understanding of Music

* Ohio University, Athens, **OH**
  History and Literature of Music I
  History and Literature of Music II
  Jazz History

Rose State College, Midwest City, **OK**
  Music in Life

* Pennsylvania State University, University Park, **PA**
  An Introduction to Western Music
  Evolution of Jazz
  Rudiments of Music

Tarrant County Junior College, Fort Worth, **TX**
  Music Appreciation

* Texas Tech University, Lubbock, **TX**
  Elementary Theory (1403)
  Elementary Theory (1404)
  Intermediate Theory (2403)
  Intermediate Theory (2404)

* Brigham Young University, Provo, **UT**
  Guitar for Everyone, Part 1
  Guitar for Everyone, Part 2

* University of Utah, Salt Lake City, **UT**
  Basic Concepts of Music

* Utah State University, Logan, **UT**
  Enjoying Music
  Fundamentals of Music

* Weber State University, Ogden, **UT**
  Evolution of Jazz

Northern Virginia Community College, Annandale, **VA**
  Music Appreciation I
  Music Appreciation II

University of Wisconsin (UW), Madison, **WI**
  Appreciation and History of Music I
  Appreciation and History of Music II
  Basic Concepts of Music

* University of Wyoming, Laramie, **WY**
  Introduction to Music

United States Ethnic Music
The Classical Period
The Romantic Period

Neuroscience

* City University, Bellevue, **WA**
  An Introduction to Neuroscience: Brain, Mind, and Behavior

Norwegian

* University of North Dakota, Grand Forks, **ND**
  Beginning Norwegian 101

University of Wisconsin (UW), Madison, **WI**
  Beginning Norwegian I
  Beginning Norwegian II

Nursing

University of Alabama, Tuscaloosa, **AL**
  Cardiac Electrophysiology
  Introduction to Nursing Research
  Human Pathology, 1st and 2nd Terms
  AIDS: A Caring Response
  Pharmacology

University of Maine at Augusta, Augusta, **ME**
  Fundamentals of Nursing

* University of Minnesota, Minneapolis, **MN**
  Life Span Growth and Development I
  Life Span Growth and Development II

North Dakota Interactive Video Network, Bismarck, **ND**
  Introduction to Adult Nursing
  Adult Nursing
  Adult Health Nursing
  Childbearing Nursing I
  Child Health Nursing I
  Trends and Issues
  Nursing in the Community
  Nursing in the Community Clinic
  Nursing Research
  Research Design and Methods in Nursing
  Epidemiology in Nursing
  Advanced Nursing Practice for Rural Cultures I

* University of South Carolina, Columbia, **SC**
  Geriatric Nutrition

University of Texas at Austin, Austin, **TX**
  Concepts of Professional Nursing

* Washington State University, Pullman, **WA**
  Profession of Nursing

University of Wisconsin (UW), Madison, **WI**
  Adult Patient Assessment: Subjective and Objective Data Base
  Interpersonal Relations—Utilizing the Basics: Effective and
    Therapeutic Communications in Nursing
  Writing for Nursing Publications

* University of Wyoming, Laramie, **WY**
  Development Influences on Health

*Institute provides nationwide or worldwide course access

Nutrition

University of Maine at Augusta, Augusta, **ME**
Human Nutrition

* Empire State College, Saratoga Springs, **NY**
Human Nutrition

North Dakota Interactive Video Network, Bismarck, **ND**
Nutrition and Introduction to Diet Therapy

* Pennsylvania State University, University Park, **PA**
Diet Therapy and Nutrition Care in Disease
Independent Studies: Nutrition in Action

University of Texas at Austin, Austin, **TX**
Introductory Nutrition

Oceanography

INTELECOM, Pasadena, **CA**
Oceanus: The Marine Environment

Northern California Telecommunications Consortium, Sacramento, **CA**
Oceanus: The Marine Environment

Florida West Coast Public Broadcasting, Inc., Tampa, **FL**
Oceanus: The Marine Environment

Harold Washington College, Chicago, **IL**
Introduction to Oceanography

College of the Air, Owings Mills, **MD**
Oceanus: The Marine Environment

Prince George's Community College, Largo, **MD**
Introduction to Oceanography

* Utah State University, Logan, **UT**
Oceanography

Office Systems Technology

Northern Virginia Community College, Annandale, **VA**
Word Processing I: Introduction to WordPerfect
Word Processing II: Advanced WordPerfect

Online Retrieval Systems

* New School for Social Research, New York, **NY**
Introduction to Online Retrieval Systems

Optical Sciences

* University of Arizona, Tucson, **AZ**
Electromagnetic Waves
Fourier and Statistical Optics
Digital Image Processing

Paralegal Studies

North Dakota Interactive Video Network, Bismarck, **ND**
Legal System and Ethics

* Texas Tech University, Lubbock, **TX**
Introduction to the Legal Assistant Profession

Pastoral Ministries

* Southeastern College, Lakeland, **FL**
Church Jurisprudence
Youth Ministries

Pastoral Studies

* Columbia Bible College and Seminary, Columbia, **SC**
Biblical Counseling by Encouragement
Principles of Personal Discipling
Marriage and Family Counseling (*Graduate Level*)
Management of Christian Organizations (*Graduate Level*)
Biblical Marriage (*Graduate Level*)
Biblical Parenting (*Graduate Level*)
Principles of Personal Discipling (*Graduate Level*)

Persian

* University of Utah, Salt Lake City, **UT**
Persian

Personal Development

* Brigham Young University, Provo, **UT**
How to Handle Conflict at Home and Other Places
Spiritual Roots of Human Relations
Ancient Documents and the Pearl of Great Price

Personnel Administration

* Western Michigan University - MITN, Office of Telecourse Programs, Kalamazoo, **MI**
Economic Analysis for Administrators

Petroleum Technology

* University of Alaska, Fairbanks, **AK**
Fundamentals of Petroleum

Pharmacy

North Dakota Interactive Video Network, Bismarck, **ND**
Drugs Subject to Abuse

* University of Tennessee, Knoxville, **TN**
Environmental Monitoring for Aseptic Processing Areas in Pharmacies

Philosophy

* Rio Salado Community College, Phoenix, **AZ**
Business Ethics

*Institute provides nationwide or worldwide course access

Northern California Telecommunications Consortium, Sacramento, **CA**
Ethics in America
Joseph Campbell: Transformations of Myth Through Time

* Colorado State University, Fort Collins, **CO**
Ethics in America

KRMA/Denver, Denver, **CO**
Ethics in America

Metropolitan State College of Denver, Englewood, **CO**
Ethics in America

* Mind Extension University, Englewood, **CO**
Ethics in America

Pikes Peak Community College, Colorado Springs, **CO**
Transformations of Myth

Connecticut Community-Technical College System, Hartford, **CT**
Ethics in America

* Southeastern College, Lakeland, **FL**
Principles of Ethics
History of Philosophy

Belleville Area College, Belleville, **IL**
Ethics

Harold Washington College, Chicago, **IL**
General Course

* University of Iowa, Iowa City, **IA**
Ethics in America

* University of Kansas, Lawrence, **KS**
Introduction to Logic

University of Maine at Augusta, Augusta, **ME**
Introduction to Philosophy

Prince George's Community College, Largo, **MD**
Introduction to Philosophy
Contemporary Moral Values

Wayne County Community College, Detroit, **MI**
Comparative Religions II

* Western Michigan University, Department of Distance Education, Kalamazoo, **MI**
Philosophy and Public Affairs: Ethics in America

* University of Missouri, Columbia, **MO**
Ethics and the Professions

University of New Hampshire, Durham, **NH**
Critical Thinking

* New School for Social Research - DIAL, New York, **NY**
Philosophical Dilemmas of Technological Society

* New York Institute of Technology, Old Westbury, **NY**
Problems of Philosophy
Ethics and Social Philosophy

Rockland Community College, Suffern, **NY**
Six Great Thinkers
Ethics in America

* Ohio University, Athens, **OH**
Islam

* Oklahoma State University, Stillwater, **OK**
Philosophies of Life

Rose State College, Midwest City, **OK**
Introduction to Philosophy

* Pennsylvania State University, University Park, **PA**
Major Figures in Philosophy
Ethics and Social Issues

Tarrant County Junior College, Fort Worth, **TX**
Ethics in America

Northern Virginia Community College, Annandale, **VA**
Introduction to Philosophy I
Introduction to Philosophy II
Logic I
Logic II

* Western Washington University, Bellingham, **WA**
Ethics in America
Ethics in America, Advanced

West Virginia Higher Education Instructional Television Consortium, Morgantown, **WV**
Ethics in America

University of Wisconsin (UW), Madison, **WI**
Ethics in Business

Photography

Northern California Telecommunications Consortium, Sacramento, **CA**
The Photographic Vision

Physical Education

* Western Michigan University, Department of Distance Education, Kalamazoo, **MI**
Beginning Bowling
Intermediate Bowling
Beginning Golf
Beginning Racquetball
Intermediate Racquetball
Beginning Tennis
Intermediate Tennis

Rockland Community College, Suffern, **NY**
Wellness for Life: Aerobics
Wellness for Life: Strength Building
Wellness for Life: Diet and Exercise

North Carolina State University, Raleigh, **NC**
Body Conditioning and Aerobics

Physics

* University of California, Berkeley, **CA**
General Physics

* Mind Extension University, Englewood, **CO**
Basic Physics and Physical World View

*Institute provides nationwide or worldwide course access

* University of Minnesota, Minneapolis, **MN**
  The Changing Physical World

* University of Missouri, Columbia, **MO**
  The Mechanical Universe

* New Jersey Institute of Technology, Newark, **NJ**
  Physics I

* Pennsylvania State University, University Park, **PA**
  Introduction to Quantum Physics

* Washington State University, Pullman, **WA**
  General Physics

Polish

* Pennsylvania State University, University Park, **PA**
  Beginning Polish

Political Science

* University of Alaska, Fairbanks, **AK**
  Introduction to American Government and Politics

Arkansas Telecommunications Consortium, Russellville, **AR**
  Government By Consent

Northern California Telecommunications Consortium, Sacramento, **CA**
  Government By Consent

* University of California, Berkeley, **CA**
  American Institutions

KRMA/Denver, Denver, **CO**
  Government by Consent
  The Pacific Century

Metropolitan State College of Denver, Englewood, **CO**
  American National Government
  Contemporary Latin America

* Mind Extension University, Englewood, **CO**
  Gender and Politics
  Problems of Government

Florida West Coast Public Broadcasting, Inc., Tampa, **FL**
  Government by Consent

Harold Washington College, Chicago, **IL**
  The National Government

* Indiana University, Bloomington, **IN**
  American Politics through Film and Fiction

* University of Iowa, Iowa City, **IA**
  Pacific Century
  Government by Consent

College of the Air, Owings Mills, **MD**
  Pacific Century

Prince George's Community College, Largo, **MD**
  American National Government

North Central Michigan College, Petoskey, **MI**
  Government By Consent

Northwestern Michigan College, Traverse City, **MI**
  Government by Consent

Wayne County Community College, Detroit, **MI**
  Introduction to Political Science

* University of Minnesota, Minneapolis, **MN**
  Contemporary Political Ideologies

* University of Missouri, Columbia, **MO**
  Congressional Politics
  The American Constitution

University of New Hampshire, Durham, **NH**
  The Pacific Century

* Empire State College, Saratoga Springs, **NY**
  The American Political System: An Introduction to American Government
  Theories of the Labor Movement
  The Constitution: The Judiciary and Public Policy
  Citizen Participation in the Political Process
  Politics and Leadership in the Bureaucracy

* New School for Social Research, New York, **NY**
  Democracy and the 21st Century

* New York Institute of Technology, Old Westbury, **NY**
  American Government and Politics
  Government and Business
  Comparative Government
  Basic Legal Concepts and Administration of Justice
  Politics of Technical Assistance

* Rochester Institute of Technology, Rochester, **NY**
  American Politics
  Government and Politics of Russia and the CIS

Rockland Community College, Suffern, **NY**
  American Government
  The Constitution

North Dakota Interactive Video Network, Bismarck, **ND**
  Problems in Political Science: Politics and Policy Making in North Dakota
  Research Methods
  Seminar: Problems in State and Local Government

* Oklahoma State University, Stillwater, **OK**
  American Government
  Problems of Government, Politics, and Public Policy: War and Peace in the Nuclear Age

Rose State College, Midwest City, **OK**
  American National Government

University of Oklahoma, Norman, **OK**
  Government of the U.S.

* Pennsylvania State University, University Park, **PA**
  The Constitution: That Delicate Balance

University of South Dakota, Vermillion, **SD**
  Government

Dallas County Community College District, Dallas, **TX**
  Government By Consent: A National Perspective
  Government By Consent: A Texas Perspective

University of Texas at Austin, Austin, **TX**
  American Foreign Relations

*Institute provides nationwide or worldwide course access

* University of Utah, Salt Lake City, **UT**
Political Science

Northern Virginia Community College, Annandale, **VA**
U.S. Government I
U.S. Government II

* City University, Bellevue, **WA**
Interpreting the American Constitution

* University of Washington, Seattle, **WA**
Introduction to American Politics
The Politics of Mass Communication in America

West Virginia Higher Education Instructional Television
Consortium, Morgantown, **WV**
The Pacific Century

Wisconsin Educational Communications Board, Madison,
WI
Americas

Central Wyoming College, Riverton, **WY**
American and Wyoming Government

Portuguese

* University of Minnesota, Minneapolis, **MN**
The Everpresent Past in Spanish and Portuguese Culture

Practical Nursing

Indiana Vocational Technical College, South Bend, **IN**
Nutrition for PNs
Anatomy and Physiology for PNs

Preaching

* Taylor University, Fort Wayne, **IN**
Introduction to Preaching

Psychology

* Southeastern Bible College, Birmingham, **AL**
Introduction to Psychology
Educational Psychology

* University of Alaska, Fairbanks, **AK**
Introduction to Psychology
Developmental Psychology in Cross-Cultural Perspective
Drugs and Drug Dependence

* Rio Salado Community College, Phoenix, **AZ**
Introduction to Psychology

Arkansas Telecommunications Consortium, Russellville,
AR
The World of Abnormal Psychology
Psychology: The Study of Human Behavior

INTELECOM, Pasadena, **CA**
Psychology: The Study of Human Behavior

Northern California Telecommunications Consortium, Sac-
ramento, **CA**
Discovering Psychology
Psychology: Study of Human Behavior
The World of Abnormal Psychology

* University of California, Berkeley, **CA**
Psychology of Communication
Developmental Psychology
Social Psychology

* Colorado State University, Fort Collins, **CO**
General Psychology
Computer-Mediated Instruction for General Psychology
Developmental Psychology Across the Life Span
Abnormal Psychology

KRMA/Denver, Denver, **CO**
Discovering Psychology
Seasons of Life
The World of Abnormal Psychology

Metropolitan State College of Denver, Englewood, **CO**
Introductory Psychology
Abnormal Psychology

* Mind Extension University, Englewood, **CO**
Industrial Psychology
General Psychology
Psychology Across the Life Span

Connecticut Community-Technical College System, Hartford, **CT**
Time to Grow

Florida West Coast Public Broadcasting, Inc., Tampa, **FL**
Discovering Psychology

Miami-Dade Community College, Miami, **FL**
Introduction to Psychology
Individual in Transition

* Southeastern College, Lakeland, **FL**
Applied and Community Psychology
Theories of Personality
Psychological Foundations of Education
Developmental Psychology
Psychology of Religion
Integration of Psychology and Theology
Psychotherapy: Theory and Practice
Social Psychology
Physiological Psychology
Experimental Psychology
Marital and Family Therapy
Directed Readings and Research in Psychology

* University of Florida, Gainesville, **FL**
General Psychology

Belleville Area College, Belleville, **IL**
General Psychology
Child Development

Governors State University, University Park, **IL**
Principles of Psychology
Personality Theories
Social Psychology
Adulthood

*Institute provides nationwide or worldwide course access

Harold Washington College, Chicago, **IL**
General Psychology
Child Psychology

* Western Illinois University, Macomb, **IL**
Seasons of Life

* Indiana State University, Terre Haute, **IN**
General Psychology

Indiana Vocational Technical College, South Bend, **IN**
Psychology

North Iowa Area Community College, Mason City, **IA**
Discovering Psychology
Time to Grow

* University of Iowa, Iowa City, **IA**
The World of Abnormal Psychology

* University of Kansas, Lawrence, **KS**
Brain and Behavior
The Mind

Elizabethtown Community College, Elizabethtown, **KY**
Discovering Psychology

Kentucky Telecommunications Consortium, Lexington, **KY**
Discovering Psychology

Murray State University, Murray, **KY**
Discovering Psychology

Northern Kentucky University, Highland Heights, **KY**
Discovering Psychology

Paducah Community College, Paducah, **KY**
Discovering Psychology

University of Maine at Augusta, Augusta, **ME**
Introduction to Psychology
Introduction to Community Health Care
Psychosocial Rehabilitation I
Crisis Identification and Intervention
Topics: Models of Addiction
Human Development
Psychology of Childhood

College of the Air, Owings Mills, **MD**
The World of Abnormal Psychology

Prince George's Community College, Largo, **MD**
General Psychology
Abnormal Psychology
Child Psychology

WGBH/Boston, Boston, **MA**
Discovering Psychology

North Central Michigan College, Petoskey, **MI**
Discovering Psychology

Northwestern Michigan College, Traverse City, **MI**
Discovering Psychology

Wayne County Community College, Detroit, **MI**
Introductory Psychology

* Western Michigan University, Department of Distance
Education, Kalamazoo, **MI**
Brain, Mind, and Behavior

* University of Missouri, Columbia, **MO**
Brain, Mind, and Behavior

University of Nebraska at Kearney, Kearney, **NE**
General Psychology
Abnormal Psychology

University of New Hampshire, Durham, **NH**
Abnormal Psychology
The Mind

* New Jersey Institute of Technology, Newark, **NJ**
Discovering Psychology

* Empire State College, Saratoga Springs, **NY**
Introduction to Psychology
Seasons of Life
Social Psychology
The Abnormal Personality

* New York Institute of Technology, Old Westbury, **NY**
Introductory Psychology
Physiological Basis of Behavior
Learning Theory
Social Psychology
Measurement Concepts
Educational Psychology
Marriage and the Family
Quantitative Methods for the Behavioral Sciences
American Urban Minorities
Social Stratification
Child Psychology
Adolescent Psychology
Psychology of Adulthood and Aging
Theories of Personality
Introduction to Sociological Theory
Behavioral Sciences in Marketing
Occupational Psychology
The Institutional Community
Community Mental Health
Urban Society
Job Satisfaction and Job Stress
Organizational Behavior
Communication and Interviewing Techniques
Introduction to Effective Communication
Abnormal Psychology
Psychology of Salesmanship
Introductory Research Methods for Behavior Sciences
Juvenile Delinquency
Environmental Psychology
Occupations
Introduction to Counseling
Rehabilitation Psychology

* Rochester Institute of Technology, Rochester, **NY**
Introduction to Psychology
Abnormal Psychology

Rockland Community College, Suffern, **NY**
General Psychology
Life Span and Psycho-Social Development
Psychology of Childhood
Abnormal Psychology

* University of North Carolina, Chapel Hill, **NC**
General Psychology

*Institute provides nationwide or worldwide course access

North Dakota Interactive Video Network, Bismarck, **ND**
   Psychological and Pathological Effects of Drugs
   Introduction to Personality
   Elementary Counseling

Edison State Community College, Greenville, **OH**
   Introduction to Psychology I
   Introduction to Psychology II

Rose State College, Midwest City, **OK**
   General Psychology

* Pennsylvania State University, University Park, **PA**
   Psychology

Community College of Rhode Island, Lincoln, **RI**
   General Psychology
   Developmental Psychology
   Abnormal Psychology

University of South Dakota, Vermillion, **SD**
   Psychology of Abnormal Behavior
   Human Development Through the Life Span

San Antonio College, San Antonio, **TX**
   Child Psychology
   General Psychology

Tarrant County Junior College, Fort Worth, **TX**
   Introduction to Psychology
   Child Growth and Development
   Life Span Growth and Development

* Texas Tech University, Lubbock, **TX**
   General Psychology

University of Texas at Austin, Austin, **TX**
   Abnormal Psychology

* University of Utah, Salt Lake City, **UT**
   Psychology of Infancy and Childhood

Northern Virginia Community College, Annandale, **VA**
   Introduction to Psychology I

Milwaukee Area Technical College, Milwaukee, **WI**
   Introductory Psychology
   Abnormal Psychology

Wisconsin Educational Communications Board, Madison,
WI
   Discovering Psychology

Central Wyoming College, Riverton, **WY**
   General Psychology

* University of Wyoming, Laramie, **WY**
   General Psychology
   Child Psychology
   Cognitive Psychology
   The Adolescent
   Abnormal Psychology
   Theories of Personality

Public Administration

* Empire State College, Saratoga Springs, **NY**
   Introduction to Public Administration
   Introduction to Public Policy

North Carolina State University, Raleigh, **NC**
   Introduction to Public Administration

Public Health

* University of Minnesota, Minneapolis, **MN**
   Toward an Understanding of Child Sexual Abuse
   Child Abuse and Neglect

Reading

* Rio Salado Community College, Phoenix, **AZ**
   Critical and Evaluative Reading

* University of California, Berkeley, **CA**
   Literature for Children

Real Estate

University of Maine at Augusta, Augusta, **ME**
   Real Estate Practice

Religious Studies

* Southeastern Bible College, Birmingham, **AL**
   Bible Study Methods
   Bible Survey I
   Bible Survey II: Old Testament
   Bible Survey III: New Testament
   Bible Exposition: Acts
   Bible Exposition: Daniel
   Bible Exposition: Exodus
   Bible Exposition: Genesis
   Bible Exposition: Hebrews
   James and Galatians
   Bible Exposition: Gospel of John
   Bible Exposition: Joshua
   Luke and John
   Bible Exposition: Revelation
   Bible Exposition: Romans
   I & II Thessalonians, Philippians
   I & II Timothy Practicum
   Life of Christ
   Missionary Methods in Acts
   Personal Evangelism
   Pastoral Practicum
   Introduction to Missions
   Doctrine: Bible Introduction Practicum
   Doctrine: Eschatology
   Doctrine: Spiritual Life
   Doctrinal Summary

KRMA/Denver, Denver, **CO**
   Beliefs and Believers

* Southeastern College, Lakeland, **FL**
   Isaiah
   Old Testament History II
   Genesis
   Jeremiah
   Hebrew Wisdom Literature
   Exodus

*Institute provides nationwide or worldwide course access

Leviticus
Ezekiel
The Book of Job
Apocalyptic Literature of the Old Testament
Matthew
Luke
Earlier Epistles of Paul
Mark
Prison Epistles
Pastoral Epistles
Biblical Introduction
General Epistles
Revelation
Epistle to the Hebrews

Governors State University, University Park, **IL**
Studies in Religion

* Emmaus Bible School, Dubuque, **IA**
Bible Prophecy
What the Bible Teaches
Guide to Christian Growth
Personal Evangelism
The Gospel of Mark
The Gospel of Luke
The Book of Acts
The Epistle to the Romans
First Corinthians
Philippians, Colossians, and Philemon
The Thessalonian Epistles
Timothy and Titus
Revelation
The Holy Spirit at Work
The Lord's Supper
How to Teach

* University of Kansas, Lawrence, **KS**
History of Judaism

* Home Study International, Silver Spring, **MD**
Prophetic Guidance

Prince George's Community College, Largo, **MD**
Thinking About Religion

* University of Minnesota, Minneapolis, **MN**
Religions of South Asia

* Empire State College, Saratoga Springs, **NY**
Islam: Religion and Culture
Religious Perspectives I
Religious Perspectives II

North Carolina State University, Raleigh, **NC**
Religious Traditions of the World

* Pennsylvania State University, University Park, **PA**
An Introduction to the Religions of the East

Tarrant County Junior College, Fort Worth, **TX**
Great Religions of the World

Rural Sociology

KRMA/Denver, Denver, **CO**
Rural Communities

Boise State University, Boise, **ID**
Rural Sociology: Legacy and Change

WGBH/Boston, Boston, **MA**
Rural Communities

West Virginia Higher Education Instructional Television Consortium, Morgantown, **WV**
Rural Communities: Legacy and Change

Russian

* University of Arizona, Tucson, **AZ**
Russian Civilization and Culture: Pre-Christian Era to the Present

* University of Iowa, Iowa City, **IA**
First-Year Russian

* University of Minnesota, Minneapolis, **MN**
Beginning Russian I
Beginning Russian II
Beginning Russian III

* University of Washington, Seattle, **WA**
First-Year Russian C101
First-Year Russian C102
First-Year Russian C103

Science

Harold Washington College, Chicago, **IL**
General Course

Prince George's Community College, Largo, **MD**
Science and Society

* University of Maryland University College, College Park, **MD**
Oceanus: The Marine Environment (*Video*)

* New York Institute of Technology, Old Westbury, **NY**
Introduction to the Life and Health Sciences
Environmental Sciences
Philosophy and History of Science

* Rochester Institute of Technology, Rochester, **NY**
Contemporary Science: Mechanical Universe
Contemporary Science: Oceanus
Modern Warfare Technology and Arms Control
Philosophy of Science

Science Fiction

* New School for Social Research, New York, **NY**
Science Fiction and Space Age Mythology

Small Business Management

INTELECOM, Pasadena, **CA**
Something Ventured

Northern California Telecommunications Consortium, Sacramento, **CA**
Something Ventured

*Institute provides nationwide or worldwide course access

WGBH/Boston, Boston, **MA**
 Something Ventured: Small Business Management

Wayne County Community College, Detroit, **MI**
 Small Business Management

West Virginia Higher Education Instructional Television
Consortium, Morgantown, **WV**
 Something Ventured: An Entrepreneurial Approach to Small
  Business Management

Wisconsin Educational Communications Board, Madison,
WI
 Something Ventured: An Entrepreneurial Approach to Small
  Business Management

Social Science

Miami-Dade Community College, Miami, **FL**
 The Social Environment

* Southeastern College, Lakeland, **FL**
 World Geography
 Economics
 United States Government

* Empire State College, Saratoga Springs, **NY**
 Societies in Transition
 Hispanic America

Rockland Community College, Suffern, **NY**
 Interdisciplinary Study of the Middle East
 The Pacific Century
 Latin America and the Caribbean

* Pennsylvania State University, University Park, **PA**
 Science, Technology, and Society

Social Sciences Degree Completion

* Mind Extension University, Englewood, **CO**
 Social Sciences Degree Completion Program

Social Services

University of Maine at Augusta, Augusta, **ME**
 Introduction to Social Service Systems
 Chemical Dependency Counseling
 Case Management
 Public Policy in the Chemical Dependency Field

Social Studies

* Columbia Bible College and Seminary, Columbia, **SC**
 Family Life I: Courtship and Marriage
 Family Life II: Parenting

Social Work

* Colorado State University, Fort Collins, **CO**
 Introduction to Social Work

* Western Michigan University, Department of Distance
 Education, Kalamazoo, **MI**
 The Black Struggle for Justice, 1965-Present

* New York Institute of Technology, Old Westbury, **NY**
 Introduction to Social Work
 Community Psychology
 Social Work II

North Dakota Interactive Video Network, Bismarck, **ND**
 Drugs: Addiction Dynamics

* University of South Carolina, Columbia, **SC**
 Foundations of Social Welfare

Sociology

* University of Alaska, Fairbanks, **AK**
 Introduction to Sociology
 Social Institutions
 The Family: A Cross-Cultural Perspective

* Rio Salado Community College, Phoenix, **AZ**
 Introduction to Sociology

INTELECOM, Pasadena, **CA**
 Sociological Imagination

Northern California Telecommunications Consortium, Sac-
ramento, **CA**
 The Sociological Imagination: Introduction to Sociology
 Portrait of a Family

* Colorado State University, Fort Collins, **CO**
 Sociology of Rural Life

KRMA/Denver, Denver, **CO**
 The Sociological Imagination

Metropolitan State College of Denver, Englewood, **CO**
 Introduction to Sociology
 Portrait of a Family

* Mind Extension University, Englewood, **CO**
 Law and Society
 Legal Ethics
 Dealing with Diversity

Florida West Coast Public Broadcasting, Inc., Tampa, **FL**
 Sociological Imagination

Belleville Area College, Belleville, **IL**
 Introductory Sociology
 The Family

Governors State University, University Park, **IL**
 Urban Dynamics
 Dealing with Diversity
 Vietnam, A Television History

Harold Washington College, Chicago, **IL**
 Introduction to the Study of Society
 Marriage and the Family

Sangamon State University, Springfield, **IL**
 Portrait of a Family

* Indiana State University, Terre Haute, **IN**
 Social Conflict

Teikyo Marycrest University, Davenport, **IA**
The Sociological Imagination
Faces of Culture

* University of Iowa, Iowa City, **IA**
Introduction to Sociology: Principles

Elizabethtown Community College, Elizabethtown, **KY**
The Sociological Imagination

Kentucky Telecommunications Consortium, Lexington, **KY**
Sociology

Murray State University, Murray, **KY**
The Sociological Imagination

Northern Kentucky University, Highland Heights, **KY**
The Sociological Imagination

Paducah Community College, Paducah, **KY**
The Sociological Imagination

University of Maine at Augusta, Augusta, **ME**
Introduction to Sociology
Sociology of Aging
Social Gerontology

College of the Air, Owings Mills, **MD**
Sociological Imagination
Rural Communities: Legacy and Change

Prince George's Community College, Largo, **MD**
Introduction to Sociology
Human Growth and Development
Marriage and the Family

* University of Maryland University College, College Park, **MD**
The Sociology of Gender (*ITV*)

WGBH/Boston, Boston, **MA**
The Sociological Imagination

North Central Michigan College, Petoskey, **MI**
The Sociological Imagination: Introduction to Sociology

Northwestern Michigan College, Traverse City, **MI**
The Sociological Imagination: Introduction to Sociology

Wayne County Community College, Detroit, **MI**
Sociology

* Western Michigan University, Department of Distance Education, Kalamazoo, **MI**
Death, Dying, and Bereavement

* University of Missouri, Columbia, **MO**
Criminology

University of Nebraska at Kearney, Kearney, **NE**
Marriage and Family
Introduction to Sociology

* New Jersey Institute of Technology, Newark, **NJ**
The Sociological Imagination: Introduction to Sociology

* New School for Social Research - DIAL, New York, **NY**
Identity: The Modular Construction of Personality

* New York Institute of Technology, Old Westbury, **NY**
Introduction to Sociology
Social Problems

Medical Sociology
Political Sociology
Social Policy

* Rochester Institute of Technology, Rochester, **NY**
Foundations of Sociology
Sociology of Health

Rockland Community College, Suffern, **NY**
Marriage and the Family
The Civil Rights Movement: A Socio-Historical Perspective
Principles of Sociology
Legacies of Women in America

North Dakota Interactive Video Network, Bismarck, **ND**
Drugs and Society

* Oklahoma State University, Stillwater, **OK**
Introductory Sociology

Rose State College, Midwest City, **OK**
Introduction to Sociology
Family in Society

University of Oklahoma, Norman, **OK**
Introduction to Sociology

Community College of Rhode Island, Lincoln, **RI**
General Sociology
Marriage and the Family

University of South Dakota, Vermillion, **SD**
Sociology of the Family
Rural Sociology

* University of Tennessee, Knoxville, **TN**
The City

Dallas County Community College District, Dallas, **TX**
The Sociological Imagination: Introduction to Sociology

San Antonio College, San Antonio, **TX**
Introduction to Sociology
Marriage and the Family

Tarrant County Junior College, Fort Worth, **TX**
Introduction to Sociology

* University of Utah, Salt Lake City, **UT**
Introduction to Sociology
Introduction to Research Methods
Introduction to Social Statistics
Sociology of Marriage and Family
Current Social Problems in America
Introduction to Criminology
Juvenile Delinquency
The Criminal Justice System
Law Enforcement in Society

* University of Washington, Seattle, **WA**
Survey of Sociology

Milwaukee Area Technical College, Milwaukee, **WI**
Introduction to Sociology

University of Wisconsin (UW), Madison, **WI**
Marriage and the Family
Sociological Foundations

*Institute provides nationwide or worldwide course access

Wisconsin Educational Communications Board, Madison, **WI**

    Seasons of Life
    Sociological Imagination

Central Wyoming College, Riverton, **WY**

    Introduction to Sociology

* University of Wyoming, Laramie, **WY**

    Introductory Sociology

Solid Waste Management

* Rochester Institute of Technology, Rochester, **NY**

    Principles of Municipal Solid Waste Systems
    Solid Waste Management I: Recycling

Spanish

* University of Arizona, Tucson, **AZ**

    Second-Semester Spanish
    Second Year Spanish

Arkansas Telecommunications Consortium, Russellville, **AR**

    Destinos: An Introduction to Spanish, Part 1

Northern California Telecommunications Consortium, Sacramento, **CA**

    Destinos: An Introduction to Spanish

* University of California, Berkeley, **CA**

    Spanish: Elementary Course I
    Spanish: Elementary Course II
    Spanish: Elementary Course III
    Spanish: Intermediate Course I
    Spanish for the Professions: Course I
    Spanish for the Professions: Course II

KRMA/Denver, Denver, **CO**

    Destinos

Miami-Dade Community College, Miami, **FL**

    Elementary Spanish 1
    Spanish for Native Speakers 1

* University of Georgia, Athens, **GA**

    Elementary Spanish I
    Elementary Spanish II
    Elementary Spanish III
    Intermediate Spanish

* University of Idaho, Moscow, **ID**

    Elementary Spanish C101
    Elementary Spanish C102

* Indiana University, Bloomington, **IN**

    Elementary Spanish I
    Elementary Spanish II

* University of Kansas, Lawrence, **KS**

    Elementary Spanish I
    Elementary Spanish II

Kentucky Telecommunications Consortium, Lexington, **KY**

    Destinos I

Northern Kentucky University, Highland Heights, **KY**

    Destinos I

* Louisiana State University, Baton Rouge, **LA**

    Elementary Spanish (1101)
    Elementary Spanish (1102)
    Spanish—I, 1st Semester
    Spanish—I, 2nd Semester
    Spanish—II, 1st Semester
    Spanish—II, 2nd Semester

College of the Air, Owings Mills, **MD**

    Destinos

* Home Study International, Silver Spring, **MD**

    Spanish I
    Spanish II

WGBH/Boston, Boston, **MA**

    Destinos: An Introduction to Spanish, Part 1
    Destinos: An Introduction to Spanish, Part 2

* University of Minnesota, Minneapolis, **MN**

    Beginning Spanish I
    Beginning Spanish II
    Beginning Spanish III
    Intermediate Spanish I
    Intermediate Spanish II
    Topics in Spanish-Portuguese Civilization and Culture
    The Everpresent Past in Spanish and Portuguese Culture

* University of Missouri, Columbia, **MO**

    Elementary Spanish I
    Elementary Spanish II
    Elementary Spanish III

University of Nebraska at Kearney, Kearney, **NE**

    Beginning Spanish

* University of Nebraska at Lincoln, Department of Independent Study, Lincoln, **NE**

    Spanish 1
    Spanish 2
    Spanish 3
    Spanish 4

* University of Nevada - Reno, Reno, **NV**

    Elementary Spanish I
    Elementary Spanish II

University of New Hampshire, Durham, **NH**

    Destinos: An Introduction to Spanish: Part I
    Destinos: An Introduction to Spanish: Part II

WNET/New York City, New York, **NY**

    Destinos

North Carolina State University, Raleigh, **NC**

    Intermediate Spanish II

* University of North Dakota, Grand Forks, **ND**

    Beginning Spanish 101
    Beginning Spanish 102
    Second-Year Spanish 201
    Second-Year Spanish 202

* Oklahoma State University, Stillwater, **OK**

    Elementary Spanish I
    Elementary Spanish II

*Institute provides nationwide or worldwide course access

Rose State College, Midwest City, **OK**
 Conversational Spanish I
 Conversational Spanish II

* Pennsylvania State University, University Park, **PA**
 Intermediate Spanish

* University of South Carolina, Columbia, **SC**
 Beginning Spanish I
 Beginning Spanish II

University of South Dakota, Vermillion, **SD**
 Introductory Spanish

* University of Tennessee, Knoxville, **TN**
 Elementary Spanish, First Semester
 Elementary Spanish, Second Semester
 Intermediate Spanish, First Semester
 Intermediate Spanish, Second Semester

San Antonio College, San Antonio, **TX**
 Beginning Conversational Spanish I

* Texas Tech University, Lubbock, **TX**
 Spanish Level I (1A)
 Spanish Level I (1B)
 Spanish Level II (2A)

* Brigham Young University, Provo, **UT**
 Introductory Spanish
 Second-Year Spanish

* Utah State University, Logan, **UT**
 Elementary Spanish 101
 Elementary Spanish 102
 Elementary Spanish 103
 Intermediate Spanish 201
 Intermediate Spanish 202

* University of Washington, Seattle, **WA**
 Elementary Spanish C101
 Elementary Spanish C102
 Elementary Spanish C102
 Intermediate Spanish C201
 Intermediate Spanish C202

* Washington State University, Pullman, **WA**
 First Semester Spanish
 Second Semester Spanish

West Virginia Higher Education Instructional Television
Consortium, Morgantown, **WV**
 Destinos: An Introduction to Spanish

University of Wisconsin (UW), Madison, **WI**
 First Semester College Spanish
 Second Semester College Spanish

Wisconsin Educational Communications Board, Madison,
WI
 Destinos: An Introduction to Spanish

Central Wyoming College, Riverton, **WY**
 First-Year Spanish
 Spanish II

* University of Wyoming, Laramie, **WY**
 First Year Spanish I
 First Year Spanish II

Special Education

* University of Arizona, Tucson, **AZ**
 Behavior Principles for the Handicapped
 Language Development for the Exceptional Child

* University of Idaho, Moscow, **ID**
 Augmentative and Alternative Communication Strategies for
 Persons with Moderate and Severe Disabilities

Governors State University, University Park, **IL**
 Survey of Exceptional Students

* University of Iowa, Iowa City, **IA**
 Introduction to Continuing Education

* University of Kansas, Lawrence, **KS**
 Introduction to the Psychology and Education of Exceptional
 Children and Youth

University of Maine at Augusta, Augusta, **ME**
 Curriculum and Instructional Programming for Exceptional
 Children
 Pre-Vocational Instructions for Students with Disabilities or at
 Risk

* University of Missouri, Columbia, **MO**
 The Psychology and Education of Exceptional Individuals

North Dakota Interactive Video Network, Bismarck, **ND**
 Early Intervention for Children with Special Needs

University of South Dakota, Vermillion, **SD**
 Educating Able Learners

Speech

* Southeastern Bible College, Birmingham, **AL**
 Speech

Belleville Area College, Belleville, **IL**
 American Playhouse

* Louisiana State University, Baton Rouge, **LA**
 Interpersonal Communication
 Argumentation and Debate

Speech Communication

* Indiana University, Bloomington, **IN**
 Public Speaking
 Interpersonal Communication
 Business and Professional Communication

Sport Science

* Pennsylvania State University, University Park, **PA**
 The Modern Olympic Games

Statistics

* University of Alaska, Fairbanks, **AK**
 Elementary Probability and Statistics

* Rio Salado Community College, Phoenix, **AZ**
 Business Statistics

*Institute provides nationwide or worldwide course access

* University of Arizona, Tucson, **AZ**
  Statistics for Engineering and the Physical Sciences

Northern California Telecommunications Consortium, Sacramento, **CA**
  Against All Odds: Inside Statistics

* Colorado SURGE, Fort Collins, **CO**
  Engineering Statistics
  Design and Data Analysis for Researchers II
  Mathematical Statistics
  Linear Statistical Models I

KRMA/Denver, Denver, **CO**
  Against All Odds

* Mind Extension University, Englewood, **CO**
  Elementary Statistics

Pikes Peak Community College, Colorado Springs, **CO**
  Introduction to Statistics

Governors State University, University Park, **IL**
  Statistics

Harold Washington College, Chicago, **IL**
  Introductory Statistics

College of the Air, Owings Mills, **MD**
  Against All Odds

* University of Minnesota, Minneapolis, **MN**
  Introduction to the Ideas of Statistics

University of Nebraska at Kearney, Kearney, **NE**
  Elementary Statistics

University of New Hampshire, Durham, **NH**
  Against All Odds: Inside Statistics

University of South Dakota, Vermillion, **SD**
  Introduction to Statistics

University of Texas at Austin, Austin, **TX**
  Statistical Methods in Psychology

* University of Utah, Salt Lake City, **UT**
  Elementary Statistics

University of Wisconsin (UW), Madison, **WI**
  Principles of Statistics

* University of Wyoming, Laramie, **WY**
  Fundamentals of Statistics

Stress Management

* University of Kansas, Lawrence, **KS**
  Managing Stress: Principles and Techniques for Coping, Prevention, and Wellness

Substance Abuse

Governors State University, University Park, **IL**
  Substance Abuse: Current Concepts
  The Adolescent Substance Abuser

Swedish

* University of Minnesota, Minneapolis, **MN**
  Beginning Swedish I
  Beginning Swedish II
  Beginning Swedish III
  Intermediate Swedish I
  Intermediate Swedish II

Systems and Industrial Engineering

* University of Arizona, Tucson, **AZ**
  Engineering Statistics
  Expert Systems

Technical Writing

* University of Minnesota, Minneapolis, **MN**
  Technical Writing for Engineers

Telecommunications

* New School for Social Research, New York, **NY**
  Telecommunication Applications

* Rochester Institute of Technology, Rochester, **NY**
  Data Communications and Computer Networks
  Telecommunication Fundamentals
  Voice Communications: Principles and Technology
  Switching Technologies
  Data Communications Technology
  Telecommunications Policy and Issues
  Network Management

Theatre

Governors State University, University Park, **IL**
  Creative Dramatics Workshop

* University of Minnesota, Minneapolis, **MN**
  Introduction to the Theatre
  Playwriting
  History of the American Theatre

* University of Missouri, Columbia, **MO**
  The Theatre in Society

* Ohio University, Athens, **OH**
  Theatre History I

Theology

* Southeastern Bible College, Birmingham, **AL**
  Theology I
  Theology II

* Southeastern College, Lakeland, **FL**
  The Doctrine of God
  The Doctrine of Christ
  The Doctrine of Last Things

* Columbia Bible College and Seminary, Columbia, **SC**
  Principles of the Christian Life

The Doctrine of the Church
Bibliology: Inerrancy and Authority of the Scriptures
Christian Theology I
Christian Theology II
The Theology of Jonathan Edwards (*Graduate Level*)

Transformative Learning

* California Institute of Integral Studies, San Francisco, **CA**
  Foundations of the Integral Worldview
  Design and Conduct of Inquiry
  Learning and Change in Human Systems

Travel Industry

* University of Alaska, Fairbanks, **AK**
  Tourism Principles and Practices

Virtual Work Group Communications

* New York University, New York, **NY**
  The Virtual College

Visual Arts

* University of North Dakota, Grand Forks, **ND**
  Introduction to Drawing and Color Materials

Vocational Education

* Colorado SURGE, Fort Collins, **CO**
  Human Resource Development
  HRD and Training Needs Assessment and Analysis

* University of Idaho, Moscow, **ID**
  Classroom Management and Student Motivation

Wastewater Management

* Rio Salado Community College, Phoenix, **AZ**
  Water/Wastewater Operational Concepts

Women's Studies

* University of Arizona, Tucson, **AZ**
  Women in Western Culture
  Women in Judaism

* University of Minnesota, Minneapolis, **MN**
  Northern Minnesota Women: Myths and Realities

* University of Nevada - Reno, Reno, **NV**
  Introduction to Women's Studies

Writing

Northern California Telecommunications Consortium, Sacramento, **CA**
  The Write Course

Dallas County Community College District, Dallas, **TX**
  The Write Course
  Communicating Through Literature

Zoology

* Louisiana State University, Baton Rouge, **LA**
  Human Physiology

---

*Institute provides nationwide or worldwide course access

Delivery System Index

This index is arranged alphabetically by delivery system, by state, by institution name.

Audio Conferencing

*Rio Salado Community College, Phoenix, **AZ**
*Western Michigan University, Department of Distance Education, Kalamazoo, **MI**
*Rochester Institute of Technology, Rochester, **NY**
 University of Texas at Austin, Austin, **TX**

Audiocassette

*Southeastern Bible College, Birmingham, **AL**
*Rio Salado Community College, Phoenix, **AZ**
*University of California, Berkeley, **CA**
 Miami-Dade Community College, Miami, **FL**
*University of Florida, Gainesville, **FL**
*University of Georgia, Athens, **GA**
*University of Idaho, Moscow, **ID**
*Indiana University, Bloomington, **IN**
*Taylor University, Fort Wayne, **IN**
*Emmaus Bible School, Dubuque, **IA**
*University of Iowa, Iowa City, **IA**
*University of Kansas, Lawrence, **KS**
*Louisiana State University, Baton Rouge, **LA**
*Home Study International, Silver Spring, **MD**
*University of Minnesota, Minneapolis, **MN**
*University of Missouri, Columbia, **MO**
*University of Nebraska at Lincoln, Department of Independent Study, Lincoln, **NE**
*University of Nevada - Reno, Reno, **NV**
 Rockland Community College, Suffern, **NY**
*University of North Carolina, Chapel Hill, **NC**
*University of North Dakota, Grand Forks, **ND**
*Ohio University, Athens, **OH**
*Oklahoma State University, Stillwater, **OK**
*Pennsylvania State University, University Park, **PA**
*Columbia Bible College and Seminary, Columbia, **SC**
*University of South Carolina, Columbia, **SC**
*University of Tennessee, Knoxville, **TN**
*Texas Tech University, Lubbock, **TX**
*Brigham Young University, Provo, **UT**
*Utah State University, Logan, **UT**

*Institute provides nationwide or worldwide course access

*Weber State University, Ogden, **UT**
*University of Washington, Seattle, **WA**
*Washington State University, Pullman, **WA**
*Western Washington University, Bellingham, **WA**
 University of Wisconsin (UW), Madison, **WI**
*University of Wyoming, Laramie, **WY**

Audiographic Conferencing

*Rochester Institute of Technology, Rochester, **NY**

Broadcast Television

*Rio Salado Community College, Phoenix, **AZ**
*University of Arizona, Tucson, **AZ**
 Arkansas Telecommunications Consortium, Russellville, **AR**
 INTELECOM, Pasadena, **CA**
 Northern California Telecommunications Consortium, Sacramento, **CA**
*University of California, Berkeley, **CA**
*Colorado State University, Fort Collins, **CO**
 KRMA/Denver, Denver, **CO**
 Metropolitan State College of Denver, Englewood, **CO**
*Mind Extension University, Englewood, **CO**
 Pikes Peak Community College, Colorado Springs, **CO**
 Connecticut Community-Technical College System, Hartford, **CT**
 Florida West Coast Public Broadcasting, Inc., Tampa, **FL**
 Boise State University, Boise, **ID**
 Belleville Area College, Belleville, **IL**
 Governors State University, University Park, **IL**
 Harold Washington College, Chicago, **IL**
 Sangamon State University, Springfield, **IL**
*Western Illinois University, Macomb, **IL**
 Indiana Vocational Technical College, South Bend, **IN**
 North Iowa Area Community College, Mason City, **IA**
 Teikyo Marycrest University, Davenport, **IA**
*University of Iowa, Iowa City, **IA**
 Elizabethtown Community College, Elizabethtown, **KY**
 Kentucky Telecommunications Consortium, Lexington, **KY**

Murray State University, Murray, **KY**
Northern Kentucky University, Highland Heights, **KY**
Paducah Community College, Paducah, **KY**
College of the Air, Owings Mills, **MD**
Prince George's Community College, Largo, **MD**
WGBH/Boston, Boston, **MA**
North Central Michigan College, Petoskey, **MI**
Northwestern Michigan College, Traverse City, **MI**
Wayne County Community College, Detroit, **MI**
*Western Michigan University - MITN, Office of Tele-
    course Programs, Kalamazoo, **MI**
*University of Minnesota, Minneapolis, **MN**
*University of Missouri, Columbia, **MO**
University of Nebraska at Kearney, Kearney, **NE**
University of New Hampshire, Durham, **NH**
*New Jersey Institute of Technology, Newark, **NJ**
Rockland Community College, Suffern, **NY**
WNET/New York City, New York, **NY**
North Carolina State University, Raleigh, **NC**
Ohio State University, Columbus, **OH**
University of Cincinnati, Cincinnati, **OH**
*Oklahoma State University, Stillwater, **OK**
Rose State College, Midwest City, **OK**
University of Oklahoma, Norman, **OK**
*Pennsylvania State University, University Park, **PA**
Community College of Rhode Island, Lincoln, **RI**
University of South Dakota, Vermillion, **SD**
East Tennessee State University, Johnson City, **TN**
Dallas County Community College District, Dallas, **TX**
San Antonio College, San Antonio, **TX**
Tarrant County Junior College, Fort Worth, **TX**
Northern Virginia Community College, Annandale, **VA**
West Virginia Higher Education Instructional Television
    Consortium, Morgantown, **WV**
Milwaukee Area Technical College, Milwaukee, **WI**
University of Wisconsin (UW), Madison, **WI**
Wisconsin Educational Communications Board, Madison,
    WI
Central Wyoming College, Riverton, **WY**

Computer Conferencing

*Rio Salado Community College, Phoenix, **AZ**
*University of Maryland University College, College Park,
    MD
*Empire State College, Saratoga Springs, **NY**
*New School for Social Research, New York, **NY**
*New School for Social Research - DIAL, New York, **NY**
*New York Institute of Technology, Old Westbury, **NY**
*Rochester Institute of Technology, Rochester, **NY**
Northern Virginia Community College, Annandale, **VA**

Computer Tutorials

*University of Idaho, Moscow, **ID**
*Indiana University, Bloomington, **IN**

*Institute provides nationwide or worldwide course access

Indiana Vocational Technical College, South Bend, **IN**
*University of Kansas, Lawrence, **KS**
*Emergency Management Institute, Emmitsburg, **MD**
*University of Minnesota, Minneapolis, **MN**
*University of Nebraska at Lincoln, Department of Inde-
    pendent Study, Lincoln, **NE**
*Ohio University, Athens, **OH**
*Oklahoma State University, Stillwater, **OK**
*Portland State University, Portland, **OR**
*Texas Tech University, Lubbock, **TX**
*Brigham Young University, Provo, **UT**
*University of Utah, Salt Lake City, **UT**
*Weber State University, Ogden, **UT**
*University of Washington, Seattle, **WA**

Electronic Mail

*University of Alaska, Fairbanks, **AK**
*University of California, Berkeley, **CA**
*Empire State College, Saratoga Springs, **NY**

Interactive Audio/Video

*Rio Salado Community College, Phoenix, **AZ**
Pikes Peak Community College, Colorado Springs, **CO**
Indiana Vocational Technical College, South Bend, **IN**
University of Maine at Augusta, Augusta, **ME**
*University of Maryland University College, College Park,
    MD
University of Nebraska - CorpNet, Nebraska CorpNet,
    Lincoln, **NE**
University of New Hampshire, Durham, **NH**
North Dakota Interactive Video Network, Bismarck, **ND**
Ohio State University, Columbus, **OH**
*Utah State University, Logan, **UT**
*Weber State University, Ogden, **UT**
Northern Virginia Community College, Annandale, **VA**

Online Services

*California Institute of Integral Studies, San Francisco, **CA**
*University of Phoenix - San Francisco, San Francisco, **CA**
*International School of Information Management, Inc.,
    Denver, **CO**
*Nova University, Fort Lauderdale, **FL**
*New York University, New York, **NY**
*Rochester Institute of Technology, Rochester, **NY**

Radio Broadcast

*University of Minnesota, Minneapolis, **MN**

Satellite Network

*University of Arizona, Tucson, **AZ**
National Technological University, Fort Collins, **CO**

Teleclasses

* Colorado SURGE, Fort Collins, **CO**
* Western Illinois University, Macomb, **IL**

Telephone Contact

* Southeastern College, Lakeland, **FL**
* Empire State College, Saratoga Springs, **NY**
  Community College of Rhode Island, Lincoln, **RI**

Videocassette

* Southeastern Bible College, Birmingham, **AL**
  University of Alabama, Tuscaloosa, **AL**
* University of Alaska, Fairbanks, **AK**
* Rio Salado Community College, Phoenix, **AZ**
* University of Arizona, Tucson, **AZ**
* University of California, Berkeley, **CA**
  Miami-Dade Community College, Miami, **FL**
* Southeastern College, Lakeland, **FL**
* University of Florida, Gainesville, **FL**
* University of Georgia, Athens, **GA**
* University of Idaho, Moscow, **ID**
  Belleville Area College, Belleville, **IL**
  Governors State University, University Park, **IL**
  Harold Washington College, Chicago, **IL**
* Western Illinois University, Macomb, **IL**
* Indiana State University, Terre Haute, **IN**
* Indiana University, Bloomington, **IN**
* Taylor University, Fort Wayne, **IN**
* University of Iowa, Iowa City, **IA**
* University of Kansas, Lawrence, **KS**
* Louisiana State University, Baton Rouge, **LA**
  Prince George's Community College, Largo, **MD**

* University of Maryland University College, College Park, **MD**
* Marygrove College, Detroit, **MI**
* Western Michigan University, Department of Distance Education, Kalamazoo, **MI**
* University of Minnesota, Minneapolis, **MN**
* University of Missouri, Columbia, **MO**
* University of Nevada - Reno, Reno, **NV**
* New Jersey Institute of Technology, Newark, **NJ**
* Empire State College, Saratoga Springs, **NY**
* Rochester Institute of Technology, Rochester, **NY**
  Rockland Community College, Suffern, **NY**
  North Carolina State University, Raleigh, **NC**
* University of North Carolina, Chapel Hill, **NC**
* University of North Dakota, Grand Forks, **ND**
  Edison State Community College, Greenville, **OH**
* Ohio University, Athens, **OH**
* Oklahoma State University, Stillwater, **OK**
* Portland State University, Portland, **OR**
* Pennsylvania State University, University Park, **PA**
* Columbia Bible College and Seminary, Columbia, **SC**
* University of South Carolina, Columbia, **SC**
* University of Tennessee, Knoxville, **TN**
  Tarrant County Junior College, Fort Worth, **TX**
* Texas Tech University, Lubbock, **TX**
* Brigham Young University, Provo, **UT**
* University of Utah, Salt Lake City, **UT**
* Utah State University, Logan, **UT**
* Weber State University, Ogden, **UT**
* City University, Bellevue, **WA**
* University of Washington, Seattle, **WA**
* Washington State University, Pullman, **WA**
* Western Washington University, Bellingham, **WA**
  University of Wisconsin (UW), Madison, **WI**
* University of Wyoming, Laramie, **WY**

*Institute provides nationwide or worldwide course access

Institution Name Index

Adams State College, Alamosa, CO
See KRMA/Denver

Allegany Community College, Cumberland, MD
See College of the Air

Allen Hancock College, Santa Maria, CA
See INTELECOM

American River College, Sacramento, CA
See Northern California Telecommunications Consortium

Anne Arundel Community College, Arnold, MD
See College of the Air

Antelope Valley College, Lancaster, CA
See INTELECOM

Arapahoe Community College, Littleton, CO
See KRMA/Denver

Arkansas Telecommunications Consortium, Russellville, AR

Ashland Community College, Ashland, KY
See Kentucky Telecommunications Consortium

Bakersfield College, Bakersfield, CA
See INTELECOM

Baltimore City Community College, Baltimore, MD
See College of the Air

Barstow College, Barstow, CA
See INTELECOM

Belleville Area College, Belleville, IL

Bergen County Community College, Paramus, NJ
See WNET/New York City

Bismarck State College, Bismarck, ND
See North Dakota Interactive Video Network

Bluefield State College, Bluefield, WV
See West Virginia Higher Education Instructional Television Consortium

Boise State University, Boise, ID

Bowie State University, Bowie, MD
See College of the Air

Bridgewater State College, Bridgewater, MA
See WGBH/Boston

* Brigham Young University, Provo, UT

Bristol Community College, Fall River, MA
See WGBH/Boston

Brookhaven College, Farmers Branch, TX
See Dallas County Community College District

Bunker Hill Community College, Boston, MA
See WGBH/Boston

* California Institute of Integral Studies, San Francisco, CA

Capital Community-Technical College, Hartford, CT
See Connecticut Community-Technical College System

Carroll Community College, Westminster, MD
See College of the Air

Catonsville Community College, Catonsville, MD
See College of the Air

Cecil Community College, North East, MD
See College of the Air

Cedar Valley College, Lancaster, TX
See Dallas County Community College District

Central Wyoming College, Riverton, WY

Cerritos College, Norwalk, CA
See INTELECOM

Charles County Community College, La Plata, MD
See College of the Air

Chesapeake College, Wye Mills, MD
See College of the Air

Citrus College, Glendora, CA
See INTELECOM

* City University, Bellevue, WA

Coast Community College District, Costa Mesa, CA
See INTELECOM

College of Alameda, Alameda, CA
See Northern California Telecommunications Consortium

College of Marin, Kentfield, CA
See Northern California Telecommunications Consortium

College of New Rochelle - Rosa Parks Campus, New York, NY
See WNET/New York City

College of San Mateo, San Mateo, CA

*Institute provides nationwide or worldwide course access

See Northern California Telecommunications Consortium

College of the Air, Owings Mills, MD

College of the Canyons, Santa Clarita, CA
See INTELECOM

Colorado Mountain College, Glenwood Springs, CO
See KRMA/Denver

Colorado Northwestern Community College, Rangely, CO
See KRMA/Denver

* Colorado State University, Fort Collins, CO

* Colorado SURGE, Fort Collins, CO

* Columbia Bible College and Seminary, Columbia, SC

Columbia College, Columbia, CA
See Northern California Telecommunications Consortium

Community College of Aurora, Aurora, CO
See KRMA/Denver

Community College of Denver, Denver, CO
See KRMA/Denver

Community College of Rhode Island, Lincoln, RI

Compton Community College, Compton, CA
See INTELECOM

Concord College, Athens, WV
See West Virginia Higher Education Instructional Television Consortium

Connecticut Community-Technical College System, Hartford, CT

Consumnes River College, Sacramento, CA
See Northern California Telecommunications Consortium

Contra Costa College, San Pablo, CA
See Northern California Telecommunications Consortium

County College of Morris, Randolph, NJ
See WNET/New York City

Crafton Hills College, Yucaipa, CA
See INTELECOM

Cumberland College, Williamsburg, KY
See Kentucky Telecommunications Consortium

Cuyamaca College, El Cajon, CA
See INTELECOM

Dallas County Community College District, Dallas, TX

Dean Junior College, Franklin, MA
See WGBH/Boston

DeAnza College, Cupertino, CA
See Northern California Telecommunications Consortium

Dickinson State University, Dickinson, ND
See North Dakota Interactive Video Network

Dundalk Community College, Dundalk, MD
See College of the Air

East Tennessee State University, Johnson City, TN

Eastern Kentucky University, Richmond, KY
See Kentucky Telecommunications Consortium

Eastern Wyoming College, Torrington, WY
See KRMA/Denver

Eastfield College, Mesquite, TX
See Dallas County Community College District

Edison State Community College, Greenville, OH

El Camino College, Torrance, CA
See INTELECOM

El Centro College, Dallas, TX
See Dallas County Community College District

Elizabethtown Community College, Elizabethtown, KY

* Emergency Management Institute, Emmitsburg, MD

* Emmaus Bible School, Dubuque, IA

* Empire State College, Saratoga Springs, NY

Essex Community College, Baltimore, MD
See College of the Air

Evergreen Valley College, San Jose, CA
See Northern California Telecommunications Consortium

Fairmont State College, Fairmont, WV
See West Virginia Higher Education Instructional Television Consortium

Fitchburg State College, Fitchburg, MA
See WGBH/Boston

Florida West Coast Public Broadcasting, Inc., Tampa, FL

Foothill College, Los Altos Hills, CA
See Northern California Telecommunications Consortium

Frederick Community College, Frederick, MD
See College of the Air

Front Range Community College, Westminster, CO
See KRMA/Denver

Fullerton College, Fullerton, CA
See INTELECOM

Garland County Community College, Hot Springs National Park, AR
See Arkansas Telecommunications Consortium

Garrett Community College, McHenry, MD
See College of the Air

Gateway Community-Technical College, New Haven, CT
See Connecticut Community-Technical College System

Glendale Community College, Glendale, CA
See INTELECOM

Glenville State College, Glenville, WV
See West Virginia Higher Education Instructional Television Consortium

Governors State University, University Park, IL

Hagerstown Junior College, Hagerstown, MD
See College of the Air

*Institute provides nationwide or worldwide course access

Harford Community College, Bel Air, MD
    See College of the Air

Harold Washington College, Chicago, IL

Harrisburg Area Community College, Harrisburg, PA
    See College of the Air

Hazard Community College, Hazard, KY
    See Kentucky Telecommunications Consortium

Henderson Community College, Henderson, KY
    See Kentucky Telecommunications Consortium

Henderson State University, Arkadelphia, AR
    See Arkansas Telecommunications Consortium

Hillsborough Community College, Tampa, FL
    See Florida West Coast Public Broadcasting

* Home Study International, Silver Spring, MD

Howard Community College, Columbia, MD
    See College of the Air

* Indiana State University, Terre Haute, IN

* Indiana University, Bloomington, IN

Indiana Vocational Technical College, South Bend, IN

INTELECOM, Pasadena, CA

* International School of Information Management, Inc.,
    Denver, CO

Iona College, New Rochelle, NY
    See WNET/New York City

Irvine Valley College, Irvine, CA
    See INTELECOM

Kentucky State University, Frankfort, KY
    See Kentucky Telecommunications Consortium

Kentucky Telecommunications Consortium, Lexington, KY

KRMA/Denver, Denver, CO

Laney College, Oakland, CA
    See Northern California Telecommunications Consortium

Laramie County Community College, Cheyenne, WY
    See KRMA/Denver

Lees College, Jackson, KY
    See Kentucky Telecommunications Consortium

Lehigh County Community College, Schnecksville, PA
    See College of the Air

Lexington Community College, Lexington, KY
    See Kentucky Telecommunications Consortium

Long Beach City College, Long Beach, CA
    See INTELECOM

Los Angeles Community College District, Los Angeles, CA
    See INTELECOM

* Louisiana State University, Baton Rouge, LA

Madisonville Community College, Madisonville, KY
    See Kentucky Telecommunications Consortium

Manatee Community College, Bradenton, FL
    See Florida West Coast Public Broadcasting

Manchester Community-Technical College, Manchester, CT
    See Connecticut Community-Technical College System

Marshall University, Huntington, WV
    See West Virginia Higher Education Instructional Television Consortium

* Marygrove College, Detroit, MI

Massasoit Community College, Brockton, MA
    See WGBH/Boston

Mayville State University, Mayville, ND
    See North Dakota Interactive Video Network

Mendocino College, Ukiah, CA
    See Northern California Telecommunications Consortium

Merritt College, Oakland, CA
    See Northern California Telecommunications Consortium

Metropolitan State College of Denver, Englewood, CO

Miami-Dade Community College, Miami, FL

Midway College, Midway, KY
    See Kentucky Telecommunications Consortium

Milwaukee Area Technical College, Milwaukee, WI

* Mind Extension University, Englewood, CO

Minot State University, Minot, ND
    See North Dakota Interactive Video Network

Mira Costa College, Oceanside, CA
    See INTELECOM

Mississippi County Community College, Blytheville, AR
    See Arkansas Telecommunications Consortium

Modesto Junior College, Modesto, CA
    See Northern California Telecommunications Consortium

Monterey Peninsula College, Monterey, CA
    See Northern California Telecommunications Consortium

Montgomery College, Rockville, MD
    See College of the Air

Montgomery County Community College, Blue Bell, PA
    See College of the Air

Moorpark College, Moorpark, CA
    See INTELECOM

Morehead State University, Morehead, KY
    See Kentucky Telecommunications Consortium

Morgan Community College, Fort Morgan, CO
    See KRMA/Denver

Mt. San Antonio College, Walnut, CA
    See INTELECOM

Mountain View College, Dallas, TX
    See Dallas County Community College District

Murray State University, Murray, KY

National Technological University, Fort Collins, CO

*Institute provides nationwide or worldwide course access

* Southeastern Bible College, Birmingham, AL

* Southeastern College, Lakeland, FL

Southern Arkansas University - Main Campus, Magnolia, AR
See Arkansas Telecommunications Consortium

Southern Arkansas University Tech, Camden, AR
See Arkansas Telecommunications Consortium

Southern West Virginia Community College, Logan, WV
See West Virginia Higher Education Instructional Television Consortium

Southwestern College, Chula Vista, CA
See INTELECOM

Suffolk County Community College, Selden, NY
See WNET/New York City

Tarrant County Junior College, Fort Worth, TX

* Taylor University, Fort Wayne, IN

Teikyo Marycrest University, Davenport, IA

* Texas Tech University, Lubbock, TX

Thomas More College, Crestview Hills, KY
See Kentucky Telecommunications Consortium

Towson State University, Towson, MD
See College of the Air

Trinidad State Junior College, Trinidad, CO
See KRMA/Denver

Tunxis Community-Technical College, Farmington, CT
See Connecticut Community-Technical College System

Union College, Barbourville, KY
See Kentucky Telecommunications Consortium

University of Alabama, Tuscaloosa, AL

* University of Alaska, Fairbanks, AK

* University of Arizona, Tucson, AZ

University of Arkansas at Little Rock, Little Rock, AR
See Arkansas Telecommunications Consortium

* University of California, Berkeley, CA

University of Cincinnati, Cincinnati, OH

* University of Florida, Gainesville, FL

* University of Georgia, Athens, GA

* University of Idaho, Moscow, ID

* University of Iowa, Iowa City, IA

* University of Kansas, Lawrence, KS

University of Kentucky, Lexington, KY
See Kentucky Telecommunications Consortium

University of Louisville, Louisville, KY
See Kentucky Telecommunications Consortium

University of Maine at Augusta, Augusta, ME

* University of Maryland University College, College Park, MD

* University of Minnesota, Minneapolis, MN

* University of Missouri, Columbia, MO

University of Nebraska at Kearney, Kearney, NE

* University of Nebraska at Lincoln, Department of Independent Study, Lincoln, NE

University of Nebraska - CorpNet, Nebraska CorpNet, Lincoln, NE

* University of Nevada - Reno, Reno, NV

University of New Hampshire, Durham, NH

* University of North Carolina, Chapel Hill, NC

* University of North Dakota, Grand Forks, ND

University of North Dakota - Lake Region, Devils Lake, ND
See North Dakota Interactive Video Network

University of North Dakota - Williston, Williston, ND
See North Dakota Interactive Video Network

University of Northern Colorado, Greeley, CO
See KRMA/Denver

University of Oklahoma, Norman, OK

* University of Phoenix - San Francisco, San Francisco, CA

* University of South Carolina, Columbia, SC

University of South Dakota, Vermillion, SD

* University of Tennessee, Knoxville, TN

University of Texas at Austin, Austin, TX

* University of Utah, Salt Lake City, UT

* University of Washington, Seattle, WA

University of West Virginia - College of Graduate Studies, Institute, WV
See West Virginia Higher Education Instructional Television Consortium

University of Wisconsin (UW), Madison, WI

University of Wisconsin - Eau Claire, Eau Claire, WI
See Wisconsin Educational Communications Board

University of Wisconsin - Green Bay, Green Bay, WI
See Wisconsin Educational Communications Board

University of Wisconsin - La Crosse, La Crosse, WI
See Wisconsin Educational Communications Board

University of Wisconsin - River Falls, River Falls, WI
See Wisconsin Educational Communications Board

University of Wisconsin - Stout, Menomonie, WI
See Wisconsin Educational Communications Board

University of Wisconsin - Whitewater, Whitewater, WI
See Wisconsin Educational Communications Board

* University of Wyoming, Laramie, WY

* Utah State University, Logan, UT

Valley City State University, Valley City, ND
See North Dakota Interactive Video Network

Ventura College, Ventura, CA
See INTELECOM

Victor Valley College, Victorville, CA
See INTELECOM

*Institute provides nationwide or worldwide course access

* Washington State University, Pullman, WA

Wayne County Community College, Detroit, MI

* Weber State University, Ogden, UT

West Liberty State College, West Liberty, WV
    See West Virginia Higher Education Instructional Television Consortium

West Valley College, Saratoga, CA
    See Northern California Telecommunications Consortium

West Virginia Higher Education Instructional Television Consortium, Morgantown, WV

West Virginia Institute of Technology, Montgomery, WV
    See West Virginia Higher Education Instructional Television Consortium

West Virginia Northern College, New Martinsville, WV
    See West Virginia Higher Education Instructional Television Consortium

West Virginia State College, Institute, WV
    See West Virginia Higher Education Instructional Television Consortium

West Virginia University, Morgantown, WV
    See West Virginia Higher Education Instructional Television Consortium

West Virginia University at Parkersburg, Parkersburg, WV
    See West Virginia Higher Education Instructional Television Consortium

Westark Community College, Fort Smith, AR
    See Arkansas Telecommunications Consortium

Westchester Community College, Valhalla, NY
    See WNET/New York City

* Western Illinois University, Macomb, IL

Western Kentucky University, Bowling Green, KY
    See Kentucky Telecommunications Consortium

* Western Michigan University, Department of Distance Education, Kalamazoo, MI

* Western Michigan University - MITN, Office of Telecourse Programs, Kalamazoo, MI

Western State College, Gunnsion, CO
    See KRMA/Denver

* Western Washington University, Bellingham, WA

Westmoreland County Community College, Youngwood, PA
    See College of the Air

WGBH/Boston, Boston, MA

Wisconsin Educational Communications Board, Madison, WI

WNET/New York City, New York, NY

Wor-Wic Tech Community College, Salisbury, MD
    See College of the Air

Yuba College, Marysville, CA
    See Northern California Telecommunications Consortium

Appendix
Institutions Providing Nationwide or Worldwide Course Access

Nationwide

Brigham Young University, Provo, UT
Emergency Management Institute, Emmitsburg, MD
Empire State College, Saratoga Springs, NY
Indiana State University, Terre Haute, IN
Indiana University, Bloomington, IN
Marygrove College, Detroit, MI
Mind Extension University, Englewood, CO
New School for Social Research - DIAL, New York, NY
New York Institute of Technology, Old Westbury, NY
Oklahoma State University, Stillwater, OK
Portland State University, Portland, OR
Rochester Institute of Technology, Rochester, NY
Southeastern Bible College, Birmingham, AL
Texas Tech University, Lubbock, TX
University of Arizona, Tucson, AZ
University of Florida, Gainesville, FL
University of Georgia, Athens, GA
University of Iowa, Iowa City, IA
University of Minnesota, Minneapolis, MN
University of Nebraska at Lincoln, Lincoln, NE
University of North Carolina, Chapel Hill, NC
University of Tennessee, Knoxville, TN
University of Wyoming, Laramie, WY
Utah State University, Logan, UT
Western Michigan University - MITN, Kalamazoo, MI

Worldwide

California Institute of Integral Studies, San Francisco, CA
City University, Bellevue, WA
Colorado State University, Fort Collins, CO
Colorado SURGE, Fort Collins, CO

Columbia Bible College and Seminary, Columbia, SC
Emmaus Bible School, Dubuque, IA
Home Study International, Silver Spring, MD
International School of Information Management, Inc., Denver, CO
Louisiana State University, Baton Rouge, LA
New Jersey Institute of Technology, Newark, NJ
New School for Social Research, New York, NY
New York University, New York, NY
Nova University, Fort Lauderdale, FL
Ohio University, Athens, OH
Pennsylvania State University, University Park, PA
Rio Salado Community College, Phoenix, AZ
Southeastern College, Lakeland, FL
Taylor University, Fort Wayne, IN
University of Alaska, Fairbanks, AK
University of California, Berkeley, CA
University of Idaho, Moscow, ID
University of Kansas, Lawrence, KS
University of Maryland University College, College Park, MD
University of Missouri, Columbia, MO
University of Nevada - Reno, Reno, NV
University of North Dakota, Grand Forks, ND
University of Phoenix - San Francisco, San Francisco, CA
University of South Carolina, Columbia, SC
University of Utah, Salt Lake City, UT
University of Washington, Seattle, WA
Washington State University, Pullman, WA
Weber State University, Ogden, UT
Western Illinois University, Macomb, IL
Western Michigan University, Kalamazoo, MI
Western Washington University, Bellingham, WA